W9-CXP-415

Managerial Economics

Managerial Economics

FIFTH EDITION

James R. McGuigan
JRM Investments

R. Charles Moyer
Babcock Graduate School of Management
Wake Forest University

West Publishing Company
St. Paul   New York   Los Angeles   San Francisco

Copy editor: Mary Hough
Composition: Polyglot Compositors
Cover and text design: Lois Stanfield
Cover photograph: Empire State Building, New York City; David Carol, The Image Bank

Copyright © 1975, 1979, 1983, 1986 by West Publishing Company

Copyright © 1989 by West Publishing Company
      50 West Kellogg Boulevard
      P.O. Box 64526
      St. Paul, MN 55164-1003

All rights reserved
Printed in the United States of America

96 95 94 93 92 91 90 89   8 7 6 5 4 3 2 1 0

Library of Congress Cataloging-in-Publication Data

McGuigan, James R.
  Managerial economics/James R. McGuigan, R. Charles Moyer.—5th ed.
  p. cm.
  Includes bibliographies and indexes.
  ISBN 0-314-46552-9
  1. Managerial economics.   I. Moyer, R Charles. 1945–
II. Title.
HD30.22.M32 1989
658.4–dc19   88-28268
                                                CIP

To my family
—J.R.M.

To Craig and Laura
—R.C.M.

Preface

Managerial economics is concerned with resource allocation decisions which are made by enterprise managers in the private, public and not-for-profit sectors of the economy. Managerial economists seek to achieve the objectives of the organization in the most efficient manner, while considering both explicit and implicit constraints on achieving the objective(s). The book is organized around the theme of the goal of shareholder wealth maximization for private sector enterprises. In addition, the theme of managerial efficiency provides a common basis for making resource allocation decisions in all enterprises.

Managerial economics is an *applied* branch of economics. The major emphasis is to provide the theory and tools essential to the analysis and solution of those problems which have significant economic consequences, both for the firm and society at large. Effective decision-making requires an understanding of the constraints (limitations) imposed on the decision-maker by the environment. In order to accomplish this, major issues associated with government regulation of the firm, as well as implicit constraints on the actions of private and public sector enterprises, are examined. These issues include a consideration of the externalities associated with economic decisions.

Course Content

A survey of managerial economics and business economics courses in a wide range of universities has led to a broad consensus on topic coverage in some areas, but a wide diversity of coverage in other areas. In organizing the book, we have recognized the differences existing in various curricula. The broad topic coverage provided in the text gives instructors a great deal of flexibility in designing a course suited to the needs of their students and the demands of their curricula. Alternative course structures are suggested in the section following this preface.

Part I of the book provides an overview of the field of managerial economics and introduces key economic concepts and tools. In this introductory set of chapters, the goal of the enterprise (shareholder wealth maximization) is established and the relationship between managerial economics and other areas of business and economic analysis is developed. In addition, this section reviews basic economic concepts including marginal analysis, supply-demand equilibrium relationships, the time value of money, the nature of risk, and techniques for managing risk.

For some students Part II, dealing with tools of analysis, will provide a first exposure to useful economic and analytical concepts and tools. For others, this section provides a handy reference source for the review of material encountered in previous courses.

Part III examines the areas of demand analysis and forecasting techniques. Part IV deals with production and cost analysis, and Part V focuses on price determination in theory and practice. Part VI considers long-term investment decision-making in private, public and not-for-profit enterprises. Part VII covers issues related to the regulation of private enterprise.

Although the primary focus of the book is on private sector management, the text is written with a recognition that many students in economics departments and schools of business and management have been finding their way into managerial and policy-making positions in the public and not-for-profit sectors of the economy. Consequently, we have provided the material in Chapters 18, 19, and 20 in order to introduce the philosophy of public involvement in the economy and to provide specific analytical tools which are of use in these sectors. In addition to this explicit coverage of the public and not-for-profit sectors, we have also used examples and developed problems throughout the book which illustrate the broader applications of managerial economics' tools and models. The traditional private sector-oriented business student will also find this material to be an important addition to their understanding of the operation of the economy.

Student Preparation

The text is designed for use by upper-level undergraduates and first-level graduate students in departments of economics and in business schools and schools of public administration. Students are presumed to have a background in the basic principles of economics. Prior work in statistics and quantitative methods is of value. Chapters 4, 5, and 6 provide a review (or introduction) to these areas. Although a knowledge of differential calculus is helpful (it is reviewed in Chapter 4), in all cases where calculus is presented, one or more alternative approaches, such as graphical, algebraic or tabular analysis, is also presented.

Pedagogical Features of the Book

The fifth edition of *Managerial Economics* has been extensively revised. As part of this revision a number of new pedagogical features have been added to the book in order to enhance student learning. The key features of the book are:

1. **Part Openers.** Each major section of the book opens with a brief discussion of the material contained in the following chapters. The relationship of the

material in the section to the objective of shareholder wealth maximization and efficient resource allocation is illustrated with a schematic diagram appearing on each part opener.

2. **Chapter Openers.** Each chapter begins with a brief overview of the chapter contents. These chapter openers discuss the reasons why the material contained in each chapter is important to a manager seeking to efficiently manage the resources of the enterprise in order to maximize shareholder wealth.

3. **Economic Analysis and Managerial Efficiency Sections.** Throughout the book are 16 highlighted sections that discuss actual problems faced by economic decision makers. Many of these sections emphasize creative solutions to problems facing managers seeking to make the most efficient use of the enterprise's resources. Other sections are designed to reinforce central economic concepts using tools such as experimental economics. Each *Economic Analysis and Managerial Efficiency* section ends with one or more discussion questions designed to stimulate class discussion or further analysis by individual students.

4. **Chapter Glossaries.** Each chapter contains a glossary of important new terms that are discussed in the chapter. The placement of the glossary at the beginning of each chapter insures that students will not be frustrated by encountering terms and concepts before they have been explicitly defined. When studying and reviewing a chapter, a student has ready access to the definitions of important terms from the chapter. An index to the glossary is provided at the end of the text.

5. **Point-by-Point Summaries.** Each chapters ends with a detailed, point-by-point summary of important concepts from the chapter.

6. **Selected References.** Each chapter contains a list of selected references that will help students to explore topics from the chapter in more detail. These selected references contain classic studies in an area as well as many contemporary application references.

7. **Diversity of Presentation Approaches.** Important analytical concepts are presented in several different ways, including tabular analysis, graphical analysis, and algebraic analysis. When calculus is used, at least one alternative mode of analysis is also provided for the student.

8. **Discussion Questions.** Each chapter contains an extensive set of discussion questions which cover the key points from the chapter and require the student to do some independent analysis of economic problems.

9. **Problems.** Each chapter also contains a large set of problems. These problems are generally analytical in nature. In this edition, several new problems have been added. Check answers are provided at the end of the text for selected problems.

10. **Short Cases.** Many chapters include short case problems which extend the concepts and tools developed in the text.

11. **Use of Examples.** A large number of examples, designed to illustrate important concepts and techniques, is contained in each chapter. Many of these examples come from actual firm decisions. These examples help students see how managerial economics principles can be applied to solve many different resource allocation problems.

Ancillary Materials

A complete set of ancillary materials is available to adopters to supplement the text, including the following:

- Totally new computer software is provided free to adopters of the book. This software is extremely user friendly and provides on screen help and user diagnostics. The software can be used to solve regression problems, forecasting problems, linear programming problems, and capital budgeting and cost-benefit analysis problems. Documentation for the software is included in Appendix B to this book.

- An *Instructors' Manual*, prepared by the authors, containing suggested answers to discussion questions and solutions to end-of-chapter problems and cases. The authors have taken extra care to provide an error-free manual for instructors to use.

- A *Test Bank*, containing a large collection of true-false, multiple choice, and numerical problems, is available to adopters for test use. A *Micro Test* diskette of the *Test Bank* is available in order to simplify the preparation of quizzes and exams.

- A *Study Guide*, prepared by Professor Raymond E. Spudeck of the University of Central Florida, is available from West Publishing Company for purchase by students. This *Study Guide* will assist students in reviewing and applying the material presented in the text.

- *Transparency Masters* have been prepared for over 100 key tables and figures from the book.

Significant Changes in the Fifth Edition

The fifth edition has been extensively revised to reflect new developments in the study of managerial economics and to enhance the textbook learning environment for students. Most importantly, the explicit tie between each major area of decision making and the goal of shareholder wealth maximization has been developed. This tie is reinforced in the part opening schematic diagram, used to illustrate the relationship between major areas of economic analysis and the shareholder wealth maximization goal, and in chapter opening discussions. Efficiently managing an enterprise's resources has become a central concern of the text discussion. In addition to this conceptual change in the way the material is organized and presented, many other major modifications, additions, deletions, and hundreds of minor changes have been made in response to user and reviewer suggestions. The most important of these changes are enumerated below:

- In Chapter 1, the discussion of the nature of decision problems has been expanded and clarified. The section dealing with the importance of economic model building has been revised to include more realistic examples. A "Problems" section has been added in this chapter.

- Chapter 2 is a new chapter which introduces the fundamental economic concepts of marginal analysis, equilibrium analysis, and the time value of money.

- Chapter 3 (Decision Making Under Risk and Uncertainty) has been modified by adding a major new section dealing with managing risk and uncertainty. This section presents techniques that can be used to manage risk, including diversification, hedging, and insurance.

- The marginal analysis material from Chapter 4 (Classical Optimization Techniques) has been moved to the new Chapter 2.

- In Chapter 6 (Econometrics), the distinctions between simple linear regression and multiple regression have been highlighted. There is an expanded discussion of the use of the Durbin-Watson test as both a one- and a two-tailed test for autocorrelation. The concepts of "degrees of freedom" and "level of significance" have been discussed in more detail.

- The material on demand functions under alternative market structures has been moved from Chapter 7 (Theory of Demand) to the appropriate price-output determination chapters. The discussion of the relationship between marginal revenue and price elasticity has been expanded.

- The Empirical Estimation of Demand chapter (Chapter 8) has been moved so that it follows immediately after the Theory of Demand chapter. There is an expanded discussion of the interpretation of the results of empirical demand analyses.

- The two forecasting chapters (Chapters 9 and 10) now are sequenced together. A section dealing with secular trends has been added to Chapter 9. In addition, constant rate of growth models are now discussed in Chapter 9. Also, a discussion of the use of lagged dependent variables and dummy variables has been added to Chapter 9.

- The discussion of returns to scale in Chapter 11 has been improved with additional analysis of isoquants and their relationship to returns to scale.

- In Chapter 12, a new discussion of the concept of relevant cost when a firm has unutilized facilities is presented. Appendix 12A, dealing with breakeven analysis, has been expanded to include a discussion of operating leverage and its relationship to the risk of an enterprise.

- In Chapter 14, new sections have been added dealing with the relationship between elasticities and profit maximization, monopoly and economic profits, and monopoly and efficiency.

- Chapter 15 contains new material dealing with factors affecting oligopolistic collusion. The OPEC example has been expanded and updated.

- Chapter 17 has a new section dealing with joint products produced in fixed proportions. The relationship between price discrimination and the price elasticity of demand has been enhanced. A new section dealing with limit pricing has been added to this chapter.

- The capital asset pricing model material has been condensed and simplified in Chapter 16. The profitability index model of capital investment analysis has been added to this chapter.

- Much of the descriptive material dealing with market structure has been deleted from this edition of the book. Chapter 19 now includes a section dealing with tax policy as a regulatory tool. Also the concept of "contestable markets" has been added to the discussion of structure-performance relationships. The material dealing with economic externalities has been condensed and included as an appendix to Chapter 19. This appendix views externalities as a special case of market failure.

Acknowledgments

A number of reviewers, users, and colleagues have been particularly helpful in providing us with many worthwhile comments and suggestions at various stages in the development of this and earlier editions of the book. Included among these individuals are:

William Beranek, J. Walter Elliott, William J. Kretlow, William Gunther, J. William Hanlon, Robert Knapp, Robert S. Main, Edward Sussna, Bruce T. Allen, Allen Moran, Edward Opperman, Dwight Porter, Robert L. Conn, Allen Parkman, Daniel Slate, Richard L. Pfister, J. P. Magaddino, Richard A. Stanford, Donald Bumpas, Barry P. Keating, John Wittman, Sisay Asefa, James R. Ashley, David Bunting, Amy H. Dalton, Richard D. Evans, Gordon V. Karels, Richard S. Bower, Patricia Sanderson, Massoud M Saghafi, John C. Callahan, Frank Falero, Ramon Rabinovitch, D. Steinnes, Jay Damon Hobson, Clifford Fry, John Crockett, Marvin Frankel, James T. Peach, Paul Kozlowski, Dennis Fixler, Steven Crane, Scott L. Smith, Edward Miller, Fred Kolb, Bill Carson, Jack W. Thornton, Changhee Chae, Robert B. Dallin, Christopher J. Zappe, Anthony V. Popp, Phil Sisneros, Richard Marcus, George Brower, Carlos Sevilla, Dean Bairn, Charles Callahan, Phillip Robins, Bruce Jaffee, Alwyn du Plessis, Daryl Winn, Gary Shoesmith, Roberts Bass, and Monty Palmer.

We are also indebted to Wayne State University, the University of Houston, Lehigh University, the University of New Mexico, Texas Tech University, and Wake Forest University for the support they provided. We also owe thanks to our faculty colleages at these universities for the encouragement and assistance provided on a continuing basis during the preparation of the manuscript. Finally, we wish to express our appreciation to the members of the West Publishing Company staff—particularly Ken Zeigler, Tad Bornhoft, and Suzanne Spellacy—for their help in the preparation of this book. Most of all we would like to thank our editor, Mary Schiller, who is a constant source of excellent advice and encouragement. Mary's high standards of performance and her total knowledge of the publishing field have helped immensely with this project. It is difficult to imagine doing a book without her assistance.

We are grateful to the Literary Executor of the late Sir Ronald A. Fisher, F.R.S.; to Dr. Frank Yates, F.R.S.; and to Longman Group, Ltd., London, for permission to reprint Table III from their book *Statistical Tables for Biological, Agriculture, and Medical Research* (6th ed., 1974).

Alternative Course Structures

In this text we have provided an extensive topic coverage to meet the varying needs of users across a broad range of institutions. With a few exceptions, the individual chapters in this book can stand alone. This provides the instructor with the maximum flexibility in organizing a course designed to meet the special needs of the curriculum and the students.

We have indicated below a number of alternative suggested chapter coverage configurations which are designed to meet the needs of many users. Of course, individual instructors may want to make further adjustments.

Option 1–Private Sector Focus
(Theory Emphasis)

Chapter 1.	Introduction and Goals of the Firm
Chapter 2.	Fundamental Economic Concepts
Chapter 3.	Decision-Making Under Risk and Uncertainty
Chapter 4.	Classical Optimization Techniques
Chapter 7.	Theory of Demand
Appendix 7A.	Indifference Curve Analysis of Demand
Chapter 8.	Empirical Estimation of Demand
Chapter 9.	Business and Economic Forecasting
Chapter 11.	Theory of Production
Chapter 12.	Theory of Cost
Chapter 13.	Empirical Determination of Production and Cost Functions
Chapter 14.	Price and Output Determination: Pure Competition, Monopolistic Competition, and Monopoly
Chapter 15.	Price and Output Determination: Oligopoly
Appendix 15A.	Theory of Games
Chapter 16.	Further Topics in Pricing
Chapter 17.	Capital Budgeting and the Cost of Capital
Chapter 19.	Government Regulation and Support of the Private Sector
Chapter 20.	Public Utility Regulation

Option 2 – Private Sector Focus
(Empirical Emphasis)

Option 3 – Public Sector/Regulatory Focus

Contents

Managerial Economics

Introduction I

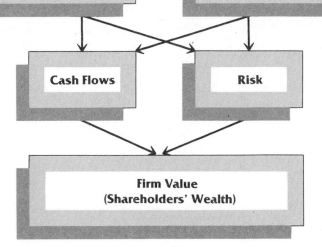

ECONOMIC ANALYSIS AND DECISIONS

1. Demand Analysis and Forecasting
2. Production and Cost Analysis
3. Pricing Analysis
4. Capital Expenditure Analysis

ECONOMIC, POLITICAL, AND SOCIAL ENVIRONMENT

1. Business Conditions (Trends, Cycles, and Seasonal Effects)
2. Factor Market Conditions (Capital, Labor, Land, and Raw Materials)
3. Competitors' Responses
4. External, Legal, and Regulatory Constraints
5. Organizational (internal) Constraints

Cash Flows

Risk

Firm Value (Shareholders' Wealth)

Part I (Introduction) presents an overview of the field of managerial economics and introduces some key economic concepts and tools. In the first chapter, the goals of the enterprise (the for-profit firm and not-for-profit organization) are developed; the decision-making process and the philosophy of optimization are introduced; and the relationship between managerial economics and other branches of economics, accounting, finance, marketing, operations management (production), and labor relations are highlighted. Chapter 2 reviews some fundamental economic concepts, including marginal analysis, supply-demand equilibrium relationships, and the time value of money. Chapter 3 discusses the concept of risk and considers techniques for managing risk. The tools and concepts developed in Part I are central to the analysis used throughout the balance of the text.

Introduction and Goals of the Firm

1

Managerial economics is a branch of economics dealing with the application of economic theory and methodology to decision-making problems faced by public, private, and not-for-profit institutions. Managerial economists assist decision makers (managers) in efficiently allocating the scarce economic resources at the command of the organization. When resource allocation is efficient, a manager is contributing to the firm's primary goal of maximizing the value of the enterprise.

What is Managerial Economics?

Managerial economics deals with the application of economic theory and methodology to decision-making problems faced by public, private, and not-for-profit institutions. The field of managerial economics has experienced rapid growth over the past three decades. This growth reflects a realization that managers can use economic theory to make decisions that will meet the goals of the organization. Managerial economics extracts from economic theory (particularly microeconomics) those concepts and techniques that enable the decision maker to allocate efficiently the resources of the organization.

The tools of managerial economics can be applied by managers in the public and not-for-profit sectors of the economy as well as by managers of profit-seeking firms because, as we shall see throughout the book, managers in all types of enterprises face a common set of problems. Despite some unique complexities, managerial problems generally follow this form:

> To identify the alternative means of achieving given objective(s), and then to select the alternative that accomplishes the objective(s) most efficiently.

For example, consider a firm that has identified two possible strategies (S1 and S2) to meet the growing demand for its products. Strategy S1 represents an internal expansion of capacity. Strategy S2 represents the purchase of a surplus plant now owned by a competitor. The objective of the firm's managers is to maximize the profits of the firm. This problem can be summarized as follows:

Objective function: Maximize profit (S1, S2)

Glossary of New Terms

Optimize
To maximize or minimize the value of some objective function, such as to maximize profits or minimize costs.

Normative objectives
Objectives that prescribe how a firm should act given some set of values, such as the desirability of making the most efficient use of a set of economic resources.

(Economic) Profit
The difference between total revenue and total economic cost. Economic cost includes a "normal" rate of return on the capital contributions of the firm's owners.

Shareholder wealth
A measure of the value of a firm. Shareholder wealth is equal to the value of a firm's common stock, which, in turn, is equal to the present value of all future cash returns expected to be generated by the firm for the benefit of its owners.

(Cont'd on next page)

Glossary of New Terms (*cont'd*)

Descriptive (positive) objectives
Objectives that illustrate how decisions are actually made by a firm or other enterprise.

Public goods
Goods that may be consumed by more than one person at the same time with little or no extra cost, such as the services of a lighthouse beacon. For most public goods, it is relatively expensive or even impossible to keep potential consumers from receiving the benefits of the good, as in the case of national defense.

Private goods
Goods that are divisible into finite units for consumption and for which it is easy to keep nonbuyers from receiving the benefits of consumption.

Agency costs
Costs associated with resolving conflicts of interest between shareholders, managers, and lenders. Agency costs include the cost of monitoring and bonding performance, the cost of constructing contracts designed to minimize agency conflicts, and the loss in efficiency resulting from unresolved agent-principal conflicts.

In this example, the following decision rules can be created:

Decision rule: Choose strategy S1 if Profit (S1) $\geq$ Profit (S2)

Choose strategy S2 if Profit (S1) $<$ Profit (S2)

Although this is a simple problem, it illustrates the essential elements of resource allocation problems. Economic theory can assist a manager in deciding upon the appropriate objective function and in clarifying the decision rules.

Managerial Economics and Economic Theory

The field of economics is traditionally divided into *microeconomics* and *macroeconomics*. Microeconomics deals with the theory of individual choice; that is, decisions made by a particular consuming and producing unit such as a business firm. Macroeconomics focuses on the overall economy and the general economic equilibrium conditions. Managerial economists draw upon both of these branches of economics during the decision-making process. Although a firm's managers can do little to affect the aggregate economy, their decisions should be consistent with the current economic outlook.

The types of decisions made by managers usually involve questions of resource allocation within the organization in both the short and the long run. In the short run, a manager may be interested in estimating demand and cost relationships in order to make decisions about the price to charge for a product and the quantity of output to produce. The areas of microeconomics dealing with demand theory and with the theory of cost and production are obviously useful in making decisions on such matters. Macroeconomic theory also enters into decision making when a manager attempts to forecast future demand based on forces influencing the overall economy.

In the long run, decisions must be made about expanding or contracting production and distribution facilities, developing and marketing new products, and possibly acquiring other firms. Basically, these decisions are concerned with economies (or diseconomies) of scale and typically require the organization to make capital expenditures; that is, expenditures made in the current period that are expected to yield returns in future periods. Economists have developed a theory of capital that can be used in deciding whether or not to undertake specific capital expenditures.

The Decision-Making Model

The ability to make good decisions is the key to successful managerial performance. Managers of profit-seeking firms are faced with a wide range of important decisions in the areas of pricing, product choice, cost control, advertising, capital investments, and dividend policy, to name but a few. Managers in the not-for-profit and the public sectors are faced with a similarly wide range of decisions. For example, the dean of your business school must decide how to allocate funds among such competing needs as travel, phone services, secretarial support, and the like. Longer-range decisions must be made about new facilities, new programs, the purchase or lease of a new computer, and the decision to establish an executive development center. Public sector managers face such decisions as the need for a "Stealth" bomber, the need to support public transit systems, the enforcement of antitrust laws, and the economic viability of passive restraint devices in automobiles.

Decision making in each of these areas shares a number of common elements. First, it is essential for the decision maker to establish or identify the objectives of the organization. The failure to identify organizational objectives correctly can result in the complete rejection of an otherwise well-conceived and well-implemented plan. Later sections of this chapter deal with the issue of organizational objectives in more detail.

Next, the decision maker must identify the problem requiring a solution. For example, the manager of a brewing plant in Milwaukee may note that the plant's profit margin on sales has been decreasing. This could be caused by pricing errors, labor force problems, or the use of outdated production equipment. Once the source or sources of the problem are identified, the manager can move to an examination of potential solutions. If the problem is the use of technologically inefficient equipment, two possible solutions are (1) updating and replacing the plant's equipment or (2) building a completely new plant. The choice between these alternatives depends on the relative costs and benefits, as well as other constraints, that may make one alternative preferable to another. For example, the decision to build a new brewery in a suburban area may not be politically desirable if it means a major inner-city facility must be closed.

The final step in the process, after all alternatives have been identified and evaluated, and the best alternative has been chosen, is the implementation of the decision. This phase often requires constant monitoring to assure that results are as expected. If they are not, corrective action needs to be taken when possible. This five-step decision-making process is illustrated in Figure 1.1.

The Importance of Economic Model Building

Economists make frequent use of economic models. Models are merely simplifications of reality designed to aid in the analysis of complex problems. Economic relationships tend to have the common feature of being highly complex.

Consider, for example, a model designed to explain the value of a share of common stock. The value of a share of common stock can be thought of as the present (or discounted) value of all expected future cash distributions from the company to its shareholders. These future cash distributions are determined largely by the earnings of the company. These earnings are determined by the productivity of the workforce, the quality of the products made by the firm, the number of current and expected future competitors, the cost of raw materials, the state of the overall economy, the effects of inflation and interest rate changes, and other similar factors. The discount rate used by investors to value these projected future cash distributions is a function of the riskiness, i.e., the potential variability of the distributions, and the general level of interest rates. The riskiness of a firm's cash distributions is determined by the volatility of its

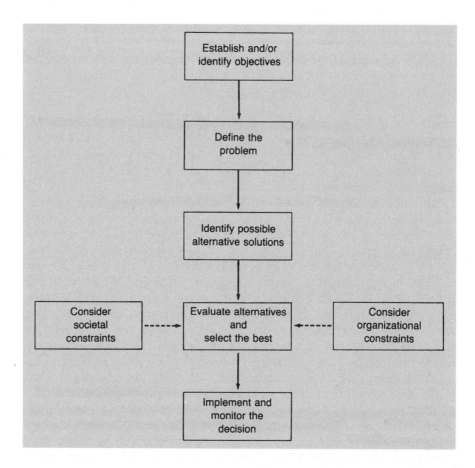

Figure 1.1
The Decision-Making Process

operating income and the additional volatility of its earnings per share due to debt financing, which has a fixed cost. (This additional earnings volatility is called financial risk.) Hence, the valuation of a share of common stock is extremely complex.

Model builders, however, may not explicitly consider each of these factors. Instead, they may make assumptions to simplify their analysis. For example, future interest rates may be assumed to remain constant or the level of future economic activity may be assumed to remain constant. In addition, the model builder may not explicitly consider all possible interactions among the individual factors known to influence share prices. Yet, in spite of these simplifications, the basic model of share valuation has been found to be extremely useful in explaining movements in the price of a company's common stock.

Thus, we can say that economic models are designed to simplify complex relationships without significant losses in explanatory ability. The first and most important step in nearly all economic analysis is to develop a model of the expected impact of important variables on the relationship being examined. Next, this model is tested with economic data to discern its explanatory and predictive capabilities.

Economic models take several forms. They can be presented as a graphical relationship such as the demand relationship pictured in Figure 1.2. This model

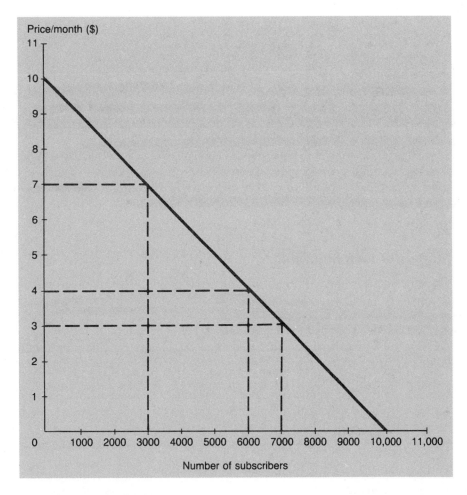

Figure 1.2
Graphic Model of the Demand for Cable TV

of the demand for cable TV services shows the quantity demanded (number of subscribers) to be related to the price (monthly charge). Other factors, such as the average age of subscribers, the amount of advertising done by the cable TV firm, program content, the cost of the initial hookup, and the marital status of potential subscribers, are all likely to have an influence on demand. However, the model builder has chosen to assume that these factors remain constant. To determine the usefulness of the model in Figure 1.2, it is necessary to test this model with actual data.

As an alternative to the graphical model, economic models can also be expressed as algebraic relationships. For example, the demand model in Figure 1.2 could be expressed as

$$Q = 10,000 - 1000\,P \qquad [1.1]$$

where Q equals the number of subscribers and P equals the monthly fee. From Figure 1.2 it can be seen that when P equals \$7, the number of monthly subscribes would be expected to be 3,000. At a price of \$4, Q would equal 6,000, and at a price of \$3, Q would equal 7,000. This same result can be obtained from Equation 1.1 by substituting various values of P into the equation. For example, when P equals \$7, Equation 1.1 becomes

$$Q = 10,000 - 1,000(7)$$
$$= 3,000 \text{ subscribers}$$

Algebraic models are quite useful in economics because they permit model builders to consider many different variables simultaneously. In contrast, graphical models are normally limited to two variables because of the difficulty in constructing graphical figures of greater than two dimensions.

In this text, we develop both graphical and algebraic models to assist in the analysis of various economic decisions. We also present a number of analytical tools to help develop and test economic models. These tools include linear programming, regression analysis, and forecasting models.

Models of Firm Behavior

The fundamental model of the firm, which was developed early by economic theorists, assumes that the objective of the owners of the firm is to maximize profits. This profit-maximization model of firm behavior has been extremely rich in its decision-making implications. The marginal (and incremental) decision rules that have been derived from this theory provide very useful guidelines for making a wide range of resource allocation decisions. For example, if incremental cost is defined as the change in total cost resulting from a decision, and if incremental revenue is defined as the change in total revenue resulting from a decision, then it should be apparent that any business decision is profitable if one of these results occurs:

1. It increases revenue more than costs

2. It decreases some costs more than it increases others (assuming revenues remain constant)

3. It increases some revenues more than it decreases others (assuming costs remain constant)

4. It reduces costs more than revenue

This rather simple enumeration of decision rules is helpful in making a wide range of economic decisions.

Profit Defined

Profit is the difference between total revenue and total economic cost. *Revenue* is measured as the sales receipts of a firm; that is, price times quantity sold.

The economic cost of any activity may be thought of as the highest valued alternative opportunity that is foregone. To attract economic resources to some activity, the firm must pay a price for these factors (land, labor, and capital) that is sufficient to convince the owners of these resources to sacrifice other alternatives and commit the resources to this use. Thus, economic costs may be thought of as *opportunity costs*, or the costs of attracting a resource from its next best alternative use.

In practice, the measurement of cost presents a number of difficult problems. Accountants typically focus only on *explicit costs*—that is, costs for which an explicit payment must be made. For example, if one firm were financed with 50 percent debt (borrowed money) and 50 percent equity (owners' funds) and another firm were financed with 100 percent owners' equity, the second firm would show lower accounting costs and higher accounting profits than the first, assuming that all other conditions of their operations are identical. This is because the first firm would report interest expense on the borrowed funds, whereas the second has no such explicit expense. The funds supplied by the owners of both firms, however, have an *implicit cost*, or *opportunity cost*, since these owners could have invested the funds elsewhere to earn a return. Numerous other differences exist between the measurement of accounting and economic costs (and profits), but the treatment of implicit costs is the most important.

From an economic perspective, cost includes not only explicit cost payments,[1] which are recognized by accountants, but also implicit costs, arising from the contribution of an owner's time and labor resources (in the case of a sole proprietorship where the owner draws no explicit salary) and the contribution of capital resources provided by the owner. Economic costs recognize that capital contributed by an owner should earn a "normal" rate of return commensurate with alternative investment opportunities and the risk of the investment. In a general sense, **economic profit** may be defined as *the difference between total revenue and total economic cost.*

Throughout this text the term *profit* refers to economic profits. Accordingly, the term *cost* includes all economic costs, both explicit and implicit, and includes in it a normal return (profit) for the owners who have contributed their financial resources. When we refer to the profit maximization objective in this book, we mean an objective of maximizing the economic profit of the firm.

Why Are Profits Necessary?

In a free enterprise system, economic profits play an important role in guiding the decisions made by the thousands of competing, independent economic units. The existence of profits (resulting from the excess of revenues over costs) determines the type and quantity of goods and services that are produced and sold. It also determines the demand for various factors of production—labor, capital, and natural resources. Because of the important role played by profits in our system, a brief review of several theories of profit is useful.

---

[1] Not all explicit costs are economic costs. For example, sunk costs (past expenditures which cannot be recovered) are not considered as economic costs for decision-making purposes. In general, the concept of economic costs is forward-looking.

Risk-Bearing Theory of Profit.   Some economists have argued that economic profits above a normal rate of return are necessary to compensate the owners of the firm for the risk they assume when making their investments. Since a firm's owners are not entitled to a fixed rate of return on their investment—that is, they are residual claimants to the firm's resources—they need to be compensated for this risk in the form of a higher rate of return. For example, investors in the bonds of Public Service Company of New Hampshire (PSNH) are promised a specific return (in the form of interest and a repayment of principal) over the life of the bonds. If these payments are not made, the bondholder may force PSNH to sell or restructure its assets to meet the claims of bondholders. PSNH's common and preferred stockholders have no such protection. During 1987 and 1988, PSNH paid no common stock dividends, and dividends on preferred stock had been suspended. In early 1988, PSNH was forced to declare bankruptcy due to its inability to meet interest payments. As a result of this bankruptcy declaration, the PSNH bonds have lost some of their value, but the common stock of PSNH has lost nearly all of its value. Because of these risks, the company's common stockholders are entitled to require a higher rate of return on their investment; otherwise, they would have no incentive to invest.

It should be noted that the risk-bearing theory of profits can be explained in the context of normal profits if *normal* is defined in terms of the relative risk of alternative investments. Normal profits for a high-risk firm, such as a wildcat oil drilling firm, should be higher than normal profits for firms of lesser risk, such as supermarkets.

Dynamic Equilibrium (Friction) Theory of Profit.   According to the dynamic equilibrium or friction theory of profits, there exists a long-run equilibrium normal rate of profit (adjusted for risk) that all firms should tend to earn. At any point in time, however, an individual firm or the firms in a specific industry might earn a rate of return above or below this long-run normal return level. This can occur because of temporary dislocations (shocks) in various sectors of the economy. For example, U.S. firms that produced insulation materials experienced a dramatic increase in demand following the beginning of the energy crisis in 1973. Rates of return for many of these firms surged upward. As new firms entered the market and as pent-up demand was satisfied, rates of return have tended to decline to normal levels.

Similarly, if a new, inexpensive, and readily available energy source were to be discovered, emphasis on energy conservation could decline considerably, reducing the demand for insulating materials. Over time, some producers would leave this increasingly unprofitable market until a normal rate of profit is restored for the remaining firms. The inability of our economic system to adjust instantaneously to changes in market conditions may result in short-term profits above or below normal levels.

Monopoly Theory of Profit.   In some industries one firm is able to effectively dominate the market and potentially earn above-normal rates of return for a long period of time. This ability to dominate the market may arise from economies of scale (a situation where one large firm can produce additional units of output at a lower cost than can smaller firms), control of essential natural resources, control of critical patents, or governmental restrictions that prohibit competition. The conditions under which a monopolist can earn above-normal profits are discussed in greater depth in Chapter 14.

Innovation Theory of Profit. The innovation theory of profit suggests that above-normal profits are the reward for successful innovations. Firms that develop unique, high-quality products (such as Apple in the computer industry) or firms that are successful in identifying unique market opportunities (such as Federal Express) are rewarded with the potential for above-normal profits. Indeed, the U.S. patent system is designed to ensure that these above-normal return opportunities furnish strong incentives for continued innovation over a long period of time.

Managerial Efficiency Theory of Profit. Closely related to the innovation theory is the managerial efficiency theory of profit. This theory maintains that above-normal profits can arise because of the exceptional managerial skills of well-managed firms. The ability to earn above-normal profits by exercising high-quality managerial skills is a continuing incentive for greater efficiency in our economic system.

No single theory of profit can explain the observed profit rates in each industry, nor are these theories necessarily contradictory. Profit performance is invariably the result of many factors, including differential risk, innovation, managerial skills, the existence of monopoly power, and chance occurrences. The important thing to remember is that profit and profit opportunities play a major role in determining the efficient allocation of resources in our economy. Without the market signals that profits give, it would be necessary to develop alternative schemes on which to base resource allocation decisions. These alternatives are often highly bureaucratic and frequently lack the responsiveness to changing market conditions that our free enterprise system provides.

Limitations of the Profit-Maximization Objective

Unfortunately, the profit-maximization goal, as operationally defined, suffers from a number of technical flaws. One significant limitation of profit maximization is its lack of precision. In its simplest form, profit maximization can be ambiguous when firms compare and rank alternative courses of action in terms of their contribution to economic efficiency. The profit-maximization goal does not define which profits are to be maximized. Should it focus on short-run or long-run profits? For example, in the short run, profits could be maximized by firing all research and development personnel and thereby eliminating a considerable immediate expense. This decision, however, would undoubtedly have a substantial impact on long-run profitability.

Furthermore, there is no generally agreed-on or understood definition of profits. Should the firm seek to maximize the amount of profit or the rate of profit? What is the appropriate measure of the rate of profit—profit in relation to total capital or profit in relation to shareholder's equity? Should traditional accounting profits be maximized or, as in the case of real estate, should cash flow be the crucial variable to be maximized?

An additional question concerns the difficulty of aggregating and comparing costs and revenues that are realized at different points in time. Most corporate undertakings involve the investment of funds that are expected to generate revenues over a number of years. The static profit-maximization criterion offers no basis for comparing alternatives that promise varying flows of revenues and expenditures over time.

An additional problem associated with the practical application of the profit-maximization concept is that it provides no explicit means of considering the risk associated with alternative decisions. Two projects generating identical future expected revenues and requiring identical outlays may differ greatly in the degree of uncertainty with which benefits are generated. The greater the uncertainty associated with benefits, the greater the risk associated with the project. An objective criterion for resource allocation in the firm must be able to incorporate this degree of risk into the analysis.

For these reasons the concept of *shareholder wealth maximization* is a useful alternative objective to guide resource allocation decisions in the firm.

Shareholder Wealth-Maximization Model of the Firm

The static profit-maximization model of firm behavior has produced a wide range of valuable insights into the efficient allocation of economic resources. In spite of these successes, the shortcomings of the model (most notably the failure to incorporate the time dimension in the decision process and the failure to deal explicitly with risk and uncertainty in decision making) led to the development of a more comprehensive model. This model, the shareholder wealth-maximization (or value-maximization) model, assumes that the objective of the firm is to maximize the value of the firm as measured in the marketplace; that is, to maximize the market value of the firm's stock.

The value of a firm's stock is equal to the discounted (or present) value of all future cash returns expected to be generated by the firm for the benefit of its owners. The stockholders of a company generally receive a portion of the income earned each period. The portion of the income earned and distributed to the common stockholders is called *dividends*. Hence the value of a firm's stock is equal to the present value of all expected future dividends (or other distributions such as the proceeds from the sale of stock by an individual investor), discounted at the stockholders' required rate of return, or

$$V_0 = \frac{D_1}{(1+k_e)^1} + \frac{D_2}{(1+k_e)^2} + \frac{D_3}{(1+k_e)^3} + \cdots \frac{D_\infty}{(1+k_e)^\infty}$$

$$V_0 = \sum_{t=1}^{\infty} \frac{D_t}{(1+k_e)^t} \qquad\qquad [1.2]$$

where V_0 is the current (present) value of a share of stock, D_t represents the dividends (distributions) expected in each of the future periods (1 through ∞), and k_e equals the investors' required rate of return. Equation 1.2 assumes that the reader is familiar with the concept of discounting and present values. (A review of this concept is found in Chapter 2.) For the purposes of analysis here, it is only necessary to recognize that $1 received one year from today is generally worth less than $1 received today because $1 today can be invested at some rate of interest, for example 15 percent, to yield $1.15 at the end of one year. Thus, an investor who requires (or has an opportunity to earn) a 15 percent annual rate of return on an investment would place a current value of $1 on $1.15 expected to be received in one year.

Equation 1.2 has some very useful properties. First, it explicitly considers the timing of future cash flows. By discounting all future distributions at the required rate of return, k_e, Equation 1.2 recognizes that a dollar received in the future is worth less than a dollar received immediately. Second, Equation 1.2 provides a conceptual basis for evaluating differential levels of risk. For example, if a series of future cash flows are highly uncertain (i.e., likely to diverge substantially from their expected values), the discount rate, k_e, can be increased to account for this risk. Hence the wealth-maximization model of the firm is capable of dealing with the two primary shortcomings of the static profit-maximization model.

Equation 1.2 also provides a unifying theme for the analysis that follows in this text. As noted, D_t represents the portion of each period's after-tax net income, Y_t, that is paid out to the firm's stockholders. Income in any period may be defined as

$$Y_t = [P_t \cdot Q_t - V_t \cdot Q_t - F_t] \, (1 - T) \qquad [1.3]$$

where P_t equals the price per unit of output sold in period t; Q_t equals the quantity of output sold in period t; V_t equals the variable cost per unit of output in period t; F_t equals fixed costs in period t; and T equals the firm's tax rate.

The first term on the right-hand side of Equation 1.3—$P_t \cdot Q_t$—represents the total revenue generated by the firm. From a decision-making perspective, this value is dependent on the nature of the firm's demand function (discussed in Chapters 7–10) and the firm's pricing decisions (see Chapters 14–16).

The firm's costs, both fixed—F_t—and variable—V_t—are discussed in Chapters 11–13. In addition, the choice of investments made by the firm—the capital budgeting decisions—determines what proportion of total cost will be fixed and what proportion will be variable. A firm that chooses a capital-intensive production technology will tend to have a higher proportion of its total costs of operation represented as fixed costs than will a firm that chooses a more labor-intensive technology. Capital budgeting decisions are considered in Chapter 17 for private sector firms and in Chapter 18 for public and not-for-profit enterprises.

The discount rate, k_e, which investors use to value the stream of income generated by a firm, is determined by the perceived risk of the firm and by conditions in the financial markets, including the level of expected inflation. Risk and its relationship to required rates of return are discussed in Chapters 3 and 17.

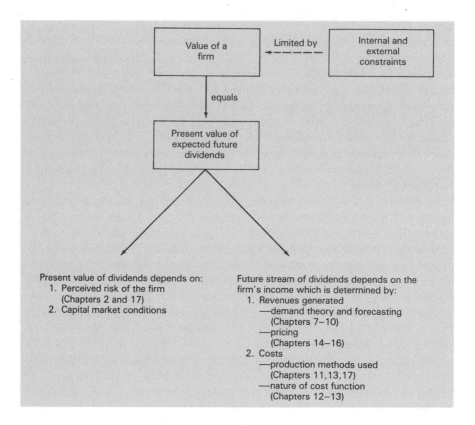

Figure 1.3
Determinants of Firm Value

In making its pricing, output, production, and cost decisions, management is faced with a number of legal, behavioral, value-based, and environmental constraints on its actions. These constraints are briefly considered in the next section and discussed in greater detail in Chapters 19 and 20.

The integrative nature of the wealth-maximization model is illustrated in Figure 1.3.

Explicit and Implicit Constraints on Decisions

Managerial economics is oriented toward helping managers make better decisions so it does not limit the analysis solely to economic theory and methodology. As discussed previously, decision-making problems typically involve optimizing the value of some objective function subject to one or more constraints: that is, resource, legal, environmental, and behavioral restrictions. In many decision-making problems, the resource constraints are explicit and well-defined. Budgets in terms of money and personnel, are established for projects and functional areas within the organization, and the decision maker is required to operate within these limitations. But other types of constraints, such as legal, environmental, and behavioral restrictions, are typically more implicit in nature and less well defined. Economists usually find it much more difficult to quantify these constraints, but this must be done if the constraints are to be incorporated into optimization models. Often the model is solved for the optimal decisions without these constraints and then, in a subjective manner, these decisions are modified to take account of implicit constraints. In analyzing the more implicit constraints, other academic disciplines become relevant.

Alternative Objectives of the Firm

The marginal (or incremental) decision criteria, derived from the static profit maximization and the dynamic wealth maximization objectives, are useful in cases where alternative decisions are easily enumerated and outcomes (costs and revenues) associated with these alternatives can be estimated. These cases include such problems as optimal production scheduling, determining an optimal inventory policy given some pattern of sales and available production facilities, and choosing from among alternative means of achieving some desirable end result (for example, buying or leasing a machine or refunding an outstanding bond issue). In practice, the techniques of optimization suggested by the marginal decision rules and the wealth-maximization objective are frequently employed to guide decision making in the corporation.

By observing the way decisions are actually made in the firm and comparing these decisions with the efficiency criteria in the previous sections, economists have frequently found a divergence between theory and practice. What are the reasons for this divergence? As the small business enterprise grew and expanded into the modern corporation of today, the roles of ownership and management became increasingly separated.[2] Some argue that this separation permitted managers of the firm to pursue goals more consistent with their self-interests, goals subject, of course, to the constraint that the managers satisfy shareholders enough to maintain control of the corporation—that is, pay a sufficient dividend and grow at a satisfactory rate over time. A discussion of some alternative firm objectives follows.

Management Utility Maximization

Williamson's model of business behavior "focuses on the self-interest-seeking behavior of corporate managers.[3] The utility function of management, which measures the amount of satisfaction that management receives from doing its job, is a function of

1. The salaries and other forms of monetary compensation (such as bonuses and stock options) managers receive from the firm,

2. The number and quality of staff personnel who report to the managers,

---

[2] Adolf Berle and Gardiner C. Means, *The Modern Corporation and Private Property* (New York: Macmillan, 1932).

[3] O. E. Williamson, "A Model of Rational Managerial Behavior" in *A Behavioral Theory of the Firm*, ed. Richard M. Cyert and James G. March (Englewood Cliffs, N.J.: Prentice-Hall, 1963), chapter 9.

Economic Analysis and Managerial Efficiency

TAKEOVERS AND CORPORATE "RAIDERS"

The recent increase in corporate takeover activity has been led by a group of so-called corporate raiders, including T. Boone Pickens and Carl Icahn. Pickens argues that "Takeovers, on balance, increase corporate efficiency, productivity, and accountability. They redeploy undervalued assets and revitalize moribund operations."* With corporate raiders actively looking for undervalued or poorly managed firms, managers have placed increased emphasis on the shareholder wealth-maximization goal as the primary measure of corporate performance.

After the takeover bid from Sir James Goldsmith, the chairman of Goodyear Tire and Rubber, Robert E. Mercer, said, "I used to check the stock price maybe once a week, but I've started checking it every day, sometimes several times a day, after this Goldsmith thing got started."** The driving force behind corporate takeovers and restructuring has been an emphasis on increasing shareholder wealth. More and more companies are examining major increases in their stock price to determine the cause of the increase: a decline in interest rates; an increase in investor optimism about the company's earnings prospects; or the

introduction of a restructuring premium, either by the company's current management or by an acquiring firm.

In addition to putting early warning systems in place to determine if a company has become a target for takeover and/or restructuring, growing numbers of firms are putting the shareholder value creation objective at the forefront of their strategic planning process. All business strategies at Kraft and Westinghouse, for example, are evaluated in the context of their contribution to shareholder wealth creation. This approach has focused attention on those elements of the company's strategic plan that have the greatest prospect of creating value for shareholders and those units that do not seem to have the potential to make this contribution. Alternative plans are being evaluated primarily in the context of their likely contribution to shareholder wealth creation. The active takeover market of the 1980s has provided renewed incentives for managers to refocus on the primary normative goal of shareholder wealth maximization.

Questions

1. What factors do you feel have caused some managers to stray from the goal of maximizing shareholder wealth?

2. What are the pros and cons of the anti-takeover laws that have been enacted in several states?

3. What do you think is a company's best defense against a takeover attempt?

---

*T. Boone Pickens, Jr., "Takeovers and the Preservation of Shareholder Wealth," in *Contemporary Financial Management*, 3rd ed. rev. R. C. Moyer, J. R. McGuigan, and W. J. Kretlow (St. Paul, MN: West Publishing, 1988).
**Alfred Rappaport, "Taking Stock of Your Company's Real Worth," *Wall Street Journal*, 2 March 1987.

3. The extent to which the managers are able to direct the investment of the firm's resources, and

4. The type and amount of perquisites (such as expense accounts, lavishly furnished offices, and chauffeur-driven limousines) that the managers receive from the firm and that are beyond the amount strictly necessary for the firm's operations.[4]

These perquisites have often been referred to as *organizational slack.*

Growth Objectives and Size Maximization

Other experts have described slightly different management objectives. Penrose, for example, has suggested that in the modern corporation growth can become an end in itself. This growth is frequently measured in terms of increased sales, assets, and/or number of employees. Penrose observes that managers have a vital interest in growth because individuals "gain prestige, personal satisfaction in the successful growth of the firm with which they are connected, more responsible and better paid positions, and wider scope for their ambitions and abilities."[5] In a test of this "growth" hypothesis, Reid found that actively merging firms tend to be oriented to furthering managers' rather than stockholders' interests.[6] Reid's tests showed that actively merging firms performed better in comparison to nonmerging firms when considered in terms of

1. Growth in assets,

2. Growth in sales, and

3. Growth in the number of employees.

In contrast, the nonmerging firms performed significantly better than the merging firms when considered in terms of

1. The increase in the share of profits attributable to stockholders relative to assets,

2. The increase in the share of profits attributable to stockholders relative to sales, and

3. The relative change in market price per share of common stock.

The latter three variables were taken to represent shareholder interests, whereas the former three represent management interests.

Baumol has suggested a model of the firm in which the managers of the firm seek to maximize total revenue subject to a profit constraint (which presumably is satisfactory to the shareholders).

---

[4] Kalman J. Cohen and Richard M. Cyert, *Theory of the Firm* (Englewood Cliffs, N.J.: Prentice-Hall, 1965), p. 355. (See also 2d ed., 1975).

[5] Edith Penrose, *The Theory of the Growth of the Firm* (Oxford: Basil Blackwell & Mott, 1959), p. 242.

[6] Samuel Richardson Reid, *Mergers, Managers and the Economy* (New York: McGraw-Hill, 1968).

Such a goal may perhaps be explained by the businessman's desire to maintain his competitive position, which is partly dependent on the sheer size of his enterprise, or it may be a matter of the interests of management (as distinguished from shareholders), since management's salaries may be related more closely to the size of the firm's operations than to its profits, or it may be simply a matter of prestige.[7]

McGuire, Chiu, and Elbing conducted a statistical investigation of the correlations among executive incomes, sales, and profits. They found that "there is a valid relationship between sales and executive incomes as Baumol assumes, but not between profits and executive incomes."[8] Further studies by Roberts[9] and Patton[10] lend additional support to this hypothesis.

The evidence of this issue is not uniform, however. Lewellen and Huntsman found that reported profits and equity market values are more important than sales in determining executive compensation.[11]

Long-Run Survival

Another goal suggested as an alternative to the normative goal of wealth maximization is assuring long-run survival for the firm.[12] Decisions based on this criterion are designed to maximize the probability that the organization will survive into the future. Long-run survival is in the direct interests of management because its present and future compensation depends on the firm's continued existence. A short career at a bankrupt firm is hardly a strong basis for successful job mobility. The desire to ensure the long-run survival of the firm provides a basis of explanation for business decision making that is often oriented toward the avoidance or minimization of risk.[13]

The long-run survival goal of the organization may in part explain the attention business executives give to social responsibility. As the small enterprise expanded into today's modern corporate institution, the time horizon for business decision making also expanded. No longer did the lifetime of the entrepreneur or of his or her children constitute an appropriate planning horizon for future decisions. The growth of the corporation also created "sizable constituencies of people whose interests and welfare are inexorably

---

[7] William J. Baumol, *Economic Theory and Operations Analysis,* 3d ed. (Englewood Cliffs, N.J.: Prentice-Hall, 1972), p. 320.

[8] Joseph W. McGuire, John Y. S. Chiu, and Alvar O. Elbing, "Executive Incomes, Sales and Profits," *American Economic Review* 52, no. 4 (September 1962), p. 760.

[9] D. R. Roberts, *Executive Compensation* (New York: Free Press, 1959).

[10] Arch Patton, "Deterioration in Top Executive Pay," *Harvard Business Review* (November-December 1965), p. 106.

[11] Wilbur G. Lewellen and Blaine Huntsman, "Managerial Pay and Performance," *American Economic Review* (September 1970).

[12] K. W. Rothschild, "Price Theory and Oligopoly," *Economic Journal* 42 (1947), pp. 297–320.

[13] See Reid, *Mergers, Managers, and the Economy*, p. 136.

linked with the company and whose support is vital to its success."[14] These constituencies include employees, stockholders, customers and consumers, suppliers, and community neighbors. Some have argued that business should seek to balance the interests of all these constituencies rather than be concerned with the stockholders alone. As yet no satisfactory balancing mechanism has been suggested that specifies how potential conflicts of interest among these competing groups may be resolved. It can be argued, however, that a concern with the interests of all the competing constituencies of the corporation is justified on the basis that it is in the interest of the corporation to create an environment within which the goal of long-run profitability can more easily be pursued.

Satisficing and Behavioral Theories

Another model of the firm, which has been proposed by Simon[15] and extended by Cohen and Cyert,[16] assumes that the firm does not try to maximize any explicit objective function. Rather, it is built on the assumption that minimal standards of achievement have been set to provide satisfactory levels of profits and guarantee the firm's long-run existence. Instead of seeking to "maximize" some objective function, the firm is said to "satisfice," or seek acceptable levels of performance. The model incorporates the notion of *organizational slack*,[17] which increases or decreases depending on whether the aspiration levels of the firm have been achieved.

Cyert and March[18] have developed a behavioral theory of the firm that builds on the early work of Simon. The behavioral models developed by Cyert and March seek to examine how firms really act or how decisions are actually made. The models incorporate much from the body of organization theory to enrich the traditional concepts of economic decision making. In general, the behavioral models they developed portray

> the process of decision making in terms consistent with a behavioral theory of the firm. The firm uses multiple, changing aspiration-level goals; it solves problems in each of its decision areas more or less independently; it searches for solutions in a manner learned from experience; it adjusts its decision rules on the basis of feedback or experience. Decisions on price, output, and sales strategy are made on the basis of profit, inventory, production-smoothing, sales, market share and competitive position goals.[19]

---

[14] Research and Policy Committee, Committee for Economic Development, *Social Responsibilities of Business Corporations* (New York: CED, 1971), pp. 18–19.

[15] Herbert A. Simon, "Theories of Decision-Making in Economics," *American Economic Review*, 49, no. 3 (June 1959), p. 253.

[16] Cohen and Cyert, *Theory of the Firm*, pp. 363–376.

[17] See the discussion of the Williamson model above for a definition of organizational slack.

[18] Richard M. Cyert and James G. March, *A Behavioral Theory of the Firm* (Englewood Cliffs, N.J.: prentice-Hall, 1963).

[19] Ibid., p. 182.

Agency Problems

Conflicting interests among the various parties in a corporation (including management, owners, lenders, employees, suppliers, and the government) may lead to suboptimal resource allocation decisions in the firm. One important class of problems of this type arise from *agency relationships*.[20] Agency relationships occur when one or more individuals (the principals) hire another individual (the agent) to provide a service on behalf of the principals. In an agency relationship, decision-making authority is delegated to the agent from the principals. In the context of economics and finance, two of the most important agency relationships are between stockholders (owners) and managers and between creditors and owners.

Inefficiencies that arise because of the existence of agency relationships have been called "agency" problems. These problems occur because each party to a corporate transaction is assumed to act in a manner consistent with maximizing his or her own utility. Thus, in a sense, agency problems can be thought of as a natural extension of Williamson's utility maximization model. Some key examples of agency problems include the following:

1. The consumption of on-the-job perquisites by managers who have only a partial ownership interest in the firm

2. The failure of managers to vigorously pursue the goal of shareholder wealth maximization because not all of the wealth that is created will go to benefit the manager

3. The incentives of stockholders to adopt high-risk investments to extract wealth from a firms's lenders

4. The incentives of stockholders to forego profitable investments to extract wealth from a firm's lenders

These agency problems give rise to a number of *agency costs*, which are incurred by shareholders and creditors to minimize agency problems. Examples of agency costs include (1) expenditures to structure an organization in a way that will minimize the incentives for management to take actions contrary to shareholder interests (such as providing a portion of management's compensation in the form of the stock of the firm); (2) expenditures to monitor management's actions (such as paying for audits of managerial performance and internal audits of a firm's expenditures); (3) bonding expenditures to protect the owners from managerial dishonesty; (4) the opportunity cost of lost profits arising from complex organizational structures that prevent management from making timely responses to opportunities; and (5) the direct and opportunity costs associated with imposing and monitoring loan indenture restrictions on the borrowing firm to protect the interests of creditors.

Financial theory has shown that agency problems and their associated costs can be greatly reduced if the financial markets operate efficiently. Unresolved

---

[20] See Amir Barnea, R. Haugen, and L. Senbet, *Agency Problems and Financial Contracting* (Englewood Cliffs, N.J.: Prentice-Hall, 1985), for an overview of the agency problem issue.

agency problems can be reduced further by complex financial contracts that detail the priorities of claims of the various parties. Remaining agency problems give rise to costs that show up in a reduction in the value of a firm's shares in the marketplace.

Implications

The discussion presented in this section illustrates the wide difference of opinion regarding corporate goals and objectives. Clearly, however, the simple assumption that business behavior and decision making by the firm's managers may be described solely in terms of the wealth-maximization goal can no longer be accepted on faith. The actions of corporate raiders/reformers such as T. Boone Pickens have raised this issue to one of prominence among investors and lawmakers.

The purpose of this section was to introduce some of the alternative theories of corporate decision making. However, the goal of this text is not to develop a descriptive model of economic decision making but rather to present the theories, techniques, and tools that when applied can lead to an optimal or efficient allocation of the resources of the organization. The extent to which management does not act in a manner consistent with developed principles may be viewed as a constraint on the objective function, for which an opportunity cost may be estimated. Furthermore, our emphasis on the profit-maximization and shareholder wealth-maximization objectives is consistent with the manner in which a wide range of business decisions are made.

Goals in the Public Sector and the Not-For-Profit Enterprise

The value-maximization objective developed for private sector firms is not an appropriate objective in the public sector or in not-for-profit organizations.[21] These organizations pursue a different set of objectives because of the nature of the good or service they supply and the manner in which they are funded.

Not-for-profit (NFP) organizations include performing arts groups, museums, libraries, hospitals, churches, volunteer organizations, cooperatives, credit unions, labor unions, professional societies, foundations, and fraternal organizations. Some of these organizations offer services to a group of clients, such as the patients of a hospital. Others provide services primarily to members, such as the members of a country club or credit union. Finally, some NFP organizations produce public benefits, as does a local symphony or theater company.[22]

---

[21] This section draws heavily on Thomas E. Copeland and Keith V. Smith, "An Overview of Nonprofit Organizations,'" *Journal of Economics and Business* 30, no. 2 (1978).

[22] R. M. Anthony and R. Herzlinger, *Management Control in Non-Profit Organizations* (Home-wood, Ill.: Richard D. Irwin, 1975), chap. 1.

The most important feature that distinguishes NFP organizations from private sector and public (government) sector organizations is their sources of financial support. NFP organizations receive a large percentage of their externally generated funds from voluntary contributions. The greater the proportion of external funds from contributions as a percentage of total revenue, the closer the organization is to being a pure NFP organization. In contrast, the lower the percentage of contributions to total revenue, the closer the organization is to being a business firm or government agency. For example, by this criterion a credit union would be expected to have organizational objectives that are very similar to those of banks, whereas the American Economic Association, a professional association of economists, is more nearly like an NFP organization.

Another distinguishing feature of NFP organizations is their tax-exempt status (this is also true for government agencies). This feature is not sufficient, however, to identify true NFP organizations. Indeed, even if NFP organizations were subject to taxes, few would ever pay taxes because of the propensity to match revenues and costs in normal budgetary periods.

Public sector (government) agencies tend to provide services with a significant *public good* character. Public goods, as compared with private goods, may be consumed by more than one person at the same time, and the transaction cost of charging a market price for a public good exceeds the benefits that are derived from charging the price. Examples of public goods include national defense, services of a lighthouse beacon, and flood control protection. Many goods, such as the performing arts, have both public and private good characteristics.[23] For example, in addition to providing direct (private) benefits to the audience, quality performing arts groups also benefit the local community and local businesses through prestige and a perceived higher quality of life. The closer a good or service is to being a public good, the more likely it is to be provided by the government sector.

Not-for-Profit Objectives

A number of organizational objectives have been suggested for the NFP enterprise. These include the following:

1. Maximization of the quantity and quality of output subject to a break-even budget constraint

2. Utility maximization of the administrators

3. Maximization of cash flows

4. Maximization of the utility (satisfaction) of contributors

For NFP organizations that rely heavily on external contributions, the overriding objective is to satisfy current and prospective contributors. This does not mean that the other objectives are mutually exclusive. It is common to find

---

[23] William J. Baumol and W. G. Bowen, *Performing Arts: The Economic Dilemma* (Cambridge, Mass.: MIT Press, 1966).

an NFP organization that seeks to satisfy its contributors by (1) efficiently managing its resources, (2) increasing its capacity to supply high-quality goods or services, and (3) providing a rewarding work environment for its administrators. As reliance on outside contributors lessens, the other objectives gain importance to the organization.

The Efficiency Objective

Although both the public sector agency and the NFP organization may pursue many objectives, a major focus of economists is on the efficiency dimension of organizational objectives. Whatever set of objectives the organization decides to pursue, these objectives should be pursued in the most resource-efficient fashion.

The model that has been developed to provide a framework for the allocation of public and NFP resources among competing uses has primarily been the benefit-cost analysis model. This model is the analogue to the capital-budgeting model in the private sector. Benefits and costs associated with investments are estimated and discounted by an appropriate discount rate, and projects are evaluated on the basis of the magnitude of the discounted benefits in relation to the costs. Because government and NFP organization spending is normally constrained by a budget ceiling, the criterion actually used in evaluating expenditures for any public purpose may be one of the following:

1. Maximize benefits for given costs.

2. Minimize costs while achieving a fixed level of benefits

3. Maximize net benefits (benefits minus costs)

Keep in mind that future benefits and costs, which are discussed here, must be discounted in the same manner as the private costs and returns, which were discussed in regard to the corporation. Chapter 18 considers the issue of the appropriate public discount rate.

Benefit-cost analysis, as a guide to a more efficient allocation of resources by a public agency or an NFP institution, is only one input necessary to the final decision. It *does* furnish decision makers with the results of a careful analysis of the costs and returns associated with alternative actions. It *does not*, however, incorporate many of the more subjective considerations or less easily quantifiable objectives into the analysis. For example, a benefit-cost analysis does not typically consider the effect of a proposed project on income distribution. Concern for these matters must be introduced at a later stage in the analysis, generally through the political process.

NFP institutions are normally faced with decision problems not markedly different from those of a public agency; they exist to supply some good (or service) in the most efficient manner. An NFP hospital, for example, may seek to provide a certain quantity and quality of medical service to the citizens of a community, given a resource or budget constraint. Decisions about what programs to emphasize (where to allocate funds) should be based on an analysis of benefits that may be generated from competing programs. The identification of specific functional goals or objectives for both governmental and NFP institutions remains a critical problem. In some cases efficiency analyses may help to identify specific goals, whereas in other cases these goals and objectives will be established (often via a political process) before any analysis about how they might best be achieved. Once established, the *normative objective*, which is assumed in this text, is that decision makers seek to achieve the goal in the most efficient manner; that is, with the least possible expenditure of real resources. The tools and techniques presented in the following chapters are developed with this purpose in mind. Chapter 18 offers an in-depth discussion of the problems associated with resource allocation and the efficient achievement of objectives in public agencies and NFP institutions.

Other Goals in Public and Not-for-Profit Enterprises

Just as there was reason to believe that a divergence existed between the efficiency criterion for the private firm and the descriptive goals or objectives the private firm actually pursued, there is equally good reason to expect that the objectives of the managers of NFP enterprises, civil servants, and appointees of government agencies are not necessarily consistent with the efficiency criterion we have identified. Much of the discussion presented earlier concerning the divergence of interests between the stockholders and the managers in private corporations is equally applicable to the managers of NFP enterprises and the civil servants of public agencies. Whereas the interests of the general public are oriented primarily toward the fulfillment of the efficiency objective in providing any government service, there are substantial reasons why this objective may not be realized.

One reason is the lack of a clear measure of performance for most public and NFP enterprises. Cost-benefit analyses and cost-effectiveness studies give an insight into the efficiency objectives of many types of programs, but the stage of development and the degree of sophistication with which these analyses have been applied vary broadly across different areas of government services. For example, a great deal of progress has been made in the estimation of costs and benefits associated with water resources projects, whereas the estimation of costs and benefits associated with educational investment is in an earlier stage of development. Furthermore, beyond the issue of how resources are to be allocated among competing programs of government service, no consistent monitoring system is available to provide a constant check on performance compared with expectations. In private enterprise, profits and stock prices perform this monitoring task. No such measure is generally present for the NFP enterprise or public agency. As we noted, objectives for NFP organizations are likely to be closely tied to the desires of contributors. Measuring the achievement of these objectives is quite difficult.

The satisficing goal, as proposed by Simon, is also applicable to government and NFP enterprises. Because these managers frequently have no specific objective function to maximize, we may expect managers to offer a level of service that just satisfies those paying for the service (the general public) or those making the contributions to the NFP organization, thereby protecting their job. This leads us to a second possible objective that may be pursued by civil servants and NFP enterprise managers: guaranteeing the long-run survival of the organization. Only by this survival is present and future compensation ensured for the manager. Consequently, we might expect to see agencies and bureaus continuing to exist well beyond their useful life. A further objective, which is tied closely to the long-run survival of the organization, is the objective of maximizing its size. In this way prestige is gained, a sense of personal satisfaction is generated from being associated with a growing and increasingly important organization, and more responsible and better compensated positions become available as the size of the organization increases. The preoccupation with both long-run survival and growth of the NFP or government enterprise may be even more likely than that existing in private enterprise because the size of the budget, the number of employees, the amount of office space, and so forth may all become surrogates for the measure of performance of the organization. These factors are quickly measured and may be easily monitored over time. Unlike the private corporation, where profit is generally recognized as one measure of the performance of the firm, the public agency or NFP institution rarely has a clear, easily measured criterion that serves as a performance measure. Under these circumstances, it is not surprising that a goal such as long-run survival or size maximization could play a leading role in guiding the decisions made in the organization.[24]

Summary

- Managerial economics is the application of economic theory and analytical tools to decision-making problems faced by private, not-for-profit, and public institutions.

- Managerial economics draws on microeconomic theory and macroeconomic models to assist managers in making optimal resource allocation decisions.

- Economic profit is defined as the difference between total revenues and total economic costs. Economic costs include a normal rate of return on the capital contributed by the firm's owners. Economic profits exist to compensate investors for the risk they assume, because of temporary disequilibrium conditions that may occur in a market, because of the existence of monopoly power, and as a reward to firms that are especially successful in innovation or are managed in a highly efficient manner.

- As an overall objective of the firm, the shareholder wealth-maximization model is very appealing. It is flexible enough to account for differential levels of risk and timing differences in the receipt of benefits and the

---

[24] A more complete discussion of these issues is in William Niskanen, *Bureaucracy and Representative Government* (Chicago: Aldine, 1971); Gordon Tullock, *The Politics of Bureaucracy* (Washington, D. C.: Public Affairs Press, 1965); and Barry P. Keating and Maryann O. Keating, *Not-For-Profit* (Glen Ridge, N.J.: Thomas Horton, 1980).

incurring of future costs. Since shareholder wealth is defined in terms of the value of the stock, this goal provides a precise measure of performance, which is free from the problems associated with using various accounting measures.

- Managers may not always behave in a manner consistent with the wealth-maximization objective. The costs associated with these deviations from the objective are often called *agency costs*. Other objectives that may be pursued by managers are the maximization of the utility of managers, size maximization, long-run survival, and satisficing.

- Not-for-profit enterprises exist to supply a good or service desired by their primary contributors. Public sector organizations often provide services having significant public-good characteristics; that is, they may be consumed by more than one person at a time with little additional cost, and the transaction cost of charging a market price for the good or service exceeds the benefits that are derived by charging the price.

- Regardless of their specific objectives, both public and private institutions should seek to furnish their goods or services in the most resource-efficient manner. The marginal decision rules from the profit-maximization model are often very valuable in this context.

Selected References

Anthony, R. N., and R. Herzlinger. *Management Control in Non-Profit Organizations*. Homewood, Ill.: Richard D. Irwin, 1975.

Anthony, Robert N. "The Trouble with Profit Maximization." *Harvard Business Review* (November–December 1960).

Barnea, Amir, R. Haugen, and L. Senbet. *Agency Problems and Financial Contracting*. Englewood Cliffs, N. J.: Prentice-Hall, 1985.

Baumol, William J. "What Can Economic Theory Contribute to Managerial Economics?" *American Economic Review* (May 1961), pp. 142–46.

Baumol, William J., and W. G. Bowen. *Performing Arts: The Economic Dilemma*. Cambridge, Mass.: MIT Press, 1966.

Berle, Adolf, and Gardiner C. Means. *The Modern Corporation and Private Property*. New York: Macmillan, 1932.

Copeland, Thomas E., and Keith V. Smith, "An Overview of Nonprofit Organizations." *Journal of Economics and Business* 30, no. 2 (1978).

Cyert, Richard M., and James G. March. *A Behavioral Theory of the Firm*. Englewood Cliffs, N. J.: Prentice-Hall, 1963.

Friedman, Milton. "The Methodology of Positive Economics." In *Essays in Positive Economics*. Chicago: University of Chicago Press, 1953.

Harris, Robert G. "The Values of Economic Theory in Management Education." *American Economic Review* (May 1984), pp. 122–126.

Jensen, Michael C., and R. S. Ruback. "The Market for Corporate Control: The Scientific Evidence." *Journal of Financial Economics* (April 1983), pp. 5–50.

Keating, Barry P., and Maryann O. Keating. *Not-For-Profit*. Glen Ridge, N.J.: Thomas Horton 1980.

Penrose, Edith. *The Theory of the Growth of the Firm*. Oxford: Basil Blackwell & Mott, 1959.

Rappaport, Alfred. *Creating Shareholder Value: The New Standard for Business Perform-ance*. New York: Free Press, 1986.

Reid, Samuel Richardson. *Mergers, Managers and the Economy*. New York: McGraw-Hill, 1968.

Research and Policy Committee. Committee for Economic Development. *Social Responsi-bilities of Business Corporations*. New York: CED, 1971.

Weisbrod, Burton A. *The Voluntary Nonprofit Sector*. Lexington, Mass.: Lexington Books, 1977.

Discussion Questions

1. What is the relationship between the field of managerial economics and the broader fields of microeconomics and macroeconomics?

2. Frequently we hear the argument that business profits are too high. What is meant by a firm's profitability? What factors should be considered when evaluating the level of profit earned by a particular industry or firm?

3. Economic theory is often developed around the concept that firms seek to maximize profits. Compare and contrast the profit maximization objective with the objective of maximizing shareholder wealth.

4. What are the opportunity costs associated with your decision to pursue a college degree? What are the explicit costs associated with pursuing a college degree?

5. What is the difference between accounting profits and economic profits?

6. During 1987, the drug industry earned an average return on net worth of 26.9 percent. In contrast, the oil and gas industry earned an average return on net worth of 9.5 percent. The railroad industry earned a 7.0 percent average return on net worth during 1987.
   a. What conclusions, if any, can be drawn about the risk of each of these industries?
   b. Evaluate the rationale for the windfall profits tax paid by the oil and gas industry in light of these figures.
   c. Which theory or theories of profit do you think best explain(s) the performance of the drug industry?

7. What features of the shareholder wealth-maximization goal of firm performance make it operationally superior to the profit-maximization objective?

8. Performance of a firm is often measured by an accounting ratio, such as the return on equity. Return on equity is defined as the ratio of net income after tax to common stockholders' equity. What are some of the limitations of using the ratio for making performance comparisons between firms?

9. Try to define, in as operational a manner as possible, the objectives that your college or university seeks to pursue.
   a. How may success in achieving these objectives be measured?
   b. To what extent do the objectives of various subunits of your college or university complement (or contradict) each other?
   c. Who are the major constituencies served by your university? What role do they play in the formation of these objectives?
   d. You may want to talk with some of your school's administrators and compare their views on the college's goals and objectives with your own.

10. Determine the major explicit and implicit constraints that are imposed on either the college or university that you are attending or the organization within which you are employed.

11. Why do organizations frequently diverge from "optimal" performance in a normative sense and pursue some objective other than (or in addition to) the efficiency objective? Would you expect a greater divergence from the efficiency objective in
    a. Small individual proprietorships?
    b. Large corporations?
    c. Public corporations?
    d. Other government agencies?
    Why?

12. Apply the decision-making model developed in this chapter to your decision to attend college or graduate school.

13. Discuss some areas where economic decision models developed for private sector firms may be fruitfully applied in not-for-profit organizations, such as the operation of a local symphony orchestra.

14. In the context of the shareholder wealth maximization model of the firm, what is the expected impact of each of the following events on the value of the firm?
    a. New foreign competitors enter the market.
    b. Strict pollution control requirements are implemented by the government.
    c. A previously nonunion work force votes to unionize.
    d. The rate of inflation increases substantially.
    e. A major technological breakthrough is achieved by the firm, reducing its costs of production.

15. Compare the goals and objectives of a typical business firm, such as AT & T, with those of your local United Way agency. How are they different? In what ways are they the same?

16. Are agency costs likely to be higher in
    a. A sole proprietorship or a public corporation?
    b. An all equity-financed corporation or a corporation that makes extensive use of debt financing?

17. During 1988, Apple Computer was projected (by *Value Line*) to earn a 32 percent return on net worth. What factors should be considered when judging the adequacy of this level of profits for Apple's investors?

18. In early 1988, Ford Motor Company had nearly $10 billion in cash awaiting investment. Discuss the pros and cons of using these funds to (1) acquire another firm, or (2) increase distributions to shareholders.

Problems

1. Sisneros has just completed his MBA degree and is considering pursuing doctoral (Ph.D.) studies in economics. If Sisneros took a job immediately after his MBA, he could earn $50,000 during the first year, with an anticipated raise of $5,000 per year over the next four years. If Sisneros pursues the doctorate, four more years of school are required. Sisneros has been offered an assistantship paying $14,000 per year plus tuition. Books and computer purchases needed for his study will cost an average of $2,000 per year. These costs would not be incurred if Sisneros took a job immediately.

Upon graduation, Sisneros expects an annual income level of $65,000 during his first year of teaching. The growth rate in Sisneros' teaching salary is expected to equal the growth rate of his income if he had not pursued the Ph.D. How should Sisneros evaluate his decision to pursue a Ph.D.? What other information do you need? What factors other than salary should be considered?

2. The ARA Railroad owns a piece of land along one of its right-of-ways. The land originally cost ARA $100,000. ARA is considering building a new maintenance facility on this land. ARA has determined that the proposal to build the new facility is acceptable if the original cost of the land is used in the analysis, but the proposal does not meet the railroad's project acceptance criteria if the land cost is above $500,000. An investor has recently offered ARA $1 million for the land. Should ARA build the maintenance facility at this location?

3. Howard Bowen is a large cotton farmer. The land and machinery he owns has a current market value of $4,000,000. Bowen owes his local bank $3,000,000. Last year Bowen sold $5,000,000 worth of cotton. His variable operating costs were $4,500,000; accounting depreciation was $40,000, although the actual decline in value of Bowen's machinery was $60,000 last year. Bowen paid himself a salary of $50,000, which is not considered part of his variable operating costs. Interest on his bank loan was $400,000. If Bowen worked for another farmer or a local manufacturer his annual income would be about $30,000. Bowen can invest any funds that would be derived, if the farm were sold, to earn 10 percent annually. Ignore taxes.

a. Compute Bowen's accounting profits.
b. Compute Bowen's economic profits.

Fundamental Economic Concepts 2

Managerial economic analysis is based largely on a few fundamental economic concepts. Four of the most important concepts are marginal analysis, equilibrium analysis, the time value of money, and the trade-offs that must be made between risk and return. Marginal analysis tools, which are derived from an understanding of marginal, average, and total relationships, are central when a decision maker is seeking to optimize some objective, such as profits or shareholder wealth. Equilibrium analysis is valuable in understanding a wide range of pricing and production decisions made by firms. The time value of money concept is important because many economic decisions result in returns and costs (such as income, cash flows, and operating costs) that occur at different points in time. The time value of money concept provides a consistent way to compare these returns and costs. Finally, risk-return analysis is important to an understanding of the many trade-offs which decision makers must make as they plan new products, increases in capacity, pricing changes, and so on. These fundamental concepts are cornerstones to further analysis in the managerial economics arena. By understanding and applying these fundamental concepts, a manager will be able to make decisions that contribute to the ultimate goal of efficient resource allocation and shareholder wealth maximization. In this chapter the first three of these fundamental concepts are discussed. Risk-return analysis is discussed in Chapter 3.

Marginal Analysis

Marginal analysis is one of the most pervasive and useful concepts of economic decision making. Resource allocation decisions are typically expressed in terms of the marginal conditions that must be satisfied to attain an optimal solution. The familiar profit-maximization rule for the firm of setting output at the point where "marginal cost equals marginal revenue" is one such example. Long-term investment decisions (capital expenditures) are also made using marginal analysis decision rules. If the expected return from an investment project (that is, the *marginal return* to the firm) exceeds the cost of funds that must be acquired to finance the project (the *marginal cost* of capital), then the project should be undertaken. Following this important marginal decision rule leads to the maximization of shareholder wealth.

Glossary of New Terms

Marginal analysis
A basis for making various economic decisions which analyzes the additional (marginal) benefits derived from a particular decision and compares them with the additional (marginal) costs incurred.

Demand function
Describes the relationship that exists during some period of time between the number of units of a good or service that consumers are willing to buy and a given set of conditions that influence the willingness to purchase, such as price, income level, and advertising.

Supply function
Describes the relationship that exists during some period of time between the number of units of a good or service that producers are willing to place on the market and a given set of conditions that influence the willingness to place those units on the

(Cont'd on next page)

Glossary of New Terms (cont'd)

market, such as price, the prices of the resources used to produce the commodity, and the available technology which can be used to produce the commodity.

Present value
The value today of a future amount of money or a series of future payments evaluated at the appropriate discount rate.

Annuity
The payment or receipt of a series of equal amounts of money per period for a specified amount of time.

Discount rate
The rate of interest used in the process of finding present values (discounting).

In the marginal analysis framework, resource allocation decisions are made by comparing the marginal benefits of a change in the level of an activity with the marginal costs of the change. A change in the level of an economic activity is desirable and should be undertaken as long as the marginal benefits exceed the marginal costs. Therefore, in decisions involving the expansion of an economic activity, the optimal level occurs at the point where the marginal benefits are equal to the marginal costs. If we define *net marginal return* as the *difference* between marginal benefits and marginal costs, then an equivalent optimality condition is that the level of the activity should be increased to the point where the net marginal return is zero.

The use of marginal analysis in optimization problems can be illustrated with an example. Economic relationships can be presented using tabular, graphic, and algebraic frameworks. Let us first use a tabular presentation. Suppose that the total profit π_T of a firm is a function of the number of units of output produced Q, as shown in columns 1 and 2 of Table 2.1. Marginal profit, which represents the change in total profit resulting from a one-unit increase in output, is shown in column 3 of the table. (A Δ is used to represent a "change in" some variable.) The marginal profit $\Delta\pi(Q)$ of any level of output Q is calculated by taking the difference between the total profit at this level $\pi_T(Q)$ and at one unit below this level $\pi_T(Q-1)$.[1] In comparing the marginal and total profit functions, we note that for increasing output levels, the marginal profit values remain positive as long as the total profit function is increasing. Only when the total profit function begins decreasing—that is, at $Q = 10$ units—does the marginal profit become negative. The average profit function values $\pi_A(Q)$, shown in column 4 of Table 2.1, are obtained by dividing the total profit figure $\pi_T(Q)$ by the output level Q. In comparing the marginal and the average profit function values, we see that the average profit function $\pi_A(Q)$ is increasing as long as the marginal profit is greater than the average profit; that is, up to $Q = 7$ units. Beyond an output level of $Q = 7$ units, the marginal profit is less than the average profit and the average profit function values are decreasing.

By examining the total profit function $\pi_T(Q)$ in Table 2.1, we see that profit is maximized at an output level of $Q = 9$ units. Given that the objective is to maximize total profit, then the optimal output decision would be to produce 9 units. If the marginal analysis decision rule discussed earlier in this section is used, the same (optimal) decision is obtained. Applying the rule to this problem, the firm would expand production as long as the *net* marginal return—that is, marginal profit—is positive. From column 3 of Table 2.1, we can see that the marginal profit is positive for output levels up to $Q = 9$. Therefore, the marginal profit decision rule would indicate that 9 units should be produced—the same decision that was obtained from the total profit function.

The relationships among the total, marginal, and average profit functions and the optimal output decision can also be represented graphically. A set of *continuous* profit functions, analogous to those presented previously in Table 2.1 for *discrete* integer values of output (Q), is shown in Figure 2.1. At the break-even output level Q_1, both total profits and average profits are zero. The

---

[1] The marginal profit of the 0th unit—that is, $Q = 0$—is defined as zero.

Table 2.1
Total, Marginal, and Average Profit Relationships

(1) Number of Units of Output per Unit of Time Q	(2) Total Profit ($) $\pi_T(Q)$	(3) Marginal Profit ($/unit) $\Delta \pi(Q) = \pi_T(Q) - \pi_T(Q-1)$	(4) Average Profit ($/unit) $\pi_A(Q) = \pi_T(Q)/Q$
0	−200	0	—
1	−150	50	−150.00
2	− 25	125	− 12.50
3	200	225	66.67
4	475	275	118.75
5	775	300	155.00
6	1,075	300	179.17
7	1,325	250	189.29
8	1,475	150	184.38
9	1,500	25	166.67
10	1,350	−150	135.00

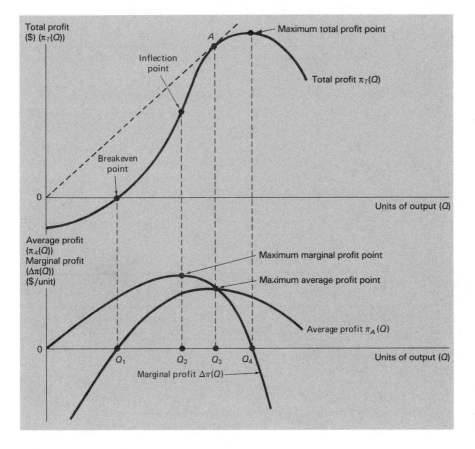

Figure 2.1
Total, Average, and Marginal Profit Functions

marginal profit function, which represents the *slope* of the total profit function, takes on its maximum value at an output of Q_2 units. This point corresponds to the *inflection point*. Below the inflection point, total profits are increasing at an increasing rate, and hence marginal profits are increasing. Above the inflection point, up to an output level Q_4, total profits are increasing at a decreasing rate and consequently marginal profits are decreasing. The average profit function, which represents the slope of a straight line drawn from the origin 0 to each point on the total profit function, takes on its maximum value at an output of Q_3 units. The average profit necessarily equals the marginal profit at this point. This follows because the slope of the 0A line, which defines the average profit, is also equal to the slope of the total profit function at point A, which defines the marginal profit. Finally, total profit is maximized at an output of Q_4 units. Beyond Q_4 the total profit function is decreasing, and consequently the marginal profit function takes on negative values.

Application of the previously discussed marginal analysis decision rule to the marginal profit function in Figure 2.1 indicates that profits are maximized by expanding output to the point where marginal profit is zero; that is, Q_4 units. Again the marginal analysis decision rule yields an optimal solution.

Another example of the application of marginal analysis is the capital budgeting expenditure decision problem facing a firm. For example, consider the Deacon Corporation that has the following schedule of potential investment projects (all assumed to be of equal risk) available to it:

Project	Investment Required ($ million)	Expected Rate of Return	Cumulative Investment ($ million)
A	$25.0	27.0%	$25.0
B	15.0	24.0	40.0
C	40.0	21.0	80.0
D	35.0	18.0	115.0
E	12.0	15.0	127.0
F	20.0	14.0	147.0
G	**18.0**	**13.0**	**165.0**
H	13.0	11.0	178.0
I	7.0	8.0	185.0

In addition, the Deacon Corporation has estimated the cost of acquiring the funds needed to finance these investment projects as follows:

Block of Funds ($ million)	Cost of Capital	Cumulative Funds Raised ($ million)
First $50.0	10.0%	$50.0
Next 25.0	10.5	75.0
Next 40.0	11.0	115.0
Next 50.0	**12.2**	**165.0**
Next 20.0	14.5	185.0

The expected rate of return on the projects listed above can be thought of as the marginal (or incremental) return available to Deacon as it undertakes each additional investment project. Similarly, the cost of capital schedule may be thought of as the marginal cost of acquiring the needed funds. Following the marginal analysis rules means that Deacon should invest in additional projects as long as the expected rate of return on the project exceeds the marginal cost of capital funds needed to finance the project.

It is clear that project A, which offers an expected return of 27 percent and requires an outlay of $25 million, is acceptable because the marginal return exceeds the marginal cost of capital (10.0 percent for the first $50 million of funds raised by Deacon). In fact, an examination of the tables indicates that projects A through G all meet the marginal analysis test because the marginal return from each of these projects exceeds the marginal cost of capital funds needed to finance these projects. In contrast, projects H and I should not be undertaken because they offer returns of 11 and 8 percent respectively, compared with a marginal cost of capital of 14.5 percent for the $20 million in funds needed to finance these projects.

In summary, the marginal analysis concept instructs the decision maker to determine the additional (marginal) costs and additional (marginal) benefits associated with a proposed action. *If the marginal benefits exceed the marginal costs* (that is, if the net marginal benefits are positive), the action should be taken. The application of the marginal analysis concept to the capital budgeting decision is illustrated in more detail in Chapter 17.

In Chapter 4, the tool of differential calculus is used to illustrate further the marginal analysis concept and its decision-making implications. The marginal analysis concept is applied throughout the book when analyzing decisions involving demand, production, cost, capital budgeting, cost-benefit, and utility analysis. By adhering to the principles of the marginal analysis concept, managers will find it easier to efficiently allocate resources and maximize shareholder wealth.

Equilibrium Analysis: Supply and Demand Relationships

Managers are repeatedly called upon to make resource allocations in their firms. For these decisions to be consistent with the objective of shareholder wealth maximization, it is imperative that managers have a solid understanding of the forces which determine equilibrium prices and quantities in the marketplace. These market forces are represented by the supply and demand functions for a particular good or service. In this section, we develop the concepts of the supply and demand functions at an intuitive level. A more rigorous development of these concepts takes place later in the text. Then we show how the supply and demand functions interact to create an equilibrium price—a price from which there is no incentive for buyers and sellers to move. Finally, we show the effects of changes in the factors affecting supply and demand on the equilibrium level of price and quantity.

The Concept of Demand

The *demand* function for a good may be defined as the various quantities of that good which consumers are willing and able to purchase during a particular period of time at all possible prices, while holding constant the effects of all other factors influencing this willingness to purchase. These other factors may include (1) the prices of related goods, (2) consumer tastes and preferences, (3) consumer income levels, (4) expectations about price changes, and (5) advertising expenditures. In analyzing demand relationships it is often useful to *hold constant* these other factors and to focus on the relationship between quantity demanded and price.

Normally we think of the quantity demanded varying inversely with price; that is, at higher prices consumers will demand less of a particular commodity and at lower prices they will demand more, while holding constant the effects of other factors. When we use the term *demand*, we are referring to the entire demand curve or schedule. For example, in Figure 2.2, the curve labeled DD may be thought of as the demand for some good or service. To say that demand has increased is equivalent to saying that the entire demand curve has moved or shifted. Thus, curve D_1D_1 represents an increase in demand from the initial demand curve represented by DD. It can be seen that at any price, the quantity demanded will be greater on curve D_1D_1 than on curve DD. A shift in the demand curve from the DD to D_1D_1 may represent an increase in consumer income levels, a growing consumer preference for the good in question (such as an increase in the popularity of Japanese cars relative to American cars), an increase in advertising expenditures, or any factor other than a change in price.

Movement along the demand curve is usually referred to as a change in *quantity demanded*. As can be seen in Figure 2.2, when the price declines from P^* to P', the quantity demanded increases from Q^* to Q'_D. For example, much of the increase in the sales of microcomputers can be attributed to a decline in the price of these computers.

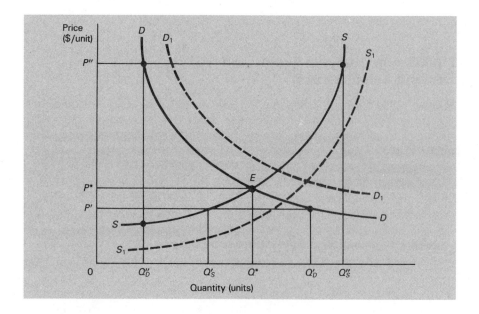

Figure 2.2
Supply and Demand Equilibrium Conditions

In summary, quantity demanded normally is inversely related to price. At higher prices consumers will normally demand less of a good or service; at lower prices consumers will normally demand more of a good or service. Movement *along* a demand curve is often referred to as *a change in the quantity demanded*, while holding constant the effects of factors other than price that affect demand. Movement *of* the entire demand curve is often referred to as *a change in demand*. Demand curve movement is caused by factors other than price that influence the desire of consumers to buy a particular product.

The Concept of Supply

The supply function of a good or service is defined as the quantities of that commodity that sellers are willing to make available to purchasers at all possible prices during some period of time. Some of the most important factors which influence the willingness of suppliers to offer goods or services to the market are (1) the price of the commodity; (2) the prices of the resources that must be used to produce the commodity, such as land, labor, and capital resources; and (3) the technology available to produce the product.

By holding constant the prices of resources used to produce the commodity and the technology available for production, we can represent the supply curve as the relationship between the quantity producers are willing to offer for sale and the various prices that could be charged. At lower price levels, less of a commodity is offered for sale because fewer producers find it profitable to sell the product at the low price. In contrast, as prices increase producers are willing to sell more of the product because their potential profits are enhanced as a result of this higher price (if the effects of all other factors are held constant). Thus, in Figure 2.2 we see that a positive relationship exists between price and quantity supplied as indicated by the curve labeled SS.

Movement *along* the supply curve is referred to as a *change in the quantity supplied*. In contrast, a movement *of* the entire supply curve is referred to as a *change in supply*. For example, curve S_1S_1 represents an increase in supply. It can be seen that for any price, the quantity that producers are willing to supply is greater on curve S_1S_1 than it is on curve SS. This supply increase may reflect a technological advance that has lowered the cost of production, a reduction in the cost of one or more of the inputs in the production of the commodity, or simply an increase in the number of firms willing to produce the good or service in question.

Equilibrium Conditions

The intersection of the supply (SS) and demand (DD) curves at point E reflects an equilibrium price (P*) and quantity (Q*). This is the price and quantity that should prevail in the marketplace, given these supply and demand curves. The reason why this is true can be demonstrated with the following examples. Suppose that the market price were temporarily at a price *below* P*. This price is represented by P′ in Figure 2.2. In this situation, consumers would demand Q'_D, but producers would only be willing to supply Q'_S. Since the quantity demanded exceeds the quantity supplied, some consumers will attempt to bid the price up. This results in upward price pressure in the direction of the equilibrium level.

For example, during much of the decade of the 1980s, limits were set on the number of Japanese autos that could be imported into the United States. The list prices of these vehicles were often set below market equilibrium levels, which resulted in many dealers charging prices of $500 to $2,000 *above* the list price. Thus, the willingness of consumers to purchase more than was being supplied at the sticker prices caused upward price pressure toward an equilibrium price level, where the quantity demanded equals the quantity supplied.

Similarly, if the price is temporarily set *above* the equilibrium price P*, price pressure would be downward toward the equilibrium. For example, at a price P″, the quantity demanded Q_D'' will be less than the quantity producers are willing to supply Q_S''. Because of this surplus of supply, buyers will put pressure on sellers to lower prices. Thus, there is pressure for the price to return to an equilibrium level.

As a current example, during much of the mid-to-late 1980s, the prices American car manufacturers and dealers placed on American-made cars were often perceived as being too high, relative to the demand for these vehicles. As a result, inventories of unsold cars built up at dealers. In order to move those inventories, manufacturers resorted to a seemingly endless stream of cash rebates and special financing offers. Manufacturers had misread the market demand and produced (supplied) more cars than consumers were willing to purchase at the listed prices. The resulting rebates brought the quantity demanded in line with the quantity supplied. At the same time, many manufacturers reduced output in order to avoid future occurrences of this problem.

In summary, the intersection of the supply and demand curves represents an equilibrium level of price and quantity. Once this equilibrium has been established, there is no economic incentive for consumers or producers to move from this position unless the other conditions affecting supply and demand cause a shift in the supply and demand curves.

Effects of an Increase or Decrease in Demand

The equilibrium level of price and quantity was determined in Figure 2.2 by the intersection of the current supply and demand curves. This equilibrium point is of some interest in its own right. The primary use of supply and demand analysis, however, is to examine the effects of changes in the factors affecting the supply and demand curves on the equilibrium price and quantity. The method of *comparative statics* in economics compares the beginning and final equilibrium points resulting from a change in supply and /or demand. The process of *how* the final equilibrium point is achieved is the concern of *economic dynamics*. The study of economic dynamics is beyond the scope of this book.

Consider, for example, the situation in Figure 2.3. The initial demand curve is DD and the supply curve is SS. At equilibrium (point E) the price is P* and the quantity demanded is Q*. Now suppose that there is suddenly an *increase in demand* caused by a change in consumer tastes or preferences, an increase in consumer income levels, an increase in the price of a substitute good, or some

Economic Analysis and Managerial Efficiency

USING LAB EXPERIMENTS TO TEST BASIC ECONOMIC PRINCIPLES

Adam Smith's theory of the operation of free markets has been a cornerstone of laissez-faire economics for over 200 years. In a free market, individuals seek to exchange goods and services in order to maximize their individual profits. The prices which result from the profit maximizing behavior of individual producing and consuming units are equilibrium prices, which give the most people the most profit. Although this fundamental economic concept has been widely accepted, there was very little direct empirical support for this proposition.

In order to test such a key economic concept, a growing number of economists have devised carefully controlled lab experiments.* One such experiment, originally devised by Professor Vernon Smith, is designed to simulate trading on the New York Stock Exchange. A group of students are given an opportunity to earn real money based upon the profit they make from trading. Half of the students are designated as buyers and half as sellers. In one trial of this exercise, the seller group is handed a slip of paper indicating the cost of each of two units of a commodity. The costs in this first trial range from $2.40 to $5. The buyer group is given similar slips indicating the prices at which they can resell any units they buy. The prices range up to $5.60. The higher the price the more profit the sellers make. The lower the price,

the more profits the buyers make. The students are not told that if all transactions take place at $4 per unit, the equilibrium price which brings supply and demand into balance, they will collectively make the greatest profit.

Trading begins as buyers and sellers shout out prices at which they are willing to transact business. The first trade is made at $3.25. After 15 minutes of transactions, the trading price is $3.90. Within another 30 minutes the price invariably settles at the equilibrium of $4, as predicted by theory. When the experiment is repeated with new slips of paper representing an increase in buyer's demands, the trading price converges on a new higher equilibrium. Similarly, on later trials in which there is an increased supply of low cost units, the trading price drops rapidly. In all repetitions, the price converges on the theoretical equilibrium price very rapidly.

Experiments such as these are being carried out by many economists to test the impact of such propositions as (1) whether the type of market used by traders (posted prices vs. open auction) affects market prices; (2) the reason why winning bids for offshore oil leases frequently lose substantial sums of money on their leases; and (3) the impact of creating a market for landing slots at airports.

These controlled economic experiments have confirmed basic economic principles and have provided valuable insights into the effects of market structure, the availability of information, and alternative pricing strategies on the functioning of markets.

Question

1. What do you think the effect would be of instituting a market for landing and take-off slots at airports by permitting airlines to trade the slots as if they were commodities?

*For a discussion of experimental economics, see H. Taylor, "Experimental Economics: Putting Markets Under the Microscope," *Business Review*, Federal Reserve Bank of Philadelphia (March–April, 1988):pp 15–25. See also Jerry Bishop, "Lab Experiments Test Old Economic Rules, Raising New Questions," *Wall Street Journal* 25 November 1986.

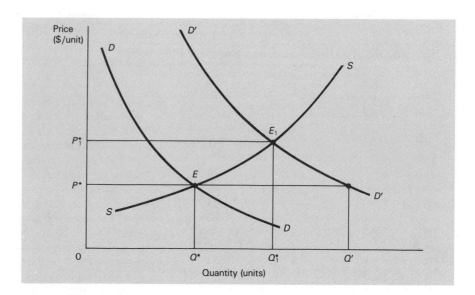

Figure 2.3
**Effect of an
Increase in
Demand**

similar factor. The demand curve DD will shift *upward to the right* and become D'D', and a new equilibrium will be established at point E_1, with a price of P_1^* and a quantity Q_1^*.

How is this new equilibrium established? When demand shifts from DD to D'D'; consumers will demand Q' units of the commodity, but suppliers only will want to supply Q* units at the current price P*. Thus, there will be pressure for a price increase due to the excess demand relative to supply. The price will ultimately be bid up to the new equilibrium level P_1^*, and a new equilibrium quantity will be supplied and consumed at Q_1^*.

Thus, an increase in demand leads to an increase in both the equilibrium price and quantity. Similarly, a decrease in demand can be expected to lead to a decrease in the equilibrium price and quantity. For example, if the Soviet Union experiences an especially poor grain harvest, it will be forced to buy grain on the world market. From the perspective of an American farmer, this is an increase in the demand for U.S. grain and it causes a shift in the demand curve upward and to the right. The effect of this increase in demand can be expected to be a higher market price for American grain and a greater level of output.

In contrast, if the campaign of the Mothers Against Drunk Driving is successful in raising public awareness of the problems associated with drunk driving and increasing legal enforcement of drunk driving laws, it is conceivable that the demand for alcoholic beverages will decline. Holding constant the effects of all other factors influencing demand, this heightened awareness of drunken driving may lead to a lower equilibrium price and quantity for alcoholic beverages.

In summary, while holding constant the effects of all other factors, an *increase* in demand leads to a new equilibrium point where both the equilibrium price and quantity are *higher* than they were at the original equilibrium point. In contrast, a *decrease* in demand results in a new equilibrium point where price and quantity are *lower* than they were at the original equilibrium point.

Effects of an Increase or Decrease in Supply

An increase in supply can be represented by a shift in the supply curve to the right. For example, in Figure 2.4 the initial equilibrium point E occurs at the intersection of the initial supply curve SS and the initial demand curve DD. Supply may increase because of many factors including a change in technology, such as the development of the computer chip that greatly increases the supply of microcomputers; a change in the amount of an available resource, such as a major oil discovery; or a change in the price or quantity of a related good, such as an increase in the price of cotton, which would surely increase the supply of cottonseed oil.

As a result of these increases in supply, a new supply curve is established, such as $S'S'$, and a new equilibrium price P_1^* and quantity Q_1^* is established at point E_1. This new equilibrium comes about because at the old price P^* the quantity demanded Q^* fell short of the quantity that producers were willing to supply Q'. In order for suppliers to move this "excess" product, prices have to be reduced until a new equilibrium point is established where the quantity demanded just equals the quantity supplied.

The rules of supply and demand analysis affect all markets, including the market for drugs. When cocaine prices increased dramatically in the early 1980s, huge crops of coca leaf, the raw material used in the production of cocaine, were planted in the producing countries. As these plants reached maturity, there were record harvests. As a result, the price of the raw crop declined by as much as 80 percent from its historically high levels. Although U.S. demand for cocaine also increased substantially, demand did not keep pace with supply. In 1983–84, a gram of 35 percent pure cocaine cost between $100 and $125. In 1985, the price declined to $100, but purity rose to about 55 percent. In 1987, the price declined to a low $50 with purity as high as 75 percent. Thus, by 1987 the marketplace had dramatically squeezed the profits of cocaine producers.

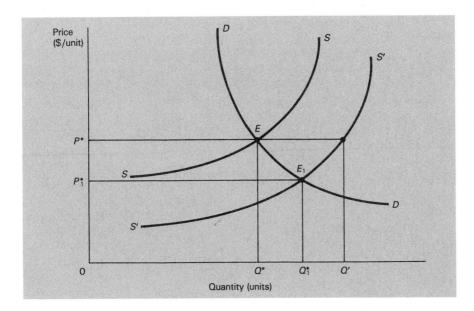

Figure 2.4
Effect of an Increase in Supply

In summary, while holding constant the effects of all other factors, an *increase* in supply results in a new equilibrium point where the price is *lower* and the quantity is *greater* than they were at the original equilibrium point. In contrast, a *decrease* in supply results in a new equilibrium point with a *higher* price and *lower* quantity than those at the original equilibrium point.

The Time Value of Money

Many economic decisions involve benefits and costs that are expected to occur at different future points in time. For example, the construction of a new office complex requires an immediate outlay of cash and results in a stream of expected cash inflows (benefits) over many future years. In order to determine if the expected future cash inflows are sufficient to justify the initial outlay, we must have a way to compare cash flows occurring at different points in time. Also, recall from Chapter 1 that the value of a firm is equal to the discounted (or present) value of all expected future (cash or equivalent) distributions (primarily dividends). These future distributions are discounted at a rate of return. consistent with the risk of the expected future cash flows. When future cash flows are more certain, the discount rate used is lower, resulting in a higher present value of the firm, *all other things being equal*. Conversely, when future cash flows are riskier or more uncertain, they are discounted at a higher rate, resulting in a lower present value of the firm, *all other things being equal*.

An explicit solution to the problem of comparing the benefits and costs of an economic transaction that occur at different points in time requires answers to the following kinds of questions: Is $1 to be received one year from today worth less than $1 in hand today? If so, why is it worth less? How much less is it worth?

The answers to these questions depend on the alternative uses available for the dollar between today and one year from today. Suppose the dollar can be invested in a guaranteed savings account paying a 6 percent annual rate of return (interest rate). The $1 invested today will return $1(1.06) = $1.06 one year from today. To receive exactly $1 one year from today, only $1/(1.06) = $.943 would have to be invested in the account today. Given the opportunity to invest at a 6 percent rate of return, we see that $1 to be received one year from today is indeed worth less than $1 in hand today, its worth being only $.943. Thus, the existence of opportunities to invest the dollar at positive rates of return makes $1 to be received at any future point in time worth less than $1 in hand today.[2] This is what is meant by the *time value of money*. The investor's required rate of return is called the *discount* rate.

---

[2] In this analysis we are abstracting from price level considerations. Changes in the level of prices (the value of the dollar in terms of the quantity of goods and services it will buy) can also affect the worth of the dollar. In theory, future price increases (or decreases) that are *anticipated* by the market will be reflected in the interest rate.

Present Value of a Single Payment

Let us generalize this result for any future series of cash flows and any interest rate. Assume that the opportunity exists to invest at a compound rate of r percent per annum. Then the *present value* (value today) of $1 to be received at the end of year n, discounted at r percent, is

$$PV = \frac{1}{(1+r)^n} \qquad [2.1]$$

For example, if an opportunity exists to invest at a compound rate of return of 12 percent, then the present value of $1 to be received four years ($n = 4$) from today is

$$PV = \frac{1}{(1+.12)^4}$$

$$= \frac{1}{1.574}$$

$$= \$.6355$$

As we see in Table 2.2, investing $.6355 today at an interest rate of 12 percent per annum will give $1 at the end of four years. Rather than performing these calculations (Equation 2.1) every time we need a present value, a present value table can be used to look up the quantity desired.

Table 4 at the end of the book contains the present values at various rates of return of $1 to be received at the end of various time periods. If we look up the present value, discounted at 12 percent, of $1 to be received in four years, we see that it is equal to $.6355—the same value as was calculated above. The present value of any amount (A_n) to be received at the end of n years, discounted at r percent, is

$$PV = \frac{A_n}{(1+r)^n} \qquad [2.2]$$

For example, the present value of $1,000(= A_4) to be received at the end of four years, discounted at 12 percent, is equal to $1,000(.63552) = $635.52.

Year	Return Received at End of Year	Value of Investment at End of Year
0 (present)	—	$.6355 ← Initial amount invested
1	.6355(.12) = $0.762	.6355 + .0762 = .7117
2	.7117(.12) = .0854	.7117 + .0854 = .7971
3	.7971(.12) = .0957	.7971 + .0957 = .8928
4	.8928(.12) = .1072	.8928 + .1072 = 1.000

Table 2.2
Present Value of $1 to Be Received at the End of 4 Years

Present Value of a Series of Equal Payments (Annuity)

The present value of a series of *equal* $1 payments to be received at the end of each of the next n years (an *annuity*), discounted at a rate of r percent, is

$$PV = \frac{1}{(1+r)^1} + \frac{1}{(1+r)^2} + \cdots + \frac{1}{(1+r)^n}$$

$$PV = \sum_{t=1}^{n} \frac{1}{(1+r)^t}$$ [2.3]

For example, the present value of $1 to be received at the end of each of the next four years, discounted at 12 percent, is

$$PV = \sum_{t=1}^{4} \frac{1}{(1+.12)^t}$$

$$= \frac{1}{(1+.12)^1} + \frac{1}{(1+.12)^2} + \frac{1}{(1+.12)^3} + \frac{1}{(1+.12)^4}$$

$$= .89286 + .79719 + .71178 + .63552 = \$3.0374$$

As shown in Table 2.3, investing $3.0374 today at 12 percent will return exactly $1 at the end of each of the next four years, with nothing remaining in the account at the end of the fourth year. Again, rather than perform the present value calculations (Equation 2.3), we can use a table to look up the values we need. Table 5 at the end of the book contains the present values at various interest rates of $1 to be received each year for various periods of time. If we look up the present value, discounted at 12 percent, of $1 to be received at the end of each of the next four years, we see that it is equal to $3.0373—the same value calculated above.[3] The present value of an amount A to be received at the end of each of the next n years, discounted at r percent, is

$$PV = \sum_{t=1}^{n} \frac{A}{(1+r)^t} = A \sum_{t=1}^{n} \frac{1}{(1+r)^t}$$ [2.4]

Table 2.3
Present Value of $1 to be Received at the End of Each of the Next 4 Years

Year	Return Received at End of Year	Amount Withdrawn at End of Year	Value of Investment at End of Year	
0 (present)	—	—	$3.0374	← initial
1	$3.0374(.12) = $.3645	$1.00	$3.0374 + .3645 − 1.00 = 2.4019	amount
2	2.4019(.12) = .2882	1.00	2.4019 + .2882 − 1.00 = 1.6901	invested
3	1.6901(.12) = .2028	1.00	1.6901 + .2028 − 1.00 = .8929	
4	.8929(.12) = .1071	1.00	.8929 + .1071 − 1.00 = .0000	

---

[3] The two figures, $3.0373 and $3.0374, differ in the last decimal place because of rounding errors introduced into the calculations.

For example, the present value of $2,000 to be received at the end of each of the next four years, discounted at 12 percent, is equal to $2,000(3.0373) = $6,074.60. Table 5 at the end of the book can only be used to find the present value of an annuity; that is, a series of *equal* payments to be received at the end of each of the next n years.

Present Value of a Series of Unequal Payments

The present value of a series of *unequal* payments (A_t, $t = 1, \dots , n$) to be received at the end of each of the next n years, discounted at a rate of r percent, is

$$PV = \sum_{t=1}^{n} \frac{A_t}{(1 + r)^t}$$

[2.5]

Table 4 at the end of the book can be used in this calculation. To illustrate, suppose $500(= A_1)$ is to be received at the end of Year 1, $1,000 (= A_2)$ at the end of Year 2, $1,000(= A_3)$ at the end of Year 3, and $2,000(= A_4)$ at the end of Year 4. The present value of this series, discounted at 12 percent, is shown in Table 2.4 to be $3,226.44.

Compounding Periods

In the discussion of present values, we assumed that the rate of return r was compounded *annually*; that is, $1 was invested at the beginning of the year and an interest return of r percent was earned at the *end* of the year. Only at the end of the second year would we earn a return on the interest earned in the first year. Often, however, the total return (for example, interest, cash flow, and dividend) is received in periodic installments throughout the year. Banks often compound and pay interest semiannually, companies pay dividends quarterly, and cash receipts and disbursements may occur monthly. In these situations, it is possible to earn a return in the next period (half-year, quarter, or month) on the return received in the previous period. The more times per year the return is compounded, the larger will be the total return and the smaller the present value.

Table 2.4
Present Value of a Series of Unequal Cash Flows

Year t	Amount Received A_t	Discount Factor (from Table 4), $\dfrac{1}{(1 + .12)^t}$	Present Value of Amount Received
1	$ 500	.89286	$ 500(.89286) = $ 446.43
2	1,000	.79719	1,000(.79719) = 797.19
3	1,000	.71178	1,000(.71178) = 711.78
4	2,000	.63552	2,000(.63552) = 1,271.04
Total			$3,226.44

Two changes must be made in the present value formulas if other than annual compounding is desired. The present value of $1 to be received at the end of year n, discounted at the rate of r percent, compounded *semiannually*, is

$$PV = \frac{1}{\left(1 + \dfrac{r}{2}\right)^{2n}}$$

For *quarterly* compounding, the present value is

$$PV = \frac{1}{\left(1 + \dfrac{r}{4}\right)^{4n}}$$

In general, the present value of $1 to be received at the end of year n, discounted at the rate of r percent, compounded m times per year, is[4]

$$PV = \frac{1}{\left(1 + \dfrac{r}{m}\right)^{mn}} \qquad [2.6]$$

With a slight modification in the procedures, Table 4 at the end of the book can be used to find present values when other than annual compounding is required. For a rate r percent compounded m times per year, the present value of $1 to be received at the end of year n is found by looking up the present value of $1 to be received in mn years discounted at a rate of r/m percent. For example, the present value of $1 to be received at the end of four years, discounted at 12 percent compounded quarterly, would be found by looking up the present value of $1 to be received in 16 years discounted at a rate of 3 percent — $.6232.

Solving for the Discount Rate

Thus far, we have been concerned with finding the present value of either a single future cash flow or a stream of future cash flows discounted at some *given*

---

[4] Continuous compounding is obtained by letting m approach infinity in Equation 2.6. Under this condition, $(1 + r/m)^m = e^r$, and the present value expression becomes

$$PV = \frac{1}{e^{rn}} = e^{-rn}$$

where e is the exponential number having the approximate value of 2.71828. For example, the present value of $1 to be received at the end of four years, discounted at the continuously compounded rate of 12 percent, is equal to $(\$1)e^{-(.12)(4)} = (\$1)e^{-.48} = \$.6188$. This compares with the values of $.6355 for annual compounding and $.6232 for quarterly compounding.

rate r. Rather than discounting the future cash flow(s) at some given rate, one is sometimes interested in *finding the rate of discount* that will equate the present value of the cash inflows with the present value of the cash outflows. In this analysis, suppose that we have a series of cash flows (inflows or outflows) over the next $n + 1$ periods—$A_0, A_1, A_2, \ldots, A_n$. In general, any of the A_t's could be positive (cash inflow) or negative (cash outflow). For a typical investment, A_0 will be negative and will represent the initial cost of the investment; and A_1, $A_2, \ldots, A_n$ will be positive and will represent the stream of benefits that are expected to be derived from the investment. We are interested in finding the rate of discount r such that

$$A_0 + \frac{A_1}{(1+r)} + \frac{A_2}{(1+r)^2} + \cdots + \frac{A_n}{(1+r)^n} = 0$$

or

$$\sum_{t=0}^{n} \frac{A_t}{(1+r)^t} = 0 \qquad [2.7]$$

In effect, we are solving Equation 2.7 for the rate r that makes the present value of the stream of cash flows equal to zero.[5] This rate r is commonly referred to as the *internal rate of return* or *yield* on an investment.

Using a trial-and-error procedure and a present value table (Table 4 at the end of the book), we can solve Equation 2.7 for the rate r for any series of A_t's. The steps in the trial-and-error procedure are as follows:

Step 1. Make an approximate estimate of the discount rate (r).

Step 2. Use this rate to compute the present value of the cash flow stream.

---

[5] Equation 2.7 is an nth degree polynomial. An nth degree polynomial has *at most n* roots (values of r that satisfy the equation). Some of these roots may be real or complex and some may be positive or negative. Among the possible n roots, the only ones of economic interest are the positive real roots. From a mathematical theorem it can be shown that the number of positive real roots is *at most equal* to the number of sign reversals in the series of cash flows (A_t, $t = 0, 1, \ldots, n$). For a typical investment, there is an initial cash outflow (negative value) followed by a series of cash inflows (positive values). Hence there is one sign reversal, from minus to plus, and at most one positive real root (internal rate of return). A sufficient condition for the existence of *at least* one positive real root is that the sum of undiscounted stream of cash flows

$$\left(\sum_{t=0}^{n} A_t \right)$$

be greater than zero. For the investment which consists of an initial cash outflow followed by a series of cash inflows, with the sum of cash inflows being greater than the initial cash outflow, there will be *exactly* one root or internal rate of return. Thus we will not have to be concerned with the multiple rates of return problem. See Chapter 2 of T. E. Copeland and J. F. Weston, *Financial Theory and Corporate Policy*, 3d ed. (Reading, Mass.: Addison-Wesley, 1988) for a discussion of multiple rates of return.

Step 3. Try a *higher* rate if a positive present value results or a *lower* rate if a negative value results.

Step 4. Repeat the process (attempting to "bracket" the discount rate) until a rate is found where the present value of the cash flow stream is equal to zero.

To illustrate this procedure, consider the following series of cash flows $A_0 = \$ - 10,000$; $A_1 = \$5,000$; $A_2 = \$4,000$; $A_3 = \$2,000$; and $A_4 = \$1,000$. The calculations are shown in Table 2.5. First, an r of 10 percent is tried, resulting in a present value for the cash flow stream of $+\$36.88$. Since the *present* value of the cash flow stream is positive, a higher value of r is tried. At 11 percent, the present value of the cash flow stream is $-\$127.91$. This indicates that the discount rate is between 10 and 11 percent. A more exact discount rate can be computed by means of interpolation:

$$r = 10\% + \frac{36.88}{36.88 + 127.91}(11\% - 10\%)$$

$$= 10\% + \frac{36.88}{164.79}(1\%)$$

$$= 10.2\%$$

For $r = 10.2$ percent, the present value of the cash flow stream is approximately equal to zero.[6,7] Thus the internal rate of return or yield on this investment is approximately 10.2 percent.

A much simpler procedure exists for finding r wherever the series of cash flows—A_1, A_2,..., A_n—are all equal. Instead of using the trial-and-error method, we can solve directly (using Table 5 at the end of the book) for the rate r that equates the discounted stream of cash flows to A_0; that is, the rate that satisfies Equation 2.7. If we let A be the uniform cash flow

Table 2.5
Trial-and-Error Procedure for Finding the Discount Rate (Internal Rate of Return)

Year t	Cash Flow A_t	$r = 10$ Percent		$r = 11$ Percent	
		Discount Factor	Present Value	Discount Factor	Present Value
0	$\$-10,000$	1.00000	$\$-10,000.00$	1.00000	$\$-10,000.00$
1	5,000	.90909	4,545.45	.90090	4,504.50
2	4,000	.82645	3,305.80	.81162	3,246.48
3	2,000	.75131	1,502.62	.73119	1,462.38
4	1,000	.68301	683.01	.65873	658.73
Total			$ +36.88		$ -127.91

---

[6] Since $r = 10.2$ percent is not in Table 4, these values would have to be calculated using Equation 2.1. A good financial calculator can do internal rate of return calculations directly.

[7] The present value is only *approximately* zero, not exactly zero, because of rounding erros in performing the calculations.

$(A = A_1 = A_2 = ,\ldots, = A_n)$, then Equation 2.7 can be written as

$$\sum_{t=1}^{n} \frac{A}{(1+r)^t} = -A_0$$

or

$$\sum_{t=1}^{n} \frac{1}{(1+r)^t} = \frac{-A_0}{A} \qquad [2.8]$$

After dividing $-A_0$ by A to determine the appropriate discount factor, we then look up this factor in the nth row of Table 5 at the end of the book to obtain the corresponding interest rate r. If the appropriate discount factor lies between two values in Table 5, interpolation can be used to give a more precise rate.

As an illustration of this procedure, consider an investment having an initial outlay $(-A_0)$ of $6,000 and providing uniform annual cash inflows (A) of $2,000 in each of the following four years. Solving Equation 2.8 for the appropriate discount factor, we obtain

$$\sum_{t=1}^{4} \frac{1}{(1+r)^t} = \frac{6,000}{2,000} = 3.0000$$

Looking up 3.0000 in the $n = 4$ row of Table 5 at the end of the book, we see that it lies between the corresponding discount factors for 12 percent and 13 percent. Interpolating between those values yields

$$r = 12\% + \frac{(3.0373 - 3.0000)}{(3.0373 - 3.0000) + (3.0000 - 2.9745)}(13\% - 12\%)$$

$$= 12\% + \frac{.0373}{.0628}(1\%) = 12\% + .6(1\%)$$

$$= 12.6\%$$

The yield or rate of return on this investment is about 12.6 percent.

Perpetuities

Occasionally, we are interested in finding the present value of an infinite number of periodic cash flows (a *perpetuity*). Assuming that we have an infinite series of equal cash flows $(A_t = A; t = 1, 2,\ldots, \infty)$, by Equation 2.4 the present value is

$$PV = \sum_{t=1}^{\infty} \frac{A}{(1+r)^t} = A \sum_{t=1}^{\infty} \frac{1}{(1+r)^t}$$

However, it can be shown that this expression reduces to

$$PV = \frac{A}{r} \qquad [2.9]$$

Thus the present value of $1,000 to be received each year in perpetuity, discounted at 6 percent, would be equal to $1,000 \div .06 = 16,666.67$.

Summary

- The marginal analysis concept requires that a decision maker determine the additional (marginal) costs and additional (marginal) benefits associated with a proposed action. If the marginal benefits exceed the marginal costs (that is, if the net marginal benefits are positive) the action should be taken.

- The *demand* for a good or service is defined as the various quantities of that good or service that consumers are willing and able to purchase during a particular period of time at all possible prices. The *supply* of a good or service is defined as the quantities that sellers are willing to make available to purchasers at all possible prices during a particular period of time.

- The intersection of the supply and demand curves represents the equilibrium price and quantity that should prevail in the marketplace, given these supply and demand curves. An increase (or decrease) in demand leads to a new equilibrium point where both the new equilibrium price and quantity are higher (or lower) than they were at the original equilibrium point. An increase (or decrease) in supply results in a new equilibrium point where the price is lower (or higher) and the equilibrium quantity is greater (or less) than those at the original equilibrium point.

- The present value of a sum of money to be received in the future is determined by the number of years in the future when the money is to be received and the interest rate that can be earned during that period. The present value concept can be applied to single amounts to be received in the future, streams of unequal periodic future receipts (such as the dividends received from owning stock) or streams of equal future receipts (annuities). In general, a dollar of benefits received in the future is worth less than a dollar of benefits in hand today.

Selected References

Hirshleifer, Jack. *Price Theory and Applications.* 4th ed. Englewood Cliffs, N.J.: Prentice-Hall, 1988.

Moyer, R. C., J. R. McGuigan, and W. J. Kretlow. *Contemporary Financial Management.* 3d rev. ed. St. Paul, Minn.: West, 1988.

Discussion Questions

1. Discuss how an airline might use the marginal analysis concept to decide on adding a new flight to its schedule. Identify the costs that should and should not be considered in this analysis.

2. To save money, the state legislature has mandated a 5 percent decrease in the enrollment at Major State University. At the same time the legislature reduced appropriations to the school by 5 percent. Evaluate this decision using the marginal analysis concepts developed in this chapter.

3. During the mid–1980s the Reagan Administration imposed a 100 percent tariff on computer chips imported from Japan. Discuss the likely impact of this decision using suppy-demand curve analysis.

4. What is the impact of restrictions on the number of Japanese automobiles that can be imported into the United States on the price of Japanese-made vehicles and American-made vehicles? Under what conditions will these effects be most significant?

5. Define the following terms:

   a. Annuity
   b. Yield
   c. Perpetuity

6. What happens to the present value of an annuity as the interest rate increases?

7. What effect does more frequent compounding have on present values?

8. Explain how to find the rate of return or yield for an uneven series of cash flows (inflows and outflows).

Problems

1. Illustrate graphically the impact of a price ceiling imposed on the sale of any commodity.

2. The Ajax Corporation has the following set of projects available to it:

Project	Investment Required ($ millions)	Expected Rate of Return
A	$500	23.0%
B	75	18.0
C	50	21.0
D	125	16.0
E	300	14.0
F	150	13.0
G	250	19.0

Ajax can raise funds with the following marginal costs:

First $250 million	14.0%
Next $250 million	15.5%
Next $100 million	16.0%
Next $250 million	16.5%
Next $200 million	18.0%
Next $200 million	21.0%

Use the marginal cost and marginal revenue concepts developed in this chapter to derive an optimal capital budget for Ajax.

3. Upon the birth of his son 20 years ago, Mr. Prudence deposited a sum of money with the bank of Indula in the form of a savings account. Today, 20 years later, the passbook shows a balance of $26,533. If the bank paid 5 percent on savings throughout the 20-year period, how much did Mr. Prudence deposit in the account?

4. A woman wishes to sell a contract that she now holds. The contract calls for the borrower to pay eight annual installments of $3,000 each. If the buyer of this contract wishes to realize a 10-percent rate of return on this contract, how much should the buyer be willing to pay for it?

5. A business firm purchases machinery priced at $26,500 and finances the purchase through a lender on a 10-year note that calls for ten annual payments of $4,690 each. What is the interest rate of this loan?

6. The Ideal Company had sales in the amount of $360,000 for the year 1988. Projected sales for the year 1993 are $750,000. What will be the annual compound rate of growth in sales over this time period?

7. Given that a 20-year corporate bond with an 11 percent coupon rate was issued this year at $1,000 (face value), and that you desire a 12 percent yield to maturity, exactly how many dollars would you offer for it?

8. A given investment will yield the following stream of earnings (cash flows) over time:

Year	Earning
1	$7,500
2	6,000
3	4,500
4	3,000
5	1,500

If a man were to pay $18,000 for this stream of earnings, what would be the rate of return on this investment?

9. Ms. Smith recently bought a new building for $100,000, payable on terms of zero down payment and 25 equal annual installment payments to include interest of 10 percent per year on the *unpaid* balance. What is the size of the equal-installment payments to be made?

10. A firm purchases a piece of land for $50,000 and agrees to remit 20 equal annual installments of $6,899.31 each. What is the interest rate on this loan?

11. The stock of Media Specific is expected to pay a dividend of $3 per share next year. This dividend rate is expected to grow by 5 percent for at least the next five years. You are considering purchasing this stock. If you buy it today, you intend to hold it for three years. You will receive the next three expected dividend payments. At the end of three years you plan to sell the stock at an expected price of $50 per share. If you demand a 15 percent rate of return on investments of this risk level, what price would you pay for the Media Specific stock?

12. The demand function for propane is:

$$Q_D = 212 - 20P$$

The supply function for propane is:

$$Q_S = 20 + 4P$$

a. What is the equilibrium price and quantity?
b. If the government establishes a price ceiling of $6, what quantity will be demanded and supplied?
c. If the government establishes a price floor (minimum price) of $9, what quantity will be demanded and supplied?
d. If supply increases to:

$$Q'_S = 20 + 6P$$

what is the new equilibrium price and quantity?

e. If demand increases to:

$$Q'_D = 250 - 19P$$

and the supply is as given in part (d), what is the new equilibrium price and quantity?

13. Your mother plans to retire this year. Her firm has offered her a lump sum retirement payment of $100,000, or a $13,000 per year lifetime annuity. Your mother is in good health and expects to live for at least fifteen more years. Which option should she choose, assuming that a 9 percent interest rate is appropriate to evaluate the annuity payments?

Decision Making under Risk and Uncertainty 3

Shareholder wealth is a function of both the expected returns and the risk of those expected returns. In general, investors will place a higher value on a more certain future stream of returns (cash flows). Conversely, the less certain (riskier) future returns are perceived to be, the lower the value assigned to these returns by investors. In the financial markets a positive relationship exists between the rate of return required by investors and the risk of the investment. Normally, high returns can only be earned by assuming high risk. In this chapter we define the concepts of risk and uncertainty, develop some approaches for making decisions under risk and uncertainty, and examine techniques designed to reduce risk efficiently. An appropriate balance of risk and expected return is an important ingredient in shareholder wealth maximization.

The Nature of a Decision Problem

A decision problem, as defined by decision theorists, consists of several basic elements. First, there must be an individual or group that is faced with the problem, that is, a *decision maker*. The decision maker must be seeking to achieve some *objective*, or desired outcome. At least two *alternative actions* or strategies, which can possibly achieve the stated objective, must be available to the decision maker. A *state of doubt* must exist within the decision maker about which alternative action is best in seeking to achieve the desired objective. Finally, the problem exists within an *environment* consisting of all factors that can influence the achievement of the objective or desired outcome but that cannot be controlled by the decision maker.

This framework is applicable in a wide variety of decision-making situations ranging from very complex management (resource allocation) problems to relatively simple problems encountered in daily life. The amount of effort expended in analyzing a decision problem using this framework clearly depends on the magnitude of the payoffs (that is, values of the outcomes) involved and the period of time available. Day-to-day routine decisions are not subjected to the same degree of analysis as are decisions that will have a long-term impact on the individual or organization. Some specific examples of decision problems are presented later in the discussions of the solution techniques of decision theory.

Glossary of New Terms

Coefficient of variation
The ratio of the standard deviation to the expected value. A relative measure of risk.

Probability
The percentage chance that a particular outcome will occur.

Expected value
The weighted average of the possible outcomes where the weights are the probabilities of the respective outcomes.

Risk
A decision-making situation in which there is variability in the possible outcomes and the probabilities of these outcomes can be specified by the decision maker.

(Cont'd on next page)

Glossary of New Terms (*Cont'd*)

Standard deviation
A statistical measure of the dispersion or variability of possible outcomes. Operationally, it is defined as the square root of the weighted average squared deviations of the possible outcomes from the expected value, where the weights are the probabilities of the respective outcomes. An absolute measure of risk.

Uncertainty
A situation in which the decision maker is either unable or unwilling to specify the probabilities of occurrence of the possible outcomes of the decision.

Game theory
A mathematical theory of group decision making for situations in which a conflict of interest exists between two or more of the participants.

Hedge
A risk reducing strategy of taking offsetting positions in the ownership of an asset.

For purposes of exposition and analysis, we can divide decision making into several parts depending on the characteristics of the decision problem. A commonly used classification scheme for decision making is described by Luce and Raiffa "according to whether a decision is made by (i) an individual or (ii) a group, and according to whether it is effected under conditions of (a) certainty, (b) risk, or (c) uncertainty."[1]

The distinction between an individual and a group is based on the compatibility of the objectives or interests of the participants in the decision-making situation. If all the participants share the same underlying objectives, then the decision problem can be analyzed *as if* the decision were going to be made by one individual. If, however, conflict exists between the objectives of two or more participants, then the decision-making situation would be analyzed as one of group decision making. Such a group decision-making situation is referred to as a "game" and is analyzed using the techniques of *game theory*.

The classification of decision-making problems among the certainty, risk, and uncertainty categories is determined by the knowledge of the possible outcomes (or payoffs) that will occur when one of the two (or more) alternative actions is chosen in a decision problem. Luce and Raiffa define a situation to be decision making under

1. *Certainty* if each action is known to lead invariably to a specific outcome;

2. *Risk* if each action leads to one of a set of possible specific outcomes, each outcome occurring with a known probability; or

3. *Uncertainty* if each action has as its consequence a set of possible specific outcomes, but where the probabilities of these outcomes are completely unknown or not even meaningful.[2]

In a game, or conflict decision-making situation, a condition of uncertainty exists because one decision maker does not know the state of knowledge, motivations, and hence the actions of the other decision makers. As we shall see later in the text, game theory seeks to reduce this element of uncertainty by postulating certain assumptions about the state of knowledge and motivations of the other decision makers in the game situation.

Based on this classification scheme, we have four possible cases to consider:

1. Individual decision making under certainty
2. Individual decision making under risk
3. Individual decision making under uncertainty
4. Group decision making; that is, games

[1] R. Duncan Luce and Howard Raiffa, *Games and Decisions* (New York: John Wiley, 1957), p 13. A fourth category considered by Luce and Raiffa was "(d) a combination of uncertainty and risk in the light of experimental evidence... statistical inference" (p. 13). We limit the analysis to the first three categories; that is, certainty, risk, and uncertainty.
[2] Luce and Raiffa, *Games and Decisions*, p. 14.

The techniques of analysis used in problems of individual decision making under certainty include such classical optimization methods as calculus and other optimization procedures such as linear and nonlinear programming. These methods of analysis are discussed and illustrated in Chapters 4 and 5. The methods used to analyze problems of individual decision making under risk and uncertainty (Cases 2 and 3) constitute the heart of decision theory and are discussed in this chapter. Game theory (Case 4) is discussed in Appendix 15A.

Meaning and Measurement of Risk

We begin the discussion of risk analysis by defining several key terms and concepts. Although the examples presented here deal primarily with investment decisions, the ideas are applicable to all other types of economic decisions, such as those of pricing and production.

The Meaning of Risk

Risk is defined as the "possibility of loss or injury; hazard; peril; danger."[3] Hence, risk implies a chance for some unfavorable event to occur. From the perspective of security analysis or the analysis of an investment project, risk is the *possibility that actual cash flows (returns) will be less than forecasted cash flows (returns).* More generally, risk refers to the chance that you will receive a return that differs from the expected return. When a range of potential outcomes is associated with a decision and the decision maker is able to assign probabilities to each of these possible outcomes, risk is said to exist.

An investment decision is said to be *risk free* if the outcome (dollar returns) from the initial investment is known with certainty. Some of the best examples of risk-free investments are United States Treasury securities. There is virtually no chance that the Treasury will fail to redeem these securities at maturity or that the Treasury will default on any interest payments owed.[4]

In contrast, Eastern Airlines bonds constitute a *risky* investment opportunity because it is possible that Eastern Airlines will default on one or more interest payments and will lack sufficient funds at maturity to redeem the bonds at face value. In other words, the possible returns from this investment are *variable*, and each potential outcome can be assigned a *probability*.

If, for example, you were considering investing in Eastern Airlines bonds, you might assign the probabilities to the three possible outcomes of this investment shown in Table 3.1. These probabilities are interpreted to mean that

---

[3] *Webster's Third New International Dictionary*, s.v. "risk" Chicago: Encyclopedia Brittanica, Inc.: 1981.

[4] Note this discussion of risk deals with *dollar returns* and ignores such other considerations as potential losses in purchasing power. In addition, it assumes that securities are held until maturity, which is not always the case. Sometimes a security must be sold before maturity for less than face value because of changes in the level of interest rates.

Table 3.1
Possible Outcomes from Investing in Eastern Airlines Bonds

Outcome	Probability
No default, bonds redeemed at maturity	0.80
Default on interest for one or more periods	0.15
No interest default, but bonds not redeemed at maturity	0.05
	1.00

an 80 percent chance exists that the bonds will not be in default over their life and will be redeemed at maturity, a 15 percent chance of interest default during the life of the bonds, and a 5 percent chance that the bonds will not be redeemed at maturity. In this example, no other outcomes are deemed possible.

Risk refers to the potential variability of outcomes from a decision alternative. The more variable these outcomes are, the greater the risk associated with the decision alternative.

Probability Distributions

The *probability* that a particular outcome will occur is defined as the *percentage chance* of its occurrence. Probabilities may be either objectively or subjectively determined. An objective determination is based on past outcomes of similar events, whereas a subjective determination is merely an opinion made by an individual about the likelihood that a given event will occur. In the case of decisions that are frequently repeated, such as the drilling of developmental oil wells in an established oil field, reasonably good objective estimates can be made about the success of a new well. In contrast, for totally new decisions or one-of-a-kind investments, subjective estimates about the likelihood of various outcomes are necessary. The fact that many probability estimates in business are at least partially subjective does not diminish their usefulness.

Using either objective or subjective methods, the decision maker can develop a probability distribution for the possible outcomes. Table 3.2 shows the probability distribution of net cash flows for two sample investments. The lowest estimated annual net cash flow for each investment—$200 for Investment I and $100 for Investment II—represents pessimistic forecasts about the investments' performance; the middle values—$300 and $300—could be considered normal performance levels; and the highest values—$400 and $500—are optimistic estimates.

Table 3.2
Probability Distributions of the Annual Net Cash Flows (NCF) from Two Investments

INVESTMENT I		INVESTMENT II	
Possible NCF	Probability	Possible NCF	Probability
$200	0.2	$100	0.2
300	0.6	300	0.6
400	0.2	500	0.2
	1.0		1.0

Expected Values

From this information, the expected value of each decision alternative can be calculated. The *expected value* is defined as the weighted average of the possible outcomes. It is the value that is expected to occur on average if the decision (such as an investment) were repeated a large number of times.

Algebraically, the expected value may be defined as

$$\bar{R} = \sum_{j=1}^{n} R_j P_j$$

[3.1]

where $\bar{R}$ is the expected value; R_j is the outcome for the jth case, where there are n possible outcomes; and P_j is the probability that the jth outcome will occur. The expected cash flows for Investments I and II are calculated in Table 3.3 using Equation 3.1. In this example both investments have expected values of annual net cash flows equaling $300.

Standard Deviation: An Absolute Measure of Risk

The *standard deviation* is a statistical measure of the dispersion of a variable about its mean. It is defined as the square root of the weighted average squared deviations of individual outcomes from the mean:

$$\sigma = \sqrt{\sum_{j=1}^{n} (R_j - \bar{R})^2 P_j}$$

[3.2]

where σ is the standard deviation.

The standard deviation can be used to measure the variability of a decision alternative. As such, it gives an indication of the risk involved in the alternative. The larger the standard deviation, the more variable the possible outcomes and the riskier the decision alternative. A standard deviation of zero indicates no variability and thus no risk. Table 3.4 shows the calculation of the standard deviations for Investments I and II.

From these calculations, it can be seen that Investment II appears to be *riskier* than Investment I because the expected cash flows from Investment II are *more variable*.

	INVESTMENT I			INVESTMENT II		
R_j	P_j	$R_j \times P_j$	R_j	P_j	$R_j \times P_j$
$200	0.2	$ 40	$100	0.2	$ 20
300	0.6	180	300	0.6	180
400	0.2	80	500	0.2	100
	Expected value: $\bar{R}_{\mathrm{I}} = \$300$				$\bar{R}_{\mathrm{II}} = \$300$

Table 3.3
Computation of the Expected Returns from Two Investments

Table 3.4
Computation of the Standard Deviations for Two Investments

	j	R_j	$\bar{R}$	$R_j - \bar{R}$	$(R_j - \bar{R})^2$	P_j	$(R_j - \bar{R})^2 P_j$
INVESTMENT I	1	$200	$300	$-100	$10,000	0.2	$2,000
	2	300	300	0	0	0.6	0
	3	400	300	100	10,000	0.2	2,000

$$\sum_{j=1}^{3}(R_j - \bar{R})^2 P_j = \$4000$$

$$\sigma = \sqrt{\sum_{j=1}^{n}(R_j - \bar{R})^2 P_j} = \sqrt{4000} = \underline{\$\ 63.25}$$

	j	R_j	$\bar{R}$	$R_j - \bar{R}$	$(R_j - \bar{R})^2$	P_j	$(R_j - \bar{R})^2 P_j$
INVESTMENT II	1	$100	$300	$-200	$40,000	0.2	$8,000
	2	300	300	0	0	0.6	0
	3	500	300	200	40,000	0.2	8,000

$$\sum_{j=1}^{3}(R_j - \bar{R})^2 P_j = \$16,000$$

$$\sigma = \sqrt{\sum_{j=1}^{n}(R_j - \bar{R})^2 P_j} = \sqrt{16,000} = \underline{\$126.49}$$

This example dealt with a *discrete* probability distribution of outcomes (net cash flows) for each investment; that is, a *limited* number of possible outcomes were identified and probabilities were assigned to them. In reality, however, many different outcomes are possible for each investment decision, ranging from losses each year to annual net cash flows in excess of the optimistic estimates of $400 and $500. To indicate the probability of *all* possible outcomes, it is necessary to construct a *continuous* probability distribution. Conceptually, this involves assigning probabilities to each possible outcome such that the sum of the probabilities over possible outcomes total 1.0 (see Figure 3.1). From this figure it can be seen that Investment I has a tighter probability distribution, indicating a lower variability of returns, and Investment II has a flatter distribution, indicating higher variability and, by extension, more risk.

Normal Probability Distribution

The outcomes from many decisions can be estimated by assuming that they follow the *normal* probability distribution. This assumption is often correct or nearly correct, and it greatly simplifies the analysis. The normal probability distribution is characterized by a symmetrical, bell-like curve. If the expected continuous probability distribution for the possible outcomes is approximately normal, a table of the *standard normal probability function* (Table 1 in Appendix A at the end of this book) can be used to compute the probability of occurrence of any particular outcome. From this table, for example, it is apparent that the actual outcome should be between plus and minus 1 standard

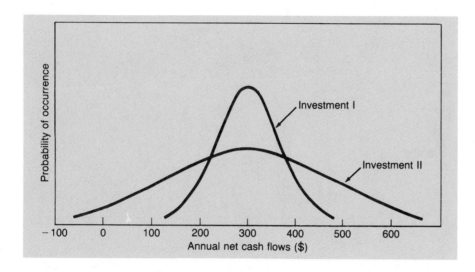

Figure 3.1
Continuous Probability Distributions for Two Investments

deviation from the expected value 68.26 percent of the time,[5] between plus and minus 2 standard deviations 95.44 percent of the time, and between plus and minus 3 standard deviations 99.74 percent of the time (see Figure 3.2).

The number of standard deviations z that a particular value of R is from the mean $\bar{R}$ can be computed as

$$z = \frac{R - \bar{R}}{\sigma}$$ [3.3]

Table 1 and Equation 3.3 can be used to compute the probability of an annual net cash flow for Investment I being less than some value R—for example, $205. First, the number of standard deviations that $205 is from the mean must be calculated. Substituting the mean and the standard deviation from Tables 3.3 and 3.4 into Equation 3.3 yields

$$z = \frac{\$205 - \$300}{\$63.25}$$

$$= -1.50$$

In other words, the annual cash flow value of $205 is 1.5 standard deviations *below* the mean. Reading from the 1.50 row in Table 1 gives a value of 0.0668. or 6.68%. Thus a 6.68 percent probability exists that Investment I will have annual net cash flows less than $205. Conversely, there is a 93.32 percent probability $(1 - 0.0668)$ that the investment will have a cash flow greater than $205.

---

[5] For example, Table 1 indicates a probability of 0.1587 of a value occurring that is greater than $+1\sigma$ from the mean *and* a probability of 0.1587 of a value occurring that is less than -1σ from the mean. Hence the probability of a value *between* $+1\sigma$ and -1σ is 68.26 percent—that is, $1.00 - (2 \times 0.1587)$.

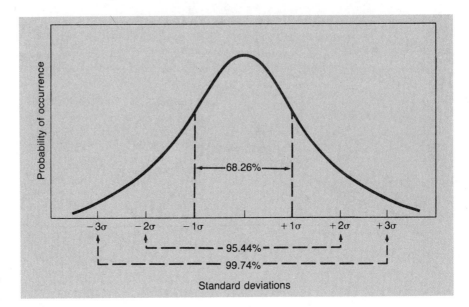

Figure 3.2
A Sample Illustration of Areas Under the Normal Probability Distribution Curve

A Practical Approach for Estimating Standard Deviations

Most business decisions have outcomes best represented by a continuous probability distribution of possible outcomes, not the discrete distribution of outcomes such as those shown in Tables 3.3 and 3.4. Under these circumstances, a simple technique can be used to derive the standard deviation of possible outcomes. Assuming that the distribution of possible outcomes is approximately normally distributed, information can be developed in a form useful for making the necessary computations.

For example, the individual responsible for making estimates of the expected return and risk from a decision, such as an investment project or the pricing of a new product, could be asked to supply the following information:

1. Estimate the most optimistic outcome. The most optimistic outcome is defined to be an outcome that would not be exceeded more than 5 percent (or any other prespecified percentage) of the time.

2. Estimate the most pessimistic outcome. The most pessimistic outcome is defined to be an outcome that you would not expect to do worse than more than 5 percent of the time.

3. With a normal distribution, the expected value will be midway between the most optimistic and the most pessimistic estimate.

4. Calculate the value of one standard deviation from Table 1, Appendix A.

For example, in pricing a new product, the product manager estimates that the most optimistic (not expected to be exceeded more than 5 percent of the time) price the firm can charge is $5.00 per unit. The most pessimistic (not expected to be less than this amount more than 5 percent of the time) estimate of the price that can be charged is $3.50. Assuming normality, the expected price is $4.25. From Table 1 in Appendix A, the z-value that leaves 5 percent in either tail of the normal distribution is approximately 1.645 standard deviations (σ) to the right or left of the expected value. This z-value corresponds to the distance between the expected value and either the most optimistic or the most pessimistic estimate of price. Hence, the probability of a price of at least $5.00 is equal to the probability of a z-value *greater* than + 1.645. To calculate the standard deviation (σ) of this distribution, use the most optimistic outcome ($5.00), the expected outcome ($4.25), and the z-value:

$$z = 1.645 = \frac{(\$5.00 - \$4.25)}{\sigma}$$

$$\sigma = \frac{\$0.75}{1.645}$$

$$= \$0.46$$

In this case the expected value is $4.25 with a standard deviation of $0.46.

This procedure can be used to derive estimates of the standard deviation of any continuous probability distribution as long as the manager is able to estimate just two numbers—the most optimistic outcome and the most pessimistic outcome.

Coefficient of Variation: A Relative Measure of Risk

The standard deviation is an appropriate measure of risk when the decision alternatives being compared are approximately equal in size (that is, have similar expected values of the outcomes) and the outcomes are estimated to have symmetrical probability distributions. Because the standard deviation is an *absolute* measure of variability, however, it is generally not suitable for comparing alternatives of differing size. In these cases the *coefficient of variation* provides a better measure of risk.

Consider, for example, two investments, T and S. Investment T has expected annual net cash flows of $500,000 and a standard deviation of $2,000, whereas Investment S has expected annual net cash flows of $4,000 and a $2,000 standard deviation. Intuition tells us that Investment T is less risky since its *relative* variation is smaller.

The coefficient of variation (v) considers relative variation and thus is well suited for use when a comparison is being made between two unequally sized decision alternatives. It is defined as the ratio of the standard deviation σ to the expected value $\bar{R}$, or

$$v = \frac{\sigma}{\bar{R}}$$

As the coefficient of variation increases, so does the relative risk of the decision alternative. The coefficients of variation for Investments T and S are computed as

Investment T:

$$v = \frac{\sigma}{R}$$

$$= \frac{\$2,000}{\$500,000}$$

$$= 0.004$$

Investment S:

$$v = \frac{\sigma}{R}$$

$$= \frac{\$2,000}{\$4,000}$$

$$= 0.5$$

Cash flows of Investment S have a *larger* coefficient of variation (0.5) than do cash flows of Investment T (0.004), therefore, Investment S is the *more* risky of the two alternatives.

In general, when comparing two equally sized decision alternatives, the standard deviation is an appropriate measure of risk. When comparing two unequally sized alternatives, the coefficient of variation is the more appropriate measure of risk.

Incorporating Risk into the Decision-Making Process

Numerous approaches have been developed for incorporating risk into the decision-making process. These range from relatively simple methods, such as the use of subjective or informal approaches, to fairly complex ones, such as the use of computerized simulation models. Five of these methods, namely, the *subjective* or *informal* approach, *utility function* approach, *decision tree approach, risk-adjusted discount rate* approach, and *simulation* approach are discussed below. This list is not exhaustive; many other risk-adjusted methods are available to the decision maker.

Subjective or Informal Approach

Decisions are frequently based on the decision maker's subjective feelings about risk in relation to expected return. For example, if a firm is evaluating two mutually exclusive investments having approximately equal net returns, the decision maker will probably choose the less risky investment. This informal approach to decision making is commonly used because it is both simple and inexpensive.

If, however, two investments under consideration have significantly different net returns as well as different levels of perceived risk, the decision becomes more complicated. In these cases the decision maker must determine—again subjectively—whether the additional risk will be offset by sufficiently higher returns.

Even though subjective decision making is often useful, more precise methods yield more valuable information in many cases.

Utility Function Approach

In decision problems whose uncertain possible outcomes constitute monetary payoffs (that is, dollars) with known probabilities of occurrence, it has been observed that a simple preference for higher dollar amounts is not sufficient to explain the choices made by many individuals. The classic example, known as the St. Petersburg paradox, was formulated by the seventeenth-century mathematician D. Bernoulli and illustrates the dilemma. The paradox consists of a gamble in which a "fair" coin—that is, a coin in which the probability of a head and tail is $\frac{1}{2}$—is tossed until the *first head* appears. The player receives or wins 2^n dollars when the first head appears on the n-th toss. The question is: How much should the player be willing to pay to participate in this gamble (that is, how much should he be willing to wager)? The *expected monetary value* of such a gamble is infinite.[6] Therefore, based on the criterion of expected monetary value, the individual should be willing to wager everything he owns in return for the chance to receive 2^n dollars. Since most individuals would choose not to participate under these conditions, we conclude that the actual monetary values of the possible outcomes of the gamble do not necessarily reveal a person's true preference for these outcomes and that the maximization of expected monetary value criterion is not necessarily a reliable guide in predicting the actions or strategies a person will choose in a given decision-making situation. Other more commonly observed examples of behavior, such as investment portfolio diversification and the simultaneous purchase of lottery tickets (that is, gambling) and insurance, also lend support to these conclusions.

If we reject maximization of expected monetary value as a valid guide in decision problems involving risky outcomes, what then is the proper criterion for decision making in such situations? In their pioneering work on game theory, Von Neumann and Morgenstern constructed a framework based on the assessment of the "utilities" of the outcomes, which provides an answer to this question.[7] Within their framework it can be shown that the *maximization of*

---

[6] This statement can be demonstrated as follows:

EMV = P(1st head on 1st toss) $\times 2^1$ + P(1st head on 2nd toss) $\times 2^2$ +

P(1st head on 3rd toss) $\times 2^3$ + ...

$= (\frac{1}{2})^1 \times 2^1 + (\frac{1}{2})^2 \times 2^2 + (\frac{1}{2})^3 \times 2^3 + ...$

$= 1 + 1 + 1 + ...$

EMV constitutes the sum of an infinitie series of 1's.

[7] See John Von Neumann and Oskar Morgenstern, *Theory of Games and Economic Behavior*, 3d ed. (Princeton, N.J.: Princeton University Press, 1953), pp. 15–30, especially pp. 26–27. Their framework consists of a series of axioms that imply the existence of a utility function. These axioms in turn yield a theorem concerning an individual's preferences for combinations of risky outcomes.

expected utility criterion will yield decisions that are in accord with the individual's true preferences, provided the individual is able to assess a consistent set of utilities over the possible outcomes in the problem. Expected utility is calculated by summing, over all the possible outcomes that may result from a decision, the product of the utility of each outcome, U_i, times its respective probability of occurrence, P_i:

$$E(U) = \sum_{i=1}^{n} U_i \times P_i$$

[3.5]

Despite the apparent attractiveness of this decision criterion, a number of difficulties arise in attempting to implement it. First, in a large organization, whose utility function do we use? In the case of a private firm do we use the managers' or the shareholders' utility functions? Suppose we use the shareholders' utility functions; since different shareholders have different utility functions, which one do we use? The utility functions of different individuals are not directly comparable, and hence it is theoretically impossible to arrive at a group utility function. Second, assuming that we have resolved the question of whose utility function to use, serious problems arise in measuring the utility function of an individual. The approaches used in attempting to empirically derive a utility function sometimes result in inconsistent utility assessments.[8] Similarly, theoretical approaches to the derivation of utility functions do not necessarily yield satisfactory results.[9] Nevertheless, if the decision makers' true preferences for the outcomes of the problem are to be incorporated into the decision-making framework, the lack of a better system for accomplishing this task forces us to attempt to make these utility assessments.

Let us illustrate how we can use utilities and the maximization of expected utility criterion in decision problems involving risk. Suppose an entrepreneur has developed a new and untested product and is considering whether to invest some capital in an effort to market the product. Suppose extensive studies of the marketing of products belonging to the same general category as this one have shown that 20 percent are successful and the remainder (that is, 80 percent) are failures. Since a subcontractor can be employed to manufacture the product, no investment in production facilities is required. The entrepreneur has determined that the cost of producing and marketing a batch of the product will be

---

[8] Frederick Mosteller and Phillip Nogee, "An Experimental Measurement of Utility," *Journal of Political Economy*, 59, no. 5 (October 1951), pp. 371–404; Donald Davidson and Patrick Suppes (in collaboration with Sidney Siegal), *Decision Making: An Experimental Approach* (Stanford, Calif.: Stanford University Press, 1957); P. E. Green, "Risk Attitudes and Chemical Investment Decisions," *Chemical Engineering Progress*, 59, no. 1 (January 1963), pp. 35–40; and C. Jackson Grayson, Jr., *Decisions Under Uncertainty: Drilling Decisions by Oil and Gas Operators* (Boston: Division of Research, Harvard Business School, 1960).

[9] One classic theoretical study was done by Milton Friedman and Leonard J. Savage, "The Utility Analysis of Choices Involving Risk," *Journal of Political Economy* 56, no. 4 (August 1948), pp. 279–304.

		STATES OF NATURE	
		Product is Successful	Product is a Failure
ALTERNATIVE ACTIONS (DECISIONS)	Invest in Product	$16,000	$ – 4,000
	Do Not Invest in Product	0	0
	Probability of occurrence	.20	.80

Figure 3.3
Payoff Table for Investment Decision Problem

$4,000. If the marketing effort is successful, a profit of $16,000 will result. Suppose further that the product can be easily copied and subsequent competition will therefore limit the profitable sales of the product to the initial production run. If the product is not initially successful and the marketing effort fails, the entrepreneur's loss will be limited to the initial $4,000 investment.

The basic characteristics of the decision problem can be summarized in a payoff table format such as Figure 3.3, where the various alternative actions (that is, decisions) are listed down the left-hand side of the payoff table, the various states of nature are listed across the top of the payoff table, and the various outcomes (that is, dollar payoffs) are listed in the payoff table for each action/state-of-nature combination. Note that the decision "Do Not Invest in Product" results in a zero return or payoff, regardless of the state of nature. The probability of occurrence of each state of nature is shown in the row below the payoff table.

The expected monetary value of the decision to "Invest in Product" is

$$EMV_1 = \$16,000 \times .20 + (\$-4,000) \times .80 = \$0$$

and for the decision "Do Not Invest" it is

$$EMV_2 = 0 \times .20 + 0 \times .80 = \$0$$

Therefore, based on the maximization of expected monetary value criterion, the entrepreneur would be *indifferent* to the two alternative actions in this problem.

Let us now introduce the entrepreneur's utility function into the decision-making framework and see how it affects preference for the two alternative actions.

In the first case, assume that the entrepreneur has the utility function (see Figure 3.4) that is characterized by *diminishing marginal utility* for money. *Marginal utility* measures the satisfaction the individual receives from a given incremental change in wealth.[10] Marginal utility is given by the *slope* of the utility function at any point on the curve.

---

[10] The terms *wealth, money*, and *return* are used interchangeably throughout the discussion of utility in this chapter.

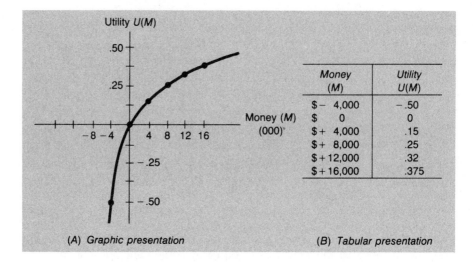

Figure 3.4
Utility Function
Exhibiting
Diminishing
Marginal Utility

The figure contains:

Money (M)	Utility U(M)
$− 4,000	−.50
$ 0	0
$+ 4,000	.15
$+ 8,000	.25
$+ 12,000	.32
$+ 16,000	.375

(A) Graphic presentation   (B) Tabular presentation

$$\text{Marginal Utility} = \text{Slope} = \frac{\Delta U(M)}{\Delta M} \qquad [3.6]$$

Diminishing marginal utility indicates that the slope of the utility function is *decreasing* as the stock of money (that is, wealth) increases. It means that as an individual's wealth increases, that individual receives *less additional satisfaction* from each equal increment of wealth.

By Equation 3.5, the expected utility, based on the utility function in Figure 3.4 of the decision to "Invest in Product," is

$$E(U_1) = U(\$16,000) \times .20 + U(\$ -4,000) \times .80$$
$$= .375 \times .20 + (-.50) \times .80 = -.325$$

and for the decision "Do Not Invest" it is

$$E(U_2) = U(0) \times .20 + U(0) \times .80$$
$$= 0 \times .20 + 0 \times .80 = 0$$

The decision "Do Not Invest" has a higher expected utility. Therefore, based on the maximization of expected utility criterion, the entrepreneur would decide *not* to invest in the new product.

In terms of expected value, the investment (that is, gamble) is fair since, as was shown earlier, it has an expected monetary value of zero. An individual who because of a diminishing marginal utility for money exhibits a definite preference for *not* undertaking fair investments such as this one is said to be *risk averse*, or to have an aversion to risk. Also, though not illustrated by this example, it is possible for the risk-averse individual to be unwilling to undertake investments having *positive* expected monetary values.

In the second case, assume that the entrepreneur has a utility function (see Figure 3.5) that is characterized by *increasing marginal utility* for money.

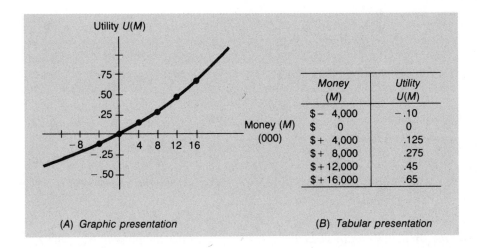

Money (M)	Utility U(M)
$- 4,000	-.10
$ 0	0
$+ 4,000	.125
$+ 8,000	.275
$+12,000	.45
$+16,000	.65

(A) Graphic presentation   (B) Tabular presentation

Figure 3.5
Utility Function Exhibiting Increasing Marginal Utility

Increasing marginal utility indicates that the slope of the utility function is increasing as the individual's wealth increases. In other words, it means that as an individual's wealth increases, that individual receives *more additional satisfaction* from each (equal) increment of wealth.

Based on the utility function in Figure 3.5 the expected utility of the decision to "Invest in the Product" is

$$E(U_1) = U(\$16,000) \times .20 + U(\$-4,000) \times .80$$
$$= .65 \times .20 + (-.10) \times .80 = +.05$$

and for the decision "Do Not Invest" it is the same as in the preceding diminishing marginal utility case; that is, $E(U_2) = 0$. Therefore, the optimal decision, based on the maximization of expected utility criterion, would be *to invest* in the product.

An individual who, because of an increasing marginal utility for money, has a definite preference for undertaking actuarially fair investments such as this one is said to be a *risk preferrer*, or to have a preference for risk. Although not illustrated by this decision problem, it is also possible for an individual with a preference for risk to be willing to undertake investments having *negative* expected monetary values.

As a final case, assume that the entrepreneur has a *linear* utility function (see Figure 3.6). In other words, the individual has a *constant marginal utility* for money, indicating that as wealth increases, the individual receives the *same additional satisfaction* from each given (equal) increment of wealth.

Although we will not illustrate the calculations for this case, it can be demonstrated that the expected utilities of both the decisions to "Invest in Product" and "Do Not Invest" are zero. Therefore, the entrepreneur with a linear utility function would be indifferent to the two alternative actions when seeking to maximize expected utility and would be said to be *risk neutral*. Note this is the same decision (that is, indifference) as was obtained earlier in this section with the maximization of expected monetary value criterion.

We will not prove the result here, but it can be shown that for an individual having a linear utility for money, *the maximization of expected monetary value*

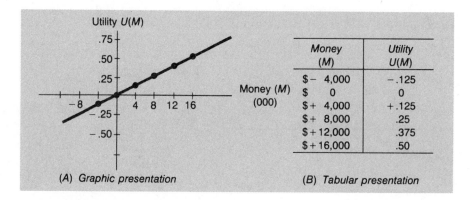

Figure 3.6
Utility Function Exhibiting Constant Marginal Utility

(A) Graphic presentation

(B) Tabular presentation

Money (M)	Utility U(M)
$- 4,000	-.125
$ 0	0
$+ 4,000	+.125
$+ 8,000	.25
$+12,000	.375
$+16,000	.50

criterion will generally yield the same decisions as the maximization of expected utility criterion. This statement has important implications for decision making. It means that if the decision maker feels his or her utility function is linear (or approximately linear) over the range of outcomes in a decision problem, then there is no need to go through the difficult task of attempting to derive his or her utility function for money. In this case, choosing the alternative with the *largest* expected monetary value will yield decisions that are in accord with the decision maker's true preferences.

In summary, we see that individuals' attitudes toward risk affect the shape of their utility function and determine the alternative that will be chosen in a decision problem involving risk.

Decision Tree Approach

Decision problems involving a reasonable number of alternative actions and states of nature can be analyzed using *decision trees*. Decision trees are an alternative approach to the use of payoff tables, such as the one illustrated earlier in Figure 3.3 for the investment decision problem. This decision problem is represented in the decision tree shown in Figure 3.7. In a decision tree, decision nodes (numbered boxes) are used to represent points at which the decision maker must choose among several alternative actions, and state-

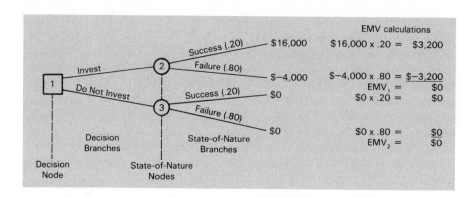

Figure 3.7
Decision Tree for Investment Decision Problem

of-nature nodes (numbered circles) are used to represent possible state-of-nature outcomes. At decision node $\boxed{1}$ are two decision branches (alternative actions)—Invest and Do Not Invest in Product. At the state-of-nature nodes ② and ③ are two state-of-nature branches (outcomes)—Product Is a Success and Product Is a Failure. The probabilities are shown along each state-of-nature branch. The outcome (payoff) is shown at the end of the branch. Using this information, we can calculate the expected monetary value for each decision branch and then select the one with the *largest* value. This yields the same results (that is, EMV and decision) as those shown in the previous section.

In the actual applications, decision trees can be much more complex than the one illustrated in Figure 3.7. They may involve sequential (or multiperiod) decision points with the opportunity to seek additional information (for example, through test market research) about the states of nature and then revise the probabilities.

When a decision tree is constructed with multiple periods, it is possible to recognize the feedback from each branch of the tree into each future period. For example, if a firm invests in a new product, the success or failure of that product in period 1 implies a great deal about its success or failure in future periods. If a product is successful during period 1, the probability of future success is greatly enhanced. Accordingly, the prospect of success in period 2 can be viewed as being closely correlated with the success in period 1. Similarly, the prospect of success in period 3 is enhanced if the product has been successful in periods 1 and 2. These *conditional* probabilities can be explicitly incorporated into a mutiperiod decision tree.

Risk-Adjusted Discount Rate Approach

When making long-term capital budgeting (investment) decisions, the risk-adjusted discount rate approach is a commonly used method for dealing with the uncertainty associated with future cash-flow estimates. In the basic net present value decision-making model (which is described in more detail in Chapter 17), net present value (NPV) is defined as

$$NPV = \sum_{t=1}^{n} \frac{NCF_t}{(1+k)^t} - NINV \qquad [3.7]$$

where NCF_t is the net cash flow in period t (for each of n periods). $NINV$ is the net investment, and k is the firm's *cost of capital*. An investment project is accepted if its NPV is greater than or equal to zero. In the risk-adjusted discount rate approach, the net cash flows for each project are discounted at a *risk-adjusted rate, k^**, rather than the firm's cost of capital (k). The magnitude of k^* depends on the risk of the project—the higher the risk, the higher the risk-adjusted discount rate.

The risk premiums (that is, $k^* - k$) applied to individual projects are commonly established *subjectively*. For example, some firms establish a small number of risk classes and then apply a different risk premium to each class. Average risk projects, such as equipment replacement decisions, might be evaluated at the firm's cost of capital; above-average-risk projects, such as facility expansions, might be assigned a risk premium of 3 percent above the firm's cost of capital; and high-risk projects, such as investments in totally new lines of business or the introduction of new products, might be assigned a risk premium of 8 percent above the firm's cost of capital. Since the risk premiums for each project are subjectively determined and no explicit consideration is given to the variation in cash flows of the project, this approach can lead to suboptimal decisions. In general, the risk-class method is most useful when evaluating relatively small projects that are frequently repeated. In these cases, much is known about the projects' potential returns, and it is probably not worth the effort to compute more "precise" risk premiums.

An example illustrating the application of the risk-adjusted discount rate approach is presented in the "Capital Budgeting and Risk" section of Chapter 17.

Simulation Approach

Computers have made it both feasible and relatively inexpensive to apply *simulation techniques* to economic decisions. Simulation is a planning tool that models some event. When simulation is used in capital budgeting, it requires that estimates be made of the probability distribution of each cash flow element (revenues, expenses, and so on). If, for example, a firm is considering introducing a new product, the elements of a simulation might include the number of units sold, market price, unit production costs, unit selling costs, the cost of the machinery needed to produce the new product, and the cost of capital. These probability distributions are then put into the simulation model to compute the project's net present value probability distribution. In any period NCF_t may be computed as

$$NCF_t = [n(p) - n(c + s) - D](1 - t) + D \qquad [3.8]$$

where n is the number of units sold, p the price per unit, c the unit production cost (excluding depreciation), s the unit selling cost, D the annual depreciation, and t the firm's marginal tax rate. Using Equation 3.8 and the previously defined NPV equation (Equation 3.7), it is possible to simulate the net present value of the project. Based on the probability distribution of each of the elements that influence the net present value, one value for each element is selected at random.

Assume, for example, that the following values for the input variables are randomly chosen: $n = 2,000$; $p = \$10$; $c = \$2$; $s = \$1$; $D = \$2,000$; and $t = 50\%$, or 0.50. Inserting these values into Equation 3.8 gives the following:

$$NCF_t = (2,000 \times \$10 - 2,000 \times \$3 - \$2,000)(1 - 0.50) + \$2,000$$
$$= (\$20,000 - \$6,000 - \$2,000) \times 0.50 + \$2,000$$
$$= \$8000$$

Assuming that the net investment is equal to the depreciable cost of the machinery ($10,000 in the example), that the net cash flows in each year of the project's life are identical, that $k = 10\%$, and that the project has a five-year life, the net present value of this particular iteration of the simulation can be

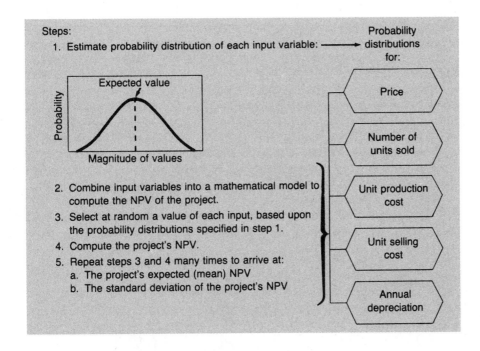

Figure 3.8
An Illustration of the Simulation Approach

computed as follows:

$$NPV = \sum_{t=1}^{5} \frac{\$8,000}{(1 + 0.10)^t} - 10,000$$

$$= \$8,000 \times 3.791 - \$10,000$$

$$= \$20,328$$

In an actual simulation the computer program is run a number of different times using different randomly selected input variables in each instance. Thus the program can be said to be repeated, or *iterated*, and each run is termed an *iteration*. In each iteration the net present value for the project would be computed accordingly. Figure 3.8 illustrates a typical simulation approach.

The results of these iterations are then used to plot a probability distribution of the project's net present values and to compute a mean and a standard deviation of returns. This information provides the decision maker with an estimate of a project's expected returns as well as its risk. Given this information, it is possible to compute the probability of achieving a net present value that is greater or less than any particular value.

For example, assume that the simulation for the previously illustrated project results in a normal distribution with an expected net present value of $12,000 and a standard deviation of $6,000. The probability of the project having a net present value of $0 or less can now be found. The value of $0 is -2.0 standard deviations below the mean:

$$z = \frac{\$0 - \$12,000}{\$6,000}$$

$$= -2.0$$

Figure 3.9
**A Sample
Illustration of the
Probability That
a Project's
Returns Will Be
Less Than $0**

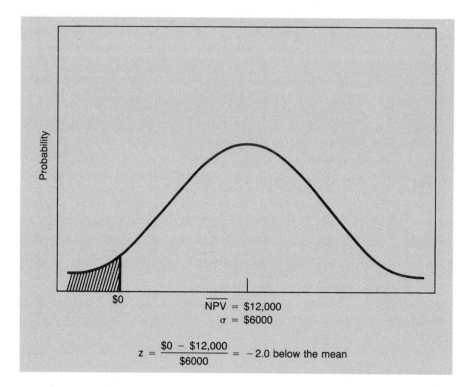

$$\text{NPV} = \$12{,}000$$
$$\sigma = \$6000$$

$$z = \frac{\$0 - \$12{,}000}{\$6000} = -2.0 \text{ below the mean}$$

It can be seen from Table 1 in the Appendix that the probability of a value less than -2.0 standard deviations from the mean is 2.28 percent. Thus there is a 2.28% chance that the actual net present value for this project will be negative. Figure 3.9 shows the probability distribution of this project's net present value. The shaded area under the curve represents the probability that the project will have a net present value of $0 or less.

The simulation approach is a powerful one because it explicitly recognizes all of the interactions among the variables that influence the outcome. It provides both a mean and a standard deviation that can help the decision maker effect trade-offs between risk and expected return. Unfortunately, considerable time and effort may be needed to gather the information for each of the input variables and to formulate the model correctly. This limits the feasibility of simulation to large projects. In addition, the simulation example illustrated here assumed that the values of the input variables were independent of one another. If this is not true—if, for example, the price of a product has a large influence on the number sold—then this interaction must be incorporated into the model, introducing even more complexity.

Decision-Making Under Uncertainty

Consider now a situation in which the decision maker is either unable or unwilling to specify the probabilities of occurrence for the various possible outcomes. Under these conditions, what is the appropriate decision criterion for

		STATES OF NATURE	
		S_1 Product Is a Success	S_2 Product Is a Failure
ALTERNATIVE ACTIONS	A_1 Invest in Product	.375	−.50
	A_2 Do Not Invest in Product	0	0

Figure 3.10
Utility (Payoff) Table for Investment Decision Problem

choosing among the alternative actions in a decision problem? As we shall see in the following analysis, a number of different decision rules are available and no single best criterion can be specified.

To illustrate various proposed decision criteria, consider again the investment decision example introduced earlier in the discussion of utility functions. Assume now that no information is available on the past success-failure rates for the marketing of similar types of products and that the entrepreneur is unable to furnish a subjective assessment of the chances of success and failure. Furthermore, assume that the entrepreneur's preferences for money are represented by the utility function shown in Figure 3.4. Using this utility function, the monetary payoffs of the investment decision problem shown in Figure 3.3 can be transformed into the utility values shown in Figure 3.10. The two decision criteria, which are illustrated in this section, are the *maximin* criterion and the *minimax regret* criterion.[11]

Maximin Criterion

The maximin criterion concentrates on the worst possible outcome (that is, *minimum* or smallest utility) across all states of nature associated with each alternative action. For the alternative A_1 ("Invest in Product"), the minimum utility in the first row of Figure 3.10 is −.50. Likewise, for the alternative A_2 ("Do Not Invest in Product") the minimum utility in the second row is 0. With the maximin criterion, the alternative action having the *maximum* of these minimum utility values is chosen. Using this criterion, we would decide not to invest in the product (that is, Action A_2) since this alternative has the largest minimum utility value.

The maximin criterion is a very conservative decision-making rule because it evaluates alternative actions solely on the worst possible outcome associated with each action. Hypothetical decision problems can be constructed in which

---

[11] Various other decision criteria (namely, Hurwicz criterion, principle of insufficient reason) have been proposed. See Luce and Raiffa, *Games and Decisions*, sec. 13.2–13.5, for a discussion of these criteria and related decision-making concepts.

this criterion will yield choices that many critics find inappropriate or unreasonable.[12]

Minimax Regret Criterion

Regret measures the loss that results from choosing the incorrect alternative action for a given state of nature. The regret associated with an alternative action is the *difference* between the *best possible* payoff (or utility) that could have been received and the *actual* payoff (or utility) that is received. For example, consider the utility entries in Figure 3.10. Suppose S_1 is true (that is, the "Product Is a Success"). The regret associated with Alternative A_2 ("Do Not Invest In Product") is the difference between largest utility in the S_1 column (that is, .375 for A_1) and the utility of A_2 in this column (that is, 0). Thus in the regret table, shown in Figure 3.11, a value of .375 has been entered into the (A_2, S_1) position. Clearly, there is no regret associated with Alternative A_1 ("Invest in Product"), since this is the correct decision when S_1 is true. Hence, a zero has been entered in the (A_1, S_1) position in Figure 3.11. Similar reasoning yields the regret values in the S_2 ("Product Is A Failure") column.

Having specified the regret table, the *maximum* regret for each alternative action is determined. For A_1 the maximum regret (in row 1) is .5. Similarly, for A_2 the maximum regret (in row 2) is .375. The decision maker then chooses the alternative action having the *minimum* of these maximum regret values. In this case he or she would choose not to invest in the product (A_2), since this alternative has the smallest maximum regret value. Although this is the same action that was chosen previously using the maximin criterion, these two decision criteria need not, in general, yield the same decisions.

As with the maximin criterion, serious questions have been raised concerning the applicability of minimax regret as a decision-making criterion. Consideration of these questions, however, is beyond the scope of this chapter.[13]

Figure 3.11
Regret Table for Investment Decision Problem

			STATES OF NATURE	
			S_1 Product Is a Success	S_2 Product Is a Failure
ALTERNATIVE ACTIONS		A_1 Invest in Product	0	.50
		A_2 Do Not Invest in Product	.375	0

---

[12] See Luce and Raiffa, *Games and Decisions*, pp. 279–280, for an example of a decision-making situation that illustrates one of the problems associated with the maximin criterion.

[13] See Luce and Raiffa, *Games and Decisions*, p. 281, for a summary of some of the objections that have been raised concerning this criterion.

The material in this and the preceding sections is only an introduction to the broad area of decision theory. The concepts discussed are designed to yield decisions in relatively simple types of problems. More complicated types, involving sequential decisions and the possibility of experimentation, require the use of more advanced analytical techniques.

Managing Risk and Uncertainty

Many avenues are open to the manager who wishes to reduce the level of risk associated with a particular decision. In this section we briefly consider some of these strategies for managing risk.

Acquisition of Additional Information

In many cases the risk facing a manager arises because of a lack of information. For example, when making the decision to develop and market a new product, there is considerable risk regarding the market's acceptance of this new product. In order to reduce this risk many firms will "test market" the product in a limited area or present the product to panels of consumers for their evaluation. These tactics provide important information to the company as it seeks to assess the probable success of the new product.

Information can also be purchased from individuals or firms that possess the knowledge the decision maker seeks. For example, a wildcat oil drilling firm will employ the services of petroleum geologists as it attempts to determine where to drill exploratory wells. Similarly, companies that plan to sell new debt securities often pay to have their bonds "rated" by one of the bond rating services, such as Moody's or Standard and Poors. The ratings applied to the bonds reduce the risk of determining the yield that will have to be offered to investors when the bonds are sold.

Normally, additional information is costly. Hence, the wealth maximizing firm would be willing to pay for additional information as long as the marginal value of that information exceeds its marginal cost.

Diversification

Diversification is the act of investing in a set of securities or assets having different risk-return characteristics. By investing in diverse assets the firm can achieve considerably more stability in returns than is possible by investing in a single asset. When a firm diversifies it holds a *portfolio* of assets or investments. *Portfolio risk* is the risk associated with collections of assets or securities. In the following examples we illustrate diversification through a portfolio of securities. The principles developed in these examples, however, are equally relevant to any collection of different assets. The diversification strategy has been used by many firms to reduce the risk associated with operating in a narrow line of business. The desire for diversification is also a major reason for many corporate mergers.

Expected Returns from a Portfolio. When two or more securities are combined into a portfolio, the expected return of the portfolio is equal to the weighted average of the expected returns from the individual securities. For example, assume a portfolio contains Acme Corporation (A) securities and Babbo Corporation (B) securities, which have expected returns of 12 percent and 8 percent, respectively. If a portion W_A of the available funds (wealth) is invested in Security A, and the remaining funds W_B is invested in Security B, the expected return of the portfolio $\bar{R}_p$ is as follows:

$$\bar{R}_p = W_A\bar{R}_A + W_B\bar{R}_B, \tag{3.9}$$

where $\bar{R}_A$ and $\bar{R}_B$ are the expected returns for Securities A and B respectively. Furthermore, $W_A + W_B = 1$, indicating that all funds are invested in either Security A or Security B.

The range of possible expected returns for a portfolio consisting of Securities A and B is 12 percent (if 100 percent of the portfolio is invested in Security A and 0 percent is invested in Security B) to 8 percent (if 100 percent is invested in Security B and 0 percent is invested in Security A). In addition, any linear weighted combination of returns for Securities A and B between 8 and 12 percent is also possible. For example, assume that 30 percent of this portfolio consists of Security A, and Security B constitutes the remaining 70 percent. In this case the expected return on the portfolio is computed as follows:

$$\bar{R}_p = 0.3(12\%) + 0.7(8\%) = 9.2\%$$

In general, the expected return from any portfolio of n securities or assets is equal to the sum of the expected returns from each security times the proportion of the total portfolio invested in that security:

$$\bar{R}_p = \sum_{i=1}^{n} W_i\bar{R}_i, \tag{3.10}$$

where $\Sigma W_i = 1$ and $0 \le W_i \le 1$.

Portfolio Risk. Although the expected returns from a portfolio of two or more securities can be computed as a weighted average of the expected returns from the individual securities, it is not sufficient merely to calculate a weighted average of the risk of each individual security to arrive at a measure of the portfolio's risk. Whenever the returns from the individual securities are not perfectly positively correlated, the risk of any portfolio of these securities may be reduced through the effects of diversification. Thus, diversification can be achieved by investing in a diverse set of securities that have different risk-return characteristics. The amount of risk reduction achieved through diversification depends on the degree of correlation between the returns of the individual securities in the portfolio. The lower the correlations among the individual securities, the greater the possibilities for risk reduction.

The risk for a two-security portfolio, measured by the standard deviation of portfolio returns, is computed as follows:

$$\sigma_p = \sqrt{W_A^2\sigma_A^2 + W_B^2\sigma_B^2 + 2W_AW_B\rho_{AB}\sigma_A\sigma_B}, \tag{3.11}$$

78

where W_A is the proportion of funds invested in Security A; W_B is the proportion of funds invested in Security B; $W_A + W_B = 1$; σ_A^2 is the variance of returns from Security A (or the square of the standard deviation for Security A, σ_A); σ_B^2 is the variance of returns from Security B (or the square of the standard deviation for Security B, σ_B); and ρ_{AB} is the correlation coefficient of returns between Securities A and B.[14]

For example, consider a portfolio containing Securities A and B as described here:

	Acme (A)	Babbo (B)
Expected return	0.12	0.08
Standard deviation of returns	0.09	0.09
Proportion invested in each security	0.5	0.5

Given various values for the correlation between the securities' returns, the risk of a portfolio containing equal proportions of the two securities can be computed.

First, consider the case where $\rho_{AB} = +1.0$ (that is, perfect *positive* correlation). The portfolio's risk is calculated as follows:

$$\sigma_p = \sqrt{(0.5)^2(0.09)^2 + (0.5)^2(0.09)^2 + 2(0.5)(0.5)(+1)(0.09)(0.09)}$$
$$= \sqrt{0.002025 + 0.002025 + 0.00405}$$
$$= \sqrt{0.0081}$$
$$= 0.09.$$

When the returns from the two securities are perfectly positively correlated, the risk of the portfolio is equal to the weighted average of the risk of the individual securities (9 percent in this example). *Thus, no risk reduction is achieved when perfectly positively correlated assets are combined in a portfolio.*

The returns from most assets are not perfectly positively correlated; this allows for risk reduction through diversification. For example, consider next the case of a low positive correlation of returns, such as $\rho_{AB} = +0.1$. The portfolio risk in this example is as follows:

$$\sigma_p = \sqrt{(0.5)^2(0.09)^2 + (0.5)^2(0.09)^2 + 2(0.5)(0.5)(+0.1)(0.09)(0.09)}$$
$$= \sqrt{0.002025 + 0.002025 + 0.000405}$$
$$= \sqrt{0.004455}$$
$$= 0.067$$

---

[14] The correlation coefficient measures the extent to which high (or low) values of one variable are associated with high (or low) values of another. Values of the correlation coefficient range from +1.0, for perfectly positively correlated variables, to −1.0, for perfectly negatively correlated variables. The *less* two variables are positively correlated, the *greater* are the potential benefits of portfolio risk reduction. See chapter 6 for additional discussion of the meaning and measurement of the correlation coefficient.

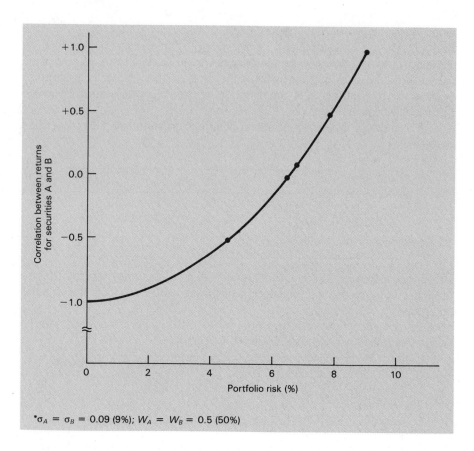

Figure 3.12
Portfolio Risk versus Correlation of Security Returns*

*$\sigma_A = \sigma_B = 0.09$ (9%); $W_A = W_B = 0.5$ (50%)

In this case diversification reduces the portfolio risk from 9 percent (the weighted average of the individual security risks) to 6.7 percent.

Finally, consider the case of a perfect *negative* correlation $\rho_{AB} = -1.0$. In this example the portfolio risk is completely eliminated.[15]

Figure 3.12 graphs the relationship between the correlation of returns for securities A and B and the risk (σ_p) of a portfolio containing equal proportions of securities A and B ($W_A = W_B = 0.5$). This figure indicates that the relationship between portfolio risk and the correlation of security returns is not linear.

One of the benefits of diversification is the reduction of total portfolio risk. This risk reduction is often cited as one of the primary reasons for corporate diversification. However, the evidence is mixed regarding the consistency of corporate diversification with the objective of shareholder wealth maximization.

---

[15] When returns from two assets are perfectly negatively correlated, *some* combination of these two assets in a portfolio can completely eliminate portfolio risk. This risk eliminating combination will only be $W_A = W_B = 0.5$ when the two assets have the same standard deviation of returns. When this is not the case, the weightings of W_A and W_B must be changed from 0.5 in order to fully eliminate portfolio risk.

Many argue that stockholders can diversify better and more cheaply than corporations can; therefore, the market will not highly value diversification undertaken at the firm level.

Hedging

A *hedge* is a transaction that limits the risk associated with market price fluctuations for a particular investment position. A hedge is accomplished by taking offsetting positions in the ownership of an asset or security, such as buying or selling a futures contract (or an option) to offset risk exposure in the cash market. A *futures contract* is a standardized contract, traded on an organized exchange, to buy or sell a fixed quantity of a defined commodity at a set price in the future. Hedging can also be accomplished using *forward contracts.* A forward contract is a contractual agreement between two parties to exchange a commodity at a set price in the future. The primary differences between futures contracts and forward contracts is that forward contracts are not actively traded on an organized exchange, such as the Chicago Board of Trade; normally forward contracts do not deal in standardized goods; and they carry the risk that one party to the contract may not perform as agreed. In contrast, futures contracts carry no such performance risk because they are essentially guaranteed by the exchange on which they are traded.

Futures and forward contracts create the legal obligation for the buyer (or seller) to purchase (or sell) the goods specified in the contract at the agreed upon price at some future point in time. In contrast, an *option* gives the buyer the *right*, but not the obligation, to either buy or sell the underlying commodity. We will confine our discussion of hedging to futures contracts. A complete discussion of hedging using forward contracts, options, and options on futures contracts is provided in several of the references listed at the end of this chapter.

Futures markets exist for many commodities, including minerals (such as copper, gold, silver, and crude oil), agricultural commodities (such as corn, wheat, live hogs, cotton, and cattle), and financial instruments (such as Treasury Bills, Treasury Bonds, foreign currencies, commercial paper, and broad-based common stock indexes like the *Standard and Poor's 500 Stock Index*). Any enterprise that normally buys or sells these commodities (or products closely related to these commodities) or is engaged in borrowing or lending operations can make use of future contracts, forward markets, and options to eliminate, or at least largely offset, the risk of future price fluctuations.

Consider the case of a corporate treasurer who projects in late September that the company's cash flows will require a $3 million bank loan in mid-December. This loan is expected to be needed for three months. The contractual agreement between the corporate borrower and its bank establishes the rate on loans such as this to be 1.5 percentage points above the three-month Eurodollar rate (also referred to as the LIBOR—London Interbank Offering Rate). The current (September) LIBOR rate is 9.5 percent. The treasurer is concerned that this rate may increase over the next three months. Therefore, the treasurer wishes to "lock-in" the current rate (11 percent) as her company's cost of borrowing in mid-December.

Eurodollar Time Deposit futures contracts are traded on the International Monetary Market (IMM), a division of the Chicago Mercantile Exchange. These Eurodollar contracts are for $1 million of three-month Eurodollar time deposits. The IMM has a pricing system that quotes these contracts on a discounted percentage basis; that is, the price of a contract is quoted as 100 minus the annualized interest rate on three-month Eurodollar Time Deposits. For example, a contract price of 91 implies an annualized interest rate of 9 percent (100 minus 91 = 9 percent).

In September, the corporate treasurer observes that the December futures contract, which can be used to "lock-in" the forward borrowing rate, is trading at 90.30, implying a forward Eurodollar rate of 9.7 percent (100.0–90.3). If the treasurer sells three December Eurodollar futures contracts ($1 million each) at 90.3, she can assure that her cost of funds in December will be 11.2 percent (9.7 percent LIBOR rate plus the 1.5 percentage points spread over LIBOR charged by the bank).

By mid-December the current Eurodollar rate has risen to 12.0 percent. The December futures price has declined to 88.00, reflecting the current 12 percent rate. Because of these higher rates, the company's quarterly interest payments to the bank are $101,250 ($3,000,000 × 13.5 percent × 0.25 years). The decline in the futures price, however, produces a profit for the corporate treasurer of $17,250 [(90.3–88.0) × $25,000 × 3 contracts]. (Each one percentage point increase in the price of a Eurodollar futures contract is equivalent to an increase in the value of that contract of $2,500, (that is, $1,000,000 × .01 × 0.25 years). Recall that the corporate treasurer sold three Eurodollar contracts in September at 90.3. The treasurer can cancel her position in the futures market by buying three contracts in December at the new lower price of 88.0.

Thus, the net interest cost to the corporate treasurer is $84,000 ($101,250 interest payment to the bank less $17,250 profit from the futures contracts), giving an effective annual rate of 11.2 percent. In this example, the treasurer has perfectly hedged her borrowing cost position. In practice, it is usually not possible to perfectly hedge one's position because of (1) differences in the size of standard future contracts and the amount of hedging desired by the firm; (2) the inability to find a futures contract in a commodity or financial instrument that has precisely the same pattern of price movements as the commodity or financial instrument in which the firm is dealing; and (3) variations in the difference (called the basis) between the spot or cash market price for a commodity or financial instrument and the futures market price. In spite of these shortcomings, hedging can be used in many situations to reduce the risk of future price changes in goods or financial instruments. Over the past decade many new financial futures and option contracts have been developed that permit financial institutions and other firms to control their future financing cost and/or to guarantee their returns on anticipated future investments.

Other Approaches for Managing Risk

In addition to hedging, acquiring additional information, and diversifying, several other techniques can be used to manage risk, such as purchasing

Economic Analysis and Managerial Efficiency

THE TORO COMPANY AND THE PROBABILITY OF SNOW*

The Toro Company makes snow blowers that remove snow from walks and driveways. According to Richard Pollick, marketing director at Toro, "We found that the big barrier to buying one of our machines was the fear that there wouldn't be enough snow to justify the cost."

The company designed a promotional campaign to overcome this problem. It agreed to refund the entire price of its machines purchased before December 10 if the snowfall during the ensuing winter was less than 20 percent of the forty-year average for the purchase location. In effect, then, the customer would get the snow blower free! If the snow fall was less than 50 percent of the forty-year average, then Toro would refund part of the purchase price. According to the marketing director, this promotion led to significantly increased early season sales.

*Based on Bill Richards, "Executives at Toro Are Dreaming Of a White Winter—Very White" *The Wall Street Journal*, 12 December 1983.

After the program ended, company management began to monitor closely reports from 172 weather stations located in the northern part of the country. Toro also hedged its bets by purchasing weather insurance from Good Weather International, a New York company. In the event of low snowfall amounts, Good Weather would reimburse Toro for its losses.

The probability that Good Weather would have to reimburse Toro under this agreement is very small. According to a meteorologist at the National Climatic Center, Minneapolis has *never* had a winter in its recorded history with a snowfall less than 20 percent of the average. Also, the city has had less than 50 percent of its average snowfall only four times in the past forty years.

Questions

1. What factors might have led Toro management to consider purchasing this type of insurance?
2. What factors would the managers at Good Weather have to consider in determining a price (i.e., insurance premium) to charge Toro for this protection?

insurance, gaining control over the operating environment, and limiting the use of firm-specific assets.

Insurance. When an individual makes a premium payment to an insurance company, that individual is exchanging the premium payment for protection against specified losses, up to the limits identified in the policy. Insurance is commonly available for losses due to fires, natural disasters, accidents occurring in the workplace, the death of key employees, fraud, product liability, and theft. Some financial instruments such as corporate bonds are backed by insurance that guarantees the payment of principal and interest. When deciding which risks should be insured externally, and which should be self-insured, efficient managers are confronted with a trade-off between a certain, small, periodic cost (the payment of the insurance premium), and the uncertainty of bearing the full cost of a loss from time to time. The willingness of managers to assume some insurable risks, the cost of the insurance, and the severity of the consequences of experiencing an uninsured loss will determine whether insurance is purchased or not.

Gaining Control Over the Operating Environment. Some business risks can be reduced by actions designed to gain control over the operating environment. For example, in order to assure adequate outlets for its products, a firm may establish a network of exclusive dealerships. If access to raw materials is uncertain, a firm may integrate backwards toward the source of supplies. The use of patents and copyrights can protect a firm against immediate competition. Legal action can also reinforce its rights under patents and copyrights. For example, in early 1988 Apple Computer sued Microsoft because many of the new programs being developed by Microsoft had "the look and feel of the Apple operating environment." This lawsuit has been widely recognized as an attempt to delay the development of operating systems for the IBM personal computer that will compete more directly with the Apple products.

Limited Use of Firm-Specific Assets. If a firm builds a plant that can only be used to produce its specific product, that firm has effectively limited its options should the product prove to be unsuccessful. The more general the purpose of the assets employed by a firm, the more flexibility that firm has to redeploy these assets to other uses. A tradeoff exists between the use of firm- or product-specific assets, which are likely to be more efficient, and the use of more general-purpose assets, which give the firm increased future flexibility. When planning new investments, this tradeoff must be carefully evaluated.

Summary

■ A decision problem consists of several basic elements—a decision maker, a set of objectives, two or more alternative actions that can possibly achieve the desired objectives, a state of doubt about which alternative is best in achieving the objectives, and an environment consisting of factors beyond the control of the decision maker.

■ For purposes of exposition and analysis, decision making is divided into several parts: *individual decision making* under *certainty, risk,* and *uncertainty,* and *group decision making.* Decision making under risk refers to the situation where the probabilities of the possible outcomes can be specified by the decision maker. In decision making under uncertainty, the decision maker is either unwilling or unable to specify these probabilities. Group decision making refers to the situation where a conflict exists among the objectives of the participants.

■ *Risk* refers to the potential variability of outcomes from a decision alternative. It can be measured either by the *standard deviation* (an absolute measure of risk) or *coefficient of variation* (a relative measure of risk).

- The decision maker's attitude toward risk affects the shape of his or her utility function and the choices he or she will make in a decision problem involving risk or uncertainty.

- Many different approaches are available for incorporating risk into the decision-making process. Five of these methods are the *informal approach, utility function approach, decision tree approach, risk-adjusted discount rate approach,* and the *simulation approach.*

- The *maximin* and *minimax regret* decision criteria can be used to choose between alternatives in decision making under uncertainty.

- Many techniques are available for managing risk, including investing in additional information, using options and futures contracts to hedge a position in the cash market, using portfolio risk reduction techniques when making investment decisions, purchasing insurance, investing in "flexible assets," and making decisions designed to gain some control over the operating environment.

Selected References

Ackoff, Russell L. *Scientific Method: Optimizing Applied Research Decisions.* New York: John Wiley, 1962.

Chernoff, H., and L. E. Moses. *Elementary Decision Theory.* New York: John Wiley, 1959.

Copeland, T. E. and J. F. Weston. *Financial Theory and Corporate Policy*, 3rd ed. Reading, Mass.: Addison-Wesley, 1988, especially chapters 8 and 9 dealing with options and futures.

Cox, J. C. and M. Rubinstein. *Option Markets.* Englewood Cliffs, N. J.: Prentice-Hall, 1985.

Davidson, Donald, and Patrick Suppes (in collaboration with Sidney Siegal). *Decision Making: An Experimental Approach.* Stanford, Calif.: Stanford University Press, 1957.

Dresher, Melvin. *Games of Strategy: Theory and Applications.* Englewood Cliffs, N.J.: Prentice-Hall, 1961.

Friedman, Milton, and Leonard J. Savage. "The Utility Analysis of Choices Involving Risk." *Journal of Political Economy*, 56, no. 4 (August 1948). Reprinted in Stephen Archer and Charles D'Ambrosio, eds., *The Theory of Business Finance: A Book of Readings.* New York: Macmillan, 1967.

Grabbe, J. O. *International Financial Markets.* New York: Elsevier, 1986.

Kolb, R. *Understanding Futures Markets*, 2nd ed. Glenview, Ill.: Scott, Foresman, 1988.

Luce, R. Duncan, and Howard Raiffa. *Games and Decisions.* New York: John Wiley, 1957.

Markowitz, Harry. *Portfolio Selection: Efficient Diversification of Investments.* New York: John Wiley, 1959.

Savage, Leonard J. *The Foundations of Statistics.* New York: John Wiley, 1954.

Schlaifer, R. *Probability and Statistics for Business Decisions.* New York: McGraw-Hill, 1959.

Von Neumann, John, and Oskar Morgenstern. *Theory of Games and Economic Behavior*, 3d ed. Princeton, N.J.: Princeton University Press, 1953.

Discussion Questions

1. Define the following terms:
   a. Probability
   b. Probability distribution

    c. Expected value

    d. Risk

    e. Standard deviation

    f. Coefficient of variation

    g. Risk-adjusted discount rate

    h. Uncertainty

    i. Maximin decision-making criterion

    j. Minimax regret decision-making criterion

2. Explain the difference between a *discrete* probability distribution and a *continuous* probabiility distribution.

3. Under what conditions is the coefficient of variation a more appropriate measure of risk than the standard deviation?

4. Illustrate by means of a graph (or table) the difference between the utility functions of individuals who have the following:

    a. Diminishing marginal utility for money

    b. Constant marginal utility for money

    c. Increasing marginal utility for money

5. Under what conditions (if any) will the maximization of expected monetary value criterion yield the same decisions as the maximization of expected utility criterion in decision problems involving risk?

6. Describe the basic elements of a decision problem.

7. Explain how payoff tables and decision trees are used in decision problems involving risk and uncertainty.

8. How much should a firm spend to acquire additional information in order to reduce the risk associated with its decisions?

9. How can a firm use the diversification principle to reduce its operating risk?

10. Distinguish between forward and futures contracts.

Problems

1. The Compatible Computer Company, a computer software developer, has estimated the probability of next year's revenues as follows:

Revenues ($000)	Probability
700	.10
800	.20
900	.40
1,000	.20
1,100	.10

    a. Compute expected annual revenues.

    b. Compute the standard deviation of annual revenues.

    c. Compute the coefficient of variation of annual revenues.

2. The demand for MICHTEC's products is related to the state of the economy. If the economy is expanding next year (an above-normal growth in GNP), the company expects sales to be $90 million. If there is a recession next year (a decline in GNP), sales are expected to be $75 million. If next year is normal (a moderate growth in GNP), sales are expected to be $85 million. MICHTEC's economists have estimated the chances that the economy will be either expanding, normal, or in a recession next year at .2, .5, and .3 respectively.

a. Compute expected annual sales.

b. Compute the standard deviation of annual sales.

c. Compute the coefficient of variation of annual sales.

3. Two investments have the following expected returns (net present values) and standard deviation of returns:

Project	Expected Returns	Standard Deviation
A	$ 50,000	$ 40,000
B	250,000	125,000

a. Based on the standard deviation, which project is riskier?

b. Based on the coefficient of variation, which project is riskier?

c. Which measure of risk do you think is appropriate to use in this case? Why?

4. An investment project has expected annual net cash flows of $100,000 with a standard deviation of $40,000. The distribution of annual net cash flows is approximately normal.

a. Determine the probability that the annual net cash flows will be negative.

b. Determine the probability that the annual net cash flows will be less than $20,000.

5. The manager of the aerospace division of General Aeronautics has estimated the price it can charge for providing satellite launch services to commercial firms. Her most optimistic estimate (a price not expected to be exceeded more than 10 percent of the time) is $2 million. Her most pessimistic estimate (a lower price than this one is not expected more than 10 percent of the time) is $1 million. The price distribution is believed to be approximately normal.

a. What is the expected price?

b. What is the standard deviation of the launch price?

c. What is the probability of receiving a price less than $1.2 million?

6. Suppose that a person is considering an investment in a new product. It is estimated that the cost of producing and marketing the product is $6,000. Three possible outcomes can result from this investment:

■ The product can be *extremely successful* and yield a *net* profit of $24,000.

■ The product can be *moderately successful* and yield a *net* profit of $12,000.

■ The product can be *unsuccessful*, in which case the loss will be equal to the initial cost of producing and marketing the product (that is, $6,000).

Additionally, assume that if the person does *not* invest in the new product, the $6,000 can be invested in another venture that is certain to yield a *net* profit of $1,500. Furthermore, suppose that he or she has assessed the chances of the product being extremely successful, moderately successful, and unsuccessful at .10, .20, and .70, respectively.

a. Determine the decision alternatives.

b. Determine the possible outcomes for each decision alternative.

c. Formulate the problem in a payoff table format (such as Figure 3.3) showing the net profit that will result from each alternative action/state-of-nature combination.
d. Determine the expected net profit of each decision alternative.
e. Assuming that the objective is to maximize expected monetary payoff, which alternative should be chosen?

7. Assume that the decision maker faced with the investment alternatives in Problem 6 is risk averse in the sense of having a diminishing marginal utility for money (return). Suppose the utility function can be specified as

Money (M)	Utility $U(M)$
−6,000	−.75
0	0.0
+1,500	.09
+6,000	.225
+12,000	.375
+24,000	.525

a. Formulate Problem 6 in a utility (payoff) table format (such as Figure 3.10), showing the utility that will result from each alternative action/state-of-nature combination.
b. Determine the expected utilities of each of the alternative actions.
c. Based on the maximization of expected utility criterion, which alternative should be chosen?

8. Consider Problem 7 again. Suppose that the decision maker is either unable or unwilling to assess the probabilities of the product being extremely successful, moderately successful, or unsuccessful.

a. Based on the *maximin* decision criterion, which alternative should be selected?
b. Based on the *minimax regret* decision criterion, which alternative should be selected?

9. Shown below is an entrepreneur's utility function for money (return) along with two alternative investment projects (A and B). Assume that the entrepreneur only has enough funds to undertake one of these investments.

Utility Function		Investment			
Return	Utility		A		B
		Return	Probability	Return	Probability
$−300,000	−4.00				
0	0.0				
300,000	.60	$−300,000	.40	$−300,000	.10
450,000	.80	1,500,000	.60	0	.20
750,000	1.00			450,000	.40
1,500,000	1.33			750,000	.30

a. Calculate the expected monetary value of each investment.
b. Assuming that the entrepreneur's investment objective is to maximize expected monetary value, which investment should be chosen?

c. Calculate the expected utility of each investment.

d. Assuming that the entrepreneur's objective is to maximize expected utility, which investment should be chosen?

e. Explain why there is a difference in the alternatives chosen in parts (b) and (d).

10. A simulation model similar to the one described in the chapter has been constructed by the HNG Corporation to evaluate the largest of its new investment proposals. After many iterations of the model, HNG's management has arrived at an expected net present value of $4.2 million with a standard deviation of $2.4 million. The net present value probability distribution is approximately normal.

a. Determine the probability that the project will have a negative net present value.

b. Determine the probability that the net present value will be less than $1.0 million.

11. A bakery is considering how many dozen hamburger buns to stock on Saturdays. From past experience, the probabilities of selling 20, 25, 30, 35, or 40 dozen are known to be .15, .20, .30, .25, and .10, respectively. The selling price is $2 per dozen and the cost is $1 per dozen. Any hamburger buns unsold at the end of the day must be sold to a surplus baked goods store for $.30 per dozen, as they cannot be sold in the bakery the following day. The bakery must decide whether to stock 20, 25, 30, 35, or 40 dozen.

a. Determine the alternative actions under consideration.

b. Determine the states of nature.

c. Formulate the problem in a payoff table format showing the net profit that will result from each alternative action/state-of-nature combination.

d. Determine the expected profit of each alternative action.

e. Based on the maximization of expected monetary value criterion, how many dozen hamburger buns should the bakery stock on Saturdays?

12. An investor is considering investing in two securities. Security A, the less risky security, has an expected return of 12 percent with a standard deviation of 3 percent. Security B has an expected return of 21 percent with a standard deviation of 11 percent. The correlation between the returns for securities A and B is +0.3. The investor plans to put 60 percent of his wealth in A and 40 percent in B.

a. Calculate the expected return from a portfolio made up of securities A and B.

b. What is the standard deviation of this portfolio's returns?

c. What is the probability of receiving a portfolio return of less than 15 percent?

13. Mammouth Mutual Fund of New York has $10 million to invest in certificates of deposit (CDs) for the next 6 months (180 days). It can buy either a Pittsburgh National Bank (PNB) CD with an annual yield of 11 percent or a Frankfurt (West Germany) Bank CD with a yield of 13.5 percent. Assume that the CDs are of comparable default risk. The analysts of the mutual fund are concerned about exchange rate risk. They were quoted the following exchange rates by the international department of a New York City bank:

West Germany *(Deutsche Marks)*	
Spot	$0.5200
30-day futures	0.5190
90-day futures	0.5170
180-day futures	0.5155

a. If the Frankfurt Bank CD is purchased and held to maturity, determine the net gain (loss) in U.S. dollars relative to the PNB CD assuming that the exchange rate in 180 days equals today's spot rate.

b. Suppose the West German mark declines in value by 5 percent relative to the U.S. dollar over the next 180 days. Determine the net gain (loss) of the Frankfurt Bank CD in U.S. dollars relative to the PNB CD for an uncovered position.

c. Determine the net gain (loss) from a covered position.

14. A corn producer can profitably produce a minimum of 10,000 bushels of corn if he is assured of a price of $2.90 per bushel at the time of planting. The corn will be harvested in late August. At the time of planting the farmer notes that the September futures price for corn is $2.90.

a. What action should the farmer take to hedge his position, that is, to "lock in" an effective price of $2.90 for his corn?

b. By late August the price of cash corn has dropped to $2.50. The September futures price has also declined to $2.50. Ignoring commissions, compute the net profits and losses from the farmer's hedged position, after the farmer closes out the hedge.

c. How does your answer to part (b) change if the late August cash price and the September futures price increase to $3.40?

Tools of Analysis

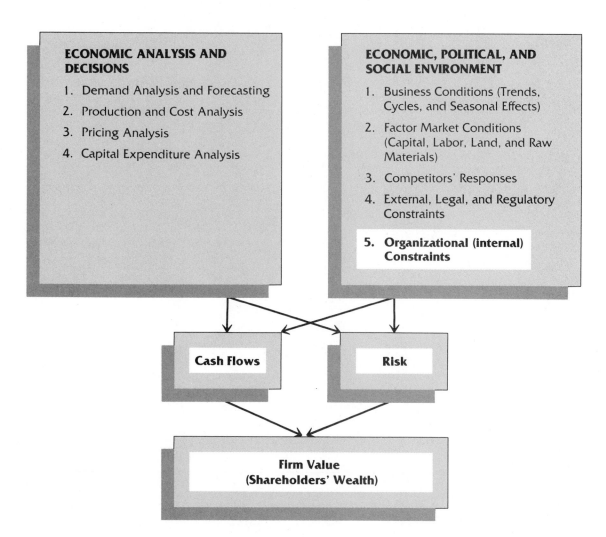

ECONOMIC ANALYSIS AND DECISIONS

1. Demand Analysis and Forecasting
2. Production and Cost Analysis
3. Pricing Analysis
4. Capital Expenditure Analysis

ECONOMIC, POLITICAL, AND SOCIAL ENVIRONMENT

1. Business Conditions (Trends, Cycles, and Seasonal Effects)
2. Factor Market Conditions (Capital, Labor, Land, and Raw Materials)
3. Competitors' Responses
4. External, Legal, and Regulatory Constraints
5. **Organizational (internal) Constraints**

Cash Flows

Risk

Firm Value (Shareholders' Wealth)

Part II (Tools of Analysis) of the book discusses tools of analysis that can assist managers in the efficient allocation of resources. Chapter 4 introduces classical optimization techniques. A review of basic calculus concepts used in the text is also provided in Chapter 4. Chapter 5 considers the linear programming optimization tool. Linear programming is a powerful analytical technique which permits managers to identify optimal resource allocation decisions in circumstances where there are constraints on the objective function. Chapter 6 provides an overview of econometric techniques, with an emphasis placed on regression analysis. Econometric tools are important in estimating demand, cost, and production relationships. In addition, econometric tools are used extensively in economic forecasting. These tools are applied throughout the text as aids in the process of efficiently allocating the resources of the enterprise.

Classical Optimization Techniques 4

Normative economic decision analysis involves determining the action that best achieves a desired goal or objective. This means finding the action that optimizes (that is, maximizes or minimizes) the value of an objective function. For example, in a price-output decision-making problem, we may be interested in determining the output level that maximizes profits. In a production problem, the goal may be to find the combination of inputs (resources) that minimizes the cost of producing a desired level of output. In capital budgeting problems, the objective may be to select those projects that maximize the net present value of the investments chosen. There are many techniques for solving optimization problems such as these. This chapter discusses some of these techniques. Optimization techniques are a powerful set of tools that are important in the process of efficiently managing an enterprise's resources and thereby maximizing shareholder wealth.

Types of Optimization Techniques

In Chapter 1 we defined the general form of a problem that managerial economics attempts to analyze. The basic form of the problem is to identify the alternative means of achieving a given objective and then to select the alternative that accomplishes the objective in the most efficient manner, subject to constraints on the means. In programming terminology, the problem is optimizing the value of some objective function, subject to any resource and/or other constraints such as legal, environmental and behavioral restrictions.

Mathematically, we can represent the problem as

$$\text{Optimize } y = f(x_1, x_2, \ldots, x_n) \qquad [4.1]$$

$$\text{subject to } g_j(x_1, x_2, \ldots, x_n) \begin{Bmatrix} \leq \\ = \\ \geq \end{Bmatrix} b_j \qquad j = 1, 2, \ldots, m \qquad [4.2]$$

where Equation 4.1 is the objective function and Equation 4.2 constitutes the set of constraints imposed on the solution. The x_i variables, $x_1, x_2, \ldots, x_n$, represent the set of decision variables, and $y = f(x_1, x_2, \ldots, x_n)$ is the objective function expressed in terms of these decision variables. Depending on the nature of the

Glossary of New Terms

First-order condition
A test to locate one or more maximum or minimum points of an algebraic function.

Second-order condition
A test to determine whether a point that has been determined from the first-order condition is either a maximum point or a minimum point.

Partial derivative
Measures the marginal effect of a change in one variable on the value of a multivariate function, while holding constant all other variables.

Derivative
Measures the marginal effect of a change in one variable on the value of a function. Graphically, it represents the slope of the function at a given point.

problem, the term *optimize* means either *maximize* or *minimize* the value of the objective function. As indicated in Equation 4.2, each constraint can take the form of an equality ($=$) or an inequality ($\leq$ or $\geq$) relationship.

A number of factors can make these problems fairly complex and difficult to solve. One such complicating factor is the *existence of multiple decision variables* in a problem. For example, as we see later in this chapter, relatively simple procedures exist for determining the profit-maximizing output level for the single-product firm. However, the typical medium- or large-size firm often produces a large number of different products, and as a result, the profit-maximization problem for such a firm requires a series of output decisions—one for each product. Another factor that may add to the difficulty of solving a problem is the *complex nature of the relationships between the decision variables and the associated outcome*. For example, in public policy decisions concerning government spending for such items as education, it is extremely difficult to determine the relationship between a given expenditure and the benefits it provides in terms of increased income, employment, and productivity. No simple relationship exists among the variables. Many of the optimization techniques discussed here are only applicable to situations in which a relatively simple function or relationship can be postulated between the decision variables and the outcome variable. A third complicating factor is the possible *existence of one or more complex constraints on the decision variables*. For example, virtually every organization has constraints imposed on its decision variables by the limited resources—such as capital, personnel, and facilities—over which it has control. These constraints must be incorporated into the decision problem. Otherwise, the optimization techniques that are applied to the problem may yield a solution that is unacceptable from a practical standpoint. Another complicating factor is the presence of *uncertainty* or *risk*. In this chapter, we limit the analysis to decision making under *certainty*, that is, problems in which each action is known to lead to a specific outcome. These factors illustrate the difficulties that may be encountered and may render a problem unsolvable by formal optimization procedures.

The mathematical techniques used to solve a problem expressed in this framework depend on the form of the criterion and constraint functions. The simplest situation to be considered is the *unconstrained* optimization problem. In such a problem no constraints are imposed on the decision variables, and the method of *differential calculus* can be used to analyze them. Another relatively simple form of the general optimization problem is the case in which all the constraints of the problem can be expressed as *equality* ($=$) relationships. The technique of *Lagrangian multipliers* can be used to find the optimal solution to many of these problems.

Often, however, the constraints in an economic decision-making problem take the form of *inequality* relationships ($\leq$ or $\geq$) rather than equalities. For example, limitations on the resources—such as personnel and capital—of an organization place an *upper bound* or budget ceiling on the quantity of these resources that can be employed in maximizing (or minimizing) the objective function. With this type of constraint, it is not necessary that all of a given resource be used in an optimal solution to the problem. An example of a *lower bound* would be a loan agreement that requires a firm to maintain a *current ratio* (that is, ratio of current assets to current liabilities) of at least 2.00. Any combination of current assets and current liabilities having a ratio greater than or equal to 2.00 would meet the provisions of the loan agreement. Such optimization procedures as the Lagrangian multiplier method are not suited to solving problems of this type efficiently; however, modern mathematical programming techniques have been developed that can efficiently solve several classes of problems with these inequality restrictions.

Linear-programming problems constitute the most important class for which efficient solution techniques have been developed. In a linear-programming problem, both the objective and the constraint relationships are expressed as linear functions of decision variables.[1] Other classes of problems include *integer-programming* problems, in which some (or all) of the decision variables are required to take on integer values, and *quadratic-programming* problems, in which the objective relationship is a quadratic function of the decision variables.[2] Generalized computing algorithms exist for solving optimization problems that meet these requirements. In addition, various other techniques—such as *geometric programming, gradient methods, direct search procedures, calculus of variations,* and *dynamic programming*—can be used in finding solutions to some types of nonlinear-programming problems.[3]

The remainder of this chapter deals with the classical optimization procedures of differential calculus and Lagrangian multipliers. Linear programming techniques are discussed in the following chapter.

Differential Calculus

In Chapter 2, marginal analysis was introduced as one of the fundamental concepts of economic decision making. In the marginal analysis framework, resource allocation decisions are made by comparing the marginal benefits of a change in the level of an activity with the marginal costs of the change. A change should be made as long as the marginal benefits exceed the marginal costs. By following this basic rule, resources can be allocated efficiently and profits/shareholder wealth can be maximized.

---

[1] A linear relationship of the variables $x_1, x_2, \ldots, x_n$ is a function of the form:

$$a_1 x_1 + a_2 x_2 + \ldots + a_n x_n$$

where all the x variables have exponents of 1.

[2] A quadratic function contains either squared terms (x_i^2) or cross-product terms $(x_i x_j)$.

[3] A discussion of nonlinear programming and other advanced optimization techniques is beyond the scope of this text. See M. Q. Anderson and R. J. Lievano, *Quantitative Management*, 2d ed. (Boston: Kent, 1986); D. M. Simmons, *Nonlinear Programming for Operations Research* (Englewood Cliffs, N.J.: Prentice-Hall, 1975); D.J. White, *Finite Dynamic Programming* (New York: Wiley, 1978); and David R. Anderson, D.J. Sweeny, and T. A. Williams, *Quantitative Methods for Business* 3d ed. (St. Paul, MN: West, 1986); Roger Hartley, *Linear and Nonlinear Programming* (New York: Halstead Press, 1985).

In the profit maximization example developed in Chapter 2, the application of the marginal analysis principles required that the relationship between the objective (profit) and the decision variable (output level) be expressed in either tabular or graphic form. This framework, however, can become somewhat cumbersome when dealing with several decision variables or with complex relationships between the decision variables and the objective. When the relationship between the decision variables and criterion can be expressed in *algebraic* form, the much more powerful concepts of differential calculus can be used to find optimal solutions to these problems.

Relationship between Marginal Analysis and Differential Calculus

Initially, let us assume that the objective we are seeking to optimize, Y, can be expressed algebraically as a function of *one* decision variable, X,

$$Y = f(X) \qquad [4.3]$$

Recall that marginal profit is defined as the change in profit resulting from a one-unit change in output. In general, the marginal value of any variable Y, which is a function of another variable X, is defined as the change in the value of Y resulting from a one-unit change in X. The marginal value of Y, M_y, can be calculated from the change in Y, ΔY, that occurs as the result of a given change in X, ΔX:

$$M_y = \frac{\Delta Y}{\Delta X} \qquad [4.4]$$

When calculated with this expression, different estimates for the marginal value of Y may be obtained, depending on the size of the change in X that we use in the computation. The nature of this difficulty can be illustrated using the output-profit function shown in Table 4.1. Suppose we are interested in the marginal profit associated with an increase in output beyond $Q = 1$ unit. Using the output-profit information from Table 4.1, the marginal profit M_π is

Table 4.1
Output-Profit Relationship

(1) Number of Units of Output per Unit of Time Q	(2) Total Profit $\$\pi$	(3) Marginal Profit ($\$/unit$) $\Delta\pi = \pi(Q) - \pi(Q-1)$
0	−200	—
1	−150	50
2	− 25	125
3	200	225
4	475	275
5	775	300
6	1,075	300
7	1,325	250
8	1,475	150
9	1,500	25
10	1,350	−150

Output Level Q_2	$\Delta Q =$ $(Q_2 - Q_1) =$ $(Q_2 - 1)$	Profit π	$\Delta \pi =$ $\pi_2 - \pi_1 =$ $\pi_2 - (-150)^a$	$M_\pi = \dfrac{\Delta \pi}{\Delta Q}$
2	1	$-25	$ 125	$125.00
3	2	200	350	175.00[b]
4	3	475	625	208.33
5	4	775	925	231.25
6	5	1,075	1,225	245.00

Table 4.2
Calculation of Marginal Profit Based on Various Size Changes in Output

[a] At $Q_1 = 1$, $\pi = -150$, from Table 4.1.
[b] For $Q_2 = 3$, M_π would be calculated as follows:

$$M_\pi = \frac{\Delta \pi}{\Delta Q} = \frac{\pi_2 - \pi_1}{Q_2 - Q_1}$$

$$= \frac{200 - (-150)}{3 - 1} = \frac{350}{2} = \$175$$

calculated for various size changes ΔQ in output in Table 4.2. From the row $Q_2 = 2$ in Table 4.2, we see that the *actual* marginal profit of a one-unit increase in output to two units is $125. We also see from the table that the calculation of the marginal profit by Equation 4.4 for various size changes in output—that is, $\Delta Q = 2, 3, 4,$ and 5 units—yields marginal estimates that differ from the actual value. In this example, these marginal estimates tend to overestimate the true marginal profit of a one-unit increase in output. In general, depending on the nature of the $Y = f(X)$ function, the calculation of the marginal figure by Equation 4.4 may either overestimate or underestimate the true marginal value.

If we examine the marginal-profit values M_π in Table 4.2, we see that the calculated values tend to approach the true marginal profit value of $125 when smaller and smaller output intervals ΔQ are used in the calculation. In other words, $M_\pi = \$175$, based on a ΔQ of two units, is closer to the true marginal profit than is $M_\pi = \$208.33$, based on a ΔQ of three units. Similar relations hold between the other M_π values. Generalizing, this suggests that the true marginal value is obtained from Equation 4.4 when ΔX is made as small as possible. In this example, since output was measured in *discrete whole units*, the smallest value that ΔQ could take on was 1. In general, however, ΔX can be thought of as a *continuous* variable that can take on *fractional* values.[4] Therefore, in calculating M_y by Equation 4.4, we can let ΔX approach 0. In concept, this is the approach taken in differential calculus. The *first derivative dY/dX,*[5] of a function is defined as the *limit* of the ratio $\Delta Y/\Delta X$ as ΔX approaches 0; that is,

$$\frac{dY}{dX} = \lim_{\Delta X \to 0} \frac{\Delta Y}{\Delta X} \qquad [4.5]$$

[4] For example, if X is a continuous variable measured in feet, pounds, and so on, then ΔX can in theory take on fractional values such as .5, .10, .05, .001, .0001 feet or pounds. When X is a continuous variable, ΔX can be made as small as desired.
[5] It is also possible to compute second, third, fourth, and so on, derivatives. Second derivatives are discussed later in this chapter.

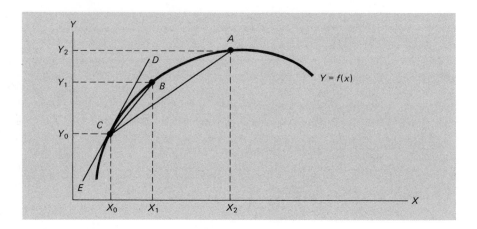

Figure 4.1
**First Derivative
of a Function**

Graphically, the first derivative of a function represents the *slope* of the curve at a given point on the curve. The definition of a derivative as the limit of the change in Y (that is, ΔY) as ΔX approaches 0 is illustrated in Figure 4.1. Suppose we are interested in the derivative of the $Y = f(X)$ function at the point X_0. The derivative dY/dX measures the slope of the tangent line ECD. An estimate of this slope, albeit a poor estimate, can be obtained by calculating the marginal value of Y over the interval X_0 to X_2. Using Equation 4.4, a value of

$$M'_y = \frac{\Delta Y}{\Delta X} = \frac{Y_2 - Y_0}{X_2 - X_0}$$

is obtained for the slope of the CA line. Now let us calculate the marginal value of Y using a smaller interval, for example, X_0 to X_1. The slope of the line C to B, which is equal to

$$M''_y = \frac{\Delta Y}{\Delta X} = \frac{Y_1 - Y_0}{X_1 - X_0}$$

gives a much better estimate of the true marginal value as represented by the slope of the ECD tangent line. Thus we see that the smaller the ΔX value, the better the estimate of the slope of the curve. Letting ΔX approach 0 allows us to find the slope of the $Y = f(X)$ curve at Point C.

Process of Differentiation

The process of differentiation—that is, finding the derivative of a function—involves determining the limiting value of the ratio $\Delta Y/\Delta X$ as ΔX approaches 0. Before offering some general rules for finding the derivative of a function, we illustrate with an example the algebraic process used to obtain the derivative without the aid of these general rules. The specific rules that simplify this process are presented in the following section.

Suppose the profit of a firm, π, can be represented as a function of the ouput level Q using the expression

$$\pi = -40 + 140Q - 10Q^2 \qquad [4.6]$$

We wish to determine $d\pi/dQ$ by first finding the marginal-profit expression $\Delta\pi/\Delta Q$ and then taking the limit of this expression as ΔQ approaches 0. Let us begin by expressing the new level of profit $(\pi + \Delta\pi)$ that will result from an increase in output to $(Q + \Delta Q)$. From Equation 4.6, we know that

$$(\pi + \Delta\pi) = -40 + 140(Q + \Delta Q) - 10(Q + \Delta Q)^2 \qquad [4.7]$$

Expanding this expression and then doing some algebraic simplifying, we obtain

$$(\pi + \Delta\pi) = -40 + 140Q + 140\Delta Q - 10[Q^2 + 2Q\,\Delta Q + (\Delta Q)^2]$$
$$= -40 + 140Q - 10Q^2 + 140\Delta Q - 20Q\,\Delta Q - 10(\Delta Q)^2 \qquad [4.8]$$

Subtracting Equation 4.6 from Equation 4.8 yields

$$\Delta\pi = 140\Delta Q - 20Q\,\Delta Q - 10(\Delta Q)^2 \qquad [4.9]$$

Forming the marginal-profit ratio $\Delta\pi/\Delta Q$, and doing some canceling, we get

$$\frac{\Delta\pi}{\Delta Q} = \frac{140\Delta Q - 20Q - 10(\Delta Q)^2}{\Delta Q}$$
$$= 140 - 20Q - 10\Delta Q \qquad [4.10]$$

Taking the limit of Equation 4.10 as ΔQ approaches 0 yields the expression for the derivative of the profit function (Equation 4.6)

$$\frac{d\pi}{dQ} = \lim_{\Delta Q \to 0} [140 - 20Q - 10\Delta Q]$$
$$= 140 - 20Q \qquad [4.11]$$

If we are interested in the derivative of the profit function at a particular value of Q, Equation 4.11 can be evaluated for this value. For example, suppose we want to know the marginal profit, or slope of the profit function, at $Q = 3$ units. Substituting $Q = 3$ in Equation 4.11 yields

$$\text{Marginal Profit} = \frac{d\pi}{dQ} = 140 - 20(3) = \$80 \text{ per unit}$$

Rules of Differentiation

Fortunately, we do not need to go through this lengthy process every time we want the derivative of a function. A series of general rules, derived in a manner similar to the process just described, exists for differentiating various types of functions.[6]

Constant Functions. A constant function can be expressed as

$$Y = a \qquad [4.12]$$

---

[6] A more expanded treatment of these rules can be found in any introductory calculus book such as John B. Fraleigh, *Calculus with Analytic Geometry,* 2d ed. (Reading, Mass.: Addison-Wesley, 1985).

where a is a constant (that is, Y is independent of X). The derivative of a constant function is equal to zero:

$$\frac{dY}{dX} = 0 \qquad\qquad [4.13]$$

For example, consider the constant function

$$Y = 4$$

which is graphed in Figure 4.2(a). Recall that the first derivative of a function (dY/dX) measures the slope of the function. Since this constant function is a horizontal straight line with zero slope, its derivative (dY/dX) is therefore equal . to zero.

Power Functions. A power function takes the form of

$$Y = aX^b \qquad\qquad [4.14]$$

where a and b are constants. The derivative of a power function is equal to b times a, times X raised to the $(b-1)$ power:

$$\frac{dY}{dX} = b \cdot a \cdot X^{b-1} \qquad\qquad [4.15]$$

A few examples are used to illustrate the application of this rule. First, consider the function

$$Y = 2X$$

which is graphed in Figure 4.2(b). Note that the slope of this function is equal to 2 and is constant over the entire range of X values. Applying the power function rule to this example, where $a = 2$ and $b = 1$, yields

$$\frac{dY}{dX} = 1 \cdot 2 \cdot X^{1-1}$$

$$= 2$$

Next, consider the function

$$Y = X^2$$

which is graphed in Figure 4.2(c). Note that the slope of this function varies depending on the value of X. Application of the power function rule to this example yields ($a = 1$, $b = 2$):

$$\frac{dY}{dX} = 2 \cdot 1 \cdot X^{2-1}$$

$$= 2X$$

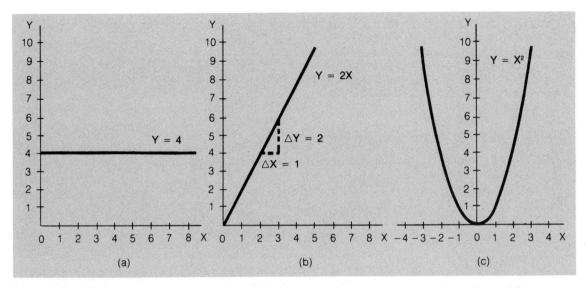

Figure 4.2
Constant, Linear, and Quadratic Functions

As we can see, this derivative (or slope) function is negative when $X < 0$, zero when $X = 0$, and positive when $X > 0$.

Sums of Functions. Suppose a function $Y = f(X)$ represents the sum of two (or more) separate functions, $f_1(X)$, $f_2(X)$, that is,

$$Y = f_1(X) + f_2(X) \qquad [4.16]$$

The derivative of Y with respect to X is found by differentiating each of the separate functions and then adding the results:

$$\frac{dY}{dX} = \frac{df_1(X)}{dX} + \frac{df_2(X)}{dX} \qquad [4.17]$$

This result can be extended to finding the derivative of the sum of any number of functions.

As an example of the application of these rules, consider again the profit function, given by Equation 4.6, that was discussed earlier:

$$\pi = -40 + 140Q - 10Q^2$$

In this example Q represents the X variable and π represents the Y variable; that is, $\pi = f(Q)$. The function $f(Q)$ is the sum of *three* separate functions—a constant function, $f_1(Q) = -40$, and two power functions, $f_2(Q) = 140Q$ and $f_3(Q) = -10Q^2$. Therefore, applying the differentiation rules yields

$$\frac{d\pi}{dQ} = \frac{df_1(Q)}{dQ} + \frac{df_2(Q)}{dQ} + \frac{df_3(Q)}{dQ}$$

$$= 0 + 1 \cdot 140 \cdot Q^{1-1} + 2 \cdot (-10) \cdot Q^{2-1}$$

$$= 140 - 20Q$$

This is the same result that was obtained earlier in Equation 4.11 by the differentiation process.

Product of Two Functions.[tt] Suppose the variable Y is equal to the product of two separate functions $f_1(X)$ and $f_2(X)$:

$$Y = f_1(X) \cdot f_2(X) \qquad [4.18]$$

In this case the derivative of Y with respect to X is equal to the sum of the first function times the derivative of the second, plus the second function times the derivative of the first.

$$\frac{dY}{dX} = f_1(X) \cdot \frac{df_2(X)}{dX} + f_2(X) \cdot \frac{df_1(X)}{dX} \qquad [4.19]$$

For example, suppose we are interested in the derivative of the expression

$$Y = X^2(2X - 3)$$

Let $f_1(X) = X^2$ and $f_2(X) = (2X - 3)$. By the above rule (and the earlier rules for differentiating constant and power functions), we obtain

$$\frac{dY}{dX} = X^2 \cdot \frac{d}{dX}[(2X - 3)] + (2X - 3) \cdot \frac{d}{dX}[X^2]$$
$$= X^2 \cdot (2 - 0) + (2X - 3) \cdot (2X)$$
$$= 2X^2 + 4X^2 - 6X$$
$$= 6X^2 - 6X$$
$$= 6X(X - 1)$$

Quotient of Two Functions.[tt] Suppose the variable Y is equal to the quotient of two separate functions $f_1(X)$ and $f_2(X)$:

$$Y = \frac{f_1(X)}{f_2(X)} \qquad [4.20]$$

For such a relationship the derivative of Y with respect to X is obtained as follows:

$$\frac{dY}{dX} = \frac{f_2(X) \cdot \dfrac{df_1(X)}{dX} - f_1(X) \cdot \dfrac{df_2(X)}{dX}}{[f_2(X)]^2} \qquad [4.21]$$

[tt] This section may be omitted without loss of continuity.

As an example, consider the problem of finding the derivative of the expression

$$Y = \frac{10X^2}{5X - 1}$$

Letting $f_1(X) = 10X^2$ and $f_2(X) = 5X - 1$, we have

$$\frac{dY}{dX} = \frac{(5X - 1) \cdot 20X - 10X^2 \cdot 5}{(5X - 1)^2}$$

$$= \frac{100X^2 - 20X - 50X^2}{(5X - 1)^2}$$

$$= \frac{50X^2 - 20X}{(5X - 1)^2}$$

$$= \frac{10X(5X - 2)}{(5X - 1)^2}$$

Functions of a Function (Chain Rule).[††] Suppose Y is a function of the variable Z, $Y = f_1(Z)$; and Z is in turn a function of the variable X, $Z = f_2(X)$. The derivative of Y with respect to X can be determined by first finding dY/dZ and dZ/dX and then multiplying the two expressions together:

$$\frac{dY}{dX} = \frac{dY}{dZ} \cdot \frac{dZ}{dX}$$

$$= \frac{df_1(Z)}{dZ} \cdot \frac{df_2(X)}{dX}$$

[4.22]

To illustrate the application of this rule, suppose we are interested in finding the derivative (with respect to X) of the function

$$Y = 10Z - 2Z^2 - 3$$

where Z is related to X in the following way:

$$Z = 2X^2 - 1$$

First, we find (by the earlier differentiation rules)

$$\frac{dY}{dZ} = 10 - 4Z$$

$$\frac{dZ}{dX} = 4X$$

and then

$$\frac{dY}{dX} = (10 - 4Z) \cdot 4X$$

[††] This section may be omitted without loss of continuity.

Table 4.3
Summary of Rules for Differentiating Functions

Function	Derivative
1. Constant Function $Y = a$	$\dfrac{dY}{dX} = 0$
2. *Power Function* $Y = aX^b$	$\dfrac{dY}{dX} = b \cdot a \cdot X^{b-1}$
3. *Sums of Functions* $Y = f_1(X) + f_2(X)$	$\dfrac{dY}{dX} = \dfrac{df_1(X)}{dX} + \dfrac{df_2(X)}{dX}$
4. Product of Two Functions $Y = f_1(X) \cdot f_2(X)$	$\dfrac{dY}{dX} = f_1(X)\dfrac{df_2(X)}{dX} + f_2(X)\dfrac{df_1(X)}{dX}$
5. Quotient of Two Functions $Y = \dfrac{f_1(X)}{f_2(X)}$	$\dfrac{dY}{dX} = \dfrac{f_2(X) \cdot \dfrac{df_1(X)}{dX} - f_1(X) \cdot \dfrac{df_2(X)}{dX}}{[f_2(X)]^2}$
6. Functions of a Function $Y = f_1(Z),\ \text{where } Z = f_2(X)$	$\dfrac{dY}{dX} = \dfrac{dY}{dZ} \cdot \dfrac{dZ}{dX}$

Substituting the expression for Z in terms of X into this equation yields

$$\frac{dY}{dX} = [10 - 4(2X^2 - 1)] \cdot 4X$$

$$= (10 - 8X^2 + 4) \cdot 4X$$

$$= 40X - 32X^3 + 16X$$

$$= 56X - 32X^3$$

$$= 8X(7 - 4X^2)$$

These rules for differentiating functions are summarized in Table 4.3.

Applications of Differential Calculus to Optimization Problems

The reason for studying the process of differentiation and the rules for differentiating functions is that these methods can be used to find optimal solutions to many kinds of maximization and minimization problems in managerial economics.

Maximization Problem

Recall from the discussion of marginal analysis, a necessary (but not sufficient) condition for finding the maximum point on a curve (for example, maximum profits) is that the marginal value or slope of the curve at this point must be equal to zero. We can now express this condition within the framework of differential calculus. Since the derivative of a function measures the slope or marginal value at any given point, an equivalent necessary condition for finding the maximum value of a function $Y = f(X)$ is that the derivative dY/dX at this point must be equal to zero.

Using the profit function (Equation 4.6)

$$\pi = -40 + 140Q - 10Q^2$$

discussed earlier, we can illustrate how to find the profit-maximizing output level Q by means of this condition. Setting the first derivative of this function (which was obtained previously) to zero, we obtain

$$\frac{d\pi}{dQ} = 140 - 20Q$$

$$0 = 140 - 20Q$$

Solving this equation for Q yields $Q^* = 7$ units as the profit-maximizing output level. The profit and first derivative functions and optimal solution are shown in Figure 4.3. As we can see, profits are maximized at the point where the function

Figure 4.3
Profit and First Derivative Functions

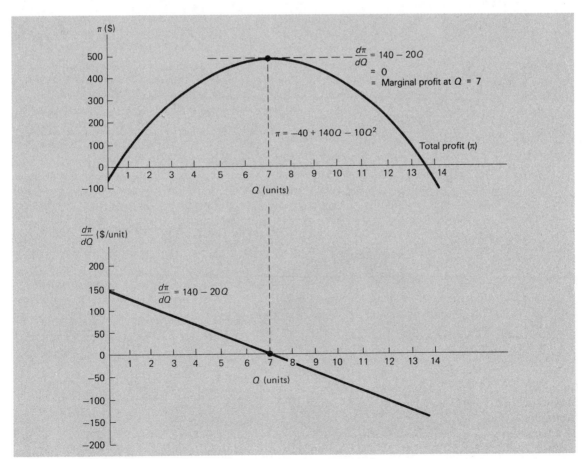

is neither increasing nor decreasing; in other words, where the slope (or first derivative) is equal to zero.

Second Derivatives and the Second-Order Condition

Setting the derivative of a function equal to zero and solving the resulting equation for the value of the decision variable does not guarantee that the point will be obtained at which the function takes on its maximum value. The slope of a U-shaped function will also be equal to zero at its low point and the function will take on its *minimum* value at the given point. In other words, setting the derivative to zero is only a *necessary* condition for finding the maximum value of a function; it is not a *sufficient* condition.

This situation is illustrated in Figure 4.4. At both points A and B the slope of the function (first derivative, dY/dX) is zero; however, only at point B does the function take on its maximum value.

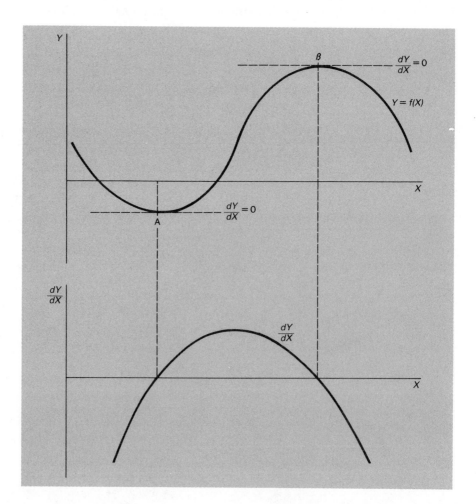

Figure 4.4
Maximum and Minimum Values of a Function

Another condition is required to assure that the maximum point has been found. We note in Figure 4.4 that the marginal value (slope) is continually *decreasing* in the neighborhood of the maximum value (point B) of the $Y = f(X)$ function. First the slope is positive up to where $dY/dX = 0$, and thereafter the slope becomes negative. Thus we must determine whether the slope's marginal value (slope of the slope) is declining. A test to see whether the marginal value is decreasing is to take the derivative of the marginal value and check to see if it is negative at the given point on the function. In effect, we need to find the derivative of the derivative—that is, the *second derivative* of the function—and then test to see if it is less than zero. Formally, the second derivative of the function $Y = f(X)$ is written as d^2Y/dX^2 and is found by applying the previously described differentiation rules to the first derivative. *A maximum point is obtained if the second derivative is negative, that is $d^2Y/dX^2 < 0$.*

Returning to the profit-maximization example, the second derivative is obtained from the first derivative as follows:

$$\frac{d\pi}{dQ} = 140 - 20Q$$

$$\frac{d^2\pi}{dQ^2} = 0 + 1 \cdot (-20) \cdot Q^{1-1}$$

$$= -20$$

Since $d^2\pi/dQ^2 < 0$ we know that a maximum-profit point has been obtained.

An opposite condition holds for obtaining the point at which the function takes on a minimum value. Note again in Figure 4.4 that the marginal value (slope) is continually *increasing* in the neighborhood of the minimum value (point A) of the $Y = f(X)$ function. First the slope is negative up to where $dY/dX = 0$, and thereafter the slope becomes positive. Therefore, we test to see if $d^2Y/dX^2 > 0$ at the given point. *A minimum point is obtained if the second derivative is positive; that is, $d^2Y/dX^2 > 0$.*

Summarizing, we see that *two* conditions are required for locating a maximum or minimum value of a function using calculus procedures. The *first-order* condition determines the points at which the first derivative dY/dX is equal to zero. Having obtained one or more points, a *second-order* condition is used to determine whether the function takes on a maximum or minimum value at the given points. The second derivative d^2Y/dX^2 indicates whether a given point is a maximum ($d^2Y/dX^2 < 0$) or a minimum ($d^2Y/dX^2 > 0$) value of the function.

Minimization Problem

In some decision-making situations, cost minimization may be the objective. As in profit-maximization problems, differential calculus can be used to locate the optimal points. For example, suppose we are interested in determining the output level that minimizes average total costs, where the average total cost function is given by the following relationship (Q represents output):

$$C = 15 - .040Q + .000080Q^2 \qquad [4.23]$$

Differentiating C with respect to Q gives

$$\frac{dC}{dQ} = -.040 + .000160Q$$

Setting this derivative equal to zero and solving for Q yields

$$0 = -.040 + .000160Q$$

$$Q^* = 250$$

Taking the second derivative, we obtain

$$\frac{d^2C}{dQ^2} = +.000160$$

Since the second derivative is positive, the output level of $Q = 250$ is indeed the value that minimizes average total costs.

Partial Differentiation and Multivariate Optimization

Thus far in the chapter, the analysis has been limited to a criterion variable Y that can be expressed as a function of *one* decision variable X. However, many commonly used economic relationships contain two or more decision variables. For example, a *production function* relates the output of a plant, firm, industry, or country to the inputs employed—such as capital, labor, and raw materials. Another example is a *demand function*, which relates sales of a product or service to such variables as price, advertising, promotion expenses, price of substitutes, and income.

Partial Derivatives

Consider a criterion variable Y that is a function of two decision variables[7] X_1 and X_2:

$$Y = f(X_1, X_2)$$

Let us now examine the change in Y that results from a given change in either X_1 or X_2. To isolate the marginal effect on Y from a given change in X_1—that is, $\Delta Y/\Delta X_1$—we must hold X_2 constant. Similarly, if we wish to isolate the marginal effect on Y from a given change in X_2—that is, $\Delta Y/\Delta X_2$—the variable X_1 must be held constant. A measure of the marginal effect of a change in any one variable on the change in Y, holding all other variables in the relationship constant, is obtained from the *partial derivative* of the function. The partial derivative of Y with respect to X_1 is written as $\partial Y/\partial X_1$ and is found by applying the previously described differentiation rules to the $Y = f(X_1, X_2)$ function, where the variable X_2 is treated as a constant. Similarly, the partial derivative of Y with respect to X_2

---

[7] The following analysis is not limited to two decision variables. Relationships containing any number of variables can be analyzed within this framework.

is written as $\partial Y/\partial X_2$ and is found by applying the differentiation rules to the function, where the variable X_1 is treated as a constant.

To illustrate the procedure for obtaining partial derivatives, let us consider the following relationship in which the profit variable, π, is a function of the output level of *two* products Q_1 and Q_2:

$$\pi = -60 + 140Q_1 + 100Q_2 - 10Q_1^2 - 8Q_2^2 - 6Q_1Q_2 \qquad [4.24]$$

Treating Q_2 as a constant, the partial derivative of π with respect to Q_1 is obtained:

$$\frac{\partial \pi}{\partial Q_1} = 0 + 140 + 0 + 2 \cdot (-10) \cdot Q_1 - 0 - 6Q_2$$

$$= 140 - 20Q_1 - 6Q_2$$

Similarly, with Q_1 treated as a constant, the partial derivative of π with respect to Q_2 is equal to

$$\frac{\partial \pi}{\partial Q_2} = 0 + 0 + 100 - 0 + 2 \cdot (-8) \cdot Q_2 - 6Q_1$$

$$= 100 - 16Q_2 - 6Q_1$$

As another example, consider the following (multiplicative) demand function, where Q = quantity sold, P = selling price, and A = advertising expenditures:

$$Q = 3.0P^{-.50}A^{.25} \qquad [4.25]$$

The partial derivative of Q with respect to P is

$$\frac{\partial Q}{\partial P} = 3.0A^{.25}(-.50P^{-.50-1})$$

$$= -1.5P^{-1.50}A^{.25}$$

Similarly, the partial derivative of Q with respect to A is

$$\frac{\partial Q}{\partial A} = 3.0P^{-.50}(.25A^{.25-1})$$

$$= .75P^{-.50}A^{-.75}$$

Maximization Problem

The partial derivatives can be used to obtain the optimal solution to a maximization or minimization problem containing two or more X variables. Analogous to the first-order conditions discussed earlier for the one-variable case, we set *each* of the partial derivatives equal to zero and solve the resulting set of simultaneous equations for the optimal X values. If we are interested in maximizing profits in the Equation 4.24 example, each of the two partial derivatives $\partial\pi/\partial Q_1$ and $\partial\pi/\partial Q_2$ would be set equal to zero:

$$0 = 140 - 20Q_1 - 6Q_2$$

$$0 = 100 - 16Q_2 - 6Q_1$$

This system of equations can be solved for the profit-maximizing values of Q_1 and Q_2.[8] The optimal values are $Q_1^* = 5.77$ units and $Q_2^* = 4.08$ units.

Having completed our discussion of some of the techniques used in solving unconstrained optimization problems, let us now consider methods for solving constrained optimization problems.

Lagrangian Multiplier Techniques[††]

As indicated earlier in the chapter, most organizations have constraints on their decision variables. The most obvious constraints, and the easiest to quantify and incorporate into the analysis, are the limitations imposed by the quantities of resources (such as capital, personnel, facilities, and raw materials) available to the organization. Other more subjective constraints include legal, environmental, and behavioral limitations on the decisions of the organization.

When the constraints take the form of equality relationships, classical optimization procedures can be used to solve the problem. One method, which can be employed when the objective function is subject to only *one* constraint equation of a relatively simple form, is to solve the constraint equation for one of the decision variables and then substitute this expression into the objective function. This procedure converts the original problem into an unconstrained optimization problem, which can be solved using the calculus procedures developed in the previous section.

As an example of this method of solving constrained optimization problems, consider again the two-product profit-maximization problem (Equation 4.24) of the last section. Suppose that the raw materials needed to make the product are in short supply and that the firm has a contract with a supplier calling for the delivery of 200 units of the given raw material during the forthcoming period. No other sources of the raw material are available. Also, assume that *all the raw material must be used during the period* and that none can be carried over to the next period in inventory. Furthermore, suppose that Product 1 requires 20 units of the raw material to produce one unit of output and Product 2 requires 40 units of raw material to produce one unit of output. The constrained optimization problem can be written as follows:

$$\text{Maximize } \pi = -60 + 140Q_1 + 100Q_2 - 10Q_1^2 - 8Q_2^2 - 6Q_1Q_2$$

$$\text{subject to} \quad 20Q_1 + 40Q_2 = 200$$

We see that the solution to the unconstrained problem obtained earlier— $Q_1 = 5.77$ and $Q_2 = 4.08$—is not a feasible solution to the constrained problem since it requires $20(5.77) + 40(4.08) = 278.6$ units of raw material when in fact only 200 units are available. Following the procedure just described, we solve

---

[8] Discussion of the second-order conditions for obtaining a maximum in the multiple variable case is beyond the scope of this chapter. See Leon Cooper and David Steinberg, *Introduction to Methods of Optimization* (Philadelphia: W. B. Saunders Company, 1970), pp. 109–112.

[††] This section may be omitted without loss of continuity.

the constraint for Q_1:

$$Q_1 = \frac{200}{20} - \frac{40Q_2}{20}$$

$$= 10 - 2Q_2$$

Substituting this expression for Q_1 in the objective function, we obtain

$$\pi = -60 + 140(10 - 2Q_2) + 100Q_2 - 10(10 - 2Q_2)^2$$
$$-8Q_2^2 - 6(10 - 2Q_2)Q_2$$
$$= -60 + 1400 - 280Q_2 + 100Q_2 - 1000 + 400Q_2$$
$$-40Q_2^2 - 8Q_2^2 - 60Q_2 + 12Q_2^2$$
$$= 340 + 160Q_2 - 36Q_2^2$$

Taking the derivative of this expression with respect to Q_2 yields

$$\frac{d\pi}{dQ_2} = 160 - 72Q_2$$

Setting $d\pi/dQ_2$ equal to zero and solving for Q_2, we obtain

$$0 = 160 - 72Q_2$$

$$Q_2^* = \frac{160}{72}$$

$$= 2.22 \text{ units}$$

In turn solving for Q_1, we obtain

$$Q_1^* = 10 - 2(2.22)$$

$$= 5.56 \text{ units}$$

Thus $Q_1^* = 5.56$ and $Q_2^* = 2.22$ is the optimal solution to the constrained profit-maximization problem.

Using the constraint to substitute for one of the variables in the objective function, as in the preceding example, will yield an optimal solution only when there is one constraint equation and it is possible to solve this equation for one of the decision variables. With more than one constraint equation and/or a complex constraint relationship, the more powerful method of Lagrangian multipliers must be employed to solve the constrained optimization problem.

With the Lagrangian multiplier technique, an additional artificial variable is created for each constraint. Using these artificial variables, the constraints are incorporated into the objective function in such a way as to leave the value of the function unchanged. This new function, called the Lagrangian function, constitutes an unconstrained optimization problem. The next step is to set the partial derivatives of the Lagrangian function for each of the variables equal to zero and solve the resulting set of simultaneous equations for the optimal values of the variables.

The Lagrangian multiplier method can be illustrated using the example discussed earlier in this section. First, the constraint equation, which is a function δ of the two variables Q_1 and Q_2, is rearranged to form an expression equal to zero:

$$\delta(Q_1, Q_2) = 20Q_1 + 40Q_2 - 200 = 0$$

Next we define an artificial variable λ (lambda) and form the Lagrangian function.[9]

$$L_\pi = \pi(Q_1, Q_2) - \lambda\delta(Q_1, Q_2)$$
$$= -60 + 140Q_1 + 100Q_2 - 10Q_1^2 - 8Q_2^2 - 6Q_1Q_2$$
$$-\lambda(20Q_1 + 40Q_2 - 200)$$

As long as $\delta(Q_1, Q_2)$ *is maintained equal to zero*, the Lagrangian function L_π will not differ in value from the profit function π. Maximizing L_π will also maximize π. L_π is seen to be a function of Q_1, Q_2, and λ. Therefore, to maximize L_π (and also π), we need to partially differentiate L_π with respect to each of the variables, set the partial derivatives equal to zero, and solve the resulting set of equations for the optimal values of Q_1, Q_2, and λ. The partial derivatives are equal to

$$\frac{\partial L_\pi}{\partial Q_1} = 140 - 20Q_1 - 6Q_2 - 20\lambda$$

$$\frac{\partial L_\pi}{\partial Q_2} = 100 - 16Q_2 - 6Q_1 - 40\lambda$$

$$\frac{\partial L_\pi}{\partial \lambda} = -20Q_1 - 40Q_2 + 200$$

Setting the partial derivatives equal to zero yields the equations

$$20Q_1 + 6Q_2 + 20\lambda = 140$$

$$6Q_1 + 16Q_2 + 40\lambda = 100$$

$$+ 20Q_1 + 40Q_2 = 200$$

After solving this set of simultaneous equations, we obtain $Q_1^* = 5.56$, $Q_2^* = 2.22$, and $\lambda^* = +.774$. Note: These are the same values of Q_1 and Q_2 that were obtained earlier in this section by the substitution method. If a problem has two or more constraints, then a separate λ variable is defined for each constraint and incorporated into the Lagrangian function.

In general, λ measures the marginal change in the value of the objective function resulting from a one-unit change in the value on the righthand side of the equality sign in the constraint relationship. In the example, λ equals $.774 and indicates that profits could be increased by this amount if one more unit of raw material were available; that is, an increase from 200 units to 201 units. The λ values are analogous to the dual variables of linear programming, which are discussed in the following chapter.

---

[9] To assist in the interpretation of the results, it is often useful to adopt the arbitrary convention that in the case of a maximization problem the lambda term should be subtracted in the Lagrangian function. In the case of a minimization problem, the lambda term should be added in the Lagrangian function.

Summary

- Within the area of decision making under certainty are two broad classes of problems—*unconstrained* optimization problems and *constrained* optimization problems.

- *Marginal analysis* is useful in making decisions about the expansion or contraction of an economic activity.

- *Differential calculus*, which bears a close relationship to marginal analysis, can be applied whenever an algebraic relationship can be specified between the decision variables and the objective or criterion variable.

- The first derivative measures the slope or rate of change of a function at a given point and is equal to the limiting value of the marginal function as the marginal value is calculated over smaller and smaller intervals, that is, as the interval approaches zero.

- Various rules are available (see Table 4.3) for finding the derivative of specific types of functions.

- A necessary, but not sufficient, condition for finding the maximum or minimum points of a function is that the first derivative be equal to zero. This is known as the *first-order condition*.

- A *second-order condition* is required to determine whether a given point is a maximum or minimum. The second derivative indicates that a given point is a maximum if the second derivative is less than zero or a minimum if the second derivative is greater than zero.

- The partial derivative of a multivariate function measures the marginal effect of a change in one variable on the value of the function, holding constant all other variables.

- In constrained-optimization problems, *Lagrangian multiplier techniques* can be used to find the optimal value of a function that is subject to *equality* constraints. Through the introduction of additional (artificial) variables into the problem, the Lagrangian multiplier method converts the constrained problem into an unconstrained problem, which can then be solved using ordinary differential calculus procedures.

Selected References

Ackoff, Russell L. *Scientific Method: Optimizing Applied Research Decisions*. New York: John Wiley, 1962.

Beightler, Charles S., and Douglass J. Wilde. *Foundations of Optimization*. Englewood Cliffs, N.J.: Prentice-Hall, 1967.

Chiang, Alpha C. *Fundamental Methods of Mathematical Economics*, 3d ed. New York: McGraw-Hill, 1984.

Cooper, Leon, and David Steinberg. *Introduction to Methods of Optimization*. Philadelphia: W. B. Saunders, 1970.

Dantzig, George B. *Linear Programming and Extensions*. Princeton, N.J.: Princeton University Press, 1964.

Diamond, Jay, and Gerald Pintel. *Applied Business Arithmetic.* Englewood Cliffs, N.J.: Prentice-Hall, 1985.

Fraleigh, John B. *Calculus with Analytic Geometry*, 2d ed. Reading, Mass.: Addison-Wesley, 1985.

Hadley, G. *Nonlinear and Dynamic Programming.* Reading, Mass.: Addison-Wesley, 1964.

Harris, D. J. *Mathematics for Business, Management and Economics.* New York: Wiley, 1985.

Yarmane, Yars. *Mathematics for Economists: An Elementary Survey.* Englewood Cliffs, N.J.: Prentice-Hall, 1962.

Discussion Questions

1. Define the following terms:
   a. Optimize
   b. Marginal analysis
   c. Derivative
   d. Partial derivative
   e. First-order condition
   f. Second-order condition

2. Discuss the factors that make optimization problems difficult to solve.

3. Explain how the first and second derivatives of a function are used to find the maximum or minimum points of a function $Y = f(X)$. Illustrate your discussion with graphs.

4. Why is the first-order condition for finding a maximum (or minimum) of a function referred to as a necessary but not sufficient condition?

5. What purpose do the artificial variables (λ's) serve in the solution of a constrained optimization problem by Lagrangian multiplier techniques?

6. What do the artificial variables (λ's) measure in the solution of a constrained optimization problem using Lagrangian multiplier techniques?

Problems

1. Defining Q to be the level of output produced and sold, suppose that the firm's total revenue (R) and total cost (C) functions can be represented in tabular form as shown below.

Output Q	Total Revenue, TR	Total Cost, TC	Output Q	Total Revenue, TR	Total Cost, TC
0	0	20	11	264	196
1	34	26	12	276	224
2	66	34	13	286	254
3	96	44	14	294	286
4	124	56	15	300	320
5	150	70	16	304	356
6	174	86	17	306	394
7	196	104	18	306	434
8	216	124	19	304	476
9	234	146	20	300	520
10	250	170			

a. Compute the marginal revenue and average revenue functions.
b. Compute the marginal cost and average cost functions.
c. On a single graph, plot the total revenue, total cost, marginal revenue, and marginal cost functions.
d. Determine the output level in the *graph* that maximizes profits (that is, profit = total revenue − total cost) by finding the point where marginal revenue equals marginal cost.
e. Check your result in part (d) by finding the output level in the *tables* developed in parts (a) and (b) that likewise satisfies the condition that marginal revenue equals marginal cost.

2. Consider again the total revenue and total cost functions shown in tabular form in the previous problem.
   a. Compute the total, marginal, and average profit functions.
   b. On a single graph, plot the total profit and marginal profit functions.
   c. Determine the output level in the graph and table where the total profit function takes on its maximum value.
   d. How does the result in part (c) in this exercise compare with the result in part (d) of the previous exercise.
   e. Determine total profits at the profit-maximizing output level.

3. Differentiate the following functions:
   a. $TC = 50 + 100Q - 6Q^2 + .5Q^3$
   b. $ATC = 50/Q + 100 - 6Q + .5Q^2$
   c. $MC = 100 - 12Q + 1.5Q^2$
   d. $Q = 50 - .75P$
   e. $Q = .40X^{1.50}$

4. Differentiate the following functions:
   a. $Y = 2X^3/(4X^2 - 1)$
   b. $Y = 2X^3 (4X^2 - 1)$
   c. $Y = 8Z^2 - 4Z + 1$, where $Z = 2X^2 - 1$ (differentiate Y with respect to X)

5. Defining Q to be the level of output produced and sold, assume that the firm's cost function is given by the relationship

$$TC = 20 + 5Q + Q^2$$

Furthermore, assume that the demand for the output of the firm is a function of price P given by the relationship

$$Q = 25 - P$$

a. Defining total profit as the difference between total revenue and total cost, express in terms of Q the total profit function for the firm. (Note: Total revenue equals price per unit times the number of units sold.)
b. Determine the output level where total profits are maximized.
c. Calculate total profits and selling price at the profit-maximizing output level.
d. If fixed costs increase from $20 to $25 in the total cost relationship, determine the effects of such an increase on the profit-maximizing output level and total profits.

6. Using the cost and demand functions in Problem 5:
   a. Determine the marginal revenue and marginal cost functions.
   b. Show that, at the profit-maximizing output level determined in part (b) of the previous exercise, marginal revenue equals marginal cost. This illustrates the economic principle that profits are maximized at the output level where marginal revenue equals marginal cost.

7. Using the cost and demand functions in Problem 5, suppose the government imposes a 20 percent *tax on the net profits* (that is, a tax on the difference between revenues and costs) of the firm.

   a. Determine the new profit function for the firm.
   b. Determine the output level at which total profits are maximized.
   c. Calculate total profits (after taxes) and the selling price at the profit-maximizing output level.
   d. Compare the results in parts (b) and (c) with the results in Problem 5 above.

8. Suppose the government imposes a 20 percent *sales tax* (that is, a tax on revenue) on the output of the firm. Answer questions (a), (b), (c), and (d) of the previous problem according to this new condition.

9. A firm's average variable cost function is given by the following relationship (where Q is the number of units produced and sold):

$$AVC = 25{,}000 - 180Q + .50Q^2$$

   a. Determine the output level (Q) that minimizes average variable cost.
   b. How does one know that the value of Q determined in part (a) *minimizes* rather than *maximizes* AVC?

10. Determine the partial derivatives with respect to all of the variables in the following functions?

   a. $TC = 50 + 5Q_1 + 10Q_2 + .5Q_1Q_2$
   b. $Q = \alpha L^{\beta_1} C^{\beta_2}$
   c. $Q_A = 2.5P_A^{-1.30} Y^{.20} P_B^{.40}$

11. A firm has determined through regression analysis that its sales (S) are a function of the amount of advertising (measured in units) in two different media. This is given by the following relationship (X = newspapers, Y = magazines):

$$S(X, Y) = 200X + 100Y - 10X^2 - 20Y^2 + 20XY$$

   a. Find the level of newspaper and magazine advertising that maximizes the firm's sales.
   b. Calculate the firm's sales at the optimal values of newspaper and magazine advertising determined in part (a).

12. Consider Problem 11 again. Suppose that the advertising budget is restricted to 20 units.

   a. Determine (using Lagrangian multiplier techniques) the level of newspaper and magazine advertising that maximizes sales subject to this budget constraint.
   b. Calculate the firm's sales at this constrained optimum level.
   c. Give an economic interpretation for the value of the Lagrangian multiplier (λ) obtained in part (a).

13. The Santa Fe Cookie Factory is considering an expansion of its retail pinon cookie business to other cities. The firm's owners lack the funds needed to undertake the expansion on their own. They are considering a franchise arrangement for the new outlets. The company incurs variable costs of $6 for each pound of cookies sold. The fixed costs of operating a typical retail outlet are estimated to be $300,000 per year. The demand function facing each retail outlet is estimated to be:

$$P = \$50 - .001Q$$

where P is the price per pound of cookies and Q is the number of pounds of cookies sold.

a. What price, output, total revenue, total cost, and total profit level will each profit-maximizing franchisee experience?

b. Assuming that the parent company charges each franchisee a fee equal to 5 percent of total revenues, recompute the values in part (a) above.

c. The Santa Fe Cookie Factory is considering a combined fixed/variable franchise fee structure. Under this arrangement each franchisee would pay the parent company $25,000 plus 1 percent of total revenues. Recompute the values in part (a) above.

d. What franchise fee arrangement do you recommend that the Santa Fe Cookie Factory adopt? What are the advantages and disadvantages of each plan?

Linear Programming 5

Most business resource allocation problems require the decision maker to take into account various types of constraints, such as capital, labor, legal, and behavioral restrictions. Linear-programming techniques can be used to provide relatively simple and realistic solutions to problems involving constrained resource allocation decisions. A wide variety of production, finance, marketing, and distribution problems have been formulated in the linear-programming framework[1]. Consequently, managers should understand the linear-programming model so they may allocate the resources of the enterprise most efficiently, particularly in situations where important constraints are placed upon the actions which may be taken. The chapter begins by developing the formulation and graphical solution to a profit-maximization production problem. The following section discusses the concept of dual variables and their interpretations. A computer solution to a cost-minimization problem is presented next. Finally, the formulation and solution of two problems from finance and distribution are presented.

A Profit-Maximization Problem

This section discusses the formulation of linear-programming problems and presents a graphical solution to a simple profit-maximization problem.

Statement of the Problem

A multiproduct firm often has the problem of determining the optimal *product mix*, that is, the combination of outputs that will maximize its profits. The firm is normally subject to various constraints on the amount of resources, such as raw

---

[1] For an extensive bibliography of linear-programming applications see David Anderson, Dennis Sweeney, and Thomas Williams, *An Introduction to Management Science* 5th ed. (St. Paul, MN: West, 1988), chapter 4; George B. Dantzig, *Linear Programming and Extensions* (Princeton, N.J.: Princeton University Press, 1963); P. G. Moore and S. D. Hodges, eds., *Programming for Optimal Decisions* (Baltimore: Penguin Books, 1974); G. Hadley, *Linear Programming* (Reading Mass.: Addison-Wessley, 1962); and the references cited at the end of this chapter.

Glossary of New Terms

Feasible solution space
The set of all possible combinations of the decision variables that *simultaneously* satisfies all the constraints of the problem.

Optimal solution
A feasible solution that maximizes or minimizes the value of the objective function.

Extreme point
Graphically, a corner point of the feasible solution space.

Slack variable
A variable that represents the difference between the right-hand side and left-hand side of a less than or equal to ($\leq$) inequality constraint. It is added to the left-hand side of the inequality to convert the constraint to an equality. It measures the amount of an unused or idle resource.

Primal problem
The original formulation of the linear-programming problem.

(Cont'd on next page)

Glossary of New Terms (*Cont'd*)

Dual problem
A linear-programming problem that is associated with the primal problem. Solution of the primal problem (by the simplex method) automatically provides a solution to the dual problem.

Dual variable
A variable that measures how much the objective function (for example, profit or cost) will change if a given constraint is increased by one unit, provided the increase in the resource does not shift the optimal solution to another extreme point of the feasible solution space.

Surplus variable
A variable that represents the difference between the right-hand side and left-hand side of a greater than or equal to (≥) inequality constraint. It is *subtracted* from the left-hand side of the inequality to convert the constraint to an equality. It measures the amount of a product (or output) in excess of the required amount.

Simplex method
A step-by-step mathematical procedure for finding the optimal solution to a linear-programming problem.

Shadow price
Measures the value (that is, contribution to the objective function) of one additional unit of a resource. It is equivalent to the dual variable.

materials, labor, and production capacity, that may be employed in the production process.

Specifically, the problem is to determine the optimal level of output (X_1 and X_2) for two products (1 and 2). Information about the problem is summarized in Table 5.1. Production consists of a machining process that takes raw materials and converts them into unassembled parts. These are then sent to one of two divisions for assembly into the final product—Division 1 for Product 1 and Division 2 for Product 2.[2] As listed in Table 5.1, Product 1 requires 20 units of raw material and 5 hours of machine-processing time, whereas Product 2 requires 40 units of raw material and 2 hours of machine-processing time. During the period, 400 units of raw material and 40 hours of machine-processing time are available. The capacities of the two assembly divisions during the period are 6 and 9 units, respectively. The profit contribution per unit or, more accurately, the per-unit contribution to profit and overhead (fixed costs) is $100 for each unit of Product 1 and $60 for each unit of Product 2. The profit contribution per unit represents the difference between the selling price per unit and the variable cost per unit. With this information, the problem can be formulated in the linear programming framework.

Formulation of the Linear-Programming Problem

Objective Function. The objective is to maximize the total profit contribution π from the production of the two products, where total profit contribution is equal to the sum of the profit contribution per unit of each product times the number of units produced. Therefore, the objective function is

$$\text{Max } \pi = 100X_1 + 60X_2 \qquad [5.1]$$

where X_1 and X_2 are, as defined earlier, the output levels of Products 1 and 2, respectively.

Constraint Relationships. The production process described has several resource constraints imposed on it. These need to be incorporated into the formulation of the problem. Consider first the raw material constraint. Production of X_1 units of Product 1 requires $20X_1$ units of raw materials. Similarly, production of X_2 units of Product 2 requires $40X_2$ units of the same raw material. The sum of these two quantities of raw materials must be less than or equal to the quantity available, which is 400 units. This relationship can be expressed as

$$20X_1 + 40X_2 \leq 400 \qquad [5.2]$$

The machine-processing time constraint can be developed in a like manner. Product 1 requires $5X_1$ hours and Product 2 requires $2X_2$ hours. With 40 hours

---

[2] This problem ignores any scheduling difficulties that may exist in the production process.

Resource	Quantity of Resources Required per Unit of Output		Quantity of Resources Available During Period
	Product		
	1	*2*	
Raw material (units)	20	40	400
Machine-processing time (hours)	5	2	40
Capacity of Assembly Division 1 (units)	1	0	6
Capacity of Assembly Division 2 (units)	0	1	9
	Product		
	1	2	
Profit contribution ($/unit)	100	60	

Table 5.1
Resource and Profit Data for the Profit-Maximization Problem

of processing time available, the following constraint is obtained:

$$5X_1 + 2X_2 \leqslant 40 \qquad [5.3]$$

The capacities of the two assembly divisions also limit output and consequently profits. For Product 1, which must be assembled in Division 1, the constraint is

$$X_1 \leqslant 6 \qquad [5.4]$$

For Product 2, which must be assembled in Division 2, the constraint is

$$X_2 \leqslant 9 \qquad [5.5]$$

Finally, the logic of the production process suggests that negative output quantities are not possible. Therefore, each of the decision variables is constrained to be nonnegative:

$$X_1 \geqslant 0 \qquad X_2 \geqslant 0 \qquad [5.6]$$

Equations 5.1 through 5.6 constitute a linear-programming formulation of the profit-maximization production problem.

Economic Assumptions of the Linear-Programming Model

In formulating this problem as a linear-programming model, it is important to understand the economic assumptions that are incorporated into the model. Basically, one assumes that a series of linear (or approximately linear) relationships involving the decision variables exist over the range of alternatives being considered in the problem. For the resource inputs, one assumes that the *prices of these resources to the firm are constant* over the range of resource quantities under consideration. This assumption implies that the firm can buy as much or as little of these resources as it needs without affecting the cost.[3] Such an assumption would rule out quantity discounts. One also assumes that there are *constant returns to scale* in the production process. In other words, in the production process, a doubling of the quantity of resources employed doubles the quantity of output obtained, for any level of resources.[4] Finally, one assumes that the *market selling prices of the two products are constant* over the range of possible output combinations.[5] These assumptions are implied by the fixed per-unit profit contribution coefficients in the objective function. If the assumptions are not valid, then the optimal solution to the linear-programming model will not necessarily be an optimal solution to the actual decision-making problem. Although these relationships need not be linear over the entire range of values of the decision variables, it is important that the linearity assumptions be valid over the full range of values being considered in the problem.

Graphical Solution of the Linear-Programming Problem

Various techniques are available for solving linear-programming problems. For larger problems involving more than two decision variables, one needs to employ algebraic methods to obtain a solution. Further discussion of these methods is postponed until later in the chapter. For problems containing only two decision variables, graphical methods can be used to obtain an optimal solution. In order to understand the nature of the objective function and constraint relationships, it is helpful to solve the preceding problem graphically. This is done by graphing the feasible solution space and objective function separately and then combining the two graphs to obtain the optimal solution.

Graphing the Feasible Solution Space. Note from Equation 5.6 that each of the decision variables must be greater than or equal to zero. Therefore, one needs only graph the upper right-hand (positive) quadrant. Figure 5.1 illustrates the raw material constraint as given by Equation 5.2. The upper limit or maximum quantity of raw materials that may be used occurs when the inequality is satisfied as an equality; in other words, the set of points that satisfies the equation:

$$20X_1 + 40X_2 = 400$$

Since it is possible to use less than the amount of raw materials available, any combination of outputs lying *on or below* this line (that is, the shaded area) will satisfy the raw materials constraint.

---

[3] This assumption involves the concept of a perfectly competitive factor or *input* market. See chapter 14 for a discussion of this type of market.

[4] "Doubling the quantity of resources" is used as an example. More generally, one would say that a given percentage increase in each of the resources would result in an equivalent percentage increase in output for any given level of resources. See chapter 11 for a further discussion of the concept of returns to scale.

[5] This assumption is satisfied in a perfectly competitive market for the two products. Further discussion of this type of market is in chapter 14.

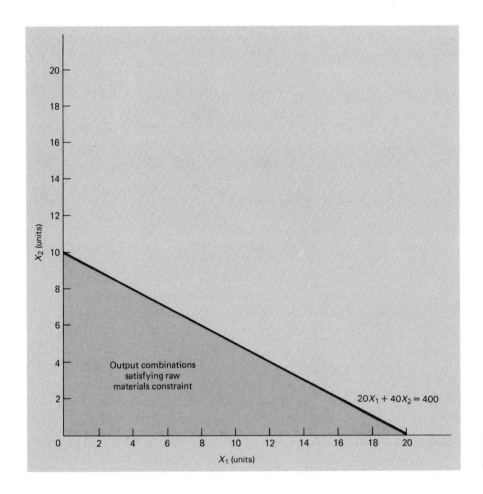

Output combinations satisfying raw materials constraint

$20X_1 + 40X_2 = 400$

X_2 (units)

X_1 (units)

Figure 5.1
Raw Material Constraint

Similarly, the constraint on the amount of machine-processing time (in hours) available (Equation 5.3) yields the combinations of X_1 and X_2 that lie on or below the line (that is, the shaded area) shown in Figure 5.2. Likewise, one can determine the set of feasible combinations of X_1 and X_2 for each of the remaining constraints (Equations 5.4 and 5.5).

Combining all the constraints (Equations 5.2–5.6) yields the *feasible solution space* (shaded area) shown in Figure 5.3, which *simultaneously* satisfies all the constraints of the problem. All possible production combinations of X_1 and X_2 that simultaneously satisfy all the resource constraints lie in or on the boundary of the shaded area.

Graphing the Objective Function. The objective function given by Equation 5.1 specifies the profit that will be obtained from any combination of output levels. The profit function can be represented graphically as a series of parallel *isoprofit* lines. Each of the lines shown in Figure 5.4 is an isoprofit line, meaning that each combination of output levels (that is, X_1 and X_2) lying on a given line has the *same* total profit. For example, the $\pi = 1200$ isoprofit line includes such output combinations as $(X_1 = 6, X_2 = 10)$ and $(X_1 = 9, X_2 = 5)$. The objective of

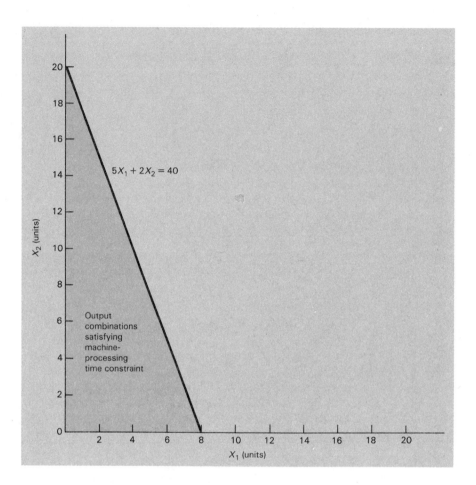

Figure 5.2
Machine-Processing Time Constraint

The graph shows $5X_1 + 2X_2 = 40$ with the shaded region labeled "Output combinations satisfying machine-processing time constraint". Axes: X_2 (units) vertical, X_1 (units) horizontal.

profit maximization can be interpreted graphically to find an output combination that falls on as high an isoprofit line as possible. The resource constraints of the problem obviously limit us from increasing output and profits indefinitely.

Graphical Solution.   Combining the graphs of the feasible solution space and objective function yields the output combination point within the feasible solution space that lies on the highest possible isoprofit line. The two graphs have been combined in Figure 5.5. From the graph it can be seen that the optimal output combination at point C is $X_1^* = 5$ units and $X_2^* = 7.5$ units, yielding a profit of

$$\pi^* = 100 \times 5 + 60 \times 7.5$$
$$= \$950$$

No other output combination within the feasible solution space will result in a larger profit.

Sometimes it is difficult to read the exact coordinates of the *optimal solution* from the graph. When this occurs (or when one wants to confirm the solution algebraically), we can determine the exact solution by solving simultaneously

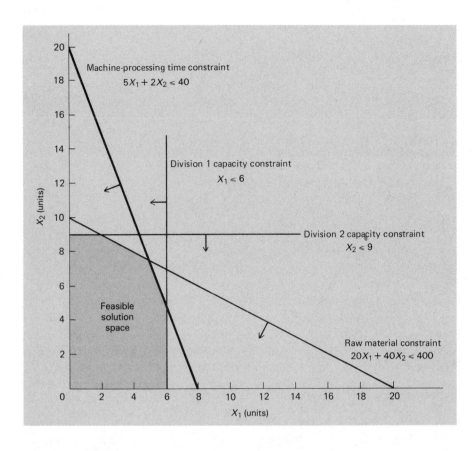

Figure 5.3
Feasible Solution Space: Profit-Maximization Problem

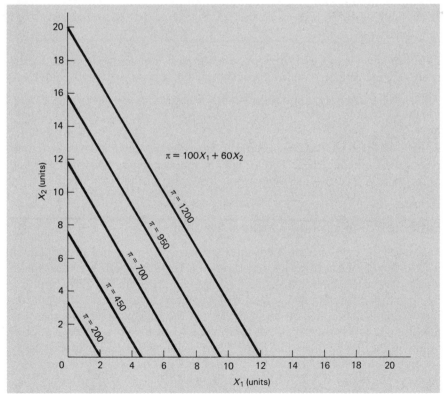

Figure 5.4
Isoprofit Lines: Profit-Maximization Problem

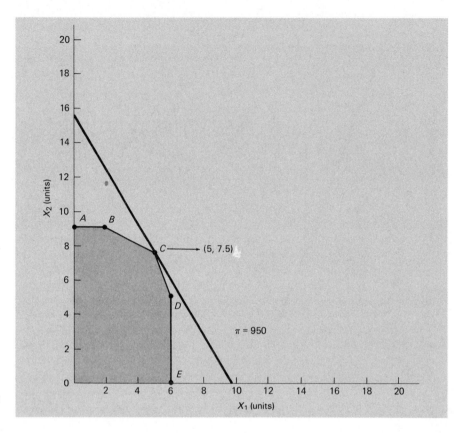

Figure 5.5
**Optimal Solution:
Profit-Maximization
Problem**

the equations of the two lines passing through the optimum point. In the preceding example, the equations of the two lines passing through point C are

$$20X_1 + 40X_2 = 400$$

$$5X_1 + 2X_2 = 40$$

which correspond to the raw material and machine-processing time constraints, respectively. Solving these two equations simultaneously does indeed yield $X_1^* = 5$ and $X_2^* = 7.5$—the same result that was obtained graphically.

Extreme Points and the Optimal Solution

This example demonstrates two important general properties of an optimal solution to a linear-programming problem. These properties are useful in developing algebraic solutions to this class of problem and they form the foundation for all computer (algorithmic) solution techniques. First, note that the optimal solution lies on the *boundary* of the feasible solution space. The implication of this property is that one can ignore the infinite number of interior points in the feasible solution space when searching for an optimal solution. Second, note that the optimal solution occurs at one of the *extreme points* (corner points) of the feasible solution space. This property reduces even further the magnitude of the search procedure for an optimal solution. For this example it means that from among the infinite number of points lying on the boundary of the feasible solution space, only six points—A, B, C, D, E, and zero—need to be examined to find an optimal solution.

Multiple Optimal Solutions

It is also possible to have *multiple* optimal solutions to a problem if the isoprofit line coincides with one of the boundaries of the feasible solution space. For example, if the objective function in the production problem were equal to

$$\pi' = 100X_1 + 40X_2 \tag{5.7}$$

then the isoprofit line $\pi' = \$800$ would coincide with the CD boundary line of the feasible solution space as illustrated in Figure 5.6. In this case both corner points C and D, along with all the output combinations falling along the CD line segment, would constitute optimal solutions to the problem.

Slack Variables

In addition to the optimal combination of output to produce (X_1^* and X_2^*) and the maximum total profit (π^*), we are also interested in the amount of each

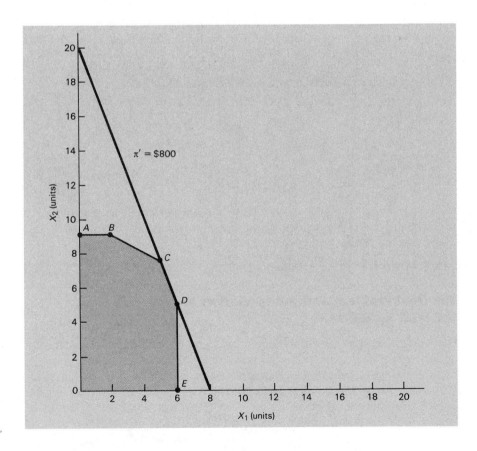

Figure 5.6
Multiple Optimal Solutions: Profit-Maximization Problem

resource used in the production process. For the production of 5 units $(=X_1^*)$ and 7.5 units $(=X_2^*)$ of products 1 and 2, respectively, the resource requirements (from Equations 5.2–5.5) are as follows:

$$20(5) + 40(7.5) = 400 \text{ units of raw materials}$$

$$5(5) + 2(7.5) = 40 \text{ hours of machine-processing time}$$

$$1(5) = 5 \text{ units of Division 1 assembly capacity}$$

$$1(7.5) = 7.5 \text{ units of Division 2 assembly capacity}$$

This information indicates that all available raw materials (400 units) and all available machine-processing time (40 hours) will be used in producing the optimal output combination. However, 1 unit of Division 1 assembly capacity $(6 - 5)$ and 1.5 units of Division 2 assembly capacity $(9 - 7.5)$ will be unused in producing the optimal output combination. These unused or idle resources associated with a less than or equal to constraint ($\leq$) are referred to as *slack*.

Slack variables can be added to the formulation of a linear-programming problem to represent this slack or idle capacity. Slack variables are given a coefficient of zero in the objective function since they make no contribution to profit. Slack variables can be thought of as representing the difference between the right-hand side and left-hand side of a less than or equal to inequality ($\leq$) constraint.

In the preceding profit-maximization problem (Equations 5.1–5.6), four slack variables (S_1, S_2, S_3, S_4) are used to convert the four (less than or equal to) constraints to equalities as follows:

$$\max \pi = 100X_1 + 60X_2 + 0S_1 + 0S_2 + 0S_3 + 0S_4$$

$$
\begin{aligned}
\text{s.t.} \quad 20X_1 + 40X_2 + 1S_1 & && && = 400 \\
5X_1 + 2X_2 & + 1S_2 && && = 40 \\
X_1 & && + 1S_3 && = 6 \\
X_2 & && && + 1S_4 = 9 \\
\end{aligned}
$$

$$X_1, X_2, S_1, S_2, S_3, S_4 \geq 0$$

As shown later in the chapter, a computer solution of a linear-programming problem automatically provides the optimal values of the slack variables as well as the original decision variables.

The Dual Problem and Interpretation of the Dual Variables

The solution of a linear-programming problem, in addition to providing the optimal values of the decision variables, contains information that can be very useful in making *marginal* resource-allocation decisions. This marginal information is contained in what are known as the *dual variables* of the linear-programming problem.

The Dual Linear-Programming Problem

Associated with every linear-programming problem is a related *dual* linear-programming problem. The *originally formulated* problem, in relation to the dual problem, is known as the *primal* linear-programming problem.[6] If the objective in the primal problem is *maximization* of some function, then the objective in the dual problem is *minimization* of a related (but different) function. Conversely, a primal minimization problem has a related dual maximization problem. The dual variables represent the variables contained in the dual problem.

Before indicating how the dual variables can be used as an aid in marginal decision making, it may be useful to illustrate, using the preceding example problem, the relation of the dual problem to the primal problem. One way to show the relationship is by means of a matrix diagram, such as the one in Figure 5.7. The primal problem is contained in the *rows* of the figure. For example, the first row (W_1) of numbers in the figure contains the Equation 5.2 constraint; that is, $20X_1 + 40X_2 \leq 400$. The last row (Constants) contains the objective function (Equation 5.1); that is, max $\pi = 100X_1 + 60X_2$.

Associated with each constraint of the primal problem is a dual variable. Since the primal problem had four constraints,[7] the dual problem has four variables—W_1, W_2, W_3, and W_4. The dual problem is contained in the *columns* of the figure. The objective of the dual problem is contained in the Constants column:

$$\text{Min } Z = 400W_1 + 40W_2 + 6W_3 + 9W_4 \qquad [5.8]$$

Similarly, the constraints of the dual problem are contained under the X_1 and X_2 columns:

$$20W_1 + 5W_2 + W_3 \geq 100 \qquad [5.9]$$

$$40W_1 + 2W_2 + W_4 \geq 60 \qquad [5.10]$$

	Variables	PRIMAL		Relation	Constants	
		X_1	X_2			
DUAL	W_1	20	40	≤	400	Equation 5.2
	W_2	5	2	≤	40	Equation 5.3
	W_3	1	0	≤	6	Equation 5.4
	W_4	0	1	≤	9	Equation 5.5
	Relation	≥	≥		min Z	
	Constants	100	60	max π		Equation 5.1
		Equation 5.9	Equation 5.10		Equation 5.8	

Figure 5.7
Primal and Dual Problems

---

[6] By symmetry, the dual of the dual problem is the primal problem.

[7] The constraints requiring each of the primal variables to be greater than or equal to zero (that is, $X_1 \geq 0$, $X_2 \geq 0$) are not included when determining the number of dual variables.

One also requires

$$W_1 \geq 0, \ W_2 \geq 0, \ W_3 \geq 0, \ W_4 \geq 0 \qquad [5.11]$$

In general, a primal problem with n variables and m constraints will have as its dual a problem with m variables and n constraints.

Economic Interpretation of the Dual Variables

In the preceding resource-constrained profit-maximization problem, a dual variable existed for each of the limited resources required in the production process. In such a problem the dual variables measure the "imputed values" or *shadow prices* of each of the scarce resources. Expressed in dollars per unit of resource, they give an indication of how much each resource contributes to the overall profit function. With this interpretation of the dual variables, the dual objective function (Equation 5.8) is to minimize the total cost or value of the resources employed in the process. The two dual constraints (Equations 5.9 and 5.10) require that the value of the resources used in producing one unit each of X_1 and X_2 be at least as great as the profit received from the sale of one unit of each product. An important linear-programming theorem, known as the *duality theorem*, indicates that the maximum value of the primal profit function will also be equal to the minimum value of the dual "imputed value" function.[8] The solution of the dual problem in effect apportions the total profit figure among the various scarce resources employed in the process.

The interpretation of the dual variables and dual problem depends on the nature and objective of the primal problem. Thus a completely different interpretation is involved whenever the primal problem is one of cost minimization.[9]

The preceding example illustrates how the dual variables can be used to make marginal resource-allocation decisions. The values of the dual variables, *which are obtained automatically in an algebraic solution of the linear-programming problem*, are $W_1^* = \$.625$ per unit, $W_2^* = \$17.50$ per unit, $W_3^* = \$0$ per unit, and $W_4^* = \$0$ per unit. Each dual variable indicates the rate of change in total profits for an incremental change in the amount of each of the various resources. In this way they are similar to the λ values used in the Lagrangian multiplier technique. The dual variables indicate how much the total profit will change (i.e., marginal profit) if one additional unit of a given resource is made available, provided the increase in the resource does not shift the optimal solution to another corner point of the feasible solution space. For example, $W_2^* = \$17.50$ indicates that profits could be increased by as much as $\$17.50$ if an additional unit (hour) of machine capacity could be made available to the production process. This type of information is potentially useful in

---

[8] See any standard linear-programming text, such as the previously cited Anderson et al., Dantzig, and Hadley books, for a complete discussion of the concept of duality and the duality theorem.

[9] See Hadley, *Linear Programming* pp. 485–487; and J. G. Kemeny, H. Mirkil, J. L. Snell, G. L. Thompson, *Finite Mathematical Structures* (Englewood Cliffs, N. J.: Prentice-Hall, 1959), pp. 364–366 and the next section, for examples of the interpretation of other types of dual problems.

making decisions about purchasing or renting additional machine capacity or using existing machine capacity more fully through the use of overtime and multiple shifts. A dual variable equal to zero, such as W_3^* and W_4^*, indicates that profits would *not* increase if additional resources of these types were made available; in fact, excess capacity in these resources exists. (Recall in the discussion of slack variables, portions of these resources were unused or idle in the optimal solution.) This discussion only indicates the type of analysis that is possible. Much more detailed analysis of this nature can be performed using parametric-programming techniques.[10]

A Cost-Minimization Problem

This section develops a cost-minimization problem and illustrates the use of computer programs for its solution.

Statement of the Problem

Large multiplant firms often produce the same products at two or more factories. Often these factories employ different production technologies and have different unit production costs. The objective is to produce the desired amount of output using the given facilities (that is, plants and production processes) to minimize production costs.

For example, suppose that a mining company owns two different mines (A and B) for producing uranium ore. The two mines are located in different areas and produce different qualities of uranium ore. After the ore is mined, it is separated into three grades—high-, medium-, and low-grade. Information concerning the operation of the two mines is shown in Table 5.2. Mine A produces .75 tons of high-grade ore, .25 tons of medium-grade ore, and .50 tons of low-grade ore *per hour*. Likewise, Mine B produces .25, .25, and 1.50 tons of high-, medium-, and low-grade ore *per hour*, respectively. The firm has contracts

Table 5.2
Output and Cost Data for the Cost-Minimization Problem

Type of Ore	Output (tons of ore per hour)		Requirements (tons per week)
	Mine		
	A	B	
High-grade ore	.75	.25	36
Medium-grade ore	.25	.25	24
Low-grade ore	.50	1.50	72
	Mine		
	A	B	
Operating cost ($/hour)	50	40	

---

[10] See Hadley, *Linear Programming*, pp. 379–400, for an explanation of such an analysis.

with uranium-processing plants to supply a minimum of 36 tons of high-grade ore, 24 tons of medium-grade ore, and 72 tons of low-grade ore *per week*. These figures are shown in the Requirements column of Table 5.2. Finally, as shown in the bottom row of Table 5.2, it costs the company $50 per hour to operate Mine A and $40 per hour to operate Mine B. The company wishes to determine the number of hours per week it should operate each mine to minimize the total cost of fulfilling its supply contracts.

Formulation of the Linear-Programming Problem

Objective Function.   The objective is to *minimize* the total cost per week (C) from the operation of the two mines, where the total cost is equal to the sum of the operating cost per hour of each mine times the number of hours per week that each mine is operated. Defining X_1 as the number of hours per week that Mine A is operated and X_2 as the number of hours per week that Mine B is operated, the objective function is

$$\text{Min } C = 50X_1 + 40X_2 \qquad [5.12]$$

Constraint Relationships.   The company's contracts with uranium-processing plants require it to operate the two mines for a sufficient number of hours to produce the required amount of each grade of uranium ore. In the production of high-grade ore, Mine A produces .75 tons per hour times the number of hours per week (X_1) that it operates, and Mine B produces .25 tons per hour times the number of hours per week (X_2) that is operates. The sum of these two quantities must be greater than or equal to the required output of 36 tons per week. This relationship can be expressed as

$$.75X_1 + .25X_2 \geq 36 \qquad [5.13]$$

Similar constraints can be developed for the production of medium-grade ore

$$.25X_1 + .25X_2 \geq 24 \qquad [5.14]$$

and low-grade ore

$$.50X_1 + 1.50X_2 \geq 72 \qquad [5.15]$$

Finally, negative production times are not possible. Therefore, each of the decision variables is constrained to be nonnegative

$$X_1 \geq 0, \; X_2 \geq 0 \qquad [5.16]$$

Equations 5.12 through 5.16 represent a linear-programming formulation of the cost-minimization production problem.

Slack (Surplus) Variables

Recall from the discussion of the maximization problem earlier in the chapter that slack variables were added to the less than or equal to inequality ($\leq$) constraints to convert these constraints to equalities. Similarly, in a minimization problem, *surplus variables* are *subtracted* from the greater than or equal to inequality ($\geq$) constraints to convert these constraints to equalities. Like the slack variables, surplus variables are given coefficients of zero in the objective function because they have no effect on the value.

In the preceding cost-minimization problem, three surplus variables (S_1, S_2, S_3) are used to convert the three (greater than or equal to) constraints to equalities as follows:

$$
\begin{aligned}
\text{Min } C = \ & 50X_1 + \quad 40X_2 + 0S_1 + 0S_2 + 0S_3 \\
\text{s.t.} \quad & .75X_1 + \ .25X_2 - 1S_1 \qquad\qquad = 36 \\
& .25X_1 + \ .25X_2 \qquad\ - 1S_2 \qquad = 24 \\
& .50X_1 + 1.50X \qquad\qquad - 1S_3 = 72 \\
& X_1, X_2, S_1, S_2, S_3 \geq 0
\end{aligned}
$$

Computer Solution of the Linear-Programming Problem

The solution of large-scale linear-programming problems typically employs a procedure (or variation of the procedure) known as the *simplex method.* Basically, the simplex method is a step-by-step procedure for moving from corner point to corner point of the feasible solution space in such a manner that successively larger (or smaller) values of the maximization (or minimization) objective function are obtained at each step. The procedure is guaranteed to yield the optimal solution in a finite number of steps. Further discussion of this method is beyond the scope of this chapter.[11]

Most practical applications of linear programming use computer programs to perform the calculations and obtain the optimal solution. Although many different programs are available for solving linear-programming problems, the output of these programs usually includes the optimal solution to the primal problem as well as the optimal values of the dual variables. The particular program illustrated here is known as "SIMPLX."[12] (Similar programs are likely to be readily available on your school's computer system. Also, the software package provided to instructors with the text contains a linear-programming routine.)

Putting the objective function and constraints (Equation 5.12 through 5.16) along with the appropriate control statements into the SIMPLX program yields the output shown in Figure 5.8. The optimal values of the decision variables are shown in the Primal Solution column—$X_1^* = 24$ and $X_2^* = 72$. The firm should operate Mine A for 24 hours per week and Mine B for 72 hours per week to *minimize* total operating costs. This yields a minimum total cost of $4,080 per week.

---

[11] Any basic linear-programming textbook, such as the previously cited Anderson et al., Dantzig, and Hadley books, contain detailed discussions of this procedure.

[12] "SIMPLX" is a terminal-oriented computer program. See E. Pearsall and B. Price, *Linear Programming and Simulation* (No. MS(350)), CONDUIT (Ames: University of Iowa).

```
:RUN "SIMPLX"

DO YOU WANT INSTRUCTIONS FOR THIS PROGRAM: YES OR NO?$NO

NUMBER OF CONSTRAINTS:        M = 3
NUMBER OF VARIABLES:          N = 2
NUMBER OF SLACKS CREATED:     S = 3
OBJECTIVE IS TO MINIMIZE COST
PRINT CONSTRAINT COEFFICIENTS: YES OR NO?$YES
PRINT OBJECTIVE ROW COEFFICIENTS: YES OR NO?$YES
PRINT RIGHT HAND SIDE ENTRIES: YES OR NO?$YES

C( 1) = 50, C( 2) = 40, B( 1) = 36, B( 2) = 24,
B( 3) = 72, A( 1, 1) = 0.75, A( 1, 2) = 0.25, A( 2, 1) = 0.25,
A( 2, 2) = 0.25, A( 3, 1) = 0.5, A( 3, 2) = 1.5,

START WITH GIVEN BASIS: YES OR NO?$NO
SUPPRESS THE PIVOT RECORD: YES OR NO?$NO

PIVOT    ENTERS    LEAVES         COST          DELTA

INVERSION PERFORMED
BEGIN PHASE I
1        X( 2)     X( 0)          1920          -2
2        X( 1)     X( 0)          3240          -0.8333333
3        X( 3)     X( 0)          4560          -0.25
BEGIN PHASE II
4        X( 5)     X( 3)          4080          -10
REINVERT BEFORE TERMINATION: YES OR NO?$YES
INVERSION PERFORMED
SOLUTION IS OPTIMAL
```

SOLUTION COST IS 4080			
PRIMAL SOLUTION		DUAL SOLUTION	
VARIABLE	VALUE	VARIABLE	VALUE
X(1)	24	W(1)	20
X(5)	48	W(2)	140
X(2)	72	W(3)	0

Figure 5.8
**SIMPLX Program
Solution of Cost-
Minimization
Problem**

Note also that the optimal value of the surplus variable S_3^* [that is, $X(5)$ on the computer output] is 48. This indicates that a surplus of 48 tons of low-grade ore (that is, 120 tons versus the required amount of 72 tons) is being produced in the optimal solution. Similarly, S_1 and S_2 are zero (all variables not listed in the primal solution are equal to zero), indicating that exactly the required amounts of high-grade and medium-grade ore (36 and 24 tons, respectively) are being produced in the optimal solution.

Recall from the earlier discussion of the dual problem and dual variables that a dual variable is associated with each constraint equation in the primal problem (excluding nonnegativity constraints). The ore-mining problem has three constraint equations—one for each of the three types of uranium ore. Conse-

Economic Analysis and Managerial Efficiency

APPLYING MATHEMATICAL PROCEDURES TO SOLVE PRACTICAL BUSINESS PROBLEMS*

The simplex algorithm is widely used in computer programs to solve constrained-optimization problems; in fact, 80 to 90 percent of linear-programming problems can be solved using this algorithm. One drawback of the simplex algorithm, however, is that in many circumstances it is too slow to be practical. The airlines, for example, make use of highly complex linear-programming models to establish the most efficient schedules for hundreds of planes, and multiple flights. American Airlines typically runs its scheduling program for crews, flights, and equipment once a month. Using the simplex algorithm, American's highly complex programming model requires several hours of computer time to obtain an optimal solution. For normal scheduling purposes, this response time poses no problems; but the program is of little use for an emergency scheduling situation like a severe storm that disrupts normal operations.

A recent development at AT&T's Bell Laboratories, however, offers potential relief to

*Based, in part, on David Stipp, "AT&T Problem-Solving Math Procedure Passes Early Tests of Its Practical Value," *Wall Street Journal*, 3 May 1985.

firms such as American Airlines, which make use of very large linear programming models and have a need for rapid updates as new constraints evolve. A researcher at Bell Labs recently announced the development of a mathematical procedure that has the potential to solve a broad range of programming problems fifty to one hundred times faster than they are currently being handled. If the early claims regarding the performance of this new procedure are correct, companies such as American Airlines will be able to use their complex programming models to make efficient adjustments rapidly in response to changing operating constraints. The new procedure may also permit small companies to use personal computers to solve complex problems that previously could only be solved on larger machines. The application of this new algorithm, however, awaits additional testing and the development of computer programs to utilize its capabilities.

Question

1. How could your university make use of linear programming to schedule courses, professors, and facilities? Try to develop explicitly the objective function and to identify the important constraints within such a linear-programming model.

quently, it has three dual variables—W_1, W_2, and W_3—associated with each of the respective constraint equations. The optimal values of the dual variables are shown in the Dual Solution column of Figure 5.8—$W_1^* = \$20$, $W_2^* = \$140$, and $W_3^* = \$0$. Each dual variable measures the change in total cost (i.e. marginal cost) that results from a one unit (ton) increase in the required output, provided that the increase does not shift the optimal solution to another corner point of the feasible solution space. For example, $W_1^* = \$20$ indicates that total costs will increase by as much as $20 if the firm is required to produce an additional ton of high-grade uranium ore. Comparison of this value to the revenue received per ton of ore can help the firm in making decisions about whether to expand or contract its mining operations.

Last, consider the interpretation of $W_3^* = \$0$. This zero value indicates that surplus low-grade ore is being produced by the firm. (Recall that $S_3^* = 48$.) At the optimal solution (operating Mines A and B at 24 and 72 hours per week, respectively), the cost of producing an additional ton of low-grade ore is $0.

Additional Linear-Programming Examples

Linear programming is useful in a wide variety of managerial resource-allocation problems. This section examines some additional applications in finance and marketing and distribution.

Finance: The Capital-Rationing Problem

Rather than letting the size of their capital budgets (expenditures that are expected to provide long-term benefits to the firm, such as plants and equipment) be determined by the number of profitable investment opportunities available (all investment projects meeting some acceptance standard), many firms place an upper limit or constraint on the amount of funds allocated to capital investment. *Capital rationing* takes place whenever the total cash outlays for all projects that meet some acceptance standard exceed the constraint on total capital investment.

For example, suppose the firm is faced with the set of nine investment projects shown in Table 5.3, requiring the outlay of funds in each of the next two years (shown in columns 2 and 3), and generating the returns (net present values) shown in column 4.[13] Furthermore, suppose the firm has decided to

**Table 5.3
Two-Period
Capital-
Rationing Problem**

Investment, j (1)	Present Value of Outlay in Year 1, C_{1j} (2)	Present Value of Outlay in Year 2, C_{2j} (3)	Net Present Value of Investment, b_j (4)
1	$12	$ 3	$14
2	54	7	17
3	6	6	17
4	6	2	15
5	30	35	40
6	6	6	12
7	48	4	14
8	36	3	10
9	18	3	12

---

[13] This problem was first formulated and solved in the mathematical programming context by Weingartner. See Martin Weingartner, *Mathematical Programming and the Analysis of Capital Budgeting Problems* (Englewood Cliffs, N.J.: Prentice-Hall, 1963).

limit total capital expenditures to $50 and $20 in each of the next two years, respectively. The problem is to select the combination of investments that provides the *largest possible return* (net present value) without violating either of the two constraints on total capital expenditures. This problem can be formulated and solved using linear-programming techniques.

Begin by defining X_j to be the fraction of project j undertaken (where $j = 1,2,3,4,5,6,7,8$, and 9). The objective is to maximize the sum of the returns (net present value) of the projects undertaken:

$$\text{Max } R = 14X_1 + 17X_2 + 17X_3 + 15X_4 + 40X_5$$
$$+ 12X_6 + 14X_7 + 10X_8 + 12X_9 \quad [5.17]$$

The constraints are the restrictions placed on total capital expenditures in each of the two years:

$$12X_1 + 54X_2 + 6X_3 + 6X_4 + 30X_5 + 6X_6 + 48X_7 + 36X_8 + 18X_9 \leq 50 \quad [5.18]$$

$$3X_1 + 7X_2 + 6X_3 + 2X_4 + 35X_5 + 6X_6 + 4X_7 + 3X_8 + 3X_9 \leq 20. \quad [5.19]$$

Also, so that no more than one of any project will be included in the final solution, all the X_j's must be less than or equal to 1:

$$X_1 \leq 1 \quad [5.20]$$
$$X_2 \leq 1 \quad [5.21]$$
$$X_3 \leq 1 \quad [5.22]$$
$$X_4 \leq 1 \quad [5.23]$$
$$X_5 \leq 1 \quad [5.24]$$
$$X_6 \leq 1 \quad [5.25]$$
$$X_7 \leq 1 \quad [5.26]$$
$$X_8 \leq 1 \quad [5.27]$$
$$X_9 \leq 1 \quad [5.28]$$

Finally, all the X_j's must be nonnegative:

$$X_1 \geq 0, X_2 \geq 0, X_3 \geq 0, X_4 \geq 0, X_5 \geq 0, X_6 \geq 0,$$
$$X_7 \geq 0, X_8 \geq 0, X_9 \geq 0 \quad [5.29]$$

Equations 5.17 through 5.29 represent a linear-programming formulation of this capital-rationing problem.

The optimal solution to this problem is shown in Table 5.4. The firm should adopt in their entirety Projects 1, 3, 4, and 9, and fractional parts of two others—97 percent of Project 6 and 4.5 percent of Project 7. There will be at most one fractional project for each budget constraint; that is, two fractional

Primal Variables	X_1^*	X_2^*	X_3^*	X_4^*	X_5^*	X_6^*	X_7^*	X_8^*	X_9^*
	1.0	0	1.0	1.0	0	.970	.045	0	1.0
Dual Variables	W_1^*	W_2^*							
	.136	1.864		Total net present value $(R^*) = \$70.27$					

Table 5.4
Optimal Solution: Two-Period Capital-Rationing Problem

projects in this problem. The total return (net present value) of the optimal solution is $70.27.

Fractional parts arise from the manner in which the linear-programming model was formulated. By allowing the X_j's to vary from 0 to 1, it was implicitly assumed that the projects were divisible; that is, the firm could undertake all or part of a project and receive benefits (cash flows) in the same proportion as the amounts invested. This assumption is somewhat unrealistic since most investments must either be undertaken in their entirety or not at all. One possible way to eliminate these fractional projects is to adjust the budget constraints upward to be able to include the entire project. Generally, total capital expenditure limits are flexible enough to allow slight upward adjustments to be made. Another method for eliminating fractional projects in the solution is to use an *integer*-programming formulation of the problem. This would be done by adding constraints to the model that require the X_j's to have integer values:

$$X_j \text{ an integer } j = 1, \ldots, 9$$

that is, $X_1, X_2, X_3, X_4, X_5, X_6, X_7, X_8, X_9$ are integers. Requiring the X_j's to be integers and also to be between 0 and 1 forces these variables to take on the values of either 1 or 0; that is, the projects would have to be accepted either in their entirety or not at all.

The solution to this primal linear-programming problem also yields a solution to the *dual* problem. There is one dual variable for every constraint in the primal problem. The optimal values of the dual variables associated with the two budget contraints (Equations 5.18 and 5.19) are shown in Table 5.4. In this problem these dual variables indicate the amount that the total present value could be increased if the budget limits (constraints) were increased to permit an additional $1 investment in the given period. In the example, if the budget constraint in Year 1 were increased from $50 to $51, then the total net present value would increase by $W_1^* = \$.136$. Similarly, if the budget constraint in Year 2 were increased from $20 to $21, the total net present value would increase by $W_2^* = \$1.864$. Since the dual variables measure the opportunity cost of not having additional funds available for investment in a given period, they can be used in deciding whether or not to shift funds from one period to another.[14] If the values of the dual variables are fairly large, indicating that total net present value could be increased significantly through additional investment, the firm may decide to increase its capital expenditure budget through such methods as new borrowing or equity financing.

---

[14] The formulation of the capital-rationing problem in a linear-programming framework creates a difficulty in interpreting the dual variables associated with budget constraints. A problem arises because two interdependent measures of the opportunity cost of investment funds are available—the dual variable value and the cost of capital (discount rate), which is used in finding the net present values (b_j's) of the investment projects. For a further discussion of the problem, see William J. Baumol and Richard E. Quandt, "Investment and Discount Rates Under Capital Rationing—A Programming Approach," *Economic Journal* 75 (June 1965), pp. 317–329.

Marketing and Distribution: The Transportation Problem

Large multiplant firms often produce their products at several different factories and then ship the products to various regional warehouses located throughout their marketing area. The objective is to minimize shipping costs subject to the contraints of meeting the demand for the product in each region and not exceeding the supply of the product available at each plant.

For example, suppose a firm has two production plants located in New England (1) and the Gulf Coast (2), and three warehouses located in the East Coast (1), Midwest (2), and West Coast (3) regions (see Figure 5.9). Shipping costs per unit of the product from each of the two plants to each of the three warehouses are shown in the center box in the figure. *Demand* for the product at each of the regional warehouses is shown in the bottom row and the *supply* of the product available at each plant is shown in the far right column of Figure 5.9. The firm wants to minimize its shipping costs.

Begin the linear-programming formulation of the problem by defining X_{ij} to be the number of units of the product shipped from Plant i to Warehouse j. This problem has six X-variables—namely, $X_{11}, X_{12}, X_{13}, X_{21}, X_{22}, X_{23}$. For example, X_{21} indicates the amount of the product shipped from the Gulf Coast plant to the East Coast warehouse. Similar interpretations apply to the other X-variables.

Total shipping costs are the sum of the number of units of the product shipped from each plant to each warehouse times the respective shipping cost per unit. The objective function is therefore

$$\text{Min } C = 20X_{11} + 35X_{12} + 65X_{13} + 25X_{21} + 15X_{22} + 50X_{23} \qquad [5.30]$$

There are two sets of constraints (plus nonnegativity constraints) in a standard transportation problem such as this one. The first set has to do with meeting the demand for the product at each of the three regional warehouses. Total shipments *to* each warehouse must be greater than or equal to demand in the region:

$$X_{11} \qquad\qquad + X_{21} \qquad \geq 2,000 \qquad\qquad [5.31]$$
$$X_{12} \qquad\qquad + X_{22} \quad \geq 1,500 \qquad\qquad [5.32]$$
$$X_{13} \qquad\qquad + X_{23} \geq 1,000 \qquad\qquad [5.33]$$

The second set of constraints is concerned with not exceeding the supply of the product at each plant. Total shipments *from* each plant must be less than or

		Regional Warehouse			
		East Coast (1)	Midwest (2)	West Coast (3)	Supply
Plant	New England (1)	$20	35	65	2000
	Gulf Coast (2)	25	15	50	2500
	Demand	2000	1500	1000	

Figure 5.9
Transportation Problem Data

Table 5.5
Optimal Solution:
Transportation
Problem

X_{11}^* 2000	X_{12}^* 0	X_{13}^* 0	X_{21}^* 0	X_{22}^* 1500	X_{23}^* 1000	C^* $112,500

equal to the supply of the product *at* the plant:

$$X_{11} + X_{12} + X_{13} \qquad\qquad \leqslant 2,000 \qquad\qquad [5.34]$$

$$X_{21} + X_{22} + X_{23} \leqslant 2,500 \qquad\qquad [5.35]$$

Finally, all the X-variables are required to be nonnegative:

$$X_{11} \geqslant 0,\ X_{12} \geqslant 0,\ X_{13} \geqslant 0,\ X_{21} \geqslant 0,\ X_{22} \geqslant 0,\ X_{23} \geqslant 0 \qquad [5.36]$$

Equations 5.30 through 5.36 constitute a linear-programming formulation of the transportation problem.

The optimal solution to this problem is shown in Table 5.5.[15] From the New England plant, the firm should ship 2000 units to the East Coast regional warehouse (X_{11}^*). From the Gulf Coast plant, the firm should ship 1500 units to the Midwest regional warehouse (X_{22}^*) and 1,000 units to the West Coast regional warehouse (X_{23}^*). Total shipping costs of the optimal solution are $112,500.

Summary

- Linear-programming problems constitute an important class of constrained-optimization problems for which efficient solution techniques have been developed.

- Linear programming has an advantage over classical optimization techniques because it can be applied to problems with inequality constraints.

- Despite the need for expressing the objective and constraint functions as linear relationships, a wide variety of problems can be formulated and solved in the linear-programming framework.

- Virtually all practical linear-programming problems are solved using computer programs that employ algebraic techniques. Graphical solution techniques are used in problems involving two decision variables to illustrate the basic linear-programming concepts.

- An important part of the solution of a linear-programming problem is the values of the *dual variables*. The dual variables are useful in making marginal resource-allocation decisions. They provide information on the resources that limit the value of the objective function and help make return-versus-cost comparisons in deciding whether to acquire additional resources.

---

[15] Special purpose computational algorithms are available for solving the transportation problem. See Dantzig, *Linear Programming and Extensions*, pp. 308–310, for a discussion of these algorithms.

Selected References

Anderson, David, Dennis Sweeney, and Thomas Williams. *An Introduction to Management Science*, 5th ed. St. Paul, Minn.: West, 1988.

Baumol, William J. *Economic Theory and Operations Analysis*, 4th ed. Englewood Cliffs, N.J.: Prentice-Hall, 1977.

Cameron, Neil. *Introduction to Linear and Convex Programming*. New York: Cambridge Univ. Press, 1985.

Dantzig, George B. *Linear Programming and Extensions*. Princeton, N.J.: Princeton University Press, 1963.

Hadley, G., *Linear Programming*. Reading, Mass: Addison-Wesley, 1962.

Hartley, Roger. *Linear and Nonlinear Programming: An Introduction to Linear Methods in Mathematical Programming*. New York: Wiley, 1985.

McNamara, John R. "A Linear Programming Model for Long-Range Capacity Planning in an Electric Utility." *Journal of Economics and Business* 28 (Spring/Summer 1976), pp. 227–235.

Thompson, Gerald E. "Linear Programming and Microeconomics." *Nebraska Journal of Economics and Business* (Autumn 1972), pp. 25–36.

Discussion Questions

1. Define the following terms:
   a. Feasible solution space
   b. Extreme point
   c. Slack variable
   d. Primal problem
   e. Dual problem
   f. Dual variable
   g. Shadow price
   h. Surplus variable
   i. Simplex method

2. Describe the relationship between the primal and dual linear-programming problems.

3. Discuss the economic assumptions necessary to formulate a profit-maximization production problem in the linear-programming framework.

4. Discuss the economic interpretation of the dual variables in the following:
   a. Profit-maximization production problem (for example, Equations 5.1–5.6)
   b. Cost-minimization production problem (for example, Equations 5.12–5.16)

5. Under what conditions (if any) will a linear-programming problem have multiple optimal solutions?

6. Describe the relationship between the slack (surplus) variables and the dual variables.

Problems

1. A manufacturer of gas dryers produces two models—a standard (STD) model and a deluxe (DEL) model. Production consists of two major phases. In the first phase, stamping and painting ($S \& P$), sheet metal is formed (stamped) into the appropriate components and painted. In the second phase, assembly and testing ($A \& T$), the sheet metal components along with the motor and controls are assembled and tested. (Ignore any scheduling problems that might arise from the sequential nature of the operations.) Information concerning the resource requirements and

availability is shown in the following table:

Resource	Quantity of Resources Required per Unit of Output		Quantity of Resources Available During Period
	Dryer Type		
	STD (1)	DEL (2)	
S & P (hours)	1.0	2.0	2,000
Motors (units)	1	1	1,400
STD Controls (units)	1	0	1,000
DEL Controls (units)	0	1	800
A & T (hours)	0.333	1.0	900
Profit Contribution ($/unit)	100	125	

Each dryer (*STD* or *DEL*) requires one motor and a respective control unit. Define X_1 and X_2 to be the number of *STD* and *DEL* dryers manufactured per period, respectively. The objective is to determine the number of *STD* and *DEL* dryers to produce so as to maximize the total profit contribution.

a. Formulate the problem in the linear-programming framework.

b. Solve for the optimal values of X_1 and X_2 graphically.

c. Determine the amount of each of the five resources that are used in producing the optimal output (X_1^* and X_2^*).

d. Based on the answer to part (c), determine the values of the five slack variables.

2. Suppose that a computer solution of Problem 1 yielded the following optimal values of the dual variables: $W_1^* = \$25$ (*S & P* constraint), $W_2^* = \$75$ (motors constraint), $W_3^* = \$0$ (*STD* controls constraint), $W_4^* = \$0$ (*DEL* controls constraint), and $W_5^* = \$0$ (*A & T* constraint). Give an economic interpretation of each of the dual variables.

3. Rework Problem 1 (a and b), assuming that the profit contributions are $75 for each standard (*STD*) dryer and $150 for each deluxe (*DEL*) dryer.

4. An urban transit authority is considering the purchase of additional buses to expand its service. Two different models are being considered. A small model would cost $100,000, carry 45 passengers, and operate at an average speed of 25 miles per hour over the existing bus routes. A larger model would cost $150,000, carry 55 passengers, and operate at an average speed of 30 miles per hour. The transit authority has $3,000,000 in its *capital* budget for purchasing new buses during the forthcoming year. However, the authority is also restricted in its expansion program by limitations imposed on its *operating* budget. Specifically, a hiring freeze is in effect and only 25 drivers are available for the foreseeable future to operate any new buses that are purchased. To plan for increased future demand, the transit authority wants at least one-half of all new buses purchased to be the larger model. Furthermore, certain bus routes require the use of the small model (because of narrow streets, traffic congestion, and so on), and there is an immediate need to replace at least five old buses with the new small model. The transit authority wishes to determine how many buses of each model to buy to maximize additional capacity measured in passenger-miles-per-hour while satisfying these constraints. Using the linear-programming framework, let X_1 be the number of small buses purchased and X_2 the number of large buses purchased.

a. Formulate the objective function.

b. Formulate the constraint relationships.

c. Using graphical methods, determine the optimal combination of buses to purchase.

d. Formulate (but do not solve) the dual problem, and give an interpretation of the dual variables.

5. Consider the cost-minimization production problem described in Equations 5.12–5.16.

a. Graph the feasible solution space.

b. Graph the objective function as a series of isocost lines.

c. Using graphical methods, determine the optimal solution. Compare the graphical solution to the computer solution given in Figure 5.8.

6. Assume that a fertilizer manufacturer wishes to determine the profit-maximizing level of output of two products, Alphagrow (X_1) and Bettergrow (X_2). Each pound of X_1 produced and sold contributes \$2 to overhead and profit, whereas X_2's contribution is \$3 per pound. Additional information:

i. The total productive capacity of the firm is 2,000 pounds of fertilizer per week. This capacity may be used to produce all X_1, all X_2, or some linear proportional mix of the two.

ii. Because of the light weight and bulk of X_2 relative to X_1, the packaging department can handle a maximum of 2,400 pounds of X_1, 1,200 pounds of X_2, or some linear proportional mix of the two each week.

iii. Large amounts of propane are required in the production process. Because of the energy shortage, the firm is limited to producing 2,100 pounds of X_2, 1,400 pounds of X_1, or some linear proportional mix of the two each week.

iv. On the average, the firm expects to have \$5,000 in cash available to meet operating expenses each week. Each pound of X_1 produced generates an initial cash outflow of \$2, whereas each pound of X_2 generates an outflow of \$4.

Questions:

a. Formulate this as a profit-maximization problem in the linear-programming framework. Be sure to clearly specify all constraints.

b. Solve for the approximate profit-maximizing levels of output of X_1 and X_2, using the graphical method.

7. Suppose a nutritionist for a United Nations food distribution agency is concerned with developing a *minimum-cost*-per-day balanced diet from two basic foods— cereal and dried milk—that meets or exceeds certain nutritional requirements. The information concerning the two foods and the requirements are summarized in the table below.

Nutrient	Fortified Cereal (units of nutrient per ounce)	Fortified Dried Milk (units of nutrient per ounce)	Minimum Requirements (units)
Protein	2	5	100
Calories	100	40	500
Vitamin D	10	15	400
Iron	1	0.5	20
Cost (cents per ounce)	3.0	2.0	

Define X_1 as the number of ounces of cereal and X_2 as the number of ounces of dried milk to be included in the diet.

a. Determine the objective function.

b. Determine the constraint relationships.

c. Using graphical methods, determine the optimal quantities of cereal and dried milk to include in the diet.

d. Determine the amount of the four nutrients used in producing the optimal diet (X_1^* and X_2^*).

e. Based on your answer to part (d), determine the values of the four surplus variables.

8. Suppose that a computer solution of Problem 7 yielded the following optimal values of the dual variables: $W_1^* = 0$ (protein constraint), $W_2^* = 0$ (calories constraint), $W_3^* = .05$ cents (vitamin D constraint), and $W_4^* = 2.5$ cents (iron constraint). Give an economic interpretation of each of the dual variables.

9. The government of Indula, in an effort to expand and develop the economy of the country, has been allocating a large portion of each year's tax revenues to capital investment projects. The Ministry of Finance has asked the various government agencies to draw up a list of possible investment projects to be undertaken over the next three years. The following list of proposals was submitted.

Investment	Present value of outlay Year 1 (in $ million)	Present value of outlay Year 2 (in $ million)	Present value of outlay Year 3 (in $ million)	Net present value of investment (in $ million)
1. Steel mill	20	80	50	50
2. Automobile manufacturing plant	75	150	100	100
3. Ship-docking facility	25	25	40	75
4. Irrigation system in Region 1	200	75	50	20
5. New hydro electric dam in Region 3	75	100	50	40
6. New hydro electric dam in Region 1	100	110	75	75
7. Oil refinery	25	40	25	60
8. Copper-smelting plant	20	50	50	50

The Ministry of Finance estimates that the present values of the amount (in millions of dollars) available for investment in each of the next three years will be 300, 325, and 350, respectively, and wishes to maximize the sum of the net present value of the projects undertaken:

a. Formulate *(but do not solve)* this problem in the linear-programming framework.

Suppose that a computer solution of this problem yields the following optimal values:

$X_1^* = 0.0$ $\quad$ $X_2^* = .667$ $\quad$ $X_3^* = 1.0$ $\quad$ $X_4^* = 0.0$ $\quad$ $X_5^* = 0.0$ $\quad$ $X_6^* = 1.0$

$X_7^* = 1.0$ $\quad$ $X_8^* = 1.0$ $\quad$ $W_1^* = 0.0$ $\quad$ $W_2^* = .667$ $\quad$ $W_3^* = 0.0$

Note: X_1—X_8 are the primal variables (i.e. proportion of each project undertaken) and W_1—W_3 are the dual variables associated with the capital budget constraints in each of the next three years.

b. Which of the investment projects should the government undertake? How should we deal with the fractional projects in the optimal solution?

c. Give an economic interpretation of the dual variables.

10. American Steel Company has three coal mines located in Pennsylvania, Tennessee, and Wyoming. These mines supply coal to its four steel-making facilities located in Ohio, Alabama, Illinois, and California. Monthly capacities of the three coal mines are 6,000, 8,000 and 12,000 tons, respectively. Monthly demand for coal at the four production facilities is 6,000, 5,000, 7,000, and 8,000 tons, respectively. Shipping costs from each of the three mines to each of the four production facilities are shown in the table below:

		Production Facilities			
		Ohio (1)	Alabama (2)	Illinois (3)	California (4)
Coal Mine	Pennsylvania (1)	3	12	12	30
	Tennessee (2)	6	3	18	25
	Wyoming (3)	20	24	15	15

The company desires to minimize its shipping costs. Let X_{ij} be the amount of coal shipped from Mine i to Production Facility j (for all i and j). Formulate (but do not solve) this problem in the linear-programming framework.

11. Mountain States Oil Company refines crude oil into gasoline, jet fuel, and heating oil. The company can process a maximum of 10,000 barrels per day at its refinery. The refining process is such that a maximum of 7,000 barrels of gasoline can be produced per day. Furthermore, there is always at least as much jet fuel as gasoline produced. The wholesale prices of gasoline, jet fuel, and heating oil are $50, $40, and $30 per barrel, respectively. The company is interested in maximizing revenue.

a. Formulate (but do not solve) this problem in the linear-programming framework. Hint: There should be three constraints in this problem.

b. Suppose that a computer solution of this problem yields an optimal value of $45 for the dual variable associated with the capacity constraint of the refinery. Give an economic interpretation of this dual variable.

Note: The following exercises require the use of a computer program to solve the linear-programming problems.

12. Solve Problem 1 using a computer program. Compare the computer solution with the graphical solution.

13. Solve Problem 4 using a computer program. Compare the computer solution with the graphical solution.

14. Solve Problem 6 using a computer program. Compare the computer solution with the graphical solution.

15. Solve Problem 7 using a computer program. Compare the computer solution with the graphical solution.

16. Solve Problem 9 using a computer program.

17. Solve Problem 10 using a computer program.

18. Solve Problem 11 using a computer program.

Econometrics

6

Econometrics is a collection of statistical techniques available for testing economic theories by empirically measuring relationships among economic variables. The measurement of economic relationships is a necessary step in using economic theories and models to obtain estimates of the numerical values of variables that are of interest to the decision maker. For example, when forecasting demand the manager must have an estimate of the responsiveness of quantity demanded to changes in other variables such as price, income levels, and advertising expenditures. Similarly, when considering the construction of a larger plant, an efficient manager must have an estimate of the impact of this new plant on the firm's cost of operations. Will the plant reduce or increase the average cost of production? The principal econometric techniques used in measuring economic relationships are regression and correlation analysis. This chapter illustrates the application of regression and correlation models and then discusses some of the problems encountered in applying these models. The simple (two-variable) linear regression model is developed first and then the more complex cases of multiple linear regression models and nonlinear models are examined. These models play a key role in our later discussions of demand, forecasting, and cost estimation. Without having good estimates of actual demand and cost relationships, it is unlikely that a manager can achieve the wealth maximization goal of the firm's owners.

Simple Linear Regression Model

Often one objective in the analysis of economic data is to discover and measure the *association* between the variables. We may also be interested in *prediction*; that is, determining the value of one variable based on the values of the other variable(s).

Suppose we want to determine the factors or variables that may affect income levels and that will help us predict or explain the income of given individuals (Y). What variables might affect an individual's income level? A list of possible demographic and psychological explanatory variables would have to include education (E), age (A), sex (S), intelligence (I), and motivation (M). In effect, the hypothesis is that some functional relationship of the form

$$Y = f(E, A, S, I, M....)$$

Glossary of New Terms

Econometrics
A collection of statistical techniques available for testing economic theories by empirically measuring relationships among economic variables.

Standard error of the estimate
The standard deviation of the error terms in a linear regression model.

Coefficient of determination
A measure of the proportion of total variation in the dependent variable, which is explained by the independent variable(s).

Autocorrelation
An econometric problem characterized by the existence of a significant pattern in the successive values of the error terms in a linear regression model.

Heteroscedasticity
An econometric problem characterized by the lack of a uniform variance of the error terms about the regression line in a linear regression.

(Cont'd on next page)

Glossary of New Terms *(Cont'd)*

Specification error
An econometric problem characterized by the omission of one or more significant explanatory variables from the regression equation.

Multicollinearity
An econometric problem characterized by a high degree of intercorrelation among some or all of the explanatory variables in a regression equation.

exists between income and the other variables. We must specify the relevant variables to include in the model and determine the form of the model to better predict an individual's income level once these variables are known. Economic theory usually provides some basis for determining which variables should be included in the model. Omitting one or more important explanatory variables may result in a *specification error*.[1]

Correlation analysis is concerned with determining the strength or degree of association between two variables. *Regression* analysis is concerned with finding the functional relationship between the variables to make estimates or predictions of a particular variable. The variable that we are trying to predict is known as the *dependent* variable (that is, Y in the preceding example). The variables that are used in predicting the value of the *dependent* variable are defined as *independent* variables (such as E, A, S, I, and M).

The analysis in this section is limited to the case of one independent and one dependent variable (two-variable case), where the form of the relationship between the two variables is *linear*.[2] In the example just given, suppose theory suggests that only education (E) is important in predicting an individual's income level (Y). The simple linear regression model that is used in this problem involves several basic underlying assumptions.

Assumptions Underlying the Simple Linear Regression Model[3]

A standard convention in regression analysis, which will be followed here, is to use X to represent the independent variable and Y to represent the dependent variable.[4]

Assumption 1. The value of the dependent variable Y is postulated to be dependent on the value of the independent variable X. Y is assumed to be a random variable, whereas X can either take on fixed values, as specified by the investigator, or can also be a random variable.

Assumption 2. A theoretical straight-line relationship (see Figure 6.1) exists between X and the expected value of Y for each of the possible values of X. This theoretical regression line

$$E(Y|X) = \alpha + \beta X \qquad [6.1]$$

---

[1] See the next to the last section of this chapter, "Problems in Applying the Linear Regression Model," for a discussion of specification error and how it can affect regression results.

[2] Nonlinear relationships are considered in the last section of this chapter.

[3] See J. Johnston, *Econometric Methods*, 3d ed. (New York: McGraw-Hill, 1984), chap. 2, for an expanded discussion of the assumptions underlying the two-variable model.

[4] Capitalized letters X and Y represent the *name* of the random variables. Lowercase x and y represent *specific values* of the random variables.

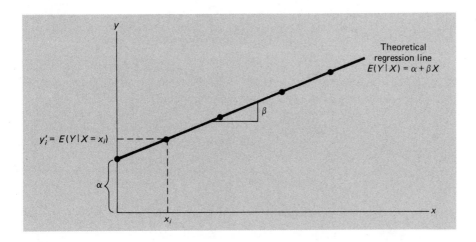

Figure 6.1
**Theoretical
Regression Line**

has a slope of β and an intercept of α. The regression coefficients α and β constitute population parameters whose values are unknown and we desire to estimate them.

Assumption 3. Associated with each value of X is a probability distribution, $f(y|x)$, of the possible values of the random variable Y. When X is set equal to some value x_i, the value of Y that is observed will be drawn from the $f(y|x_i)$ probability distribution and will not necessarily lie on the theoretical regression line (see Figure 6.2). When a sample of n pairs of observations is collected, a series of (x_i, y_i) values is obtained that is scattered around the theoretical regression line (see Figure 6.3). If ϵ_i is the *deviation* of the *observed* y_i value

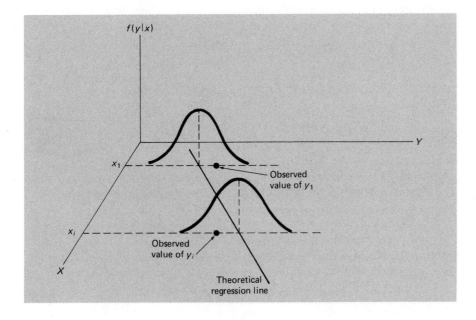

Figure 6.2
**Conditional
Probability
Distribution of
Dependent
Variable**

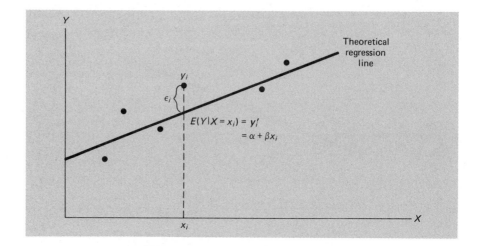

Figure 6.3
Deviation of the Observations about the Theoretical Regression Line

from the *true theoretical value* y_i', then

$$y_i = y_i' + \epsilon_i \qquad [6.2]$$

$$y_i = \alpha + \beta x_i + \epsilon_i$$

or, in general, the *theoretical regression equation* becomes

$$Y = \alpha + \beta X + \epsilon \qquad [6.3]$$

ϵ is called the *stochastic disturbance* (or *error*) *term*.

Assumption 4. The disturbance term (ϵ_i) is assumed to be an independent random variable [that is, $E(\epsilon_i \epsilon_j) = 0$ for $i \neq j$] with an expected value equal to zero [that is, $E(\epsilon_i) = 0$] and with a variance equal to σ_ϵ^2 [that is, $E(\epsilon_i^2) = \sigma_\epsilon^2$]. Futhermore, in order to perform the statistical tests of significance (i.e., t-tests and F-tests) later in the chapter, we must also assume that the disturbance term (ϵ_i) follows the normal probability distribution.

Estimating the Population Regression Coefficients

Once the regression model is specified, the unknown values of the population regression coefficients α and β are estimated by using the n pairs of sample observations (x_1, y_1), (x_2, y_2), ..., (x_n, y_n). This process involves finding a *sample regression line* that best fits the sample of observations.

The sample estimates of α and β can be designated by a and b, respectively. The estimated or predicted value of Y, y_i', for a given value of X (see Figure 6.4) is:

$$y_i' = a + bx_i$$

Letting e_i be the *deviation* of the *observed* y_i value from the *estimated value* y_i', then

$$y_i = y_i' + e_i = a + bx_i + e_i \qquad [6.4]$$

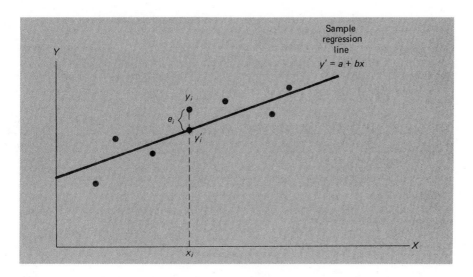

Figure 6.4
Deviation of the Observations about the Sample Regression Line

or, in general, the *sample regression equation* becomes

$$Y = a + bX + e \qquad [6.5]$$

Although there are several methods for determining the values of a and b (that is, finding the regression equation that provides the best fit to the series of observations), the best known and most widely used is the method of *least squares*. The objective of least-squares analysis is to find values of a and b that *minimize* the sum of the squares of the e_i deviations. (By squaring the errors, positive and negative errors are both counted, rather than having them cancel each other out.) From Equation 6.4, the value of e_i is given by

$$e_i = y_i - a - bx_i \qquad [6.6]$$

Squaring this term and summing over all n pairs of sample observations, one obtains

$$\sum_{i=1}^{n} e_i^2 = \sum_{i=1}^{n} (y_i - a - bx_i)^2 \qquad [6.7]$$

Using calculus it can be shown that the values of a and b that minimize this sum of squared deviations expression are given by

$$b = \frac{n\Sigma x_i y_i - \Sigma x_i \Sigma y_i}{n\Sigma x_i^2 - (\Sigma x_i)^2} \qquad [6.8]$$

$$a = \bar{y} - b\bar{x} \qquad [6.9]$$

where $\bar{x}$ and $\bar{y}$ are the arithmetic means of X and Y respectively (that is, $\bar{x} = \Sigma x/n$

Table 6.1 **Worksheet for Estimation of the Regression Equation: Income-Education Example**

Observation	Education Level	Income ($000)			
(1)	(2)	(3)	(4)	(5)	(6)
i	x_i	y_i	$x_i y_i$	x_i^2	y_i^2
1	12	15.0	180.00	144	225.00
2	12	7.6	91.20	144	57.76
3	16	21.5	344.00	256	462.25
4	12	9.0	108.00	144	81.00
5	18	27.0	486.00	324	729.00
6	10	9.5	95.00	100	90.25
7	12	12.7	152.40	144	161.29
8	12	14.0	168.00	144	196.00
9	14	17.2	240.80	196	295.84
10	9	6.7	60.30	81	44.89
11	8	8.4	67.20	64	70.56
12	12	9.1	109.20	144	82.81
13	12	11.5	138.00	144	132.25
14	12	12.1	145.20	144	146.41
15	18	19.5	351.00	324	380.25
16	16	15.5	248.00	256	240.25
17	18	32.0	576.00	324	1024.00
18	10	7.5	75.00	100	56.25
19	12	8.0	96.00	144	64.00
20	12	11.1	133.20	144	123.21
21	14	16.5	231.00	196	272.25
22	12	9.0	108.00	144	81.00
23	10	7.2	72.00	100	51.84
24	16	14.5	232.00	256	210.25
25	12	14.5	174.00	144	210.25
	$\Sigma x_i = 321$	$\Sigma y_i = 336.6$	$\Sigma x_i y_i = 4681.50$	$\Sigma x_i^2 = 4305$	$\Sigma y_i^2 = 5488.86$

$$\bar{x} = \frac{\Sigma x_i}{n} \qquad \bar{y} = \frac{\Sigma y_i}{n}$$

$$= \frac{321}{25} \qquad = \frac{336.6}{25}$$

$$= 12.84 \qquad = 13.464$$

and $\bar{y} = \Sigma y/n$) and where the summations range over all the observations ($i = 1, 2, \ldots, n$).[5]

To return to the example discussed earlier in this section, suppose that we postulate that an individual's income level is a linear function of his or her education level. Letting Y represent yearly income (measured in thousands of dollars) and X represent education (measured in years of academic or vo-

---

[5] See J. Johnston, *Econometric Methods*, sec. 2-2 for a derivation of these expressions.

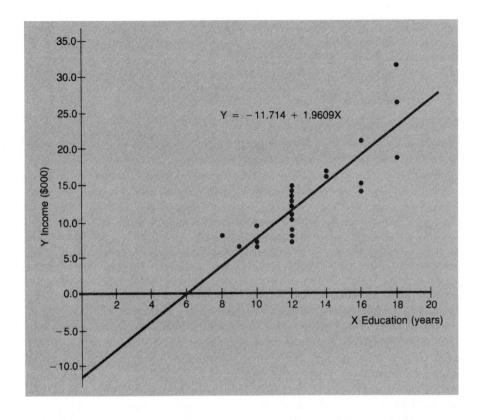

Figure 6.5
Estimated Regression Line: Income-Education Example

cational training completed beyond kindergarten), the regression model can be represented by Equation 6.3. If education is used to predict the income of an individual, estimates of α and β must be calculated from a sample of individuals. Suppose that twenty-five individuals are randomly selected from the population and their past year's income and their education levels are measured (see columns 1–3 of Table 6.1).[6] The data can also be represented graphically (see Figure 6.5). The estimated slope of the regression line is calculated as follows, using Equation 6.8:

$$b = \frac{25(4681.50) - (321)(336.6)}{25(4305) - (321)^2} = 1.9609$$

Similarly, using Equation 6.9 the intercept can be estimated as

$$a = 13.464 - (1.9609)(12.84) = -11.714$$

Therefore, the equation for estimating income based on education level becomes

$$Y = -11.714 + 1.9609X \qquad [6.10]$$

---

[6] A sample size of twenty-five was chosen to keep the arithmetic simple. In actual problems one would, if possible, select a much larger sample. The desired accuracy and the cost of sampling must be weighed in determining the best sample size to use in a given problem.

and is graphed in Figure 6.5. The coefficient of X (1.9609) indicates that for a one-unit increase in X (one additional year of education) income (Y) will increase by 1.9609 ($\times$ \$1,000) or \$1,960.90.

Using the Regression Equation to Make Forecasts

A regression equation can be used to make forecasts or predictions concerning the value of Y, given any particular value of X. This is done by substituting the particular value of X, namely x_p, into the sample regression equation (Equation 6.4):[7]

$$y' = a + bx_p \qquad [6.11]$$

For example, suppose one is interested in estimating the income of persons having fourteen years of education (as defined earlier). Substituting $x_p = 14$ into the estimated regression equation (Equation 6.10) yields

$$y' = -11.714 + 1.9609(14.00) = 15.739$$

or an annual income of \$15,739.

Caution must be exercised in using regression models for prediction, particularly when the value of the independent variable lies *outside* the range of observations from which the model was estimated. In many cases the linear relationship is not valid for extremely large or small values of the independent variable. For example, suppose we want to estimate the income of an individual having twenty-two years of education (that is, eight years of grade and middle school, four years of high school, four years of college, four years of graduate school and two years of postgraduate study). Since this value of X falls well outside of the series of observations for which the regression line was calculated, we cannot be certain that the prediction of income based on the regression model would be reasonable. Such factors as diminishing returns and the existence of saturation levels can cause relationships between economic variables to be nonlinear.

A measure of the accuracy of estimation with the regression equation can be obtained by calculating the standard deviation of the errors of prediction. The error term e_i was defined earlier in Equation 6.6 to be the difference between the observed and predicted value of the dependent variable. The standard deviation of the e_i terms is calculated as

$$s_e = \sqrt{\frac{\Sigma e_i^2}{n-2}} = \sqrt{\frac{\Sigma(y_i - a - bx_i)^2}{n-2}}$$

or, when this expression is simplified, by

$$s_e = \sqrt{\frac{\Sigma y_i^2 - a\Sigma y_i - b\Sigma x_i y_i}{n-2}} \qquad [6.12]$$

---

[7] The expected value of the error term (e) is zero, as indicated earlier in Assumption 4.

If the observations are tightly clustered about the regression line, the value of s_e (also known as the *standard error of the estimate*) will be small and prediction errors will tend to be small. Conversely, if the deviations e_i between the observed and predicted values of Y are fairly large, both s_e and the prediction errors will be large.

Substituting the relevant data from Table 6.1 into Equation 6.12 yields

$$s_e = \sqrt{\frac{5488.86 - (-11.714)(336.6) - 1.9609(4681.50)}{25 - 2}}$$

$$= 3.309$$

or a standard error of $3,309.

The standard error of the estimate (s_e) can be used to construct prediction *intervals* for Y.[8] An *approximate* 95 percent prediction interval is equal to[9]

$$y' \pm 2s_e \qquad [6.13]$$

Returning to the income-education example again, suppose we want to construct an approximate 95 percent prediction interval for the income of an individual having fourteen years of education. Substituting $y' = 15.739$ and $s_e = 3.309$ into Equation 6.13 gives

$$15.739 \pm 2(3.309)$$

or a prediction interval from 9.121 to 22.357 (that is, from $9,121 to $22,357).

Inferences about the Population Regression Coefficients

For repeated samples of size n, the sample estimates of α and β—that is, a and b—will tend to vary from sample to sample. In addition to prediction, often one of the purposes of regression analysis is testing whether the slope parameter β is equal to some particular value β_0. One standard hypothesis is to test whether β is equal to zero.[10] In such a test the concern is with determining whether X has a significant effect on Y. If β is either zero or close to zero, then the independent variable X will be of no practical benefit in predicting or explaining the value of

---

[8] An *exact* (1 − k) percent prediction interval is a function of both the sample size (n) and how close x_p is to $\bar{x}$ and is given by the following expression:

$$y' \pm t_{k/2, n-2} s_e \sqrt{1 + \frac{1}{n} + \frac{(x_p - \bar{x})^2}{\Sigma(x_i - \bar{x})^2}}$$

where $t_{k/2, n-2}$ is the value from the t-distribution (with $n - 2$ degrees of freedom) in Table 2 of the Statistical Tables (Appendix A) in the back of the book.

[9] For large n ($n > 30$), the t-distribution approximates a normal distribution and the t-value for a 95 percent prediction interval approaches 1.96 or approximately 2. For most applications, the approximation methods give satisfactory results.

[10] The intercept parameter, α, is of less interest in most economic studies and will be excluded from further analysis.

the dependent variable Y. When $\beta = 0$, a one-unit change in X causes Y to change by zero units, and hence X has no effect on Y.

To test hypotheses about the value of β, the sampling distribution of the statistic b must be known.[11] It can be shown that b has a t-distribution with $n - 2$ degrees of freedom.[12,13] The mean of this distribution is equal to the true underlying regression coefficient β, and an estimate of the standard deviation can be calculated as

$$s_b = \sqrt{\frac{s_e^2}{\Sigma x_i^2 - (\Sigma x_i)^2/n}} \qquad [6.14]$$

where s_e is the standard deviation of the error terms from Equation 6.12.

Suppose that we want to test the null hypothesis:

$$H_0: \beta = \beta_0$$

against the alternative hypothesis:

$$H_a: \beta \neq \beta_0$$

at the k percent level of significance.[14] We calculate the statistic

$$t = \frac{b - \beta_0}{s_b} \qquad [6.15]$$

and the decision is to reject the null hypothesis, if t is either less than $-t_{k/2,n-2}$ or

---

[11] In addition to testing hypotheses about β, one can also calculate confidence intervals for β. See J. Johnston, *Econometric Methods*, pp. 34–35, or any other standard econometrics text for a discussion of the procedures for calculating confidence intervals.

[12] A t-test is usually used to test for the significance of individual regression parameters when the sample size is relatively small (30 or less). For larger samples, tests of statistical significance may be made using the standard normal probability distribution.

[13] *Degrees of freedom* are the number of observations beyond the minimum necessary to calculate a given regression coefficient or statistic. In a regression model, the number of degrees of freedom is equal to the number of observations less the number of parameters (α and βs) being estimated. For example in a simple (two-variable) regression model, a minimum of two observations is needed to calculate the slope (β) and intercept (α) parameters—hence the number of degrees of freedom is equal to the number of observations minus two.

[14] The *level of significance* (k) used in testing hypotheses indicates the probability of making an incorrect decision with the decision rule—that is, rejecting the null hypothesis when indeed it is true. For example, setting $k = .05$ (i.e., 5 percent) indicates that there is one chance in 20 that the decision rule will lead to an incorrect decision.

greater than $t_{k/2,n-2}$ where the $t_{k/2,n-2}$ value is obtained from the t-distribution (with $n-2$ degrees of freedom) in Table 2 (Appendix A).[15]

In the earlier example, suppose we want to test (at the $k=.05$ level of significance) whether an individual's education level is a useful variable in predicting his or her income. In effect, we wish to perform a statistical test to determine whether the sample value—that is, $b=1.9609$—is significantly different from zero. The null and alternative hypotheses are:

$$H_0: \beta = 0 \text{ (No relationship between } X \text{ and } Y)$$

$$H_a: \beta \neq 0 \text{ (Linear relationship between } X \text{ and } Y)$$

Since there were 25 observations in the sample used to compute the regression line, the sample statistic b will have a t-distribution with $23(=n-2)$ degrees of freedom. From the t-distribution (Table 2 of Appendix A), we obtain a value of 2.069 for $t_{.025,23}$. Therefore, the decision rule is to reject H_0—in other words, to conclude that $\beta \neq 0$ and that a statistically significant relationship exists between education and income—if the calculated value of t is either less than -2.069 or greater than $+2.069$.

Using Equation 6.4, s_b is calculated as

$$s_b = \sqrt{\frac{(3.309)^2}{4305 - (321)^2/25}}$$

$$= .24437$$

The calculated value of t, from Equation 6.15, becomes

$$t = \frac{1.9609 - 0}{.24437}$$

$$= 8.024$$

Since this value is greater than 2.069, we reject H_0. Therefore, based on the sample evidence, we conclude at the 5 percent level of significance that a linear relationship exists between an individual's education level and his or her income.

Correlation Coefficient

As indicated earlier, in linear correlation analysis we can determine the strength or degree to which two variables tend to vary together. In other words, we analyze the extent to which high (or low) values of one variable tend to be

---

[15] *One-tail* tests can also be performed. In order to test $H_0: \beta \leq \beta_0$ against $H_a: \beta > \beta_0$, one calculates t using Equation 6.15 and rejects H_0 at the k level of significance if $t > t_{k,n-2}$, where $t_{k,n-2}$ is obtained from the t-distribution (Table 2) with $n-2$ degrees of freedom. Similarly, to test $H_0: \beta \geq \beta_0$ against $H_a: \beta < \beta_0$, one calculates t using Equation 6.15 and rejects H_0 at the k level of significance if $t < t_{k,n-2}$.

associated with high (or low) values of the other variable. In linear correlation analysis it is unnecessary to label the variables under consideration as being either dependent or independent. The measure of the degree of association between two variables is called the linear *correlation coefficient*. Given n pairs of observations from the population, (x_1, y_1), $(x_2, y_2), \ldots, (x_n, y_n)$, the sample correlation coefficient is defined as

$$r = \frac{\Sigma(x_i - \bar{x})(y_i - \bar{y})}{\sqrt{\Sigma(x_i - \bar{x})^2 \Sigma(y_i - \bar{y})^2}}$$

and, when this expression is simplified, calculated as

$$r = \frac{n\Sigma x_i y_i - \Sigma x_i \Sigma y_i}{\sqrt{[n\Sigma x_i^2 - (\Sigma x_i)^2][n\Sigma y_i^2 - (\Sigma y_i)^2]}} \qquad [6.16]$$

The value of the correlation coefficient (r) ranges from $+1$ for two variables with perfect positive correlation to -1 for two variables with perfect negative correlation. Figure 6.6(a) and (b) illustrate two variables that exhibit perfect positive and negative correlation respectively. Very few, if any, relationships between economic variables exhibit perfect correlation. Figure 6.6(c) illustrates the case of zero correlation—no discernible relationship exists between the observed values of the two variables. A positive correlation coefficient indicates that high values of one variable tend to be associated with high values of the other variable, whereas a negative correlation coefficient indicates just the opposite—high values of one variable tend to be associated with low values of the other variable.

The income-education sample discussed earlier can be used to illustrate the calculation of the sample correlation coefficient. Substituting the relevant quantities from Table 6.1 into Equation 6.16, we obtain a value of

$$r = \frac{25(4681.50) - (321)(336.6)}{\sqrt{[25(4305) - (321)^2][25(5488.86) - (336.6)^2]}}$$

$$= .8584$$

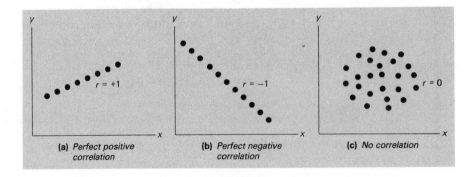

Figure 6.6
Correlation Coefficient

(a) *Perfect positive correlation* $r = +1$

(b) *Perfect negative correlation* $r = -1$

(c) *No correlation* $r = 0$

for the correlation between the sample observations of income and education level.[16]

Correlation analysis is useful in exploratory studies of the relationships among economic variables. The information obtained in the correlation analysis can then be used as a guide in building descriptive models of economic phenomena that can serve as a basis for prediction and decision making.

The Analysis of Variance

The section on "Estimating the Population Regression Coefficients," illustrated a method for testing the statistical significance of individual regression coefficients. Now we will examine some techniques for evaluating the overall "fit" of the regression line to the sample of observations.

We begin by examining a typical observation (y_i) (see Figure 6.7). Suppose we want to predict the value of Y for a value of X equal to x_i. While ignoring the regression line for the moment, what error is incurred if we use the average value of Y (that is, $\bar{y}$) as the best estimate of Y? The graph shows that the error involved, labeled the "total error," is the difference between the observed value (y_i) and $\bar{y}$. Suppose we now use the sample regression line to estimate Y. The best estimate of Y, given $X = x_i$, is y_i'. As a result of using the regression line to estimate Y, the estimation error has been reduced to the difference between the observed value (y_i) and y_i'. In the graph, the total error ($y_i - \bar{y}$) has been partitioned into two parts—unexplained error ($y_i - y_i'$) and the explained error

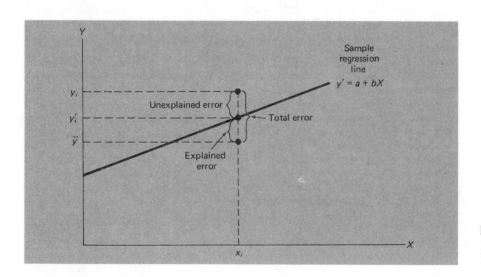

Figure 6.7
Partitioning the Estimation Error

---

[16] Statistical techniques exist for testing whether the degree of correlation within the population is significantly different from zero. See Wayne W. Daniel and James C. Terrell, *Business Statistics: Basic Concepts and Methodology*. 2d ed. (Boston: Houghton Mifflin, 1979), pp. 330–332, for a discussion of these techniques.

$(y_i' - \bar{y})$; that is,

Total error = Unexplained error + Explained error

$$(y_i - \bar{y}) = (y_i - y_i') + (y_i' - \bar{y})$$

If we decompose the total error of each observation in the sample using this procedure and then sum the squares of both sides of the equation, we obtain (after some algebraic simplification):[17]

Total SS = Unexplained SS + Explained SS

$$\Sigma(y_i - \bar{y})^2 = \Sigma(y_i - y_i')^2 + \Sigma(y_i' - \bar{y})^2 \qquad [6.17]$$

This equation indicates that the sum of the squared errors, over all the observations in the sample, can be partitioned into two independent parts—the Unexplained SS and the Explained SS.

By using this sum-of-squares analysis, we can now illustrate two techniques for evaluating the overall explanatory power of the regression equation. One measure of the fit of the regression line to the sample observations is the sample *coefficient of determination*. The coefficient of determination (r^2) is equal to the ratio of the Explained SS to the Total SS:

$$r^2 = \frac{(y_i' - \bar{y})^2}{(y_i - \bar{y})^2} \qquad [6.18]$$

It measures the proportion of the variation in the dependent variable that is explained by the regression line (the independent variable). The coefficient of determination ranges in value from 0—when none of the variation in Y is explained by the regression—to 1—when all the variation in Y is explained by regression.

Table 6.2 shows the calculation of the Explained, Unexplained, and Total SS for the income-education example that was introduced earlier.[18] The Explained SS is 705.02 and the Total SS is 956.87 (see Table 6.2), and therefore, by Equation 6.18 the coefficient of determination is

$$r^2 = \frac{705.02}{956.87}$$

$$= .7368$$

The regression equation, with education as the independent variable, explains 74 percent of the variation in incomes of the individuals in the sample. Note also

---

[17] A standard convention in statistics is to let "SS" represent the "Sum of Squares" or, more accurately the "Sum of Squared Errors."

[18] Only two of the three SS need to be calculated in the manner shown in Table 6.2, since the third SS can be obtained from Equation 6.17 once the other two SS are calculated.

Table 6.2 Calculation of Explained, Unexplained, and Total SS for Income–Education Example

i	x_i	y_i	$y_i' = -11.714 + 1.9609x_i$	Explained SS $(y_i' - \bar{y})$	$(y_i' - \bar{y})^2$	Unexplained SS $(y_i - y_i')$	$(y_i - y_i')^2$	Total SS $(y_i - \bar{y})$	$(y_i - \bar{y})^2$
1	12	15.0	11.817	-1.647	2.713	3.183	10.131	1.536	2.359
2	12	7.6	11.817	-1.647	2.713	-4.217	17.783	-5.864	34.386
3	16	21.5	19.660	6.196	38.390	1.840	3.386	8.036	64.577
4	12	9.0	11.817	-1.647	2.713	-2.817	7.935	-4.464	19.927
5	18	27.0	23.582	10.118	102.374	3.418	11.683	13.536	183.223
6	10	9.5	7.895	-5.569	31.014	1.605	2.576	-3.964	15.713
7	12	12.7	11.817	-1.647	2.713	.883	.780	-.764	.584
8	12	14.0	11.817	-1.647	2.713	2.183	4.765	.536	.287
9	14	17.2	15.739	2.275	5.176	1.461	2.135	3.736	13.958
10	9	6.7	5.934	-7.530	56.701	.766	.587	-6.764	45.752
11	8	8.4	3.973	-9.491	90.079	4.427	19.598	-5.064	25.644
12	12	9.1	11.817	-1.647	2.713	-2.717	7.382	-4.364	19.044
13	12	11.5	11.817	-1.647	2.713	-.317	.100	-1.964	3.857
14	12	12.1	11.817	-1.647	2.713	.283	.080	-1.364	1.860
15	18	19.5	23.582	10.118	102.374	-4.082	16.663	6.036	36.433
16	16	15.5	19.660	6.196	38.390	-4.160	17.306	2.036	4.145
17	18	32.0	23.582	10.118	102.374	8.418	70.863	18.536	343.583
18	10	7.5	7.895	-5.569	31.014	-.395	.156	-5.964	35.569
19	12	8.0	11.817	-1.647	2.713	-3.817	14.569	-5.464	29.855
20	12	11.1	11.817	-1.647	2.713	-.717	.514	-2.364	5.588
21	14	16.5	15.739	2.275	5.176	.761	.579	3.036	9.217
22	12	9.0	11.817	-1.647	2.713	-2.817	7.935	-4.464	19.927
23	10	7.2	7.895	-5.569	31.014	-.695	.483	-6.264	39.238
24	16	14.5	19.660	6.196	38.390	-5.160	26.626	1.036	1.073
25	12	14.5	11.817	-1.647	2.713	2.683	7.198	1.036	1.073
					705.022		251.813		956.872*

*"Total SS" differs slightly from the sum of "Explained SS" and "Unexplained SS" because of rounding errors.

Table 6.3
Analysis of Variance Table for Regression Model

Source of Variation	Sum of Squares	Degrees of Freedom	Mean Squares
Regression $\left(\begin{array}{c}\text{explained}\\\text{variation}\end{array}\right)$	$SSR = \Sigma \ (y_i' - \bar{y})^2$	1	$MSR = SSR \div 1$
Residual $\left(\begin{array}{c}\text{unexplained}\\\text{variation}\end{array}\right)$	$SSE = \Sigma \ (y_i - y_i')^2$	$n - 2$	$MSE = SSE \div (n - 2)$
Total	$SST = \Sigma \ (y_i - \bar{y})^2$	$n - 1$	

that, in the two-variable linear regression model, the coefficient of determination is equal to the square of the correlation coefficient, i.e., $r^2 = .7368 = (r)^2 = (.8584)^2$.

A second technique for evaluating the explanatory power of the regression equation is an F-test of the sources of variation within the sample data.[19] Using the sum-of-squares framework discussed above, an analysis of variance table is constructed as shown in Table 6.3. The F ratio

$$F = \frac{MSR}{MSE}$$

[6.19]

can then be used to test whether the estimated regression equation explains a significant proportion of the variation in the dependent variable. The decision is to reject the null hypothesis of no relationship between X and Y (that is, no explanatory power) at the k level of significance if the calculated F ratio is greater than the $F_{k,1,n-2}$ value obtained from the F-distribution in Table 3 of the Statistical Tables (Appendix A).

An analysis of variance table for the income-education example appears in Table 6.4. Forming the F ratio, we obtain

$$F = \frac{705.02}{10.948}$$

$$= 64.397$$

The value of $F_{.05,1,23}$ from the F-distribution (Table 3 of Appendix A) is 4.28. Therefore, we reject, at the .05 level of significance, the null hypothesis that there is no relationship between the education of individuals and their incomes. In other words, we conclude that the regression model *does* explain a significant proportion of the variation in the incomes of individuals in the sample.

---

[19] For the simple (two-variable) regression model, the F-test can be shown to be equivalent to the t-test discussed in the section, "Inferences About the Population Regression Coefficients," for testing whether $\beta = 0$. See Johnston, *Econometric Methods op. cit.*, section 2.6. For the multiple linear regression model (discussed in the section, "Multiple Linear Regression Model"), the F-test is used to test the hypothesis that *all* the regression coefficients are zero.

Source of Variation	Sum of Squares	Degrees of Freedom	Mean Squares
Regression	705.02	1	705.02
Residual	251.81	23	10.948
Total	956.87*	24	

Table 6.4
Analysis of Variance Table: Income-Education Example

*Total SS differs slightly from the sum of Regression SS and Residual SS because of roundoff error.

Association and Causation

Based on the finding of a statistically significant regression relationship, one may be tempted to conclude that a causal economic relationship exists—the independent variable being the cause and the dependent variable being the effect. It should be emphasized, however, that *the presence of association does not necessarily imply causation*. Statistical tests can only establish whether association exists between the variables. The existence of a cause-and-effect economic relationship can only be inferred from economic reasoning.

An association relationship may not imply a causal relationship for many reasons. First, the association between two variables may result simply from pure chance. Second, the association between two variables may be the result of the influence of a third common factor. For example, although per capita expenditures for food and clothing exhibit a close relationship over time, one cannot conclude that increases in food expenditures cause increases in clothing expenditures. The high degree of association between these variables can be attributed to a third variable—namely, per capita income. As per capita income increases over time, people tend to spend more on both food and clothing. Finally, both variables may be the cause and the effect at the same time. In other words, a simultaneous or interdependent relationship may exist between the variables. For example, in the income-education example described earlier, it was hypothesized that a person's income is a function of his or her level of education—the more years of schooling the person has, the higher will be the income. However, one could argue that the opposite relationship is also true—namely, that education level is a function of income. A higher income increases the likelihood that a person will be able to afford additional college or vocational education.

Multiple Linear Regression Model

Consider again the problem, introduced in the section "Simple Linear Regression Model," of determining the variables that affect an individual's income level. Rather than limiting the analysis to one independent variable, suppose we now decide to use two explanatory variables, namely education (E) and age (A) in predicting an individual's income level. Furthermore, we hypothesize that the effects of education and age on income are independent, linear, and additive.[20]

---

[20] More complex relationships—that is, nonlinear or multiplicative—are discussed in the section, "Nonlinear Regression Models," in this chapter.

Designating the dependent variable (income) by Y and two independent variables (education and age) by X_1 and X_2, respectively, we hypothesize a functional relationship of the form

$$Y = \alpha + \beta_1 X_1 + \beta_2 X_2 + \epsilon$$

where α, β_1 and β_2 are the regression parameters to be estimated and ϵ is the stochastic disturbance term.

A functional relationship of this form, containing two or more independent variables, is known as a multiple linear regression model. In the (completely) general multiple linear regression model, the dependent variable Y is hypothesized to be a function of m independent variables $X_1, X_2, \ldots, X_m$, and to be of the form

$$Y = \alpha + \beta_1 X_1 + \beta_2 X_2 + \cdots + \beta_m X_m + \epsilon \qquad [6.20]$$

Assumptions Underlying the Multiple Linear Regression Model

In addition to satisfying a set of four assumptions (or postulates) similar to those for the simple linear regression model (discussed earlier in the chapter), the application of the least-squares estimation procedure to the multiple linear regression model requires two further assumptions.

Assumption 5. The number of observations (n) must exceed the number of parameters to be estimated $(m + 1)$.

Assumption 6. No exact linear relationships can exist among any of the independent variables.

Use of Computer Programs

Using matrix algebra, procedures similar to those explained for the simple linear regression model can be employed for calculating the estimated regression coefficients $(a, b\text{'s})$ of Equation 6.20 and testing the statistical significance of the individual independent variables and overall explanatory power of the regression equation.[21] In most practical applications of multiple regression analysis, generalized computer programs are used in performing these procedures on a given set of data.

Although many different programs are available for doing multiple regression analysis, the output of these programs is fairly standardized. The output normally includes the estimated regression coefficients, t-statistics of the in-

---

[21] See Johnston, *Econometric Methods*, chap. 5, for a discussion of the multiple linear regression model.

Observation	Income ($000) Y	Education level X_1	Age X_2	Sex X_3
1	15.0	12	40	1
2	7.6	12	22	0
3	21.5	16	45	1
4	9.0	12	35	0
5	27.0	18	55	1
6	9.5	10	24	0
7	12.7	12	31	0
8	14.0	12	33	0
9	17.2	14	32	1
10	6.7	9	19	0
11	8.4	8	22	0
12	9.1	12	45	0
13	11.5	12	27	1
14	12.1	12	30	1
15	19.5	18	36	1
16	15.5	16	33	1
17	32.0	18	52	1
18	7.5	10	19	0
19	8.0	12	25	0
20	11.1	12	24	0
21	16.5	14	37	1
22	9.0	12	35	0
23	7.2	10	45	0
24	14.5	16	32	1
25	14.5	12	25	1

Table 6.5
**Input Data:
Income Example**

dividual coefficients, R^2, analysis of variance, and F-test of overall significance. The particular program that is illustrated here is a *SAS* (Statistical Analysis System) subroutine called "SYSREG."[22]

Suppose we hypothesize that income (Y) is a linear function of education (X_1), age (X_2), and sex (X_3), expressed as follows:

$$Y = \alpha + \beta_1 X_1 + \beta_2 X_2 + \beta_3 X_3 + \epsilon \qquad [6.21]$$

Data were collected on the four variables for twenty-five randomly selected individuals (same individuals as in Table 6.1) and are shown in Table 6.5. Note that variable X_3 (Sex) takes on only two values, $X_3 = 0$ if the individual is female and $X_3 = 1$ if the individual is male. A *categorical* variable, such as this one, is known as a *dummy* variable.[23] Putting these data along with the appropriate control statements into the SYSREG program yields the output shown in Figure 6.8.

---

[22] See SAS User's Guide (Cary, N.C.: SAS Institute, 1979).
[23] See Johnston, *Econometric Methods*, section 6–3, for a further discussion of dummy variables.

Figure 6.8
**Computer Output:
Income Example**

MODEL:	MODEL01		SSE	189.668960	F RATIO	28.31
			DFE	21	PROB>F	0.0001
DEP VAR:	INCOME (Y)		MSE	9.031855	R-SQUARE	0.8018
			PARAMETER	STANDARD		
VARIABLE		DF	ESTIMATE	ERROR	T RATIO	PROB>|T|
INTERCEPT		1	−8.668425	3.552673	−2.4400	0.0236
EDUCATION (X_1)		1	1.168708	0.378332	3.0891	0.0056
AGE (X_2)		1	0.172465	0.082034	2.1024	0.0478
SEX (X_3)		1	3.018047	1.709616	1.7653	0.0920

Standard Error of the Estimate (SE) = 3.005

Estimating the Population Regression Coefficients

From the computer output (Parameter Estimate column) the following regression equation is obtained:

$$Y = -8.6684 + 1.1687X_1 + .17247X_2 + 3.0180X_3 \qquad [6.22]$$

The coefficient of the X_1 variable (1.1687) indicates that, *all other things being equal*, an additional year of education increases an individual's expected income by $1,168.70. The coefficient of X_3 (3.0180), the dummy variable, indicates that, *all other things being equal*, being male rather than female increases an individual's expected income by $3,018.

Using the Regression Model to Make Forecasts

As in the simple linear regression model, the multiple linear regression model can be used to make point or interval forecasts. Point forecasts can be made by substituting the particular values of the independent variables into the estimated regression equation. For example, suppose we are interested in estimating the income of persons having the following characteristics: $x_1 = 16$, $x_2 = 27$, and $x_3 = 1$. Substituting these values into Equation 6.22 yields

$$y' = -8.6684 + 1.1687(16) + .17247(27) + 3.0180(1)$$
$$= 17.705$$

or $17,705 in income.

The standard error of the estimate (s_e) from the output (labeled SE) can be used to construct prediction intervals for y. An *approximate* 95 percent prediction interval is equal to

$$y' \pm 2s_e \qquad [6.23]$$

For a person having the characteristics cited in the previous paragraph, an *approximate* 95 percent prediction interval is equal to

$$17.705 \pm 2(3.005)$$

or from $11,695 to $23,715.

Inferences About the Population Regression Coefficients

Most regression programs test whether *each* of the independent variables (X's) is statistically significant in explaining the dependent variable (Y). This tests the null hypothesis:

$$H_0: \beta_i = 0$$

against the alternative hypothesis:

$$H_a: \beta_i \neq 0$$

The decision rule is to reject the null hypothesis at the k level of significance if the t-value (labeled T RATIO) from the computer output ($t = b/s_b$) is either less than $-t_{k/2,n-m-1}$ or greater than $t_{k/2,n-m-1}$ where the $t_{k/2,n-m-1}$ is obtained from the t-distribution (with n-m-1 degrees of freedom) in Table 2 in the Tables (Appendix A).[24]

To test the null hypothesis of no relationship between income (Y) and each of the independent variables at the .05 significance level, we would reject the null hypothesis if the respective t-value for each variable is less than $-t_{.025,21} = -2.080$ or greater than $t_{.025,21} = +2.080$. As shown in Figure 6.8, all the calculated t-values except for the X_3 variable are greater than 2.080. Hence, we can conclude that education (X_1) and age (X_2) are statistically significant (at the .05 level) in explaining income.

The Analysis of Variance

Techniques similar to those described for the simple linear regression model are used to evaluate the *overall* explanatory power of the multiple linear regression model.

The multiple coefficient of determination (r^2) is a measure of the overall "fit" of the model. The R-SQUARE value of .8018 in Figure 6.8 indicates that the three-variable regression equation explains 80 percent of the total variation in the dependent variable (income).

The F-value (labeled F-RATIO in the computer output) is used to test the hypothesis that the independent variables ($X_1, X_2, \ldots, X_m$) explain a significant proportion of the variation in the dependent variable (Y). One is using the F-value to test the null hypothesis:

$$H_0: \text{All } \beta_i = 0$$

against the alternative hypothesis:

$$H_a: \text{At least one } \beta_i \neq 0$$

---

[24] Rather than having to look up the $t_{k/2,n-m-1}$ in the table, SAS calculates the significance level at which one can reject the null hypothesis ($\beta_i = 0$). For example, if we are testing the null hypothesis at the $k = .05$ significance level, we would reject the null hypothesis (no relationship between Y and X_i) if the PROB>|T| value from the computer output is less than .05.

In other words, we are testing whether at least one of the explanatory variables contributes information for the prediction of Y. The decision is to reject the null hypothesis at the k level of significance if the F-value from the computer output is *greater* than the $F_{k,m,n-m-1}$ value from the F-distribution (with m and n-m-1 degrees of freedom). Table 3 of the Tables (Appendix A) provides F values.

In the preceding computer example, suppose we want to test whether the three independent variables explain a significant (at the .05 level) proportion of the variation in income. The decision rule is to reject the null hypothesis (no relationship) if the calculated F-value is greater than $F_{.05,3,21} = 3.07$. Since the F-value of 28.31 (from Figure 6.8) exceeds 3.07, we reject the null hypothesis and conclude that the independent variables *are* useful in explaining income.[25]

Problems in Applying the Linear Regression Model

When the simple linear and multiple linear regression models were discussed earlier in this chapter, several assumptions were made about the nature of the relationships among the variables. Questions naturally arise on the applicability or validity of these assumptions in the actual analysis of economic relationships and data. How can we determine if the assumptions are being violated in a given situation? How does the violation of the assumptions affect the parameter estimates and prediction accuracy of the model? What methods (if any) exist for overcoming the difficulties caused by the inapplicability of the assumptions in a given situation?

The science of econometrics provides answers to some, but not all, of these questions. A thorough treatment of them is beyond the scope of this introductory chapter. The (more limited) objective in this section is to make the reader aware of some of the potential problems that can arise in actual applications of the regression models and, in a few instances, to suggest possible techniques for overcoming the problems. Some of the problems that may invalidate the regression results include the following:

1. Autocorrelation

2. Heteroscedasticity

3. Specification and measurement errors

4. Multicollinearity

5. Simultaneous equation relationships

6. Nonlinearities

The first five of these problems are discussed in this section, and the problem of nonlinear relationships is treated in the following section.

---

[25] Rather than having to look up the $F_{k,m,n-m-1}$ value in the table, SAS calculates the significance level at which we can reject the null hypothesis (all $\beta_i = 0$). This is shown in the PROB>F value below the F-RATIO value.

Autocorrelation

In many economic modeling and prediction problems, empirical data are in the form of a *time series*—a series of observations taken on the variables at different points in time. For example, we may be interested in predicting total (domestic U.S.) television sales by using disposable income as the independent variable. The data used to calculate estimates of the regression parameters (that is, a and b) might consist of a series of yearly (or quarterly) measurements of the number of television sets sold and disposable income for a period of ten to fifteen years. In working with time-series data, a problem known as autocorrelation can arise.

Recall that one of the assumptions underlying the regression model (specifically, Assumption 4) is that the disturbance term must be an independent random variable. In other words, we assume that the regression equation produces no predictable pattern in the successive values of the disturbance term e_t. The existence of a significant pattern in the successive values of the error term constitutes *autocorrelation*. Successive values of the disturbance term can exhibit either positive or negative autocorrelation. Positive autocorrelation, as shown in Figure 6.9(a), is inferred whenever successive positive (or negative) disturbances tend to be followed by disturbances of the *same* sign. Negative autocorrelation, as shown in Figure 6.9(b), is inferred whenever successive positive (or negative) disturbances tend to be followed by disturbances of the *opposite* sign.

Autocorrelation can result from several factors. One is the existence of trends and cycles in economic variables. The overall growth of the economy coupled with business cycles causes most economic time series to have an overall upward trend with periodic upturns and downturns around this trend. These trends and cycles tend to produce positive autocorrelation. Autocorrelation may also result if significant explanatory variables are not included in the regression equation or if nonlinear relationships exist.

As a safeguard when working with time-series data, the deviation e_t for each observation should be computed and then the e_t values should be examined for randomness. Statistical tests are also available to check for autocorrelation. One commonly used technique is the Durbin-Watson statistic. It is calculated

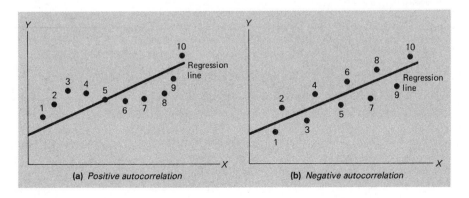

Figure 6.9
Types of Autocorrelation (Numbers 1, 2, 3, ..., 10 refer to successive time periods.)

as follows:[26]

$$d = \frac{\sum_{t=2}^{n} (e_t - e_{t-1})^2}{\sum_{t=1}^{n} e_t^2}$$

[6.23]

where e_t is the estimated error term in period t and e_{t-1} is the error term in period $t - 1$. The Durbin-Watson statistic tests for first-order autocorrelation, that is, whether the error in period t is dependent on the error in the preceding period $t - 1$. The value of d ranges from 0 to 4. If there is *no* first-order autocorrelation, the expected value of d is 2. Values of d *less* than 2 indicate the possible presence of *positive* autocorrelation, whereas values of d *greater* than 2 indicate the possible presence of *negative* autocorrelation.

Formal hypothesis tests for first-order autocorrelation can be performed using the d statistic and the Durbin-Watson table (Table 6 in the Tables of Appendix A). The critical value of d from the table (at the .025 significance level for a one-tail test, that is, a test for positive autocorrelation or a test for negative autocorrelation, or at the .05 significance level for a two-tail test) is a function of both the number of observations (n) and the number of independent variables (m). The decision rules are summarized in Figure 6.10.

For example, suppose we wish to test for the presence of positive autocorrelation (at the .025 level of significance) in a regression equation with four independent variables (not counting the constant term) estimated from twenty-

Figure 6.10
Testing for the Presence of First-Order Autocorrelation

Type of Autocorrelation	One-tail Tests		Two-tail Test*
	Positive autocorrelation	Negative autocorrelation	Positive *and* Negative
Hypothesis			
Null	Ho: No positive autocorrelation	Ho: No negative autocorrelation	Ho: No positive or negative autocorrelation
Alternative	Ha: Positive autocorrelation	Ha: Negative autocorrelation	Ha: Positive or negative autocorrelation
Decision Rule			
Reject Ho	$d < d_L$	$d > (4 - d_L)$	$d < d_L$ or $d > (4 - d_L)$
Do not reject Ho	$d > d_U$	$d < (4 - d_U)$	$d_U < d < (4 - d_U)$
Test is inconclusive (No conclusion can be made concerning the possible presence of autocorrelation)	$d_L \le d \le d_U$	$(4 - d_U) \le d \le (4 - d_L)$	$d_L \le d \le d_U$ or $(4 - d_U) \le d \le (4 - d_L)$

*Note that for a two-tail test, the significance level is *double* that shown in Table 6 of the Statistical Tables.

---

[26] Most computer regression programs will compute the Durbin-Watson statistic when specified by the user on the control statements.

five observations. For $m = 4$ and $n = 25$, the values of d_L and d_U are 0.94 and 1.65, respectively (see Table 6, Appendix A). If the calculated d value is less than $d_L = 0.94$, we would *reject* H_0 and conclude that there is statistically significant evidence of the presence of positive autocorrelation. If the calculated d value is between 0.94 and 1.65, no conclusion could be drawn concerning the possible presence of positive autocorrelation. Finally, if the calculated d value is greater than 1.65, one would *not reject* H_0 and conclude that there is *no* statistically significant evidence of the presence of positive autocorrelation.

The presence of autocorrelation leads to several undesirable consequences in the regression results. First, although the estimates of α and β will be unbiased, the least-squares procedure will tend to underestimate the sampling variances of these estimates. [An estimator is unbiased if its expected value is identical to the population parameter being estimated. The computed a and b values are unbiased estimators of α and β, respectively, since $E(a) = \alpha$ and $E(b) = \beta$.] As a result, the use of the t-statistic to test hypotheses about these parameters may yield incorrect conclusions about the importance of the individual predictor (that is, independent) variables. Second, overall measures of the fit and explanatory power of the regression model, such as the coefficient of determination (r^2) and F-test, will no longer provide reliable information about the significance of the economic relationships obtained. Finally, the use of the regression equation for forecasting purposes will yield predictions with unnecessarily large sampling variances.

Several procedures are available for dealing with autocorrelation.[27] If one can determine the functional form of the dependence relationship in the successive values of the residuals, then the original variables can be transformed to remove this pattern. Another technique that may help to reduce autocorrelation is to include a new linear trend or time variable in the regression equation.[28] A third procedure is to calculate the first differences in the time series of each of the variables (that is, $Y_{t+1} - Y_t, X_{1,t+1} - X_{1,t}, X_{2,t+1} - X_{2,t}$, and so on) and then calculate the regression equation using these transformed variables. This method assumes that the autocorrelation follows a very simple pattern and will not always yield satisfactory results. A fourth method is to include additional variables of the form $X_1{}^2$ or $X_1 X_2$ in the regression equation.

Heteroscedasticity

In developing the regression model, one of the assumptions (Assumption 4) is that the error terms, which are independent random variables, have a constant variance. In other words, we assume that the observations have uniform variability about the theoretical regression line. This property is referred to as *homoscedasticity*. Departure from this assumption is known as *heteroscedasticity*,

---

[27] See Johnston, *Econometric Methods*, or any standard econometrics text, for a much more detailed discussion of procedures for dealing with autocorrelation.

[28] A linear trend variable is one in which each observation in the time series is given a successively larger integer value, such as, 1, 2, 3, ..., n, when n is the number of observations.

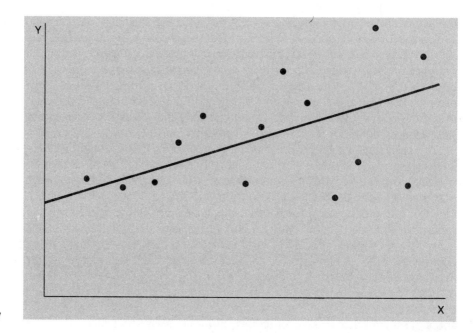

Figure 6.11
**Illustration of
Heteroscedasticity**

which is indicated whenever there is a systematic relationship between the absolute magnitude of the error term and the magnitude of one (or more) of the independent variables. Graphic or tabular comparisons between the absolute values of disturbance terms and the values of each of the independent variables will help to detect the existence of significant heteroscedasticity.

The presence of heteroscedasticity causes the estimate of the variance of the error term (s_e) to be dependent on the particular set of values of the independent variables that was chosen. Another set of observations may yield a much different estimate of this variance. As a result, tests of the statistical significance of the individual regression coefficients (the t-test) and overall explanatory power of the regression equation (the F-test, r^2) may prove to be misleading.

One form of heteroscedasticity occurs when the variance of the error term increases with the size of the independent variable (see Figure 6.11). For example, consider a regression model in which savings by households is postulated to be a function of household income. In this case it is likely that more variability will be found in the savings of high-income households compared with low-income households simply because high-income households have more money available for potential savings. In some cases this form of heteroscedasticity can be reduced or eliminated by dividing all the variables in the regression equation by the independent variable that is thought to be causing the heteroscedasticity and then applying the least-squares analysis to the resulting set of transformed variables. This transformation, however, *does* alter the form of the hypothesized relationship among the variables and thus may be inappropriate in some situations. Another method for dealing with heteroscedasticity might be to take logarithms of the data. Again, this transformation alters the form of the hypothesized relationship among the variables.

Specification and Measurement Errors

Specification errors can result whenever one or more significant explanatory variables are not included in the regression equation. If the missing variable is moderately or highly correlated with one of the explanatory variables included in the regression equation, then the effect of the missing variable will be represented in the coefficient (b value) of the included variable. This may lead to overestimating the economic significance of the explanatory variable included in the regression equation. If, on the other hand, the missing variable is independent of (that is, uncorrelated with) all the other explanatory variables included in the regression equation, then the effect of the missing variable will be to increase the magnitude of the residual errors and the resulting estimated standard deviation of the residuals (s_e). The exclusion of a significant explanatory variable from the regression equation may also produce autocorrelation problems.[29]

The estimation of the parameters of the regression equation requires that a series of measurements be made on both the dependent and independent variables that are to be included in the relationship. Despite the many precautions taken, errors in the measurement of economic variables can arise. For example, the values of many economic variables (such as, unemployment GNP, and prices) are obtained from samples, and sampling error is inherent in the data. Also, data based on a complete census of the population can contain errors caused by missing observations, interviewer biases, recording errors, and so forth. Measurement errors in the dependent variable do not affect the validity of the assumptions underlying the regression model or the parameter estimates obtained by the least-squares procedure since these errors become part of the overall residual or unexplained error. However, measurement errors in the explanatory variables (that is, X's) cause the values of the error term e_i to be dependent on the observed values of the explanatory variables. Consequently, the assumption that the disturbance terms are independent random variables (Assumption 4) is violated, and the resulting least-squares estimates of the regression coefficients (α, β's) are biased.[30]

Multicollinearity

Whenever a high degree of intercorrelation exists among some or all of the explanatory variables in the regression equation, it becomes difficult to determine the separate influences of each of the explanatory variables on the dependent variable.[31] Under such a condition, known as *multicollinearity*, the least-squares procedure tends to yield highly unreliable estimates of the

---

[29] See J. Walter Elliot, *Economic Analysis for Management Decisions* (Homewood, III.: Richard D. Irwin, 1973), pp. 63–64, for an example of this problem.

[30] See Johnston, *Econometric Methods*, section 10.6, for a discussion of this problem and some suggested procedures for overcoming the difficulty.

[31] See Lawrence Klein, *An Introduction to Econometrics* (Englewood Cliffs, N.J.: Prentice-Hall, 1962), pp. 62–64, for a geometric interpretation of the problem of multicollinearity.

Table 6.6
Correlation
Coefficients:
Income Example

	Y	X_1	X_2	X_3	X_4
Y (Income)	1.00				
X_1 (Education)	.60	1.00			
X_2 (Age)	.55	.25	1.00		
X_3 (Intelligence)	.65	.90	.05	1.00	
X_4 (Sex)	.65	.40	.10	.05	1.00

regression coefficients. Multicollinearity is indicated whenever two or more explanatory variables are highly correlated and the standard deviations (s_b's) of their respective regression coefficients become large.

The presence of multicollinearity, through its effects on both the estimates of the regression coefficients and their respective standard deviations, means that the t-test is no longer a reliable indicator of the statistical significance of the individual explanatory variables. The presence of high intercorrelation among the independent variables, however, does not necessarily invalidate the use of the regression equation for prediction purposes. Provided that the intercorrelation pattern among the explanatory variables persists into the future, the equation can produce reliable forecasts of the value of the dependent variable.

A number of techniques exist for dealing with multicollinearity. One technique is to alter the model by removing all but one of the set of highly intercorrelated variables. For example, consider some of the variables that affect income (Y)—namely, education (X_1), age (X_2), intelligence (X_3), and sex (X_4). Suppose that the correlation coefficients are calculated between each of the variables, as shown in Table 6.6. The correlations between each of the possible pairs of explanatory (independent) variables are shown in the enclosed area in the table. Note the high degree of intercorrelation between education (X_1) and intelligence (X_3), indicating that estimates of the regression coefficients (b's) may be unreliable. Therefore, the analyst may want to consider dropping one of these variables from the regression equation. When working with time-series data, another technique is to use cross-sectional data to obtain independent estimates of some of the regression parameters. Finally, the elimination of trends, through deflation procedures such as using a trend variable or first differences, will often reduce the multicollinearity problem.

Simultaneous Equation Relationships

The direction of this chapter has been on building single equation models of economic phenomena in which we attempt to explain or predict the value of one dependent variable using one or more independent variables. However, as Johnston emphasizes:

> It would appear that the most serious defect of the single-equation model is that attention is focused on a *single* equation, when the essence of economic theory is the interdependence of economic phenomena and the determination of the values of economic variables by the simultaneous interaction of relationships.[32]

---

[32] Johnston, *Econometric Methods*, 1st ed. (New York: McGraw-Hill, 1963), p. 146.

The problems that are encountered in attempting to estimate the parameters in simultaneous equation relationships are beyond the scope of this introductory econometrics chapter; however, one aspect, namely the *identification* problem, is discussed in the section of Chapter 8 dealing with the statistical estimation of demand functions.[33]

Nonlinear Regression Models

Although the relationships among many economic variables can be satisfactorily represented using a linear regression model, situations do occur in which a nonlinear model is clearly required to portray adequately the relationship over the relevant range of observations. For example, economic theory postulates the existence of nonlinear diminishing returns relationships among many production and consumption variables. Also, many economic time series tend to exhibit a constant percentage rate of growth and thus yield a nonlinear relationship when plotted against time. Finally, although no underlying theoretical reasons may suggest the presence of nonlinearities, a plot of the variables in a scatter diagram may yield some form of nonlinear relationship, such as the one shown in Figure 6.9(a).

Various nonlinear models are available to deal with these situations. Through an appropriate transformation of the variables in the model, the standard linear regression procedures can be used to estimate the values of the parameters of these nonlinear models. The transformations that are discussed here include the semilogarithmic transformation, the double-log transformation, reciprocal transformation, and polynomial transformations. These transformations can normally be handled with an appropriate instruction to the regression analysis computer program.

Semilogarithmic Transformation

Frequently, the relationship between one or more of the independent variables and the dependent variable can be best estimated by taking the logarithm of one or more of the independent variables. This transformation is often useful when problems of heteroscedasticity exist with respect to one of the independent variables. For example, cross-section regression models, which use firm size as one of the independent variables, often take the log of firm size because of the potential problems caused by including in the same equation firms of $10 million in assets with firms of $10 billion in assets.

A semilog transformation would be of the form

$$Y = a + b \log S + cX + dZ \qquad [6.24]$$

---

[33] See Johnston, *Econometric Methods*, 3d ed., chap. 11; and Elliot, *Economic Analysis for Management Decisions*, chap. 4, for a discussion of simultaneous equation relationships.

where Y is the dependent variable, X and Z are independent variables expressed in a normal form, and $log\ S$ is an independent variable expressed in a logarithmic form. Standard least-squares techniques can be used to estimate Equation 6.24.

Double-Log Transformation

As will be seen later in Chapter 13, a useful model for relating the quantities of various inputs used in a production process to the quantity of output obtained is the *power function*. A three-variable power regression function can be represented as

$$Z = AV^{\beta_1} W^{\beta_2} u \tag{6.25}$$

where V and W are the explanatory variables; α, β_1, and β_2 are the parameters to be estimated; and u is the (multiplicative) disturbance term. Taking logarithms of both sides of Equation 6.25 yields

$$\log Z = \log A + \beta_1 \log V + \beta_2 \log W + \log u$$

By defining the following transformations: $Y = \log Z$, $\alpha = \log A$, $X_1 = \log V$, $X_2 = \log W$, and $\epsilon = \log u$, the ensuing multiple linear regression model is obtained:

$$Y = \alpha + \beta_1 X_1 + \beta_2 X_2 + \epsilon$$

Again, least-squares procedures can be used to estimate these regression coefficients.

Reciprocal Transformation

Another transformation, which is useful in relationships that exhibit an asymptotic behavior, is the reciprocal transformation. The two possible cases are shown in Figure 6.12. In Figure 6.12(a) the relationship is of the form

$$Y = \alpha + \frac{\beta}{Z} \tag{6.26}$$

and in Figure 6.12(b), it is of the form

$$Y = \alpha - \frac{\beta}{Z} \tag{6.27}$$

Defining the transformation $X = 1/Z$, Equations 6.26 and 6.27 yield the following respective simple linear regression models:

$$Y = \alpha + \beta X + \epsilon$$

and

$$Y = \alpha - \beta X + \epsilon$$

whose parameters can be estimated by the usual least-squares procedures.

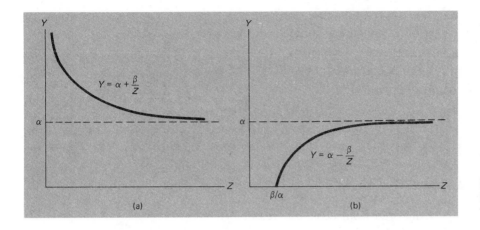

Figure 6.12
Reciprocal Transformations

Polynomial Transformation

As will be seen in Chapter 13, the cost-output function for the firm is often postulated to follow a quadratic or cubic pattern. This type of relationship can be represented by means of a *polynomial function*. For example, a third-degree (that is, cubic) polynomial function can be represented as

$$Y = \alpha + \beta_1 Z + \beta_2 Z^2 + \beta_3 Z^3 \qquad [6.28]$$

Letting $X_1 = Z$, $X_2 = Z^2$, $X_3 = Z^3$, Equation 6.28 can be transformed into the following multiple linear regression model:

$$Y = \alpha + \beta_1 X_1 + \beta_2 X_2 + \beta_3 X_3$$

Again, standard least-squares procedures can be used in estimating the parameters of this model.

The transformations discussed illustrate the possibilities that are available to the model builder. These various transformations may, of course, be combined and used in the same equation. Further discussions of these and other more complex transformations are found in most econometrics books.

Summary

- The objective of *regression analysis* is to develop a functional relationship between the dependent and independent (explanatory) variables. Once a functional relationship (that is, regression equation) is developed, the equation can be used to make forecasts or predictions concerning the value of the dependent variable for given values of the independent variables.

- The *least-squares* technique is used to estimate the regression coefficients. Least squares minimizes the sum of the squares of the differences between the observed and estimated values of the dependent variable over the sample of observations.

- The t-test is used to test the hypothesis that a *given* independent variable is useful in explaining variation in the dependent variable.

- The F-test is used to test the hypothesis that *all* the independent variables $(X_1, X_2, \ldots, X_m)$ in the regression equation explain a significant proportion of the variation in the dependent variable.

- The *coefficient of determination* (r^2) measures the proportion of the variation in the dependent variable that is explained by the regression equation (that is, independent variables).

- The presence of association does not necessarily imply causation. Statistical tests can only establish whether or not an association exists between variables. The existence of a cause-and-effect economic relationship can only be inferred from economic reasoning.

- Various methodological problems can occur when applying the single-equation linear regression model. These include autocorrelation, heteroscedasticity, specification and measurement errors, multicollinearity, simultaneous equation relationships, and nonlinearities. Many of these problems can invalidate the regression results. In some cases methods are available for detecting and overcoming these problems.

Selected References

Anderson, David R., Dennis J. Sweeney and Thomas A. Williams. *Statistics for Business and Economics*, 2d ed. St. Paul: West Publishing Company, 1984.
Johnston, J. *Econometric Methods*, 3rd ed. New York: McGraw-Hill, 1984.
Theil, Henri. *Introduction to Econometrics*. Englewood Cliffs, N. J.: Prentice-Hall, 1978.

Discussion Questions

1. Define the following terms:
   a. Econometrics
   b. Standard error of the estimate
   c. Correlation coefficient
   d. Coefficient of determination
   e. Autocorrelation
   f. Heteroscedasticity
   g. Specification error
   h. Multicollinearity

2. Discuss the assumptions underlying the following:
   a. Simple linear regression model
   b. Multiple linear regression model

3. Discuss the *least-squares* procedure for estimating the regression coefficients.

4. Explain each of the terms in the following expression:

   Total sum of squares = Unexplained sum of squares + Explained sum of squares

   Illustrate your answer with a graph.

5. Explain why it is risky to use a sample regression equation to make forecasts outside the range of values of the independent variable represented in the sample.

6. Explain why, in a regression analysis, an association relationship between two variables may not imply a causal relationship.

7. Explain the hypotheses tested when applying the t-test and F-test in the following:
   a. Simple linear regression model
   b. Multiple linear regression model

8. How do specification and measurement errors affect the results of a regression analysis; that is, regression coefficients, t values, r^2 statistic, residuals, and usefulness of the model for forecasting?

9. Suppose an appliance manufacturer is doing a regression analysis, using quarterly *time-series* data, of the factors affecting its sales of appliances. A regression equation was estimated between appliance sales (in dollars) as the dependent variable and disposable personal income and new housing starts as the independent variables. The statistical tests of the model showed large t values for both independent variables, along with a high r^2 value. However, analysis of the residuals indicated that substantial autocorrelation was present.
   a. What are some of the possible causes of this autocorrelation?
   b. How does this autocorrelation affect the conclusions concerning the significance of the individual explanatory variables and the overall explanatory power of the regression model?
   c. Given that a person uses the model for forecasting future appliance sales, how does this autocorrelation affect the accuracy of these forecasts?
   d. What techniques might be used to remove this autocorrelation from the model?

10. Suppose the appliance manufacturer discussed in Question 9 also developed another model, again using time-series data, where appliance sales were the dependent variable and disposable personal income and retail sales of durable goods were the independent variables. Although the regression coefficients are statistically significant and the r^2 statistic is high, the manufacturer also suspects that serious multicollinearity exists between the two independent variables.
   a. In what ways does the presence of this multicollinearity affect the results of the regression analysis?
   b. Under what conditions might the presence of multicollinearity cause problems in the use of this regression equation in forecasting future appliance sales.

Problems

1. A university is typically required to prepare operating budgets well in advance of actually receiving its revenues and incurring the expenditures. An important source of revenue is student tuition, which is obviously a function of the number of students enrolled. A university was having problems in preparing accurate budgets because past forecasts of enrollment, made each February before the start of the academic year in September, were subject to considerable error. One aspect of the problem was determining the relationship between the numbers of applications received by February 1 and the number of new students entering the university in the following September. The data tabulated below were collected on September registrations and February 1 applications.

Year	Number of applications received by February 1 (hundreds)	Number of new students enrolled in September (hundreds)
19X0	28	24
19X1	26	20
19X2	28	18
19X3	28	22
19X4	36	32
19X5	36	33
19X6	42	34
19X7	46	34
19X8	46	35
19X9	50	38

a. Given the nature of the forecasting problem, which variable would be the dependent variable and which would be the independent variable?

b. Plot the data.

c. Determine the estimated regression line. Give an economic interpretation of the slope (b) coefficient.

d. Test the hypothesis that there is no relationship (that is, $\beta = 0$) between the variables.

e. Calculate the coefficient of determination.

f. Perform an analysis of variance on the regression, including an F-test of the overall significance of the results.

g. Suppose 4,200 applications are received by February 1. What is the best estimate, based on the regression model, of the number of new students that will be enrolled in the following September? Construct an approximate 95 percent prediction interval.

h. Suppose that as the result of changes in the deadlines for scholarship and loan selection requests, applications received by February 1 increase to 6,000. What would be the estimate of enrollment for the following September?

i. Would the estimate of enrollment in part (h) be reliable? Why or why not?

2. Executive Insurers, Inc. is examining the factors that affect the amount of life insurance held by executives. The following data on the amount of insurance and annual incomes of a random sample of twelve executives was collected:

Observation	Amount of life insurance ($\times$ \$1,000)	Annual income ($\times$ \$1,000)
1	90	50
2	180	84
3	225	74
4	210	115
5	150	104
6	150	96
7	60	56
8	135	102
9	150	104
10	150	108
11	60	65
12	90	58

a. Given the nature of the problem, which would be the dependent variable and which would be the independent variable?

b. Plot the data.

c. Determine the estimated regression line. Give an economic interpretation of the slope (b) coefficient.

d. Test the hypothesis that there is no relationship (i.e., $\beta = 0$) between the variables.

e. Calculate the coefficient of determination.

f. Perform an analysis of variance on the regression, including an F-test of the overall significance of the results.

g. Determine the best estimate, based on the regression model, of the amount of life insurance held by an executive whose annual income is $80,000. Construct an approximate 95 percent prediction interval.

3. The county assessor is interested in developing a regression model to estimate the market value (i.e., selling price) of residential property within his jurisdiction. The assessor feels that the most important variable affecting selling price (measured in thousands of dollars) is the size of house (measured in hundreds of square feet). He randomly selected fifteen houses and measured both the selling price and size as shown in the table below.

Observation i	Selling price ($\times$ 1000) Y	Size ($\times$ $100\,ft^2$) X_1
1	65.2	12.0
2	79.6	20.2
3	111.2	27.0
4	128.0	30.0
5	152.0	30.0
6	81.2	21.4
7	88.4	21.6
8	92.8	25.2
9	156.0	37.2
10	63.2	14.4
11	72.4	15.0
12	91.2	22.4
13	99.6	23.9
14	107.6	26.6
15	120.4	30.7

a. Plot the data.

b. Determine the estimated regression line. Give an economic interpretation of the estimated slope (b) coefficient.

c. Determine if size is a statistically significant variable in estimating selling price.

d. Calculate the coefficient of determination.

e. Perform an F-test of the overall significance of the results.

f. Construct an *approximate* 95 percent prediction interval for the selling price of a house having an area (size) of 15 (hundred) square feet.

4. Cascade Pharmaceuticals Company developed the following regression model, using time-series data from the past 33 quarters, for one of its nonprescription cold remedies:

$$Y = -1.04 + .24X_1 - .27X_2$$

where

Y = quarterly sales (in thousands of cases) of the cold remedy

X_1 = Cascade's quarterly advertising ($\times$ $1000) for the cold remedy

X_2 = competitors' advertising for similar products ($\times$ $10,000).

Additional information concerning the regression model:

$$s_{b_1} = .032 \qquad s_{b_2} = .070$$
$$R^2 = .64 \qquad s_e = 1.63 \qquad F\text{-statistic} = 31.402$$
$$\text{Durbin-Watson } (d) \text{ statistic} = .4995$$

a. Which of the independent variables (if any) appear to be statistically significant (at the .05 level) in explaining sales of the cold remedy?

b. What proportion of the total variation in sales is explained by the regression equation?

c. Perform an F-test (at the .05 level) of the overall explanatory power of the model.

d. What conclusions can be drawn from the data about the possible presence of autocorrelation?

e. How do the results in part (d) affect your answers to parts (a), (b), and (c)?

f. What additional statistical information (if any) would you find useful in the evaluation of this model?

5. Suppose an appliance manufacturer (of refrigerators, washers, dryers, ranges, and so on) is seeking to develop a model for forecasting future appliance sales of the firm. The firm decides to test the following (single-equation) model:

$$S_t = \alpha + \beta_1 A_t + \beta_2 H_t + \beta_3 L_t + \epsilon_t$$

where S_t is the firm's sales in dollars in period t; A_t is its *a*dvertising expenditures; H_t is an index of new *h*ousing starts; L_t is an index of *l*iquid asset holdings by consumers; and ϵ_t is the disturbance term.

a. Develop a hypothesis concerning the sign (plus or minus) of each of the β parameters (that is, predict whether sales will increase or decrease as the result of an increase in each of the independent variables in the model).

Suppose that the following regression equation was estimated from quarterly time-series data:

$$S_t = 20.2 + 6.1A_t + 4.1H_t - 3.3L_t$$

Additional information about the equation includes:

$$n = 20 \text{ (sample size, that is, number of quarters)}$$
$$r^2 = .79$$

Standard errors of the coefficients:

$$s_{b_1} = 2.21$$
$$s_{b_2} = 1.23$$
$$s_{b_3} = 1.22$$

Standard error of the estimate: $s_e = 25.3$

b. Would any of the statistical results appear to be inconsistent with the hypothesis developed in part (a)? What statistical factors might explain any inconsistencies?

c. What additional statistical information would you find useful in the evaluation of this model?

d. What practical difficulties would be encountered in using this model to forecast sales for the next four quarters?

6. A product manager has been reviewing selling expenses (that is, advertising, sales commissions, and so on) associated with marketing a line of household cleaning products. The manager suspects that there may be some sort of diminishing marginal returns relationship between selling expenses and the resulting sales generated by these expenditures. After examining the selling expense and sales data for various regions (all regions are similar in sales potential) shown in the following table and graph, however, the manager is uncertain about the nature of the relationship.

Region	Selling Expense ($000)	Sales (100,000 units)	Log (selling expense)	Log (sales)
A	5	1	3.6990	5.0000
B	30	4.25	4.4771	5.6284
C	25	4	4.3979	5.6021
D	10	2	4.0000	5.3010
E	55	5.5	4.7404	5.7404
F	40	5	4.6021	5.6990
G	10	1.75	4.0000	5.2430
H	45	5	4.6532	5.6990
I	20	3	4.3010	5.4771
J	60	5.75	4.7782	5.7597

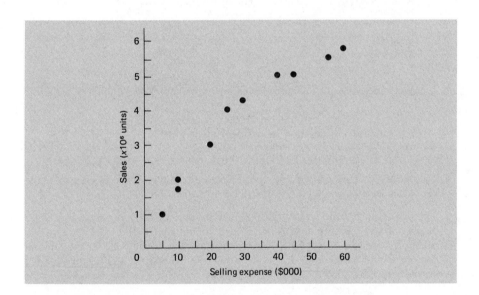

a. Using the linear regression model

$$Y = \alpha + \beta X + \epsilon$$

where Y is sales and X is selling expenses, estimate α, β, and the r^2 statistic by the least-squares technique.

b. Using the power function model

$$Y = \alpha X^{\beta} \epsilon$$

apply the double logarithmic transformation to obtain a linear relationship that can be estimated by the least-squares technique.

c. Applying the least-squares technique, estimate α, β, and the r^2 statistic for the transformed (linear) model in part (b). (Note that the logarithms of the X and Y variables needed in the calculations are given in the table.)

d. Based on the r^2 statistics calculated in parts (a) and (c), which model would appear to give a better fit of the data?

e. What implications does the result in part (d) have for the possible existence of a diminishing marginal returns relationship between sales and selling expenses as suggested by the manager?

f. What other transformations of the variables might we try to give a better fit to the data?

7. a Fill in the missing information (blanks) in the following multiple regression computer output.

DEPENDENT VARIABLE: SALES

VARIABLE	DF	PARAMETER ESTIMATE	STANDARD ERROR	T-RATIO
INTERCEPT	1	_____	1.105	2.205
PRICE	1	− .3750	_____	−1.570
INCOME	1	_____	.140	2.780
ADVERTISING	1	−6.2500	1.950	_____

SOURCE OF VARIATION	DF	SUM OF SQUARES	MEAN SQUARES
REGRESSION	_____	1187.343	_____
RESIDUAL	_____	_____	18.625
TOTAL	25	_____	

R-SQUARE: _____
F-RATIO: _____

b. Determine which of the variables (if any) are statistically significant (at the .05 level).

c. Determine whether the independent variables explain a significant (.05 level) proportion of the variation in the dependent variable.

Note: The following problems require the use of a regression computer program.

8. Solve Problem 1 using a computer program. Compare the computer solution to the one calculated by the methods described in the chapter.

9. Executive Insurers, Inc. (see Problem 2) feels the use of more independent variables might improve the overall explanatory power of the regression model. Data on two additional variables (age of the executive and number of children) for the random sample of twelve executives are shown along with the original data from Problem 2 in the following table:

Observation	Amount of life insurance (× $1,000)	Annual income (× $1,000)	Age (years)	Number of children
1	90	50	34	2
2	180	84	40	4
3	225	74	46	3
4	210	115	63	3
5	150	104	62	4
6	150	96	54	2

Observation	Amount of life insurance (× $1,000)	Annual income (× $1,000)	Age (years)	Number of children
7	60	56	31	1
8	135	102	57	3
9	150	104	40	3
10	150	108	42	4
11	60	65	45	2
12	90	58	35	1

a. Using a computer regression program, determine the estimated regression equation with the three explanatory variables shown in the table.

b. Give an economic interpretation of each of the regression coefficients.

c. Which of the independent variables (if any) are statistically significant (at the .05 level) in explaining the amount of insurance held by executives?

d. What proportion of the total variation in the amount of insurance is explained by the regression model?

e. Perform an F-test (at the .05 significance level) of the overall explanatory power of the model.

f. Construct an *approximate* 95 percent prediction interval for the amount of insurance held by an executive whose annual income is $90,000, whose age is 50, and who has three children.

10. The county assessor (see Problem 3) feels that the use of more independent variables in the regression equation might improve the overall explanatory power of the model.

Observation i	Selling price (× $1000) Y	Size (× $100\,ft^2$) X_1	Total no. of rooms X_2	Age X_3	Attached garage (No = 0, Yes = 1) X_4
1	65.2	12.0	6	17	0
2	79.6	20.2	7	18	0
3	111.2	27.0	7	17	1
4	128.0	30.0	8	18	1
5	152.0	30.0	8	15	1
6	81.2	21.4	8	20	1
7	88.4	21.6	7	8	0
8	92.8	25.2	7	15	1
9	156.0	37.2	9	31	1
10	63.2	14.4	7	8	0
11	72.4	15.0	7	17	0
12	91.2	22.4	6	9	0
13	99.6	23.9	7	20	1
14	107.6	26.6	6	23	1
15	120.4	30.7	7	23	1

In addition to size, the assessor feels that the total number of rooms, age, and whether or not the house has an attached garage might be important variables affecting selling price. This data for the fifteen randomly selected dwellings is shown in the table above.

a. Using a computer regression program, determine the estimated regression equation with the four explanatory variables shown in the table.

b. Give an economic interpretation of each of the estimated regression coefficients.

c. Which of the independent variables (if any) are statistically significant (at the .05 level) in explaining selling price?

d. What proportion of the total variation in selling price is explained by the regression model?

e. Perform an F-test (at the .05 significance level) of the overall explanatory power of the model.

f. Construct an *approximate* 95 percent prediction interval for the selling price of a 15-year-old house having 1,800 square feet, 7 rooms, and an attached garage.

11. The county assessor (see Problem 10) is concerned about possible multicollinearity between the size (X_1) and total number of rooms (X_2) variables. Calculate the correlation coefficient between these two variables. Check the computer solution by calculating the correlation coefficient using the methods described in the chapter.

12. The following table presents data on sales (S), advertising (A), and price (P):

Observation	Sales (S)	Advertising (A)	Price (P)
1	495	900	150
2	555	1200	180
3	465	750	135
4	675	1350	135
5	360	600	120
6	405	600	120
7	735	1500	150
8	435	750	150
9	570	1050	165
10	600	1200	150

a. Estimate the following functional relationships

(i) $S = \alpha + \beta_1 A + \beta_2 P$

(ii) $S = \alpha A^{\beta_1} P^{\beta_2}$

b. Determine whether the estimated values of β_1 and β_2 are statistically significant (at the .05 level).

c. Based on the value of R^2 and the F-ratio, which model gives the best fit?

Demand and Forecasting III

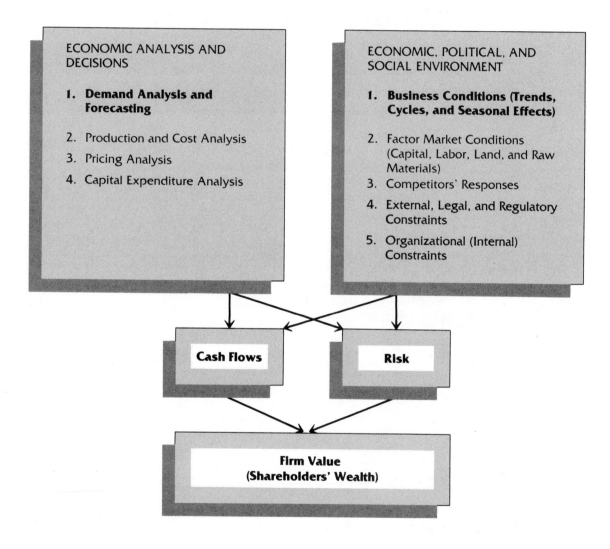

ECONOMIC ANALYSIS AND
DECISIONS

1. **Demand Analysis and Forecasting**

2. Production and Cost Analysis
3. Pricing Analysis
4. Capital Expenditure Analysis

ECONOMIC, POLITICAL, AND
SOCIAL ENVIRONMENT

1. **Business Conditions (Trends, Cycles, and Seasonal Effects)**

2. Factor Market Conditions (Capital, Labor, Land, and Raw Materials)
3. Competitors' Responses
4. External, Legal, and Regulatory Constraints
5. Organizational (Internal) Constraints

Cash Flows

Risk

**Firm Value
(Shareholders' Wealth)**

Part III (Demand and Forecasting) considers the elements determining the demand for a firm's output. Chapter 7 develops the theory of demand and introduces the elasticity properties of the demand function. Chapter 8 examines the procedures that may be used in making empirical estimates of the demand relationships developed in Chapter 7. Business and economic forecasting is the topic in Chapter 9. We consider forecasting at both the level of the firm and the overall economy. Chapter 10 discusses the use of input-output analysis as a forecasting tool. Technological forecasting is also discussed in Chapter 10. Understanding the determinants of demand is central to estimating the level and risk of the cash flows facing a firm. Forecasts of future economic activity and assessments of the impact of differing levels of economic activity on the demand of a firm are important inputs in the pricing, production, and resource allocation decisions that wealth-maximizing managers must make.

Theory of Demand 7

Demand analysis serves two major managerial objectives. First, it provides the insights necessary for the effective manipulation of demand. Second, it aids in forecasting sales and revenues. This chapter develops the theory of demand and introduces the elasticity properties of the demand function. The chapter begins by examining only the relationship between price and quantity, thereby assuming that the other factors that influence demand, such as income levels and advertising, remain unchanged or are held constant. Later the effects of these other factors are added to the analysis. The appendix to the chapter derives the demand function from consumer indifference curves. One of the most important concepts from the theory of demand, the concept of elasticity, is developed in this chapter. In the general context of demand analysis, elasticity is a measure of the responsiveness of quantity demanded to a change in one of the factors influencing demand, such as price, advertising, income levels, or the price of substitute and complementary goods. A thorough understanding of demand theory and its applications is central to effective, wealth-maximizing decision making by a firm's managers because demand relationships determine the revenue portion of a firm's cash flow stream.

Demand Relationships: The Demand Schedule and the Demand Curve

Demand relationships can be represented in the form of a schedule (table), graph, or algebraic function. Each of these forms of presentation provides insights into demand relationships. This section focuses on schedules and graphs; the next section discusses algebraic functions.

The Demand Schedule Defined

The demand schedule is the simplest form of the demand relationship. It is merely a list of prices and corresponding quantities of a commodity that would be demanded by some individual or group of individuals at those prices. For example, Table 7.1 shows the demand schedule for Product A at some point in time. This demand schedule indicates that *if* the price of A were $9, 60 units of A would be purchased by consumers. Note that the lower the price, the greater the

Glossary of New Terms

Durable good
A good that yields benefits to the owner over a number of future time periods.

Producers' good
A good that is not produced for direct consumption but rather is the raw material or capital equipment that is used to produce a consumer good (or some other producers' good).

Price elasticity
The ratio of the percentage change in quantity demanded to the percentage change in price, assuming that all other factors influencing demand remain unchanged. Also called *"own"* price elasticity.

Income elasticity
The ratio of the percentage change in quantity demanded to the percentage change in income, assuming that all other factors influencing demand remain unchanged.

(Cont'd on next page)

Table 7.1
Simplified Demand Schedule

Price of A ($)	Quantity of A demanded (units per time period)
10	50
9	60
8	70
7	80
6	90

Glossary of New Terms (Cont'd)

Cross elasticity
The ratio of the percentage change in the quantity demanded of Good A to the percentage change in the price of Good B, assuming that all other factors influencing demand remain unchanged. Also called *cross price elasticity*.

Substitute goods
Two goods, A and B, are substitutes if the quantity demanded of Good A *increases* (decreases) when the price of Good B is *increased* (decreased), assuming all other factors affecting demand remain unchanged.

Complementary goods
Two goods, A and B, are complementary if the quantity demanded of Good A *decreases* (increases) when the price of Good B is *increased* (decreased), assuming all other factors affecting demand remain unchanged.

Marginal revenue
The change in total revenue that results from a one-unit change in quantity demanded.

quantity of A that would be demanded. This inverse or negative relationship between price and quantity demanded is generally referred to as the "law of demand." At lower prices people will be able and willing to purchase more of a commodity than at a higher price because that commodity becomes cheaper in relation to possible alternatives or substitutes. For example, if the price of sirloin steak declined from $5 per pound to $2 per pound, all other things remaining equal, individuals would very likely increase the amount of steak in their diet at the expense of other substitute food items.

Income and Substitution Effects

Economists have identified two basic reasons for the increase in quantity demanded as a result of a price reduction. First, when the price of some commodity—steak, for example—declines, the effect of this decline is that the real income of the consumer has increased. This has been called the *income effect*. For example, if an individual normally consumed two pounds of sirloin steak per week at $5 per pound, a price decline to $2 per pound would enable the consumer to purchase the same total amount of steak for $6 less. This savings of $6 represents an increase in real income of $6, which may be spent to purchase greater quantities of steak (as well as all other goods) each week.

The second reason that explains the inverse relationship between price and quantity is that a decline in the price of one good, A, makes it less expensive in relation to other goods.[1] Consequently, as is demonstrated in the following example, the rational consumer should switch some portion of his or her total expenditure from the relatively higher-priced item to the relatively lower-priced items. This has been called the *substitution effect*. The income and substitution effects are developed in more detail using indifference curve analysis in the appendix to this chapter.

Law of Diminishing Marginal Utility

One of the basic assumptions of economic theory is that consumers are rational. As rational individuals they seek to maximize the satisfaction gained from their consumption or expenditure decisions. This satisfaction may be defined as

---

[1] The terms *commodity, good,* and *product* are used interchangeably throughout the text to describe both physical goods and services.

utility. To maximize utility, consumers should allocate their consumption dollars in such a manner that they receive the same marginal, or additional, satisfaction for the last dollar spent on each commodity they consume. Specifically, marginal utility may be defined as *the rate of change in total utility per unit change in the consumption of a given commodity, holding constant the quantity consumed of other commodities.* In order to maximize utility, the ratio of marginal utility MU to price P for all commodities purchased must be equal:[2]

$$\frac{MU_A}{P_A} = \frac{MU_B}{P_B} = \frac{MU_C}{P_C}\cdots \qquad\qquad [7.1]$$

If this condition does not hold (perhaps because of a price change for one of the commodities), it would be possible for a consumer to reallocate expenditure dollars in a manner that would result in an increase in total satisfaction (utility). If, for example $MU_A/P_A > MU_B/P_B$, and if Product A costs \$10, $(1/10)\, MU_A$ represents the satisfaction (utility) that an additional dollar spent on A will yield. Consequently, a transfer of resources from B to A will result in an increase in total utility, since the satisfaction received from the last dollar spent on A exceeds the satisfaction obtained from the last dollar spent on B.

This short digression illustrates the disequilibrating effects that a price decline may have. Assume once again that the consumer is presently in equilibrium:

$$\frac{MU_A}{P_A} = \frac{MU_B}{P_B}$$

If the price of A were to decline, equilibrium would be disrupted, resulting in

$$\frac{MU_A}{P_A} > \frac{MU_B}{P_B}$$

To restore equilibrium the consumer would be directed to reallocate some resources from B to A. The additional satisfaction (marginal utility) derived from successive units of a commodity is thought to decline—the *law of diminishing marginal utility.* Hence, the consumer will buy less of B—thereby increasing the marginal utility derived from the last unit of B—and more of A—thereby decreasing the marginal utility derived from the last unit of A—until equilibrium is restored and MU_A/P_A once again equals MU_B/P_B.

For example, if the marginal utility derived from a unit of product A (MU_A) is 15 and the price of $A(P_A)$ is 15, the ratio of MU_A/P_A is 1.0. Similarly, if the marginal utility from a unit of B is 20 and the price of B is 20, the ratio of MU_B/P_B is also 1.0 and equilibrium will exist. Suppose, however, that the price of A decreases to 10. Now the ratio of MU_A/P_A is 1.5 and it exceeds the ratio of MU_B/P_B. Thus the consumer will have an incentive to use more of A and less of B. As the consumer demands more of A and less of B, the marginal utility from

---

[2] See Appendix 7A for a further discussion of this optimality condition. See also Jack Hirshleifer, *Price Theory and Applications*, 4th ed. (Englewood Cliffs, N.J.: Prentice-Hall, 1988), chap. 4, for a detailed proof of this utility maximization proposition.

an additional unit of A will decline, while the marginal utility from B will increase. If many consumers make similar substitutions of A for B, the price of A will be bid up and the price of B will decline. These two effects will continue until a new equilibrium of $MU_A/P_A = MU_B/P_B$ is reached.

In summary, because of the combined impact of the income and substitution effects, a decline in the price of some commodity, A, will always have an impact on the quantity demanded for that commodity. This impact specifies that the relationship between price and quantity will necessarily be inverse; that is, more will be demanded at lower prices, and vice versa. Both the substitution and income effects dictate an increase in quantity demanded at lower prices, except in the case of inferior goods.[3] The net effect of both actions, even in the case of inferior goods, is that more will likely be demanded at lower prices.[4]

The Demand Curve Defined

The demand relationship may be represented graphically in the form of a demand curve. Using the data from the preceding example (Table 7.1), we may plot and hence define the demand curve for Commodity A. In graphing demand relationships, it is common practice to plot the quantity demanded on the horizontal axis and the price level on the vertical axis. Figure 7.1 shows a

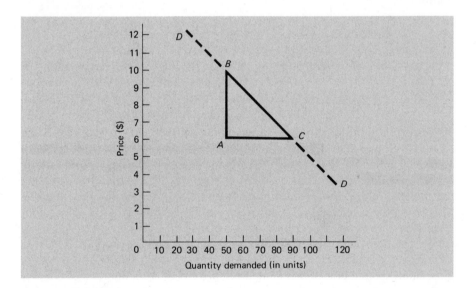

Figure 7.1
Straight Line Demand Curve

---

[3] Inferior goods are those that are consumed less as income rises, and vice versa.

[4] As Baumol has noted, "In practice, the income effect for most consumers' goods is likely to be small because a buyer's outlay on any one commodity constitutes a relatively small proportion of his budget, so that a fall in the price of that item alone will not increase his real income significantly." This suggests that more will be demanded at lower prices, even for inferior goods. See William J. Baumol, *Economic Theory and Operations Analysis*, 4th ed. (Englewood Cliffs, N.J.: Prentice-Hall, 1977), p. 210.

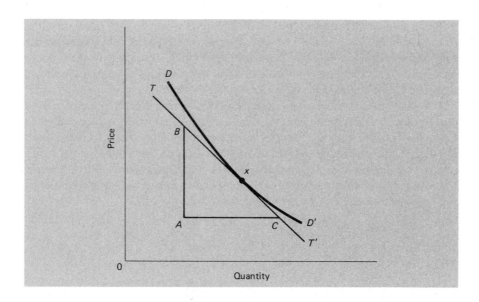

Figure 7.2
**Nonlinear
Demand Curve**

demand curve. The curve indicates that at a price of $8, for example, 70 units of A would be demanded.

One of the more important properties of the demand curve is its slope. The slope of a straight line, as in this example, is constant along the length of that line. In general, we may think of the slope of a line as a measure of its steepness. It is defined as the change in the variable on the vertical axis (rise) divided by the corresponding change in the variable on the horizontal axis (run) or as $AB \div AC$ (see Figure 7.1). In this example, since $AB = -4$ and $AC = 40$, the slope is equal to $-1/10$. The slope is negative because as price declines, the quantity demanded increases.

In the case where the demand curve is not a straight line, the slope is uniquely defined for every point along the line (see Figure 7.2). At any point, X, along the demand curve, DD', the slope of the curve at that point may be found by calculating the slope of the tangent, TT' to DD' at point X. The slope of the demand curve DD' at point X is given by $AB \div AC$. As in the previous example, the slope is negative since more is demanded at lower prices. In general, the slope of any line is a measurement of the rate of change in that line. Since the derivative of any function is also equivalent to the rate of change in that function, we may generalize that the inverse of the slope of any demand function is equivalent to the first derivative of that function with respect to price, or dQ/dP. The concept of the slope of a curve will be useful in the discussion of demand functions and the elasticity of demand.

Demand Relationships: The Demand Function

The demand schedule and the demand curve specify the relationship between prices and the quantity of a commodity that will be demanded at those prices at some point in time, *holding constant the influence of all other factors*. A number of these factors may effect a change in the shape as well as the position of the demand curve as time passes. In other words, quantity demanded is a function of a number of factors in addition to price. Traditionally, economists have placed an extremely heavy emphasis on price as a factor influencing demand. This emphasis may be well founded in some industries, such as in the commodities markets. However, in many manufacturing industries, price may be one of the last decision variables that management will consider altering because of the likelihood of price retaliation from competitors. In these cases the design and packaging of products, the amount and distribution of the firm's advertising budget, the size of the sales force, and promotional expenditures may be the more significant variables manipulated by management. Algebraically, the demand function can be represented as

$$Q_D = f\ (P,\ P^S,\ P^C,\ Y,\ A,\ A^C,\ N,\ C^P,\ P^E, \ldots) \tag{7.2}$$

where Q_D = quantity demanded of the product
P = price of the product
P^S = price of substitute product(s)
P^C = price of complementary product(s)
Y = income of consumers
A = advertising expenditures
A^C = competitors' advertising expenditures on the product
N = population
C^P = consumer preferences for the product
P^E = expected (future) changes in price

This representation of the demand function indicates that quantity demanded is a function of a number of different factors (i.e. independent variables). Table 7.2 summarizes some of the factors that affect the shape and/or position of the demand curve. The variables listed above represent only some of the possible explanatory variables affecting demand. For any given product, other variables may be equally important in explaining demand.

It is important to remember that the demand schedule or demand curve merely deals with the price-quantity relationship. *Changes in the price (i.e, P) of the commodity will result only in movement along the demand curve whereas changes in any of the other independent variables (i.e., P^S, P^C, Y, A, A^C, N, C^P, P^E, ...) in the demand function are likely to result in a shift of that curve.*

This is illustrated graphically in Figure 7.3. The initial demand relationship is line DD'. If the original price were P_1, quantity Q_1 would be demanded. If the price declined to P_2, the quantity demanded would increase to Q_2. If, however, changes occurred in the other independent variables, we would expect to have a shift in the entire curve. If, for example, a tax reduction were approved and consumer disposable income increased, the new demand curve might become D_1D_1'. At any price, P_1, along D_1D_1', a greater quantity, Q_3, will be demanded than at the same price on the original curve DD'. Similarly, if the prices of substitute products were to decline, the demand curve would shift downward and to the left. At any price, P_1, along the new curve D_2D_2', a smaller quantity, Q_4, would be demanded than at the same price on either DD' or D_1D_1'.

The demand function given in Equation 7.2 expresses the general relationship between quantity demanded and the various explanatory variables. An

Factor	Effect
Increase (decrease) in price of substitute goods[a] (P^S)	Increase (decrease) in demand (Q_D)
Increase (decrease) in price of complementary goods[b] (P^C)	Decrease (increase) in Q_D
Increase (decrease) in consumer income levels[c] (Y)	Increase (decrease) in Q_D
Increase (decrease) in the amount of advertising and promotional expenditures (A)	Increase (decrease) in Q_D
Increase (decrease) in level of advertising and promotion by competitors (A^C)	Decrease (increase) in Q_D
Increase (decrease) in population (N)	Increase (decrease) in Q_D
Increase (decrease) in consumer preferences for Q_D good or service (C^P)	Increase (decrease) in Q_D
Expected price increases (decreases) for Q_D good (P^E)	Increase (decrease) in Q_D

**Table 7.2
Partial List of
Factors Affecting
Demand**

[a] Two goods are substitutes if an increase (decrease) in the price of Good 1 results in an increase (decrease) in the quantity demanded of Good 2, holding other factors constant, such as the price of Good 2, other prices, income, and so on: or vice versa. For example, margarine may be viewed as a rather good substitute for butter. As the price of butter increases, more and more people will decrease their consumption of butter and increase their consumption of margarine.

[b] Goods that are used in conjunction with each other, either in production or consumption, are called *complementary goods*. For example, magnetic tapes are used in conjunction with tape recorders. An increase in the price of tape recorders would have the effect of decreasing the demand for magnetic tapes, *ceteris paribus*. In other words, two goods are complementary if a decrease in the price of Good 1 results in an increase in the quantity demanded of Good 2, *ceteris paribus*. Similarly, two goods are complements if an increase in the price of Good 1 results in a decrease in the quantity demanded of Good 2.

[c] The case of inferior goods—that is, those goods which are purchased in smaller total quantities as income levels rise—will be discussed below in a consideration of the concept of income elasticity.

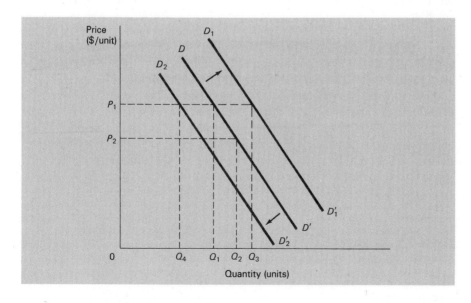

**Figure 7.3
Shifting Demand**

example of a specific demand function is the following linear[5] demand equation for Christmas trees in a given city:[6]

$$Q_D = 15,000 - 2500P + 2.50Y \qquad [7.3]$$

where Q_D = number of trees (quantity) sold
P = price of trees (measured in dollars)
Y = per capita disposable personal income (measured in dollars)

Note that this demand function contains only two explanatory variables—namely, price (P) and income (Y).

Other Factors Affecting Demand

Up to this point it has been implicitly assumed that we are considering the demand for consumer goods of a nondurable nature. These are goods purchased largely to meet current needs, and they generally provide service on a short-term basis. Food items, cleaning products, and virtually all services fall in this category. Although much of the foregoing discussion is relevant to the demand for durable as well as producers' goods, some unique characteristics about the demand for these items can be noted.

Durable Goods. *Durable goods* may be broadly defined as those that *yield services to their owners over a number of future time periods*. Because of the relatively long-term nature of the services provided by durables, the demand for these items is generally more volatile. One reason for this is that by their very nature durable goods *may be stored for periods of time*. If distributors, producers, and consumers (both final or intermediate) have accumulated large inventories of some durable good, an increase in the demand for that good may not show up in production for a considerable period of time, until inventories are worked off. Conversely, when inventories of the durable good are low, a small increase in demand may be magnified as distributors and producers increase inventories to accommodate even larger demand increases in the future. Another reason for this volatility is that the *replacement of a durable item may be delayed* from period to period by performing additional maintenance on existing items or by merely tolerating an old model. For example, an automobile may be repaired (or its out-of-date styling merely endured); an electric range may be fixed (at considerably less cost than buying a new range); or the discomforts of old furniture may be tolerated for "one more year." Thus an analysis of the demand for durable items must take account of both consumer desires and needs to expand the total stock of the durable good and the replacement of old, worn-out, or out-of-style products.[7]

---

[5] It is also possible to develop nonlinear demand functions, such as logarithmic models. The following chapter contains a discussion of these models.

[6] The procedures for estimating the slope and intercept parameters of demand equations are examined in the following chapter.

[7] Joel Dean, *Managerial Economics* (New York: Prentice-Hall, 1951), pp. 148–149.

As Joel Dean has observed, obsolescence in style, convenience, and prestige value probably plays a larger role in affecting the replacement of durables than does physical deterioration. An analysis of the expansion demand for durables is not fundamentally different from an analysis of the demand for nondurables. The significant difference between the two is that nondurables are purchased for present consumption, whereas durables are consumed or provide services over successive periods in the future. Also, *consumer expectations* regarding future levels of income, product availability, and product price play a major role in explaining the demand for durable goods. For example, a consumer may ask the following sorts of questions when embarking on a personal computer purchase:

- Will my income be sufficient and steady enough to make the payments on the computer?

- Are prices likely to rise or fall over the next year?

- Will new products soon make my computer obsolete? Will adequate software be available?

To a lesser extent, these factors also come into play in evaluating replacement demand. For these reasons an analysis of the demand for durable goods is more complex than a similar analysis for nondurables. The fluctuations in demand will be greater as consumers postpone or expand purchases based on their pessimism or optimism about future economic developments.

Derived Demand. In addition to the factors just discussed, the demand functions for some goods include the demand for another good as one of the independent variables. For example, the demand for automobile loans is not determined directly. Rather, it is *derived* from the demand for automobiles. This is also the case for *producers' goods.*

Producers' goods differ from consumer goods in that they are not produced for direct consumption but rather are the raw materials, capital equipment, and parts that are combined to produce a consumer good (or some other producers' good). As such, the demand for producers' goods may be thought of as a *derived demand* since it is derived from some ultimate consumer desire. For example, the demand for aluminium, a raw material, is not solely dependent on consumer desires and tastes for aluminium but rather on consumer desires and tastes for those products that are wholly or partially made of aluminium. These consumer preferences may be completely independent of the fact that aluminium is used in the production of the good.

It is essential, then, that in an analysis of the demand for some specific producers' good, or any other good for which the demand is derived, an account be taken of two sets of factors influencing this demand. First, we must consider the criteria or specifications used by the purchasing agent of the producing company that guide the agent in selecting one material, machine, process, or product over competitive alternatives. Second, and perhaps more important, we must take account of the significant factors affecting the demand for the ultimate consumer goods for which the producers' goods are inputs. Once this has been done, a demand analysis of producers' goods is conceptually the same as an analysis for a consumer good.

Price Elasticity of Demand

From a decision-making perspective the firm needs to know the effect of changes in any of the independent variables in the demand function on the quantity demanded. Some of these variables are under the control of management, such as price, advertising, product quality, and customer service. For these variables, management must know the effects of changes on quantity to assess the desirability of instituting the change. Other variables, including income, prices of competitors' products, and expectations of consumers regarding future prices, are outside the direct control of the firm. Nevertheless, effective forecasting of demand requires that the firm be able to measure the impact of changes in these variables on the quantity demanded.

Price Elasticity Defined

The most commonly used measure of the responsiveness of quantity demanded to changes in any of the variables that influence the demand function is *elasticity*. In general, *elasticity* may be thought of as a ratio of the percentage change in one quantity (or variable) to the percentage change in another, *ceteris paribus* (all other things remaining unchanged). In other words, how responsive is some dependent variable to changes in a particular variable? With this in mind, we define the *price elasticity of demand* (E_D) as the ratio of the percentage change in quantity demanded to a percentage change in price:

$$E_D = \frac{\%\Delta Q}{\%\Delta P}, \; ceteris \; paribus \qquad [7.4]$$

where ΔQ = change in quantity demanded
ΔP = change in price

Because of the normal inverse relationship between price and quantity demanded, the sign of the price elasticity coefficient will usually be negative. Occasionally, price elasticities are referred to as absolute values. In the passages that follow, the use of absolute values will be indicated where appropriate.

Arc Price Elasticity

The *arc* price elasticity of demand is a technique for calculating price elasticity between two prices. It indicates the effect of a change in price, from P_1 to P_2, on the quantity demanded. The following formula is used to compute this elasticity measure:

$$E_D = \frac{\dfrac{Q_2 - Q_1}{\left(\dfrac{Q_2 + Q_1}{2}\right)}}{\dfrac{P_2 - P_1}{\left(\dfrac{P_2 + P_1}{2}\right)}} \qquad [7.5]$$

where Q_1 = quantity sold before a price change
Q_2 = quantity sold after a price change
P_1 = original price
P_2 = price after a price change

The fraction $(Q_2 + Q_1)/2$ represents average quantity demanded in the range over which the price elasticity is being calculated. $(P_2 + P_1)/2$ also represents the average price over this range. Since both the numerator and denominator are divided by 2, the formula may be simplified to

$$E_D = \frac{\dfrac{Q_2 - Q_1}{Q_2 + Q_1}}{\dfrac{P_2 - P_1}{P_2 + P_1}}$$

[7.6]

or

$$E_D = \frac{Q_2 - Q_1}{P_2 - P_1} \cdot \frac{P_2 + P_1}{Q_2 + Q_1}$$

[7.7]

From this equation it is apparent that the elasticity measurement depends on the inverse of the *slope* of the ordinary demand curve

$$\frac{Q_2 - Q_1}{P_2 - P_1}$$

as well as the *position* on the curve or schedule where elasticity is calculated

$$\frac{P_2 + P_1}{Q_2 + Q_1}$$

Since the slope (or its inverse) remains constant over the entire schedule (*assuming linearity*), but the value of $(P_2 + P_1)/(Q_2 + Q_1)$ changes, depending on where on the demand curve elasticity is being calculated, *the value of the elasticity measure generally changes throughout the length of the demand curve*.

The calculation and use of price elasticity is illustrated in the following examples.

Example 1. Consider the demand schedule shown in Table 7.3. Calculate the price elasticity between an original price of $19 (14 units are demanded) and a new price of $18. Substituting the relevant data from Table 7.3 into Equation 7.6 yields:

$$E_D = \frac{\dfrac{16 - 14}{16 + 14}}{\dfrac{18 - 19}{18 + 19}}$$

$$= -2.46$$

Table 7.3
Demand Schedule:
Example 1

Price, P (dollars)	Quantity, Q_D (units)
20	12
19	14
18	16
17	18
16	20
12	28
11	30

A price elasticity of demand coefficient of -2.46 means that a 1 percent increase (decrease) in price can be expected to result in a 2.46 percent decrease (increase) in quantity demanded, *ceteris paribus*.

Now assume the original price was $12, and a new price of $11 is set. Determine the price elasticity of demand. Employing Equation 7.7 and the relevant data from Table 7.3 yields:

$$E_D = \frac{30 - 28}{11 - 12} \cdot \frac{11 + 12}{30 + 28} = -0.79$$

A price elasticity of demand of $-.79$ means that a 10 percent increase (decrease) in price can be expected to result in a 7.9 percent decrease (increase) in quantity demanded, *ceteris paribus*.

Example 2. We can also use Equation 7.6 to compute a price that would have to be charged to achieve a particular level of sales. Consider the NBA Corporation, which had monthly sneaker sales of 10,000 pairs (at $10 per pair) before a price cut by its major competitor. After this competitor's price reduction, NBA's sales declined to 8,000 pairs a month. From the past experience NBA has estimated the price elasticity of demand to be about -2.0 in this price-quantity range. If NBA wishes to restore its sales to 10,000 pairs a month, determine the price that must be charged.

Letting $Q_2 = 10,000$, $Q_1 = 8,000$, $P_1 = \$10$, and $E_D = -2.0$, the required price, P_2, may be computed using Equation 7.6:

$$-2.0 = \frac{\dfrac{10,000 - 8,000}{10,000 + 8,000}}{\dfrac{P_2 - 10}{P_2 + 10}}$$

$$P_2 = \$8.95$$

A price cut to $8.95 would be required to restore sales to 10,000 pairs a month.

Point Price Elasticity

The preceding formula measures the *arc elasticity* of demand; that is, elasticity is computed over a discrete range of the demand curve or schedule. Since the elasticity is normally different at each point on the curve, arc elasticity is a measure of the average elasticity over that range.

By employing some elementary calculus, the elasticity of demand at any *point* along the curve may be calculated with the following expression:

$$E_D = \frac{\partial Q_D}{\partial P} \cdot \frac{P}{Q_D}$$

[7.8]

where $\dfrac{\partial Q_D}{\partial P}$ = the partial derivative of quantity with respect to price (that is, the inverse of the slope of the demand curve)

Q_D = the quantity demanded at price P

P = the price at some specific point on the demand curve

The partial derivative of quantity with respect to price, $\partial Q_D/\partial P$, is merely an indication of the rate of change in quantity demanded as price changes. It is analogous to

$$\frac{Q_2 - Q_1}{P_2 - P_1}$$

in the arc elasticity measure.

The algebraic demand function for Christmas trees (Equation 7.3) introduced in the previous section can be used to illustrate the calculation of the point price elasticity. Suppose one is interested in determining the point price elasticity when the price (P) is equal to $8 and per capita disposable personal income (Y) is equal to $6,000. Taking the partial derivative of Equation 7.3 with respect to P yields:

$$\frac{\partial Q_D}{\partial P} = -2500$$

Substituting the relevant values for P and Y into Equation 7.3 gives:

$$Q_D = 15,000 - 2500(8) + 2.50(6,000) = 10,000$$

From Equation 7.8 one obtains:

$$E_D = -2500 \left(\frac{8}{10,000} \right) = -2.0$$

Interpreting the Price Elasticity: Relationship between the Price Elasticity and Revenues

Once the price elasticity of demand has been calculated, it is necessary to interpret the meaning of the number obtained. The elasticity coefficient may take on *absolute values* over the range from 0 to ∞ (infinity). Values in the indicated ranges are described in Table 7.4.

When demand is *unit* elastic, a percentage change in price P is matched by an equal percentage change in quantity demanded Q_D. When demand is *elastic*, a percentage change in P is exceeded by the percentage change in Q_D. For

Table 7.4
**Price Elasticity of
Demand in
Absolute Values**

Range	Description
$E_D = 0$	Perfectly inelastic
$0 < |E_D| < 1$	Inelastic
$|E_D| = 1$	Unit elastic
$1 < |E_D| < \infty$	Elastic
$|E_D| = \infty$	Perfectly elastic

inelastic demand, a percentage change in P results in a smaller percentage change in Q_D. The theoretical extremes of perfect elasticity and perfect inelasticity are illustrated in Figure 7.4. (These extremes are rarely encountered. Rather they illustrate the limits of price elasticity.)

The price elasticity of demand indicates the effect a change in price will have on the total revenue that is generated. Since total revenue TR is equal to price (average revenue) times the number of units sold, Q_D, we may determine, from our knowledge of demand elasticity, the effect on total revenue when price changes.

When demand elasticity is less than 1 in absolute value (or inelastic), an increase (decrease) in price will result in an increase (decrease) in total consumer expenditures $(P \cdot Q_D)$. This occurs because an inelastic demand indicates that a given percentage increase in price results in a smaller percentage decrease in quantity sold, the net effect being an increase in the total expenditures, $P \cdot Q_D$. Table 7.5 illustrates this point. It may be seen that when demand is *inelastic*—that is, $|E_D| < 1$—an increase in price from \$2 to \$3, for example, results in an increase in total revenue from \$18 to \$24.[8]

In contrast, when demand is *elastic*—that is, $|E_D| > 1$—a percentage increase (decrease) in price is more than offset by a larger percentage decrease (increase) in quantity sold. An increase in price from \$9 to \$10 results in a reduction in total consumer expenditure from \$18 to \$10 (see Table 7.5).

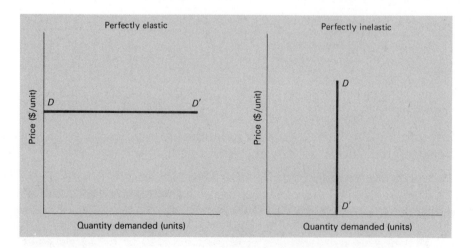

Figure 7.4
**Perfectly Elastic
and Inelastic
Demand Curves**

---

[8] The symbol $|E_D| < 1$ indicates that we are talking about the absolute value of the elasticity coefficient, rather than its actual negative value. This symbol (| |) is used whenever we refer to absolute values.

Price, P (dollars)	Quantity, Q_D (units)	Elasticity E_D	Total Revenue $P \cdot Q_D$ (dollars)	Marginal Revenue (dollars)
10	1		10	
9	2	−6.33	18	8
8	3	−3.40	24	6
7	4	−2.14	28	4
6	5	−1.44	30	2
5	6	−1.00	30	0
4	7	−0.69	28	−2
3	8	−0.46	24	−4
2	9	−0.29	18	−6
1	10	−0.15	10	−8

Table 7.5
Relationship between Elasticity and Marginal Revenue

When demand is *unit elastic*, a percentage change in price is exactly offset by the same percentage change in quantity demanded, the net result being a constant total consumer expenditure. If the price is increased from $5 to $6, total revenue would remain constant at $30, since the decrease in quantity demanded at the new price just offsets the price increase (see Table 7.5). It may be noted that when the price elasticity of demand $|E_D|$ is equal to 1 (or is unit elastic), the total revenue function is maximized. In the example, total revenue equals 30 when price P equals either 5 or 6 and quantity demanded Q_D equals either 6 or 5.

The relationship among price, quantity, elasticity measures, marginal revenue, and total revenue is illustrated graphically in Figure 7.5. When total revenue is maximized, marginal revenue equals zero and demand is unit elastic. At any price higher than P_1 (unit elasticity), the demand function is elastic. At lower prices the demand function is inelastic. Hence, successive equal percentage increases in price may be expected to generate greater and greater percentage decreases in quantity demanded because the demand function is becoming increasingly elastic (see Figure 7.5). Alternatively, successive equal percentage reductions in price may be expected to generate even lower percentage increases in quantity demanded because the demand function is more inelastic at lower prices.

The relationship between marginal revenue and price elasticity can be expressed algebraically as follows:[9]

$$MR = P \left(1 + \frac{1}{E_D}\right)$$

[7.9]

[9] This equation can be derived from the definitions of marginal revenue and price elasticity. Marginal revenue is equal to the first derivative of total revenue:

$$MR = \frac{d(TR)}{dQ_D} = \frac{d(P \cdot Q_D)}{dQ_D}$$

(*continued*)

Using this equation, one can demonstrate that when demand is unit elastic, marginal revenue is equal to zero. Substituting $E_D = -1$ into Equation 7.9 yields:

$$MR = P\left(1 + \frac{1}{-1}\right)$$
$$= P(0)$$
$$= 0$$

The fact that total revenue is maximized (and marginal revenue is equal to zero) when $|E_D| = 1$ can be shown with the following example. Given the demand function

$$Q_D = 150 - 10P \qquad [7.10]$$

one may rewrite the demand curve in terms of P as a function of Q_D.

$$P = 15 - \frac{Q_D}{10} \qquad [7.11]$$

Total revenue (TR) is equal to price times quantity sold.

$$TR = P \cdot Q_D$$
$$= \left(15 - \frac{Q_D}{10}\right)Q_D$$
$$= 15\,Q_D - \frac{Q_D^2}{10}$$

Footnote 9 (*Cont'd*)

Using the rule for taking the derivative of a product yields:

$$MR = P \cdot \frac{dQ_D}{dQ_D} + Q_D\frac{dP}{dQ_D}$$
$$= P + Q_D\frac{dP}{dQ_D}$$

This equation may be rewritten as

$$MR = P\left(1 + \frac{Q_D}{P} \cdot \frac{dP}{dQ_D}\right)$$

Recalling that the point price elasticity of demand is

$$E_D = \frac{dQ_D}{dP} \cdot \frac{P}{Q_D}$$

it can be seen that the term $\frac{Q_D}{P} \cdot \frac{dP}{dQ_D}$ is the reciprocal of the point price elasticity measure.

Hence, substituting $\frac{1}{E_D}$ for $\frac{Q_D}{P} \cdot \frac{dP}{dQ_D}$, results in Equation 7.9:

$$MR = P\left(1 + \frac{1}{E_D}\right)$$

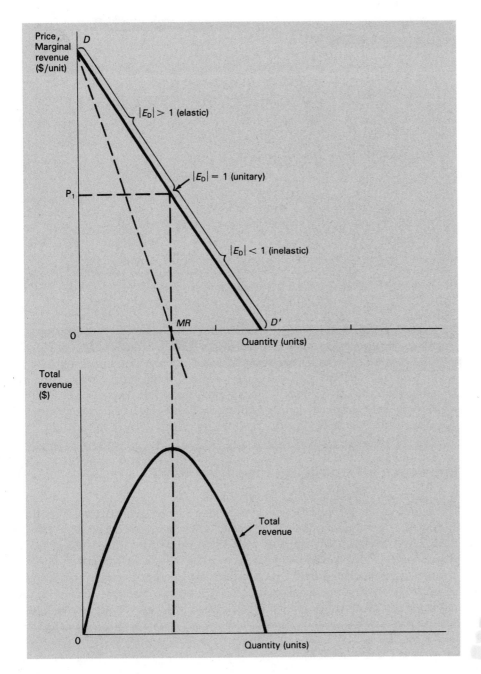

Figure 7.5
Price Elasticity over the Demand Function

Marginal revenue (MR) is equal to the first derivative of total revenue with respect to Q_D:

$$MR = \frac{d(TR)}{dQ_D} = 15 - \frac{Q_D}{5}$$

In order to find the value of Q_D where total revenue is maximized, set marginal revenue equal to zero:[10]

$$MR = 0$$

$$15 - \frac{Q_D}{5} = 0$$

$$Q_D^* = 75 \text{ units}$$

Substituting this value into Equation 7.11 yields

$$P^* = 15 - \frac{75}{10} = \$7.50 \text{ per unit}$$

Thus, total revenue is maximized at $Q_D = 75$ and $P = \$7.50$.
Checking:

$$E_D = \frac{\partial Q_D}{\partial P} \cdot \frac{P}{Q_D} = (-10)\frac{(7.5)}{75} = -1$$

$$|E_D| = 1$$

In addition to showing that $|E_D| = 1$ when the total revenue function is at its maximum, this example also demonstrates that marginal revenue MR is equal to zero when total revenue is maximized. This finding is not surprising when reminded that the definition of marginal revenue is the increase in total revenue resulting from the sale of one additional unit. Beyond the output level where total revenue is maximized, marginal revenue becomes negative and total revenue declines; that is, $|E_D| < 1$.

Importance of Elasticity-Revenue Relationships

It is extremely important for decision makers to be aware of the relationship between price, elasticity, and total revenue. For example, an urban transit system faced with large, continuous operating deficits may be tempted to raise its fares to increase revenues. This strategy will only be successful if the current fare structure is such that demand is inelastic. In the unhappy case that total revenues are already being maximized by present fares—that is, the elasticity of demand is unitary—any further increases in fares will be self-defeating, leading to a reduction in total revenues and increased losses if service levels are maintained.

Empirical Price Elasticities

Economists have made many estimates of the price elasticity of demand for a wide variety of goods and services. A number of empirically determined price

---

[10] To be certain one has found values for P and Q_D, where total revenue is maximized rather than minimized, check the second derivative of TR to see that it is negative. In this case $d^2TR/dQ_D^2 = -1/5$, so the total revenue function is maximized.

Commodity	Price Elasticity
Corn	-0.77^a
Beef	-0.50^b
Butter	-0.70^b
Milk	-0.31^b
Wheat	-0.03^a
Air transportation	-1.10^c
Wool	-1.32^d
Furniture	-3.04^e
School lunches	-0.47^f
Outdoor recreation	-0.12 to $-.56^g$

Table 7.6
Empirical Price Elasticities

Sources:

[a] Henry Schultz, *The Theory and Measurement of Demand* (Chicago: University of Chicago Press 1938).

[b] Herman Wold, *Demand Analysis* (New York: John Wiley, 1953).

[c] Ragnar Frisch, "A Complete Scheme for Computing All Direct Cross Demand Elasticities in a Model with Many Sectors," *Econometrica* 28 (1959), pp. 177–96.

[d] C. E. Ferguson and M Polasek, "The Elasticity of Import Demand for Raw Apparel Wood in the United States," *Econometrica* 30 (1962), pp. 670–99.

[e] Richard D. Stone and D. A. Rowe, "The Durability of Consumers' Durable Goods", *Econometrica* 28 (1960), pp. 407–16.

[f] George A. Braley and P. E. Nelson, Jr., "Effect of a Controlled Price Increase on School Lunch Participation: Pittsburgh, 1973," *American Journal of Agricultural Economics* (February, 1975), pp. 90–96.

[g] Russell L. Gum and W. E. Martin, "Problems and Solutions in Estimating the Demand for and Value of Rural Outdoor Recreation," *American Journal of Agricultural Economics* (November 1975), pp. 558–566.

elasticities are shown in Table 7.6. This table indicates that the demand for furniture, a durable good, is extremely price elastic (-3.04), whereas the demand for wheat (-0.03) is extremely price inelastic. Additional empirically determined elasticities are discussed in the next chapter.

A study by Huang, Siegfried, and Zardoshty on the demand for coffee confirms the relationship between price levels and the price elasticity of demand shown in Figure 7.5.[11] After studying coffee demand for the period 1963–1977, they found that the price elasticity of demand for that period ranged from -0.10 for price levels prevailing throughout most of the period to -0.89 for the peak price level, which occurred in the second quarter of 1977. Thus coffee users are nearly nine times more sensitive to price changes at high prices than at lower price levels.

Factors Affecting the Price Elasticity of Demand

As shown in Table 7.6, price elasticities vary greatly among different products and services. Some of the factors that account for the differing responsiveness of consumers to price changes are examined below.

---

[11] Cliff J. Huang, J. J. Siegfried, and F. Zardoshty, "The Demand for Coffee in the United States, 1963–1977," *Quarterly Review of Economics and Business* (Summer 1980), pp. 36–50.

Availability of Substitutes. The most important determinant of the price elasticity of demand is the availability and closeness of substitutes. The greater the number of substitute goods, the more price elastic is the demand for a product because a customer can easily shift to a substitute good if the price of a product in question increases. The availability of substitutes relates not only to different products, such as butter and margarine or beef and pork, but also to the availability of the same product from different producers. For example, the demand for Chevrolets is likely to be very price elastic because of the ready availability of close substitutes such as Fords, Plymouths, and Volkswagens.

Durable Goods. The demand for durable goods tends to be more price elastic than the demand for nondurables. This is true because of the ready availability of a relatively inexpensive substitute in many cases; that is, repairing a worn-out durable good, such as a TV, car, or refrigerator, rather than buying a new one. Consumers of durable goods are often in a position to wait for a more favorable price, a sale, or a special deal when buying these items. This accounts for some of the volatility in the demand for durable goods.

Relative Size of Expenditures. The demand for relatively high-priced goods tends to be more price elastic than the demand for inexpensive items. This is true because expensive items account for a greater portion of a person's income and potential expenditures than do low-priced items. Consequently, we would expect the demand for automobiles to be more price elastic than the demand for children's toys.

Time Frame of Analysis. Over time, the demand for many products tends to become more elastic because of the increase in the number of effective substitutes that become available. For example, in the short run, the demand for gasoline may be relatively price inelastic because the only available alternatives are not taking a trip or using some form of public transportation. Over time, as consumers replace their cars, they find another excellent substitute for gasoline—namely, more fuel-efficient vehicles. Also, other product alternatives may come available, such as electric cars or cars powered by natural gas or coal.

Income Elasticity of Demand

Among the variables that affect demand, income is often one of the most important. Analogous to the price elasticity of demand, one can also compute an income elasticity of demand.

Income Elasticity Defined

Income elasticity of demand measures the responsiveness of a change in quantity demanded of some commodity to a change in income. It can be

Economic Analysis and Managerial Efficiency

SELLING VANITY LICENSE PLATES

Many states offer drivers an opportunity to express their individuality with their automobile license plates. For the privilege of having your license plate imprinted with your own custom message—such as SINGLE, PISCES, AG OF 81, PLIBIT, MY BENZ, B-PHIT—drivers normally pay a small premium to the state.

In 1965 when vanity license plates were introduced in Texas, they could be acquired for a mere $10 over the cost of a normal license plate. By 1985 the price had jumped to $25. At this price 154,000 Texans invested in "their own automotive identity." As Texas entered the oil price recession of the mid-eighties, however, legislative leaders frantically scrambled for new sources of revenue.

In 1986 the Texas legislature tripled the price to $75. Sales tumbled to only 56,000 custom plates. Faced with this sudden decline in demand, the legislature cut the price to $40 for 1987. The Texas legislators learned a quick lesson in the concept of price elasticity.

Questions

1. What assumptions do you believe led the legislature to increase the price in 1986?

2. Compute the arc price elasticity of demand between $25 and $75, assuming no other factors affecting the demand for license plates changed between 1985 and 1986. Given this calculation, why do you feel the legislature cut the price to $40 for 1987?

3. What other factors should be considered in future pricing decisions by the legislature?

expressed as

$$E_y = \frac{\%\Delta Q_D}{\%\Delta Y}, ceteris\ paribus \qquad [7.12]$$

where ΔQ_D = change in quantity demanded

ΔY = change in income

Various measures of income can be used in the analysis. One commonly used measure is consumer disposable income, calculated on an aggregate, household, or per capita basis.

Arc Income Elasticity

The *arc* income elasticity is a technique for calculating income elasticity between two income levels. It is computed as

$$E_y = \frac{\dfrac{Q_2 - Q_1}{Q_2 + Q_1}}{\dfrac{Y_2 - Y_1}{Y_2 + Y_1}} \qquad [7.13]$$

or

$$E_y = \frac{Q_2 - Q_1}{Y_2 - Y_1} \cdot \frac{Y_2 + Y_1}{Q_2 + Q_1}$$ [7.14]

where Q_2 = quantity sold after an income change
Q_1 = quantity sold before an income change
Y_2 = new level of income
Y_1 = original level of income

The income elasticity calculation can be illustrated with the following example. Assume that an increase in disposable personal income from \$100 million to \$110 million is associated with an increase in boat sales from 50,000 to 60,000 units. Determine the income elasticity over this range. Substituting the relevant data into Equation 7.13 yields:

$$E_y = \frac{\dfrac{60,000 - 50,000}{60,000 + 50,000}}{\dfrac{110 - 100}{110 + 100}}$$

$$= 1.91$$

Thus, a 10 percent increase in income would be expected to result in a 19.1 percent increase in quantity demanded, *ceteris paribus*. Recall that this calculation assumes that all other factors influencing quantity demanded have remained unchanged. If this assumption (*ceteris paribus*) is not met, the calculated elasticity measure may be quite misleading. This warning applies to all elasticity calculations.

Point Income Elasticity

The arc income elasticity measures the responsiveness of quantity demanded to changes in income levels over a range. In contrast, the *point* income elasticity provides a measure of this responsiveness at a specific point on the demand function. The point income elasticity is defined as

$$E_y = \frac{\partial Q_D}{\partial Y} \cdot \frac{Y}{Q_D}$$ [7.15]

where Y = income
Q_D = quantity demanded of some commodity
$\dfrac{\partial Q_D}{\partial Y}$ = the partial derivative of quantity with respect to income

The algebraic demand function for Christmas trees (Equation 7.3) introduced earlier in the chapter can be used to illustrate the calculation of the point income elasticity. Suppose one is interested in determining the point income elasticity when the price is equal to $8 and per capita personal disposable income is equal to $6,000. Taking the partial derivative of Equation 7.3 with respect to Y yields:

$$\frac{\partial Q_D}{\partial Y} = 2.50$$

Recall from the point price elasticity calculation described earlier in the chapter that substituting $P = \$8$ and $Y = \$6000$ into Equation 7.3 gave Q_D equal to 10,000 units.

Therefore, from Equation 7.15, one obtains

$$E_y = 2.50 \left(\frac{6,000}{10,000}\right) = 1.50$$

Interpreting the Income Elasticity

For most products, income elasticity is expected to be positive; that is, $E_y > 0$. Such goods are referred to as *normal* goods. Those goods having a calculated income elasticity that is negative are called *inferior* goods. Inferior goods are those that are purchased in smaller absolute quantities as the income of the consumer increases. Such food items as pork and beans and mush are frequently cited as examples of inferior goods. They may compose a large part of a low-income diet but may virtually disappear from the diet as income levels increase.

Income elasticity is typically defined as being *low* when it is between 0 and 1 and *high* if it is greater than 1. Goods that are normally considered luxury items generally have a high income elasticity, whereas goods that are necessities (or perceived as necessities) have low income elasticities.

Knowledge of the magnitude of the income elasticity of demand for a particular product is especially useful in relating forecasts of economic activity, such as an expected increase in disposable personal income, to the effects it will have on a particular industry. In industries that produce goods having high income elasticities (such as most durable goods producers) a major increase or decrease in economic activity will have a significant impact on the performance of firms in that industry during the period of projection.[12] Knowledge of income elasticities is also useful in developing marketing strategies for products. For example, products having a high income elasticity can be promoted as being luxurious and stylish, whereas goods having a low income elasticity can be promoted as being economical.

Empirical Income Elasticities

As an example of a study of income elasticities, Roistacher found that low-income renters have an income elasticity for housing of 0.22, whereas

---

[12] This could be measured in a number of ways, such as changes in GNP, national income, disposable personal income, or some other variable judged especially relevant to the industry being examined.

households that switch from renting to owning have a higher elasticity of 0.34.[13] This means that in the case of low-income renters, a 10 percent increase in income will result in an increase of 2.2 percent in their annual expenditures on housing. In the case of households switching from renting to owning, a 10 percent increase in income will result in a 3.4 percent increase in annual expenditures on housing.

It should be emphasized, however, that demand is a function of more than just consumer income levels. For example, an expected increase in industry sales brought about by anticipated increases in consumer income might be more than offset by a decline in the price of a close substitute product or by some other factor. As will become more apparent in Chapters 8 and 9, a meaningful analysis and forecast of demand requires a consideration of all major variables influencing the demand for a particular commodity.

Cross Elasticity of Demand

Another variable that often affects the demand for a product is the price of a related (substitute or complementary) product.

Cross Elasticity Defined

The *cross elasticity of demand*, E_x, (also called *cross-price elasticity*) is a measure of the responsiveness of changes in the quantity demanded (Q_{DA}) of Product A to price changes for Product $B(P_B)$.

$$E_x = \frac{\%\Delta Q_{DA}}{\%\Delta P_B}, \text{ ceteris paribus} \qquad [7.16]$$

where ΔQ_{DA} = change in quantity demanded of Product A
P_B = change in price of Product B

Arc Cross Elasticity

The *arc* cross elasticity is a technique for computing cross elasticity between two price levels. It is calculated as

$$E_x = \frac{\dfrac{Q_{A2} - Q_{A1}}{Q_{A2} + Q_{A1}}}{\dfrac{P_{B2} - P_{B1}}{P_{B2} + P_{B1}}} \qquad [7.17]$$

---

[13] Elizabeth A. Roistacher, "Short-Run Housing Responses to Changes in Income," *American Economic Review* (February 1977), pp. 381–386.

or

$$E_x = \frac{Q_{A2} - Q_{A1}}{P_{B2} - P_{B1}} \cdot \frac{P_{B2} + P_{B1}}{Q_{A2} + Q_{A1}}$$

[7.18]

where Q_{A2} = quantity demanded of A after a price change in B
Q_{A1} = original quantity demanded of A
P_{B2} = new price for Product B
P_{B1} = original price for Product B

For example, suppose the price of butter P_B increases from \$1 to \$1.50 per pound. As a result, the quantity demanded of margarine Q_A increases from 500 pounds to 600 pounds a month at a local grocery store. Compute the arc cross elasticity of demand. Substituting the relevant data into Equation 7.17 yields:

$$E_x = \frac{\dfrac{600 - 500}{600 + 500}}{\dfrac{1.50 - 1.00}{1.50 + 1.00}}$$

$$= 0.45$$

This indicates that a 1 percent increase in the price of butter will lead to a 0.45 percent increase in the quantity demanded of margarine, which is, of course, a butter substitute, *ceteris paribus*.

Point Cross Elasticity

In similar fashion, the *point* cross elasticity between Products A and B may be computed as

$$E_x = \frac{\partial Q_A}{\partial P_B} \cdot \frac{P_B}{Q_A}$$

[7.19]

where P_B = price of Product B
Q_A = quantity demanded of Product A when the price of Product B equals P_B
$\dfrac{\partial Q_A}{\partial P_B}$ = the partial derivative of Q_A with respect to P_B

Interpreting the Cross Elasticity

If the cross elasticity measured between items A and B is *positive* (as might be expected in our butter/margarine example or between such products as plastic wrap and aluminium foil), the two products are referred to as *substitutes* for each other. The higher the cross elasticity, the closer the substitute relationship. A *negative* cross elasticity, on the other hand, indicates that the two products are

Table 7.7
Electricity-Use
Elasticities

	Price Elasticity	Income Elasticity	Cross Elasticity (gas)
Residential Market	−1.3	0.3	0.15
Commercial Market	−1.5	0.9	0.15
Industrial Market	−1.7	1.1	0.15

complementary. For example, a decrease in the price of prerecorded cassettes would probably result in an increase in the demand for cassette recorders.

The number of close substitutes that a product has may be an important determinant of market structure. The fewer and poorer the number of close substitutes that exist for a product, the greater the amount of monopoly power that is possessed by the producing or selling firm (and conversely, the more and better substitutes, the closer the market structure approximates a competitive market).

An Empirical Example of Price, Income, and Cross Elasticities

Economists have done much empirical work to estimate the various elasticity measures for a wide range of goods and services. With the increased emphasis on the price and availability of energy resources in the United States, an obvious need exists for accurate elasticity measures of the demand for such goods as electric power.

A study by Chapman, Tyrrell, and Mount examined the elasticity of energy use by residential, commercial, and industrial users during the period 1946–1972.[14] They hypothesized that the demand for electricity was determined by the price of electricity, income levels, and the price of a substitute good—natural gas.

Table 7.7 summarizes the electricity-use elasticities with respect to price, income, and natural gas prices. As shown in the table, price elasticity of demand for electricity is relatively elastic in all markets, with the highest price elasticity being in the industrial market. The significant decline in the growth rate in demand for electricity since the energy crisis-induced price increases is consistent with these results. The income elasticity figures indicate that electricity use tends to increase with increases in income. The positive cross-elasticity values show that electricity and natural gas are, indeed, substitute goods.

Other Demand Elasticity Measures

Price, income, and cross-elasticity measures are the most common applications of the elasticity concept to demand analysis. It should be remembered, however, that elasticity is a general concept relating the responsiveness (or relative

---

[14] D. Chapman, T. Tyrell, and T. Mount, "Electricity Demand Growth and the Energy Crisis," *Science*, 17 November 1972, p. 705.

change) of one variable to changes in another variable. With this in mind, this section briefly defines some less common elasticities.[15]

Advertising Elasticity

Advertising elasticity measures the responsiveness of sales to changes in advertising expenditures. It is measured by the ratio of the percentage change in sales to a percentage change in advertising expenditures. The higher the advertising elasticity coefficient, the more responsive sales are to changes in the advertising budget. An awareness of this elasticity measure may assist advertising or marketing managers in their determination of appropriate levels of advertising outlays.

Elasticity of Price Expectations

In an inflationary environment, the elasticity of price expectations may provide helpful insights. It is defined as the percentage change in *future* prices expected as a result of current percentage price changes. When the coefficient exceeds unity, it indicates that buyers expect future prices to rise (or fall) by a greater percentage amount than current prices. A positive coefficient that is less than unity indicates that buyers expect future prices to increase (or decrease), but by a lesser percentage amount than current price changes. A zero coefficient indicates that consumers feel that current price changes have no influence on future changes. Finally, a negative coefficient indicates that consumers believe an increase (decrease) in current prices will lead to a decrease (increase) in future prices.

A positive coefficient of price expectations (especially one greater than unity) suggests that current price increases may shift the demand function to the right. This may result in the same or greater sales at the higher prices as consumers try to beat future price increases by stockpiling the commodity. The sugar price rise of 1975 can be explained, at least in part, by the effects of a high elasticity of price expectations. Eventually a competitor's reactions or the large inventory of the product in the consumers' hands will tend to lower the price expectations elasticity, perhaps turning it negative, and result in a shift to the left in the demand function.

---

[15] In addition to demand elasticities, one can also define a price elasticity of *supply*. The price elasticity of supply measures the responsiveness of quantity supplied by producers to changes in prices. An inelastic supply function is one whose price elasticity coefficient is less than unity. It indicates that a 1 percent change in price will lead to a less than 1 percent change in quantity supplied. An elastic supply function has an elasticity coefficient greater than unity, indicating that a 1 percent change in price will result in a greater-than-1-percent change in quantity supplied. Since producers are normally willing to supply more at higher prices, the sign of the price elasticity coefficient of supply will normally be positive.

Combined Effect of Demand Elasticities

When two or more of the factors that affect demand change simultaneously, one is often interested in determining their combined impact on quantity demanded. For example, suppose that a firm plans to increase the price of its product next period and anticipates that consumers' incomes will also increase next period. Other factors affecting demand, such as advertising expenditures and competitors' prices are expected to remain the same in the next period. From the formula for the price elasticity (Equation 7.4), the effect on quantity demanded of a price increase would be equal to

$$\%\Delta Q_D = E_D(\%\Delta P)$$

Similarly, from the formula for the income elasticity (Equation 7.12), the effect on quantity demanded of an increase in consumers' incomes would be equal to

$$\%\Delta Q_D = E_y(\%\Delta Y)$$

Each of these percentage changes (divided by 100 to put them in a decimal form) would be multiplied by current period demand (Q_1) to get the respective changes in quantity demanded caused by the price and income increases. Assuming that the price and income effects are *independent* and *additive*, the quantity demanded next period (Q_2) would be equal to current period demand (Q_1) plus the changes caused by the price and income increases:

$$Q_2 = Q_1 + Q_1 [E_D(\%\Delta P)] + Q_1 [E_y(\%\Delta Y)]$$

$$Q_2 = Q_1 [1 + E_D(\%\Delta P) + E_y(\%\Delta Y)] \qquad [7.20]$$

An example can be used to illustrate the application of this concept. Consider the case of a firm that is planning to increase the price of its product by 10 percent in the coming year. Economic forecasters expect real disposable personal income to increase by 6 percent during the same period. From past experience, the price elasticity of demand has been estimated to be approximately -1.3 and the income elasticity has been estimated at 2.0. These elasticities are assumed to remain constant over the range of price and income changes anticipated. The firm currently sells two million units of its product per year. Determine the forecasted demand for next year (assuming that the percentage price and income effects are independent and additive). Substituting the relevant data into Equation 7.20 yields:

$$Q_2 = 2,000,000 [1 + (-1.3)(.10) + (2.0)(.06)]$$
$$= 1,980,000 \text{ units}$$

The forecasted demand for next year is 1.98 million units assuming that other factors that influence demand, such as advertising and competitors' prices, remain unchanged. In this case, the positive impact of the projected increase in income is more than offset by the decline in quantity demanded associated with a price increase.

The combined use of income and price elasticities, illustrated here for forecasting demand, can be generalized to include any of the elasticity concepts that were developed in the preceding sections of this chapter.

Summary

- Demand relationships can be represented in the form of a schedule (table), graph, or algebraic function. Each of these methods of presentation provides insights into the demand concept.

- The demand curve is typically downward sloping, indicating that consumers are willing to purchase more units of a good or service at lower prices. The downward-sloping demand curve can be explained by the law of diminishing marginal utility.

- Changes in price result in *movement* along the demand curve, whereas changes in any of the other variables in the demand function result in *shifts* of the entire demand curve. Thus changes in quantity demanded along a particular demand curve result from price changes. In contrast, when one speaks of changes in demand, one is referring to shifts in the entire demand curve.

- Some of the factors that cause a shift in the entire demand curve are changes in the income level of consumers, the price of substitute and complementary goods, the level of advertising, competitors' advertising expenditures, population, consumer preferences, and price expectations.

- Elasticity refers to the responsiveness of one economic variable to changes in another, related variable. Thus *price elasticity* of demand refers to the percentage change in quantity demanded associated with a percentage change in price, holding constant the effects of other factors thought to influence demand. Demand is said to be relatively price *elastic* if a percentage change in price results in a greater percentage change in quantity demanded. Demand is said to be relatively price *inelastic* if a percentage change in price results in a lesser percentage change in quantity demanded.

- When demand is unit elastic, marginal revenue equals zero and total revenue is maximized. When demand is elastic, an increase (decrease) in price will result in a decrease (increase) in total revenue. When demand is inelastic, an increase (decrease) in price will result in an increase (decrease) in total revenue.

- *Income elasticity* of demand refers to the percentage change in quantity demanded associated with a percentage change in income, holding constant the effects of other factors thought to influence demand.

- *Cross elasticity* of demand refers to the percentage change in quantity demanded of some good *A* associated with a percentage change in the price of some other good *B*.

- An understanding of the magnitude of various elasticity measures for a product can be extremely helpful when forecasting demand for that product.

Selected References

Baumol, William J. *Economic Theory and Operations Analysis*, 4th ed. Englewood Cliffs, N.J.: Prentice-Hall, 1977.

Chapman, D., T. Tyrell, and T. Mount. "Electricity Demand Growth and the Energy Crisis," *Science*, 17 November 1972, p. 705.

Cohen, Kalman J., and Richard M. Cyert. *Theory of the Firm: Resource Allocation in a Market Economy*, 2nd ed. Englewood Cliffs, N.J.: Prentice-Hall, 1975.

Dean, Joel. *Managerial Economics*. New York: Prentice-Hall, 1951.

Gahvari, Firoz. "Demand and Supply of Housing in the U.S., 1929–1978." *Economic Inquiry* (April 1986), pp. 333–347.

Henderson, James M., and Richard E. Quandt. *Microeconomic Theory*, 2d ed. New York: McGraw-Hill, 1971.

Hirshleifer, Jack. *Price Theory and Application*, 2nd ed. Englewood Cliffs, N.J.: Prentice-Hall, 1980.

Hoffer, G. E., and R. J. Reilly. "Automobile Styling as a Shift Variable: An Investigation by Firm and by Industry." *Applied Economics* 16 (1984), pp. 291–297.

Kimball, James N. "The Price Elasticity of Demand and Its Effect on Public Utility Revenues." *Public Utilities Fortnightly*, 4 December 1980, pp. 53–54.

Leftwich, Richard H., and Ross D. Eckert. *The Price System and Resource Allocation*, 9th ed. New York: Dryden Press, 1985.

Reckie, W. D. "The Price Elasticity of Demand for Evening Newspapers." *Applied Economics* (March 1976), pp. 69–79.

Suits, D. B. "The Elasticity of Demand for Gambling." *Quarterly Journal of Economics* (February 1979), pp. 155–162.

Discussion Questions

1. What is meant by a *change in quantity demanded* as opposed to a *shift in demand?*

2. What is the difference between a *point elasticity* measure and an *arc elasticity* measure of demand?

3. What is the relationship between the price elasticity of demand and the effect of price changes on the total revenues received by a firm?

4. Over long periods of time the demand for most products tends to become relatively more price elastic. Why?

5. Prove that a linear demand curve cannot have a constant price elasticity.

6. "Because of the American love affair with driving and the automobile, increases in the price of gasoline will not affect consumption." What type of demand curve is implied by this statement? Do you believe this is true? Why?

7. Some proposals for tax reform would eliminate the interest deduction for second homes. Explain the impact this would have on the disposable income of owners of second homes and on the price of second homes in the marketplace.

8. What do you think the cross price elasticity of demand is between propane and fuel oil used for home heating?

9. How do the income and substitution effects help to determine the shape of the typical demand curve?

10. In the early 1970s, Southwest Airlines entered the Texas intrastate air service market providing service between Houston, Dallas, and San Antonio. Southwest dramatically

reduced its airfares below those charged by its major competitors. Since this initial entry into the market, Southwest has grown and prospered and become one of the most profitable airlines in the United States.

What factors led to Southwest's phenomenal success? How did Southwest perceive the demand function for airline travel? How did its competitors perceive this demand function?

11. Given your knowledge of factors that influence the price elasticity of demand, how would you describe the price elasticity of demand for the following items: (Justify your answer.)

   a. Automatic dishwashers
   b. Salt
   c. Morton's brand of salt
   d. Vacation air travel
   e. Business air travel
   f. New automobiles
   g. Chevrolet Caprice automobiles
   h. Gasoline (over the next year)
   i. Gasoline (over the next five years)
   j. Bread

12. Explain or show graphically in what portion of its demand curve (elastic, inelastic, or unit elastic) a firm is most likely to operate. Under what circumstances might a firm violate this principle?

13. The total demand for gasoline is quite price inelastic, whereas the demand for branded gasoline is highly elastic. In view of this situation:

   a. How important is price competition among sellers of name-brand gasolines?
   b. What is the likely effect of a gas price war on gasoline companies?
   c. What type of competition is most frequently observed in the retail gasoline market?
   d. What is the major appeal of the independent gasoline retailer? Why have these retailers been able to sell gas below the branded price and generally not precipitate competitive price cutting from the branded majors?

14. What would you expect the advertising elasticity of demand to be for a firm in a purely competitive market? What would you expect it to be in an oligopoly market characterized by highly differentiated products, such as automobiles?

15. The concept of elasticity is very general. Describe what might be meant by the temperature elasticity of demand when used in the context of electric utilities or natural gas distribution utilities.

16. Table 7.7 reports the price elasticity of demand for electricity use in the residential, commercial, and industrial markets. Why do you think demand is more price elastic in the industrial market than in the residential market?

17. If the price of VCRs declines by 20 percent and the total revenue from the sale of VCRs rises, what can you say about the price elasticity of demand for VCRs? Will this price reduction necessarily lead to an increase in profits for VCR manufacturers?

18. The cross-price elasticity of demand for Washington State apples relative to Pennsylvania apples is +0.7. What can be said about the perceived differences in quality between the two apple varieties? How would your answer change if the cross price elasticity were only +0.1?

Problems

1. Jenkins Photo Co. manufactures an automatic camera that currently sells for $90. Sales volume is about 2,000 cameras per month. A close competitor, the B.J. Photo Company, has cut the price of a similar camera it makes from $100 to $80. Jenkins' economist has estimated the cross elasticity of demand between the two firms' products at about 0.4, given current income and price levels.

   What impact, if any, will the action by B.J. have on total revenue generated by Jenkins, if Jenkins leaves its current price unchanged?

2. The Potomac Range Corporation manufactures a line of ultrasonic ovens costing $500 each. Its sales have averaged about 6,000 units per month during the past year. In August, Potomac's closest competitor, Spring City Stove Works, cut their price for a closely competitive model from $600 to $450. Potomac noticed that its sales volume declined to 4,500 units per month after Spring City announced its price cut.

   a. What is the arc cross elasticity of demand between Potomac's oven and the competitive Spring City model?

   b. Would you say that these two firms are very close competitors? What other factors could have influenced the observed relationship?

   c. If Potomac knows that the arc price elasticity of demand for its ovens is -3.0, what price would Potomac have to charge to sell the same number of units it did before the Spring City price cut?

3. The price elasticity of demand for personal computers is estimated to be -2.2. If the price of personal computers declines by 20 percent, what will be the expected percentage increase in the quantity of computers sold?

4. The Olde Yogurt Factory has reduced the price of its popular Mmmm Sundae from $2.25 to $1.75. As a result, the firm's daily sales of these sundaes have increased from 1,500/day to 1,800/day. Compute the arc price elasticity of demand over this price and consumption quantity range.

5. The subway fare in your town has just been increased from a current level of 50 cents to $1.00 per ride. As a result, the transit authority notes a decline in ridership of 30 percent.

   a. Compute the price elasticity of demand for subway rides.

   b. If the transit authority reduces the fare back to 50 cents, what impact would you expect on the ridership? Why?

6. The demand for mobile homes in Azerpajama, a small, oil-rich sheikdom, has been estimated to be $Q_D = 250,000 - 35P$. If this relationship remains approximately valid in the future:

   a. How many mobile homes would be demanded at a price of $2,000? $4,000? $6,000?

   b. What is the *arc* price elasticity of demand between $2,000 and $4,000? Between $4,000 and $6,000?

   c. What is the *point* price elasticity of demand at $2,000, $4,000, and $6,000?

   d. If 25,000 mobile homes were sold last year, what would you expect the average price to have been?

   e. In a move to increase his popularity (and in the face of rapidly accumulating oil royalties) Sheik Archie has decided to subsidize the price of mobile homes and offer them to all who want them at a price of only $1,000. As the sheik's chief adviser, how many homes would you expect to be bought at this bargain-basement price? At this price, how confident are you of the estimated demand equation?

f. Without subsidy, what is the highest theoretical price that anyone would pay for a mobile home in the sheikdom?

7. A number of empirical studies of automobile demand have been made yielding the following estimates of income and price elasticities:

Study	Income Elasticity	Price Elasticity
Chow	+3.0	−1.2
Alkinson	+2.5	−1.4
Roos and Von Szeliski	+2.5	−1.5
Suits (as reworked)	+3.9	−1.2

Assume also that income and price effects on automobile sales are *independent* and *additive*. Assume also that the auto companies intend to increase the average price of an automobile by about 6 percent in the next year and that next year's disposable personal income is expected to be 4 percent higher than this year's. If this year's automobile sales were 11 million units, how many would you expect to be sold under each pair of price and income demand elasticity estimates?

8. A typical consumer behaved in the following manner with respect to purchases of butter over the past eight years:

Year	Price of butter ($/pound)	Quantity of butter purchased (pounds)	Real income (dollars)	Price of margarine ($/pound)
1	$ .95	200	$11,000	$ .65
2	1.10	180	11,000	.65
3	1.10	190	11,500	.65
4	1.10	200	11,500	.90
5	1.15	170	11,500	.90
6	.99	190	11,500	.90
7	.99	175	10,500	.90
8	.99	150	10,500	.65

Compute all meaningful price, income, and cross-elasticity coefficients. (Remember that the effects of other factors need to be held constant when computing any one of these coefficients.)

9. If the marginal revenue from a product is $15 and the price elasticity of demand is −1.2, what is the price of the product?

10. If the price elasticity of demand for cable TV connections is high (for example, greater than 1.5) and the price elasticity of demand for movies shown in theaters is less than 1, what strategy would you expect cable TV firms to follow in arranging for initial hookups?

11. The demand function for bicycles in Holland has been estimated to be:

$$Q = 2,000 + 15Y - 5.5P$$

where Y is income in *thousands* of dollars, Q is the quantity demanded in units, and P is the price unit. When $P = \$150$ and $Y = \$15(000)$, determine the following:

a. Price elasticity of demand

b. Income elasticity of demand

12. Two goods have a cross-price elasticity of $+1.2$.

    a. Would you describe these goods as substitutes or complements?

    b. If the price of one of the goods increases by 5 percent, what will happen to the demand for the other product, holding constant the effects of all other factors?

13. In an attempt to increase revenues and profits, a firm is considering a 4 percent increase in price and an 11 percent increase in advertising. If the price elasticity of demand is -1.5 and the advertising elasticity of demand is $+0.6$, would you expect an increase or decrease in total revenues?

14. During 19X5 the demand for a firm's product has been estimated to be:

$$Q = 1000 - 200P$$

During 19X6 the demand for that same firm's product has been estimated to be

$$Q = 1150 - 225P$$

If the price was $2 during 19X5 and $3 during 19X6, has the price elasticity of demand for this product been increasing or decreasing?

15. Between 19X1 and 19X2, the quantity of automobiles produced and sold declined by 20 percent. During this period the real price of cars increased by 5 percent, real income levels declined by 2 percent, and the real cost of gasoline increased by 20 percent. Knowing that the income elasticity of demand is $+1.5$ and the cross price elasticity of gasoline and cars is -0.3,

    a. Compute the impact of the decline in real income levels on the demand for cars.

    b. Compute the impact of the gasoline price increase on the demand for cars.

    c. Compute the price elasticity of the demand for cars during this period.

16. Compute the price elasticity of demand and the income elasticity of demand at the prices and income specified in the following demand function:

$$Q = 25 - 4P + 6I$$

    a. When $I = 10$ and $P = 4$

    b. When $I = 4$ and $P = 6$

17. The demand function for school lunches in Pittsburgh has been estimated to be

$$Q = 16{,}415.21 - 262.743P$$

where $Q =$ lunches served

$P =$ price in cents

    a. Compute the point elasticity of demand for school lunches at a price of

      (i) 40 cents per lunch

      (ii) 50 cents per lunch

    b. What is the arc price elasticity of demand between a price of 40 cents and 50 cents?

18. Over the past six months Heads-Up Hair Care, Inc. has normally had sales of 500 bottles of A-6 Hair Conditioner per week. On the weeks when Heads-Up ran sales on its B-8 Hair Conditioner, cutting the price of B-8 from $10 to $8, sales of A-6 declined to 300 bottles.

    a. What is the arc cross elasticity of demand between A-6 and B-8?

    b. If the price of B-8 were increased to $12, what effect would you expect this to have on the quantity demanded of A-6?

    c. What does the evidence indicate about the relationship between B-8 and A-6?

19. Ms. Jones consumes three products, A, B, and C. She has decided that her last purchase of A gave her 8 units of satisfaction, her last purchase of B gave her 10 units of satisfaction, and her last purchase of C gave her 5 units of satisfaction. The prices of A, B and C are $4, $5 and $3 per unit, respectively.

    As a rational consumer, what should Ms. Jones purchase?

20. The income elasticity of demand for residential use of electricity has been estimated as 0.3. If the price of electricity is expected to remain constant and the price of substitute goods is expected to remain constant, what would you expect to happen to the demand for electricity by residential customers if disposable personal income were expected to decline by 10 percent over the next year?

21. A study of the long-term income elasticity of demand for housing by renters is in the range of 0.8 to 1.0, whereas the income elasticity for owner-occupants is between 0.7 and 1.15.

    a. If income levels are expected to increase at a compound annual rate of 4 percent per year for the next five years, forecast the impact of this increase in income levels on the quantity of housing demanded in the two markets (rental and owner-occupants) in five years (assume that the price of housing does not change over this period).

    b. What would be the impact of price increases during this period on the levels of demand forecasted in part (a)?

22. Given the following demand function:

Price $P(\$)$	Quantity Q_D (units)	Arc Elasticity E_D	Total Revenue ($)	Marginal Revenue ($/unit)
$12	30	—	—	
11	40	—	—	—
10	50	—	—	—
9	60	—	—	—
8	70	—	—	—
7	80	—	—	—
6	90	—	—	—
5	100	—	—	—
4	110	—	—	—

    a. Compute the associated arc elasticity, total revenue, and marginal revenue values.

    b. On separate graphs, plot the demand function, total revenue function, and marginal revenue function.

23. The Stopdecay Company sells an electric toothbrush for $25. Its sales have averaged 8,000 units per month over the last year. Recently, its closest competitor, Decayfighter, reduced the price of its electric toothbrush from $35 to $30. As a result, Stopdecay's sales declined by 1,500 units per month.

    a. What is the arc cross elasticity of demand between Stopdecay's toothbrush and Decayfighter's toothbrush? What does this indicate about the relationship between the two products?

    b. If Stopdecay knows that the arc price elasticity of demand for its toothbrush is -1.5, what price would Stopdecay have to charge to sell the same number of units as it did before the Decayfighter price cut? Assume that Decayfighter holds the price of its toothbrush constant at $30.

c. What is Stopdecay's average monthly total revenue from the sale of electric toothbrushes before and after the price change determined in part (b)?

d. Is the result in part (c) necessarily desirable? What other factors would have to be taken into consideration?

24. The demand for renting motor boats in a resort town has been estimated to be $Q_D = 5000 - 50P$ where Q_D is the quantity of boats demanded (boat-hours) and P is the average price per hour to rent a motor boat. If this relationship holds true in the future:

a. How many motor boats will be demanded at a rental price of $10, $20, and $30 per hour?

b. What is the *arc* price elasticity of demand between $10 and $20? Between $20 and $30?

c. What is the *point* price elasticity of demand at $10, $20, and $30?

d. If the number of boat rental hours was 4,250 last year, what would you expect the average rental rate per hour to have been?

25. The following table gives hypothetical data for the weekly purchase of sirloin steak by a college fraternity house. Compute all meaningful arc elasticity coefficients (price, cross, and income). Remember that the effects of the other factors must be held constant when computing any of these elasticities.

Week	Price per Pound of Steak	Quantity of Steak Purchased (pound)	Income (Member Dues)	Price per Pound of Hamburger
1	$1.50	100	$500	$ .90
2	1.60	95	500	.90
3	1.60	100	550	.90
4	1.60	105	550	.95
5	1.50	115	550	.95
6	1.50	105	550	.90
7	1.50	100	500	.90
8	1.65	90	500	.90
9	1.65	110	500	1.00
10	1.65	90	400	1.00

26. The Reliable Aircraft Company manufactures small, pleasure-use aircraft. Based on past experience, sales volume appears to be affected by changes in the price of the planes and by the state of the economy as measured by consumers' disposable personal income. The following data pertaining to Reliable's aircraft sales, selling prices, and consumers' personal income were collected:

Year	Aircraft Sales	Average Price	Disposable Personal Income (in constant 1980 dollars— billions)
19X3	525	$7200	$610
19X4	450	8000	610
19X5	400	8000	590

a. Estimate the arc price elasticity of demand using the 19X3 and 19X4 data.

b. Estimate the arc income elasticity of demand using the 19X4 and 19X5 data.

c. Assume that these estimates are expected to remain stable during 19X6. Forecast 19X6 sales for Reliable asssuming that their aircraft prices remain constant at 19X5 levels and that disposable personal income will increase by $40 billion. Also assume the arc income elasticity computed in (b) above is the best available estimate of income elasticity.

d. Forecast 19X6 sales for Reliable given that their aircraft prices increase by $500 from 19X5 levels and that disposable personal income will increase by $40 billion. Assume that the price and income effects are *independent* and *additive* and that the arc income and price elasticities computed in parts (a) and (b) are the best available estimates of these elasticities to be used in making the forecast.

Indifference Curve Analysis of Demand

Indifference Curves Defined

Consider the situation of a consumer who wishes to allocate an available amount of income between two commodities, A and B. The utility, U, or satisfaction the consumer receives from the two goods, can be expressed as:

$$U = U(A, B) \qquad [7A.1]$$

The utility received from consuming various combinations of A and B can be ranked in an ordinal fashion. That is, it is possible to indicate that a consumer prefers 8 units of A and 3 units of B to an alternative combination, such as 4 units of A and 1 unit of B. This notion of ordinal utility can be depicted by *indifference curves*. An indifference curve is a plotting of points representing various combinations of two goods, for example A and B, such that the consumer is *indifferent* among any combinations along a specific indifference curve.

Figure 7A.1 shows two indifference curves, U_1 and U_2. The consumer is indifferent among Combinations 1, 2, and 3 on curve U_1, but prefers any combination of A and B, such as points 4 and 5 on curve U_2 to any combination available on curve U_1. The most important properties of indifference curves are:

1. Any combination of commodities lying on an indifference curve (U_2, for example) which is above and to the right of another indifference curve (such as U_1) is the preferred combination.

2. Indifference curves have a negative (downward) slope to the right, indicating that more of A can only be obtained by consuming less of B.

3. Indifference curves never intersect.

4. Indifference curves are convex to the origin. The absolute value of the slope of an indifference curve is the marginal rate of substitution of B for A. The convex shape of an indifference curve indicates that the slope diminishes as one moves to the right; i.e., the consumer is willing to give up fewer and fewer units of B in order gain an increasing number of units of A. This is consistent with the law of diminishing marginal utility discussed in this chapter.

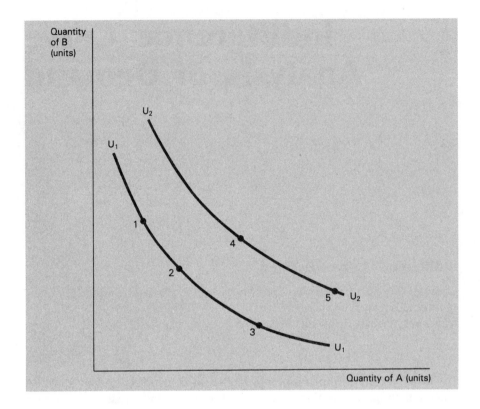

Figure 7A.1
**Illustrative
Indifference
Curves**

Deriving the Demand Function

Indifference curves can be used to derive the demand curve discussed in this chapter. Consider the two-commodity case represented by the utility function:

$$U = U(A, B) \tag{7A.1}$$

The consumer also faces a budget constraint of the form:

$$Y = P_A A + P_B B \tag{7A.2}$$

where Y represents the amount of income available to the consumer to be spent on goods A and B. P_A and P_B represent the price of a unit of A and B respectively. The amount spent on A—$P_A A$—plus the amount spent on B—$P_B B$—equals the total amount of income available, Y.

Given this budget constraint, the consumer's problem is to choose the combination of A and B which *maximizes* the utility derived without overspending the budget. This occurs at the point of *tangency* between the budget constraint and the highest consumer indifference curve as illustrated in Figure 7A.2. Given three possible indifference curves, U_1, U_2, and U_3, and a budget constraint (the straight line running from Y/P_B—the number of units of B purchased if all income is spent on B—to Y/P_A—the number of units of A purchased if all income is spent on A), the optimal combination of A and B for this consumer is given at point D. At this point the consumer can achieve a U_2 level of satisfaction by consuming A_1 units of A and B_1 units of B. These levels provide the highest utility without violating the budget constraint.

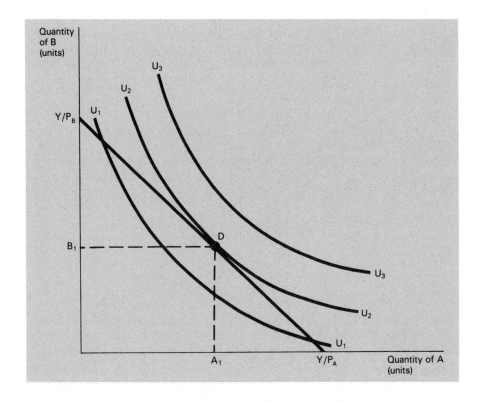

Figure 7A.2
Equilibrium Given a Budget Constraint

At the point of tangency of the indifference curve (U_2) and the budget line in Figure 7A.2, the slope[16] of the indifference curve is equal to the slope of the budget line. The slope of the indifference curve ($\Delta B/\Delta A$) at any point measures the consumer's *marginal rate of substitution* (*MRS*) of commodity B for commodity A (holding utility constant). This slope is equal to the ratio of the marginal utility of A ($MU_A = \partial U/\partial A$) to the marginal utility of B ($MU_B = \partial U/\partial B$), that is,

$$\frac{\Delta B}{\Delta A} = MRS = \frac{MU_A}{MU_B} \qquad [7A.3]$$

The slope ($\Delta B/\Delta A$) of the budget line is equal to the ratio of the price of commodity A (P_A) to the price of commodity B (P_B); that is,

$$\frac{\Delta B}{\Delta A} = \frac{P_A}{P_B} \qquad [7A.4]$$

At the equilibrium (tangency) point, setting Equation 7A.3 equal to Equation 7A.4 yields

$$\frac{MU_A}{MU_B} = \frac{P_A}{P_B} \qquad [7A.5]$$

---

[16] Note that the slopes of the indifference curves and budget line are both negative. In the remainder of this appendix, slope will be taken to mean *absolute value.*

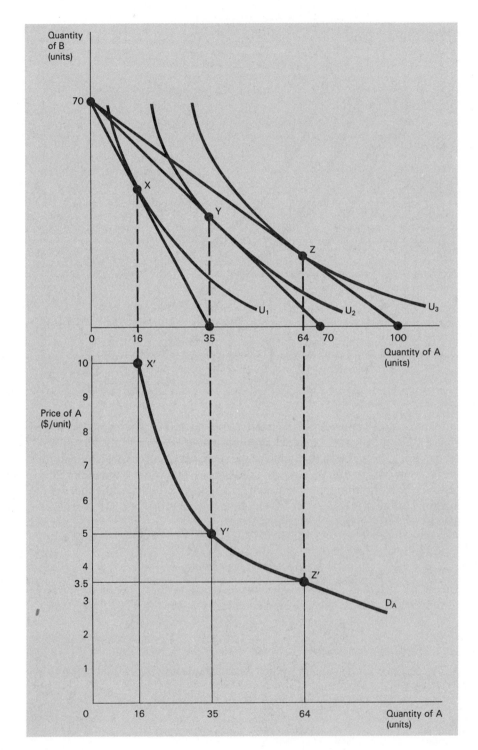

Figure 7A.3
**Derivation of a
Demand Function**

or

$$\frac{MU_A}{P_A} = \frac{MU_B}{P_B} \qquad [7A.6]$$

which is equivalent to (for the two-commodity case) the optimality condition (Equation 7.1) presented earlier in Chapter 7.

The demand function for a commodity such as A can be derived in a straightforward manner from the previous analysis. This is illustrated in Figure 7A.3. Assume a consumer has $350 to spend on products A and B. The initial price of B is $5 and the initial price of A is $10. Under these conditions, the consumer could acquire 70 units of B or 35 units of A, or any combination thereof, (illustrated in the lower budget line). Three indifference curves are plotted, U_1, U_2, and U_3. Given the income constraint of $350 and the initial prices of A ($10) and B ($5), the consumer would choose Combination X on Curve U_1. At this point the consumer would acquire 16 units of A. Hence at a price of $10 per unit, the consumer would demand 16 units of A. This point is now plotted on the lower panel of Figure 7A.3 as point X'.

If the price of A declines to $5, a new budget line is defined which intersects the A axis at 70 units. The new optimum occurs at point Y with 35 units of A being demanded at a price of $5. This point is plotted on the lower panel at Y'.

Finally, at a price of $3.50 for a unit of A, a new optimum point occurs at Z with 64 units of A being demanded. By plotting in the lower panel of Figure 7A.3, the three prices and associated quantities demanded, the familiar demand curve, D_A, for good A is derived. This is illustrated by the curve that connects points X', Y', and Z'.

Income and Substitution Effects

Indifference curve analysis can also be used to illustrate the income and substitution effects of a price decline. Consider the case of a consumer who consumes two products, A and B. The consumer has Y dollars to allocate among the two commodities. Given an initial set of prices for A and B and an initial level of income, the budget constraint is given in Figure 7A.4 as XV. The consumer will buy Q_1 units of A and Q_4 units of B, as indicated at Point 1.

If the price of A declines such that the new budget line becomes XV', Point 2 represents the new optimum for the consumer. This point falls on the higher of the two indifference curves, U_2, plotted on the figure. Given the new lower price for A, the consumer demands Q_2 units of A.

Next, we construct a new, artificial budget line, ZW, which is parallel to XV' and tangent to the original indifference curve U_1. From the original optimum, Point 1, to the artificial optimum, Point 3, "real" income of the consumer has remained the same in the sense that the consumer experiences the same utility at Point 1 and Point 3. The shift in demand for A from Q_1 to Q_3 may be thought of as representing the "pure" substitution effect of A for B resulting from the price change in A. In contrast, the increased consumption of A measured from Points Q_3 to Q_2 may be thought of as the "pure" income effect. This is so because the only difference between ZW and XV' is the level of income that each reflects. In

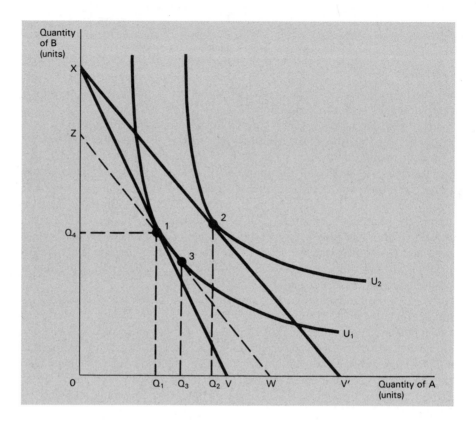

Figure 7A.4
**Income and
Substitution
Effects**

summary, a decline in price for A results in the consumer demanding $Q_3 - Q_1$ more units of A because of the substitution effect, and $Q_2 - Q_3$ more units of A because of the income effect.

Discussion Questions

1. Which factor, the income effect or the substitution effect, do you think has the greater impact on determining the demand function for most products? Why?

2. What is the most important characteristic of an indifference curve?

3. What role does the budget constraint play in determining the demand curve for a product?

Problems

1. Suppose an individual's utility (that is, satisfaction) received from two goods can be represented by the following relationship:

$$U(X_1, X_2) = 2X_1 + 2X_2 - .5X_1^2 + X_1X_2 - .6X_2^2,$$

where X_1 and X_2 are the amounts consumed of the respective goods. Furthermore, assume that the cost per unit of Good 1 is $4 and the cost per unit of Good 2 is $6. The individual has $48 available to spend on the two goods and desires to maximize the utility received from consumption of the two goods subject to his budget constraint.

a. Formulate the problem in a programming format.
b. Convert this constrained-optimization problem into an unconstrained problem by forming the Lagrangian function.
c. Solve this unconstrained problem using the techniques of differential calculus.
d. Defining $MU_1 = \partial U/\partial X_1$ and $MU_2 = \partial U/\partial X_2$ to be the marginal utility functions, show that the ratio of the marginal utilities

$$\frac{MU_1}{MU_2}$$

evaluated at optimal values of X_1 and X_2 obtained in part (c), is equal to the ratio of the prices of the two goods.

This illustrates the economic principle that in equilibrium the ratio of the prices of two goods must be equal to the ratio of the marginal utilities (i.e., Equation 7A.5).
e. Give an economic interpretation of the value of the Lagrangian multiplier (λ) obtained in part (c).

Empirical Estimation of Demand 8

The preceding chapter developed the theory of demand, including the concepts of price elasticity, income elasticity, and cross elasticity of demand. A manager who is contemplating an increase in the price of one of the firm's products needs to know the impact of this increase on quantity demanded, total revenue, and profits. Is the demand elastic, inelastic, or unit elastic with respect to price over the range of the contemplated price increase? What will happen to demand if consumer incomes increase or decrease as a result of an economic expansion or contraction? These types of problems face managers every day. A concern for empirical demand relationships is not limited to profit-seeking enterprises. Governments and not-for-profit institutions are faced with similar relationships. What will be the impact of an increase in cigarette taxes? Will tax revenue increase, decrease, or remain constant? What effect will a tuition increase have on local state university revenues? These and a multitude of similar questions illustrate the importance of developing empirical estimates of demand relationships. This chapter discusses some of the techniques and problems associated with making such estimates. The better the knowledge a manager has regarding the demand for his or her firm's product, the more likely that manager will be to take actions that can maximize the cash flows accruing to the firm and therefore contribute to the goal of maximizing shareholder wealth.

Glossary of New Terms

Identification problem A difficulty encountered in empirically estimating a demand function by regression analysis. This problem arises from the simultaneous relationship between two functions such as supply and demand.

Approaches to Gathering Data

Before examining some of the statistical models that are useful in estimating demand relationships, this section briefly looks at three alternative approaches to gathering data which will help in the analysis—consumer surveys, consumer clinics, and market experiments.

Consumer Surveys

Consumer surveys involve questioning a sample of consumers to determine such factors as their willingness to buy, their sensitivity to price changes or relative price levels, and their awareness of advertising campaigns. For example, recently American Airlines conducted an extensive survey of its passengers.

Some of the questions asked in this survey were as follows:

1. All things considered, how would you describe the value of the transportation and service received on today's flight in relation to your fare?
   a. The flight is a real bargain.
   b. The flight is priced about right.
   c. The price is too high for what is received.
   (Responses to this question can be helpful to American Airlines when considering future price strategies.)

2. Are you traveling with other family members on American Airlines' Family Fare?

3. If the Family Fare had NOT been available, how many of these family members (including yourself) would still have taken THIS TRIP ON AMERICAN AIRLINES AT THIS TIME?
   (Responses to Questions 2 and 3 will help American to assess the effectiveness of its Family Fare plan.)

4. If you are traveling on a discount fare and the discount had not been available for your trip today, would you personally still have taken this trip by air?
   (Question 4 is designed to measure the impact of American's discount fares on demand.)

5. What is the main purpose of this trip?
   (Respondents to this question could choose among a variety of business, personal, and vacation reasons for travel. When the responses to this question are combined with those from Question 4, it is possible for American to structure future discount fare programs to have the greatest impact on its revenues without giving discounts to individuals who would travel whether or not discounts are offered).

6. How many commercial airline trips have you made during the twelve months before this trip?

7. Your total annual family income before taxes:
   (Questions 6 and 7 can help American to assess the income elasticity of demand for air travel.)

Consumer surveys can provide a great deal of useful information to a firm; however, many consumers are not able or not willing to give accurate answers to these types of questions. Can you specify what your response would be to a 25-cent rise in the price of hamburgers at your favorite fast-food restaurant? How many fewer hamburgers would you buy per month? Do you know how many you buy now? It should be obvious that the approach of direct consumer interviewing has many potential pitfalls. As unrealistic as it may be to expect even the most earnest of consumers to be able to specify his or her response to hypothetical price changes, questions about reactions to changes in the quantity or emphasis of advertising and to changes in income levels produce responses that may be even more suspect.

This is not to say that nothing can be learned from consumer interviews. Consumer expectations about future business and credit conditions may provide significant insights into their propensity to purchase many items, especially durable goods. Using a little imagination and asking less direct questions may also offer insights. If questioning reveals that consumers are unaware of price differences among several competing goods, it might be concluded that at least within the current range of prices, consumers are not terribly price conscious; that is, demand may be price inelastic. Also, the effectiveness of advertising campaigns may be tested by sampling the awareness of a group of consumers to the campaign.

Consumer Clinics

Another means of recording consumer responses to changes in factors affecting demand is through the use of *consumer clinics*. In these situations, for example, experimental groups of consumers are given a small amount of money with which to buy certain items. The experimenter can observe the impact on actual purchases as price, prices of competing goods, and other variables are manipulated.[1]

Although consumer clinics of this sort are considerably more realistic than the hypothetical situations facing consumers in the direct interview method, they still have shortcomings. First, the costs of setting up and running such a clinic are substantial, and consequently the number of consumers actually participating is likely to be quite small. Second, the participants are generally aware that their actions are being observed, and hence they may seek to act in a manner somewhat different from normal—the Hawthorne effect.[2] An individual taking part in a consumer clinic may suspect that the experimenter is interested in sensitivity to prices and may be significantly more price conscious than otherwise would be the case.

In spite of these problems, interview and consumer clinic approaches often furnish useful information to aid in the decision-making process. It should be evident after the discussion of direct-market experimentation and the use of regression techniques that sometimes interviews and consumer clinics offer the only usable information.

Market Experiments

Another approach that is sometimes used to garner information about the demand function is the *market experiment*, which examines the way consumers behave in real-market situations. A firm may vary one or more of the

---

[1] An excellent example of the use of laboratory experimentation to estimate demand elasticities is given in E. A. Pessemier, "An Experimental Method for Estimating Demand," *Journal of Business* (October 1960). See also E. A. Pessemier, *Experimental Methods for Analyzing Demand for Branded Consumer Goods with Applications to Problems of Marketing Strategy* (Pullman: Washington State University Press, 1963).

[2] F. J. Roesthlisberger and W. J. Dickson, *Management and the Worker* (Cambridge, Mass.: Harvard University Press, 1939), chap. 18.

determinants of the amount sold, such as price and advertising, and observe the impact on quantity demanded. This may be done in a number of ways. The Bic Pen Company might determine that Houston and Dallas are markets sufficiently similar to permit comparison. Prices could be raised in Houston for three months and held constant in Dallas and the impact on Houston's sales observed versus Dallas's sales over the same period of time. Similar tests could vary quantity or emphasis of advertising in two similar markets. Another alternative is to make price changes in the Houston market alone. If prices were increased for two months and then decreased for two months, the impact on sales could be observed.

This approach may be especially useful in developing a feel for the price elasticity or cross elasticity of demand for a product. Dean reports such an experiment conducted by the Simmons Mattress Company.[3] Two identical types of mattresses, some with the Simmons label and others with an unknown brand name, were offered for sale at the same prices and varying price spreads to determine cross elasticity. It was found that with identical prices, Simmons outsold the unknown brand 15 to 1; with a $5 premium over the unknown label, Simmons's margin was reduced to 8 to 1; and with a 25 percent premium over the unknown label, sales were about the same.

Market experimentation has several serious shortcomings. If done on a scale large enough to generate a high degree of confidence in the results, it may be quite risky. Customers lost by a change in advertising strategy or an increase in price may never be regained. Market experimentation is also extremely expensive on such a large scale. And its cost is even higher when a controlled experiment is attempted. As a result, few of these well-controlled, expensive experiments are conducted, so results can be unreliable. Observed changes that occur in an uncontrolled experiment may be due to all sorts of disturbance factors, such as unusually bad weather, competitive advertising or competitive price reductions, and even local strikes or large layoffs that change consumer incomes significantly. Because of the high cost and risk of a market experiment, the duration of the test is likely to be short and the number of possible variations in parameters, such as price or advertising outlays, are likely to be few. Hence long-run decisions must be made on the basis of a few short-run observations.

In spite of these limitations, direct market experimentation may be useful in a number of situations. Statistical demand studies may be impossible when the marketing of a new product is being considered, but market experiments may provide important data for verifying the results of a statistical study or for providing information about a few points on the demand curve where other statistical data are not available. The information that a statistical demand analysis can provide, however, is generally more comprehensive and often significantly lower in cost than the alternatives outlined above. Hence, this method is usually superior to consumer surveys, clinics, or market experimentation. The following section discusses the application of regression analysis to the estimation of demand functions.

---

[3] Joel Dean, *Managerial Economics* (Englewood Cliffs, N.J.: Prentice-Hall, 1960).

Statistical Estimation of the Demand Function

Chapter 6 introduced econometric techniques, the best-known and most frequently used techniques in developing estimates of the demand function. Because the method of regression analysis and the statistics useful in interpreting regression results were discussed in Chapter 6, along with some of the common statistical problems that may be encountered in regression studies, this section is limited to a consideration of how the technique may be applied to demand studies. The *identification problem*, often encountered in demand analyses, is also discussed.

Developing the Model

As discussed in Chapter 7, the demand function may be viewed as the relationship between quantity demanded (the dependent variable) and several independent variables. The first task in developing a statistical demand model is to identify the independent variables that are likely to influence quantity demanded. These might include such factors as price of the good in question, price of competing or substitute goods, population, per capita income, and advertising and promotional expenditures. The researcher should seek to learn as much as possible about factors that may influence the demand for a product before specifying which independent variables are to be used in the initial demand equation. If an important variable is omitted in the specification process, the regression statistics that are ultimately computed may be badly distorted; that is, the significance of the coefficients of the variables that are included in the model may be overestimated or underestimated. When the model is being formulated, it is most important that the researcher attempt to include *all* the *important* variables. However, because the inclusion of additional independent variables requires that more data be collected, and because these data are not always readily available or are expensive to generate, one must frequently be content with a model containing relatively few variables. Rarely will an empirical demand equation be encountered that contains more than six or seven independent variables.

Once the variables have been identified, the next task is to collect the data. If time-series analysis is being used, much of the data that are required must be gathered from past records of the firm, published statistics of governmental agencies, trade associations, and so on. Some variables, such as consumer expectations about future prices or business conditions, may have to be generated using survey techniques. Frequently, data will not be available in the form originally desired. This may require that some variables in the model be respecified or transformations be made to put the data in the required form.

The next step is to specify the form of the equation, or model, that indicates the relationship between the independent variables and the dependent variable(s). For example, if one decided to estimate the demand for cigarettes in Transylvania and decided to use time-series data, one might hypothesize that the number of cartons of cigarettes sold in Transylvania in any year (the dependent variable) is a function of the average retail price per carton, the disposable personal income of consumers, the size of the population, and the amount of cigarette advertising (the independent variables). Assume that sales are measured in *millions of cartons*, price in *dollars per carton*, disposable personal income in *dollars per capita*, size of the population in *thousands of people* eighteen years or older, and advertising expenditures in *millions of dollars*. Two of the most commonly used functional relationships in demand studies are the *linear model* and the *multiplicative model*. These models are examined below.

Linear Model. The most common form of estimation equation in demand studies is a linear relationship. In the cigarette industry demand function example, a linear model would be specified as follows:

$$Q_D = \alpha + \beta_1 P + \beta_2 Y + \beta_3 N + \beta_4 A + \Sigma \qquad [8.1]$$

where Q_D is the number of cartons of cigarettes demanded each year, P is the average price per carton, Y is the per capita disposable income for the residents of Transylvania, N is the population of Transylvania, A is the advertising expenditures of the cigarette companies, and Σ is the error term.[4] Based on economic theory, one would hypothesize that price (P) would have a negative impact on quantity demanded (Q_D) (i.e., as the price rises, quantity sold declines, holding constant all other variables) and that all the other independent variables (Y,N,A) would have a positive impact on cigarette sales. The values of the parameters ($\alpha, \beta_1, \beta_2, \beta_3$, and β_4) in the demand function are estimated by the method of least squares.[5] Since that method was discussed in Chapter 6, the reader is referred to that chapter for a review of the technique. In actual demand studies, computer regression programs are used to estimate the value of the parameters, thus simplifying the estimation procedure considerably.

The parameter estimates may be interpreted in the following manner. The constant or intercept term, α, generally has little economic significance because it represents the quantity of cigarettes demanded when all the independent variables (i.e., price, income, population, and advertising) are equal to zero. Clearly, this is an absurd assumption. It points out the caution that must be exercised when making estimates or forecasts of demand that lie too far beyond the range of observed values used to estimate the model's parameters.

The value of each β coefficient provides an estimate of the change in quantity demanded associated with a *one-unit* change in the given independent variable, holding constant all other independent variables. The β coefficients are equivalent to the partial derivatives of the demand function:

$$\frac{\partial Q_D}{\partial P} = \beta_1, \frac{\partial Q_D}{\partial Y} = \beta_2, \frac{\partial Q_D}{\partial N} = \beta_3, \frac{\partial Q_D}{\partial A} = \beta_4 \qquad [8.2]$$

---

[4] Recall from Chapter 6 that the error term (ϵ), or stochastic disturbance term, represents the deviation of the observed value of the dependent variable from its true theoretical value and has an expected value equal to zero.
[5] The use of ordinary least-squares estimation techniques is not always appropriate for equations that form part of a simultaneous system, such as the standard demand function. This point is discussed in further detail later in the section dealing with the identification problem.

Thus, each independent variable has a *constant marginal impact* on quantity demanded, regardless of the level of the other independent variables (i.e., regardless of the point on the demand curve where it is measured). Note also that the elasticity of demand with respect to each independent variable is *not* constant, but instead varies with the point on the demand curve where it is measured. This can be shown as follows for the price elasticity. Recalling from Chapter 7 that the point price elasticity was defined as (Equation 7.8)

$$E_D = \frac{\partial Q_D}{\partial P} \cdot \frac{P}{Q_D} \qquad [8.3]$$

and substituting Equation 8.2 into Equation 8.3 yields

$$E_D = \beta_1 \cdot \frac{P}{Q_D} \qquad [8.4]$$

Equation 8.4 shows that price elasticity is a function of the values of price (P) and quantity demanded (Q_D).

The cigarette demand function example can be used to illustrate the concepts discussed above. Suppose the following demand function was estimated with actual data using the least-squares method:

$$Q_D = -51.5 - 15.0P + .024Y + .0125N + 1.10A \qquad [8.5]$$

(Note that the sign [+ or −] of the coefficient of each of the independent variables is consistent with the hypothesized relationship given earlier.) The coefficient of the price variable (P) indicates that for a one dollar increase in price, quantity demanded will *decline* by 15.0 (million) cartons. Similarly, a fifty dollar increase in per capita disposable personal income will result in a 1.2 million carton (i.e., .024 × 50) increase in quantity demanded. Note that these values are constant regardless of the quantity demanded. Next, suppose one is interested in calculating the price elasticity of demand when $P = \$10.00$, $Y = \$5,000$, $N = 5,000$ (i.e., 5,000,000), and $A = \$200$ (i.e., \$200,000,000). From Equation 8.5,

$$Q_D = -51.5 - 15.0(10.00) + .024(5,000) + .0125(5,000) + 1.10(200)$$

$$= 201 \text{ (million cartons)}$$

Substituting this value along with $P = \$10.00$ and $\beta_1 = -15.0$ into Equation 8.4 yields

$$E_D = -15.0 \left(\frac{10.00}{201} \right) = -0.746$$

indicating that for a one percent increase in cigarette prices, demand will decline by 0.746 percent. Note also that when $P = \$11.00$, with the values of all the other independent variables remaining the same as in the above E_D calculation, E_D is now equal to -0.887—indicating that it is indeed a function of P and Q_D.

Linear demand equations have been used extensively in empirical work because of their ease of estimation and the realism with which they approximate many true demand relationships.

Multiplicative Model. Another commonly used demand relationship is the multiplicative model

$$Q_D = \alpha P^{\beta_1} Y^{\beta_2} N^{\beta_3} A^{\beta_4} \epsilon \qquad [8.6]$$

This model is popular both because of its ease of estimation and its intuitive appeal. For instance, Equation 8.6 may be transformed to a simple linear relationship in logarithms as follows:

$$\log Q_D = \log \alpha + \beta_1 \log P + \beta_2 \log Y + \beta_3 \log N + \beta_4 \log A + \log \epsilon \qquad [8.7]$$

and the parameters α, β_1, β_2, β_3, β_4 may be estimated by the standard least-squares technique. Most computer regression packages allow the transformation from Equation 8.6 to Equation 8.7 by merely changing one or two commands, thus making it unnecessary for the researcher to convert all data to logarithmic values by hand.

The intuitive appeal of this multiplicative form is based on the fact that the marginal impact of any one independent variable is not constant but is *dependent on* the value of that independent variable, as well as on the value of all other independent variables in the equation. For example, the marginal impact of a change in price on quantity demanded is dependent not only on the price change but also on the level of income, population, and advertising expenditures.

Demand functions in the multiplicative form possess the useful feature that the *elasticities are constant* over the range of data used in estimating the parameters and are equal to the estimated values of the respective parameters. For example, the income elasticity of demand was defined in Chapter 7 as

$$E_y = \frac{\partial Q_D}{\partial Y} \cdot \frac{Y}{Q_D} \qquad [8.8]$$

Differentiating Equation 8.6 with respect to income results in (dropping the disturbance term)

$$\frac{\partial Q_D}{\partial Y} = \beta_2 \alpha P^{\beta_1} Y^{\beta_2 - 1} N^{\beta_3} A^{\beta_4} \qquad [8.9]$$

Hence

$$E_y = \beta_2 \alpha P^{\beta_1} Y^{\beta_2 - 1} N^{\beta_3} A^{\beta_4} \left(\frac{Y}{Q_D} \right) \qquad [8.10]$$

Substituting Equation 8.6 for Q_D yields

$$E_y = \beta_2 \alpha P^{\beta_1} Y^{\beta_2 - 1} N^{\beta_3} A^{\beta_4} \left(\frac{Y}{\alpha P^{\beta_1} Y^{\beta_2} N^{\beta_3} A^{\beta_4}} \right) \qquad [8.11]$$

By canceling and combining terms where possible, Equation 8.11 becomes

$$E_y = \frac{\beta_2 \alpha P^{\beta_1} Y^{\beta_2} N^{\beta_3} A^{\beta_4}}{Y} \cdot \frac{Y}{\alpha P^{\beta_1} Y^{\beta_2} N^{\beta_3} A^{\beta_4}} = \beta_2 \qquad [8.12]$$

The property of constant elasticity is useful, since it means that a given percentage change in one of the independent variables, such as income, will result in the same proportionate percentage change in quantity demanded at all points on the demand curve. This is a peculiar property of the multiplicative demand function in comparison with the more typical linear demand function. As was shown earlier, the elasticity of a linear function changes over the entire range of the demand curve.

The cautions against extrapolating the results from the estimated equation too far beyond the values of the data used in obtaining the original parameter estimates are just as applicable for the multiplicative, or any other specified form of the demand equation, as for the linear equation.

The specific form of the demand function, which the econometrician estimates, is normally chosen to depict the true relationships as closely as possible. In addition to the pure linear and multiplicative forms, many alternatives and variations may be tried. Since there is often no a priori reason for expecting one form to model the true relationship better than another, many variations are usually estimated to obtain the best fit between the data for the dependent and independent variables.[6] A clue to which functional format should initially be tried may be gained by graphing such relationships as the dependent variable over time and each independent variable against the dependent variable. The results of this preliminary analysis will often tell whether a linear equation is most appropriate or whether logarithmic, exponential, or other transformations are more appropriate.

The Identification Problem

The statistical problems of multicollinearity (the inclusion of mutually correlated independent variables in the model) and serial correlation of the residuals or error terms (or autocorrelation, as it is called when time-series data are being used) were discussed in Chapter 6. In addition to these problems, the econometrician developing demand functions from empirical data is faced with problems arising because of the simultaneous relationship between the demand function and the supply function.[7] It is the interaction of the demand and supply functions that determines the price at which a product is sold.[8]

This may pose a problem when estimating the shape of an empirical demand function since one may observe only one actual price-output combination at any point in time. If, for example, one sought to estimate the demand curve for Product Z, one might observe historical data on quantity bought (sold) and the

---

[6] Any standard econometrics text, such as R. S. Pindyck and D. L. Rubinfeld, *Econometric Models and Economic Forecasts*, 2d ed. (New York: McGraw-Hill, 1981), may be consulted to suggest some of the alternative forms that may be tried.

[7] Many economic relationships are characterized by simultaneous interactions. A recognition of simultaneous relationships is at the heart of national-income analysis. The input-output tables discussed in Chapter 10 show in great detail the interactions among the demand for outputs of various industries. For instance, the demand for steel depends on the demand for automobiles, but the steel industry also *uses* automobiles, which ultimately affects the demand for steel.

[8] The supply function or curve shows the relationship between the amount of a commodity that producers will make available for sale and a set of prices for which it may be sold, *holding constant all other factors that influence the supply function*.

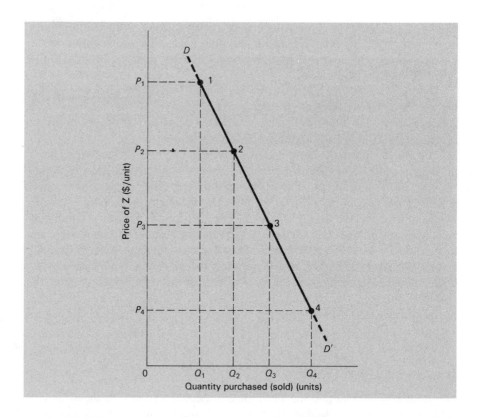

Figure 8.1
**Quantity of Z
Purchased (Sold)**

price at a specific time. A next step would be to plot these data on a graph (see Figure 8.1).

Is the line DD', drawn by connecting the four observed price-output combinations, equivalent to the demand curve for Z? Not necessarily. Although it does have the traditional negative slope of a demand curve, one cannot conclude that it represents the true demand-price relationship.

To see why this is so, recall that the price-output combinations actually observed result from an interaction of the supply and demand curves at a point in time. This is illustrated in Figure 8.2. If D_1, D_2, D_3, and D_4 represent the true demand curves at four different points in time and S_1, S_2, S_3, and S_4 the corresponding supply curves, one would have been seriously misled to conclude that the true demand relationship was depicted by DD' and was generally inelastic, when in fact demand was quite elastic and shifting (as was the supply curve). During the four successive time periods in which price-output combinations were observed, both the demand and supply curves had shifted. Recall from Chapter 7 that the simple demand function, relating price to quantity demanded, assumed that all other variables affecting the position of the functions were held *constant*. Hence to obtain a true estimate of the actual demand function, one must hold constant the effects of all other variables in the demand functions, allowing only price and quantity demanded to vary.

Under what circumstances may valid empirical estimates of the demand function be made? If both curves retain their original shape and position from one time period to the next, nothing could be learned of the true demand curve since all observed price-output combinations would coincide or at least be

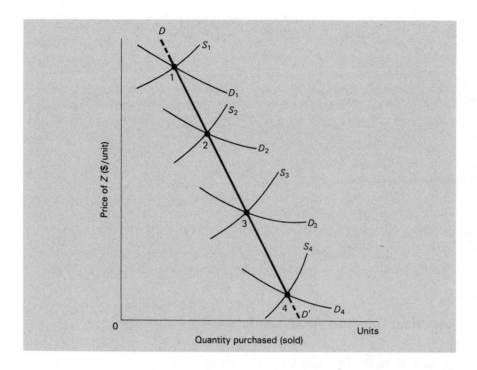

Figure 8.2
Quantity of Z Purchased (Sold) with Supply-Demand Interaction

closely clustered. If, however, the supply curve shifts but the demand curve remains constant, observed price-output combinations will trace out the true demand curve. This is illustrated in Figure 8.3. If, for example, a technological advance were being introduced in the production of Commodity Z during periods 1, 2, 3, and 4, then the supply curve would shift downward and to the right, from S_1 to S_4, tracing out the actual demand curve.

A final possibility is that both curves have shifted during the time period under consideration, but one has enough information to *identify* how each curve has shifted. When simultaneous relationships such as this occur, the ordinary least-squares (OLS) curve-fitting techniques discussed in Chapter 6 and earlier in this chapter may very well *break down and yield results that bear little or no relationship to the actual equation being sought*. Separating the effects of simultaneous relationships in demand analysis requires that more than just price-output data be available. In other words, other variables, such as income and advertising which may cause a shift in the demand function, must also be included in the model. Alternative statistical estimation techniques, such as two-stage least-squares (2SLS), must often be used to separate supply curve shifts from shifts in the demand curve.[9]

---

[9] A discussion of these alternative estimation procedures is beyond the scope of this book. The reader is referred to William J. Baumol, *Economic Theory and Operations Analysis*, 4th ed. (Englewood Cliffs, N.J.: Prentice-Hall, 1977), chap. 10 and its Appendix, for a further discussion of the identification problem and alternative estimation techniques. See also J. Johnston, *Econometric Methods*, 3d ed. (New York: McGraw-Hill, 1984), chap. 11, for a discussion of simultaneous equation relationships and the two-stage least-squares estimation procedure.

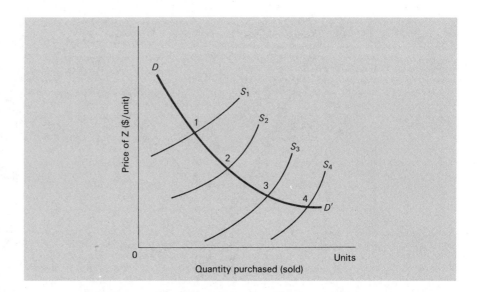

Figure 8.3
Stable Demand, Shifting Supply

Empirical Demand Analysis: Some Applications

The preceding sections of this chapter discussed the general procedure for developing empirical estimates of the demand function. This section summarizes the results of five empirical demand studies and presents a conceptual model to estimate the demand for an outdoor recreation area.

The Demand for Coffee in the United States

Hughes examined the U.S. demand for coffee for the periods 1920–1941 and 1947–1966.[10] The following equation was estimated for the two time periods:

$$Q = f(Y_d, rP) \qquad [8.13]$$

where

Q = per capita consumption (14 years and older) of green beans (pounds)

Y_d = per capita (14 years and older) disposable income in thousands of 1957–1959 dollars

rP = the average retail price of coffee in cents per pound (weighted by amounts of regular and instant coffee purchased), deflated by the consumer price index

Q' = an adjusted Q to correct for instant coffee consumption and the increasing efficiency of the extraction rate required in conversion to instant coffee. Q' converts actual Q into the number of green beans required for regular coffee consumption only. When Q' is used, Equation 8.13 is estimated as $Q' = f(Y_d, rP)$.

Some of the results obtained by Hughes are given in Table 8.1.

---

[10] John J. Hughes, "Note on the U.S. Demand for Coffee," *American Journal of Agricultural Economics* (November 1969), pp. 912–914.

Equation^a	by^b	Ey^c	brp^b	Erp^c	$\bar{R}^{2d}$	DW^e
1. 1920–1941	3.92	0.315	−0.104	−0.271	0.707	2.38
Q	$(4.31)^f$		(-6.88)			
2. 1947–1966	−2.79	−0.315	−0.033	−0.113	0.59	2.14
Q	(-5.48)		(-3.41)			
3. 1947–1966	−0.731	−0.078	−0.039	−0.125	0.28	1.84
Q'	(-1.19)		(-3.31)			

Table 8.1
Coffee Demand Equations

^{a} The means for Equations 1 through 3 are 24.1, 22.4, and 23.6.
^{b} by and brp are regression coefficients for Y_d and rP respectively.
^{c} Ey and Erp are the elasticities of quantity with respect to income and relative price, respectively, evaluated at the means.
^{d} $\bar{R}^2$ is the coefficient of multiple determination, adjusted for degrees of freedom. It indicates the percentage of the total variation in the dependent variable that can be explained by the independent variable(s).
^{e} DW is the Durbin-Watson statistic, which is used to test for the presence of autocorrelation.
^{f} Numbers in parentheses refer to the value of the t-test for the significance of the coefficients which are reported above.

This coffee demand study illustrates a number of problems that may be encountered in any time-series study of demand. One problem is evident in the shift in the sign of the income variable from positive in the prewar period (Equation 1) to negative in the postwar period (Equations 2 and 3). Hughes hypothesizes that coffee has become an inferior good while incomes have risen and the consumption of wine and distilled spirits has increased. However, it was impossible to test directly for the effect that alcoholic beverages have on coffee consumption because of a multicollinearity problem between disposable personal income and a distilled spirits and wine variable. (The simple correlation coefficient between the two variables was .93.) When such multicollinearity exists, it is impossible to sort out the relative effects of the collinear variables. Users of this model should be aware, however, that the included income variable reflects both the effect of income and the effect of a shift to greater consumption of alcoholic beverages on the quantity of coffee consumed.

Another problem evident in this study is the change in the product that occurred over the study period. The introduction of instant coffee (which uses less green coffee beans per cup because of a greater efficiency in extraction) in the postwar period required that the dependent variable be adjusted to account for the differential extractive efficiency. The adjusted results, Q', are reported in Equation 3.

Finally, the Durbin-Watson statistic is reported as a test for autocorrelation; that is, a serial correlation of the residuals over time.[11] When autocorrelation exists, significance tests on the individual independent variables become unreliable. The values reported in this case indicate that autocorrelation is probably not a serious problem.

Note that in all three equations the price elasticity coefficient is negative and less than unity, indicating that demand is highly inelastic. Given the price inelasticity of coffee demand, it seems reasonable to conclude that as a result of

[11] A discussion of the Durbin-Watson statistic may be found in Chapter 6.

the 1976–1977 coffee price increases, the revenues for coffee producers should increase dramatically. It also suggests that efforts to hold some product off the market to drive up prices are likely to be profitable.

More recently, Huang, Siegfried, and Zardoshty estimated the demand for regular and soluble (instant) coffee in the U.S. during the period 1963–1977.[12] They found regular coffee demand to be quite price inelastic (about −0.16) for the period studied. The demand for instant coffee was also price inelastic, but the elasticity was somewhat higher (about −0.45) than the demand for regular coffee. Income was not found to be a significant variable in explaining coffee demand during this period. Finally, this study incorporated seasonal effects in the demand equation. In spring and summer a significant negative seasonal effect was observed; that is, demand tended to be lower during these periods.

The Demand for Shoes in the United States

Houthakker and Taylor have made estimates of the demand functions for some eighty-four different goods and services.[13] Their study provides one of the richest sources for studying empirical demand analyses. The model for the demand for shoes and other footwear was of the following functional relationship:

$$Q_t = f(X_t, P_t, C_t, D_t) \tag{8.14}$$

where

Q_t = per capita personal consumption expenditure on shoes and other footwear during year t (1954 dollars)
X_t = total per capita consumption expenditure during year t (1954 dollars)
P_t = relative price of shoes in year t (1954 dollars)
C_t = automobile stocks per capita in year t
D_t = dummy variable used to separate the pre–WW II years from those following; $D_t = 0$ for 1929–1941; $D_t = 1$ for 1946–1961

The equation was estimated as follows:

$$Q_t = 19.575 + .0298X_t - .0923P_t - 99.568C_t - 4.06D_t \tag{8.15}$$
$$(4.163) \quad (.0032) \quad (.0522) \quad (10.061) \quad (1.16)$$

$$r^2 = .857$$

The standard deviations of each coefficient are shown in parentheses. Total per capita expenditures and automobile stocks per capita are the most impor-

---

[12] Cliff J. Huang, John J. Siegfried, and Farangis Zardoshty, "The Demand for Coffee in the United States, 1963–1977," *Quarterly Review of Economics and Business* (Summer 1980), pp. 36–50.

[13] H. S. Houthakker and Lester D. Taylor, *Consumer Demand in the United States, 1929–1970—Analyses and Projections* (Cambridge, Mass.: Harvard University Press, 1966). See also H. S. Houthakker and Lester D. Taylor, *Consumer Demand in the United States*, 2d ed. (Cambridge, Mass.: Harvard University Press, 1970), for an updated study of the demand functions for eighty-one different products.

tant explanatory variables. The value for the coefficient of the dummy variable indicates a significant difference between levels of the prewar and postwar periods. The price variable has the expected negative sign. Demand was found to be rather price inelastic, with a calculated elasticity of -0.3878. The r^2 of .857 indicates that the model explains about 86 percent of the observed variation in the dependent variable, Q_t. Demand models (such as Equation 8.15) can be useful to shoe manufacturers and retailers in forecasting future demand for shoes.

The Demand for New Automobiles in the United States

A classic example of a multi-equation demand analysis is Suits's study of the demand for new automobiles in the United States.[14] The automobile market was represented by a system of four equations including (a) the demand for new cars, (b) the supply of new cars by retail dealers, (c) the supply of used cars by retail dealers, and (d) the demand for used cars by the public. The four equations were specified as follows:

(a) Demand for new cars:

$$R = \alpha_0 + \alpha_1 \frac{P - U}{M} + \alpha_2 Y + \alpha_3 \Delta Y + \epsilon_1 \qquad [8.16]$$

(b) Supply of new cars at retail:

$$R = \beta_0 + \beta_1 P + \beta_2 W + \beta_3 T + \epsilon_2 \qquad [8.17]$$

(c) Supply of used cars:

$$R' = \gamma_0 + \gamma_1 R + \epsilon_3 \qquad [8.18]$$

(d) Demand for used cars:

$$R' = \eta_0 + \eta_1 \frac{U}{M} + \eta_2 Y + \eta_3 \Delta Y + \eta_4 S + \epsilon_4 \qquad [8.19]$$

where

R = retail sales of new cars
R' = supply of used cars to the public
Y = real disposable income
P = real retail price of new cars
U = average real price of used cars
M = average credit terms
S = stock of used cars
W = real wholesale price of new cars
T = retailers' operating costs
$\epsilon_1, \epsilon_2, \epsilon_3,$ and ϵ_4 = disturbance terms
$(P - U)/M$ = net real monthly outlay a buyer must make.

---

[14] Daniel B. Suits, "The Demand for New Automobiles in the United States, 1929–1956," *Review of Economics and Statistics* 40, no. 3 (August 1958), pp. 273–280.

After manipulating these four equations, Suits found annual sales of new passenger automobiles to be a function of the following:

1. Real disposable income

2. The stock of passenger cars on the road, January 1

3. The average retail price of new passenger automobiles divided by the average number of months' duration of automobile credit contracts

The elasticities of demand for new passenger automobiles at the mean levels of each variable were computed as follows:

Variable	Demand Elasticity
Real disposable income	4.16
Stock of cars, January 1	−3.65
Index of real monthly payment	−0.58

Computed demand elasticities such as these could be useful to automobile manufacturers in their pricing and marketing strategies.

The Demand for Airline Travel in the North Atlantic Market

Cigliano has estimated the demand for airline travel across the North Atlantic.[15] His study looks at two submarkets: the U.S./Europe market and the Canada/Europe market. In addition, Cigliano estimated separate demand functions by class of service. The basic demand function estimated by Cigliano was the following:

$$\ln(USPAX) = a_1 + a_2 \ln(USGNP) + a_3 \ln(USFARE) \qquad [8.20]$$

where

$USPAX$ = total passengers traveling from the United States to Europe between 1965 and 1978 on International Air Transport Association (IATA) carriers

$USGNP$ = U.S. gross national product adjusted for inflation

$USFARE$ = an average weighted (by seasonal distribution of traffic) fare between New York and London, adjusted for inflation

A similar equation was estimated for the Canadian market. Since this model is estimated in a logarithmic form, the coefficients provide direct elasticity estimates.

As can be seen in Table 8.2, the income elasticity is greater than 1.0 in both markets, indicating the sensitivity of airline traffic in both the U.S./Europe and Canada/Europe markets to the level of economic activity. For example, in the

[15] J. M. Cigliano, "Price and Income Elasticities for Airline Travel: The North Atlantic Market," *Business Economics* (September 1980), pp. 17–21.

Table 8.2
Air Travel Demand

Independent Variable	U.S./Europe Market	Canada/Europe Market
Constant	2.737	3.923
	(−0.873)	(1.015)
USGNP	1.905	—
	(7.286)	
USFARE	−1.247	—
	(−5.071)	
CANADIAN GNP	—	1.765
		(5.891)
CANADIAN FARE	—	−0.824
		(−2.192)
Adjusted R^2	0.97	0.98
Durbin-Watson statistic	1.831	2.106
Standard error of regression	0.64	.073

Note: t-ratios in parentheses.

U.S./Europe market, the coefficient of 1.9 indicates that a 5 percent increase in real U.S. GNP will result in a 9.5 percent increase in air traffic.

The U.S. price elasticity coefficient of −1.25 indicates that demand is relatively price elastic. A 5 percent general fare increase will result in a 6.25 percent decline in traffic. The price elasticity coefficient in the Canadian market is −0.824, indicating that demand in that market is relatively price inelastic, perhaps because of a different passenger mix in that market—more business travel relative to vacation travel.

Cigliano also estimated price elasticities by class of service in the U.S./ Europe market. He found that demand for first-class travel is highly price inelastic (coefficient of −0.447). The price elasticity for regular economy travel is −1.30, for long excursion travel it is −1.826, and for short excursion travel it is −2.181. From these results it can be seen that demand is relatively price elastic for a large segment of the market because of the number of nonbusiness travelers in the market.

Cigliano concluded that these results indicate the potential value of segmenting travel according to various market sectors and preferences for frequency of travel and using lower fares to take advantage of the different price elasticities. Estimates of income and price elasticities are also useful to airlines in forecasting future demand based on income and price trends.

The Demand for Public Goods[16]

Gibson has used survey data to estimate demand elasticities for various public goods.[17] Gibson's study examines the demand for (1) aid to needy people,

---

[16] A public good may be defined as a good that may be consumed by more than one person at the same time at little or no extra cost and whose exclusion of use by potential consumers proves expensive.

[17] Betty Blecha Gibson, "Estimating Demand Elasticities for Public Goods from Survey Data," *American Economic Review* (December 1980), pp. 1069–1076.

Economic Analysis and Managerial Efficiency

PRICE ELASTICITY ISSUES IN THE SETTING OF ELECTRIC UTILITY RATES

Electric utilities in the United States are regulated on a cost reimbursement basis in most regulatory jurisdictions. The utility normally is permitted an opportunity to earn a rate of return sufficient to cover all reasonable and prudently incurred costs plus provide a return to the investors (primarily the common stockholders and bondholders) equal to the cost of capital. This allowed rate of return is multiplied by the assets owned by the firm (rate base assets) which are used in providing service to customers.

As the cost of building new plants has increased (for example, some nuclear power plants have added more than $4 billion to the rate base assets of a utility), utility companies and their regulators have been faced with a difficult pricing problem. On one hand, the utility company would like to have the plant enter rate base as quickly as possible so that the company will have an immediate opportunity to recover its costs. On the other hand, placing a very large plant into rate base can result in "rate shock," that is, very large

increases in rates. In order to make a rational decision regarding the best way to bring a large plant into service, utility managers must have a feel for the price elasticity of the demand for electric service. For example, Bohi and Zimmerman (D. R. Bohi and M. Zimmerman, "An Update on Economic Studies of Energy Demand Behavior," *Annual Review of Energy* 9 (1984), pp. 105–154) found that the mean short-term (up to one year) price elasticity obtained from a sample of twenty-three studies was -0.2; however, the long-term price elasticity was estimated to be five times larger.

Questions

1. What customer groups do you think have the most price elastic demand function for electric power supplied by a utility company?

2. Why do you think the long-term price elasticity of demand is five times as large as the short-term elasticity?

3. What pricing strategies do you think this evidence regarding price elasticity suggests for an electric utility that is about to bring a costly, large plant into service?

(2) pollution control, (3) colleges and universities, (4) elementary school aid, (5) parks and recreational areas, and (6) highway construction and maintenance. Variables thought to influence the demand for each of these public goods were (1) price (measured by perceived tax payment), (2) income, and (3) taste. The taste variable was based on responses to a series of questions designed to identify the respondents' attitude toward state expenditures. The dependent variable was a measure of benefits derived from each activity. Respondents were asked to rank the benefits they felt they derived from each of the six activities. The model was estimated in a logarithmic form, with the coefficients representing the various elasticities.

Table 8.3 summarizes the results of the Gibson study. It is interesting to note the high income elasticity for education, parks, and highway construction, and the low income elasticity for aid to needy people and pollution control expenditures. The price elasticity is negative and close to -1.0 in all cases. Taste differences were found to have a significant impact on the demand for public goods. One should note that the estimation of the demand for public goods is

Table 8.3 **The Demand for Public Goods**

Activity	Constant	Price Elasticity	Income Elasticity	Taste Coefficient	R	Number of Cases
Aid to Needy People	5.89	−.83 (.15)	.26 (.27)	.45 (.35)	.44	47
Pollution Control	1.17	−.99 (.19)	.77 (.34)	.84 (.43)	.37	32
Colleges and Universities	−1.19	−.87 (.11)	.92 (.19)	.96 (.28)	.49	51
Elementary School Aid	−1.29	−1.16 (.12)	1.14 (.20)	.87 (.28)	.41	52
Parks and Recreational Areas	.20	−1.02 (.10)	1.06 (.18)	.32 (.21)	.22	50
Highway Construction and Maintenance	1.02	−1.09 (.08)	.99 (.06)	.42 (.29)	.32	33

Note: Standard errors are shown in parentheses

considerably more difficult than the estimation of demand for private goods. (The disbelieving reader is referred directly to the Gibson article referenced in Footnote 17.)

A Conceptual Model of the Demand for Outdoor Recreation[18]

Increasing population, urbanization, more leisure time, higher incomes, and individual mobility have caused an increase in the demand for recreation. In deciding how resources are to be allocated among competing public uses, a model must be developed to enable us to place values on resources allocated to recreational purposes and to study the demand relationships that help determine these values. Because outdoor recreational resources—such as national parks, wildlife refuges, and open-space areas near urban centers—are normally made available to the public free or at a nominal charge, one does not have the market-price mechanism available to measure the value the public places on these resources.

The method suggested requires that cost data be used as an indirect means of determining appropriate prices by which economic value may be determined. Data may be collected on the numbers and origins of park visitors to construct a demand curve for the recreation area. The cost of visiting a park area might include such things as transportation, lodging, and food costs above those incurred if the visit were not made.

Clawson has derived demand curves for outdoor recreation that assume that cost is the only determinant of the number of visits individuals make to a recreational area.[19] Using a simple example, one might observe the visitation

---

[18] This example is based on Jack L. Knetsch, "Outdoor Recreation Demands and Benefits," *Land Economics* 39, no. 4 (November 1963), pp. 387–396.

[19] Marion Clawson, "Methods of Measuring the Demand for and Value of Outdoor Recreation," Reprint 10 (Washington, D.C.: Resources for the Future, 1959).

Table 8.4
Data for Construction of Demand Schedule for Park Visits

City	Population	Cost of a Visit (dollars)	Visits per 1,000 Population	Visits Made to Park by Total Population
A	1,000	$1	400	400
B	2,000	3	200	400
C	4,000	4	100	400
				1,200

rate of people from each of three different urban centers located at varying distances from a free recreational area. The observed data are summarized in Table 8.4.

These data show that visits, per unit of population, decline as cost increases. For simplicity, one may assume that the length of each stay at the park is identical for all visitors, although in an actual application this assumption could easily be discarded. The relationship may be given in equation form as

$$V = 5 - C \qquad [8.21]$$

where C is the cost per visit and V is the rate of visits in hundreds per thousand population. At a cost C of $3 per visit, 200 visits per thousand population would be made. Although the relationship illustrated here is conveniently linear, data in an actual case may indicate that a dollar's change in cost may have little or no effect on high-cost visits but a significant impact on low-cost visits.

At a zero-user charge, 1,200 visits are presently being made. This is one point on the demand curve in Figure 8.4. According to Equation 8.21, a $1 increase in the cost of visiting the park would result in a drop in the expected visit rate to 300 per thousand in City A, 100 per thousand in B, and zero in C. Multiplying these figures by the population in each city and making corresponding calculations for

Figure 8.4
Demand Function: Outdoor Recreation

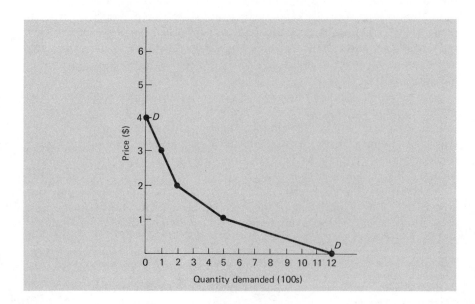

Table 8.5
**Demand Schedule
for Park Visits**

Price (added cost)	Quantity (total visits)
0	1,200
1	500
2	200
3	100
4	0

cost or price additions of $2, $3, or $4 yields the demand schedule presented in Table 8.5 and graphed in Figure 8.4. Table 8.5 approximates the true demand schedule by indicating how people would react to increases in the cost of visitation (our proxy for price).

Knetsch has expanded Clawson's model by including some factors other than costs that may affect visitation rates. These might include the availability of close substitutes (both locationally and in size and quality), the congestion of people at the recreation area, and the income level of potential visitors. The total demand function would be

$$V = f(C, Y, S, G) \qquad [8.22]$$

where V and C are defined as before, Y is income of various population groups, S is substitute areas, and G is a measure of congestion.

The value of the recreational area is the value it has for the consumer and is measured by the consumer's willingness to pay for its use. Whether a payment is actually made is irrelevant. The demand schedule in Table 8.5 enables one to calculate the worth of the park to the individuals who use it. The total area under the demand curve (see Figure 8.4) represents the yearly benefits of the project to those who use it. Since individuals may have a preference for being near a park area, the increase in the value of land near the park should be added to the economic worth of the recreational area. This preference to be near park areas is often evident at lakefront and seashore properties.

The discussion above has outlined a conceptual model that may be adapted for use in estimating the demand for and value of a specific public good, that is, outdoor recreation. This model merely illustrates the possibility of broader applications of microeconomic models developed primarily for use in analyzing the profit sector of our economy.

Summary

- Empirical estimates of the demand for a good or service are essential if the firm is to achieve its goal of shareholder wealth maximization. Without good estimates of the demand function facing a firm, it is impossible for that firm to make profit-maximizing price and output decisions.

- Consumer surveys involve questioning a sample of consumers to determine such factors as their willingness to buy, their sensitivity to price changes or levels, and their awareness of promotional campaigns.

- Consumer clinics make use of experimental groups of consumers. These consumers are given money to spend in a closely monitored environment and their purchasing behavior is then analyzed. Consumer clinics tend to be expensive to operate, and they may be influenced by significant experimental bias if the consumers are aware that their behavior is being monitored.

- Market experiments observe consumer behavior in real-market situations. By varying product characteristics, price, advertising, or other factors in some markets but not in others, the effects of these variables on demand can be determined. Market experiments are very expensive.

- Statistical techniques are often found to be of great value and relatively inexpensive as a means to make empirical demand function estimates. Regression analysis is often used to estimate statistically the demand function for a good or service.

- The linear model and the multiplicative model are the two most commonly used functional relationships in demand studies.

- In a *linear* demand model, the coefficient of each independent variable provides an estimate of the change in quantity demanded associated with a one-unit change in the given variable, holding constant all other variables. This marginal impact is constant at all points on the demand curve. The elasticity of a linear demand model with respect to each independent variable (e.g., price elasticity, and income elasticity) is not constant, but instead varies over the entire range of the demand curve.

- In a multiplicative demand model, the marginal impact of each independent variable on quantity demanded is not constant, but instead varies over the entire range of the demand curve. The elasticity of a multiplicative demand curve with respect to each independent variable is constant and is equal to the estimated value of the respective parameter.

- Because of the simultaneous equation relationship that exists between the demand function and the supply function in determining the market clearing price and quantity, econometricians must exercise great care when estimating and interpreting empirical demand functions.

Selected References

Buchanan, James M. *The Demand and Supply of Public Goods*. Chicago: Rand McNally, 1968.

Chow, Gregory C. *Econometrics*. New York: McGraw-Hill, 1983.

Gillingham, R., and R. P. Hagemann. "Household Demand for Fuel Oil." *Applied Economics* 16 (1984), pp. 475–482.

Houthakker, H. S., and Lester D. Taylor. *Consumer Demand in the United States, 1929–1970—Analyses and Projections*. Cambridge, Mass.: Harvard University Press, 1966. See also 2d and enlarged ed. (1970).

Johnston, Jack. *Econometric Methods*, 3d ed. New York: McGraw-Hill, 1984.

Morgan, W. D., and J. D. Vasché. "A Note on the Elasticity of Demand for Wagering." *Applied Economics* 14 (1982), pp. 469–474.

Neter, J., and W. Wasserman. *Applied Linear Regression Analysis* Homewood, III.: Richard D. Irwin, 1983.

Pindyck, R. A., and D. L. Rubinfeld. *Econometric Models and Economic Forecasts*. New York: McGraw-Hill, 1981.

Discussion Questions

1. Discuss some of the primary shortcomings of consumer surveys as an approach to gathering information for demand forecasting.

2. Discuss how consumer clinics can help to overcome some of the shortcomings of consumer surveys. What are the primary limitations of consumer clinics?

3. Discuss the relative strengths and weaknesses of market experiments as an approach to gathering information about the demand function of a firm.

4. Explain the difference in the economic interpretation of the β coefficients in linear and non-linear multiplicative demand models.

5. What is meant by the *identification problem?* How would you expect the estimation of the advertising and demand relationship to be affected by the identification problem?

6. What rationale can you give for the low income elasticity of demand for aid to needy people found in the study by Gibson, discussed in the chapter?

7. The following equation was estimated as the demand function for gasoline (number of observations equals 100, and standard errors are in parentheses):

$$\ln Q = 3.95 - 0.582\ \ln P + 0.401\ \ln Y - 0.211\ \ln P_c$$
$$(0.105) \quad\ \ (0.195) \quad\ \ (0.156)$$

where Q = gallons of gas demanded, P = price per gallon of gasoline, Y = income level of consumers, and P_c = an index of the price for automobiles.

a. Interpret the coefficients of the various variables in the preceding demand equation.
b. How much confidence do you have in each of these coefficient estimates?

8. You wish to design an experiment aimed at estimating the price elasticity of demand for your firm's new Convertible Monster (CONMON) toy. The toy currently sells for $14.95 and is sold exclusively at FloorMart discount stores throughout the country. Design an experiment that will enable you to estimate the price elasticity of demand for these toys at the lowest possible cost to your firm.

9. Regression analysis of the demand for Cabbage Field Dolls has resulted in the following demand function:

$$Q = 48.5 + 6.5P + 0.65Y$$

where Q = number of dolls demanded, P = price per doll, and Y = per capita income level. All coefficients are statistically significant at the 1 percent level.

a. What problems can you observe in this estimated demand function?
b. What are some possible causes for the observed problems?

Problems

1. General Cereals is using a regression model to estimate the demand for Tweetie Sweeties, a whistle-shaped, sugar-coated breakfast cereal for children. The following (multiplicative) demand function is being used:

$$Q_D = 6{,}280 P^{-2.15}\ A^{1.05}\ N^{3.70}$$

where

Q_D = quantity demanded, in 10 oz. boxes

P = price per box, in dollars

A = advertising expenditures on daytime television, in dollars

N = proportion of the population under twelve years old

a. Determine the point price elasticity of demand for Tweetie Sweeties.

b. Determine the advertising elasticity of demand.

c. What interpretation would you give to the exponent of N?

2. The following demand function has been estimated for Product A:

$$Q_A = a P_A^b I^c P_B^d P_{op}^e A_B^f A_A^g$$

where

Q_A = quantity of A demanded in units

P_A = price of A

P_B = price of B

I = per capita income

P_{op} = total population

A_A = advertising expenditures for A

A_B = advertising expenditures for B

a. Determine the cross elasticity between A and B. Determine the price elasticity of A. Determine the income elasticity of A.

b. How would you interpret the values for e, f, and g?

c. If $c = -.8$, what could you say about Product A?

d. If $f = -.3$ and $d = .9$, what can you say about Products A and B?

3. Moyer Winery is the maker of a high-quality champagne. A linear regression model used to estimate the demand function for Moyer's champagne yielded the following results:

$$Q_D = 10,425 - 2,910P_x + .028A + 11,100P_{op}$$
$$\quad\quad\quad (1,010) \quad (.004) \quad (3,542)$$

where

Q_D = quantity of Moyer champagne demanded

P_x = price of Moyer champagne

A = Moyer Winery advertising in dollars

P_{op} = percentage of the U.S. population over twenty-one years of age

a. Determine the point price elasticity for prices of $5 and $10, when $A = \$1,000,000$ and $P_{op} = .5$.

b. Determine the point advertising elasticity at an advertising level of $2,000,000, if price remains at $5 and $P_{op} = .5$.

c. The standard error for each coefficient is given in parentheses. If you know that the demand function was estimated using twenty-five observations, can you reject at the 95 percent confidence level the hypothesis that there is no relationship between each of the independent variables and Q_D?

4. An early estimate of the demand function for household furniture produced the following results:

$$F = .0036 Y^{1.08} R^{0.16} P^{-0.48} \quad\quad r^2 = .996$$

where

F = furniture expenditures per household

Y = disposable personal income per household

R = value of private residential construction per household

P = ratio of the furniture price index to the consumer price index

a. Determine the point price and income elasticities for household furniture.

b. What interpretation would you give to the exponent for R? Why do you suppose R was included in the equation as a variable?

c. If you were a furniture manufacturer, would you have preferred to see the analysis performed in physical (constant dollar) sales units rather than actual dollar units? If you change F to constant dollar terms, what other variable should you also change?

5. In an article entitled "A Coherence Approach to Estimates of Price Elasticities in the Vacation Travel Market," Taplin reports the following regression equation for vacation leisure travel expenditures in Australia.[20] The dependent variable in the equation (X_1) is dollars spent on vacation travel overseas. The independent variables are household disposable income in dollars per week (Y), and age of household head in years (Z).

$$\log X_1 = -0.6858 + 0.7407 \, \log Y + 0.6267 \, \log Z$$
$$(2.181) \qquad (0.432)$$

$$r^2 = 0.519$$

(*Note:* t values in parentheses; 8 degrees of freedom).

a. What interpretation would you give to the coefficient of the Y variable; that is, 0.7407?

b. What interpretation would you give to the coefficient of the Z variable; that is, 0.6267?

c. What conclusions can you draw about the significance of the income variable and the age variable?

d. What interpretation can you give to r^2 from this equation?

6. The Pilot Pen Company has decided to use fifteen test markets to examine the sensitivity of demand for its new product to various prices. Advertising effort was identical in each market. Each market had approximately the same level of business activity and population.

Test Market	Price Charged	Quantity Sold (thousand of pens)
1	50 ¢	20.0
2	50 ¢	21.0
3	55 ¢	19.0
4	55 ¢	19.5
5	60 ¢	20.5
6	60 ¢	19.0
7	65 ¢	16.0

---

[20] John Taplin, "A Coherence Approach to Estimates of Price Elasticities in the Vacation Travel Market," *Journal of Transport Economic Policy* 14 (1980).

Test Market	Price Charged	Quantity Sold (thousand of pens)
8	65 ¢	15.0
9	70 ¢	14.5
10	70 ¢	15.5
11	80 ¢	13.0
12	80 ¢	14.0
13	90 ¢	11.5
14	90 ¢	11.0
15	40 ¢	17.0

a. Using a linear regression model, estimate the demand function for Pilot's new pen.

b. Evaluate this model by computing the coefficient of determination and by performing a t-test of the significance of the price variable.

c. What is the price elasticity of demand at a price of 50 cents?

7. The demand for gasoline sold by the Black Gold Refining Company has been estimated as

$$Q_B = .22 P_B^{-.95} I^{1.4} A_B^{.3} P_C^{.2} P_{op}^{.6}$$

where

Q_B = number of gallons of gas sold each month (millions).

P_B = price per gallon charged by Black Gold

I = level of per capita disposable personal income in Black Gold's market area

A_B = dollar amount of advertising expenditures made by Black Gold

P_C = price per gallon charged by competitors

P_{op} = driving age population in Black Gold's market area

a. What interpretation can you give to the exponents of P_B, I, A_B, P_C, P_{op}?

b. Are these values consistent with your expectations?

c. If Black Gold ceased advertising, what would be the impact on demand according to this demand equation? What problem does this illustrate in an interpretation of demand functions?

8. The demand for haddock has been estimated as[21]

$$\log Q = a + b \log P + c \log I + d \log P_m$$

where

Q = quantity of haddock sold in New England

P = price per pound of haddock

I = a measure of personal income in the New England region

P_m = an index of the price of meat and poultry.

---

[21] F. W. Bell, "The Pope and the Price of Fish," *American Economic Review* (December 1958).

If $b = -2.174$, $c = .461$, and $d = 1.909$,

a. Determine the price elasticity of demand.

b. Determine the income elasticity of demand.

c. Determine the cross elasticity of demand.

d. How would you characterize the demand for haddock?

e. Suppose disposable income is expected to increase by 5 percent next year. Assuming all other factors remain constant, forecast the percentage change in the quantity of haddock demanded next year.

9. The demand for tea has been estimated as

$$Q = 7,000 - 550P + 210I + 425P_c$$

where

Q = thousands of pounds of tea sold

P = price per pound of tea

I = per capita disposable personal income in thousands of dollars

P_c = price per pound of coffee

a. If next year's tea price is forecast to be $3, per capita disposable personal income is estimated to be $15,000 (that is, 15), and the price per pound of coffee is estimated to be $4, compute the expected quantity demanded for the coming year.

b. Economic forecasters think there is a high probability of a major recession next year that would reduce per capita income to $13,000 (13). In addition, a frost in Brazil is likely to increase the price of coffee to $7 per pound. What impact would these changes in the economic outlook have on the demand for tea?

10. A Department of Energy report showed that during the period between March 19X0 and March 19X1, energy consumption per U.S. household dropped 9 percent. During the same period, energy prices rose by 24 percent.

a. Assuming all other factors influencing demand remained constant during this period, what was the price elasticity of demand for household energy consumption?

b. What other factors may have influenced the results for this period?

c. If household energy consumption had been increasing at a rate of 2 percent per year before this price increase, what impact would this have on the computed price elasticity?

11. In 19X2 the fare on Chicago's transit system was 60 cents per ride. This resulted in 711.6 million trips being taken on the system. In 19X3 the fare was increased to 80 cents and ridership declined to 692.4 million trips.

a. Compute the arc price elasticity of demand for transit ridership in Chicago assuming that all other factors influencing demand remained constant during this period.

b. Based on your answer to part (a), do you believe the fare increase was a rational action for the Chicago Transit Authority?

c. What other factors do you feel may have had an impact on ridership during this period? Do you believe the decline in ridership experienced in 19X3 tends to overstate or understate the actual impact of the fare increase?

d. In 19X4 the fare increased to 90 cents and ridership declined to 640 million trips. Compute the arc price elasticity between 19X3 and 19X4. How can you account for the differences between the 19X2–19X3 elasticity coefficient and the 19X3–19X4 elasticity coefficient?

12. JCR Corporation produces small garden tractors. JCR's economist has estimated the demand function for its Little Hustler line of tractors as follows:

$$Q = -11,000 - 1.1P + 75A - 400i + .6P_c + 250Y$$
$$(7,000) \quad (0.25) \quad (31) \quad (5.5) \quad (0.2) \quad (110)$$

where Q = quantity demanded, P = price per unit, A = thousands of dollars of advertising by JCR, i = annual percentage rate of interest charged by JCR Finance Company when a customer borrows to buy the tractor, P_c = price of a competitor's tractor, and Y = thousands of dollars of per capita disposable personal income of individuals living in the states where JCR sells its tractors.

The R^2 of this equation is 0.91 and the standard error of the estimate is 950. The standard errors for each of the regression coefficients are shown in parentheses.

a. How much of the variability in demand for the Little Hustler tractor is *not* accounted for by this model?

b. If P = $3,000, A = $400(000) i = 10%, P_c = $3,200 and Y = $13,000, what is the expected demand that JCR faces?

c. Using a normal distribution to estimate probabilities, what is the chance that the value of the coefficient relating advertising expenditures to quantity demanded is at least 25?

d. What is the impact of a $100,000 increase in advertising on JCR's sales, if all else remains constant?

e. What is the point price elasticity of demand if each of the variables in the demand function assume values equal to those in part (b)?

13. The supply function for Gooseberry Patch Dolls has been estimated to be

$$Q_s = -35,000 + 4,000P + 2000T$$

where T is a trend variable with a value $T = 0$ during 19X0, $T = 1$ during 19X1, $T = 2$ during 19X2 and so on. P is the price per doll and Q_s is the quantity supplied. Over the past ten years, actual price and quantity sold have been as follows:

Year	Price	Quantity Sold
19X0	$15.00	25,000
19X1	14.00	23,100
19X2	13.50	22,700
19X3	13.20	24,100
19X4	12.50	22,700
19X5	12.00	23,200
19X6	12.00	24,600
19X7	11.50	25,700
19X8	11.20	25,800
19X9	11.00	26,800

a. Plot the supply curves year by year by first letting $T = 0$ for 19X0, then setting $T = 1$ for 19X1, and so on.

b. On the same graph with the ten supply curves, plot the actual price and quantity sold data.

c. Estimate the demand function using the preceding data and a simple regression routine. What is the slope of the regression line? [Alternatively, you may visually fit a regression line through the points plotted on the graph paper in part (b).]

d. What assumptions must you make to be confident about the demand function estimated in part (c)?

14. The Sure-Fire Spark Plug Co. performed a regression analysis to determine the demand for its spark plugs in the "aftermarket" (replacement) and obtained the following results:

$$Q_D = 1060 - 2.86 P + 36.3 A + 2.3 N - .172 Y$$

where

Q_D = quantity demanded (millions of units)

P = price index of automobile replacement parts (1977–79 = 100)

A = advertising expenditures (millions of vehicles)

N = number of used cars registered (millions of vehicles)

Y = per capita disposable income (dollars)

a. Economists estimate that for next year $P = 125$, $N = 98.5$, and $Y = \$3,300$. If the company wishes to sell 450 million spark plugs next year, how much should it spend on advertising?

b. For the information given (and computed) in part (a), compute the point elasticity of demand for advertising.

c. Using the answer obtained in part (D), predict the effect on quantity of spark plugs demanded of a 5 percent cutback in Sure-Fire's advertising budget for next year.

**Case Problem 1
Demand
Estimation**

Early in 1989, the Southeastern Transportation Authority (STA), a public agency responsible for serving the commuter rail transportation needs of a large Eastern city, was faced with rising operating deficits on its system. Also, because of a fiscal austerity program at both the federal and state levels, the hope of receiving additional subsidy support was slim.

The board of directors of STA asked the system manager to explore alternatives to alleviate the financial plight of the system. The first suggestion made by the manager was to institute a major cutback in service. This cutback would result in no service after 7 P.M., no service on weekends, and a reduced schedule of service during the midday period Monday through Friday. The board of STA indicated that this alternative was not likely to be politically acceptable and could only be considered as a last resort.

The board suggested that because it had been over five years since the last basic fare increase, a fare increase from the current level of $1 to a new level of $1.50 should be considered. Accordingly, the board ordered the manager to conduct a study of the likely impact of this proposed fare hike.

The system manager has collected data on important variables thought to have a significant impact on the demand for rides on STA. These data have been collected over the past twenty-four years and include the following variables:

1. Price per ride (in cents)—This variable is designated P in Table 1. Price is expected to have a negative impact on the demand for rides on the system.

2. Population in the metropolitan area serviced by STA—It is expected that this variable has a positive impact on the demand for rides on the system. This variable is designated T in Table 1.

3. Disposable per capita income—This variable was initially thought to have a positive impact on the demand for rides on STA. This variable is designated I in Table 1.

4. Parking rate per hour in the downtown area (in cents)—This variable is expected to have a positive impact on demand for rides on the STA. It is designated H in Table 1.

The transit manager has decided to perform a multiple regression on the data to determine the impact of the fare increase.

Table 1
Data on Transit Ridership

Year	Weekly Riders (Y) $(\times\ 1,000)$	Price (P) per Ride (cents)	Population (T) $(\times\ 1,000)$	Income (I)	Parking Rate (H) (cents)
1962	1,200	15	1,800	2,900	50
1963	1,190	15	1,790	3,100	50
1964	1,195	15	1,780	3,200	60
1965	1,110	25	1,778	3,250	60
1966	1,105	25	1,750	3,275	60
1967	1,115	25	1,740	3,290	70
1968	1,130	25	1,725	4,100	75
1969	1,095	30	1,725	4,300	75
1970	1,090	30	1,720	4,400	75
1971	1,087	30	1,705	4,600	80
1972	1,080	30	1,710	4,815	80
1973	1,020	40	1,700	5,285	80
1974	1,010	40	1,695	5,665	85
1975	1,010	40	1,695	5,800	100
1976	1,005	40	1,690	5,900	105
1977	995	40	1,630	5,915	105
1978	930	75	1,640	6,325	105
1979	915	75	1,635	6,500	110
1980	920	75	1,630	6,612	125
1981	940	75	1,620	6,883	130
1982	950	75	1,615	7,005	150
1983	910	100	1,605	7,234	155
1984	930	100	1,590	7,500	165
1985	933	100	1,595	7,600	175
1986	940	100	1,590	7,800	175
1987	948	100	1,600	8,000	190
1988	955	100	1,610	8,100	200

Questions

1. What is the dependent variable in this demand study?
2. What are the independent variables?
3. What are the expected signs of the variables thought to affect transit ridership on STA?
4. Using a multiple regression program available on a computer to which you have access, estimate the coefficients of the demand model for the data given in Table 1.
5. Provide an economic interpretation for each of the coefficients in the regression equation you have computed.
6. What is the value of the coefficient of determination? How would you interpret this result?
7. Calculate the price elasticity using 1988 data.
8. Calculate the income elasticity using 1988 data.
9. What is the Durbin-Watson statistic for this regression? What does this indicate about the presence of autocorrelation in the data?
10. Based on an analysis of the correlation matrix of the independent variables, what can you say about the presence of multicollinearity in the model?
11. If the fare is increased to $1.50, what is the expected impact on weekly revenues to the transit system if all other variables remain at their 1988 levels?

Roses have an almost universal identification with the act of sending flowers, and consequently, they are one of the major products that the retail florist sells either by itself or as part of floral arrangements. The wholesale cut flower supplier must therefore be able to supply roses to retail florists; however, a number of recent factors have affected the growth in demand for roses. First, there has been a general breakdown of "old country social customs" such as the tradition of always sending flowers for a funeral. Second, there has been a growth in demand for competing products, such as carnations, which live longer than roses. Likewise, retailers increasingly use other flowers that are larger and require smaller quantities per arrangement. (Also, growth in the demand for green plants has accelerated. Green plant sales accounted for only 22 percent of the total sales for the floral industry in 1977 but are predicted to go to 50 percent by 1989.) Third, the costs of growing roses, particularly fuel and labor costs, have been increasing significantly.

**Case Problem 2
Demand
Estimation**

Matthews & Sons is a wholesale supplier of flowers to retail florists in the Beloit metropolitan area. This firm is concerned with developing a model that will aid in forecasting its rose sales (Q_t). Data on Matthews's rose sales over the past eighteen quarters were available from their monthly sales summaries. The variables that are thought to influence Matthews's rose sales included (1) its average wholesale price of roses, (2) its average wholesale price of carnations, (3) the average unemployment rate in the Beloit area, (4) the total number of "flower events" which, as defined here, means the total number of births, deaths, and marriages occuring during the quarter, (5) average weekly family disposable income, and (6) a "trend" variable. Price data for roses and carnations were available from Matthews's billing records. All other data were obtained from government documents for the Beloit SMSA. Table 2 (page 266) summarizes all of the relevant data.

Questions

1. Develop a linear demand model for Matthews's rose sales in terms of the six variables that are hypothesized to affect sales. From your knowledge of economic theory, develop a hypothesis concerning the sign (+ or −) for each of the explanatory variables (excluding the "trend" variable) in the demand model.

2. Using a multiple linear regression program, estimate the coefficients of the demand model for the data in Table 2.

3. Interpret each of the regression coefficients. Are the actual signs of the coefficients consistent with your hypothesized signs? Are the coefficients statistically significant?

4. What is the coefficient of determination for this model? Give an interpretation of its magnitude.

5. Calculate the price elasticity using the second quarter data for 1987. Give an economic interpretation of this figure.

6. Calculate the cross elasticity of demand using second quarter data for 1987. Give an economic interpretation of this figure.

7. In the preceding demand model we have ignored the competitive aspects of the metropolitan Beloit wholesale florist market. How might we go about incorporating this factor into the demand model?

8. What problems could arise in developing a demand model using *quarterly* data?

9. How does the possible presence of autocorrelation and multicollinearity in the data affect our interpretation of the results?

10. What are some of the shortcomings of using this model to forecast Matthews's future rose sales?

Table 2 **Raw Data for Rose Demand Study**

(1) Quarter	(2) Year	(3) Quantity of Roses Sold (Dozen) Q_t	(4) Average Wholesale Price of Roses ($\$/Doz$) P_t	(5) Average Wholesale Price of Carnations ($\$/doz$) C_t	(6) Average Unemployment Rate (%) U_t	(7) Births (B)	(8) Deaths (D)	(9) Marriages (M)	(10) Total "Flower Events" $(B + D + M)$ E_t	(11) Average Weekly Family Disposable Income ($\$/week$) Y_t	(12) Trend T
3	83	11,484	2.26	3.49	8.8	19,284	8,819	11,919	40,022	258.11	1
4	83	9,348	2.54	2.85	7.1	18,062	9,334	9,600	36,996	273.36	2
1	84	8,429	3.07	4.06	8.1	17,207	9,828	7,000	34,035	265.26	3
2	84	10,079	2.91	3.64	9.0	16,771	8,900	10,926	36,597	272.92	4
3	84	9,240	2.73	3.21	8.6	17,118	9,008	11,958	38,084	278.46	5
4	84	8,862	2.77	3.66	6.3	16,533	9,217	9,454	35,204	298.62	6
1	85	6,216	3.59	3.76	6.2	16,160	9,570	7,381	33,111	286.28	7
2	85	8,253	3.23	3.49	7.0	16,059	8,931	11,257	36,247	288.98	8
3	85	8,038	2.60	3.13	7.1	16,844	9,165	11,666	37,675	280.49	9
4	85	7,476	2.89	3.20	5.4	15,518	9,165	9,431	34,114	283.33	10
1	86	5,911	3.77	3.65	8.8	14,819	8,983	6,475	30,277	281.87	11
2	86	7,950	3.64	3.60	9.1	15,033	8,924	10,664	34,621	285.00	12
3	86	6,134	2.82	2.94	9.4	16,178	8,618	11,140	35,936	284.00	13
4	86	5,868	2.96	3.12	9.9	15,190	9,956	9,005	34,151	288.20	14
1	87	3,160	4.24	3.58	15.7	14,455	9,057	6,455	29,967	275.67	15
2	87	5,872	3.69	3.53	15.9	14,769	8,324	10,814	33,907	288.00	16
3	87	6,190	3.51	3.25	14.5	14,815	9,111	11,001	34,927	301.00	17
4	87	5,725	4.10	3.10	13.0	14,215	9,210	7,522	30,947	297.11	18

Business and Economic Forecasting 9

One of the central concerns of managers in all enterprises is forecasting the future demand for their products, forecasting the cost of producing this product, and forecasting the price at which the product will be sold. The forecasts at the firm level depend upon the performance of the overall economy, including the growth rate in gross national product, the level of interest rates, the rate of unemployment, the value of the dollar in foreign exchange markets, and the rate of inflation. These macroeconomic forecasts are provided by economists employed by the government, large firms, and economic forecasting organizations. The forecasting models used to forecast the future macroeconomic environment are very complex and require considerable judgment in their use. Other forecasting techniques are more suitable for use at the firm level. In this chapter we discuss several classes of forecasting techniques and consider the strengths and weaknesses of each. Because the value of a firm depends upon expected levels of future cash flows, it can be seen that forecasting the components of these future cash flows is very important if managers wish to make shareholder wealth-maximizing decisions.

Significance of Forecasting

Since management in both public and private enterprise typically operates under conditions of uncertainty, one of the most important functions of the managerial economist is that of forecasting. A forecast is merely a prediction concerning the future and is required in virtually all areas of the enterprise. Sales estimates are necessary to plan the proper future levels of production. The financial manager requires estimates of the future cash flows of the firm. This in turn requires a forecast of probable future levels of sales, production, receipts, and disbursements, as well as capital expenditures. In planning for capital investments, predictions about future economic activity are required so that returns accruing from the capital investment may be estimated. Forecasts of money and credit conditions must also be made so that the cash needs of the firm may be met at the lowest possible cost.

Public administrators and managers of not-for-profit institutions must also make forecasts. City government officials, for example, forecast the level of services that will be required of their various departments during a budget period. How many police officers will be needed to handle the public safety

Glossary of New Terms

Time-series data
A series of observations taken on an economic variable at various past points in time.

Cross-sectional data
A series of observations taken on different observation units (for example, households, states, or countries) at the same point in time.

Secular trends
Long-run changes (growth or decline) in an economic time-series variable.

Cyclical variations
Major expansions and contractions in an economic series that usually are longer than a year in duration.

Seasonal effects
Variations in a time series during a year that tend to appear regularly from year to year.

problems of the community? How many streets will require repair next year, and how much will this cost? What will next year's school enrollment be at each grade level? Government officials continually make estimates of the revenues that a specific tax or package of taxes will generate. This requires an evaluation of the level of economic activity that will prevail during the budget period. The hospital administrator faces such problems as forecasting the health-care needs of the community and the amount and cost of charity patient care the hospital will provide. To do this effectively, an estimate has to be made, not only of the growth in absolute size of population, but also of the changes in the number of people in various age groups and of the varying medical needs that these different age groups will have. Universities forecast student enrollments, costs of operations, and in many cases the level of funds that will be provided by tuition and government appropriations.

Obviously, good forecasting is essential to reduce the uncertainty of the environment in which most managerial decisions are made. The level of sophistication required in forecasting techniques varies directly with the significance of the problem being examined. Many decisions require that only very simple assumptions be made about the future. In cases where the decision is relatively insignificant (the potential gains or losses are small) and the decision has a short-run impact, an appropriate forecast may simply be based on the assumption that the future will be similar to the present. When the costs of an erroneous forecast increase and when the period of time over which the forecast is to be made increases, the use of more formal and sophisticated methodology becomes justifiable.

Although most of the examples developed in this chapter relate to the private sector, the methodology used is equally applicable to the problems faced in the public and not-for-profit sectors.

Selection of a Forecasting Technique

The forecasting technique used in any particular situation depends on a number of factors.[1] One dimension that helps determine the appropriate technique is the level of aggregation of the items being forecast. The highest level of economic aggregation that is normally forecast is that of the national economy, although world economic forecasts have become increasingly common. The usual measure of overall economic activity is gross national product (GNP), however, a firm may be more interested in forecasting some subset of GNP. For example, a machine tool firm may be more concerned about expected plant and equipment expenditures than about the GNP as a whole. Retail establishments are more concerned about future levels and changes in disposable personal income than about the overall GNP estimate.

The next level in the hierarchy of economic forecasts is the industry sales forecast. This is usually dependent on the expected performance of the overall

[1] This and the following section are based to a considerable extent on Roger K. Chisholm and Gilbert R. Whitaker, *Forecasting Methods* (Homewood, Ill.: Richard D. Irwin, 1971).

economy or on some major sector. Last are individual firm sales forecasts, which are in turn dependent on industry sales forecasts. For example, a simple, single firm forecast might take the industry sales estimate and relate this to the expected market share of the individual firm. Future market share might be estimated on the basis of historical market shares as well as on changes that are anticipated because of new marketing strategies, new products and model changes, and relative prices.

Within the firm, a hierarchy of forecasts also exists. The firm may estimate future total dollar sales, dollar and unit sales by product line, or regional sales in total dollars and units of specified product lines. These forecasts are used in planning orders for raw materials, employee-hiring needs, shipment schedules, and production runs. In addition, marketing managers use sales forecasts to determine optimal sales force allocations, to set sales goals, and to plan promotions. The sales forecast constitutes a crucial part of the financial manager's forecast of the cash needs of the firm. Long-term forecasts for the economy, the industry, and the firm are used in planning long-term capital expenditures for plant and equipment and for charting the general direction of the firm.

The managerial economist may choose from a wide range of forecasting techniques. These can be classified in the following general categories:[2]

1. Naïve forecasting techniques

2. Smoothing techniques

3. Barometric techniques

4. Survey and opinion polling

5. Econometric techniques

6. Input-output analysis

7. Technological forecasting

Some of these techniques are quite simple and rather inexpensive to develop and use, whereas others are extremely complex, require significant amounts of time to develop, and may be quite expensive. Some are best suited for short-term projections, whereas others are better for preparing intermediate- or long-term forecasts. The technique used in any specific instance depends on a number of factors, including the following:

1. The cost associated with developing the forecasting model compared with potential gains resulting from its use

2. The complexity of the relationships that are being forecast

3. The time period of the forecast (long-term or short-term)

4. The accuracy required of the model

5. The lead time necessary for making decisions dependent on the variables estimated in the forecast model

---

[2] Appendix 9A considers double exponential smoothing models.

This chapter examines the first five categories of forecasting techniques. Chapter 10 discusses the use of input-output analysis in forecasting and technological forecasting.

Naïve Forecasting Techniques

Naïve forecasting models are based *solely* on historical observations of the values of the variable being forecast. Naïve models do not attempt to explain underlying causal relationships that produce the observed outcome. For example, if a university were interested in predicting student enrollments for the coming term, only past student enrollment figures would be used in developing the forecast.

The term *naïve forecasting* should not be misinterpreted to mean simple. As will be shown later, the data manipulations that are undertaken in time-series analysis may actually be somewhat complex.

In their simplest form, the naïve forecasting models assume that historical values of some variable, such as sales, furnish the best basis for estimating current or future values of that variable. Letting $\hat{Y}$ denote the forecast value of the variable of interest, Y denote an actual observed value of the variable, and the subscript t identify the time period, one may identify the following simple models.

Some Elementary Models

The simplest model states that the forecast value of the variable for the next period will be the same as the value of that variable for the present period:

$$\hat{Y}_{t+1} = Y_t \qquad [9.1]$$

To forecast monthly beer sales (see Table 9.1), for example, the model uses *actual* beer sales from March 19X3 of 2,433 barrels as the forecast value for April. A model such as this is quite easy to use and simple to understand. It is particularly useful for forecasting over a short time period when historical evidence indicates no dramatic short-run changes in the data being forecast. Thus where changes occur slowly and the forecast is being made for a relatively short period in the future, such a model may be quite useful. One of the obvious problems that might exist with such a model is the availability of data. Since a forecast of next month's sales requires a knowledge of this month's sales, the forecaster may be faced with the task of speeding up the collection of actual data. Another problem with this model is that it makes no provision for incorporating the effects of known changes in the environment that may affect sales. Special promotions by the firm (or its competitors) could cause such great distortion in the observed values of the variable for one or more time periods that past data will be of little use in predicting future values.

An examination of Table 9.1 indicates that monthly sales are not totally random. Sales are high during the summer months and low during the winter. Failure to recognize and incorporate this information into the model will result in consistently high or low forecast values. If a recognizable pattern exists, it may

	Year			
Month	*19X1*	*19X2*	*19X3*	
January	2,370	2,446	2,585	
February	2,100	2,520	2,693	
March	2,412	2,898	2,433	
April	2,376	2,333		
May	3,074	3,250		
June	3,695	3,446		
July	3,550	3,986		
August	4,172	4,222		
September	3,880	3,598		
October	2,931	2,441		
November	2,377	2,180		
December	2,983	2,878		

Table 9.1
Monthly Beer Sales (thousands of barrels)

be incorporated by adjusting Equation 9.1 slightly to yield this equation:

$$\hat{Y}_{t+1} = Y_t + (Y_t - Y_{t-1}) \qquad [9.2]$$

In the example, the forecast value for April 19X3 would be

$$\hat{Y}_{t+1} = 2{,}433 + (2{,}433 - 2{,}693)$$
$$= 2{,}433 - 260 = 2{,}173$$

The use of this model, however, is still somewhat inappropriate for the data in Table 9.1. Although the forecast value for April is probably within reason, the forecast for May would probably seriously understate actual sales in May due to strong seasonality. A better forecast might be that May 19X3 beer sales will assume the same value as May 19X2 sales or that May 19X3 sales will be some specified percentage above average sales of the first four months of the year. This percentage adjustment used in making the May forecast is frequently called a *seasonal adjustment*. It is discussed in more detail below.

The foregoing merely suggests the types of naïve forecasting models that may be developed. With the use of a little imagination, the forecaster may increase the complexity of these simple models to fit the requirements of the situation. Naïve models are especially useful in making short-term forecasts about some variable when the values of that variable are relatively stable (or changing slowly or uniformly). Many problems, however, require more complex analysis to obtain reliable estimates.

Adjusting the Data

Data collected for use in forecasting the value of a particular variable may be classified into two major subsets: time-series and cross-sectional data. *Time-series data* are defined as a sequential array of the values of an economic variable. The data in Table 9.1 form an economic time series. *Cross-sectional data* are an array of the values of an economic variable observed at the same time. Data collected in a census are cross-sectional because they consist of a

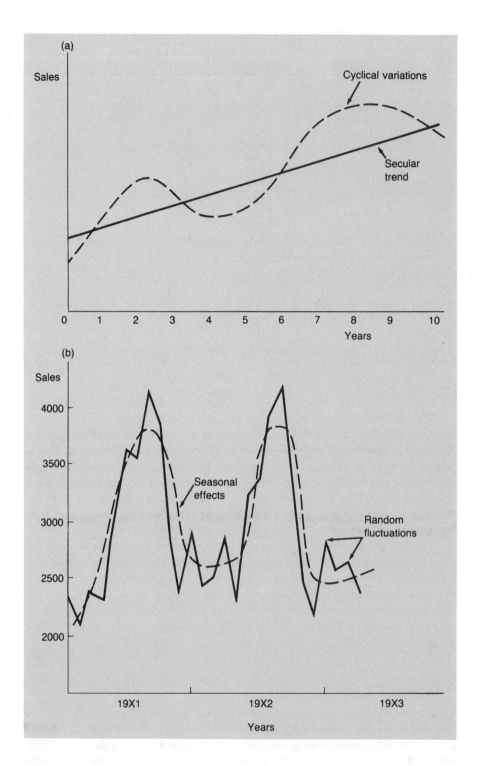

Figure 9.1
Secular, Cyclical, Seasonal, and Random Fluctuations in Beer Sales

series of observations taken at approximately the same time on various aspects of the population. No matter what type of forecasting model is being used, it is important to decide whether time-series or cross-sectional data are most appropriate (and available).

It is common to plot time-series data (as in Figure 9.1a, b) on a graph where time (in years, months, and so on) is represented on the horizontal axis and the values of the variable are on the vertical axis. The variations that are evident in the time series on Figure 9.1 (and in virtually all economic time series) may be caused by these four factors:

1. *Secular trends*—These are long-run changes in a series of data over time (*solid line* in Figure 9.1a). For example, in empirical demand analyses, such factors as increasing population size (or changes in its makeup) and changing consumer tastes may result in general increases or decreases of a demand series over time.

2. *Cyclical variations*—These are major expansions and contractions in an economic series that are usually greater than a year in duration (*broken line* in Figure 9.1a). For example, the housing industry appears to experience regular, relatively long-term expansions and contractions in demand. In most industries, however, cyclical variations are not consistent or predictable over time. In addition, to make valid statistical adjustments for cyclical fluctuations in an economic series over time, one must assume that secular trend and cyclical fluctuations result from two different sets of causal factors. This is often difficult to establish. For these reasons, methods of adjusting time-series forecast models for cyclical variations will not be discussed here.

3. *Seasonal effects*—These cause variations during a year that tend to be more or less consistent from year to year. The data in Figure 9.1(b) (broken line) on the demand for beer show significant seasonal variation. Beer consumption, for example, is normally much higher during the hot summer months.

4. Finally, an economic series may be influenced by random factors that are by and large not predictable (*solid line* in Figure 9.1b), such as wars, natural disasters, and extraordinary government actions (for example, a wage-price freeze).

Secular Trends

Long-run changes in an economic time series can follow a number of different types of trends. Three possible cases are shown in Figure 9.2. A *linear* trend is shown in Panel (a). Panels (b) and (c) depict *nonlinear* trends. In Panel (b), the economic time series follows a *constant rate of growth* pattern. The earnings of many corporations follow this type of trend. Panel (c) shows an economic time series that exhibits a declining rate of growth. Sales of a new product may follow this pattern. As market saturation occurs, the rate of growth will decline over time. Linear and constant rate of growth trends are examined in more detail below.

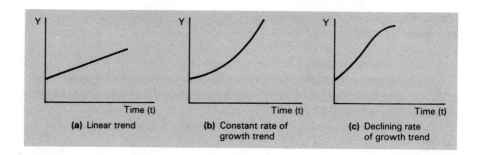

Figure 9.2
Time-Series
Growth Patterns

(a) Linear trend

(b) Constant rate of growth trend

(c) Declining rate of growth trend

Linear trends. A linear trend factor in a time series may be estimated in a number of ways. The easiest is to visually fit a straight line through the observed points in a graph relating the variable to points in time, but this method lacks sophistication and consistency since two different forecasters will rarely fit identical trend lines to the same set of data. The use of *least-squares* analysis, however, will provide an equation of a straight line of "best fit." (See Chapter 6 for a further discussion of the least-squares technique.) The equation of a linear trend line is given in the general form

$$\hat{Y}_t = \alpha + \beta t \qquad [9.3]$$

where $\hat{Y}_t$ is the forecast or predicted value for period t, α is the y intercept or constant term, t is a unit of time, and β is an estimate of this trend factor. Typically, some year, quarter, or month is identified as the starting time period. If, for example, one sought to forecast monthly ice cream sales of the Prizer Creamery, a least-squares trend line could be estimated on the basis of ice cream sales during the past several years. Assume that the equation of this line is calculated to be

$$\hat{Y}_t = 30,950 + 87.5t$$

where

$\hat{Y}_t$ = predicted monthly ice cream sales in gallons in month t

$30,950$ = number of gallons sold when $t = 0$

t = time period (months) (where December 19X0 = 0, January 19X1 = 1, February 19X1 = 2, March 19X1 = 3,...)

The coefficient (87.5) of t indicates that sales may be expected to increase by 87.5 gallons on the average each month.

Constant Rate of Growth Trends. The formula for the constant rate of growth forecasting model is

$$\hat{Y}_t = Y_0(1 + g)^t \qquad [9.4]$$

where $\hat{Y}_t$ is the forecasted value for period t, Y_0 is the initial ($t = 0$) value of the time series, g is the constant growth rate per period, and t is a unit of time. The predicted value of the time series in period t ($\hat{Y}_t$) is equal to the initial value of the series (Y_0) compounded at the growth rate (g) for t periods. Since Equation 9.4 is a nonlinear relationship, the parameters cannot be estimated directly with the least-squares method. However, taking logarithms of both sides of the equation gives

$$\log \hat{Y}_t = \log Y_0 + \log(1 + g) \cdot t$$

or

$$\hat{Y}'_t = \alpha + \beta t \qquad\qquad [9.5]$$

where $\hat{Y}'_t = \log \hat{Y}_t$, $\alpha = \log Y_0$, and $\beta = \log(1 + g)$. Equation 9.5 is a linear relationship whose parameters can be estimated using standard linear regression techniques.

For example, suppose that annual earnings data for the Fitzgerald Company for the past ten years have been collected and that Equation 9.5 was fitted to the data using least-squares techniques. The annual rate of growth of company earnings was estimated to be 6 percent. If the company's earnings this year ($t = 0$) are \$600,000, then next year's ($t = 1$) forecasted earnings would be

$$\hat{Y}_1 = 600,000 \ (1 + .06)^1$$
$$= \$636,000$$

Similarly, forecasted earnings for the year after next ($t = 2$) would be[3]

$$\hat{Y}_2 = 600,000 \ (1 + .06)^2$$
$$= \$674,160$$

Seasonal Variations

When *seasonal* variations are introduced into a naïve forecasting model, it may be possible to improve significantly its short-run predictive power. Seasonal variations may be estimated in a number of ways. The best known of these is the ratio-to-trend method.[4] If the trend analysis of ice cream demand at the Prizer Creamery, for example, forecasts August 19X5 sales of 35,850 gallons, this estimate may be adjusted for seasonality. Assume that over the past four years the trend model predicted the August sales patterns shown in Table 9.2 and that actual sales are as indicated.

These data indicate that on the average August sales have been 10 percent higher than the trend value. Hence, the August 19X5 sales forecast should be

---

[3] For large values of t, such calculations can become quite cumbersome. In these cases, present value (and/or compound value) tables or financial calculators can be used in performing the calculations.

[4] Another time-series forecasting model that is often very effective in generating forecasts when there is a significant seasonal component is the exponentially weighted moving-average (EWMA) forecasting model. At each point in time, the EWMA model estimates a smoothed average from past data, an average trend gain, and the seasonal factor. These three components are then combined to compute a forecast. See William Mendenhall and James E. Reinmuth, *Statistics for Management and Economics*, 3d ed. (North Scituate, Mass.: Duxbury Press, 1978), chap. 15, for a detailed discussion of EWMA models, including example applications.

Table 9.2
August Ice Cream Sales

Year (August)	Forecast	Actual	Actual/Forecast (percent)
19X1	31,650	33,865	107
19X2	32,700	36,624	112
19X3	33,750	36,450	108
19X4	34,800	39,324	113
19X5	35,850	—	—
			Average = 110

seasonally adjusted upward by 10 percent to 39,435. If, however, the model predicted the following February's sales to be 36,375 but similar data indicated February sales to be 20 percent below trend on the average, the forecast would be adjusted downward to $36,375 \ (1 - .2) = 29,100$.

Trend projections such as this are most useful for intermediate- and long-term forecasting while a simplified trend model is generally inappropriate for estimating short-term variations and predicting the turning points in an economic series. Simple trend projections (as well as other naïve forecasting models) assume that historical relationships will continue into the future and do not try to discover the underlying causes that produced those historical relationships. If the causal factors change, a poor forecast may result.[5] The introduction of seasonality factors into a forecasting model, however, should significantly improve the model's ability to predict short-run turning points in the data series, provided the historical causal factors have not changed significantly.

The naïve models of time-series forecasting discussed in this section may have substantial value in many areas of business. It is essential, however, that the business forecaster not rely too heavily on time-series models alone. These naïve models do not seek to relate changes in a data series to the causes underlying observed values in the series, so they are highly susceptible to making poor predictions when the underlying causal factors have been altered.

Smoothing Techniques

Smoothing techniques are a higher form of naïve forecasting models which assume that an underlying pattern can be found in the historical values of a variable that is being forecast. It is assumed that these historical observations represent not only the underlying pattern but also random variations. By taking some form of an average of past observations, smoothing techniques attempt to eliminate the distortions arising from random variation in the series and to base the forecast on a smoothed average of several past observations.

In general, smoothing techniques work best when a data series tends to change slowly from one period to the next and when no frequent changes occur

---

[5]A more flexible (and more complex) technique for short-term time-series forecasting is the Box-Jenkins technique. See G. E. Box and G. M. Jenkins, *Time Series Analysis: Forecasting and Control*, rev. ed. (San Francisco: Holden Day 1976).

in the direction of the underlying pattern. Smoothing techniques, like other naïve forecasting models, are cheap to develop, relatively inexpensive with respect to data storage needs, and inexpensive to operate; that is, they use up very little computer time.

Moving Averages

Moving averages are one of the simplest of the smoothing techniques. If a data series possesses a large random factor, a naïve forecast like those discussed in the previous section will tend to generate forecasts having large errors from period to period. In an effort to eliminate the effects of this randomness, a series of recent observations can be averaged to arrive at a forecast. This is the moving average method. A number of observed values are chosen, their average is computed, and this average serves as a forecast for the next period. In general, a moving average may be defined as

$$\hat{Y}_{t+1} = \frac{Y_t + Y_{t-1} + \cdots + Y_{t-N+1}}{N} \qquad [9.6]$$

where

$$\hat{Y}_{t+1} = \text{forecast value of } Y \text{ for one period in the future}$$

$$Y_t, Y_{t-1}, Y_{t-N+1} = \text{observed values of } Y \text{ in periods } t, t-1, \cdots, t-N+1,$$
$$\text{respectively}$$

$$N = \text{number of observations in the moving average.}$$

The greater the number of observations N used in the moving average, the greater the smoothing effect because each new observation receives less weight $(1/N)$ as N increases. Hence, generally, the greater the randomness in the data series and the slower the change in the underlying pattern, the more preferable it is to use a relatively large number of past observations in developing the forecast.

The use of Equation 9.6 can be illustrated with the data in Table 9.3. The forecast for period 4 is computed by averaging the observed values for periods 1, 2, and 3.

$$\hat{Y}_4 = \frac{Y_3 + Y_2 + Y_1}{N} \qquad [9.7]$$

$$= \frac{1,925 + 1,400 + 1,950}{3}$$

$$= 1,758$$

Similarly, the forecast for period 5 is computed as

$$\hat{Y}_5 = \frac{Y_4 + Y_3 + Y_2}{N} \qquad [9.8]$$

$$= \frac{1,960 + 1,925 + 1,400}{3}$$

$$= 1,762$$

Table 9.3
Three-Period Moving Average Forecast

Time Period	Observation	Three-Period Moving Average Forecast
1	1,950	—
2	1,400	—
3	1,925	—
4	1,960	1,758
5	2,800	1,762
6	1,800	2,228
7	1,600	2,187
8	1,450	2,067
9	2,000	1,617
10	2,250	1,683

Note that if one subtracts $\hat{Y}_4$ from $\hat{Y}_5$, the result is the change in the forecast from $\hat{Y}_4$, or

$$\Delta \hat{Y}_4 = \hat{Y}_5 - \hat{Y}_4$$

$$= \frac{Y_4 + Y_3 + Y_2}{N} - \frac{Y_3 + Y_2 + Y_1}{N}$$

$$= \frac{Y_4}{N} - \frac{Y_1}{N} \qquad [9.9]$$

Adding this change to $\hat{Y}_4$, the following alternative expression for $\hat{Y}_5$ can be derived:

$$\hat{Y}_5 = \hat{Y}_4 + \frac{Y_4}{N} - \frac{Y_1}{N} \qquad [9.10]$$

or, in general,

$$\hat{Y}_{t+1} = \hat{Y}_t + \frac{Y_t}{N} - \frac{Y_{t-N}}{N} \qquad [9.11]$$

which indicates that each moving average forecast is equal to the past forecast, $\hat{Y}_t$, plus the weighted effect of the most recent observation, Y_t/N, minus the weighted effect of the oldest observation that has been dropped, Y_{t-N}/N. As N becomes larger, the smoothing effect increases because the new observation, Y_t, has a small impact on the moving average.

The choice of an appropriate moving average period, that is, the choice of N, should be based on a comparison of the results of the model in forecasting past observations. For example, the forecaster might try a three-period average, a five-period average, and a seven-period average, and compare the accuracy of the alternatives. One criterion that is often used for such comparative purposes is the minimization of the sum of squared errors, or

$$\text{Min} \sum_{t=1}^{m} (\hat{Y}_t - Y_t)^2 \qquad [9.12]$$

where m is the number of time periods. The difference between each forecast value, $\hat{Y}_t$, and each actual value, Y_t, is calculated and squared for each period when historical values are available. The best moving average is chosen on the basis of the value of N that minimizes the sum of squared errors (Equation 9.12).

First-Order Exponential Smoothing

Two primary criticisms of weighted averages as smoothing techniques can be made. First, they normally give equal weight (a weight of $1/N$) to all observations used in preparing the forecast, even though intuition often indicates that the most recent observation probably contains more immediately useful information than more distant observations. Second, weighted averages require the storage of the N observations needed to make each forecast. For large values of N, or in the case where many such forecasts are being made for several data series, these data storage problems can become cumbersome and expensive. Exponential smoothing is designed to overcome both of these objections.

Consider the following alternative forecasting model:

$$\hat{Y}_{t+1} = wY_t + (1 - w)\hat{Y}_t \qquad [9.13]$$

This model weights the most recent observation by w (some value between 0 and 1 inclusive), and the past forecast by $(1 - w)$. A large w indicates that a heavy weight is being placed on the most recent observation.

Using Equation 9.13, a forecast for $\hat{Y}_t$ may also be written as:

$$\hat{Y}_t = wY_{t-1} + (1 - w)(\hat{Y}_{t-1}) \qquad [9.14]$$

By substituting Equation 9.14 into 9.13, we get

$$\hat{Y}_{t+1} = wY_t + w(1 - w) Y_{t-1} + (1 - w)^2\hat{Y}_{t-1} \qquad [9.15]$$

By continuing this process of substitution for past forecasts, we obtain the general equation

$$\hat{Y}_{t+1} = wY_t + w(1 - w)Y_{t-1} \\ + w(1 - w)^2Y_{t-2} + w(1 - w)^3Y_{t-3} + \cdots \qquad [9.16]$$

Equation 9.16 shows that the general formula (Equation 9.13) for an exponentially weighted moving average is a weighted average of all past observations, with the weights defined by the geometric progression:

$$w, (1 - w)w, (1 - w)^2w, (1 - w)^3w, (1 - w)^4w, (1 - w)^5w,\ldots \qquad [9.17]$$

For example, a w of 2/3 would produce the following series of weights:

$$w = .667$$

$$(1 - w)w = .222$$

$$(1 - w)^2w = .074$$

$$(1 - w)^3w = .024$$

$$(1 - w)^4 w = .0082$$

$$(1 - w)^5 w = .0027$$

.
.
.

With a high initial value of w, heavy weight is placed on the most recent observation, and rapidly declining weights are being placed on older values.

Another way of writing Equation 9.13 is

$$\hat{Y}_{t+1} = \hat{Y}_t + w(Y_t - \hat{Y}_t) \qquad [9.18]$$

This indicates that the new forecast is equal to the old forecast plus w times the error in the most recent forecast. A w that is close to 1 indicates a desire to quickly adjust for any error in the preceding forecast. Similarly, a w closer to zero, suggests little desire to adjust the current forecast for last period's error.

It should be apparent from Equations 9.18 and 9.13 that exponential forecasting techniques can be very easy to use. All that is required is last period's forecast, last period's observation, plus a value for the weighting factor, w. The optimal weighting factor is normally determined by making successive forecasts using past data with various values of w and choosing the w that minimizes the sum of squared errors in Equation 9.12.

Using the data from Table 9.4, one can apply the exponential technique to generate forecast estimates. To illustrate the approach, an exponential weight w of .5 will be used. To get the process started, one needs to make an initial forecast of the variable. This forecast might be a weighted average or some naïve forecast, such as

$$\hat{Y}_{t+1} = Y_t$$

The latter approach will be used. Hence the forecast for period 2 made in period 1 would be 1,950 ($\hat{Y}_{t+1} = 1,950$). The period 3 forecast value is (using Equation 9.18)

$$\hat{Y}_3 = 1,950 + .5(1,400 - 1,950)$$
$$= 1,950 - 275 = 1,675$$

Table 9.4
Exponential
Forecasting
Example

Time Period	Observation	Exponential Forecast
1	1,950	—
2	1,400	1,950
3	1,925	1,675
4	1,960	1,800
5	2,800	1,880
6	1,800	2,340
7	1,600	2,070
8	1,450	1,835
9	2,000	1,642
10	2,250	1,821

Similarly, the period 4 forecast equals

$$\hat{Y}_4 = 1,675 + .5(1,925 - 1,675)$$
$$= 1,800$$

The remaining forecasts are calculated in a similar manner. This process is normally repeated for several different values of w until a w is found that minimizes the sum of squared errors. The optimal w is then used to generate future forecasts.

Exponential smoothing gives the forecaster a great deal of flexibility in choosing the appropriate weights for past values. Furthermore, this approach only requires that two pieces of data be stored for each series being forecast—the observed value for the last period and the last period forecast.

Appendix 9A to this chapter discusses double exponential smoothing models. These models generally give more satisfactory results than first-order exponential smoothing models when the data possess a linear trend over time.

Barometric Techniques

The naïve forecasting models discussed earlier assume that future patterns in an economic time series may be predicted by projecting past data from that same series. Recall that in our discussion of time-series analysis, cyclical variations were largely ignored because very few economic time series exhibit consistent enough cyclical variations to make simple projection forecasting of these variations a reliable tool. Economists, however, have long recognized that if it were possible to isolate sets of time series which exhibited a close correlation of their movements over time, and if one or more of these time series normally *led* (in a consistent manner) the time series in which the forecaster has interest, then this leading series could be used as a predictor or barometer for short-term changes in the series of interest.

Although the concept of leading or barometric forecasting is not new,[6] current barometric forecasting is based largely on the work done at the National Bureau of Economic Research by Burns, Moore, Shiskin, and Mitchell. The barometric forecasting model they have developed is used primarily to identify potential future changes in *general business conditions*, rather than conditions for a specific industry or firm.

Economic indicators may be classified as leading, coincident, or lagging indicators (see Figure 9.3). The *Business Conditions Digest*, a monthly publication of the Department of Commerce, provides an extensive list of leading, lagging, and coincident indicators. The long list of indicators includes more than three hundred time series that are useful to business analysts and forecasters.

A short list of indicators is also developed that includes twelve series that tend to lead the peaks and troughs of business cycles, four series of roughly

---

[6] Andrew Carnegie used to count the number of smoke-belching chimneys in Pittsburgh to forecast the level of business activity and consequently the demand for steel.

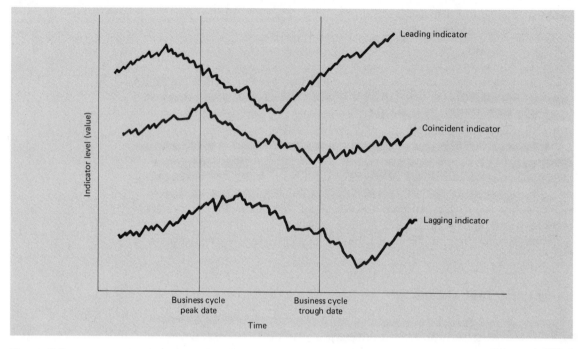

Figure 9.3
**Barometric
Indicators**

coincident indicators of economic activity, and six series that tend to lag peaks and troughs of economic activity. Table 9.5 lists the economic series included in the short list. This table lists the series name, the mean lead or lag of the series in relation to peaks and troughs of economic activity, the standard deviation of this lead or lag, and the score assigned to the indicator on the basis of its performance in the following areas:

1. Overall economic significance

2. Statistical adequacy

3. Conformity with the direction and magnitude of changes in the level of economic activity

4. Smoothness

5. Currency in the availability of data

6. Consistency with respect to turning points in economic activity

A perfect score for an indicator according to these criteria would be 100.

The rationale for the use of many of the series listed in this table is obvious. Many of these series represent commitments to future levels of economic activity. Building permits precede housing starts, and orders for durable goods precede their actual production. For some of the other indicators, the nature of the causal relationships involved is not quite so clear. The value of any particular time series as a predictor of future changes in another series depends on a number of factors. First, the user must be concerned with the success of the series in predicting the turning points in economic activity. Even the best series

Table 9.5 **Short List of Leading, Coincident, and Lagging Indicators**

Indicator	Mean Lead (+) or Lag (−) in Months	Standard Deviation	Overall Score
Leading indicators (12 series)			
Average work week of production workers, manufacturing	−7.3	6.6	73
Layoff rate, manufacturing (inverted)	−8.6	8.5	76
New orders, consumer goods and materials, 1972 dollars	−6.7	7.1	75
Vendor performance, slower deliveries	−7.3	6.2	69
Index of net business formation	−7.4	7.8	73
Contracts and orders, plant and equipment, 1972 dollars	−5.5	3.7	76
New building permits, private housing	−10.9	7.7	76
Net change in inventories on hand and on order, 1972 dollars (smoothed)	−5.6	3.8	76
Change in sensitive commodity prices (smoothed)	−8.8	6.8	72
Index of stock prices, 500 common stocks	−7.0	3.2	80
Change in total liquid assets (smoothed)	−8.5	5.1	73
Money supply (M2), 1972 dollars	−11.8	5.4	78
Roughly coincident indicators (4 series)			
Employees on nonagricultural payrolls	−0.3	2.4	88
Personal income, less transfer payments, 1972 dollars	−0.6	1.7	85
Index of industrial production, total	−1.6	2.2	86
Manufacturing and trade sales, 1972 dollars	−2.3	2.2	80
Lagging indicators (6 series)			
Average duration of unemployment (inverted)	+4.9	5.2	86
Manufacturing and trade inventories, 1972 dollars	+4.0	2.7	84
Labor cost per unit of output, manufacturing	+9.0	3.7	73
Average prime rate charged by banks	+7.1	5.2	85
Commercial and industrial loans outstanding	+3.9	3.7	83
Ratio, consumer installment debt to personal income	+5.6	4.6	76
Composite Indexes			
Twelve leading indicators	−8.2	5.9	80
Four roughly coincident indicators	−1.2	2.1	89
Six lagging indicators	+4.8	4.0	87

Source: U.S. Department of Commerce, Bureau of Economic Analysis, *Handbook of Cyclical Indicators* (Washington, D.C.: U.S. Government Printing Office, May 1977).

exhibit only 80 to 90 percent accuracy. In addition, a series is more valuable not only if it consistently leads (lags) business cycles but also if it lacks a large variability in the *length* of the lead (lag). Data for the series must also be available on a current basis. Finally, a series that is free of large random or seasonal fluctuations should be rated high since it will not give as many false signals.

The main value of leading and lagging indicators is in predicting the *direction* of future change in economic activity. These indicators reveal little or nothing about the *magnitude* of the changes.

To overcome some of the weaknesses associated with forecasting based on leading series, economists have developed the *diffusion index*. The primary advantage of this index is that it reduces the chances of making a false prediction based on a short-term fluctuation in one series alone. When all indicators in the index are rising, the diffusion index equals 100; when all are falling it equals 0; and when one-fourth are rising it equals 25. During business cycle expansions, Moore has found that this index is normally above 50 percent and during contractions it is normally below 50 percent. Diffusion indexes may be constructed using any combination of indicator series that the forecaster feels is appropriate.

Composite indexes, which are weighted averages of several indicators, are also designed to overcome the problem of making false predictions based on short-term fluctuations in a single series. The performance of the composite indexes for the twelve leading, four coincident, and six lagging indicators is summarized in Table 9.5. Figure 9.4 graphs the performance of these indexes over the major business cycles since 1948. The markings along the top of the figure indicate the month (above) of the peak (P) and trough (T) of an economic cycle. The values on the graph at each peak period and trough period on the graph indicate the lead ($-$) or lag ($+$) in the series relative to the actual peak or trough. For example, the lead for the leading indicator series was four months before the July 1953 peak and six months before the May 1954 trough.

In summary, barometric forecasting provides a better basis for predicting short-run turning points in an economic series than the naïve methods discussed earlier. Nevertheless, barometric forecasting still suffers from the major weakness that it is generally incapable of predicting the magnitude of forecast changes.

Survey and Opinion-Polling Techniques

Survey and opinion-polling techniques are other forecasting tools that may be helpful in making short-period forecasts. These techniques may be used for forecasting the overall level of economic activity (or some special portion of it), or they may be used within the firm for forecasting future sales. The rationale for the use of survey and opinion-polling techniques is that certain attitudes having an impact on economic decisions may be identified in advance of the actual implementation of the decision. If individuals who are responsible for making these decisions are polled, they may provide insights into their intended actions. Business firms normally plan additions to plant and equipment well in advance of the actual expenditures; consumers plan expenditures for many durable goods (as well as most other large expenditures such as vacations and education) in advance of the actual purchase; and governments at all levels prepare budgets indicating priorities and amounts of intended expenditures.

Survey techniques furnish a substantial amount of qualitative information that may be useful in economic forecasting. These techniques are usually used to supplement the other quantitative forecasting methods discussed in this chapter. The greatest value of survey and opinion-polling techniques is that they may help to uncover changes in past relationships that the quantitative

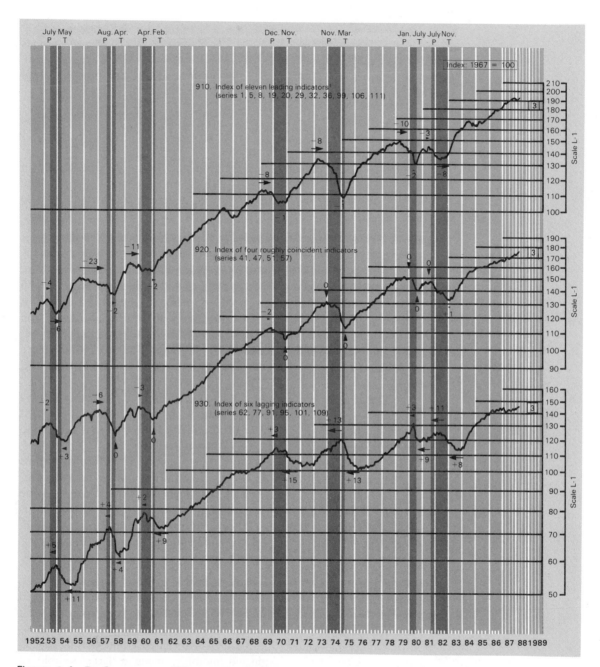

Figure 9.4 **Performance of Composite Series**

Note: Numbers entered on the chart indicate length of leads ($-$) and lags ($+$) in months from reference turning dates.

[1] Values of this index prior to January 1984 include a twelfth component, series 12, which has been suspended from the current index.

Source: Business Conditions Digest, US. Dept. of Commerce (April 1988).

techniques assume will remain stable. If consumer tastes are changing or if business executives begin to lose confidence in the economy, survey techniques may be able to uncover these trends before their impact is felt. In addition, survey techniques may provide the only source of data for predicting the demand for new products.

Forecasting Economic Activity

As mentioned, survey and opinion-polling techniques are used as an aid in forecasting economic activity in various sectors of the economy. Some of the best-known surveys available from private and governmental sources include the following:

1. *Plant and equipment expenditure plans*—Surveys of business intentions regarding plant and equipment expenditures are conducted by McGraw-Hill, the National Industrial Conference Board, the U.S. Department of Commerce, *Fortune* magazine, the Securities and Exchange Commission, and a number of individual trade associations. The McGraw-Hill survey, for example, is conducted twice yearly and covers all large corporations and many medium-sized firms. The survey reports plans for expenditures on fixed assets, as well as for expenditures on research and development. More than 50 percent of all new investment is accounted for by the McGraw-Hill survey.

   The Department of Commerce-Bureau of Economic Analysis plant and equipment expenditures survey is conducted quarterly and published regularly in the *Survey of Current Business*. The sample used is larger and more comprehensive than that used by McGraw-Hill.

   The National Industrial Conference Board surveys capital appropriations commitments made by the board of directors of one thousand manufacturing firms. The survey picks up capital expenditure plans that are to be made sometime in the future and for which funds have been appropriated. It is especially useful to firms that sell heavily to manufacturers and may aid in picking turning points in plant and equipment expenditures. This survey is published in the *Survey of Current Business*.

2. *Plans for inventory changes and sales expectations*—Business executives' expectations about future sales and their intentions about changes in inventory levels are reported in surveys conducted by the U.S. Department of Commerce, McGraw-Hill, Dun and Bradstreet, and the National Association of Purchasing Agents. The National Association of Purchasing Agents survey, for example, is conducted monthly, using a large sample of purchasing executives from a broad range of geographical locations and industrial activities in manufacturing firms.

3. *Consumer expenditure plans*—Consumer intentions to purchase specific products—including household appliances, automobiles, and homes—are reported by the Survey Research Center at the University of Michigan and by the Census Bureau. The Census Bureau survey, for example, is aimed at uncovering varying aspects of consumer expenditure plans, including

income, holdings of liquid and nonliquid assets, the likelihood of making future durable goods purchases, and consumer indebtedness.

Sales Forecasting

Opinion polling and survey techniques are also used on a micro level within the firm for forecasting sales. Some of the variations of opinion polling that are used include the following:

1. *Jury of executive opinion model*—The subjective views of top management are averaged to generate one forecast about future sales. Usually, this method is used in conjunction with some quantitative method, such as trend extrapolation. The management jury then modifies the resulting forecast based on their own expectations and insights regarding the sales environment.

2. *Sales force polling*—Some firms survey their own salespeople in the field about their expectations for future sales by specific geographical area and product line. The idea is that the employees who are closest to the ultimate customers may have significant insights to the state of the future market. Forecasts based on sales force polling may then be used to modify other quantitative or qualitative forecasts that have been generated internally in the firm.

3. *Surveys of consumer intentions*—Some firms conduct their own surveys of specific consumer purchases. Such surveys are common in durable goods industries but too expensive or infeasible for less expensive items. A furniture company may conduct a mail survey of a sample of consumers to estimate consumers' intentions of purchasing new furniture. Among other things, the firms may analyze the intentions to buy in relation to the consumers' income. The results of such a survey are then used to project national or regional furniture sales and to predict the impact that changes in income will have on furniture sales.

Econometric Methods

Another forecasting tool that is available to the managerial economist is econometric methodology. Econometrics is a combination of theory, statistical analysis, and mathematical model building to explain economic relationships. Econometric models may vary in their level of sophistication from the simple to the extremely complex. Econometric techniques were discussed in detail in Chapters 6 and 8. The discussion in this section deals with the application of these techniques to economic forecasting.

Advantages of Econometric Forecasting Techniques

Forecasting models based on econometric methodology possess a number of significant advantages over naïve or trend projection models, barometric models, and survey or opinion poll-based models. The most significant advantage of econometric models is that they seek to actually *explain* the economic phenomenon being forecast. Because management frequently is able to manipulate some of the independent variables embodied in the model (such as price or advertising expenditures in a demand model), econometric models enable management to assess quantitatively the impact of changes in its policies.

Another advantage of econometric models is that they predict not only the direction of change in an economic series but also the magnitude of that change. This represents a substantial improvement over the naïve models, which failed to identify turning points, and the barometric models, which did not forecast the magnitudes of expected changes.

A third advantage of econometric models is their adaptability. On the basis of a comparison between forecast values and actual values, the model can be modified (that is, existing parameters may be reestimated and new variables or relationships developed) to improve future forecasts.

Single-Equation Models

The simplest form of econometric model is the single-equation model. This is the type that is frequently used in empirical demand analysis. For example, in the previous chapter, a single-equation model was developed for explaining the demand for cigarettes in Transylvania. Cigarette demand (Q_D), the dependent variable, was hypothesized to be a function of four independent variables —price (P), disposable personal income (Y), size of the population (N), and advertising expenditures (A). The linear demand model (Equation 8.1) was given as

$$Q_D = \alpha + \beta_1 P + \beta_2 Y + \beta_3 N + \beta_4 A + \epsilon \qquad [9.19]$$

In order to use this model in forecasting the future demand of cigarettes, the parameters of the model (i.e., α, β_1, β_2, β_3, β_4) must first be estimated. The estimated cigarette demand model (Equation 8.5) was given as

$$Q_D = -51.5 - 15.0P + .024Y + .0125N + 1.10A \qquad [9.20]$$

Once the parameters of the model have been estimated, the forecaster must obtain estimates for the future values of the independent variables in the model. Substituting these values into the model yields a forecast value for the dependent variable. Clearly, if this model is to be used in forecasting, the future values of the independent variables must be easily obtainable. In some cases, this requires that forecasts first be made of some of the independent variables (such as P, Y, N, and A) and that these forecast values be incorporated into the model.

The cigarette demand model can be used to illustrate how such an equation can be used in forecasting future (e.g., next year's) demand. Suppose that the price of cigarettes is expected to rise to $11.00 per carton next year, disposable personal income per capita is expected to increase to $5300 next year, population is expected to increase to 5,020(000) next year, and advertising expenditures are expected to increase to $215(000,000) next year. Based on Equation 9.20, next year's cigarette sales in Transylvania are then forecasted to be

$$Q_D = -51.5 - 15.0(11.00) + .024(5300) + .0125(5020) + 1.10(215)$$
$$= 209.95 \text{ (million cartons)}$$

Applications of Single-Equation Forecasting Models

Single-equation econometric models have been widely used by firms to aid in forecasting the demand for their products. Three examples of single-equation forecasting models are presented below to illustrate the form and substance of many such models.

Example 1. Palda reports a forecasting equation used for Lydia Pinkham's Vegetable Compound.[7] The firm spent 40–60 percent of its sales revenue on advertising during the period 1908–1960. Hence the model that was developed focused on the effect of this advertising effort. The following prediction equation was estimated:

$$\hat{Y}_c = -3,649 + .665X_1 + 1,180(\log X_2) + 774X_3 + 32X_4 - 2.83X_5$$

where

$\hat{Y}_c$ = predicted yearly sales ($ thousands)

X_1 = last year's sales ($ thousands)

X_2 = current year's budgeted advertising expenditures ($ thousands)

X_3 = a dummy variable $\begin{cases} 1 = 1908\text{--}1925 \\ 0 = 1926\text{--}1960 \end{cases}$

X_4 = a trend variable (1908 = 0; 1909 = 1; 1910 = 2; 1911 = 3;...)

X_5 = current year's disposable personal income ($ billions)

The model explains about 94 percent of the variance in yearly sales and has been used in future forecasting efforts. Several characteristics of this model should be noted. First, the model uses a *lagged dependent variable*, namely, last year's sales (X_1), in predicting yearly sales. Second, a *trend variable* (X_4) is used in the forecasting equation. Third, a *dummy variable* (X_3) is used in the demand model. The dummy variable is used here to distinguish between two different time periods (i.e., before 1926 versus 1926 and afterward). Finally, note that the current year's budgeted advertising expenditures (X_2) are included in the model in *logarithmic* form. This may have been done because of a nonlinear relationship between sales (Y_c) and the raw (untransformed) independent variable.

---

[7] Kristian S. Palda, *The Measurement of Cumulative Advertising Effects* (Englewood Cliffs, N.J.: Prentice-Hall, 1964), pp. 67–68.

Example 2. Parker and Segura report the form of an equation used by American Can Company to forecast the demand for beer cans:[8]

$$\hat{Y}_{t+1} = a + b_1\hat{I}_{t+1} + b_2D_t + b_3A_t$$

where

$\hat{Y}_{t+1}$ = forecast sales for the coming year

$\hat{I}_{t+1}$ = estimated disposable personal income for the coming year

D_t = number of drinking establishments in the current year

A_t = a variable representing the age distribution in the current year

A characteristic of this model is the use of another forecasted variable as an independent variable. For beer can sales to be forecasted, a forecast of disposable personal income for the coming year, $\hat{I}_{t+1}$, must be made. This forecast is most likely obtained from one of the many multi-equation econometric models discussed later in this section.

Example 3. Du Pont has used a regression model to forecast its market share for a product in a region.[9] The results of this model were used to reallocate advertising expenditures for the product studied. The model takes the form

$$\hat{MS} = a + b_1AVL + b_2DP + b_3ADV$$

where

$\hat{MS}$ = Du Pont market share

AVL = product availability (percent of outlets in a territory that stock the Du Pont product)

DP = dealer push (percent of sales people specifying the Du Pont product)

ADV = percent change in advertising expenditures from last year

Forecast values from this market share equation are then multiplied by total estimated industry sales to determine expected Du Pont sales. In the cases tested by Du Pont, actual market share was found to be within 1 percent of the model's forecast.

Multiple-Equation Models

Although in many cases single-equation models may accurately specify the relationship that is being examined, frequently the interrelationships may be so complex that a system of several equations becomes necessary. Before examin-

---

[8] G. E. S. Parker and E. C. Segura, "How to Get a Better Forecast," *Harvard Business Review* (March–April 1971), p. 101.

[9] Robert D. Buzzell, "E. I. Du Pont de Nemours and Co., Inc.," in *Mathematical Models and Marketing Management* (Boston: Harvard Business School Division of Research, 1964), pp. 157–179.

ing a simple five-equation model of the national economy, it may be helpful to define some of the more important terms encountered in a discussion of econometric models. *Endogenous* variables are those that the model seeks to explain, or predict, via the solution of the system of equations. *Exogenous* variables are explained outside the model. Exogenous variables are determined by factors external to the model and may include such things as the level of government expenditures or the level of exports. They may also include variables that are specified by earlier data. If corporate investment were expressed as a function of corporate profits lagged by one period, the corporate profit variable would be considered an exogenous variable. Remember that every econometric model may have a different set of endogenous and exogenous variables and that a variable considered exogenous in one model may be endogenous in another.

An econometric model consists of two types of equations: *structural* (or *behavioral*) equations and *definitional* equations. A structural equation explains the relationship between a particular endogenous variable and other variables in the system. In addition, a number of definitional equations will be included in the model that specify relationships that are true by definition. The statement that gross national product (GNP) equals consumption expenditures C plus gross capital investment I plus government expenditures G is an example of a definitional equation:

$$GNP = C + I + G$$

An econometric model based on a system of equations can best be illustrated by examining a simple model of the national economy:

$$C = \alpha_1 + \beta_1 Y + \epsilon_1 \qquad [9.21]$$

$$I = \alpha_2 + \beta_2 P_{t-1} + \epsilon_2 \qquad [9.22]$$

$$T = \beta_3 GNP + \epsilon_3 \qquad [9.23]$$

$$GNP = C + I + G \qquad [9.24]$$

$$Y = GNP - T \qquad [9.25]$$

where

C = consumption expenditures

I = investment

P_{t-1} = profits, lagged one period

GNP = gross national product

T = taxes

Y = national income

G = government expenditures

Equations 9.21, 9.22, and 9.23 are behavioral or structural equations, whereas Equations 9.24 and 9.25 are identities or definitional equations. Once the system of equations has been specified, the next task is to estimate the value of the parameters ($\alpha_1, \alpha_2, \beta_1, \beta_2, \beta_3$) based on historical data. The ϵ's are included in Equations 9.21, 9.22, and 9.23 to reflect the fact that the theoretical relationships

Economic Analysis and Managerial Efficiency

USING MACROECONOMIC FORECASTS

Most firms do not have the internal resource capabilities to generate their own forecasts of the performance of the macroeconomy. Consequently, managers rely heavily on the forecasts provided by individual economists employed by very large firms, government agencies, and econometric forecasting services. Summaries of these forecasts are carried regularly in publications such as *Business Week* and the *Wall Street Journal*. For example, at year-end 1987, a survey of forty economists from large banks, investment banking firms, and corporations revealed an expected annual growth rate in real gross national product (GNP) of 1.9 percent (with a range of estimates from −3.5 percent to +5.5 percent) from the fourth quarter of 1987 to the fourth quarter of 1988.* Over the same period, prices were expected to increase at a 4 percent annual rate (with a range of estimates from +2.0 percent to +5.5 percent), and the unemployment rate was expected to increase slightly to 6.2 percent (with a range from 5.0 percent to 9.2 percent) by the fourth quarter of 1988. The large econometric forecasting models provided a similar range of forecasts for the same period.

When choosing among the various economic forecasting models, it is important for managers to understand the relative complexity of the models used by various forecasting organizations and the techniques being used in deriving the forecast. For example, the Chase Econometric Associates model generates monthly forecasts of about seven hundred macroeconomic variables. The basis for the forecasts is a complex, multi-equation econometric model, which receives about 70 percent of the weight, judgment (with a 20 percent weight), times-series methods (with a 5 percent weight), and current data analysis (with a 5 percent weight). In contrast, the Wharton Econometric Forecasting Associates model generates monthly forecasts of about one thousand macroeconomic variables, placing 60 percent weight on a complex econometric model, a 30 percent weight on judgment, and a 10 percent weight on current data analysis. The Townsend-Greenspan model provides quarterly forecasts of about eight hundred macroeconomic variables, placing a 45 percent weight on a complex econometric model, a 45 percent weight on judgment, and a 10 percent weight on current data analysis.** Thus, some of the large econometric models still rely heavily on the judgment of their staffs of economists and on a subjective interpretation of current economic data. In choosing an econometric model, a manager should determine that the model provides *timely* forecasts of variables of particular importance to the firm. The manager should also check the past forecasting accuracy of the model compared with alternative, available models.

Question

1. As an exporter of machine tools from the United States, what macroeconomic variables would you be especially interested in forecasting?

---

* "The Forecasts for 1988: From Economists and From Econometric Services," *Business Week* (28 December 1987), p. 111.

** For an excellent summary discussion of the major econometric forecasting models see Stephen K. McNees, "The Recent Record of Thirteen Forecasters," *New England Review* (September-October 1981), pp. 5–21.

are not exact. To make unbiased estimates of the model's parameters, one must assume that the ϵ's (disturbance terms) are randomly distributed with an expected value of zero.[10] The econometric techniques used to solve for the values of the parameters in a system of equations are beyond the scope of this book.[11]

Once parameters have been estimated, forecasts may be generated by substituting known or estimated values for the exogenous variables into the system and solving for the endogenous variables.

A number of complex econometric models of the U.S. economy have been developed and are used to forecast business activity. The Wharton annual and industry forecasting model, for instance, consists of at least 155 structural equations and 191 definitional identities. To make forecasts based on these models, estimates must be made for a large number of exogenous variables. The Wharton annual model requires that estimates be made of at least ninety exogenous variables before forecasts may be generated. The accuracy of forecasts that may be generated from these models depends, to a certain degree, on the forecaster's skill (or luck) in predicting the exogenous variables.

Summary

- A forecast is a prediction concerning the future.

- The choice of a forecasting technique depends on the cost of developing the forecasting model relative to the potential benefits to be derived, the complexity of the relationship being forecast, the time period for the forecast, the accuracy required of the model, and the lead time required to obtain inputs for the forecasting model.

- Data used in forecasting may be in the form of a time series—that is, a series of observations of a variable over a number of past time periods—or they may be cross-sectional—that is, observations are taken at a single point in time for a sample of individuals, firms, geographic regions, communities, or some other set of observable units.

- *Naïve* forecasting models are based on an extrapolation of past values into the future. Naïve forecasting models may be adjusted for seasonal, secular, and cyclical trends in the data.

- When a data series possesses a great deal of randomness, *smoothing techniques,* such as moving averages and exponential smoothing, may improve the forecast accuracy.

- Neither naïve models nor smoothing techniques are capable of identifying major future changes in the direction of an economic data series.

---

[10] See J. Johnston, *Econometric Methods*, 3d ed. (New York: McGraw-Hill, 1984), chap. 2, for a discussion of unbiased estimators.

[11] See, for example, William J. Baumol, *Economic Theory and Operations Analysis*, 4th ed. (Englewood Cliffs, N. J.: Prentice-Hall, 1977), chap. 10. See also Johnston, *Econometric Models*, 3d ed., chap. 11.

- *Barometric techniques,* which employ leading, lagging, and coincident indicators, are designed to forecast changes in the direction of a data series but are poorly suited to forecasting the magnitude of the change.

- *Survey and opinion-polling techniques* are often useful in forecasting such variables as business capital spending and major consumer expenditure plans and for generating product-specific or regional sales forecasts for a firm.

- *Econometric methods* seek to explain the reasons for a change in an economic data series and to use this quantitative, explanatory model to make future forecasts. Econometric models are one of the most useful business forecasting tools, but they tend to be expensive to develop and maintain.

- The ultimate measure of the effectiveness of a forecast is not its level of mathematical or theoretical sophistication but rather its ability to generate cost-effective estimates of the future that are sufficiently accurate to meet the needs of the decision maker.

Selected References

Armstrong, J. Scott. "Research on Forecasting: A Quarter Century Review, 1960–1984." *Interfaces* (January–February 1986), pp. 89–109.

Chambers, J. C., S. K. Mullick, and D. D. Smith. "How to Choose the Right Forecasting Technique." *Harvard Business Review* (July–August 1971), pp. 45–74.

Chisholm, Roger K., and Gilbert R. Whitaker. *Forecasting Methods.* Homewood, III.: Richard D. Irwin, 1971.

Cicarelli, James, and J. Narayan. "The Performance of Eleven Economic Forecasting Models in the 1970s." *Business Economics* (September 1980), pp. 12–16.

"Keys for Business Forecasting." Federal Research Bank of Richmond, 1980.

McNees, Stephen K. "The Rationality of Economic Forecasts." *American Economic Review* (May 1978), pp. 301–305.

Moore, G. H., and J. Shiskin. *Indicators of Business Expansions and Contractions.* New York: National Bureau of Economic Research, 1967.

Wheelwright, Steven C., and Spyros Makridakis. *Forecasting Methods for Management,* 2d ed. New York: John Wiley, 1977.

Wheelwright, Steven C. and Spyros Makridakis. *Interactive Forecasting,* 2d ed. San Francisco: Holden-Day, 1978.

Zarnowitz, Victor. "Recent Work on Business Cycles in Historical Perspective," *Journal of Economic Literature* (June 1985), pp. 523–580.

Discussion Questions

1. "The best forecasting model is one that most realistically considers the underlying causal factors in an economic relationship and that therefore has the best 'track record' in generating forecasts." Evaluate this statement. What criteria can you develop for assessing the worth of a forecasting model?

2. Based on an examination of Figure 9.4, by how many months did the Index of Twelve Leading Indicators
   a. Lead the 1969 peak?
   b. Lead the 1973 peak?
   c. Lead the 1981 peak?

d. Lead the 1970 trough?
e. Lead the 1975 trough?
f. Lead the 1982 trough?

3. Based on an examination of Figure 9.4, by how many months did the Index of Six Lagging Indicators

a. Lag the 1969 peak?
b. Lag the 1970 trough?
c. Lag the 1981 peak?
d. Lag the 1982 trough?

4. Distinguish among secular trends, cyclical variations, seasonal variations, and random variations in a time-series set of data.

5. Large-scale, multiequation econometric models are capable of accounting for many complex interrelationships of economic variables. Because of the increased realism these models provide, they are often thought to be superior to less complex models. What are the major limitations in the use of multiequation models?

6. When using first-order exponential smoothing techniques, how is the smoothing or weighting coefficient selected?

7. Distinguish between *exogenous* and *endogenous* variables in multiequation econometric models.

8. Distinguish between *structural* equations and *definitional* equations in multiequation econometric models.

9. Forecast errors can usually be reduced by increasing the amount of time and money spent on preparing the forecast. Under what circumstances might such an increase in expenditures not be undertaken by profit-maximizing managers?

10. In industries that have a high, positive income elasticity of demand for their products, what is the relationship between economic growth and demand forecasts for these industries? How does this change if the income elasticity of demand is very low?

Problems

1. An economist for Pittsburgh Brewing Company has hypothesized a forecasting model in which the sales in any particular month are directly proportional to the square of the wages of Pittsburgh steelworkers in the previous month, plus a random error.

a. If S = sales, W = steelworkers' wages, t = time, and e = the random error term, formulate an equation for this month's sales and another equation to forecast next month's sales.
b. If the random errors average out to zero, and if sales this month are $900,000 and wages last month were $2,000, what should next month's sales be if this month's wages decline to $1,800?

2. The forecasting staff for the Prizer Corporation has developed a model to predict sales of its air-cushioned-ride snowmobiles. The model specifies that sales S vary jointly with disposable personal income Y and the population between ages 15 and 40, Z, and *inversely* with the price of the snowmobiles P. Based on past data, the best estimate of this relationship is

$$S = k \frac{YZ}{P}$$

where k has been estimated (with past data) to equal 100.

a. If $Y = \$11,000$, $Z = \$1,200$, and $P = \$20,000$, what value would you predict for S?
b. What happens if P is reduced to $17,500?
c. How would you go about developing a value for k?
d. What are the potential weaknesses of this model?

3. The Genessee Transportation Company operates an urban bus system in the city of Genessee, Pennsylvania. Economic analysis performed by the firm indicates that two major factors influence the demand for its services: fare levels and downtown parking rates. Table 1 presents information available from 19X1 operations. Forecasts of future fares and daily parking rates are presented in Table 2.

Table 1

Average Daily Transit Riders (19X1)	Round-Trip Fare	Average Downtown Parking Rate
5,000	$1.00	$5.50

Table 2

Year	Round-Trip Fare	Average Parking Rates
19X2	$1.00	$6.50
19X3	$1.25	$6.50

Genessee's economists supplied the following information so that the firm can estimate ridership in 19X2 and 19X3. Based on past experience, the coefficient of cross elasticity between bus ridership and downtown parking rates is estimated at 0.2, given a fare of $1.00, round trip. This is not expected to change for a fare increase to $1.25. The price elasticity of demand is currently estimated at -1.1, given daily parking rates of $5.50. It is estimated, however, that the price elasticity will change to -1.2 when parking rates increase to $6.50. Using these data, estimate the average daily ridership for 19X2 and 19X3.

4. Stowe Automotive is considering an offer from Indula to build a plant making automotive parts for use in that country. In preparation for a final decision, Stowe's economists have been hard at work constructing a basic econometric model for Indula to aid the company in predicting future levels of economic activity. Because of the cyclical nature of the automotive parts industry, forecasts of future economic activity are quite important in Stowe's decision process.

Corporate profits (P_{t-1}) for all firms in Indula were about $100 billion. GNP for the nation is composed of consumption C, investment I, and government spending G. It is anticipated that Indula's federal, state, and local governments will spend in the range of $200 billion next year. On the basis of an analysis of recent economic activity in Indula, consumption expenditures are assumed to be $100 billion plus 80 percent of national income. National income is equal to GNP minus taxes T. Taxes are estimated to be at a rate of about 30 percent of GNP. Finally, corporate investments have historically equaled $30 billion plus 90 percent of last year's corporate profits (P_{t-1}).

a. Construct a five-equation econometric model of the state of Indula. There will be a consumption equation, an investment equation, a tax receipt equation, an equation representing the GNP identity, and a national income equation.

b. Assuming that all random disturbances average to zero, solve the system of equations to arrive at next year's forecast values for C, I, T, GNP, Y. (*Hint*: It is easiest to start by solving the investment equation and then working through the appropriate substitutions in the other equations.)

5. a. Fred's Hardware and Hobby House expects its sales to increase at a constant rate of 8 percent per year over the next three years. If current sales are $100,000, what will they be three years from now?

b. If sales in 19X0 were $60,000 and they grew to $100,000 by 19X4 (a four-year period), what was the actual annual compound growth rate?

6. Metropolitan Hospital has estimated its average monthly bed needs as

$$N = 1,000 + 9X$$

where

$$X = \text{time period (months); January } 19X6 = 0$$
$$N = \text{monthly bed needs}$$

Assume that no new hospital additions are expected in the area in the foreseeable future. The following monthly seasonal adjustment factors have been estimated, using data from the past five years:

Month	Adjustment Factor
January	+5%
April	−15%
July	+4%
November	−5%
December	−25%

a. Forecast Metropolitan's bed demand for: January, April, July, November and December of 19X8.

b. If the following actual and forecast values for June bed demands have been recorded, what seasonal adjustment factor would you recommend be used in making future June forecasts?

Year	Forecast	Actual
19X6	1,045	1,096
19X5	937	993
19X4	829	897
19X3	721	751
19X2	613	628
19X1	505	560

7. A firm has experienced the demand shown in the table below over the past ten years.

a. Fill in the following table by preparing forecasts based upon a 5-year moving average, a 3-year moving average, and exponential smoothing (with a $w = .9$ and a $w = .3$). *Note*: The exponential smoothing forecasts may be begun by assuming $\hat{Y}_{t+1} = Y_t$.

Year	Demand	5-Year Moving Average	3-Year Moving Average	Exponential Smoothing $(w = .9)$	Exponential Smoothing $(w = .3)$
19X0	800	xxxxx	xxxxx	xxxxx	xxxxx
19X1	925	xxxxx	xxxxx	—	—
19X2	900	xxxxx	xxxxx	—	—
19X3	1025	xxxxx	—	—	—
19X4	1150	xxxxx	—	—	—
19X5	1160	—	—	—	—
19X6	1200	—	—	—	—
19X7	1150	—	—	—	—
19X8	1270	—	—	—	—
19X9	1290	—	—	—	—
19Y0	*	—	—	—	—

*Unknown future value to be forecast

b. Using the forecasts from 19X5 through 19X9, compare the accuracy of each of the forecasting methods using the minimization-of-sum-of-squared-errors criterion.

c. Which forecast would you use for 19Y0? Why?

8. The economic analysis division of Mapco Enterprises has estimated the demand function for its line of weed trimmers as

$$Q_D = 18,000 + 0.4N - 350P_M + 90P_S$$

where

N = number of new homes completed in the primary market area

P_M = price of the Mapco trimmer

P_S = price of its competitor's Surefire trimmer

In 19X1, 15,000 new homes are expected to be completed in the primary market area. Mapco plans to charge $50 for its trimmer. The Surefire trimmer is expected to sell for $55.

a. What sales are forecast for 19X1 under these conditions?

b. If its competitor cuts the price of the Surefire trimmer to $50, what effect will this have on Mapco's sales?

c. What effect would a 30 percent reduction in the number of new homes completed have on Mapco's sales (ignore the impact of the price cut of the Surefire trimmer)?

9. The sales of Cycle City, a large motorcycle and moped distributor, have been growing significantly over the past ten years. This past history of sales growth is indicated in the table below:

Year	Sales
19X0	$100,000
19X1	130,000
19X2	166,400
19X3	209,664
19X4	259,983
19X5	317,180
19X6	380,615

Year	Sales
19X7	449,126
19X8	520,986
19X9	593,924
19Y0	665,195

a. What has been the compound annual rate of growth in sales for Cycle City over this 10-year period?

b. Based upon your answer in part (a), what sales do you forecast for the next year (19Y1)?

c. Graph the growth in sales over the past ten years. What has been happening to the rate of growth over this period?

d. Based on your answer to part (c), what sales do you forecast for 19Y1?

10. The Questor Corporation has experienced the following sales pattern over the past ten years:

Year	Sales ($000)
19X0	121
19X1	130
19X2	145
19X3	160
19X4	155
19X5	179
19X6	215
19X7	208
19X8	235
19X9	262
19Y0	*

*Unknown future value to be forecast.

a. Compute the equation of a trend line (similar to Equation 9.3) for these sales data to forecast sales for the next year. (Let $19X0 = 0$, $19X1 = 1$, etc., for the time variable.) What does this equation forecast for sales in the year 19Y0?

b. Use a first-order exponential smoothing model with a w of 0.9 to forecast sales for the year 19Y0.

11. The following table provides corporate average bond yields for each month of 19X4:

Month	Yield
January	12.92%
February	12.88
March	13.33
April	13.59
May	14.13
June	14.40
July	14.32
August	13.78

Month	Yield
September	13.56
October	13.33
November	12.88
December	12.74

a. Use the models in Equations 9.1, 9.2, 9.3, plus a three-month moving average to forecast the interest rate for January 19X5.

b. Compare the results of each of these forecasts with the actual January 19X5 figure of 12.64 percent.

12. Bell Greenhouses has estimated its monthly demand for potting soil to be the following:

$$N = 400 + 4X$$

where

N = monthly demand for bags of potting soil

X = time periods in months (March 19X4 = 0)

Assume this trend factor is expected to remain stable in the foreseeable future. The following table contains the monthly seasonal adjustment factors, which have been estimated using actual sales data from the past five years:

Month	Adjustment Factor
March	+2%
June	+15%
August	+10%
December	−12%

a. Forecast Bell Greenhouses' demand for potting soil in March, June, August, and December 19X6.

b. If the following table shows the forecasted and actual potting soil sales by Bell Greenhouses for April in each of the past five years, determine the seasonal adjustment factor to be used in making an April 19X6 forecast.

Year	Forecast	Actual
19X5	500	515
19X4	452	438
19X3	404	420
19X2	356	380
19X1	308	320

13. The manager of the Midwestern University Bookstore is attempting to forecast next year's demand for "Whizzo," a mini, wristwatch-size calculator. She hypothesizes that the number of units sold (S) in any period should be directly proportional to the engineering enrollment at the university in hundreds of students (E), average professors' salaries at the university in thousands of dollars (I), and inversely proportional to the price of these calculators (P) and expresses the relationship in the following form:

$$S = k\frac{EI}{P}$$

a. Estimate k given the following data from the previous year: $S = 150$ units, $E = 25$ (hundred) students, $I = \$18$ (thousand) and $P = \$200$.

b. Use the equation in (a) to forecast next year's calculator sales assuming that the price of the calculators declines to $150 and that the other variables remain unchanged.

c. Use the equation in (a) to forecast next year's calculator sales assuming that the price declines to $150, engineering enrollment increases by 10 percent to 27.5, and average professors' salaries increase by 5 percent to $18.9.

d. What other factors might the manager want to consider in analyzing the demand for Whizzo calculators?

Double Exponential Smoothing Models[12]

APPENDIX

9A

Data that are collected over time frequently exhibit a linear trend, either upward or downward. When a linear trend is not apparent in the data, single exponential smoothing is well suited as a forecasting technique. However, if a trend is present in the data, double exponential smoothing is more appropriate for obtaining forecasts than is single exponential smoothing.

The Model

The double exponential smoothing technique is closely related to the trend analysis technique of simple linear regression, in which the forecast for Y_{t+1}, given historical data up to and including time t is $\hat{Y}_{t+1} = a + b(t + 1)$, where a and b are the usual least-squares regression coefficients. In double exponential smoothing, the coefficients a and b are considered to be functions of time (thus labeled a_t and b_t) and are updated as each successive observation becomes available. These updated coefficients are given by the following expressions:

$$b_t = [w/(1 - w)](S_t - S_t^{(2)}) \qquad [9A.1]$$

and

$$a_t = 2S_t - S_t^{(2)} - tb_t \qquad [9A.2]$$

where w is a smoothing constant chosen to minimize the sum of the squared forecast errors,
      S_t is the single smoothed statistic computed recursively as

$$S_t = w Y_t + (1 - w) S_{t-1} \qquad [9A.3]$$

and $S_t^{(2)}$ is the double smoothed statistic also computed recursively as

$$S_t^{(2)} = wS_t + (1 - w)S_{t-1}^{(2)} \qquad [9A.4]$$

---

[12] This appendix was prepared in large part by Professor Gary Kelley of West Texas State University.

The initial values S_o and $S_o^{(2)}$ are obtained using the equations

$$S_o = a_o - [(1 - w)/w] b_o \qquad \text{[9A.5]}$$

and

$$S_o^{(2)} = a_0 - 2 [(1 - w)/w] b_o \qquad \text{[9A.6]}$$

The quantities a_o and b_o are initial values of the regression coefficients. If data are available, say, to time t, a_o and b_o are simply regression coefficients computed using the model $Y_t = a_o + b_o t$. If no data are available, values for a_o and b_o are assigned subjectively, or if this is not possible S_o and $S_o^{(2)}$ are both assigned the initial value of the series, Y_o.

Assuming that S_t and $S_t^{(2)}$ have been computed recursively from time 0, the double exponentially smoothed forecast for Y_{t+1} is given by

$$\hat{Y}_{t+1} = a_t + b_t(t + 1)$$

where a_t and b_t are as given in Equations 9A.1 and 9A.2.

A Numerical Example

Consider the following time series:

	t	Y_t
	0	2
	1	6
	2	5
	3	8

Given these data, we choose to forecast Y_4 using double exponential smoothing. Since four data points are available, they will be used to calculate the initial regression coefficients a_o and b_o. Simple regression techniques with t as the independent variable and Y_t as the dependent variable yield the following equation: $\hat{Y}_t = 2.7 + 1.7t$. Hence $a_o = 2.7$ and $b_o = 1.7$. Suppose w is initially chosen to be .20. S_o and $S_o^{(2)}$ can now be calculated using Equations 9A.5 and 9A.6 as follows:

$$S_o = a_o - [(1 - w)/w] b_o$$
$$= 2.7 - [(1 - .2)/.2] 1.7$$
$$= - 4.10$$

and

$$S_o^{(2)} = a_o - 2 [(1 - w)/w] b_o$$
$$= 2.7 - 2[(1 - .2)/.2] 1.7$$
$$= - 10.90$$

S_1, S_2, and S_3 are found using Equation 9A.3:

$$S_1 = (.2)(6) + (.8)(-4.10)$$
$$= -2.08$$

$$S_2 = (.2)(5) + (.8)(-2.08)$$
$$= -.66$$

and

$$S_3 = (.2)(8) + (.8)(-.66)$$
$$= 1.07$$

Likewise, $S_1^{(2)}$, $S_2^{(2)}$, and $S_3^{(2)}$ are found using Equation 9A.4:

$$S_1^{(2)} = (.2)(-2.08) + (.8)(-10.90)$$
$$= -9.14$$

$$S_2^{(2)} = (.2)(-.66) + (.8)(-9.14)$$
$$= -7.44$$

and

$$S_3^{(2)} = (.2)(1.07) + (.8)(-7.44)$$
$$= -5.74$$

The updated coefficients a_t and b_t for $t = 3$ given in Equations 9A.1 and 9A.2 are

$$b_3 = (.2/.8)(1.07 - (-5.74))$$
$$= 1.70$$

and

$$a_3 = 2(1.07) - (-5.74) - 3(1.70)$$
$$= 2.78.$$

Thus, the double exponentially smoothed forecast for Y_4 is

$$\hat{Y}_4 = 2.78 + 4(1.70)$$
$$= 9.58$$

The one remaining point that needs to be addressed is the selection of the smoothing constant, w. It is important to realize that each time S_t and $S_t^{(2)}$ are computed, a_t and b_t can be computed. Hence $\hat{Y}_{t+1}$ can be forecasted, and when Y_{t+1} actually is observed the forecast error $Y_{t+1} - \hat{Y}_{t+1}$ can be calculated. The smoothing constant is chosen so that $\Sigma(Y_t - \hat{Y}_t)^2$ is minimized, where the summation extends over all historical data. The actual process of choosing w is iterative; that is, choose an initial value, compute $\Sigma(Y_t - \hat{Y}_t)^2$, and so forth until a value for w is found that minimizes this sum.

Discussion Question

1. Under what circumstances is a double exponential smoothing model likely to yield a better forecast from a time-series of data than is a single exponential smoothing model?

Problem

1. The following data represent the number of bond issues floated by electric utility firms over six consecutive months:

Month (t)	Bonds Floated (Y_t)
0	6
1	7
2	11
3	15
4	17
5	20

Using double exponential smoothing with $w = 0.1$, forecast the number of bonds expected to be issued in period 6 ($\hat{Y}_6$). What is the sum of the squared forecast errors for months 1 through 5 $\left(\sum_{t=1}^{5} (Y_t - \hat{Y}_t)^2 \right)$? Use simple regression trend analysis on the data above to obtain starting values.

Forecasting: Additional Topics

10

This chapter discusses additional forecasting techniques. Input-output analysis considers the significant demand interactions between major sectors of the economy. Input-output models permit managers to trace the effects of an increase in demand for one product through to other industries. As such, input-output analysis provides an excellent bridge between overall economy and market sector forecasts, and the forecasts for specific industries and individual firms. Technological forecasting tools are used to provide insights into the pace of development and implementation of new technology. This is particularly important as the speed of technological advance has quickened. By developing accurate forecasting tools, managers can reduce the risk associated with the decisions they make. A reduction in risk leads to better estimates of future cash flows and a higher market valuation for those cash flows. Accordingly, good forecasting is a central concern to managers seeking to utilize efficiently the resources of the enterprise and to maximize shareholder wealth.

Glossary of New Terms

Delphi technique
A forecasting technique in which a panel of experts is used to predict the future occurrence of various types of events (such as technological innovations).

Forecasting with Input-Output Analysis[1]

One of the most sophisticated and promising forecasting methods is based on Leontief's input-output model of the economy.[2] Input-output analysis enables the forecaster to trace the effects of an increase in demand for one product to other industries. An increase in the demand for automobiles will first lead to an increase in the output of the auto industry. This in turn will lead to an

---

[1] This section is based primarily on "The Input-Output Structure of the U.S. Economy: 1972," *Survey of Current Business* (February 1979), pp. 34–72 and "The Input-Output Structure of the U.S. Economy, 1977" *Survey of Current Business* (May 1984), pp. 42–78.

[2] See Wassily W. Leontief et al., *Studies in the Structure of the American Economy* (New York: Oxford University Press, 1953), especially chap. 3. An advanced discussion is contained in Robert Dorfman, Paul Samuelson, and Robert Solow, *Linear Programming and Economic Analysis* (New York: McGraw-Hill, 1955). An excellent elementary discussion of the mathematics of input-output analysis is found in Henri Theil, J. C. G. Boot, and Teum Kloeck, *Operations Research and Quantitative Economics* (New York: McGraw-Hill, 1965), chap. 3.

increase in the demand for steel, glass, plastics, tires, and upholstery fabric. In addition, secondary impacts will occur as the increase in the demand for upholstery fabric, for example, requires an increase in the production of fibers used to make the fabric. The demand for machinery may also increase as a result of the fabric demand, and so the pattern continues. Input-output analysis permits the forecaster to trace through all the interindustry effects that occur as a result of the initial increase in the demand for automobiles.

Input-output forecasting requires the use of a complicated set of tables specifying the interdependence among the various industries in the economy. The construction of these tables is a massive undertaking. Fortunately for most managerial economists, it is done periodically and made available by the Bureau of Economic Analysis (BEA) of the Department of Commerce.

This section discusses, by using a simple example, the construction of an input-output matrix for the U.S. economy. The potential uses of input-output analyses are then examined.

Construction of Input-Output Tables

The most recent input-output table for the United States uses 1977 data from eighty-five industries; earlier tables are also available for 1972, 1967, 1963, 1958, and 1947.[3]

To understand the mass of data contained in the input-output tables, we develop an example illustrating an economy consisting of two industries (A and B), a consumer sector, and a government sector. We begin the example with simplified income statements for Industries A and B using the "T" account format shown in Table 10.1. Receipts for each industry are recorded in column 1

**Table 10.1
Industry
Production
Accounts**

Receipts		Expense + Profits	
		Industry A	
Sales to Industry A	20	Purchases from Industry A	20
Sales to Industry B	40	Wages	90
Sales to consumers	55	Depreciation	15
Sales to government	35	Profits	25
	150		150
		Industry B	
Sales to Industry B	10	Purchases from Industry B	10
Sales to consumers	30	Purchases from Industry A	40
Sales to government	30	Wages	10
	70	Depreciation	5
		Profits	5
			70

---

[3] The most recent input-output tables may be found for eighty-five industries in "The Input-Output Structure of the U.S. Economy: 1977," *Survey of Current Business* (May 1984), pp. 42–78. These tables have been slightly modified from time to time to reflect changes in the computation of the National Income and Product Accounts and other minor changes.

Wages	100	Personal consumption expenditure	85
Profits	30	Government	65
Depreciation	20	GNP	150
GNP	150		

Table 10.2
National Income and Product Accounts

and show the sale of goods to intermediate industries, as well as sales to final users (consumers and the government). In column 2, expenses are recorded that illustrate the consumption of intermediate goods, as well as the value added. The expense side may be thought of as inputs, whereas the receipts side reflects the industry's output. In the simple model developed in the table, Industry A provides raw materials for itself and for Industry B, in addition to selling to consumers and the government. Industry B sells to itself, consumers, and the government. In Table 10.2, the transactions for our simple two-industry economy are aggregated into the national income and product accounts. Interindustry transactions are not included in these summary accounts, since that would involve double counting.

The information from Tables 10.1 and 10.2 is then combined to develop Table 10.3, the transactions table or input-output flow table. Reading across the rows, we can see that producers in Industry A sell $20 of output to other firms in Industry A, $40 to firms in Industry B, $55 to consumers, and $35 to government. The column for Industry B shows the sources of the goods and services purchased by firms in Industry B for use in production, as well as its value added by producers in Industry B. Extracting interindustry transactions once again, we

Table 10.3 **Input-Output Flow Table**

		Producer		Final Markets		
		A	B	Personal Consumption	Govern-ments	Row Totals
Producer	A	20	40	55	35	150
Producer	B	0	10	30	30	70
Value added	Wages	90	10			100
	Profit plus depreciation	40	10			50
Column total		150	70	85	65	

GNP = 150 (Value added bracket)

GNP = 150 (Final markets bracket)

**Table 10.4
Output
Distribution
Table**

Producing Industry	Industry A	Industry B	Consumers	Government	Total
A	.13	.27	.37	.23	1.00
B	.00	.14	.43	.43	1.00

can see that GNP may be computed either by summing the value added by Industries A and B or by summing the final markets (demand) columns.

For forecasting purposes, we are primarily interested in three other tables that may be derived from the basic information in Table 10.3. One such table is the *output-distribution table*. It may be used to examine the pattern of sales by the industry and for comparisons between the industry pattern and an individual firm's pattern. It also indicates how dependent each industry is on other sectors of the economy. The output distribution table (see Table 10.4) may be derived by dividing the *rows* of the input-output flow table (Table 10.3) by the *row totals*. Thus, Industry A sells 13 percent of its output to other firms in the industry, 27 percent to firms in Industry B, 37 percent to consumers, and 23 percent to government. Column totals have no significance.

The *direct requirements table* (see Table 10.5) relates each of the inputs of an industry to its total output. The entries in each column show the dollar inputs required directly from each industry named at the beginning of each row to produce a dollar of output. The values in the direct requirements table (Table 10.5) are found from Table 10.3 by dividing each entry in the *columns* for the producers (A and B) by the *column total*.

The direct requirements matrix shows the interdependencies that exist in our simple two-industry economy. If B experienced a sales increase of $1,000,000, there would be a required increase in inputs from A of $580,000, $140,000 from B, $140,000 in additional labor, and $140,000 of other inputs (profits plus depreciation).

It should be apparent, however, that total labor requirements resulting from the initial demand increase will be in excess of $140,000. Industry A will require $348,000 ($580,000 × .6) more labor; and Industry B needs $19,600 ($140,000 × .14) more labor. Thus, the total increase in labor requirements as a result of the initial $1 million increase in sales to B will be $507,000.

The direct requirements table does not account for all the interactions that occur throughout the system as a result of an increase in demand. Re-

**Table 10.5
Direct
Requirements
Table**

	Producing Industry	
Supplying Industry	A	B
A	.13	.58
B	.00	.14
Wages	.60	.14
Profit + depreciation	.27	.14
Total	1.00	1.00

	Producer		
Supplier	A	B	
A	1.15	.78	
B	0	1.16	

Table 10.6
Total Requirements Table (per dollar of output for final consumption)

turning to the initial increase in demand of $1,000,000 for Industry B, $580,000 of output would be demanded from Industry A (.58 × $1,000,000) and $140,000 would be required from itself (.14 × $1,000,000). This demand for inputs from itself and Industry A, however, also requires additional inputs from both industries, and so on. These interactions among industries become quite complex as the number of industries increases.

To account for these interactions, we prepare the *total requirements table*. The proces of preparing the total requirements table involves computing the following matrix $(I - A)^{-1}$, where I is the identity matrix (in this case $\begin{pmatrix} 1 & 0 \\ 0 & 1 \end{pmatrix}$) and A is the direct requirements matrix of requirements between industries, $\begin{pmatrix} .13 & .58 \\ 0 & .14 \end{pmatrix}$. The exponent, -1, on the $(I - A)$ matrix indicates that we need to find the inverse of that matrix. Although the mathematics of matrix inversion is beyond the scope of this book, the inverse of a matrix is similar in concept to the reciprocal of a whole number. Fortunately, the total requirements table prepared as a part of the BEA input-output tables has already been computed, so it is not necessary to trace through all the impacts of a change in demand in one sector each time. The total requirements table (Table 10.6) for our simple hypothetical economy shows the direct, as well as indirect, requirements of each industry listed in the left-hand column to produce one dollar's worth of output for the industry identified at the top of each column.

The total requirements table makes it possible to compute the impacts on various industries in the economy that result from changes in the final demand for products of one or more industries. By reading Table 10.6, we see that if Industry B is to produce $1 million of output for final demand, it must produce a total of $1,160,000 in output. In addition, $780,000 of output would be demanded from Industry A. The construction of the total requirements table becomes much more complex as the number of industries and the interactions increase.

Table 10.7 reproduces a portion of the total requirements table from the 1977 input-output tables. From Table 10.7 it can be seen that to provide for the final demand from an additional expenditure of $1,000 on printing and publishing (column 26) requires $1,131 [$1,000 × 1.131 (row 26)] from the printing and publishing industry and $226 [$1,000 × .226 (row 24)] from the paper and allied products industry.

Each row of the total requirements table indicates the requirements of an industry due to the final demand in other industries. For example, line 65 (transportation and warehousing) shows the demand for transportation and warehousing associated with a one-dollar increase in final demand for the

Table 10.7 Total Requirements, Direct and Indirect, per Dollar of Delivery to Final Demand (at Producer's Prices), 1977

Each entry represents the output required, directly and indirectly, of the commodity named at the beginning of the row for each dollar of delivery to final demand of the commodity named at head of the column

Commodity Number	Commodity	15 Tobacco Manufactures	16 Broad and Narrow Fabrics, Yarn and Thread Mills	17 Miscellaneous Textile Goods and Floor Coverings	18 Apparel	19 Miscellaneous Fabricated Textile Products	20 Lumber and Wood Products, Except Containers	21 Wood Containers	22 Household Furniture	23 Other Furniture and Fixtures	24 Paper and Allied Products, Except Containers	25 Paperboard Containers and Boxes	26 Printing and Publishing	27 Chemicals and Selected Chemical Products	28 Plastics and Synthetic Material
1	Livestock and livestock products	0.00835	0.01187	0.01433	0.00528	0.00766	0.00313	0.00268	0.00418	0.00216	0.00417	0.00268	0.00349	0.00492	0.00415
2	Other agricultural products	25269	10214	02944	03072	04254	00378	00268	01008	00291	00545	00333	00337	00660	00993
3	Forestry and fishery products	00068	00085	00114	00789	00113	14143	04909	01816	01002	01342	00594	00293	00171	00137
4	Agricultural, forestry, and fishery services	01068	00550	00279	00278	00280	01594	00620	00311	00181	00256	00152	00116	00372	00262
5	Iron and ferroalloy ores mining	00047	00104	00123	00064	00086	00142	00137	00311	00888	00099	00142	00070	00427	00249
6	Nonferrous metal ores mining	00076	00253	00338	00136	00162	00127	00088	00225	00347	00186	00192	00121	01415	00769
7	Coal mining	00339	01020	00948	00546	00674	00504	00573	00766	01349	01558	00996	00525	01675	01685
8	Crude petroleum and natural gas	02359	05442	05644	03091	03505	03125	02864	02797	02607	05864	04639	02694	18130	11402
9	Stone and clay mining and quarrying	00136	00201	00202	00111	00134	00158	00133	00173	00193	00526	00292	00154	00694	00380
10	Chemical and fertilizer mineral mining	00083	00294	00348	00138	00174	00080	00055	00096	00091	00211	00161	00107	02104	00897
11	New construction	01417	02829	02575	01983	02153	02796	02681	02381	02398	03257	03046	01946	03998	03557
12	Maintenance and repair construction	00005	00006	00005	00006	00005	00020	00010	00010	00011	00006	00005	00006	00006	00006
13	Ordnance and accessories	00601	01063	01227	01046	01309	00856	00922	01297	00695	01552	01006	01337	01776	01401
14	Food and kindred products	—	—	—	—	—	—	—	—	—	—	—	—	—	—
15	Tobacco manufactures	1.25721	(*)	(*)	(*)	(*)	(*)	(*)	(*)	(*)	00005	00002	00001	00001	00001
16	Broad and narrow fabrics, yarn and thread mills	00230	1.46526	25979	39273	47152	00346	00261	10352	01255	02687	01204	00807	00275	01563
17	Miscellaneous textile goods and floor coverings	00163	01618	1.06037	00854	09288	00535	00237	02339	02596	00933	00430	00443	00131	00272
18	Apparel	00041	00226	01742	1.26189	01888	00091	00105	00599	00212	00116	00081	00066	00050	00074
19	Miscellaneous fabricated textile products	00037	00077	00216	01711	1.03096	00059	00042	00355	00094	00046	00036	00045	00084	00059
20	Lumber and wood products, except containers	00530	00538	00723	00453	00710	1.44506	49556	18244	10011	12776	05563	02491	00879	00848
21	Wood containers	00108	00032	00015	00013	00016	00020	1.00883	00104	00060	00013	00008	00006	00010	00010
22	Household furniture	00001	00002	00004	00002	00002	00004	00003	1.00222	00037	00003	00003	00002	00003	00003
23	Other furniture and fixtures	00002	00004	00006	00003	00004	00007	00005	00005	1.00773	00009	00007	00004	00006	00005
24	Paper and allied products, except containers	03158	02107	02918	01926	02382	00821	03672	01892	01708	1.23393	51626	22657	02489	03646
25	Paperboard containers and boxes	01034	01578	01420	01139	01749	00526	06174	01700	01636	02138	1.05392	01003	00860	01457
26	Printing and publishing	01667	00427	00460	00461	00550	00308	00538	00569	00477	00507	00504	1.13135	00540	00464
27	Chemicals and selected chemical products	04875	16261	18988	07425	09551	04360	02843	04870	04238	08879	07921	05610	1.31548	46903
28	Plastics and synthetic materials	00845	22453	27691	10904	11934	01255	00088	04004	02155	04560	03319	01390	01880	1.07644
29	Drugs, cleaning and toilet preparations	00197	00549	00513	00580	00362	00083	00088	00151	00101	00358	00206	00142	00763	00880
30	Paints and allied products	00063	00166	00202	00110	00128	00751	00344	01292	01073	00217	00355	00141	00345	00393
31	Petroleum refining and related industries	02623	04241	04061	02725	02892	03641	03414	02852	02616	06386	05065	02747	06707	06092
32	Rubber and miscellaneous plastics products	03147	02572	04571	01735	04125	01449	00937	06057	05030	03654	02102	01924	01753	02979
33	Leather tanning and finishing	00002	00012	00014	00605	00958	00013	00019	00398	00045	00006	00004	00018	00005	00004
34	Footwear and other leather products	00005	00042	00015	00034	00026	00043	00019	00015	00010	00013	00011	00012	00018	00015

#	Industry														
35	Glass and glass products	00200	00191	00101	00098	00141	00316	00729	00132	00261	00320	00213	00497	00572	00062
36	Stone and clay products	00580	00670	00306	00527	00684	00877	00948	00832	01124	00305	00263	00398	00382	00202
37	Primary iron and steel manufacturing	01999	02940	01038	02237	01371	16150	05328	02295	02192	01114	00796	01325	01116	00650
38	Primary nonferrous metals manufacturing	02581	04400	01014	01733	01329	04501	02662	00892	01315	00882	00800	01942	01100	00484
39	Metal containers	04400	01307	00148	00194	00211	00151	00198	00106	00148	00215	00178	00366	00313	00094
40	Heating, plumbing, and structural metal products	00971	00335	00157	00244	00283	00226	00244	00377	00683	00168	00150	00209	00218	00109
41	Screw machine products and stampings	00277	00288	00188	00242	00314	02182	01092	00618	01429	00190	00144	00198	00169	00113
42	Other fabricated metal products	00232	01005	00768	01494	01682	04417	06687	01911	03485	00441	00432	00552	00502	00939
43	Engines and turbines	00832	00289	00084	00136	00151	00180	00121	00130	00142	00100	00088	00140	00139	00072
44	Farm and garden machinery	00201	00030	00021	00019	00025	00027	00034	00053	00058	00054	00044	00048	00109	00233
45	Construction and mining machinery	00028	00383	00076	00120	00168	00162	00116	00088	00109	00089	00075	00132	00131	00060
46	Materials handling machinery and equipment	00249	00052	00024	00031	00041	00045	00045	00049	00097	00071	00059	00049	00142	00021
47	Metalworking machinery and equipment	00041	00217	00123	00587	00211	00676	00359	00414	00481	00164	00127	00207	00178	00092
48	Special industry machinery and equipment	00193	01049	00677	00722	00578	00139	00278	00333	00193	00617	00563	01464	01023	00085
49	General industrial machinery and equipment	00691	00777	00167	00266	00309	00606	00271	00206	00293	00196	00182	00321	00285	00142
50	Miscellaneous machinery, except electrical	00606	00372	00214	00451	00373	00777	00495	00691	00539	00333	00272	00424	00392	00136
51	Office, computing, and accounting machines	00352	00042	00060	00031	00038	00075	00046	00038	00028	00042	00038	00036	00040	00037
52	Service industry machines	00041	00210	00062	00080	00091	00128	00081	00101	00165	00069	00064	00085	00085	00040
53	Electric industrial equipment and apparatus	00145	00448	00151	00222	00222	00662	00244	00203	00288	00158	00141	00239	00208	00092
54	Household appliances	00305	00029	00022	00113	00026	00025	00024	00024	00026	00025	00113	00022	00023	00013
55	Electric lighting and writing equipment	00026	00119	00067	00087	00096	00120	00092	00105	00127	00072	00068	00084	00087	00043
56	Radio, TV, and communication equipment	00098	00108	00073	00054	00052	00086	00094	00052	00051	00054	00069	00051	00059	00031
57	Electronic components and accessories	00053	00057	00182	00092	00107	00165	00168	00138	00083	00112	00119	00120	00141	00082
58	Miscellaneous electrical machinery and supplies	00128	00136	00051	00052	00054	00082	00056	00061	00099	00055	00052	00051	00090	00150
59	Motor vehicles and equipment	00047	00054	00257	00299	00310	00893	00361	00383	00543	00258	00211	00225	00237	00185
60	Aircraft and parts	00268	00277	00046	00063	00054	00066	00045	00048	00046	00033	00028	00047	00036	00025
61	Other transportation equipment	00085	00094	00073	00117	00122	00118	00121	00226	00514	00060	00071	00071	00058	00038
62	Scientific and controlling instruments	00157	00177	00055	00089	00104	00099	00123	00117	00080	00075	00067	00083	00094	00039
63	Optical, ophthalmic, and photographic equipment	00107	00110	01122	00106	00111	00102	00108	00102	00077	00098	00093	00122	00102	00093
64	Miscellaneous manufacturing	00106	00119	00492	00113	00113	00114	00260	00124	00129	00363	01983	00131	00120	00073
65	Transportation and warehousing	07557	08370	05617	09184	07674	05464	05561	06435	05594	04451	03675	06355	04816	02693
66	Communications, except radio and TV	00865	00921	01603	00890	00883	01086	01264	00935	00674	01152	01766	00944	01291	00562
67	Radio and TV broadcasting	00008	00009	00009	00008	00006	00008	00007	00007	00005	00007	00007	00007	00008	00009
68	Electric, gas, water, and sanitary services	10043	11811	03878	06271	08862	04750	04317	04234	04087	05183	04457	07095	07612	02375
69	Wholesale and retail trade	08091	07739	07698	07628	10505	08298	09888	10664	09157	09957	08964	09093	09927	04023
70	Finance and insurance	01912	02214	02159	01593	01741	02612	02975	03327	01996	01949	01926	01782	01831	02120
71	Real estate and rental	03544	04041	03590	02330	02497	02568	02676	02345	01875	03142	02818	02754	03343	03763
72	Hotels; personal and repair services (exc. auto)	00607	00586	00975	00521	00669	00629	00688	00633	00425	00832	00676	00524	00509	00284
73	Business services	07318	07096	08602	05158	05994	07648	07626	06087	04265	06713	06466	06688	07885	08636
74	Eating and drinking places	01371	01403	02590	01082	00991	01178	01334	01565	00938	01251	01236	01167	01280	00593
75	Automobile repair and services	00850	00730	00860	00918	00878	01041	01109	00996	00982	00723	00704	00733	00762	00563
76	Amusements	00163	00170	00211	00120	00144	00208	00274	00150	00138	00148	00146	00145	00172	00179
77	Health, educ., & social serv. and nonprofit org	00260	00260	00306	00153	00205	00290	00369	00505	00268	00472	00223	00199	00298	00153
78	Federal Government enterprises	00368	00398	01949	00399	00388	00612	00562	00545	00304	00567	00782	00507	00471	00506
79	State and local government enterprises	00082	00090	00073	00109	00148	00055	00068	00080	00052	00065	00073	00111	00103	00049
80	Noncomparable imports	00765	00997	00434	00505	00531	00463	00586	00311	00311	01054	00449	01946	00488	00226
81	Scrap, used, and secondhand goods	00280	00437	00393	00853	01766	00721	00342	00176	00165	00227	00136	00870	00262	00098

commodities listed at the top of the columns. For example, a one-dollar increase in the demand for household furniture results in a 5.56-cent increase in the demand for transportation and warehousing services. A one-dollar increase in the demand for tobacco manufactures results in a 2.69-cent increase in the demand for transportation and warehousing services.

Uses of Input-Output Tables

Input-output tables have been used in a variety of applications, from forecasting sales for an individual firm to evaluating the impacts of major economic programs. The major contribution of input-output analysis is that it facilitates a detailed tracing and measurement of the effects of all the demands (both direct and indirect) on the output of each industry influenced by an initial change in some final demand. Industry outputs derived in this manner may be used to estimate related industry requirements. With supplementary data, the output estimates for each industry may be translated into labor force requirements or future capital expenditure requirements. Input-output analysis has also been used by individual firms to forecast requirements for inputs (by analyzing the sales outlook for the industry) to make certain they have adequate sources of supply; and it has been useful in evaluating market prospects for established products and in identifying potential markets for new products.

Input-output analysis is also an aid for determining the impact of energy shortages and changing patterns of energy use. Input-output analysis has also facilitated the study of the environmental impact of industrial pollution that may be associated with various levels and compositions of final demand. The federal government has used the input-output tables to study the long-term growth of the economy and the implications for personnel requirements. The impacts of imports and exports on employment in various industries and regions of the nation has also been explored. State and local governments have constructed and used input-output tables to evaluate the effects of alternative means for economic development and to study the industrial impacts of various tax programs. Concern for our water resources has led to the use of input-output tables to identify activities that generate significant requirements for water resources, not only as direct users but also because of indirect impacts on their suppliers of raw materials, energy, and so on, which also require water. This information is then used to develop a rational scheme for regional development.

A 1966 study by Almon illustrates the use of input-output analysis for long-range forecasting.[4] Almon constructed an input-output table for 1975 based on projections about the size of the labor force and the expected final demands in 1975 and on forecasted input-output coefficients. To arrive at these forecasts, Almon considered trends in work habits and attitudes, trends in consumption patterns, and trends in technological development. Almon compared expected

---

[4] Clopper Almon, Jr., *The American Economy to 1975* (New York: Harper & Row, 1966).

1975 industry outputs with actual 1963 outputs and was able to estimate projected growth rates for various industries.

Other uses of input-output analysis include an application by Mohn, who used this model for sales forecasting for the Montreal Expos baseball team.[5] Van Auken has also used the model as an aid to small business planning.[6]

Some Final Cautions

Input-output analysis has limitations. We have already mentioned the high cost of developing area-specific or product-specific input-output models; however, government-prepared input-output tables are available at little or no cost to aid in macroforecasting efforts. Another limitation is that the user must recognize that the final demand forecast plays a crucial role in the usefulness of an input-output forecast of the direct and indirect consequences of that final demand. A poor final demand forecast will lead to poor forecasts of related industry requirements.

A third limitation is the assumption used in the construction of the technical coefficients that as output increases, input proportions will remain constant; for example, a 50 percent increase in output will require a 50 percent increase in all inputs. If this assumption does not hold, then expansion in one industry may not have the effects on their industries that input-output analysis indicates. Furthermore, because input-output tables are normally prepared with a considerable time lag (1988 Department of Commerce tables are based on 1977 data), the chance that input proportions may have changed as technology changes or as the prices of various inputs increase, causing input substitutions, becomes a real possibility. This is especially true for rapidly growing and technologically advancing industries.

A fourth limitation is the avoidance of an explicit recognition of prices. The tables are constructed based upon the *dollar* value of outputs in various industries. But if relative prices change between individual industries, as they are likely to do when the lag increases between the base year tables and the forecast year, then the tables will give a somewhat distorted representation of various industry relationships.

In spite of these problems, input-output analysis often can provide insights that are useful in the forecasting process. In many cases, in fact, input-output analysis is used in conjunction with or as a part of other forecasting models. For example, the Wharton econometric model incorporates input-output relationships in its system of forecasting equations.[7] Also, many centrally planned economies have used input-output techniques to help them set quotas for various products.

---

[5] N. Carroll Mohn et al., "Input-Output Modeling: New Sales Forecasting Tool," *University of Michigan Business Review* (July 1976), pp. 7–15.

[6] M. Van Auken and R. D. Ireland, "Input-Output Approach to Small Business Planning," *Journal of Small Business Management* (January 1980), pp. 44–50.

[7] Ross S. Preston, *The Wharton Annual and Industry Forecasting Model* (Philadelphia: Wharton School, 1972).

Technological Forecasting[8]

The forecasting techniques we have reviewed to this point are based on the assumption that historical data are available and that these data will be of use in predicting future values of the variable in question. In some important instances, however, no such historical data are available or data are insufficient to permit the use of traditional forecasting techniques. One such instance is a forecast of when a new process or product will become widely accepted. For example, the technology for using solar energy for power generation has been in existence for some time; but the adaptation of this technology to practical use depends on a number of factors such as alternative energy costs, proven reliability based on prototype plant performance, and public acceptance of the environmental consequences of the technology. A firm that moves too rapidly in its efforts to bring this technology to the marketplace may find itself with no viable economic market for its output. Conversely, a laggard firm may completely miss a promising market.

A second area where traditional forecasting may be of little use is in predicting new discoveries and developments in such a field as medical research, fusion reactor research, superconductivity, or space travel. Both situations require the use of experts in the preparation of forecasts. In this section we consider some of the techniques that can be used to assist these experts in making their forecasts.

The Importance of Technological Forecasting

Qualitative or technological forecasting techniques were developed during the 1950s. Their use has expanded substantially during the past thirty years and is now rather widely practiced. For example, one study estimated that about six hundred medium- to large-sized American firms had an identifiable technological forecasting function as part of their operations.[9] Another study found that 70 percent of medium- to large-sized companies used some form of technological forecasting as part of their long-range planning process. In addition, Gerstenfeld found that the use of technological forecasting is most prevalent in rapidly growing industries, where a failure to be technologically progressive may lead to firm failure.[10]

The primary incentive for the growing use of technological forecasting is the increased rate of technological innovation and the decreasing time interval between discovery and commercial use. Jantsch, for example, found that "before 1900 it was not uncommon for twenty years or more to elapse between the time of invention and its commercial use."[11] In contrast, he found the current gap to

---

[8] This section is primarily based on Steven C. Wheelwright and Spyros Makridakis, *Forecasting Methods for Management* (New York: John Wiley, 1973), chap. 11. An excellent source of research on technological forecasting is the journal *Technological Forecasting and Social Change* published by Elsevier Science Publishing Company.

[9] Erich Jantsch, *Technological Forecasting in Perspective* (Paris: OECD, 1976).

[10] Arthur Gerstenfeld, "Technological Forecasting," *Journal of Business* (January 1971), pp. 10–18.

[11] Jantsch, *Technological Forecasting in Perspective*, pp. 41–46.

Economic Analysis and Managerial Efficiency

SUPERCONDUCTIVITY AND TECHNOLOGICAL PROGRESS*

The development of materials capable of the resistance-free movement of electrical current at comparatively high temperatures has set off an explosion of theoretical and applied research aimed at harnessing and using the superconductive properties of newly developed compounds. Perhaps more than any other development of the past quarter century, the progress of research in superconductivity promises vast, significant technological changes in many industries.

Electric utilities may be able to use giant electromagnets to store power for use during peak hours. A superconducting power line could transmit power without losses. Power losses on the current generation of copper and aluminium power lines equal the power supply for the entire West Coast. Power plants using superconductive materials will be vastly more efficient than current power plants. Superconductive motors will be more powerful and much more efficient than the best motors available today. In electronics,

superconductivity holds the promise of future microcomputer systems with one hundred times the computing power of today's most powerful systems. Superconductors can also create huge magnetic fields for magnetic levitation systems, capable of moving trains at speeds of up to 300 miles per hour. Equally exciting prospects exist in the health care area, where new imaging machines could provide vastly improved diagnostic capabilities at a much reduced cost. Advances in controlled fusion research hold out the promise of virtually limitless future supplies of pollution-free energy.

In the face of these potential developments, few firms can ignore the impact of superconductivity on the future operating environment of their firms. In many industries making long-lived investments, such as the electric utility industry, developing realistic forecasts of the time frame within which superconductivity can be applied in a cost-effective manner will have an important impact on the type and profitability of new investments made by the firms. This kind of long-range forecasting is becoming increasingly important in well-managed firms, seeking to maximize shareholder wealth.

Question
1. What impact do you think the promise of superconductivity applications will have on the construction programs of electric utilities?

*Based in part on "The New World of Superconductivity," *Business Week* (6 April 1987).

---

be only two years. The rapid pace of developments in the microcomputer industry and superconductivity is strong evidence of this trend. This pace has tremendous implications for both the timing for new products and the making of long-term investment decisions that may commit the firm to a course of action for many years.

Techniques Used in Technological Forecasting

There are two general classes of technological forecasting techniques. The *exploratory approach* begins with today's knowledge, projects potential future progress, and then considers the effects of this future technological environment on the firm's decisions. In contrast, the *normative approach* attempts to assess future goals and objectives and then to identify the technological requirements for meeting these goals. The final step of normative models is to identify limits and barriers in the current state of technology that preclude the achievement of the identified objectives. These technological gaps become prime candidates for research and development efforts by the firm.

Some of the specific technological forecasting methods that have been used include the Delphi technique, curve fitting, and analogy. Each of these approaches is examined briefly here.

Delphi Technique. The Delphi technique was developed by Olaf Helmer at the Rand Corporation.[12] A panel of experts is selected by the technological forecaster with the objective of studying a specific issue. Rather than engaging in direct debate, the experts respond to a closely monitored series of written questionnaires. The following actual case illustrates the use of the method:[13]

- First round: The panel members were requested to list inventions and scientific breakthroughs that they thought were both urgently needed and achievable in the next fifty years. From these answers, a list of forty-nine items was prepared. Normally, the first-round questionnaire is worded in an open-ended fashion to permit the experts to consider a wide range of relevant factors that may influence the forecast.

- Second round: The panel members were asked in a second questionnaire to locate the 50–50 probability of achievement of each of the forty-nine items in one of several time intervals into which the 50-year time period had been divided.

- Third round: The third-round letter and questionnaire identified to the panel those items on which the group had reached a consensus. Those panel members who did not agree with the consensus view were asked to state their reasons for disagreement. For those items on which no consensus had been reached, the participants were asked to present the reasons for their choices. Some members reevaluated past estimates, and a narrower time range was estimated.

- Additional rounds: The third-round procedure was repeated, providing panel members with a summary of their responses and the rationale for these responses. Finally, a list of thirty-one items was arrived at on which near consensus was obtained. For those items on which no consensus could
- be reached, the forecaster had the benefit of the reasons given by various panelists for divergent forecasts.

Advocates of the Delphi approach argue that it is superior to conventional approaches designed to achieve consensus through open discussion because direct contact between the panelists is eliminated. This eliminates the influences of such factors as the persuasive ability of individual panel members, the

---

[12] Olaf Helmer, *Social Technology* (New York: Basic Books, 1969).
[13] Gerstenfeld, "Technological Forecasting," pp. 10–11.

reluctance to abandon publicly stated opinions, and the bandwagon effect of majority opinions.

The disadvantages of this approach are that (1) the experts may be unable to reach a consensus view; (2) the results may be widely divergent if different panels of experts are used; (3) it is difficult to take into account the unexpected; and (4) the technique is very sensitive to the ambiguity of the questions initally posed. To a large extent, these limitations exist for other techniques as well. In spite of these disadvantages, the Delphi approach has been successfully used to forecast the need for new products and processes and to determine the most attractive possibilities and the best time for introduction. For such new product or process forecasting in a firm, the panel may consist of knowledgeable individuals from both inside and outside the firm. It is usually preferable to have a wide range of expertise represented on the panel.

Curve Fitting. Curve-fitting techniques can be used for qualitative forecasting even if the number of historical data points available is not sufficient to apply regression analysis or some other form of trend analysis. The S-type curve is one of the most common (but not the only) curves used in technological forecasting. It implies a slow beginning, a period of rapid growth, and finally a plateau of the trend. The S-curve represents many technological developments, such as incandescent and fluorescent lighting efficiency, the maximum speed of aircraft, and the efficiency of commercial electric power plants, as well as the sales of many new products including CB radios, small calculators, and microcomputers. Although many technologies (or new products) seem to be experiencing exponential growth at the outset, as illustrated by the solid portion of the curve in Figure 10.1, they may approach some physical limit, such as the theoretical

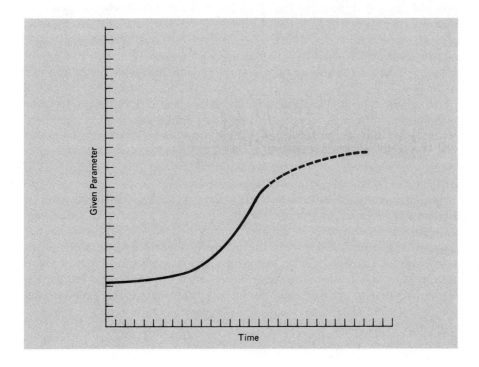

Figure 10.1
Technological Curve Fitting

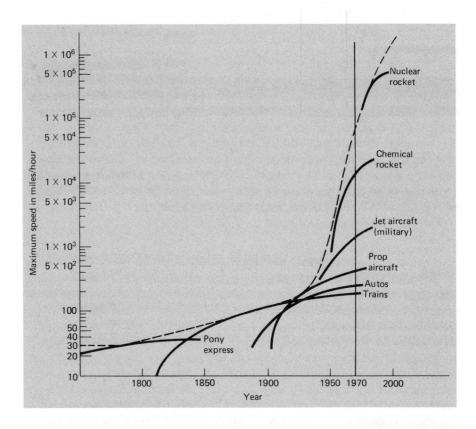

Figure 10.2
**Envelope
Forecasting
Example**

efficiency of light, a 100 percent limit for the efficiency of energy conversion processes or a zero limit for the control of pollutants. Similarly, new product sales may grow rapidly until market saturation is approached. Beyond this saturation point, new sales will be largely determined by growth in the market and replacement demand. This phenomenon often causes a linear or exponential growth curve to assume an S-shape as the variable asymptotically approaches its limit.

In addition to applying curve-fitting techniques to specific products or technological processes, we can also apply them more generally to a family of technologies, such as the maximum speed of transportation. When used in this way, the curve-fitting technique is called *envelope forecasting*. As illustrated in Figure 10.2, an envelope S-curve can be obtained by connecting the tangents of each of the individual technological growth curves.

Although the S-curve technique has proven to be useful in many instances, it is often difficult to identify the point on the curve where a product or technology is located at a particular time. Another limitation is that the S-curve is not the only possible functional form that may be applied to a product or technology being forecast. In some cases an exponential or logarithmic form may be more appropriate, and yet it is difficult to make an a priori determination of this fact. These problems emphasize the importance of having experts detail all the assumptions and identify any theoretical or practical limits to the expansion of the series being forecast.

Analogy Techniques. We can often forecast developments in one area based on developments in another related area. Lenz found that maximum speeds of military aircraft seem to be useful in forecasting the speed of commercial aircraft in later years.[14] Figure 10.3 illustrates the nature of this relationship. From this diagram the forecaster may conclude that the rate of increase in the speed of military planes is such that it tends to double every ten years, whereas civilian aircraft speed doubles only about every twelve years. Lenz found the lag between military and civilian aircraft speeds to be six years in 1920 and eleven years in 1959. This finding highlights some of the major problems with analogy techniques. First, the lag structure in the relationship may change over time.

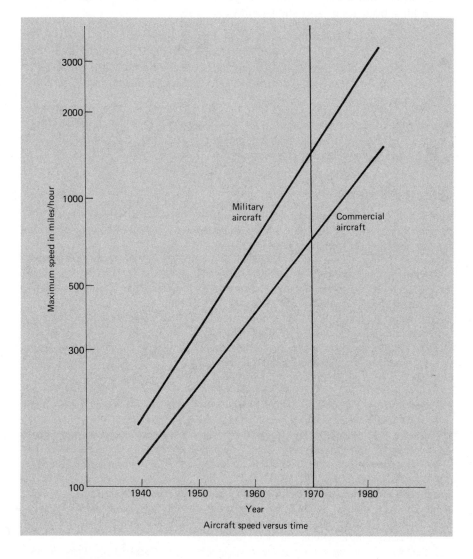

Figure 10.3
Analogy Forecasting Example

---

[14] Ralph C. Lenz, Jr., *Technological Forecasting*, 2d ed., Technical Report ASD-TDR-62-414, USAF Aeronautical Systems Division (June 1962).

Also, it may be difficult to find some reliable precursor to be used in analogy forecasts. Finally, the number of data points relating the precursor trend with the trend to be forecast may be insufficient, resulting in unreliable estimates of the lag relationship.

Summary

- *Input-output analysis* is a forecasting model that permits the forecaster to trace the effects of a change in demand for one product through to related products and industries. Input-output analysis has been used to assist in making both long- and short-range forecasts.

- *Technological forecasting* techniques attempt to predict the need for, or possibility of, new product or process developments. These techniques have also been used to identify the likely date of acceptance of new products or technological processes. Technological forecasting tends to have a medium- or long-range focus.

- No single forecasting method is generally superior to all others. The choice of a method is dependent on cost, required accuracy, data availability, and the time perspective of the forecast.

Selected References

Almon, Clopper, Jr. *The American Economy to 1975*. New York: Harper & Row, 1966.

Almon, Clopper, Jr. et al. *1985: Interindustry Forecasts of the American Economy*. Lexington Mass.: Lexington Books, 1974.

Armstrong, J. Scott. "Research on Forecasting: A Quarter Century Review 1960–1984." *Interfaces* (January–February 1986), pp. 89–109.

Bright, James R., ed. *Technological Forecasting for Industry and Government*. Englewood Cliffs, N.J.: Prentice-Hall, 1968.

Bright, James R., and Milton E. F. Schoeman, eds. *A Guide to Practical Technological Forecasting*. Englewood Cliffs, N.J.: Prentice-Hall, 1973.

Dofman, Robert, Paul Samuelson, and Robert Solow. *Linear Programming and Economic Analysis*. New York: McGraw-Hill, 1955.

Duckel, Earl B. et al. *The Business Environment of the Seventies: A Trend Analysis for Business Planning*. New York: McGraw-Hill, 1970.

Feldman, Stanley J. "Structural Change in the United States: Changing Input-Output Coefficients." *Business Economics* (January 1985), pp. 39–54.

Harmeston, F. K., and R. E. Lund. *Application of an Input-Output Framework to a Community Economic System*. Columbia: University of Missouri Press, 1967.

"The Input-Output Structure of the U.S. Economy, 1977." *Survey of Current Business* (May 1984), pp. 42ff.

Jantsch, Eric. *Technological Forecasting in Perspective*. Paris: OECD, 1967.

Kahn, Herman, and A. J. Weiner. *The Year 2000*. New York: Macmillan, 1967.

Lenz, Ralph C., Jr. *Technological Forecasting*, 2d ed. Technical Report ASD-TDR-62-414, USAF Aeronautical Systems Division (June 1962).

Leontief, Wassily W. *Input-Output Economics*. New York: Oxford Univ. Press, 1985.

Miernyk, W. H. "Long-Range Forecasting with a Regional Input-Output Model." *Western Economic Journal* 6 (June 1968).

Miller, Ronald E., and P. D. Blair. *Input-Output Analysis: Foundations and Extensions*. Englewood Cliffs, N.J.: Prentice-Hall, 1985.

Rosenberg, Nathan. *Technology and American Economic Growth*. New York: Harper & Row, 1972.

Use of Input-Output Analysis as an Aid in Forecasting in the Capital Goods Industries. New York: Machinery and Allied Products Institute, 1968.

Wills, Gordon, David Ashton, and Bernard Taylor, eds. *Technological Forecasting and Corporate Strategy*. New York: American Elsevier, 1969.

Discussion Questions

1. Define technological forecasting. What type of firm would most likely be involved in some form of technological forecasting?

2. Explain how the Delphi technique can be used in technological forecasting.

3. What is the difference between analogy techniques and curve-fitting techniques used in technological forecasting?

4. Distinguish between the *direct requirements table* and the *total requirements table* in input-output analysis.

5. What is the value of the *output-distribution table* in input-output analysis?

6. What are the major limitations of input-output analysis tables for use in forecasting?

Problems

1. The Borgner Manufacturing Corporation is interested in assessing its competitive position and marketing strategy within the industrial machinery industry. A new MBA executive has suggested that the Department of Commerce input-output tables might help to provide some insights. Borgner's sales are currently broken down as follows:

Sales to	Percentage
Industry A	8%
Industry B	27
Industry C	30
Other Industries	5
Individuals	10
Government	20

The relevant portion of the output-distribution table for Borgner's industry (A) from the input-output tables is as follows:

Producing Industry	A	B	C	Other	Individuals	Government
A	.20	.05	.10	.10	.25	.30

a. Based on this information, indicate where you believe Borgner's marketing effort has been weakest.

b. Before reaching any conclusions about possible market strategies that might be developed in light of these data, what additional information would you like to have?

2. International Farmer is a large farm equipment manufacturer. Because of the current high demand for agricultural products at present prices, government economists, as well as International's own economic forecasters, anticipate farm equipment sales to increase by nearly 10 percent next year. Current final demand farm equipment sales are about $1 billion. Assume the economy is dominated by three industries: Industry X (farm equipment) and two others, Y and Z. The following table represents the *total requirements* (direct and indirect) per dollar of final consumption:

	Producer (*Industry*)		
Supplier (*industry*)	X	Y	Z
X	1.21	.31	.54
Y	.06	1.02	1.7
Z	.06	.12	1.09

   a. If the 10 percent increase in final consumption demand for farm equipment occurs, what will be the total required output from Industry X? Y? Z?
   b. If International accounts for 30 percent of industry sales, what would you estimate International's output to be next year?
   c. If total consumption demand for Industry Z were expected to increase by $30 million, what impact would you expect this to have on the demand for products in Industry X?

3. Refer to Table 10.7 in the chapter. Assume that expenditures on household furniture are expected to increase by $30 million. In order to provide for this final demand, what expenditures must be made by the Household Furniture industry (22), the Lumber and Wood Products industry (20), the Fabrics industry (16) and the Steel industry (37)?

4. Refer to Table 10.7. What effect does a $10 million increase in the demand for Wood Containers (21), Household Furniture (22), Printing and Publishing (26), and Tobacco Manufacture (15) have on the demand for:
   a. Primary Nonferrous Metals Manufacturing (38)?
   b. Electric Lighting and Wiring Equipment (55)?
   c. Finance and Insurance (70)?
   d. Real Estate and Rental (71)?

5. Refer to Table 10.7. What effect does a $20 million increase in final demand for Apparel (18) have on the demand for
   a. Chemicals (27)?
   b. Electric, Gas, Water and Sanitary Services (68)?
   c. Business Services (73)?
   d. Wholesale and Retail Trade (69)?

6. As a major producer of Lumber and Wood Products (20), you are interested in the impact of the forecasted economic recession. Economists expect that current final demand output of $10 billion will decline to $9 billion when the economy softens.
   a. What will be the new total required output from the lumber and wood products industry during the recession? (Refer to Table 10.7).
   b. If your firm currently has a 10 percent market share, to what level must this market share be increased to retain the current dollar volume of sales?

Production and Cost IV

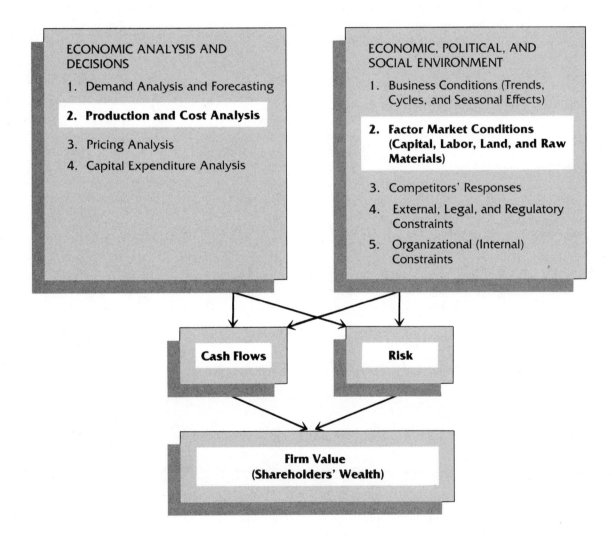

ECONOMIC ANALYSIS AND DECISIONS

1. Demand Analysis and Forecasting
2. **Production and Cost Analysis**
3. Pricing Analysis
4. Capital Expenditure Analysis

ECONOMIC, POLITICAL, AND SOCIAL ENVIRONMENT

1. Business Conditions (Trends, Cycles, and Seasonal Effects)
2. **Factor Market Conditions (Capital, Labor, Land, and Raw Materials)**
3. Competitors' Responses
4. External, Legal, and Regulatory Constraints
5. Organizational (Internal) Constraints

Cash Flows

Risk

Firm Value (Shareholders' Wealth)

Part IV deals with the production and cost analysis decisions facing managers of an economic enterprise. In Chapter 11 the theory of production decisions is developed. Production decisions include the determination of the type and amount of resources—such as land, labor, materials, capital equipment, and managerial skills—that are used in the production of a desired amount of output. The objective is to combine these inputs in the most efficient manner to produce the output of the enterprise. In Appendix 11A linear programming techniques are applied to the production planning problem. In Chapter 12 the theory of cost analysis is developed. When appropriate costs are assigned to the various inputs in the production process, a manager can determine the true economic cost of the enterprise's outputs. These cost figures are combined with revenue estimates to determine optimal (wealth-maximizing) levels and mixes of output. Appendix 12A illustrates the use of important cost theory concepts in the context of breakeven analysis and operating leverage analysis. Chapter 13 deals with the problems encountered when empirically estimating production and cost relationships. The learning curve effect encountered in manufacturing is the topic of Appendix 13A.

Theory of Production 11

The manager of a firm is required to make decisions about the employment of the various types of resources within the firm. Traditionally, these have been classified into production, marketing, financing, and personnel decisions. Although these decisions are interrelated, it is useful to discuss each of them separately. Production decisions include the determination of the type and amount of resources or inputs—such as land, labor, raw and processed materials, factories, machinery, equipment, and managerial talent—to be used in the production of a desired quantity of output. The objective of the private sector manager is to combine the resources of the firm in the most efficient manner to contribute to the goal of maximizing shareholder wealth. In government agencies and other not-for-profit institutions, managers are often faced with binding budget constraints. In this context, their goal is to maximize output (the provision of services) given the budget constraint. This can be accomplished by finding the lowest cost combination of inputs to produce the organization's output. This chapter and Chapter 12 discuss the use of the economic theories of production and cost in making wealth-maximizing production decisions.

Production Defined

In a very general sense, *production* is the creation of any good or service that has economic value to either consumers or other producers. This definition includes more than just the physical processing or manufacturing of material goods. It also includes production of transportation services, legal advice, education (teaching students), and invention (research and development). The list of goods and services produced by industry, not-for-profit organizations, and government is endless. The economic theory of *production* consists of a formal framework to assist the manager in deciding how to combine most efficiently the various inputs[1] needed to produce the desired output (product or service), given the existing technology. This technology consists of available production processes, equipment, labor and management skills, and information-processing capabilities. The economic theory of *cost* consists of a framework for

Glossary of New Terms

Production
The creation of any good or service that has value to either consumers or other producers.

Production function
A mathematical model, schedule (table), or graph that relates the maximum quantity of output that can be produced from given amounts of various inputs.

Short run
The period of time in which one (or more) of the resources employed in a production process is fixed or incapable of being varied.

Long run
The period of time in which *all* the resources employed in a production process can be varied.

Marginal product
The incremental change in total output that can be obtained from the use of one more unit of an input in the production process (while holding constant all other inputs).

(Cont'd on next page)

---

[1] The terms *input, factor,* and *resource* are used interchangeably throughout the chapter. They all have the same meaning in production theory.

Glossary of New Terms (*Cont'd*)

Input
A resource or factor of production, such as a raw material, labor skill, or piece of equipment, that is employed in a production process.

Marginal factor cost
The amount that an additional unit of the variable production input adds to total cost.

Marginal revenue product
The amount that an additional unit of the variable production input adds to total revenue.

Production isoquant
An algebraic function or a geometric curve representing all the various combinations of two inputs that can be used in producing a given level of output.

Marginal rate of technical substitution
The *rate* at which one input may be substituted for another input in producing a given quantity of output.

Returns to scale
The proportionate increase in output that results from a given proportionate increase in *all* the inputs employed in the production process.

assigning costs to the various output levels in order to be able to compare costs with revenues and thus make optimal production decisions.

The Production Function

The theory of production is centered around the concept of a production function. A *production function* relates the maximum quantity of output that can be produced from given amounts of various inputs for a given technology. It can be expressed in the form of a mathematical model, schedule (table), or graph. A change in technology, such as the introduction of more automated equipment or the substitution of skilled for unskilled workers, results in a new production function. The production of most outputs (goods and services) requires the use of large numbers of inputs. The production of a house, for example, requires the use of many different labor skills (carpenters, plumbers, and electricians), raw materials (lumber, cement, bricks, and insulating materials), and types of equipment (bulldozers, saws, and cement mixers). Also, many production processes result in more than one output. For example, in the meat-processing industry, the slaughtering of a steer results in the output of various cuts of meat, hides, and fertilizer. To simplify the analysis and to illustrate the basic theory, the following discussion is limited to a two-input, one-output production function.[2]

Letting X and Y represent the quantities of two inputs used in producing a quantity Q of output, a production function can be represented in the form of a mathematical model as

$$Q = f(X, Y)$$

[11.1]

The function f incorporates the existing state of technology in producing Q from X and Y. The general function, f, can take many different forms. One commonly used function is

$$Q = \alpha L^{\beta_1} K^{\beta_2}$$

[11.2]

where L is the amount of labor and K is the amount of capital used in the production process (α, β_1, and β_2 are constants). This particular multiplicative model is known as the *Cobb-Douglas production function* and is examined in more detail in Chapter 13.

Production functions can also be expressed in the form of a *schedule* (or table), as illustrated in the following ore-mining example. Suppose that equipment of various sizes, as measured by its horsepower rating, exists to mine ore. Suppose also that the amount of ore mined during a given shift is a function only of the number of workers assigned to the crew operating a given piece of

---

[2] A more advanced text on microeconomic theory can be consulted for a treatment of the general case of m inputs and n outputs. See, for example, James M. Henderson and Richard E. Quandt, *Microeconomic Theory: A Mathematical Approach*, 2d ed. (New York: McGraw-Hill, 1971), chap. 3.

equipment. The data in Table 11.1 show the amount of ore produced (measured in tons) when various sizes of crews are used to operate the equipment efficiently. In this example, the two inputs are labor, X—that is, number of workers—and capital, Y—that is, size of equipment—and the output Q is the number of tons of ore produced with the given combination of inputs.

A two-input, one-output production function can also be represented *graphically* as a three-dimensional production surface, where the height of the bar associated with each input combination indicates the amount of output produced. The production surface for the ore-mining example is shown in Figure 11.1.

In deciding how to combine the various inputs (X and Y) to produce the desired output, inputs are usually classified as being either fixed or variable. A *fixed* input is defined as one required in the production process but whose quantity employed in the process is constant over a given period of time regardless of the quantity of output produced. The costs of a fixed input must be incurred regardless of whether the production process is operated at a high or a low level. A *variable* input is defined as one whose quantity employed in the process changes, depending on the desired quantity of output to be produced.

The *short run* corresponds to the period of time in which one (or more) of the inputs is fixed. This means that to increase output, the firm must employ more of the variable inputs with the given quantity of fixed inputs. Thus, for example, with a production plant of fixed size and capacity, the firm can increase output only by employing more labor, such as by paying workers overtime or by scheduling additional shifts.

As the time period under consideration (planning horizon) is lengthened, however, more of the fixed inputs become variable. Over a planning horizon of about six months or more, the firm could possibly acquire or build additional plant capacity and order more manufacturing equipment. Production facilities would no longer be a fixed factor. In lengthening the planning horizon, a point is eventually reached where all inputs are variable. The *long run* corresponds to this period of time in which *all* the inputs of the production function are variable.

Table 11.1
Total Output —
Table Ore-Mining
Example

		Capital Input, Y (horsepower)							
		250	500	750	1,000	1,250	1,500	1,750	2,000
	1	1	3	6	10	16	16	16	13
	2	2	6	16	24	29	29	44	44
	3	4	16	29	44	55	55	55	50
Labor Input, X	4	6	29	44	55	58	60	60	55
(number of	5	16	43	55	60	61	62	62	60
workers)	6	29	55	60	62	63	63	63	62
	7	44	58	62	63	64	64	64	64
	8	50	60	62	63	64	65	65	65
	9	55	59	61	63	64	65	66	66
	10	52	56	59	62	64	65	66	67

Figure 11.1
**Ore-Mining
Production
Function**

In the short run, since some of the inputs are fixed, only a subset of the total possible input combinations are available to the firm. By contrast, in the long run all possible input combinations are available to the firm. Consequently, in the long run the firm can choose between increasing production through the use of more labor (overtime or hiring more workers) or through plant expansion, depending on which combination of labor and plant size is most efficient at producing the desired output.

In developing some of the concepts of production theory, a production function with one fixed and one variable input is examined first. The objective of the analysis is to determine how to combine different quantities of the variable input with a given amount of the fixed input to produce various quantities of output. The total, average, and marginal products are defined and illustrated and the law of diminishing returns and marginal revenue product are discussed. Then a slightly more complex situation is considered—a production function with two variable inputs. The objective in this situation is to determine how to combine the two variable inputs, based on the relative costs of producing a desired output by different input combinations. This situation is used to illustrate isoquants and returns to scale.

Production Functions with One Variable Input

Suppose in the ore-mining example of the previous section that the amount of capital input Y—that is, the size of mining equipment—employed in the production process is a fixed factor. Specifically, suppose that the firm owns or leases a piece of mining equipment having a 750-horsepower rating. Depending on the amount of labor input X—that is, number of workers—used to operate the 750-horsepower equipment, varying quantities of output will be obtained, as shown in the "$Y = 750$" column of Table 11.1 and again in the "Q" column of Table 11.2. This *total product* function can be represented graphically, as shown in Figure 11.2 where output Q is measured along the vertical axis and the variable input, labor (X), is measured along the horizontal axis.

Labor Input X (number of workers)	Total Product, $TP_x (= Q)$ (tons of ore)	Marginal Product of Labor, MP_x ($\Delta Q \div \Delta X$)	Average Product of Labor, AP_x ($Q \div X$)	Elasticity, E_x ($MP_x \div AP_x$)
0	0	—	—	—
1	6	+ 6	6	1.0
2	16	+10	8	1.25
3	29	+13	9.67	1.34
4	44	+15	11	1.36
5	55	+11	11	1.0
6	60	+ 5	10	.50
7	62	+ 2	8.86	.23
8	62	0	7.75	0.0
9	61	− 1	6.78	− .15
10	59	− 2	5.90	− .34

Table 11.2
Total Product, Marginal Product, Average Product, and Elasticity: Ore-Mining Example

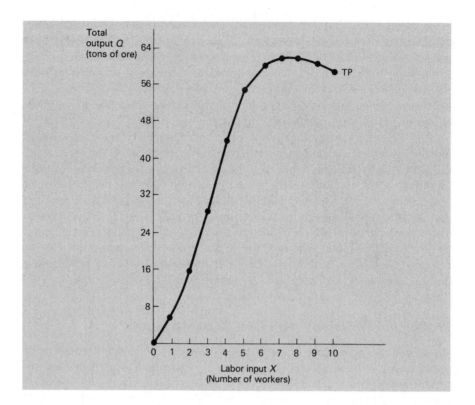

Figure 11.2
Total Product Curve: Ore-Mining Example

Marginal and Average Product Functions

Once the total product function is given (either in tabular, graphic, or algebraic form), the marginal and average product functions can be derived. The *marginal product* is defined as the incremental change in total output that can be produced by the use of one more unit of the variable input in the production process. Letting ΔQ be the change in total output brought about by a change in the variable input, while Y remains fixed, then the *marginal product* is equal to[3]

$$MP_x = \frac{\Delta Q}{\Delta X}$$

[11.3]

The marginal product of labor in the example is shown in the MP_x column of Table 11.2 and in Figure 11.3.

If input X is infinitely divisible, and hence a continuous variable, then the marginal product can be obtained by taking the partial derivative of Q (Equa-

---

[3] Strictly speaking, the ratio $\Delta Q/\Delta X$ represents the *incremental* product rather than the *marginal* product. For clarity, we continue to use the term *marginal*, even though this and similar ratios throughout the text are calculated on an incremental basis.

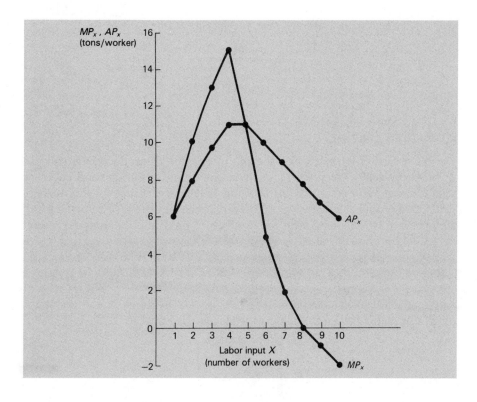

Figure 11.3
**Marginal and
Average Product
Curves: Ore-
Mining Example**

tion 11.1) with respect to X:

$$MP_x = \frac{\partial Q}{\partial X} \qquad [11.4]$$

For example, consider the following short-run algebraic production function

$$Q = 6X^2 - .2X^3 \qquad [11.5]$$

Taking the derivative of Equation 11.5 with respect to X yields the following marginal product function:

$$MP_x = 12X - .6X^2 \qquad [11.6]$$

The *average product* is defined as the ratio of total output to the amount of the variable input used in producing the output. For the quantities that have been defined, the average product is equal to

$$AP_x = \frac{Q}{X} \qquad [11.7]$$

The average product of labor for the ore-mining example is shown in the AP_x column of Table 11.2 and in Figure 11.3. For the algebraic production function given in Equation 11.5, the average product function is equal to

$$AP_x = \frac{6X^2 - .2X^3}{X}$$

$$= 6X - .2X^2 \qquad [11.8]$$

Production Elasticity

The discussion of the theory of demand in Chapter 7 introduced the concept of price elasticity. The price elasticity at any point on the demand curve or schedule was defined as the ratio of the percentage change in the quantity demanded brought about by a given percentage change in the price of the good, all other factors remaining the same. Similarly in production analysis, it is useful to define a production elasticity. The elasticity of production is defined as the percentage change in output Q resulting from a given percentage change in the amount of the variable input X employed in the production process, with Y remaining constant. The production elasticity indicates the responsiveness of output to changes in the given input. Expressed in terms of the quantities previously defined, the elasticity of production is equal to

$$E_x = \frac{\%\Delta Q}{\%\Delta X} \qquad [11.9]$$

$$= \frac{\dfrac{\Delta Q}{Q}}{\dfrac{\Delta X}{X}}$$

Rearranging terms yields

$$E_x = \frac{\dfrac{\Delta Q}{\Delta X}}{\dfrac{Q}{X}}$$

or, since $MP_x = \Delta Q/\Delta X$ and $AP_x = Q/X$:

$$E_x = \frac{MP_x}{AP_x} \qquad [11.10]$$

which shows that the elasticity of production is equal to the ratio of the marginal product to the average product of input X.

The elasticity of production for the ore-mining example is shown in the E_x column of Table 11.2. A production elasticity greater than (less than) 1.0 indicates that output increases more than (less than) proportionately with a given percentage increase in the variable input. An elasticity of zero indicates that no change takes place in output as a result of a given percentage increase in the input, and a negative elasticity indicates that output *decreases* with a given percentage increase in the input. The elasticity-of-production concept is discussed further in Chapter 13.

Law of Diminishing Marginal Returns

The tabular production function just discussed illustrates the production law of diminishing marginal returns. Initially, the assignment of more workers to the crew operating the mining equipment (the fixed factor) allows greater labor specialization in the use of the equipment. As a result, the marginal output of each worker added to the crew at first increases, and total output increases at an increasing rate. Thus, as shown in Table 11.2, the addition of a second worker to the crew results in 10 additional tons of output; the addition of a third worker results in 13 additional tons of output; and the addition of a fourth worker yields 15 additional tons. However, in adding more workers to the crew, a point is eventually reached where the marginal increase in output for each worker added to the crew begins to decline. This occurs because only a limited number of ways exist to increase significantly the output of the equipment through greater labor specialization. Thus, the addition of a fifth worker to the crew yields a marginal increase in output of 11 additional tons, compared with the marginal increase of 15 additional tons for the fourth worker. Similarly, the additions of the sixth and seventh workers to the crew yield successively smaller increases of 5 and 2 tons, respectively. Note, however, the total output is still increasing. It still may be profitable to operate a crew of five, six, or seven workers.

In some cases, total output may level off or decline when even larger crew sizes are used to operate the equipment. Under these conditions the marginal product of each additional worker becomes zero or even negative. Note that the eighth, ninth, and tenth workers have marginal products of 0, -1, and -2 tons, respectively. A zero or negative marginal product for labor may result, for example, from the inability to supervise adequately the excessive number of workers operating the equipment.

The law of diminishing marginal returns (sometimes also known as the diminishing marginal productivity law, or law of variable proportions) can be formally stated as follows:

Given that the amount of all other productive factors remains unchanged, the use of increasing amounts of a variable factor in the production process beyond some point will eventually result in diminishing marginal increases in total output.

Note that the law does not state that each and every increase in the amount of the variable factor used in the production process will yield diminishing marginal returns. As the preceding illustrates, it is possible that initial increases in the amount of the variable factor used in the production process may yield increasing marginal returns. However, by increasing the amount of the variable factor used, a point will always be reached where the marginal increases in total output will begin declining.

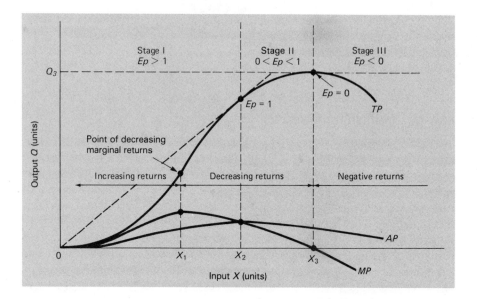

Figure 11.4
Relationships among Total, Average, and Marginal Product Curves

The law of diminishing marginal returns is *not* a mathematical theorem that can be proved or disproved logically. Rather it is an empirical assertion about the physical relationship between inputs and outputs that has been observed to be true in every economic production process. To illustrate some additional properties of production functions with one variable input, assume now that the variable input, rather than being composed of finitely divisible units (workers), is infinitely divisible. In other words, the variable input is now considered to be a *continuous* variable rather than a discrete variable, as in the example discussed previously. Figure 11.4 illustrates a production function (TP) with a continuously variable input exhibiting the properties described in the previous two paragraphs. Also shown are the average product (AP) and marginal product (MP) functions.

Several relationships among the TP, AP, and MP curves can be seen in the graph. In the first region labeled "increasing returns," the TP function (total output) is increasing at an *increasing rate*. Since the MP curve measures the slope of the TP curve ($MP = \partial Q/\partial X$), the MP curve is increasing up to X_1. In the region labeled "decreasing returns," the TP function is increasing at a *decreasing rate*, and the MP curve is decreasing up to X_3. In the region labeled "negative returns," the TP function is *decreasing*, and the MP curve continues decreasing and becomes negative beyond X_3. An *inflection point* occurs at X_1. At this point the TP curve switches from being *convex* to the horizontal axis (U-shaped) to being *concave* to the horizontal axis (inverted U-shaped). X_3 is the point of maximum output for the given or fixed amount of other inputs, Y, employed in the production process. Next, if a line is drawn from the origin 0 to any point on the TP curve, it can be seen that the slope of this line, Q/X, is at a maximum when the line touches the TP curve at an input value of X_2. The slope of this line, Q/X, measures the average product AP. Hence we see that the AP curve reaches a maximum at this point. Note also that the marginal product MP equals the average product AP at X_2. This follows because the marginal product MP is equal to the slope of the TP curve ($MP = \partial Q/\partial X$), and at X_2 the average product AP is also equal to the slope of the TP curve.

Three Stages of Production

In analyzing the production function, economists have identified three different stages of production based on the relationships among the TP, AP, and MP functions. Stage I is defined as the *range of X over which the average product is increasing*. This occurs from the origin (0) up to X_2. Stage II corresponds to the *range of X from the point at which the average product is a maximum (X_2) to the point where the marginal product (MP) declines to zero (X_3)*. The endpoint of Stage II thus corresponds to the point of maximum output on the TP curve. Stage III encompasses the *range of X over which the total product is declining* or, equivalently, *the marginal product is negative*. Stage III thus corresponds to all values of X greater than (i.e., to the right of) X_3.

The determination of the optimal quantity of input X to be used in producing a given amount of output Q is described in the next section; however, one can eliminate several values of X from consideration at this point. First, the rational producer would not operate the production process over the range of values of input X contained in Stage III. In Stage III an excessive amount of the variable input, relative to the fixed input Y, is being used to produce the desired output. In other words, since the marginal product of input X is negative beyond X_3, using more than X_3 units would cause a *reduction* in total output. Any desired output (up to the maximum obtainable with the given amount of the fixed input, that is, Q_3) could be produced by using less than X_3 units of the variable input. Consequently, even if the variable input was free, the rational producer would not want to operate in Stage III. As we demonstrate later in the chapter, the rational producer also would not want to operate the production process over the range of values of input X contained in Stage I.

Determining the Optimal Use of the Variable Input

With one of the inputs (Y) fixed in the short run, the producer must determine the optimal quantity of the variable input (X) to employ in the production process. Such a determination requires the introduction into the analysis of product (output) prices and factor costs. Therefore, the analysis begins by defining *marginal revenue product* and *marginal factor cost*.

Marginal Revenue Product

Marginal revenue product (MRP_x) is defined as *the amount that an additional unit of the variable input adds to total revenue*, or

$$MRP_x = \frac{\Delta TR}{\Delta X}$$

[11.11]

Table 11.3   **Marginal Revenue Product and Marginal Factor Cost—Ore-Mining Example**

Labor Input X (number of workers)	Total Product $Q = (TP_x)$ (tons of ore)	Marginal Product of Labor MP_x (tons per worker)	Total Revenue $TR = P \cdot Q$ ($)	Marginal Revenue $MR_Q = \dfrac{\Delta TR}{\Delta Q}$ ($/ton)	Marginal Revenue Product $MRP_x = MP_x \cdot MR_Q$ ($/worker)	Marginal Factor Cost MFC_x ($/worker)
0	0	—	0	—	—	—
1	6	6	60	10	60	50
2	16	10	160	10	100	50
3	29	13	290	10	130	50
4	44	15	440	10	150	50
5	55	11	550	10	110	50
6*	60	5	600	10	$\boxed{50}$	$\boxed{50}$
7	62	2	620	10	20	50
8	62	0	620	10	0	50

where ΔTR is the change in total revenue associated with the given change (ΔX) in the variable input. MRP_x is equal to the marginal product of X (MP_x) times the marginal revenue (MR_Q) resulting from the increase in output obtained:

$$MRP_x = MP_x \cdot MR_Q \qquad \text{[11.12]}$$

For example, consider again the ore-mining example (Table 11.2) of the previous section where Y (capital) is fixed at 750 horsepower. Suppose that the firm can sell all the ore it can produce at a price of $10 per ton (that is, in a *perfectly competitive market*). The marginal revenue product of labor (MRP_x) is computed using Equation 11.12 and is shown in Table 11.3.[4] Note that in a perfectly competitive market, marginal revenue is equal to the selling price.[5]

Marginal Factor Cost

Marginal factor cost (MFC_x) is defined as *the amount that an additional unit of the variable input adds to total cost*, or

$$MFC_x = \frac{\Delta TC}{\Delta X} \qquad \text{[11.13]}$$

where ΔTC is the change in cost associated with the given change (ΔX) in the variable input.

---

[4] Input levels in Stage III ($MP_x < O$) have been eliminated from consideration.
[5] This relationship is discussed further in chapter 14.

Returning again to the ore-mining example, suppose that the firm can employ as much labor (X) as its needs by paying the workers $50 per day ($C_x$). In other words, the labor market is assumed to be *perfectly competitive*. Under these conditions, the marginal factor cost (MFC_x) is equal to C_x, or $50 per worker. It is constant regardless of the level of operation of the mine (see Table 11.3).

Optimal Input Level

Given the marginal revenue product and marginal factor cost, we can compute the optimal amount of the variable input to use in the production process. Recall from the discussion of marginal analysis in Chapter 3 that an economic activity (for example, production) should be expanded as long as the marginal benefits (revenues) exceed the marginal costs. The optimal level occurs at the point where the marginal benefits are equal to the marginal costs. For the short-run production decision, the optimal level of the variable input occurs where

$$MRP_x = MFC_x \qquad\qquad [11.14]$$

As can be seen in Table 11.3, the optimal input is $X^* = 6$ workers since $MRP_x = MFC_x = \$50$ at this point. At less than six workers, $MRP_x > MFC_x$ and the addition of more labor (workers) to the production process will increase revenues more than it will increase costs. Beyond six workers the opposite is true—costs increase more than revenues.

Having completed the discussion of production functions with one variable input, we now examine the slightly more complex situation of a production function with two variable inputs.

Production Functions with Two Variable Inputs

Using the ore-mining example, suppose now that both capital—as measured by the horsepower rating of the equipment—and labor—as measured by the number of workers—are variable inputs to the ore-mining process. The firm can choose to operate the production process using any of the capital-labor combinations shown previously in Table 11.1. Note that the law of diminishing returns holds true in every row and column of the table. If one holds the number of workers X fixed and increases the size of the equipment Y, total output eventually increases at a decreasing rate, and for some (but not all) values of X, total output also declines. Similarly, if one holds the size of the equipment Y fixed and increases the number of workers X, total output eventually increases at a decreasing rate; and in some cases it also declines.

Production Isoquants

A production function with two variable inputs and one output can be represented graphically in either two or three dimensions. (A three-dimensional example was shown earlier in Figure 11.1.) Since a two-dimensional graph is

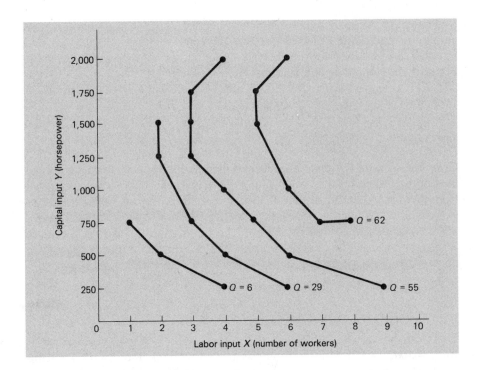

Figure 11.5
Production Isoquants: Ore-Mining Example

more amenable to further analysis, this method of illustration will be used. A production function is represented by a set of two-dimensional *production isoquants*. A *production isoquant* is either a geometric curve or an algebraic function representing all the various combinations of the two inputs that can be used in producing a given level of output. In the ore-mining example, a production isoquant shows all the alternative ways in which labor input (number of workers) and capital input (size of equipment) can be combined to produce any desired level of output (tons of ore). Several of the production isoquants for the ore-mining example are shown in Figure 11.5. Each production isoquant is constructed by plotting all the various labor-capital combinations that can be used in producing a given level of output and then connecting these points by a series of straight lines. For example, an output of 6 tons can be produced using any of three different labor-capital combinations—by either 1 unit of labor (1 worker) and 750 units of capital (750-horsepower mining equipment), by 2 units of labor and 500 units of capital, or by 4 units of labor and 250 units of capital. Similarly, as seen in the graph, an output of 62 tons can be produced using any one of six different labor-capital combinations. Each isoquant indicates how quantities of the two inputs may be *substituted* for one another in producing the desired level of output.

To develop further the concept of input substitution, assume that the two inputs are infinitely divisible and can be represented as continuous variables. Under this assumption, the production isoquants become smooth continuous curves, as shown in Figure 11.6. Four isoquants are sketched corresponding to the output levels of $Q^{(1)}$, $Q^{(2)}$, $Q^{(3)}$, and $Q^{(4)}$. Each point along the isoquant labeled $Q^{(1)}$ represents an alternative combination of inputs X and Y that when used together in the production process will yield $Q^{(1)}$ units of output.

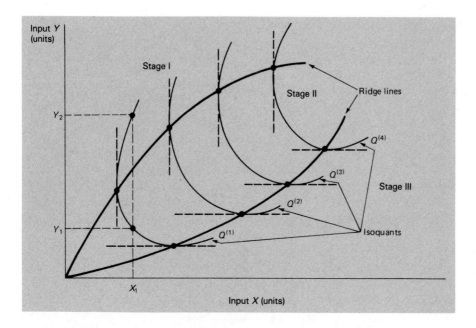

Figure 11.6
Production Isoquants: Infinitely Divisible Inputs

The other isoquants labeled $Q^{(2)}$, $Q^{(3)}$, and $Q^{(4)}$ represent the alternative ways in which the two inputs (X and Y) may be combined to produce $Q^{(2)}$, $Q^{(3)}$, and $Q^{(4)}$ units of output, respectively. For clarity, only four of the large number of possibilities are shown; that is, one isoquant exists for every possible level of output Q. Also shown in Figure 11.6 are the two *ridge lines* that are the boundaries of the set of efficient combinations of inputs X and Y. The ridge lines are constructed by drawing horizontal and vertical tangents to each of the isoquants and then connecting each of the vertical tangency points and each of the horizontal tangency points with smooth curves. The set of efficient combinations consists of all the points in the graph that lie *between* the two ridge lines. Recall from the earlier discussion of production functions with one variable input that we deduced a rational range of values for input X, called Stage II, outside of which the firm would not want to operate the production process. Similarly, in the two-variable input case, the firm would want to avoid producing a given amount of output using a combination of inputs X and Y that falls outside of the area bounded by the two ridge lines.

By using the production isoquants and total product curve shown in Figure 11.7, one can demonstrate that the firm would not want to operate its production process over the range of values of input X contained in Stage I. In Stage I an excessive amount of the fixed input Y, relative to the variable input X, is being used to produce the desired amount of output. As can be seen in Figure 11.7, if Y_2 units of the fixed input Y are used in combination with X_1 units of the variable input X, then $Q^{(1)}$ units of output will be obtained. However, $Q^{(1)}$ units of output could also be produced using a smaller amount (Y_1) of the fixed input. Hence, X_1 units of the variable input along with Y_2 units of the fixed input is not a rational combination of inputs to use in the production process. Similar reasoning can be used to eliminate from consideration all the other values of input X contained in Stage I.

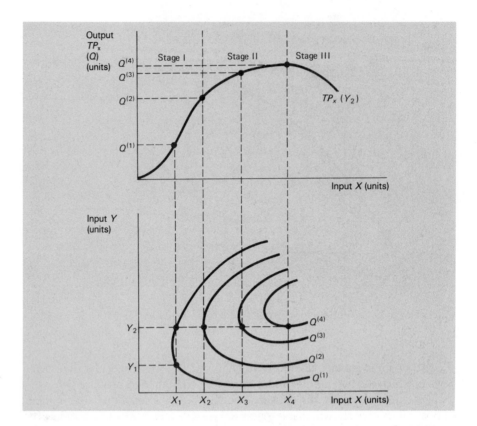

Figure 11.7
Production Isoquants and the Three Stages of Production

Marginal Rate of Technical Substitution

At this point an individual isoquant from the isoquant map in Figure 11.5 for the discrete case and one from Figure 11.6 for the continuous case are examined. In addition to indicating the quantity of output that can be produced with any of the various input combinations that lie on the isoquant curve, the isoquant also indicates the *rate* at which one input may be substituted for the other input in producing the given quantity of output. Suppose one considers the meaning of a shift from Point A to Point B on the isoquant labeled "$Q = 29$" in Figure 11.8. At Point A, 3 workers and a 750-horsepower machine are being used to produce 29 tons of output, whereas at Point B, 4 workers and a 500-horsepower machine are being used to produce the same amount of output. In moving from Point A to Point B one has substituted one additional unit of labor for 250 units of capital. The rate at which capital has been replaced with labor in producing the given output is equal to 250/1 or 250 units of capital per unit of labor. The rate at which one input may be substituted for another input in the production process, while total output remains constant, is known as the *marginal rate of technical substitution*, or *MRTS.*[6]

---

[6] Some books use the term *marginal rate of substitution* or *technical rate of substitution*.

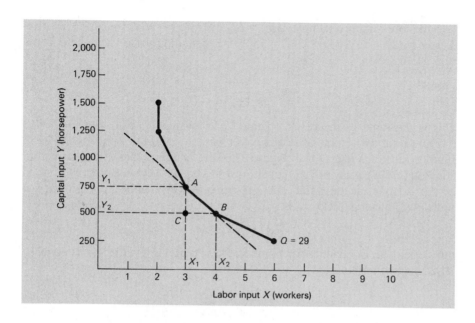

Figure 11.8
Production Isoquant Curve: Ore-Mining Example

The rate of change of one variable with respect to another variable is given by the slope of the curve relating the two variables. Thus, the rate of change of input Y with respect to input X—that is, the rate at which Y may be substituted for X in the production process—is given by the slope of the curve relating Y to X—that is, the slope of the isoquant. The slope of the AB segment of the isoquant in Figure 11.8 is equal to the ratio of AC to CB. Algebraically, $AC = Y_1 - Y_2$ and $CB = X_1 - X_2$; therefore the slope is equal to $(Y_1 - Y_2) \div (X_1 - X_2)$. Since the slope is negative and one wishes to express the substitution rate as a positive quantity, a negative sign is attached to the slope:

$$MRTS = -\frac{Y_1 - Y_2}{X_1 - X_2} = -\frac{\Delta Y}{\Delta X} \qquad [11.15]$$

In the ore-mining example, $\Delta X = 3 - 4 = -1$, $\Delta Y = 750 - 500 = 250$. Substituting these values into Equation 11.15 yields

$$MRTS = \frac{250}{-1} = 250$$

It can be shown that the $MRTS$ is equal to the ratio of the marginal products of X and Y by using the definition of the marginal product (Equation 11.3). This definition yields $\Delta X = \Delta Q/MP_x$ and $\Delta Y = \Delta Q/MP_y$. Substituting these expressions into Equation 11.15 (and dropping the minus sign) yields:

$$MRTS = \frac{Q/MP_y}{Q/MP_x}$$

$$MRTS = \frac{MP_x}{MP_y} \qquad [11.16]$$

For the ore-mining example, $MP_x = \Delta Q/\Delta X = (29 - 16)/(4 - 3) = 13$, $MP_y = \Delta Q/\Delta Y = (29 - 16)/(750 - 500) = 13/250$. Substituting these values into Equation 11.16 yields

$$MRTS = \frac{13}{13/250} = 250$$

This is the same as the result obtained previously.

When the two inputs are continuous variables and the isoquants are continuous functions like $Q^{(2)}$ in Figure 11.9, the marginal rate of technical substitution ($MRTS$) at any point on the isoquant is equal to the negative of the slope of the isoquant at the point. For our general two-variable input production function (Equation 11.1)

$$Q = f(X, Y)$$

the slope of an isoquant at any point, such as Point A in Figure 11.9, is equal to dY/dX, and therefore

$$MRTS = -\frac{dY}{dX} \qquad [11.17]$$

In a manner analogous to that described earlier for the case of discrete input variables (Equation 11.16), it can be shown that the marginal rate of technical substitution in the continuous input variables case is likewise equal to the ratio of the marginal products of the two inputs where

$$MP_x = \frac{\partial Q}{\partial X} \qquad [11.18]$$

and

$$MP_y = \frac{\partial Q}{\partial Y} \qquad [11.19]$$

As will be seen later in the chapter, the marginal rate of technical substitution is a very important concept in the derivation of the optimum combination of inputs to be used in producing a given quantity of output.

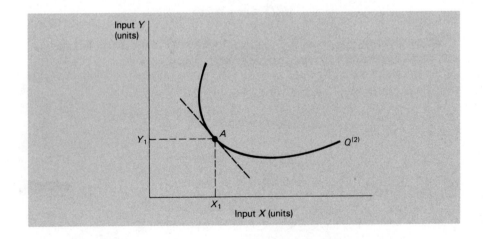

Figure 11.9
**Production
Isoquant Curve:
Infinitely
Divisible Inputs**

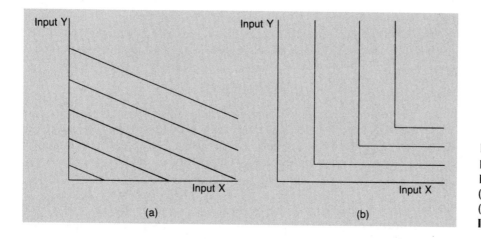

Figure 11.10
Production Isoquants: Perfect (a) Substitute and (b) Complementary Inputs

Perfect Substitute and Complementary Inputs

Production inputs vary in the degree to which they can be substituted for one another in a given process. The extreme cases are *perfect substitutes* and *perfect complements*. Isoquants for these two cases are shown in Figure 11.10. The isoquants for inputs that are *perfect substitutes* for one another consist of a series of parallel lines, as shown in Figure 11.10 (a). Examples of perfect substitutes are the use of alternative fuels (inputs) such as oil or coal in the production of electricity or the use of soybeans or oats in the production of nutrients in animal feeds. The isoquants for inputs that are *perfect complements* for one another consist of a series of right angles, as shown in Figure 11.10 (b). Such inputs are said to have zero substitutability. Examples of perfect complements include component parts that must be combined in fixed proportions, such as wheels and frames for automobiles or foundations and roofs for houses.

Most production inputs fall somewhere between the extreme cases of perfect complements and perfect substitutes. The isoquants for most production functions are curves that are convex to the origin as shown earlier in Figure 11.7. This shape implies that the production inputs are imperfectly substitutable and that the rate of substitution declines as one input is substituted for another.

Determining the Optimal Combination of Inputs

As shown in the previous section, a given level of output can be produced using any of a large number of possible combinations of two inputs. Given that positive prices exist for these resources, differing total costs will be incurred in producing the desired output, depending on which combination of inputs is used. The firm is thus faced with determining the optimal combination of resources to employ in the production process.

Isocost Lines

The total cost of each possible input combination is a function of the market prices of these inputs. Assuming that inputs are purchased by the firm in *perfectly competitive markets*, the per unit price of each input will be constant, regardless of the amount of the input that is purchased. Letting C_x and C_y be the per unit prices of inputs X and Y, respectively, then the total cost (C) of any given input combination is

$$C = C_x X + C_y Y \qquad [11.20]$$

In the ore-mining example discussed earlier, suppose that workers are paid $50 per day ($C_x$) and that mining equipment can be leased at a cost of $.20 per horsepower per day (C_y). The total cost of using X workers and equipment having Y horsepower to produce a given amount of output is

$$C = 50X + .20Y \qquad [11.21]$$

From this relationship, it can be seen that the mining of 55 tons of ore using 5 workers (X) and equipment having 750 horsepower (Y) would cost $50(5) + .20(750) = \$400$. However, this is not the only combination of workers and equipment costing $400. Any combination of inputs satisfying the equation

$$400 = 50X + .20Y$$

would cost $400. Solving this equation for Y yields

$$Y = \frac{\$400}{.20} - \frac{50}{.20}X = \$2,000 - 250X$$

Thus the combinations $X = 1$ and $Y = 1,750$, $X = 2$ and $Y = 1,500$, $X = 3$ and $Y = 1,250$ (plus many other combinations) all cost $400.

The combinations of inputs costing $400 can be represented as the line in Figure 11.11 labeled "$C = \$400$." This line is called an *isocost* line, since it shows

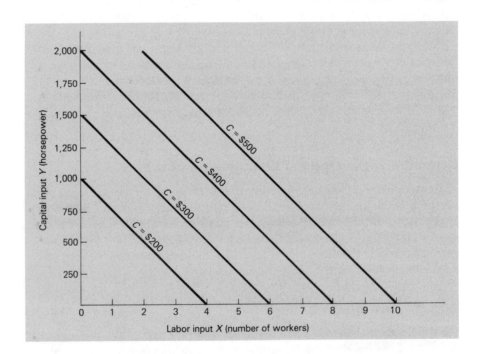

Figure 11.11
Isocost Lines: Ore-Mining Example

all the combinations of inputs having *equal* total costs. An isocost line exists for every possible total cost C. Solving Equation 11.21 for Y gives the equation of each isocost line

$$Y = \frac{C}{.20} - 250X \qquad [11.22]$$

A series of isocost lines are shown in Figure 11.11. Note that all the isocost lines are parallel, each one having a slope of -250. In general, the set of isocost lines consists of the set of equations given by the solution of Equation 11.20 for various values of C:

$$Y = \frac{C}{C_y} - \frac{C_x}{C_y} X \qquad [11.23]$$

Once the isoquants and isocosts are specified, it is possible to solve for the optimum combination of inputs. The production decision problem can be formulated in two different ways, depending on the manner in which the production objective or goal is stated. It is possible to solve for the combination of inputs that either

1. minimizes total cost subject to a given constraint on output or

2. maximizes output subject to a given total cost constraint.

It should be noted that constrained cost minimization is the dual problem to constrained output maximization problem. To illustrate the general conditions for an optimum solution to each of these two types of production problems, it is necessary to assume, as was done earlier in this chapter, that the two inputs X and Y are infinitely divisible and can be represented as continuous variables. A graphic solution can be obtained by combining the isoquant and isocost curves on one set of axes. A set of isoquants for the general two-variable input production function and a set of isocosts are shown together in Figures 11.12 and 11.13.

Minimizing Cost Subject to an Output Constraint

Consider first the problem of minimizing the total cost of producing a given desired quantity of output. Suppose it is desired to produce at least $Q^{(2)}$ units of output. As shown in Figure 11.12, this constraint requires that the solution be in the feasible region containing the input combinations that lie either on the $Q^{(2)}$ isoquant or on isoquants that fall above and to the right having larger output values (the shaded area). The total cost of producing the required output is minimized by finding the input combinations within this region that lie on the lowest cost isocost line. Combination D on the $C^{(2)}$ isocost line satisfies this condition. Combinations E and F, which also lie on the $Q^{(2)}$ isoquant, yield higher total costs, since they fall on the $C^{(3)}$ isocost line. No other point within the feasible region lies on an isocost line with a lower total cost than does Point D. Thus, the use of X_1 units of input X and Y_1 units of input Y will yield a (constrained) minimum cost solution of $C^{(2)}$ dollars.

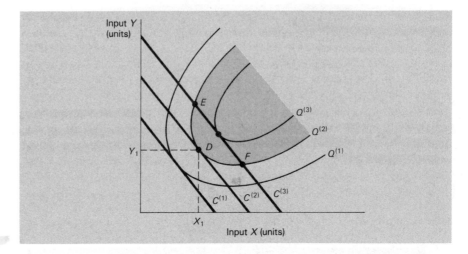

Figure 11.12
Cost Minimization Subject to an Output Constraint

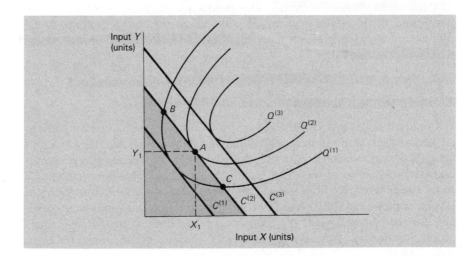

Figure 11.13
Output Maximization Subject to a Cost Constraint

Two important characteristics of this solution permit us to state the necessary algebraic conditions needed to solve for the particular combination of inputs (X_1, Y_1).[7] First, note that the optimal solution occurs at the *boundary* of the feasible region of input combinations. Hence, one needs only to examine the $Q^{(2)}$ isoquant and the $C^{(2)}$ isocost in solving for an optimal solution. Second, note that the optimal solution occurs at the point where the isoquant is *tangent* to the isocost line. At the optimal input combination, the slope of the isoquant must equal the slope of the isocost line. As in the previous section, the slope of an isoquant is equal to dY/dX and

$$-\frac{dY}{dX} = MRTS = \frac{MP_x}{MP_y}$$

[11.24]

---

[7] A set of *sufficient* conditions for an optimal solution must also include that the isoquants be convex to the origin.

Taking the derivative of the isocost equation (Equation 11.23), the slope of the isocost line is given by

$$\frac{dY}{dX} = -\frac{C_x}{C_y}$$

[11.25]

Multiplying Equation 11.25 by (-1), and setting the result equal to Equation 11.24 yields

$$-\frac{dY}{dX} = -\left(-\frac{C_x}{C_y}\right)$$

$$= \frac{MP_x}{MP_y}$$

Thus the following condition, the "equimarginal criterion,"

$$\frac{MP_x}{MP_y} = \frac{C_x}{C_y}$$

or equivalently,

$$\boxed{\frac{MP_x}{C_x} = \frac{MP_y}{C_y}}$$

[11.26]

must be satisfied in order that an input combination be an optimal solution to the problem of minimizing cost subject to an output constraint. Equation 11.26 indicates that the ratio of the marginal product of a factor to its associated cost must be equal to the ratio of the marginal product of the other factor to its associated cost. Note that the logic of this optimality condition is equivalent to that developed in Chapter 7 (Equation 7.1) dealing with demand theory.

The ore-mining example can be used to illustrate the graphic approach to finding an optimal solution to a cost-minimization problem. Suppose one is interested in finding the combination of labor input (workers) and capital input (horsepower) that minimizes the cost of producing at least 29 tons of ore. Assume that the isocost lines are the ones defined by Equation 11.21 and graphed in Figure 11.11 earlier in this section. Figure 11.14 combines several isoquants and isocost lines for the ore-mining problem. The shaded area in the graph represents the set of feasible input combinations; that is, those labor and capital input combinations that yield at least $Q = 29$ tons of output. From the graph, note that the "$C = \$300$" isocost line is tangent to the boundary of the feasible region; that is, the "$Q = 29$" isoquant. In this case there are two optimal (minimum cost) input combinations—3 workers and a 750 horsepower machine or 4 workers and a 500-horsepower machine. Both input combinations yield the desired 29 tons of output at a minimum cost of $300.

Maximizing Output Subject to a Cost Constraint

Consider next the problem of maximizing output subject to an upper limit or constraint on the total cost to be incurred in producing the output. Suppose that

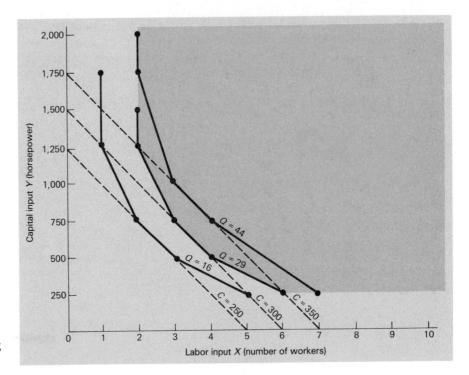

Figure 11.14
Isoquant Curves and Isocost Lines for the Ore-Mining Example

a total cost constraint of $C^{(2)}$ dollars is imposed on the production process. As shown in Figure 11.13, this constraint requires that the solution fall in the feasible region consisting of the input combinations that lie on or below the $C^{(2)}$ isocost line (the shaded area). Output is maximized by finding the input combinations within the feasible region that lie on the isoquant with the largest output value. Combination A on the $Q^{(2)}$ isoquant satisfies this condition. Combinations B and C, which also lie on the $C^{(2)}$ isocost line, yield lower outputs, since they fall on the $Q^{(1)}$ isoquant. No other point within the feasible region lies on an isoquant with a larger output value than does Point A. Thus the use of X_1 units of input X and Y_1 units of input Y will yield a (constrained) maximum output of $Q^{(2)}$ units.

As in the previously discussed cost-minimization problem, the optimal input combination occurs at the boundary of the feasible region of input combinations and at a point of tangency between the isocost and isoquant curves. As before, the slope of the isocost line is equal to the slope of the isoquant at the optimal input combination point. From this characteristic of the solution, and using similar reasoning, it can be shown that the same condition

$$\boxed{\frac{MP_x}{C_x} = \frac{MP_y}{C_y}}$$

[11.27]

that had to be satisfied in the cost-minimization problem must also hold true for an input combination to be an optimal solution to the problem of output maximization subject to a cost constraint.[8]

Effect of a Change in Input Prices

As shown above, the optimal combination of inputs in both the cost-minimization and output-maximization problems is a function of the relative prices (or costs) of the inputs, that is, C_x and C_y. As the price of the input X rises, one would expect the firm to use less of this input and more of the other input Y in the production process, all other things being equal. This shift is demonstrated in Figure 11.15. The firm is interested in minimizing the cost of producing a given quantity of output $Q^{(0)}$. Initially, the costs of inputs X and Y are C_x and C_y, respectively, resulting in the isocost line $C = C_xX + C_yY$. Given these conditions, the firm would operate at tangency point A—using X_1 units of input X and Y_1 units of input Y. Now suppose that the price of input X is increased to C_x'. This has the effect of increasing the slope of the isocost lines, such as isocost line $C' = C_x'X + C_yY$ shown in the graph. To produce the same $Q^{(0)}$ units of output at minimum cost, the firm would operate at tangency point B—using X_2 units of input X and Y_2 units of input Y.

---

[8] This condition can be demonstrated using Lagrangian multiplier techniques. Given the production function $Q = f(X, Y)$ and cost constraint $C_xX + C_yY = C$, form the Lagrangian function:

$$L = f(X, Y) + \lambda(C_xX + C_yY - C) \tag{1}$$

Differentiate L, with respect to X, Y, and λ and set the derivatives equal to 0 (condition for maximum):

$$\frac{\partial L}{\partial X} = \frac{\partial f(X, Y)}{\partial X} + \lambda C_x = 0 \tag{2}$$

$$\frac{\partial L}{\partial Y} = \frac{\partial f(X, Y)}{\partial Y} + \lambda C_y = 0 \tag{3}$$

$$\frac{\partial L}{\partial \lambda} = C_xX + C_yY - C = 0 \tag{4}$$

Recognizing that $\dfrac{\partial f(X, Y)}{X} = MP_x$ and $\dfrac{\partial f(X, Y)}{Y} = MP_y$, solve Equations [2] and [3] for λ

$$\lambda = -\frac{MP_x}{C_x} \tag{5}$$

$$\lambda = -\frac{MP_y}{C_y} \tag{6}$$

Set Equations [5] and [6] equal to each other to obtain the optimality condition:

$$\frac{MP_x}{C_x} = \frac{MP_y}{C_y} \tag{7}$$

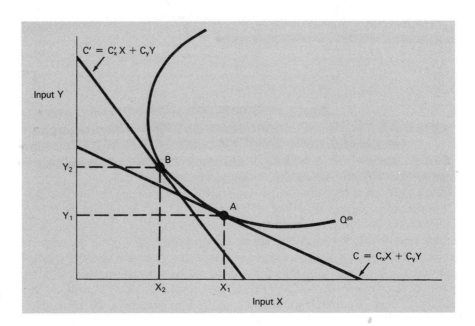

Figure 11.15
Effect of a Change in Input Prices

From this analysis one can see that as the price of one input increases, the firm will substitute away from this input and use more of the relatively less expensive input. Historically, this phenomenon has been observed in the shift toward more capital-intensive production processes (that is, greater use of labor-saving equipment) because the price of labor has increased relative to the price of capital.

This and the previous sections have been concerned with the effect on production output of arbitrary changes in either or both of the two inputs and in finding the optimal combination of inputs. The following section examines the effects on output of proportional changes in both inputs simultaneously. In other words, an investigation of the effects of a change in the scale of production.

Returns to Scale

This section begins with a definition of returns to scale, followed by discussions of measurement of returns to scale, increasing and decreasing returns to scale, and homogeneous production functions and returns to scale.

Definition of Returns to Scale

In addition to providing a framework for determining the optimal combination of inputs to use in producing a desired level of output, production theory also offers a means for analysis of the effects on output of changes in the *scale* of production. An increase in the scale of production consists of a simultaneous proportionate increase in *all* the inputs used in the production process. The proportionate increase in the output of the production process that results from

Economic Analysis and Managerial Efficiency

A HIGH TECH RESCUE OF AMERICAN MANUFACTURERS*

After nearly two decades of neglect, corporate America is placing new emphasis on reviving the competitiveness of America's factories. This revival has been spurred by a decline in the market share enjoyed by many of America's industries. For example, in the electronics area the market share of American firms declined to less than 10 percent in 1985, from over 30 percent in 1965. The steel and automotive industries have witnessed similar market share declines.

Recent major advances in technology, however, have caused many American firms to rediscover the factory. For example, many firms have embarked upon aggressive automation programs. General Electric is spending $1 billion to automate its large appliance plant in Louisville, Kentucky. And IBM is spending more than $15 billion to automate its factories and make them more competitive in the world market. PPG Industries is constructing a new glass plant designed to be 50 percent more productive than any other existing glass plant. The plant will be completely paperless—all record keeping will be done by computer. Many of these new factories can also produce customized products almost overnight. By

*Based, in part, on "High Tech to the Rescue," *Business Week* (16 June 1986), pp. 100–108.

using integrated systems of computer-aided designs, computer-aided engineering, and computer-aided manufacturing, firms can produce low-cost products in record time, while meeting higher quality standards than were common in the past.

For smaller companies, automation not only poses major challenges but also offers exciting opportunities. These companies must often custom design their own automation programs; however, many of these companies have been able to market their internally developed automation expertise to other firms facing similar challenges.

Managers seeking to maximize shareholder wealth face new challenges as rapid advances in computer assisted manufacturing technology require large new capital investments to keep the firm competitive. Perhaps now, more so than at any time in the recent past, managers are confronting major decisions regarding the choice of inputs (i.e., the selection of a production technology) necessary to remain competitive.

Questions

1. What effect do you believe the decline in the value of the dollar that occurred during 1987 and 1988 will have on the drive to automate America's factories and restore them to a position as viable world competitors?

2. How will the new drive toward increased automation affect American labor unions?

the given proportionate increase in all the inputs is defined as the physical *returns to scale*. Suppose, in the ore-mining example introduced earlier, one is interested in determining the effect on the number of tons of ore produced (output) of a 1.50 factor increase in the scale of production from a given labor-capital combination of 4 workers and equipment having 500 horsepower. A 1.50 factor increase in the scale of production would constitute a labor-capital combination of $4 \times 1.5 = 6$ workers and equipment having $500 \times 1.5 = 750$ horsepower. From Table 11.1 note that the labor-capital combination of 4 workers and 500 horsepower yields 29 tons of output, whereas the combination of 6 workers and 750 horsepower yields 60 tons of output. Output has increased by the ratio of $60/29 = 2.07$. Thus, a 1.50 factor increase in input use has resulted in more than a 1.50 factor increase (that is, 2.07) in the quantity of output produced. Clearly, this relationship between the proportionate increases in inputs and outputs is not required to be the same for all increases in the scale of production. A 1.50 factor increase in the scale of production from 6 workers and 500 horsepower to 9 workers and 750 horsepower results in an increase in output from 55 to 61 tons—an increase by a factor of only 1.10.

Measurement of Returns to Scale

To present a general framework for analyzing physical returns to scale, assume, as in previous sections, that the two inputs of the production function can be represented as continuous variables. An increase in the scale of production can be represented graphically in a two-dimensional isoquant map, as is shown in Figure 11.16. Increasing the scale of production by a factor of λ from the combination of X_1 units of input X and Y_1 units of input Y (Point A on the graph) constitutes a shift to the combination consisting of $X_2 = \lambda X_1$ units of input X and $Y_2 = \lambda Y_1$ units of input Y (Point B on the graph). Any increase (or decrease) in the scale of production from a given point must lie along a line from the origin through the given point on the isoquant map. This follows because an increase in the scale of production requires that the inputs in the production process continue to be combined in the same proportion as that at the given point. At Point A in the graph, the inputs are being combined in the proportion X_1/Y_1. At Point B, the inputs are being combined in the same proportion since

$$\frac{X_2}{Y_2} = \frac{\lambda X_1}{\lambda Y_1} = \frac{X_1}{Y_1}$$

The increase in the quantity of output from $Q^{(1)}$ to $Q^{(2)}$ represents the returns to scale of an increase in the amounts of both inputs employed in the production process by a factor of λ. Three possible relationships exist between the increase in inputs and the increase in outputs. For an increase in all inputs

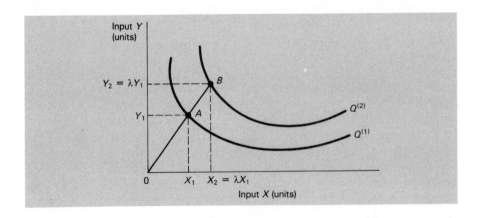

Figure 11.16
Returns to Scale

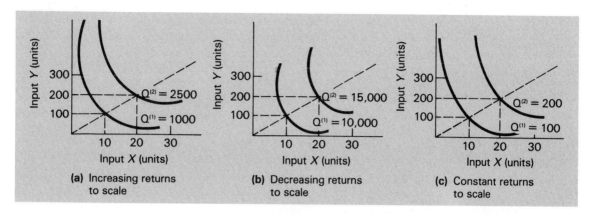

(a) Increasing returns to scale

(b) Decreasing returns to scale

(c) Constant returns to scale

Figure 11.17
Production Isoquants Exhibiting Increasing, Decreasing, and Constant Returns to Scale

by a factor of λ:

1. *Increasing* returns to scale case: Output increases by *more than* λ; that is, $Q^{(2)} > \lambda Q^{(1)}$

2. *Decreasing* returns to scale case: Output increases by *less than* λ; that is, $Q^{(2)} < \lambda Q^{(1)}$.

3. *Constant* returns to scale case: Output increases by *exactly* λ; that is, $Q^{(2)} = \lambda Q^{(1)}$.

Depending on whether $Q^{(2)}$ is more than, less than, or equal to $\lambda Q^{(1)}$, the production function is said to exhibit increasing, decreasing, or constant physical returns to scale over the range of input combinations from A to B in Figure 11.16.

Figure 11.17 illustrates three different production functions that exhibit these types of returns to scale. In Panel (a), showing increasing returns to scale, doubling input X from 10 to 20 units and input Y from 100 to 200 units yields more than double the amount of output—an increase from 1000 to 2500 units. In Panel (b), showing decreasing returns to scale, a similar doubling of the two inputs yields less than double the amount of output—an increase from 10,000 to 15,000 units. Finally in Panel (c), showing constant returns to scale, a similar doubling of inputs X and Y yields exactly double the amount of output—an increase from 100 to 200 units.

As one makes successive increases in the scale of production, it is not necessary that the production function exhibit the same type (increasing, decreasing, or constant) of scale relationship. Suppose that starting from the labor-capital combination of 2 workers and 500 horsepower in the ore-mining example discussed earlier, we successively double ($\lambda = 2.0$) the scale of production. From Table 11.1 note that output first increases from 6 tons to 55 tons, a 9.17 factor increase, and then increases from 55 tons to 65 tons, which is only a 1.18 factor increase. Over the given change in the scale of production, this production function first exhibits increasing and then decreasing returns to scale.

If the production function is given in algebraic form, returns to scale can be measured by increasing each of the inputs by a factor of λ and determining the effect on output. For example, suppose one is interested in determining the returns to scale of a production process having the following Cobb-Douglas power production function:

$$Q = .5L^{.6}K^{.3} \tag{11.28}$$

First, increase each of the inputs by a factor of λ; that is, $L' = \lambda L$ and $K' = \lambda K$. Next, substitute these values into the production function as follows:

$$
\begin{aligned}
Q' &= .5L'^{.6}K'^{.3} \\
&= .5(\lambda L)^{.6}(\lambda K)^{.3} \\
&= .5(\lambda^{.6}L^{.6})(\lambda^{.3}K^{.3}) \\
&= \lambda^{.9}(.5L^{.6}K^{.3}) \\
&= \lambda^{.9}Q
\end{aligned}
$$

Since output increases by less than λ—by a factor of $\lambda^{.9}$—this production process exhibits *decreasing* returns to scale.

Increasing and Decreasing Returns to Scale

In addition to satisfying the law of diminishing marginal returns discussed earlier, the production function of economic theory is also often hypothesized to have a shape characterized by first increasing and then decreasing physical returns to scale. A number of arguments have been presented to justify this characteristic of the production function. The major argument given for initial increasing returns, as the scale of production is first increased, is the opportunity for *specialization in the use of capital and labor*. As the scale of production is increased, equipment that is more efficient in performing a limited set of tasks can be substituted for less efficient all-purpose equipment. Similarly, the efficiency of workers in performing a small number of related tasks is greater than that of less highly skilled but more versatile workers. Practical limits on the degree of specialization, however, may prevent increasing returns from being realized in producing ever-larger quantities of output.

A principal argument given for the existence of decreasing returns to scale is the increasingly complex *problems of coordination and control* faced by management as the scale of production is increased. Limitations on the ability of management to transmit and receive information (such as decisions and reports on performance) may diminish the effectiveness of management in exercising control and coordination of increasingly larger scales of production. As a result, proportionate increases in all of the inputs of the production process, including the input labeled "management," may eventually yield less than proportionate increases in total output. However, the combination of large-scale, high-speed data communications and processing equipment, along with modern methods of production planning and control raises questions about whether decreasing physical returns to scale do in fact occur.

Whether a production function for a particular production process exhibits any one or a combination of increasing, decreasing, and constant returns to scale is a question that probably can best be answered by statistical methods.

Chapter 13 examines some of the approaches that have been used in empirically measuring the shape and characteristics of production functions.

Homogeneous Production Functions and Returns to Scale

Many of the algebraic production functions used in analyzing production processes, such as the Cobb-Douglas power function (Equation 11.2), are said to be homogeneous.[9] Homogeneous functions have certain mathematical properties that make them desirable in modeling production processes. If each input in the production function is multiplied by an arbitrary constant λ and if this constant can be factored out of the function, then the production function is defined as *homogeneous*.

One can also measure the degree of homogeneity of a production function. A production function $Q = f(x, y)$ is said to be *homogeneous of degree n* if

$$f(\lambda x, \lambda y) = \lambda^n f(x, y) \, for \, \lambda \neq 0 \qquad [11.29]$$

where λ is some constant. For example, the following production function

$$f(x, y) = .6x + .2y \qquad [11.30]$$

is homogeneous of degree 1.0 since

$$f(\lambda x, \lambda y) = .6(\lambda x) + .2(\lambda y)$$
$$= \lambda^1(.6x + .2y)$$
$$= \lambda^1 f(x, y)$$

If the degree of homogeneity (n) is equal to 1.0, then the production function is said to be *linearly homogeneous*. The following Cobb-Douglas power production function

$$Q = 2.0 L^{.7} K^{.3} \qquad [11.31]$$

is also linearly homogeneous. The degree of homogeneity (n) indicates the type of returns to scale (i.e., increasing, decreasing, or constant) that characterize a production function. If $n = 1$, the production function exhibits constant returns to scale: if $n > 1$ the production function exhibits increasing returns to scale, and if $n < 1$ the production function exhibits decreasing returns to scale.

Summary

■ A *production function* is a schedule, graph, or mathematical model relating the maximum quantity of output that can be produced from various quantities of inputs.

---

[9] The mathematical properties of the Cobb-Douglas production function are examined in Chapter 13.

- For a production function with one variable input, the *marginal product* is defined as the incremental change in total output that can be produced by the use of one more unit of the variable input in the production process.

- For a production function with one variable input, the *average product* is defined as the ratio of total output to the amount of the variable input used in producing the output.

- The *law of diminishing marginal returns* states that, with all other productive factors held constant, the use of increasing amounts of the variable factor in the production process beyond some point will result in diminishing marginal increases in total output.

- In the short run, with one of the productive factors fixed, the optimal output level (and optimal level of the variable input) occurs where marginal revenue product equals marginal factor cost. *Marginal revenue product* is defined as the amount that an additional unit of the variable input adds to total revenue. *Marginal factor cost* is defined as the amount that an additional unit of the variable input adds to total cost.

- A *production isoquant* is either a geometric curve or algebraic function representing all the various combinations of inputs that can be used in producing a given level of output.

- The *marginal rate of technical substitution* is the rate at which one input may be substituted for another input in the production process, while total output remains constant. It is equal to the ratio of the marginal products of the two inputs.

- In the long run, with both inputs being variable, minimizing cost subject to an output constraint (or maximizing output subject to a cost constraint) requires that the production process be operated at the point where the ratios of the marginal product of each factor to its associated cost are equal.

- Physical *returns to scale* is defined as the proportionate increase in the output of a production process that results from a given proportionate increase in all the inputs.

- The production function of economic theory, in addition to satisfying the law of diminishing marginal returns, is hypothesized to have a shape characterized by first increasing and then decreasing physical returns to scale.

Selected References

Baumol, William J. *Economic Theory and Operations Analysis*, 4th ed. Englewood Cliffs, N. J.: Prentice-Hall, 1977.

Douglas, Paul H. "Are There Laws of Production?" *American Economic Review* (March 1948), pp. 1–41.

Ferguson, C. E., and J. P. Gould. *Microeconomic Theory*, 4th ed. Homewood, Ill.: Richard D. Irwin, 1975.

Henderson, James M., and Richard E. Quandt. *Microeconomic Theory: A Mathematical Approach*, 2d ed. New York: McGraw-Hill, 1971.

Walters, A. A. "Production and Cost Functions: An Econometric Survey." *Econometrica* (January–April 1963), pp. 1–66.

Discussion Questions

1. Define the following terms:
   a. Input
   b. Production function
   c. Production elasticity
   e. Marginal factor cost
   f. Production isoquant
   g. Ridge lines
   h. Isocost line
   i. Marginal rate of technical substitution

2. Explain the difference between the short run and long run in production analysis.

3. Explain the difference between diminishing marginal returns and decreasing returns to scale.

4. Explain the necessary conditions that must be satisfied in determining the combination of inputs that minimizes cost subject to an output constraint.

5. Define and give examples of the following inputs:
   a. Perfect substitutes
   b. Perfect complements

6. What is meant by a homogeneous production function? How is the degree of homogeneity related to returns to scale?

7. Explain how to determine the boundaries of the three stages of production.

8. Explain the primary reason(s) given for the existence of:
   a. increasing returns to scale
   b. decreasing returns to scale

9. Suppose the short run total product curve (TP_x) is a linear function of the variable input over some range of values. Determine the shape of the corresponding marginal product (MP_x) and average product (AP_x) functions.

10. Suppose that as the result of recent labor negotiations, wage rates are *reduced* by 10 percent in a production process employing only capital and labor. Assuming that other conditions (for example, productivity) remain constant, determine what effect this decrease will have on the desired proportions of capital and labor used in producing the given level of output at minimum total cost. Illustrate your answer with an isoquant-isocost diagram.

Problems

1. In the ore-mining example described in the chapter (Table 11.1), suppose again that labor is the variable input and capital is the fixed input. Specifically, assume that the firm owns a piece of equipment having a 500-horsepower rating.

a. Complete the following table:

Labor Input X (no. of workers)	Total Product $TP_x(=Q)$	Marginal Product MP_x	Average Product AP_x	Elasticity of Production E_x
1	_____	_____	_____	_____
2	_____	_____	_____	_____
3	_____	_____	_____	_____
4	_____	_____	_____	_____
5	_____	_____	_____	_____
6	_____	_____	_____	_____
7	_____	_____	_____	_____
8	_____	_____	_____	_____
9	_____	_____	_____	_____
10	_____	_____	_____	_____

b. Plot the (i) total product, (ii) marginal product, and (iii) average product functions.
c. Determine the boundaries of the three stages of production.

2. From your knowledge of the relationships among the various production functions, complete the following table:

Variable Input X	Total Product $TP_x(=Q)$	Average Product AP_x	Marginal Product MP_x
0	0	—	—
1	_____	_____	8
2	28	_____	_____
3	_____	18	_____
4	_____	_____	26
5	_____	20	_____
6	108	_____	_____
7	_____	_____	−10

3. The amount of fish caught per week on a trawler is a function of the crew size assigned to operate the boat. Based on past data, the following production schedule was developed:

Crew Size (number of men)	Amount of Fish Caught per Week (hundreds of pounds)
2	3
3	6
4	11
5	19
6	24
7	28

Crew Size (number of men)	Amount of Fish Caught per Week (hundreds of pounds)
8	31
9	33
10	34
11	34
12	33

a. Over what ranges of workers are there (i) increasing, (ii) constant, (iii) decreasing, and (iv) negative returns?

b. How large a crew should be used if the trawler owner is interested in maximizing the total amount of fish caught?

c. How large a crew should be used if the trawler owner is interested in maximizing the average amount of fish caught per man?

4. Consider Problem 3 again. Suppose the owner of the trawler can sell all the fish he can catch for $75 per hundred pounds and can hire as many crew members as he wants by paying them $150 per week. Assuming that the owner of the trawler is interested in maximizing profits, determine the optimal crew size.

5. In the ore-mining example described in the chapter (Table 11.1), suppose one is interested in maximizing output subject to a cost constraint. Assume that the per-unit costs of labor and capital are $45 and $.24 respectively. Total costs (the sum of labor and capital costs) are constrained to $360 or less.

a. Using graphical isoquant-isocost analysis, determine the optimal combination of labor and capital to employ in the ore-mining process and the optimal output level.

b. Determine the optimal combination of labor and capital and optimal output level if the per-unit costs of labor and capital are $60 and $.18, respectively.

6. Consider the following short-run production function where X = variable input, Q = output:

$$Q = 6X^2 - .4X^3$$

a. Determine the marginal product function (MP_x).

b. Determine the average product function (AP_x).

c. Find the value of X that maximizes Q.

d. Find the value of X at which the marginal product function takes on its maximum value.

e. Find the value of X at which the average product function takes on its maximum value.

f. Plot the (i) total, (ii) marginal, and (iii) average product functions for values of $X = 0, 1, 2, 3, \ldots, 12$.

7. Consider the following short-run production function (where X = variable input, Q = output):

$$Q = 10X - .5X^2$$

Suppose that output can be sold for $10 per unit. Also assume that the firm can obtain as much of the variable input (X) as it needs at $20 per unit.

a. Determine the marginal revenue product function.

b. Determine the marginal factor cost function.

c. Determine the optimal value of X, given that the objective is to maximize profits.

8. A firm uses two variable inputs, labor (L) and raw materials (M) in producing its output. At its current level of output:

$$C_L = \$10/\text{unit} \qquad MP_L = \$25/\text{unit}$$
$$C_M = \$2/\text{unit} \qquad MP_M = \$4/\text{unit}$$

a. Determine whether the firm is operating efficiently, given that its objective is to minimize the cost of producing the given level of output.

b. Determine what changes (if any) in the relative proportions of labor and raw materials need to be made to operate efficiently.

9. Suppose that a firm's production function is given by the following relationship:

$$Q = 2.5 \sqrt{LC} \qquad (\text{i.e., } Q = 2.5L^{.5}C^{.5})$$

where

$$Q = \text{output}$$
$$L = \text{labor input}$$
$$C = \text{capital input}$$

a. Determine the percentage increase in output if labor input is increased by 10 percent (assuming that capital input is held constant).

b. Determine the percentage increase in output if capital input is increased by 25 percent (assuming that labor input is held constant).

c. Determine the percentage increase in output if *both* labor and capital are increased by 20 percent.

10. *Lagrangian multipliers*: The output (Q) of a production process is a function of two inputs (X and Y) and is given by the following relationship:

$$Q = .50XY - .10X^2 - .05Y^2$$

The per-unit costs of inputs X and Y are $20 and $25, respectively. The firm is interested in maximizing output subject to a cost constraint of $500.

a. Formulate the Lagrangian function (*Hint*: See footnote 8):

$$L_Q = Q - \lambda(C_x X + C_y Y - C)$$

b. Take the partial derivatives of L_Q with respect to X, Y, and λ and set them equal to zero.

c. Solve the set of simultaneous equations in part (b) for the optimal values of X, Y, and λ.

d. Based on your answers to part (c), how many units of X and Y should be used by the firm? What is the total output of this combination?

e. Give an economic interpretation of the λ value determined in part (c).

11. Determine whether each of the following production functions exhibits increasing, constant, or decreasing returns to scale:

a. $Q = 1.5X^{.70}Y^{.30}$ c. $Q = 2.0XY$

b. $Q = .4X + .5Y$ d. $Q = 1.0X^{.6}Y^{.5}$

12. Determine if the following production functions are homogeneous and, if so, the degree of homogeneity:

a. $Q = 2X^{.7} + 3Y^{.7}$ d. $Q = 3X^2Y^2 - .1X^3Y^3$

b. $Q = 2X^{.5}Y^{.5}$ e. $Q = 2X^{.8} + 3Y^{.7}$

c. $Q = \dfrac{2X^3 + 3Y^3}{6X^2 - 2Y^2}$

Production and Linear Programming[10]

The application of linear programming to production described in chapter 5 was concerned with multiple products. The problem involved determining the combination of products (output) that maximized profits, given restrictions on the resources (inputs) employed in the production process. The focus of the analysis was on *output*; recall that the horizontal and vertical axes of the graphs measured the quantities of the respective products (outputs) and that resources (inputs) were represented only as a series of constraint lines on the outputs.

In contrast, the following discussion of linear programming and production is concerned with a single product. The focus of the analysis is on *inputs* and the alternative production processes within which the inputs can be used to obtain the product. The production problem involves determining the combination of production processes that maximizes output (or profits), subject to the restrictions on the required resources (inputs).[11] When the problem is stated in this form, the production isoquant framework of production theory can be used to illustrate the alternative production processes and the concept of input substitution. First, the output-maximization problem is formulated and solved. Later, the profit-maximization problem is examined.

Algebraic Formulation of the Output-Maximization Problem

A manufacturer of lamps employs capital (machine-hours) and labor (work-hours) in its operation. Three different production processes ($P_1, P_2,$ and P_3) are available for manufacturing a certain type of lamp. Each process involves a different combination of labor and capital—process P_1 requires 1 machine-hour of capital and 4 work-hours of labor to produce each lamp; process P_2

---

[10] The student who is unfamiliar with linear programming should read Chapter 5 before proceeding with this material.

[11] The linear-programming analysis described here can be expanded to cover the case of multiple products (outputs) and multiple production processes; however, this more general problem is beyond the scope of the text.

requires 2 machine-hours and 2 work-hours to produce each lamp; and process P_3 requires 5 machine-hours and 1 work-hour to produce each lamp. Production resources are limited—5 machine-hours of capital and 8 work-hours of labor are available per day to manufacture these lamps.

Define Q_1, Q_2, and Q_3 to be the number of lamps produced per day by processes P_1, P_2, and P_3, respectively. Given that the objective is to maximize output subject to the input (capital and labor) constraints, the problem can be formulated in the linear-programming framework as follows:

Max	$Q_1 + Q_2 + Q_3$	(objective function)
Subject to	$Q_1 + 2Q_2 + 5Q_3 \le 5$	(capital constraint)
	$4Q_1 + 2Q_2 + Q_3 \le 8$	(labor constraint)
	$Q_1, Q_2, Q_3 \ge 0$	(nonnegativity constraint)

The objective function represents the total output obtained from the three production processes. The first two constraints represent the respective limitations on the amounts of capital and labor that are available to operate the three production processes. The coefficients of the Q_i variables in these constraints represent the number of units of the given resource required to manufacture one lamp by the ith production process. For example, the coefficient of Q_3 in the capital constraint indicates that 5 machine-hours of capital are required to produce one lamp using process P_3. The other coefficients have similar interpretations. The final constraint rules out negative production quantities.

Graphical Representation and Solution of the Output-Maximization Problem

The linear-programming problem just described can be illustrated and solved graphically, using *process rays* to represent the production processes, *production isoquants* to represent the objective function, and a *feasible region* to represent the resource constraints.

Process Rays

A production process can be defined as one in which the inputs are combined in *fixed proportions* to obtain the output. By this definition, a production process can be represented graphically as a ray through the origin having a slope equal to the ratio of the number of units of the respective resources required to produce one unit of output. The three production process rays for the example problem are shown in Figure 11A.1. Along ray P_1, the inputs are combined in the ratio of 4 work-hours of labor to 1 machine-hour of capital. Hence, ray P_1 has a slope of 4. Similarly, along ray P_2, the inputs are combined in the ratio of 2 work-hours of labor to 2 machine-hours of capital. Process ray P_3 shows the inputs combined in the ratio of 1 to 5.

Each production process is assumed to exhibit *constant returns to scale*. This means that output along each ray increases proportionately with increases in the inputs. For example, at Point A on process ray P_1, 1 machine-hour of capital and 4 work-hours of labor are used to produce one unit of output.

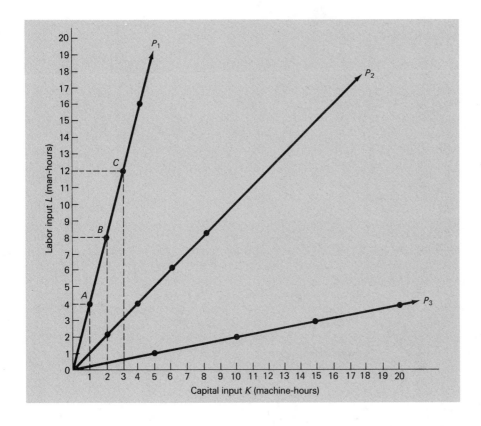

Figure 11.A1
Process Rays

Doubling the amount of capital and labor yields two units of output (Point B), and tripling the amount of capital and labor yields three units of output (Point C).

Production Isoquants

A production isoquant was defined earlier in the chapter as a curve representing all the various combinations of the two inputs that can be used in producing a given level of output. The production isoquants for the example problem can be constructed by drawing straight lines between the points of equal output on *adjacent* process rays. Four production isoquants, representing output levels Q of 1, 2, 3, and 4 lamps, respectively, are shown in Figure 11A.2.[12] Note that these linear-programming production isoquants have the same basic shape as the isoquants of production theory. The primary difference is that these isoquants consist of a series of line segments, whereas the isoquants of production theory consist of smooth curves (see Figure 11.6). Note also that the linear-programming production isoquants have parallel line segments between adjacent process rays. For example, line segment AB is parallel to DE, and line

---

[12] Production isoquants for *noninteger* output levels can also be constructed, although none is shown here.

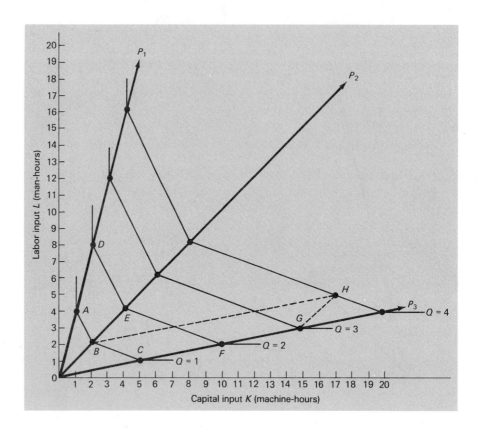

Figure 11.A2
**Production
Isoquants**

segment BC is parallel to EF. This occurs because the coefficients of the Q_1 variables in the resource constraints are constants.

As indicated earlier, points *along* each process ray represent the output obtained if the two inputs (labor and capital) are combined in the ratio of the respective number of units of each resource required to produce a given unit of output. However, the points that lie on isoquants *between* adjacent process rays have a slightly different interpretation. These points represent a combination of output from each of the adjacent production processes. For example, Point H on the "$Q = 4$" isoquant in Figure 11A.2 represents a production combination using both processes P_2 and P_3. The quantity of output that is produced by each process can be obtained by constructing a parallelogram such as the one shown in Figure 11A.2.[13] A line is drawn from Point H parallel to process ray P_2, intersecting process ray P_3 at Point G. Another line is drawn from Point H parallel to process ray P_3, intersecting process ray P_2 at Point B. From the parallelogram $OBHG$, we can determine both the quantity of output produced by each process and the respective amount of inputs used in each process. The firm should produce one unit of output using P_2, since Point B is on the "$Q = 1$"

---

[13] See William J. Baumol, *Economic Theory and Operations Analysis*, 4th ed. (Englewood Cliffs, N.J.: Prentice-Hall, 1977), footnote 5, p. 305, for a geometrical proof of this assertion.

isoquant, and three units of output using process P_3, since Point G is on the "$Q = 3$" isoquant. This combination will yield the four units of output. At Point B, 2 machine-hours of capital and 2 work-hours of labor are used in process P_2; and at Point G, 15 machine-hours of capital and 3 work-hours of labor are used in process P_3. Total capital and labor resources used in producing the four units of output are 17 machine-hours and 5 work-hours, respectively. All other points that lie between process rays can be interpreted in a similar manner.

Feasible Region

The feasible region consists of all the capital and labor input combinations that simultaneously satisfy all constraints of the linear-programming problem. The shaded rectangle $OABC$ shown in Figure 11A.3 represents the feasible region for the example problem. Since a maximum of 5 machine-hours of capital is available per day to produce lamps, only input combinations on or to the left of the BC line represent possible solutions to the linear-programming problem. Similarly, since a maximum of 8 work-hours of labor is available per day, possible solutions must lie on or below the AB line. Finally, the nonnegativity constraints preclude input combinations to the left of the OA line and below the horizontal axis.

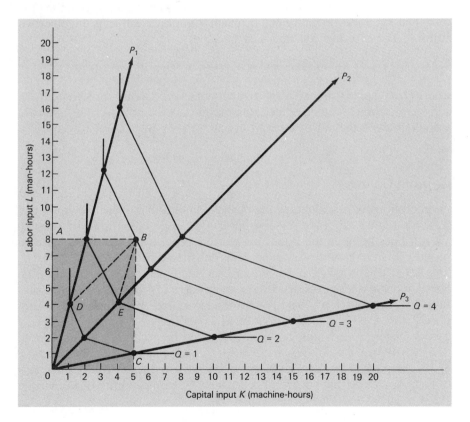

Figure 11.A3
Solution of Output-Maximization Problem

Optimal Solution

The combination of production processes that maximizes output subject to the resource constraints occurs at the point on the boundary of the feasible region that lies on the highest production isoquant. For the example problem shown in Figure 11A.3, the optimal solution occurs at Point B. At Point B, three units of output (lamps) are obtained by using 5 machine-hours of capital and 8 work-hours of labor. Constructing the parallelogram $ODBE$ shows that one unit of output should be produced using process P_1 and two units of output using process P_2. Production process P_1 should employ 1 machine-hour of capital and 4 work-hours of labor, and process P_2 should use 4 machine-hours of capital and 4 work-hours of labor.

Profit-Maximization Problem

The production problem can also be formulated as a profit-maximization problem. Assume that the firm has analyzed the costs of the three different production processes in the example problem described earlier in the appendix. It has been determined that each unit of output produced by process P_1 contributes $6 to profit and overhead; that is, revenue less variable cost is $6 per unit. Similarly, the profit contribution of output produced by processes P_2 and P_3 are $5 and $4 per unit, respectively.

Given that the firm desires to maximize profits rather than output, the only change in the linear-programming problem formulated earlier is the objective function. The objective function now becomes

$$\text{Max } \pi = 6Q_1 + 5Q_2 + 4Q_3$$

where Q_1, Q_2, and Q_3 are the respective quantities produced by processes P_1, P_2, and P_3. An optimal solution of the profit-maximization problem can be obtained graphically with the aid of *isoprofit* curves.

Isoprofit Curves

An isoprofit curve represents all the various combinations of the two inputs that yield the same total profit. An isoprofit curve can be constructed by drawing straight lines between the points on adjacent process rays having equal total profits. To show how this is done, consider the "$Q = 1$" isoquant from Figure 11A.3. This isoquant is reproduced in Figure 11A.4 and is labeled ECA. Suppose one wishes to construct an isoprofit curve (π) corresponding to a profit of $4. Point A is clearly on this isoprofit curve, since one unit of output produced by process P_3 yields a profit of $4. Point C also represents one unit of output; however, each unit of output produced by process P_2 yields a profit of $5. Therefore, the point on process ray P_2 having profit of $4 must be $4 ÷ $5 = 80 percent of the distance from the origin (0) to Point C. This corresponds to Point B. Similarly, the point on process ray P_1 having a profit of $4 must be

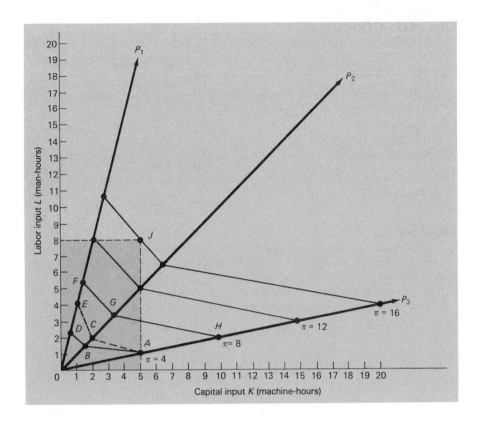

Figure 11.A4
Solution of Profit-Maximization Problem

$4 ÷ $6 = 67 percent of the distance from the origin (0) to Point E. This occurs at Point D. By connecting the points on adjacent process rays with straight-line segments, one obtains the "$\pi = 4$" isoprofit curve. The profit curves corresponding to profits of $8, $12, and $16 are also shown in Figure 11A.4. Like the production isoquants described earlier, the isoprofit curves have parallel line segments between adjacent process rays. For example, line segment DB is parallel to FG, and line segment BA is parallel to GH. This occurs because the coefficients of the Q_i variables in the objective function are constants.

Optimal Solution

The combination of production processes that maximizes total profits subject to the resource constraints occurs at the point on the boundary of the feasible region that lies on the highest isoprofit curve. For the example problem shown in Figure 11A.4, the optimal solution is at point J, which lies on the "$\pi = 16$" isoprofit curve. Recalling that this solution corresponds to Point B in Figure 11A.3, the firm should produce one lamp using process P_1 and two lamps using process P_2 to maximize profits. Substituting these values for Q_1 and Q_2, respectively ($Q_3 = 0$), into the objective function shows that a profit of $(6 \times 1) + (5 \times 2) + (4 \times 0) = \$16$ is obtained.

Discussion Questions

1. Explain how the production linear-programming maximization problem solved in this appendix differs from the production linear-programming maximization problem solved in Chapter 5.

2. Explain how the following concepts are used in solving a production linear-programming maximization problem:
   a. Process rays
   b. Production isoquants
   c. Feasible region

3. Explain how the linear-programming production isoquants differ from the production isoquants developed in Chapter 11.

Problem

1. In the output-maximization problem described in the Appendix, assume that production resources are limited to 14 machine-hours of capital and 6 work-hours of labor.
   a. Formulate the problem algebraically in the linear programming framework.
   b. Determine graphically the optimal amount of resources (capital and labor) to employ in each of the production processes and the total output obtained.

Theory of Cost 12

Economic cost refers to the sacrifice that is made whenever an exchange or transformation of resources takes place. Economic costs are measured as opportunity costs. The opportunity cost of a resource is the cost of attracting that resource from its next best alternative use. Managers seeking to make the most efficient use of the enterprise's resources in order to maximize the value of the enterprise must be concerned both with short- and long-run cost/output relationships. Short-run cost/output relationships help the managers to plan for the most profitable level of output, given the capital resources that are immediately available. Long-run cost/output relationships are important inputs into the decision to expand or contract the size of the enterprise. By making the most efficient use of resources in the short-run and by making prudent long-run investment decisions, managers can contribute to the objective of maximizing the value of the enterprise.

The Meaning and Measurement of Cost

In its most elementary form, *cost* refers to the sacrifice incurred whenever an exchange or transformation of resources takes place. Many of the difficulties and controversies associated with the concept of cost arise when one attempts to measure this sacrifice. The appropriate manner to measure costs is a function of the purpose for which the information is to be used.

Accounting versus Economic Costs

Accountants have been primarily concerned with measuring costs for *financial reporting* purposes. As a result, they define and measure cost by the *historical outlay of funds* that takes place in the exchange or transformation of a resource. Thus, whenever A sells a product or commodity to B, the *price* paid by B, expressed in dollars, measures the cost of the product to B. When A exchanges labor services for money or other items of value, the *wages* that A receives represent the cost of A's services to the employer. Similarly, the *interest* paid to the bondholder or lending institution is used to measure the cost of funds to the borrower.[1]

Glossary of New Terms

Cost
The sacrifice incurred whenever an exchange or transformation of resources takes place.

Sunk cost
A cost incurred regardless of the alternative action chosen in a decision-making problem.

Cost function
A mathematical model, schedule, or graph that shows the cost (such as total, average, or marginal cost) of producing various quantities of output.

Opportunity cost
The value of a resource in its next best alternative use. Opportunity cost represents the return or compensation that must be foregone as the result of the decision to employ the resource in a given economic activity.

Marginal cost
The incremental increase in total cost that results from a one-unit increase in output.

(*Cont'd on next page*)

---

[1] See Chapter 17 for a discussion of the costs of debt and equity capital.

Glossary of New Terms (*Cont'd*)

Economies of scale Declining long-run average costs as the level of output for the firm (or production plant) is increased.

Diseconomies of scale Rising long-run average costs as the level of output is increased.

Operating leverage The use of assets having fixed costs (e.g., depreciation) in an effort to increase expected returns.

Economists have been mainly concerned with measuring costs for *decision-making* purposes. The objective is to determine the present and future costs of resources associated with various alternative courses of action. Such an objective requires a consideration of the opportunities foregone (or sacrificed) whenever a resource is used in a given course of action. Cost is a function of the value of a resource in its best alternative use. Consequently, the outlay of funds incurred in obtaining a resource may not always be the appropriate measure of cost in a decision problem.

The *opportunity cost* of using a given quantity of resources (inputs) to produce a unit of Good A is the number of units of the *next best* alternative that must be sacrificed or foregone as a result of the decision to produce A. If the resources (labor, materials, equipment) needed to build ten houses (of a specified size and quality) can also be used to build one office building (likewise of a specified size and quality), then the opportunity cost of the decision to build the office building is equal to the ten houses that have to be foregone. With a fixed quantity of resources available to the organization, resources used in the production of one good cannot be used in the production of other goods.

In calculating the cost to the firm of producing a given quantity of output, economists include some additional costs that are typically not reflected in the cost figures appearing in the financial reports of the firm. Both the accounting cost and the economic cost of a product will include such *explicit* costs as labor, raw materials, supplies, rent, interest, and utilities. Economists also include several *implicit* costs. The implicit costs consist of the opportunity costs of time and capital that the owner-manager has invested in producing the given quantity of output. The opportunity cost of the owner's time is measured by the most attractive salary or other form of compensation that the owner could have received by operating or managing a similar kind of firm for another investor. The opportunity cost of the capital employed in producing the given quantity of output is measured by the profit or return that could have been received if the owner had chosen to employ capital in the best alternative investment of comparable risk.

Relevant Cost Concept

The cost that should be used in a given decision-making problem is known as the *relevant cost*. The concept of relevant cost will be illustrated with four examples.

Depreciation Cost Measurement. The production of a good or service, in addition to labor, raw materials, and other resources, typically requires the use of capital assets; that is, plant and equipment. As these assets are used in producing output, their service life is expended; the assets wear out or become obsolete. Depreciation is the cost of using these assets in producing the given output. If a machine has a current market value of $8,000 and is expected to have a value of $6,800 after one more year of use, the opportunity cost of using the machine for one year (the depreciation cost) is $8,000 − $6,800 = $1,200.

Assuming that 2,000 units of output were produced during the year, the depreciation cost would be $1,200 \div 2,000$ units $= \$.60/$per unit. Ideally, this is the depreciation cost that the economist would include in calculating the cost to the firm of the output produced. Unfortunately, it is very difficult, if not impossible in most cases, to determine the *actual value* of the service life of an asset that is consumed in producing a given quantity of output.[2] To overcome these measurement problems, accountants have adopted certain procedures for allocating a portion of the acquisition cost of an asset to each accounting time period and in turn to each unit of output that is produced within the time period. This is typically done by estimating the service life of the asset and then charging a portion of the cost of the asset against income during each year of the service life. If a machine is purchased for $10,000 and is expected to have a ten-year life and no salvage value, using the straight-line method of depreciation,[3] $10,000 \div 10 = \$1,000$ would be the depreciation cost of this asset each year. Assuming that 2,000 units of output are produced in a given year, then $\$1,000 \div 2,000 = \$.50$ would be allocated to the cost of each unit produced. Note from this example that the method described for allocating depreciation costs is arbitrary and the calculated depreciation cost may not represent the actual depreciation cost incurred.

Inventory Valuation. Whenever materials are stored in inventory for a period of time before being used in the production process, the accounting and economic costs may differ if the market price of these materials has changed from the original purchase price. The accounting cost is equal to the actual acquisition cost, whereas the economic cost is equal to the current *replacement* cost. As the following example illustrates, the use of the acquisition cost can lead to incorrect production decisions. Assume that a firm is offered a contract for $10,000 to provide the plumbing for a new building. The labor and equipment costs are calculated to be $6,000 for fulfilling the contract. Also suppose that the firm has the materials in inventory to complete the job. The materials originally cost the firm $5,000; however, prices have since declined and the materials could now be purchased for $3,750. Material prices are not expected to increase in the near future and hence no gains can be anticipated from holding the materials in inventory. The question is: Should the firm accept the contract? An analysis of the contract under both methods for measuring the cost of the materials is shown in Table 12.1. Assuming that the materials are valued at the acquisition cost, the firm would not accept the contract, since an apparent loss of $1,000 results. By using the replacement cost as the value of the materials,

---

[2] This cost of the portion of the asset consumed should be measured in terms of the *current replacement* cost of the asset rather than the *historical acquisition* cost of the asset. For a discussion of the replacement cost versus historical cost issue, see Sidney Davidson et al., *An Income Approach to Accounting Theory: Readings and Questions* (Englewood Cliffs, N. J.: Prentice-Hall, 1964), sec. IV.

[3] The *straight-line* depreciation method allocates an equal amount of the cost of the asset to each period during the life of the asset. Other *accelerated* depreciation methods are also used. See R. Charles Moyer, James R. McGuigan, and William J. Kretlow. *Contemporary Financial Management*, 3d rev. ed. (St. Paul, Minn.: West, 1988), chap. 9 and appendix 9A.

Table 12.1
Effect of Inventory Valuation Methods on Measured Profit

		Acquisition cost		*Replacement cost*
Value of contract			$10,000		$10,000
Costs					
Labor, equipment, and so on	$6,000			$6,000	
Materials	5,000			3,750	
			11,000		9,750
Profit (or loss)			$(1,000)		$ 250

however, the contract would be accepted, since a profit of $250 results. To see which method is correct, examine the income statement of the firm at the end of the accounting period. If the contract *is not* accepted, then at the end of the accounting period the firm would have to reduce the cost of its inventory by $1250 ($5,000–$3,750) to reflect the lower market value of this unused inventory. The firm would thus incur a loss of $1,250. If the contract *is* accepted, then the firm would make a profit of $250 on the contract, but would also incur a loss of $1,250 on the materials used in completing the contract. The firm would thus incur a *net* loss of only $1,000. Hence, acceptance of the contract results in a smaller overall loss to the firm than does rejection of the contract. In this example, replacement cost is the appropriate measure of the cost of materials for decision-making purposes.

Unutilized Facilities. A manufacturing firm recently discontinued a product line and is left with 50,000 square feet of unused and unneeded (for the foreseeable future) warehouse space. The firm rents the entire warehouse (200,000 square feet) from the owner for $1,000,000 per year (i.e., $5 per square foot) under a long-term (10-year) lease agreement. A nearby company that is expanding its operations offered to rent the 50,000 square feet of unneeded space for one year for $125,000 (i.e., $2.50 per square foot). Should the manufacturing company accept the offer to rent the unused space? (Assume that no other higher offers for the warehouse space are expected to be received in the foreseeable future and that no additional costs will be incurred if the space is rented.)

One could argue that the manufacturing company should reject the offer since the additional rent (revenue) of $2.50 per square foot is less than the lease payment (cost) of $5 per square foot. Such reasoning, however, will lead to an incorrect decision. The lease payment ($5 per square foot) represents a *sunk cost* that must be paid regardless of whether or not the manufacturing company rents the unneeded warehouse space. As shown in Table 12.2, renting the unneeded warehouse space *reduces* the net cost of the warehouse from $1,000,000 to $875,000, a savings of $125,000 per year to the manufacturing firm. The relevant comparison is between the incremental revenue ($125,000) and the incremental costs ($0 in this case). Thus, sunk costs (such as the lease payment of $5 per square foot in this example), which are independent of the alternative action chosen, should not be considered in making the optimal decision.

	Decision	
	Do Not Rent	Rent
Total Lease Payment	$1,000,000	$1,000,000
Less: Rent Received on Unused Space	—	125,000
Net Cost of Warehouse to Manufacturing Company	$1,000,000	$ 875,000

Table 12.2
Warehouse Rental Decision

Measuring Profitability.   Suppose that an entrepreneur owns and operates a specialty clothing store. A traditional income statement for the business is shown in Panel (a) of Table 12.3. The mortgage on the store has been paid and therefore no interest expenses are shown on the income statement. Also, the building has been fully depreciated and thus no depreciation charges are shown. From an *accounting* standpoint and from the perspective of the Internal Revenue Service, the entrepreneur is earning a *positive accounting profit* of $40,000 (before taxes).

(a) Accounting Income Statement		
Net sales		$500,000
Less: Cost of goods sold		250,000
Gross profit		250,000
Less: Expenses		
Employee compensation*	150,000	
Advertising	30,000	
Utilities and maintenance	20,000	
Miscellaneous	10,000	
Total		210,000
Net profit before taxes		$ 40,000
(b) Economic Profit Statement		
Total revenues		$500,000
Less: Explicit costs		
Cost of goods sold	250,000	
Employee compensation*	150,000	
Advertising	30,000	
Utilities and maintenance	20,000	
Miscellaneous	10,000	
Total		460,000
Accounting profit before taxes		40,000
Less: Implicit costs		
Salary (manager)	30,000	
Rent on building	18,000	
Total		48,000
Economic profit before taxes		$−8,000

Table 12.3
Profitability of Clothing Store

*Employee compensation does not include any salary to the entrepreneur.

However, consider the store's profitability from an *economic* standpoint. Recall from chapter 1 that economic profit was defined as the difference between total revenues and total economic costs. Algebraically, economic profit is given by:

$$\frac{Economic}{Profit} = \frac{Total}{Revenue} - \frac{Explicit}{Costs} - \frac{Implicit}{Costs} \qquad [12.1]$$

As indicated earlier in the chapter, implicit costs include the opportunity costs of time and capital that the entrepreneur has invested in the firm. Suppose the entrepreneur could go to work as a clothing department manager for a large department or specialty store chain and receive a salary of $30,000 per year. Also assume that the entrepreneur could rent his building to another merchant for $18,000 (net) per year. Under these conditions, as shown in Panel (b) of Table 12.3, the entrepreneur is earning a *negative economic profit* ($–8,000 before taxes). By renting his store to another merchant and going to work as manager of a different store, he could make $8,000 more than he is currently earning from his clothing store business.[4] Thus, accounting profits, which do not include opportunity costs, are not always a valid indication of the economic success of an enterprise.

Several conclusions can be drawn from this discussion of the concept of cost:

1. Costs can be measured in different ways, depending on the purpose for which the cost figures are to be used.

2. The costs of an economic activity (production), which are obtained for financial reporting purposes, are not always appropriate for decision-making purposes. Typically, changes and modifications have to be made to reflect the opportunity costs of the various alternative actions that can be chosen in a given decision problem. The *relevant cost* in economic decision making is the opportunity cost of the resources rather than the outlay of funds required to obtain the resources.

3. Sunk costs, which are incurred regardless of the alternative action chosen, should not be considered in making the optimal decision.

4. It is sometimes very difficult to measure the opportunity cost of a given action in a decision problem. Cost estimates can be highly subjective and arbitrary.

Short-Run Cost Functions

In addition to measuring the costs of producing a given quantity of output, economists are also concerned with determining the behavior of costs as output is varied over a range of possible values. The relationship between cost and output serves as an important building block in theories of resource allocation

---

[4] In deciding whether to continue operating the clothing store, the entrepreneur may feel that noneconomic factors, such as the "desire to be one's own boss," outweigh the profitability issue.

and pricing within the firm. The behavior of costs is expressed in terms of a *cost function*—a schedule, graph, or mathematical relationship showing the minimum achievable total cost of producing various quantities of output. The shape of the firm's long-run cost function has important implications for decisions to expand the scale of operations, and the shape of its short-run cost function has a crucial impact on decisions about the quantities of inputs that are employed in the production process at any point in time.

The discussion in Chapter 11, concerning the inputs used in the production process, distinguished between fixed and variable inputs. A fixed input was defined as an input that is required in the production process but whose quantity used in the process is constant over a given period of time regardless of the level of output produced. A variable input was defined as an input whose amount is varied in response to the desired quantity of output to be produced. Short-run questions relate to a situation in which one or more of the inputs to the production process is fixed or incapable of being varied. Long-run questions relate to a situation in which *all* inputs are variable; that is, no restrictions are imposed on the amount of a resource that can be employed in the production process.

The actual period of time corresponding to the long run for a given production process will depend on the nature of the inputs employed in the production process. Generally, the more capital equipment used relative to labor and other inputs (that is, the more capital intensive the process), the longer will be the period of time required to increase significantly all the factors of production and the scale of operations. A period of five or more years may be required for a new or expanded electric utility generating facility, steel mill, or oil refinery to be constructed and put into operation. Before completion of the expansion (the short run), increases in production output can only be achieved by operating existing production facilities at higher rates of use through the utilization of greater amounts of labor and other inputs. In comparison, a service-oriented production process (such as an employment agency, consulting firm, or government agency), which uses a relatively small amount of capital equipment, may have a long-run planning horizon of only a few months. A significant expansion of the scale of operations can be achieved in a relatively short period of time by leasing additional office space and equipment and by hiring and training additional staff personnel.

Associated with the short-run and long-run planning periods are short-run and long-run cost functions. This section discusses the development and interpretation of short-run costs and cost functions. The next section contains a similar discussion of cost functions associated with long-run decisions.

Total Cost Function

The total cost of producing a given quantity of output is equal to the sum of the costs of each of the inputs used in the production process. In discussing short-run cost functions, it is useful to classify costs as either *fixed* or *variable costs*. *Fixed costs* represent the costs of all the inputs to the production process that are fixed or constant over the short run. These costs will be incurred regardless of whether a small or large quantity of output is produced during the period. *Variable costs* consist of the costs of all the variable inputs to the production process. Whereas variable costs may not change in direct proportion to the quantity of output produced, they will increase (or decrease) in some manner as output is increased (or decreased).[5]

To illustrate the nature of short-run costs and show how the short-run cost function can be derived from the production function for the firm, consider again the ore-mining example that was discussed in Chapter 11. It was assumed that two inputs, capital and labor, are required to produce or mine ore. Various-sized pieces of capital equipment, as measured by their horsepower rating Y, are available to mine the ore. Each of these pieces of equipment can be operated with various-sized labor crews X. The amount of output (tons of ore) that can be produced in a given work shift with each capital-labor input combination is shown again in Table 12.4. It was also assumed that the rental cost of using the mining equipment during a given shift is $.20 per horsepower and that the cost of each worker (labor) employed during a shift is $50. This yielded the following total cost equation for any given combination of labor X and capital Y (Equation 11.21):

$$C = 50X + .20Y$$

Suppose that the firm has signed a lease agreeing to rent, for the next year, a 750-horsepower piece of mining equipment (capital). During the ensuing year (the short run), the amount of capital that the firm can employ in the ore-mining process is fixed at 750 horsepower. Therefore, during each shift a fixed cost of $.20 \times 750 = $150 will be incurred, regardless of the quantity of ore that is produced. The firm must operate the production process at one capital-labor

Table 12.4
Production Function-Ore Mining Example

					Capital Input, Y (horsepower)				
		250	500	750	1000	1250	1500	1750	2000
	1	1	3	6	10	16	16	16	13
	2	2	6	16	24	29	29	44	44
	3	4	16	29	44	55	55	55	50
Labor Input, X	4	6	29	44	55	58	60	60	55
(number of	5	16	43	55	60	61	62	62	60
workers)	6	29	55	60	62	63	63	63	62
	7	44	58	62	63	64	64	64	64
	8	50	60	62	63	64	65	65	65
	9	55	59	61	63	64	65	66	66
	10	52	56	59	62	64	65	66	67

[5] A third category, *semivariable costs* can also be considered. Semivariable costs are costs that increase (decrease) in a stepwise manner as output is increased (decreased). Semivariable costs are constant when output varies within a given range. They increase or decrease only when output moves outside this range. In general, cost theory can be developed without employing semivariable costs in the analysis. Such costs can be included with fixed costs.

Table 12.5 **Short-Run Cost Functions: Mining Example**

Output	Variable Cost		Fixed Cost		Total Cost	Average Fixed Cost	Average Variable Cost	Average Total Cost	Marginal Cost
Q	Labor Input X	$VC = \$50 \cdot X$	Capital Input Y	$FC = \$150$	$TC = FC + VC$	$AFC = \dfrac{FC}{Q}$	$AVC = \dfrac{VC}{Q}$	$ATC = \dfrac{TC}{Q}$	$MC = \dfrac{\Delta TC}{\Delta Q}$
0	0	$ 0	750	$150	$150	—	—	—	
6	1	50	750	150	200	$25.00	$8.33	$33.33	$\dfrac{50}{6} = \$8.33$
16	2	100	750	150	250	9.38	6.25	15.63	$\dfrac{50}{10} = 5.00$
29	3	150	750	150	300	5.17	5.17	10.34	$\dfrac{50}{13} = 3.85$
44	4	200	750	150	350	3.41	4.55	7.95	$\dfrac{50}{15} = 3.33$
55	5	250	750	150	400	2.73	4.55	7.27	$\dfrac{50}{11} = 4.55$
60	6	300	750	150	450	2.50	5.00	7.50	$\dfrac{50}{5} = 10.00$
62	7	350	750	150	500	2.42	5.65	8.06	$\dfrac{50}{2} = 25.00$

combination in the "$Y = 750$" column of Table 12.4. Output can be increased (decreased) by employing more (less) labor in combination with the given 750-horsepower capital equipment. Labor is thus a variable input to the production process.

The short-run cost functions for the example are shown in Table 12.5.[6] The various possible output levels Q and the associated capital-labor input combinations X and Y are obtained from Table 12.4. The short-run variable cost VC is equal to $50 times the number of workers (X) employed in the mining process. The short-run fixed cost FC is equal to the rental cost of the 750-horsepower equipment ($150). The total cost in the short run is the sum of the fixed and variable costs:

$$TC = FC + VC \qquad [12.2]$$

In Figure 12.1 the three curves from the data given in Table 12.5 are plotted. Note that the TC curve has an identical shape to that of VC, being shifted upward by the FC of $150.

---

[6] The rational producer would not employ more than seven workers in the short-run, since the use of additional workers will not result in any increase in the quantity of ore that is produced.

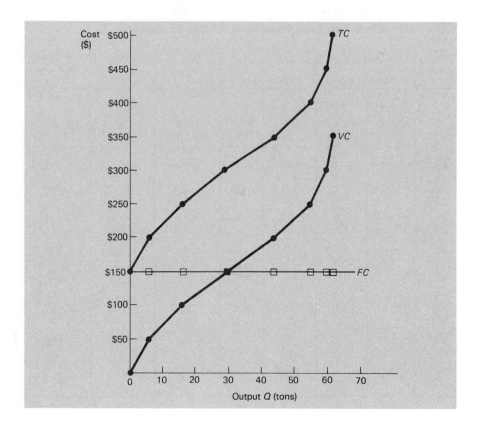

Figure 12.1
**Short-Run
Variable, Fixed,
and Total Cost
Functions: Ore-
Mining Example**

Average and Marginal Cost Functions

Once the total cost function is determined, one can then derive the average and
marginal cost functions. The average fixed cost *AFC*, average variable cost *AVC*,
and average total cost *ATC* are equal to the respective fixed, variable, and total
costs divided by the quantity of output produced:

$$AFC = \frac{FC}{Q}$$ [12.3]

$$AVC = \frac{VC}{Q}$$ [12.4]

$$ATC = \frac{TC}{Q}$$ [12.5]

Also,

$$ATC = AFC + AVC \qquad [12.6]$$

Marginal cost is defined as the incremental increase in total cost that results from a one-unit increase in output, and is calculated as[7]

$$MC = \frac{\Delta TC}{\Delta Q}$$
$$= \frac{\Delta VC}{\Delta Q} \qquad [12.7]$$

or in the case of a continuous *TC* function:

$$MC = \frac{d(TC)}{dQ} \qquad [12.8]$$
$$= \frac{d(VC)}{dQ} \qquad [12.9]$$

The average and marginal costs that were calculated in Table 12.5 are plotted in the graph in Figure 12.2. Except for the *AFC* curve, which is continually declining, note that all other average and marginal cost curves are U-shaped.

The ore-mining example illustrated the derivation of the various cost functions when the cost data are given in the form of a schedule (that is, tabular data). Consider another example where the cost information is represented in the form of an algebraic function. Suppose fixed costs for a production process are equal to $100 and variable costs are given by the following relationship (where Q = output):

$$VC = 60Q - 3Q^2 + .10Q^3 \qquad [12.10]$$

Given this information, one can derive the total cost function using Equation 12.2:

$$TC = 100 + 60Q - 3Q^2 + .10Q^3$$

Next, *AFC*, *AVC*, and *ATC* can be found using Equations 12.3, 12.4, and 12.5,

---

[7] The ratio $\Delta TC/\Delta Q$ represents the *incremental* cost rather than the true *marginal* cost; however, we will use the term *marginal cost* even though the ratio is presented here on an incremental basis.

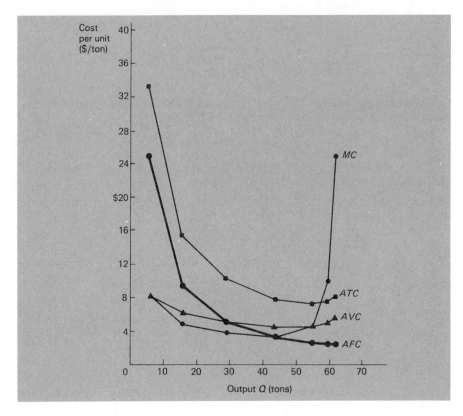

Figure 12.2
Short-Run Average and Marginal Cost Functions: Ore-Mining Example

respectively, as follows:

$$AFC = \frac{100}{Q}$$

$$AVC = 60 - 3Q + .10Q^2$$

$$ATC = \frac{100}{Q} + 60 - 3Q + .10Q^2$$

Finally, the marginal cost function can be obtained by differentiating the variable cost function (Equation 12.10) with respect to Q:

$$MC = \frac{d(VC)}{dQ} = 60 - 6Q + .30Q^2$$

Relationships among the Various Cost and Production Curves

To investigate further the properties of and relationships among the various cost and production curves, assume now that the cost and production curves can be represented by smooth continuous functions as shown in Figure 12.3. Also assume that input X is the variable factor, with an associated variable cost VC;

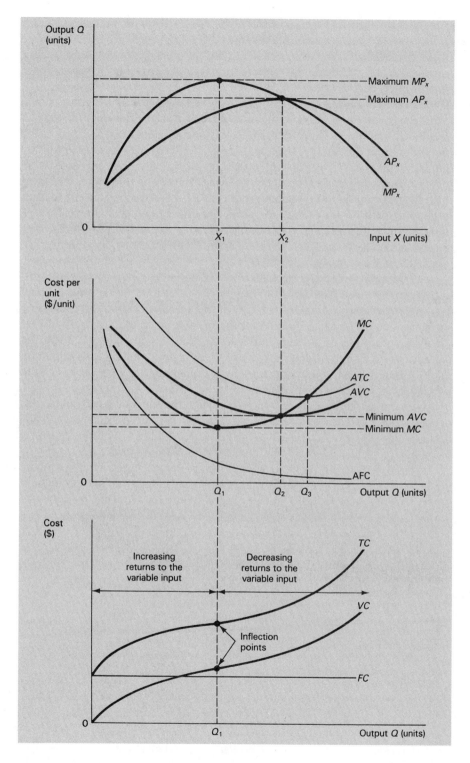

Figure 12.3
Short-Run Cost and Production Functions

that the per-unit price of each of the factors of production (i.e., C_X and C_Y) is *constant* over all usage levels,[8] and that input Y is the fixed factor, with an associated fixed cost FC. First, note that variable costs (and total costs) initially increase at a decreasing rate as output Q is increased up to Q_1. Correspondingly, the marginal cost function MC is declining. Over this range of output, the marginal product of the variable input X is increasing. Since it has been assumed that the unit cost of X is constant, an increasing marginal product for input X necessarily implies that the marginal cost function must be declining.[9] The minimum point on the MC curve at Q_1 corresponds to the maximum point on the MP_X curve at X_1. Beyond Q_1, variable (and total) costs increase at an increasing rate and, correspondingly, the marginal cost curve is increasing. Over this range of output, the marginal product of X is decreasing and, for reasons analogous to those just noted, marginal cost must necessarily be rising.

Examining the average variable cost curve, AVC, note that it is declining over output levels to Q_2 and is increasing thereafter. The shape of the average variable cost function, like the shape of the marginal cost function, is closely related to the production function defined in Chapter 11. *Given that the unit cost of the variable input is constant*, an increasing (or decreasing) average product for input X necessarily implies that the average variable cost will be decreasing (or increasing).[10] The minimum point on the AVC curve at Q_2 corresponds to the maximum point on the AP_X curve at X_2. Note also in Figure 12.3 that the marginal cost curve intersects the average variable cost function at its minimum value. This necessarily follows because the marginal product curve intersects the average product curve at its maximum value.

The average total cost curve, which is equal to the sum of the vertical heights of the average fixed cost and average variable cost curves, likewise initially declines and subsequently begins rising beyond some level of output. At a level of output of Q_3 the average total cost curve is a minimum.

As discussed in the previous chapter, more intensive use of the variable inputs (specialization) in combination with fixed inputs to the production process is believed to yield initially more than proportionate increases in output. Subsequently, due to the law of diminishing returns, more intensive use

---

[8] This is the same assumption that was employed in the section, "Determining the Optimal Combination of Inputs," in Chapter 11.

[9] The relationship can be shown algebraically in the following way: MC is defined as $\Delta TC/\Delta Q$, which is also equal to $\Delta VC/\Delta Q$. ΔVC is equal to $C_X \Delta X$, where C_X is the unit cost of the variable input X. Thus, $MC = C_X(\Delta X/\Delta Q)$. However, the marginal product of input X, MP, was defined in Equation 11.3 as $\Delta Q/\Delta X$, or, in reciprocal form, $1/MP = \Delta X/\Delta Q$. Substituting $1/MP$ in the relationship for MC, we obtain $MC = C_X(1/MP)$. Since the marginal productivity of X is increasing, the marginal cost must be decreasing, in order for the equation to be valid.

[10] This relationship can be shown using the previously defined expressions for the average product AP and average variable cost AVC. AVC is equal to VC/Q. VC is equal to $C_X \cdot X$ where C_X is the unit cost of the variable input. Thus $AVC = (C_X \cdot X)/Q$. In the previous chapter the average product was defined as Q/X (Equation 11.7) or, in reciprocal form $1/AP = X/Q$. Substituting this in the expression for AVC, we obtain $AVC = C_X(1/AP)$. Thus if the average product is increasing, the average variable cost must be decreasing and vice versa.

yields less than proportionate increases. This reasoning is used to explain the U-shaped pattern of the *ATC*, *AVC*, and *MC* curves. Initially, specialization in the use of the variable resources results in increasing returns and declining average and marginal costs. With one or more fixed inputs in the production process, increased specialization will begin to yield successively smaller returns, and then marginal and average costs will begin increasing. The actual shape of the cost functions for a specific production process is a question that can best be answered by attempting to measure empirically the functions for a given set of cost-output observations. Chapter 13 continues the discussion of this topic.

Long-Run Cost Functions

Over the long-run planning horizon, the firm can choose the combination of inputs that minimizes the cost of producing a desired level of output. Using the existing production methods and technology, the firm can choose the plant size, types and sizes of equipment, labor skills, and raw materials that, when combined, yield the lowest cost of producing the desired amount of output. Once the optimum combination of inputs is chosen to produce the desired level of output, some of these inputs (plant and equipment) become fixed in the short run. Correspondingly, a short-run average cost function exists for this set of inputs. In theory, there exists an optimum combination of inputs and a minimum total cost for each level of output. Associated with the fixed inputs in each of these optimum combinations is a short-run average cost function. Several of these short-run average cost functions (SAC_1, SAC_2, SAC_3, SAC_4) are shown in Figure 12.4.

The long-run average cost function shown consists of the *lower boundary* or *envelope* of all the (infinitely many) short-run curves. No other combination of inputs exists for producing each level of output Q at an average cost below the cost that is indicated by the *LAC* curve. From the graph one can see that the long-run average cost of producing any given level of output, in general, does *not* occur at the point where short-run average costs are minimized. Only at

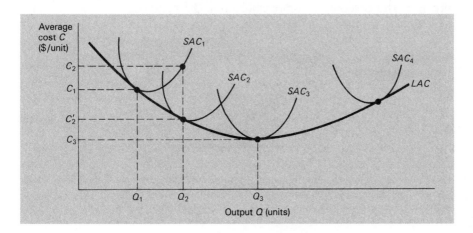

Figure 12.4
Long-Run and Short-Run Average Cost Functions

the output level Q_3, corresponding to the minimum cost point on the LAC curve, does the long-run average cost equal the minimum short-run average cost.

The relationship between the short-run and long-run average cost functions can be further illustrated by examining the effect on costs of an expansion in output from Q_1 to Q_2 in Figure 12.4. Assume that the firm has been producing Q_1 units of output using a plant of size "1," having a short-run average cost curve of SAC_1. The average cost of producing Q_1 units is therefore C_1. Suppose that the firm wishes to expand output to Q_2. What will the average cost of producing this higher volume of output be? In the short run, with some inputs (the plant) being fixed at size "1," the average cost would be C_2. However, in the long run, it would be possible for the firm to build a plant of size "2," having a short-run average cost curve of SAC_2. With this larger plant, the average cost of producing Q_2 units of output would be only C'_2. Thus it can be seen that the firm has more options available to it in the long run. The inputs and costs of production that are fixed in the short run can be altered in the long run to obtain a more efficient allocation of resources.

The long-run cost function can also be obtained directly from the production function by first finding the *expansion path* for the given production process. The *expansion path* for a production process consists of the combinations of inputs X and Y for each level of output Q that satisfy the optimality criterion developed in the section "Determining the Optimal Combination of Inputs" in Chapter 11.

Recall, in that section, we derived the condition that the marginal rate of technical substitution between the two inputs ($MRTS = MP_x/MP_y$) must be equal to the ratio of the unit costs of the two inputs (C_x/C_y) for a given input combination to be an optimal solution to either the output-maximization or cost-minimization problems. Graphically, the optimal input combination occurred at the point where the production isoquant was tangent to the isocost line.[11] As shown in Figure 12.5, the expansion path can be represented by a line that connects these various tangency points between the isoquants and isocost lines. After the expansion path is determined, the long-run total cost function can be obtained from the corresponding cost and output values of each tangency point along the expansion path. Thus, for example, from Point "1" in Figure 12.5 one obtains the cost-output combination (C_1, $Q^{(1)}$), which is then plotted in Figure 12.6. The cost-output combinations (C_2, $Q^{(2)}$) and (C_3, $Q^{(3)}$) are obtained in a similar manner. Connecting these points yields the long-run total cost (LTC) curve shown in Figure 12.6. The long-run average (LAC) and marginal cost (LMC) curves are defined and calculated in a manner similar to their short-run counterparts:

$$LAC = \frac{LTC}{Q}$$

[12.11]

---

[11] As in the development of the short-run cost functions in the previous section, it is assumed that the per-unit price of each factor is constant regardless of the quantity used in the production process. We comment further on this assumption in the next section.

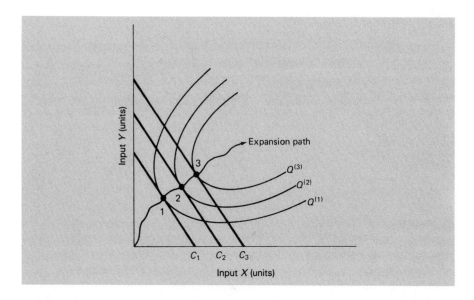

Figure 12.5
Expansion Path

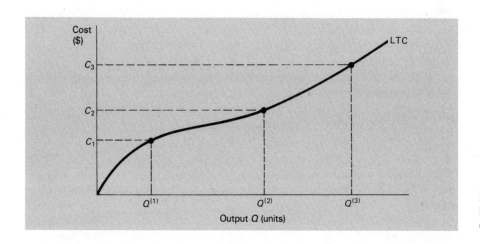

Figure 12.6
**Long-Run Total
Cost Function**

$$LMC = \frac{\Delta LTC}{\Delta Q}$$

[12.12]

Economies and Diseconomies of Scale

The long-run average cost function of economic theory is hypothesized to be U-shaped. This is shown in Figure 12.4—long-run average costs are declining for output levels up to Q_3 and are increasing for output levels beyond Q_3.

Economies of Scale

Declining long-run average costs over the lower part of the range of possible outputs are usually attributed to *economies of scale*. Economies of scale occur over the range of the long-run cost function which corresponds to increasing returns to scale of the production function, assuming constant factor input costs. In the following discussion, it is useful to distinguish between economies of scale associated with an individual production *plant* and economies of scale associated with the entire *firm*.[12]

Plant Economies. Within a production plant are a number of different possible sources of scale economies. First, as discussed in the previous chapter, increasing physical returns to scale can be realized from *greater specialization in the use of capital and labor*. As the scale of production is increased, special-purpose equipment, which is more efficient in performing a limited set of operations, can be substituted for less efficient general-purpose equipment. Also, as the scale of production is increased, the production process can be broken down into a series of small tasks, and workers can be assigned to the tasks for which they are most qualified. Workers are then able to acquire additional proficiency through repetition of the tasks to which they are assigned. Generally, the productivity of workers who specialize in performing a given task repetitively is greater than that of more versatile workers who perform a variety of different tasks.

Scale economies can also be realized from the *indivisible nature of many types of capital equipment*. For example, consider a relatively small plant that requires the use of a forklift truck in its operation for only four hours of the eight-hour daily production period. Although the plant only needs the forklift half the time, it cannot purchase one-half of a forklift to meet its needs. It must either purchase one entire unit or forgo the use of this piece of equipment. A large plant that can use the forklift truck for the full eight hours is able to spread the initial cost over a larger volume of output and hence achieve lower average costs.

A third source of scale economies arises from the relative productivity and purchase prices of different sizes of capital equipment. Generally, *the productive capacity of capital equipment rises much faster than its purchase price*. In other words, a machine that costs twice as much as a smaller one will typically produce more than twice as much output.

Finally, scale economies can be realized in equipment maintenance. *Reserves of replacement parts and maintenance personnel* needed to deal with randomly occurring equipment breakdowns normally *increase less than proportionately with increases in the size of the plant*.

---

[12] For a more detailed discussion of scale economies, including a summary of the empirical evidence, see F. M. Scherer, "Economies of Scale and Industrial Concentration," in *Industrial Concentration: The New Learning*, ed. H. Goldschmid, H. Mann, and J. Weston (Boston: Little, Brown, 1974).

Firm Economies. In addition to the plant economies of scale are other scale economies associated with the overall size of the firm. Often these latter scale economies can only be realized by the large multiproduct, multiplant firm. One possible source of scale economies to the firm is in *materials procurement*. Firms that purchase large quantities of goods and services from suppliers are often able to negotiate *quantity discounts*, which result in lower average costs to the large-volume buyer as compared with the small-volume buyer. Also, order preparation and shipping costs per unit are generally lower for large quantities of materials.

A second possible source of scale economies to the firm is in *raising capital funds*. Since flotation costs increase less than proportionately with the size of the security (stock or bond) issue, average flotation costs per dollar of funds raised is smaller for larger firms.[13] Also, the securities of larger firms are generally less risky than those of smaller firms. Statistical studies have shown that both the relative variability in profits and the relative frequency of bankruptcy and securities default tend to vary inversely with the size of firms. Since most investors are averse to risk, they are often willing to pay a higher price (relative to earnings) for the less risky securities of larger firms. Hence, all other things being equal, the larger firm will have a lower cost of capital than the smaller firm.

Possible scale economies also exist in *sales promotion*. These scale economies can take such forms as quantity discounts in securing advertising media space and time and the ability of the large firm to spread the fixed costs of advertising preparation over greater output volumes. In addition, the large firm may be able to achieve a relatively greater degree of brand recognition and brand loyalty from its higher level of sales promotion expenditures over an extended period of time.

Another possible source of scale economies is in *technological innovation*. Unlike smaller firms, large firms can afford sizable research and development (R&D) laboratories and costly specialized equipment and research personnel. Also, the large firm is better able to undertake a diversified portfolio of R&D projects and can thus reduce the risk associated with the failure of any one (or small number) of the projects. The smaller firm, in contrast, may be unwilling to undertake a large R&D project, since failure of the project could result in bankruptcy. Finally, the costs of many R&D projects may be so high that only large firms, which are in a position to capture a sizable share of the market for the product, can justify the initial R&D investment.

One other possible source of scale economies is *management*. Compared with a small firm, a large firm can normally make greater use of various specialized types of such in-house managerial talent as tax accountants, market researchers, and labor contract negotiators. The smaller firm must either hire outside consultants as the need arises or do without these specialized managerial skills.

---

[13] *Flotation costs* are the costs paid to the investment underwriter or securities dealer who arranges the sale of the securities issue to investors.

Economic Analysis and Managerial Efficiency

FORD MOTOR COMPANY'S FLAT ROCK PLANT: SOMETIMES A PLANT CAN BE TOO BIG*

Ford Motor Company spent an estimated $200 million in the early 1970s to construct a plant in Flat Rock, Michigan to build engine blocks. The plant was built exclusively to manufacture engine blocks in the fastest, most efficient manner possible. In fact, it could produce 500,000 tons of cast iron blocks per year. The plant was designed to take advantage of economies of scale—the principle that large-scale production would result in lower costs per unit of output.

In 1981, however, Ford executives decided to close the plant and move the production of engine blocks to a much older plant in Cleveland. The Flat Rock plant originally was built to make V–8 engine blocks on five ultra-high-speed production lines. As George Booth, iron-operations manager for the casting division at Ford, explained, "Flat Rock was built to make a few parts at very high volumes. But the plant turned out to be very inflexible for conversion to making new types and different sizes of engine blocks. It wound up costing us a lot of money."

During the 1970s, cars started getting smaller and fuel efficient four- and six-cylinder engines became more popular. In 1978 Ford spent $36

*Based on an article in the *Wall Street Journal*, 16 September 1981.

million to convert just one of the five production lines at the Flat Rock plant to begin making four-cylinder engines for its Escort and Lynx subcompact models. After these changes were made, however, the plant's efficiency declined because much of the remaining machinery was designed to handle larger amounts of iron than required by the smaller, lighter engines.

Compared with the Flat Rock plant, Ford's Cleveland plant had ten smaller and slower production lines. When operating at full capacity, the Cleveland plant was the less efficient of the two factories; however, Ford executives decided to keep it operating rather than the Flat Rock plant for two reasons. First, it would cost less to convert its smaller production lines into lines for building new engines. Second, with ten production lines, it had the ability to produce more than five types of engines at one time, the capacity of the Flat Rock plant.

The Flat Rock plant is a rare example of what can occur when a plant is too highly specialized. As David Lewis, a University of Michigan business professor noted, "Flat Rock was efficient at producing what it was originally designed to make, but as soon as the product changed, the plant became outmoded by its own size. It was just too big to convert to other uses. Its closing is a lesson in mass production. Sometimes you really can be too big."

Question

1. What factors that led to its closing did Ford managers fail to consider when deciding to build the Flat Rock plant?

Diseconomies of Scale

Rising long-run average costs at higher levels of output are usually attributed to *diseconomies of scale*. A primary source of diseconomies of scale associated with an individual production plant is *transportation costs*. If the firm's customers are geographically scattered, then the transportation costs of distributing output from one large plant will be greater than the transportation costs of distributing output from a series of strategically located smaller plants. Another possible source of plant diseconomies is *imperfections in the labor market*. As a plant expands and its labor requirements increase, the firm may have to pay higher wage rates or engage in costly worker recruiting and relocation programs to attract the necessary personnel, particularly if the plant is located in a sparsely populated area.

Disagreement exists among economists about whether long-run average costs for the firm remain constant once scale economies are exhausted or whether these costs begin rising. The existence of diseconomies of scale for the firm is hypothesized by some economists to result from *problems of coordination and control encountered by management* as the scale of operations is increased. These coordination and control problems impose rising costs on the firm in a number of different ways. First, the size of management staffs and their associated salary costs may rise more than proportionately as the scale of the firm is increased. Also, less direct and observable costs may occur, such as the losses arising from delayed or faulty decisions and weakened or distorted managerial incentives.

The degree to which an actual production process, plant, or firm is subject to economies or diseconomies of scale is a question that can probably best be answered by examining the empirical evidence.[14] The next chapter discusses some of the techniques that have been used in attempting to answer this question.

Summary

- *Cost* is defined as the sacrifice incurred whenever an exchange or transformation of resources takes place.

- Different approaches are used in measuring costs, depending on the purposes for which the information is to be used. For financial reporting purposes, the historical outlay of funds is usually the appropriate measure of cost, whereas for decision-making purposes it is often appropriate to measure cost in terms of the opportunities foregone or sacrificed.

- A *cost function* is a schedule, graph, or mathematical relationship showing the minimum achievable cost (such as total, average, or marginal cost) of producing various quantities of output.

---

[14] See Jack Johnson, *Statistical Cost Analysis* (New York: McGraw-Hill, 1960), pp. 23–24, for a further discussion of the issues involved. For some excellent representative examples, see William Longbrake, "Statistical Cost Analysis," *Financial Management* (Spring 1973), pp. 49–55, and Barry Keating and Maryann Keating, "Nonprofit Firms, Decision Making and Regulation," *Review of Social Economy* (April 1975), pp. 26–42.

- Short-run *total costs* are equal to the sum of *fixed* and *variable costs*.

- *Marginal cost* is defined as the incremental increase in total cost that results from a one-unit increase in output.

- The theoretical short-run average variable and marginal cost functions of economic theory are hypothesized to be U-shaped, first falling and then rising as output is increased. Falling costs are attributed to the gains available from specialization in the use of capital and labor. Rising costs are attributed to diminishing returns in production.

- The theoretical long-run average cost function, like its short-run counterpart, is also postulated to be U-shaped. This is due to the presence of economies and diseconomies of scale. *Economies of scale* are attributed primarily to the nature of the production process or the factor markets, whereas *diseconomies of scale* are attributed primarily to problems of coordination and control in large-scale organizations.

Selected References

Black J. H. *Cost Engineering Planning Techniques for Management*. New York: Marcel Dekker, 1984.

Gold, Bela. "Changing Perspectives on Size, Scale, and Returns: An Interpretive Survey." *Journal of Economic Literature* 19 (March 1981).

Henderson, James M., and Richard E. Quandt. *Microeconomic Theory: A Mathematical Approach*, 3d ed. New York: McGraw-Hill, 1980.

Johnston, Jack. *Statistical Cost Analysis*. New York: McGraw-Hill, 1960.

Longbrake, William. "Statistical Cost Analysis." *Financial Management* (Spring 1973), pp. 49–55.

Keating, Barry, and Maryann Keating. "Nonprofit Firms: Decision Making and Regulation." *Review of Social Economy* (April 1975), pp. 26–42.

Morrison, Thomas A., and Eugene Kaczka. "A New Application of Calculus and Risk Analysis to Cost-Volume-Profit Changes." *Accounting Review* 44 (April 1969).

Reinhardt, U. E. "Breakeven Analysis for Lockheed's Tri-Star: An Application of Financial Theory." *Journal of Finance* 28 (September 1973).

Scherer, F. M. "Economies of Scale and Industrial Concentration" in *Industrial Concentration: The New Learning*, edited by H. Goldschmid, H. Mann, and J. Weston. Boston: Little, Brown, 1974.

Discussion Questions

1. Define the following terms:
   a. Cost
   b. Opportunity cost
   c. Cost function
   d. Fixed costs
   e. Variable costs
   f. Marginal cost
   g. Expansion path
   h. Economies of scale
   i. Diseconomies of scale

2. Explain the difference(s) between accounting and economic costs.

3. Define depreciation. Explain why it is generally difficult to measure true depreciation costs.

4. What is a sunk cost and how does it affect economic decisions?

5. Explain the difference between the accounting profit and economic profit of a firm. How would one go about determining the economic profit of a firm, once its accounting profit is known?

6. How does one distinguish between the long run and the short run and the associated long-run and short-run cost functions?

7. Explain how the shape of the firm's short-run cost functions is related to its short-run production function and the law of diminishing returns.

8. Explain how the short-run and long-run cost functions are related to each other.

9. Explain how the long-run cost function can be derived from the long-run production function.

10. What economic factors give rise to economies and diseconomies of scale?

Problems

1. In the ore-mining example described earlier in the chapter (Table 12.4), suppose again that labor (X) is a variable input and capital (Y) is a fixed input. Specifically, assume that the firm has a piece of equipment having a 500-horsepower rating.

   a. Complete the following table.

Output Q	Input X	Variable Cost VC	Input Y	Fixed Cost FC	Total Cost TC	Avg. Variable Cost AVC	Avg. Fixed Cost AFC	Avg. Total Cost ATC	Marginal Cost MC
___	0	___	___	___	___	___	___	___	___
___	1	___	___	___	___	___	___	___	___
___	2	___	___	___	___	___	___	___	___
___	3	___	___	___	___	___	___	___	___
___	4	___	___	___	___	___	___	___	___
___	5	___	___	___	___	___	___	___	___
___	6	___	___	___	___	___	___	___	___
___	7	___	___	___	___	___	___	___	___
___	8	___	___	___	___	___	___	___	___

   b. Plot the variable, fixed, and total cost functions on one graph.
   c. Plot the marginal, average variable, average fixed, and average total cost functions on another graph.

2. From your knowledge of the relationships among the various cost functions, complete the following table

Q	TC	FC	VC	ATC	AFC	AVC	MC
0	125	___	___	—	—	—	—
10	___	___	___	___	___	___	5
20	___	___	___	10.50	___	___	___
30	___	___	110	___	___	___	___
40	255	___	___	___	___	___	___
50	___	___	___	___	___	3	___
60	___	___	___	___	___	___	3
70	___	___	___	5	___	___	___
80	___	___	295	___	___	___	___

3. Economists at General Industries have been examining operating costs at one of its parts manufacturing plants in an effort to determine if the plant is being operated efficiently. From weekly cost records, the economists developed the following cost-output information concerning the operation of the plant:

a. AVC (average variable cost) at an output of 2,000 units per week is $7.50.

b. At an output level of 5,000 units per week AFC (average fixed cost) is $3.

c. TC (total cost) increases by $5,000 when output is increased from 2,000 to 3,000 units per week.

d. TVC (total variable cost) at an output level of 4,000 units per week is $23,000.

e. AVC (average variable cost) decreases by $.75 per unit when output is increased from 4,000 to 5,000 units per week.

f. AFC plus AVC for 8,000 units per week is $7.50 per unit.

g. ATC (average total cost) decreases by $.50 per unit when output is decreased from 8,000 to 7,000 units per week.

h. TVC increases by $3,000 when output is increased from 5,000 to 6,000 units per week.

i. TC decreases by $7,000 when output is decreased from 2,000 to 1,000 units per week.

j. MC (marginal cost) is $16 per unit when output is increased from 8,000 to 9,000 units per week.

Given the preceding information, complete the following cost schedule for the plant. *Hint:* Proceed sequentially through the list, *filling in all the related entries before proceeding to the next item of information in the list.*

Output (units per week)	TFC	TVC	TC	AFC	AVC	ATC	MC
0	___	___	___	X	X	X	X
1,000	___	___	___	___	___	___	___
2,000	___	___	___	___	___	___	___
3,000	___	___	___	___	___	___	___

Output (units per week)	TFC	TVC	TC	AFC	AVC	ATC	MC
4,000	——	——	——	——	——	——	——
5,000	——	——	——	——	——	——	——
6,000	——	——	——	——	——	——	——
7,000	——	——	——	——	——	——	——
8,000	——	——	——	——	——	——	——
9,000	——	——	——	——	——	——	——

4. Consider the following variable cost function (Q = output);

$$VC = 200Q - 9Q^2 + .25Q^3$$

Fixed costs are equal to $150.
   a. Determine the total cost function.
   b. Determine the (i) average fixed, (ii) average variable, (iii) average total, and (iv) marginal cost functions.
   c. Determine the value of Q where the average variable cost function takes on its minimum value. *Hint:* Take the first derivative of the *AVC* function, set the derivative equal to 0, and solve for Q. Also use the second derivative to check for a maximum or minimum.
   d. Determine the value of Q where the marginal cost function takes on its minimum value.

5. Consider Problem 4 again.
   a. Plot the (i) *AVC* and (ii) *MC* functions on a single graph for the values of $Q = 2, 4, 6, \ldots, 24$.
   b. Based on the cost functions graphed in part (a), determine the value of Q that minimizes (i) *AVC* and (ii) *MC*.
   c. Compare your answers in part (b) with those obtained earlier in 4(c) and 4(d).

6. Suppose a firm's variable cost function is given by the relationship:

$$VC = 150Q - 10Q^2 + .5Q^3$$

where Q is the quantity of output produced.
   a. Determine the output level Q where the *average* variable cost function takes on its minimum value.
   b. What is the value of the variable cost and average variable cost functions at the output level in part (a)?
   c. Determine the output level Q where the *marginal* cost function takes on its minimum value.
   d. What is the value of the variable cost and marginal cost functions at the output level in part (c)?

7. A manufacturing plant has a potential production capacity of 1,000 units per month (capacity can be increased by 10 percent if subcontractors are employed). The plant is normally operated at about 80 percent of capacity. Operating the plant above this level significantly increases variable costs per unit because of the need to pay the skilled workers higher overtime wage rates. For output levels up to 80 percent of capacity, variable cost per unit is $100. Above 80 and up to 90 percent, variable costs on this *additional* output *increase* by 10 percent. When output is above 90 and up to 100 percent of capacity, the *additional* units cost an *additional* 25 percent over the unit variable costs for outputs up to 80 percent of capacity. For production above 100 percent and up to 110 percent of capacity, extensive subcontracting work is used and the unit variable costs of these *additional* units are 50 percent above those at output levels up to 80 percent of capacity. At 80 percent of capacity, the plant's fixed costs per unit are $50. Total fixed costs are not expected to change within the production range under consideration. Based on the preceding information, complete the following table.

Q	TC	FC	VC	ATC	AFC	AVC	MC
500	____	____	____	____	____	____	____
600	____	____	____	____	____	____	____
700	____	____	____	____	____	____	____
800	____	____	____	____	____	____	____
900	____	____	____	____	____	____	____
1000	____	____	____	____	____	____	____
1100	____	____	____	____	____	____	____

8. The Blair Company has three assembly plants located in California, Georgia, and New Jersey. Currently, the company purchases a major subassembly, which becomes part of the final product, from an outside firm. Blair has decided to manufacture the subassemblies within the company and must now consider whether to rent one centrally located facility (for example, in Missouri, where all the subassemblies would be manufactured) or to rent three separate facilities, each located near one of the assembly plants, where each facility would manufacture only the subassemblies needed for the nearby assembly plant. A single, centrally located facility, with a production capacity of 18,000 units per year, would have fixed costs of $900,000 per year, and a variable cost of $250 per unit. Three separate decentralized facilities, with production capacities of 8,000, 6,000, and 4,000 units per year, would have fixed costs of $475,000, $425,000, and $400,000, respectively, and variable costs per unit of only $225 per unit owing primarily to the reduction in shipping costs. The current production rates at the three assembly plants are 6,000, 4,500, and 3,000 units, respectively.

   a. Assuming that the current production rates are maintained at the three assembly plants, which alternative should management select?

   b. If demand for the final product were to increase to production capacity, which alternative would be more attractive?

   c. What additional information would be useful before making a decision?

9. Kitchen Helper Company has decided to produce and sell food blenders and is considering three different types of production facilities ("plants"). Plant *A* is a labor-intensive facility, employing relatively little specialized capital equipment. Plant *B* is a semiautomated facility that would employ less labor than *A* but would also have higher capital equipment costs. Plant *C* is a completely automated facility using much more high-cost, high-technology capital equipment and even less labor than *B*. Information about the operating costs and production capacities of these three different types of plants is shown in the following table.

		Plant Type	
	A	B	C
Unit variable costs			
Materials	$3.50	$3.25	$3.00
Labor	4.50	3.25	2.00
Overhead	1.00	1.50	2.00
Total	$9.00	$8.00	$7.00
Annual fixed costs			
Depreciation	$ 60,000	$100,000	$200,000
Capital	30,000	50,000	100,000
Overhead	60,000	100,000	150,000
Total	$150,000	$250,000	$450,000
Annual capacity	75,000	150,000	350,000

a. Determine the average total cost schedules for each plant type for annual outputs of 25,000, 50,000, 75,000, ... , 350,000. For output levels beyond the capacity of a given plant, assume that multiple plants of the same type are built. For example, in order to produce 200,000 units with plant A, three of these plants would be built.

b. Based on the cost schedules calculated in part (a), construct the long-run average total cost schedule for the production of blenders.

The Leisure Time Products Company (LTP) manufactures lawn and patio furniture. Most of its output is sold to wholesalers and to retail hardware and department store chains (for example, True-Value and Montgomery Ward), who then distribute the products under their respective brand names. LTP is not involved in direct retail sales. Last year the firm had sales of $35 million.

Case Problem
Cost Analysis

One of LTP's divisions manufactures folding (aluminum and vinyl) chairs. Sales of the chairs are highly seasonal, with 80 percent of the sales volume concentrated in the January–June period. Production is normally concentrated in the September–May period. Approximately 75 percent of the hourly work force (unskilled and semiskilled workers) is laid off (or take their paid vacation time) during the June–August period of reduced output. The remainder of the work force, consisting of salaried plant management (foremen and supervisors), maintenance, and clerical staff, are retained during this slow period. Maintenance personnel, for example, perform major overhauls of the machinery during the slow summer period.

LTP planned to produce and sell 500,000 of these chairs during the coming year at a projected selling price of $7.15 per chair. The cost per unit was estimated as follows:

Direct labor	$2.25
Materials	2.30
Plant overhead*	1.15
Administrative and selling expense*	.80
TOTAL	$6.50

*These costs are allocated to each unit of output based on the projected annual production of 500,000 chairs.

A 10 percent markup ($.65) was added to the cost per unit in arriving at the firm's selling price of $7.15 (plus shipping).

In May, LTP received an inquiry from Southeast Department Stores concerning the possible purchase of folding chairs for delivery in August. Southeast indicated that they would place an order for 30,000 chairs if the price did not exceed $5.50 each (plus shipping). The chairs could be produced during the slow period using the firm's existing equipment and work force. No overtime wages would have to be paid to the work force in fulfilling the order. Adequate materials are on hand (or can be purchased at prevailing market prices) to complete the order.

LTP's management was considering whether to accept the order. The firm's chief accountant felt that the firm should *not* accept the order since the price per chair was less than the total cost and contributed nothing to the firm's profits. The firm's chief economist argued that the firm should accept the order *if* the incremental revenue exceeds the incremental cost.

The following cost accounting definitions may be helpful in analyzing this decision:

- Direct labor—labor costs incurred in converting the raw material into the finished product.
- Material—raw materials that enter into and become part of final product.
- Plant overhead—all costs other than direct labor and materials that are associated with the product, including wages and salaries paid to employees who do not work directly on the product but whose services are related to the production process (such as foremen, maintenance, and janitorial personnel), heat, light, power, supplies, depreciation, taxes, and insurance on the assets employed in the production process.
- Selling and distribution costs—costs incurred in making sales (for example, billing and salesmen's compensation), storing the product, and shipping the product to the customer. (In this case the customer pays all shipping costs.)
- Administrative costs—items not listed in the preceding categories, including general and executive office costs, research, development, engineering costs, and miscellaneous items.

Questions

1. Calculate the incremental (that is, marginal) cost per chair to LTP of accepting the order from Southeast.
2. What assumptions did you make in calculating the incremental cost in Question 1? What additional information would be helpful in making these calculations?
3. Based on your answers to Questions 1 and 2, should LTP accept the Southeast order?
4. What additional considerations might lead LTP to reject the order?

Breakeven Analysis and Operating Leverage: An Application of Cost Theory

Many of the planning activities that take place within a firm are based on anticipated levels of output. The study of the interrelationships among a firm's sales, costs, and operating profit at various output levels is known as *cost-volume-profit analysis*, or *breakeven analysis*. The use by a firm of assets having fixed operating costs (e.g., depreciation) results in *operating leverage*—that is, an increase in the possible returns (as well as risks) to the owners of the firm. The measurement and implications of operating leverage will be examined after the discussion of breakeven analysis is completed.

The term *breakeven analysis* is somewhat misleading, since this type of analysis is typically used to answer many other questions besides those dealing with the breakeven output level of a firm. For example, breakeven analysis is also used to evaluate the financial profitability of new firms and new product lines. In addition, it is a valuable analytical tool for measuring the effects of changes in selling prices, fixed costs, and variable costs on the output level that must be achieved before the firm can realize operating profits.

Breakeven analysis is based on the revenue-output and cost-output functions of microeconomic theory. These functions are shown together in Figure 12A.1. Total revenue is equal to the number of units of output sold multiplied by the price per unit. Assuming that the firm can sell additional units of output only by lowering the price, the total revenue curve *TR* will be concave (inverted U-shaped), as is indicated in Figure 12A.1. The total cost curve *TC* shown is a static short-run cost function analogous to that shown earlier in Figure 12.3. It indicates the relationship between costs and output for a given production process in which one or more of the factors of production (for example, plant and production technology) are fixed. As discussed earlier in the chapter, short-run total costs consist of a fixed-cost component and a variable-cost component.

The difference between total revenue and total cost at any level of output represents the total profit that will be obtained.[15] In Figure 12A.1, total profit *TP*

---

[15] An additional assumption of breakeven analysis is that all the units produced during the period are sold during the period; that is, no inventories exist.

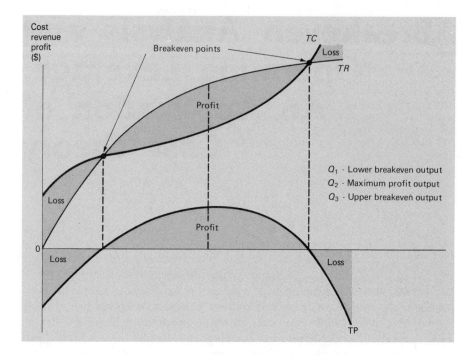

Figure 12A.1
**Generalized
Breakeven
Analysis**

at any output level is given by the vertical distance between the total revenue TR and total cost TC curves. A breakeven situation (zero profit) occurs whenever total revenue equals total cost. In Figure 12A.1, note that a breakeven condition occurs at two different output levels—Q_1 and Q_3. Below an output level of Q_1, losses will be incurred since $TR < TC$. Between Q_1 and Q_3, profits will be obtained, since $TR > TC$. At output levels above Q_3, losses will occur again, since $TR < TC$. Total profits are maximized within the range of Q_1 to Q_3, where the vertical distance between the TR and TC curves is greatest; that is, at an output level of Q_2.

Linear Breakeven Analysis

In the application of economic breakeven analysis to practical decision-making problems, the nonlinear revenue-output and cost-output relationships of economic theory are often replaced by linear functions.[16] A linear breakeven analysis can be developed either graphically or algebraically (or as a combination of the two).

---

[16] In addition, there is a shift in objectives of the analysis. In economic theory the cost-output and revenue-output relationships are used primarily to determine the profit-maximizing price and output levels. In contrast, the main objective of linear breakeven analysis is usually to determine the output level required to either "break even" or earn a "target profit."

Graphic Method

Figure 12A.2 is an example of a basic linear breakeven analysis chart. Costs and revenues (measured in dollars) are plotted on the vertical axis, whereas output (measured in units) is plotted on the horizontal axis. The *total revenue* function *TR* represents the total revenue that the firm will realize at each output level, given that the firm charges a constant selling price *P* per unit of output. Similarly, the *total* (operating) *cost* function *TC* represents the total cost the firm will incur at each output level. Total cost is computed as the sum of the firm's fixed costs *F*, which are independent of the output level, plus the variable costs, which increase at a constant rate per unit of output *V*. Earnings before interest and taxes, or EBIT, is equal to the difference between total revenues (TR) and total (*operating*) costs (TC). Note that this measure of profits *excludes* financing costs (e.g., interest on debt) as well as taxes.[17]

The assumptions of a constant selling price per unit *P* and a constant variable cost per unit *V* yield *linear* relationships for the total revenue and total cost functions. These linear relationships are only valid, however, over some *relevant range* of output values, such as from Q_1 to Q_2 in Figure 12A.2. (The relevant range of output is that range where the linearity assumptions of breakeven analysis are assumed to hold.)

The breakeven point occurs at point Q_b in Figure 12A.2 where the total revenue and the total cost functions intersect. If a firm's output level is below

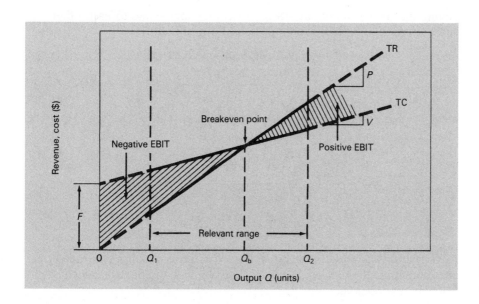

Figure 12A.2
Linear Breakeven Analysis Chart

---

[17] See R. Charles Moyer, James R. McGuigan, and William J. Kretlow. *Contemporary Financial Management*, 3d rev. ed. (St. Paul, MN: West Publishing Company, 1988), chapter 7 for a discussion of how financial leverage (i.e., use of fixed cost sources of financing) can be incorporated into the analysis.

this breakeven point—that is, if $TR < TC$—it incurs *operating losses*, defined as a *negative EBIT*. If the firm's output level is above this breakeven point—that is, if $TR > TC$—it realizes *operating profits*, defined as a *positive EBIT*.

Determining a firm's breakeven point graphically involves three steps:

1. Drawing a line through the origin with a slope of P to represent the TR function

2. Drawing a line that intersects the vertical axis at F and has a slope of V to represent the TC function

3. Determining the point where the TR and TC lines intersect, dropping a perpendicular line to the horizontal axis, and noting the resulting value of Q_b

Algebraic Method

To determine a firm's breakeven point algebraically, it is necessary to set the total revenue and total (operating) cost functions equal to each other and solve the resulting equation for the breakeven volume.

Total revenue is equal to the selling price per unit times the output quantity:

$$TR = P \times Q \tag{12A.1}$$

Total (operating) cost is equal to fixed plus variable costs, where the variable cost is the product of the variable cost per unit times the output quantity:

$$TC = F + (V \times Q) \tag{12A.2}$$

Setting the total revenue and total cost expressions equal to each other and substituting the breakeven output Q_b for Q results in:

$$TR = TC$$

or

$$PQ_b = F + VQ_b \tag{12A.3}$$

Finally, solving Equation 12A.3 for the breakeven output Q_b yields.

$$PQ_b - VQ_b = F$$

$$(P - V)Q_b = F$$

$$Q_b = \frac{F}{P - V} \tag{12A.4}$$

Breakeven analysis also can be performed in terms of dollar *sales* rather than units of output. The breakeven dollar sales volume S_b can be determined by the following expression:

$$S_b = \frac{F}{1 - V/P} \tag{12A.5}$$

where V/P is the variable cost ratio (that is, the variable cost per dollar of sales).

The *difference* between the selling price per unit and the variable cost per unit, $P - V$, is sometimes referred to as the *contribution margin per unit*. It measures how much each unit of output contributes to meeting fixed costs and operating profits. Thus it can also be said that the breakeven output is equal to the fixed cost divided by the contribution margin per unit.

Occasionally the analyst is interested in determining the output quantity at which a *target profit* (expressed in dollars) is achieved. An expression similar to Equation 12A.4 can be used to find such a quantity:

$$\text{Target volume} = \frac{\text{fixed cost} + \text{target profit}}{\text{contribution margin per unit}} \qquad [12A.6]$$

Examples of Breakeven Analysis

The equations defined in the preceding section can be used to perform a breakeven analysis for the Allegan Manufacturing Company. Assume that the firm manufactures one product which it sells for $250 per unit ($P$). Variable costs ($V$) are $150 per unit. The firm's fixed costs (F) are $1,000,000. Substituting these figures into Equation 12A.4 yields the following breakeven output:

$$Q_b = \frac{\$1,000,000}{\$250 - \$150}$$

$$= 10,000 \text{ units}$$

Allegan's breakeven output can also be determined graphically, as shown in Figure 12A.3.

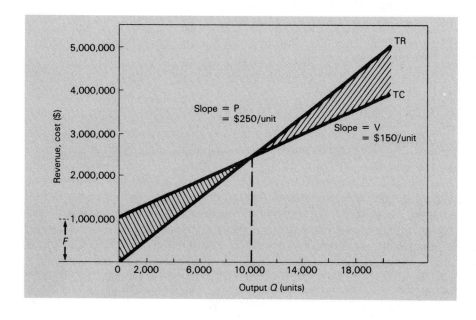

Figure 12A.3
Linear Breakeven Analysis Chart for the Allegan Manufacturing Company

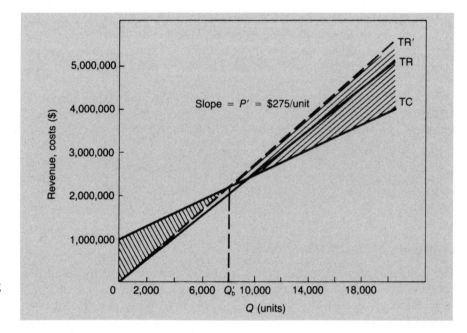

Figure 12A.4
Linear Breakeven Analysis Chart for the Allegan Manufacturing Company Showing the Effects of a Price Increase

Since a firm's breakeven output is dependent on a number of variables—in particular, the price per unit, variable (operating) costs per unit, and fixed costs—the firm may wish to analyze the effects of changes in any one (or more) of the variables on the breakeven output. For example, it may wish to consider either of the following:

1. Changing the selling price

2. Substituting fixed costs for variable costs

Assume that Allegan increased the selling price per unit P' by \$25 to \$275. Substituting this figure into Equation 12A.4 gives a new breakeven output:

$$Q'_b = \frac{\$1,000,000}{\$275 - \$150}$$

$$= 8,000 \text{ units}$$

This can also be seen in Figure 12A.4, in which an increase in the price per unit increases the slope of the total revenue function TR' and reduces the breakeven output.

Rather than increasing the selling price per unit, Allegan's management may decide to substitute fixed costs for variable costs in some aspect of the company's operations. For example, as labor wage rates increase over time, many firms seek to reduce operating costs through automation, which in effect represents the substitution of fixed-cost capital equipment for variable-cost labor. Suppose that Allegan determines that it can reduce labor costs by \$25 per unit by purchasing \$1,000,000 in additional equipment. Assume that the new equipment is depreciated over a 10-year life using the straight-line method.

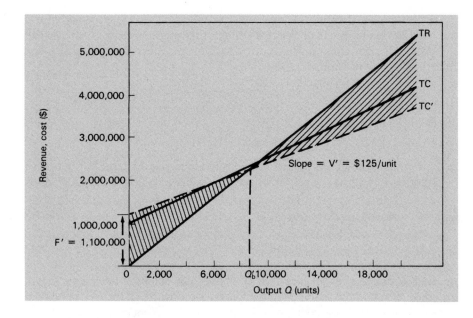

Figure 12A.5
Linear Breakeven Analysis Chart for the Allegan Manufacturing Company Showing the Effects of Substituting Fixed Costs for Variable Costs

Under these conditions, annual depreciation of the new equipment would be $1,000,000/10 = \$100,000$, and the firm's new level of fixed costs F' would be $\$1,000,000 + \$100,000 = \$1,100,000$. Variable costs per unit V' would be $\$150 - \$25 = \$125$. Substituting $P = \$250$ per unit, $V' = \$125$ per unit, and $F' = \$1,100,000$ into Equation 12A.4 yields a new breakeven output:

$$Q'_b = \frac{\$1,100,00}{\$250 - \$125}$$

$$= 8,800 \text{ units}$$

As we can see in Figure 12A.5, the effect of this change in operations is to raise the intercept on the vertical axis, decrease the slope of the total (operating) cost function TC', and reduce the breakeven output.

Breakeven Analysis and Risk Assessment

The information generated from a breakeven analysis can be used to assess the operating risk to which a firm is exposed. Consider the example represented in Figure 12A.3. With fixed costs of $\$1,000,000$, a price per unit of $\$250$, and variable costs per unit of $\$150$, the breakeven output was computed to be 10,000 units. If one adds to this set of information the *expected* (mean) level of sales (in units) for some future period of time, the standard deviation of the distribution of sales, and the assumption that actual sales are normally distributed, it is possible to compute the probability that the firm will have operating losses (that is, it will sell fewer units than the breakeven level) and the probability that the firm will have operating profits (that is, it will sell more units than the breakeven level).

For example, if expected unit sales for Allegan are 15,000 units with a standard deviation of 4,000, the probability of having operating losses (that is, the probability of selling fewer than 10,000 units) can be computed using the following equation (Equation 3.3):

$$z = \frac{R - \bar{R}}{\sigma}$$

[12A.7]

and the probability values from Table 1 (Appendix A at the back of the book). Substituting $R = 10,000$, $\bar{R} = 15,000$, and $\sigma = 4,000$ into Equation 12A.7 yields

$$z = \frac{10,000 - 15,000}{4,000}$$

$$= -1.25$$

In other words, a sales level of 10,000 units is 1.25 standard deviations *below* the mean. From Table 1, the probability associated with -1.25 standard deviations is .1056 or 10.56 percent. Thus, there is a 10.56 percent chance that Allegan will incur operating losses and an 89.44 percent chance (100 percent minus the 10.56 percent chance of losses) that the firm will record operating profits (that is, it will sell more than the breakeven number of units of output).

Some Limitations of Breakeven Analysis

Breakeven analysis has a number of limitations that arise from the *assumptions* made in constructing the model and developing the relevant data. The application of breakeven analysis is of value only to the extent that these assumptions are valid.

Constant Selling Price and Variable Cost per Unit. In the breakeven analysis model the assumptions of a constant selling price and variable cost per unit yield *linear* relationships for the total revenue and total cost functions. In practice these functions tend to be nonlinear for the reasons discussed earlier. The assumption of a constant selling price and variable cost per unit is probably valid over some relevant range of output levels; however, consideration of output levels outside this range will normally require modifications in the breakeven chart.

Composition of Operating Costs. Another assumption of breakeven analysis is that costs can be classified as either fixed or variable. In fact, fixed and variable costs are dependent on both the time period and the output range. As mentioned earlier, all costs are variable in the long run. In addition, some costs are partly fixed and partly variable. Futhermore, some costs increase in a stepwise manner as output is increased—they are *semivariable*—and are constant only over relatively narrow ranges of output.

Multiple Products.   The breakeven model also assumes that a firm is producing and selling either a *single* product or a *constant mix* of different products. In many cases the product mix changes over time, and problems can arise in allocating fixed costs among the various products.

Uncertainty.   Still another assumption of breakeven analysis is that the selling price and variable cost per unit, as well as fixed costs, are known at each level of output. In practice these parameters are subject to uncertainty. Thus the usefulness of the results of breakeven analysis depends on how accurate the estimates of these parameters are.

Short-Term Planning Horizon.   Finally, breakeven analysis is normally performed for a planning period of one year or less; however, the benefits received from some costs may not be realized until subsequent periods. For example, research and development costs incurred during a specific period may not result in new products for several years. For breakeven analysis to be a dependable decision-making tool, a firm's operating costs must be matched with resulting revenues for the planning period under consideration.

Operating Leverage

Operating leverage involves the use of assets having fixed costs. A firm uses operating leverage in the hope of earning returns in excess of the fixed costs of the assets, thereby increasing the returns to the owners of the firm. A firm's degree of operating leverage (DOL) is defined as the multiplier effect resulting from the firm's use of fixed operating costs. More specifically, DOL can be computed as the *percentage change* in earnings before interest and taxes (EBIT) resulting from a given *percentage change* in sales (output):

$$\text{DOL at } X = \frac{\text{Percentage change in EBIT}}{\text{Percentage change in Sales}}$$

This can be rewritten as follows:

$$\text{DOL at } X = \frac{\dfrac{\Delta \text{EBIT}}{\text{EBIT}}}{\dfrac{\Delta \text{Sales}}{\text{Sales}}} \qquad [12A.8]$$

where Δ EBIT and Δ Sales are the changes in the firm's EBIT and Sales, respectively. Since a firm's DOL differs at each sales level, it is necessary to indicate the sales point, X, at which operating leverage is measured. The degree of operating leverage is analogous to the elasticity of demand concept (for example, price and income elasticities) because it relates percentage changes in one variable (EBIT) to percentage changes in another variable (sales). Equation 12A.8 requires the use of two different values of sales and EBIT. Another equation (derived from Equation 12A.8) that can be used to compute a firm's DOL more easily is

$$\text{DOL at } X = \frac{\text{Sales-Variable Costs}}{\text{EBIT}} \qquad [12A.9]$$

The variables defined in the previous section on breakeven analysis can also be used to develop a formula for determining a firm's DOL at any given output level. Since sales are equivalent to TR(or $P \times Q$), variable cost is equal to $V \times Q$, and EBIT is equal to total revenue (TR) less total (operating) cost, or $(P \times Q) - F - (V \times Q)$, these values can be substituted into Equation 12A.9 to obtain the following:

$$\text{DOL at } Q = \frac{(P \times Q) - (V \times Q)}{(P \times Q) - F - (V \times Q)}$$

or

$$\text{DOL at } Q = \frac{(P - V)Q}{(P - V)Q - F} \qquad [12A.10]$$

In the earlier discussion of breakeven analysis for the Allegan Manufacturing Company, the parameters of the breakeven model were determined as $P = \$250/\text{unit}$, $V = \$150/\text{unit}$, and $F = \$1,000,000$. Substituting these values into Equation 12A.10 along with the respective output (Q) values yields the DOL values shown in Table 12A.1. For example, a DOL of 6.00 at an output level of 12,000 units indicates that, from a base output level of 12,000 units, EBIT will increase by 6.00 percent for each one percent increase in output.

Note that Allegan's DOL is largest (in absolute value terms) when the firm is operating near the breakeven point (that is, where $Q = Q_b = 10,000$ units). Note also that the firm's DOL is negative below the breakeven output level. A negative DOL indicates the percentage *reduction* in operating *losses* that occurs as the result of a one percent *increase* in output. For example, the DOL of -1.50 at an

Table 12A.1
DOL at Various Output Levels for Allegan Manufacturing Company

Output Q	Degree of Operating Leverage DOL
0	0
2,000	-0.25
4,000	-0.67
6,000	-1.50
8,000	-4.00
10,000	(undefined) Breakeven level
12,000	$+6.00$
14,000	$+3.50$
16,000	$+2.67$
18,000	$+2.25$
20,000	$+2.00$

output level of 6,000 units indicates that, from a base output level of 6,000 units, the firm's operating *losses* will be *reduced* by 1.5 percent for each one percent *increase* in output.

A firm's DOL is a function of the nature of the production process. If the firm employs large amounts of labor-saving equipment in its operations, it tends to have relatively high fixed operating costs and relatively low variable operating costs. Such a cost structure yields a high DOL, which results in large operating profits (positive EBIT) if sales are high and large operating losses (negative EBIT) if sales are depressed.

Discussion Questions

1. Explain how a linear breakeven chart is constructed when a firm's selling price, variable cost per unit, and fixed costs are known.

2. Define *contribution margin*. What is its relationship to breakeven analysis?

3. What are some of the limitations of linear breakeven analysis?

4. Define *operating leverage* and explain how it is measured.

5. Assuming that all other factors remain unchanged, determine how a firm's breakeven point is affected by each of the following:
   a. The firm finds it necessary to reduce the price per unit because of increased foreign competition.
   b. The firm's direct labor costs are increased as the result of a new labor contract.
   c. The Occupational Safety and Health Administration (OSHA) requires the firm to install new ventilating equipment in its plant. (Assume that this action has no effect on worker productivity.)

Problems

Refer to the following data when working Problems 1-4 below. East Publishing Company is doing an analysis of a proposed new finance text. The following data have been obtained:

Fixed costs (per edition):	
Development (reviews, class testing, etc.)	$15,000
Copy editing	4,000
Selling and promotion	7,500
Typesetting	23,500
Total	$50,000
Variable costs (per copy):	
Printing and binding	$ 6.65
Administrative costs	1.50
Salesmen's commission (2% of selling price)	.55
Author's royalties (12% of selling price)	3.30
Bookstore discounts (20% of selling price)	5.50
Total	$17.50
Projected selling price	$27.50

1. Using the data presented above:
   a. Determine the company's breakeven volume for this book in
      (i) Units
      (ii) Dollar sales
   b. Develop a breakeven chart for the text.
   c. Determine the number of copies East must sell in order to earn an (operating) profit of $30,000 on this text.
   d. Determine total (operating) profits at sales levels of
      (i)   3000 units
      (ii) 5000 units
      (iii) 10,000 units

2. Determine the degree of operating leverage (DOL) and give an economic interpretation of the value at the following sales levels:
   a. 3,000 units
   b. 7,000 units

3. Suppose expected sales (per edition) are 10,000 units with a standard deviation of 2,000 units:
   a. Determine the probability that East will incur operating losses on the finance text.
   b. Determine the probability that East will have operating profits on the proposed text.

4. Suppose East feels that $27.50 is too high a price to charge for the new finance text. It has examined the competitive market and determined that $25 would be a better selling price. What would the breakeven volume be at this new selling price?

Empirical Determination of Production and Cost Functions

13

In order to make wealth-maximizing decisions based upon the costs of operation, it is important for a manager to have good estimates of the cost structure facing the firm. This chapter examines some of the techniques that have been developed for estimating the production and cost functions of actual production processes and firms. In the short run, a knowledge of the firm's cost function is essential when deciding whether to accept an additional order, perhaps at less than "full cost," whether to schedule overtime for workers, whether to temporarily close the plant, and similar short-run decisions. In the long run, a knowledge of cost and production function relationships will determine the capital investments that the firm makes, the production technology the firm chooses, the markets that the firm may choose to enter, and the new products the firm may produce. Because capital expenditures often cannot be reversed without significant losses, it is essential that a wealth-maximizing manager gather the cost information needed to make these long-term investment decisions. The first part of the chapter contains a discussion of the methodology and problems involved in using regression techniques to fit power production functions[1] to production input and output data, along with two examples of statistically estimated production functions. The second part of the chapter examines various techniques for empirically estimating short-run and long-run cost functions. Appendix 13A examines learning curves—a cost estimation technique.

Glossary of New Terms

Technical progress
The increase in productivity over time that results from the development and use of more efficient capital equipment, labor skills, and production methods.

Cobb-Douglas production function
A particular type of mathematical model, known as a power function, which is used to represent the relationship between the inputs employed in a production process and the output obtained from the process.

Statistical Estimation of Production Functions

The production function was defined in Chapter 11 as a schedule, graph, or mathematical model relating the maximum quantity of output that can be produced with the existing technology from various quantities of inputs. A production function is therefore a physical transformation relationship between the inputs and outputs of a process. The process under consideration may consist of an *individual* unified operation or economic unit—such as a plant or firm—or of an *aggregation* of economic units—such as an industry,

---

[1] Power functions are also referred to as Cobb-Douglas functions—they are named after the economists who pioneered the use of these functions.

geographical region, or entire economy. The reason for distinguishing between individual and aggregate economic units is that the development and interpretation of the production function differs for the two cases.

Individual Firm Production Functions

For the individual firm producing a relatively *homogeneous* product, a production function can be developed between gross output Q_G, measured in actual physical units, and the various inputs—labor L, capital K, and raw materials M:

$$Q_G = f(L, K, M) \qquad [13.1]$$

Suppose we are interested in developing a production function for a cement plant. The product is relatively homogeneous, and therefore the output of the plant can be measured in tons produced during a given time period. Since output is measured as a *flow* variable, ideally the inputs should also be measured as flow variables. Data on flow variables are not always available however, and *stock* variables must sometimes be used instead.[2] Labor input could be measured as a flow variable using the number of hours worked in the plant during the time period under consideration. In the absence of such data, labor input could be measured as a stock variable using the average number of workers employed in the plant over a period of time. Capital input is a much more difficult quantity to define and measure. What is desired is a measure of the capital consumed in producing the given output during the period. The capital assets of a firm, consisting of such items as buildings and equipment, are highly durable in nature and are of varying ages and quality. As a result, estimating the actual value of such assets consumed in producing a given quantity of output is a highly subjective procedure. Rather than attempting to measure capital use, a capital stock variable is often used in the production function. Possible capital stock variables include fixed assets or total assets of the plant or firm. Raw materials and other intermediate goods should also be included in the production function of a plant or firm. For the concrete firm, principal raw materials would include sand, gravel, and lime. Since these items are relatively homogeneous, a variable measuring the total tonnage of such inputs could be used. Also, if fuels or other sources of energy are significant inputs in a production process, these too could be included, either in the raw materials variable or as a separate variable in the production function.

For the plant or firm that produces a series of *nonhomogeneous* products, the sum of the number of physical units of the various products may not be a meaningful measure of output. An example might be an electronics manufacturer who produces a whole product line of components for various consumer, industrial, and military applications. In such a case some measure of the *value* of the various products manufactured or shipped during the period could be used

---

[2] The difference between a *flow* and a *stock* variable is that a flow variable measures the amount of a resource *used or consumed per unit of time*, whereas a stock variable measures the amount of a resource *in existence or available for use at a given point in time*.

as the output variable. Because of the problems associated with changing price levels over time and differing supply and demand conditions in the markets for inputs and outputs, it is generally preferable to measure the variables in the production function, as far as possible, in terms of physical units rather than monetary values. This is not always possible, as the example just given illustrates. When attempting to estimate a production function from value data collected over various time periods (*time-series* data), it is necessary to deflate the input and output variables by some type of price index (for example, consumer price index, wholesale price index, or other appropriate indices). Similarly, when working with value data collected from firms located at various points in a country or region (that is, *cross-sectional* data), it is useful to adjust the input and output variables by indices that reflect the relative prices or wage rates prevailing in different geographical areas.

In some studies, a production function is developed using *value-added* data to measure the output of a firm, industry, or region. The value added by the entity under consideration represents the difference between the gross value of output produced by the entity and the value of all intermediate goods consumed in producing the given output. Value-added data on a concrete firm (or the concrete industry) would measure the difference between total sales for the firm (or industry) and the cost of materials (for example, sand, gravel, and lime) used in producing the given level of sales. Value-added data therefore measures the *net* output for the entity. The use of a net output variable simplifies the production function since the raw materials variable(s) need not be included, explicitly, in the functional relationship. Therefore, the production function to be estimated using net output (Q_N) data becomes

$$Q_N = f(L, K) \qquad [13.2]$$

Aggregate Production Functions

It is also possible to develop a production function for an *aggregate* of economic entities such as an industry, geographical region, sector of the economy, or the entire economy. Conceptually, in an aggregate production function for the entire economy (or large component thereof), the output (Q), labor (L), and capital (K) variables each would consist of thousands of individual elements. The output variable would be a vector of the quantities of all the various final outputs produced:

$$Q = (q_1, q_2, \ldots, q_m)$$

Similarly, labor would be a vector of the amounts (for example, work-hours) of all the various labor inputs employed:

$$L = (l_1, l_2, \ldots, l_n)$$

And capital would be a vector of the amounts of all the various types of capital inputs used:

$$K = (k_1, k_2, \ldots, k_p)$$

Because of the difficulties of specifying and measuring such a complex functional relationship, the model is simplified by using indices to represent each of the Q, L, and K vectors. For the entire economy, an appropriate index for the output variable Q might be the gross national product figures compiled by the Commerce Department. If time-series GNP data are being used to measure the functional relationship, then the figures would have to be deflated by a suitable price index, such as the GNP deflator. In estimating a production function for the industrial sector of the economy, an index of industrial production, such as the figures compiled by the Federal Reserve Board, could be used as the output variable. Statistical data on the labor variable L (for example, employment or work-hours) are available from the Bureau of Labor Statistics. A capital stock variable K can be constructed from gross investment and depreciation data published by the Commerce Department. However, for reasons outlined earlier in the discussion of the measurement of capital for the individual firm, reliable estimates of capital are likewise difficult to obtain for the economy and its components. Possible sources of statistical data on the output, labor, and capital variables for various industries include company annual reports, trade association publications, and the periodic *censuses of manufacturers* and *businesses* by the Commerce Department.

Although the functional form and procedures for estimating the parameters of an aggregate production relationship generally are similar to those used in estimating the corresponding relationships for individual firms, it is more difficult to give a meaningful physical interpretation to the aggregate relationship. For the individual firm, the production function is an expression of the specific technological process employed in transforming inputs into outputs. In contrast, a production function for the entire economy (or major sector of it), in which aggregate variables are used to represent the thousands of different inputs and outputs, constitutes a descriptive model of the many different technological processes employed by all the productive entities within the economy. Because of the aggregative nature of the variables, the resulting model is not representative of the production process of either an "average" firm or any specific individual firm.[3]

An aggregate relationship that comes closer to representing the production process of an individual firm would be the industry production function. Within a given industry (for example, steel, aluminum, and shipbuilding) the productive processes of most firms are somewhat similar. Also, the input and output variables in an industry production function, whether measured from cross-sectional or time-series data, would be relatively homogeneous; that is, the types and mix of products, labor skills, capital equipment, and raw materials would be similar among the firms in the industry.

Despite the similarities, one must exercise care in making inferences about the production function of an individual firm within the industry based on the

---

[3] Although the aggregate production function may not be representative of any specific firm, it still can be useful as a descriptive or predictive *macroeconomic* model of the economy. The emphasis of the discussion (and the book), however, is on the usefulness of such models as *microeconomic* decision-making tools.

aggregate production function for the entire industry.[4] For example, some inputs, such as specialized labor skills, may constitute a *fixed* factor (input) of production from the standpoint of the industry and yet be a *variable* factor from the standpoint of the individual firm.[5] Also, even if all the firms in the industry are faced with increasing returns to scale, it does not necessarily follow that the industry as a whole will encounter similar returns to scale. Returns to scale for the industry may be limited by such factors as a lack of suitable production or marketing sites and limited supplies of raw materials.

Technical Progress

One important factor in the specification and measurement of production functions, which has not been discussed thus far, is how to incorporate *technical progress* into the relationship. Technical progress constitutes the changes in the production process that occur over time as the result of the development and use of more efficient capital equipment, labor skills, and production methods. Technical progress manifests itself in increased productivity over time. In other words, the total output of an aggregate entity, such as an industry or the economy, will tend to increase over time even if the quantities of capital and labor inputs are held constant. When working with time-series data, one possible method for incorporating the effects of technical progress into the production function is to introduce a trend or time variable t into the relationship:

$$Q = f(L, K, t) \qquad [13.3]$$

Various types of trends are possible such as linear, parabolic, and exponential.

Having completed our discussion of some of the methodology and problems associated with the measurement of production functions, the next section examines the Cobb-Douglas production function.

Cobb-Douglas Production Functions

In their first studies of production functions, Cobb and Douglas used a power function of the form[6]

$$Q = \alpha L^{\beta} K^{1-\beta} \qquad [13.4]$$

where α and β are the parameters to be estimated and Q, L, and K are indices of output, labor input, and capital input, respectively. Because the exponents of the labor and capital variables sum to 1, such a model *assumes* there are no

---

[4] See pp. 8–11 of A. A. Walters, "Production and Cost Functions: An Econometric Survey," *Econometrica* 31, no. 1–2 (January-April 1963), pp. 1–66, for a more detailed summary of the problems encountered in aggregation.

[5] The individual firm can increase the use of the given factor (for example, labor) by paying more than the going market rate for the factor. This will cause a shift in some of this factor to the firm and away from other firms.

[6] C. W. Cobb and P. H. Douglas. "A Theory of Production," *American Economic Review* 16 (Suppl.) (1928), pp. 139–165.

economies or diseconomies of scale.[7] In other words, if the quantities of both labor and capital inputs are increased by a factor of λ, then output will also increase exactly by a factor of λ. This can be shown as follows:

$$\begin{aligned} Q^* &= \alpha[\lambda L]^{\beta}[\lambda K]^{1-\beta} \\ &= \alpha[\lambda^{\beta}L^{\beta}][\lambda^{1-\beta}K^{1-\beta}] \\ &= (\lambda)^{\beta+(1-\beta)}(\alpha L^{\beta}K^{1-\beta}) \\ &= (\lambda)^1 Q \end{aligned}$$

In later studies by Cobb and Douglas and others, the assumption of no economies or diseconomies of scale was relaxed by employing a function of the form

$$Q = \alpha L^{\beta_1}K^{\beta_2} \tag{13.5}$$

where β_1 and β_2 are completely independent parameters that do *not* necessarily sum to 1.

The Cobb-Douglas power function has several important mathematical and economic properties that make the function an appealing one for representing the input-output production relationship.

Nonlinear Relationship

In the Cobb-Douglas power function, output is a (nonlinear) monotonically increasing function of each of the inputs.[8] As can be seen in Figure 13.1, with capital input held constant, output increases at a decreasing rate (marginal product falls) as labor input is increased. In other words, for any given amount of capital input (for instance, $K^{(0)}$, $K^{(1)}$, $K^{(2)}$, the slope of the output-labor input curve decreases as labor is added. A similar relationship exists between output and capital input if labor input is held constant. Also, the Cobb-Douglas production function can provide a good fit to the traditional S-shaped production function of economic theory over a wide range of values for the input variables (see Figure 13.2).

Linear Logarithmic Relationship

The nonlinear Cobb-Douglas production function (Equation 13.5) can be transformed into a linear relationship by taking logarithms of all the variables:

$$\log Q = \log \alpha + \beta_1 \log L + \beta_2 \log K \tag{13.6}$$

or

$$Q' = \alpha' + \beta_1 L' + \beta_2 K'$$

---

[7] In Equation 13.4 the sum of the exponents of the L and K variables is $\beta + (1 - \beta) = 1$.

[8] A "monotonically increasing function," $Y = f(X)$, means that Y *never decreases* (either increases or remains constant) as X increases.

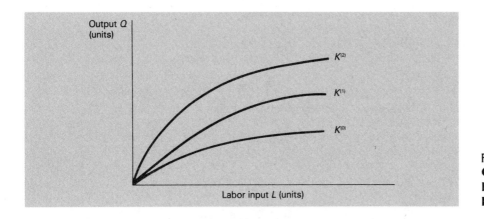

Figure 13.1
**Output as a
Function of
Labor Input**

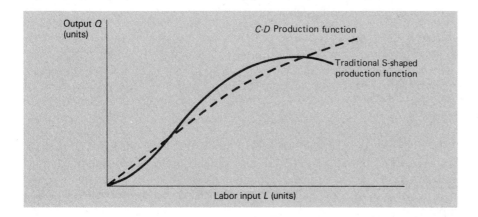

Figure 13.2
**Cobb-Douglas
Production
Function and the
Traditional
S-shaped
Production
Function**

where $Q' = \log Q$, $\alpha' = \log \alpha$, $L' = \log L$ and $K' = \log K$. With this transformation, the parameters of the model (α, β_1, β_2) can be estimated for input-output data using the standard least-squares regression techniques that were discussed in Chapter 6.

Constant Production Elasticities

In Chapter 11 the elasticity of production was defined as the percentage change in output that occurs as the result of a given percentage change in one input with all other inputs held constant. The elasticity of production was shown to be equal to the ratio of the marginal product to the average product of the given input. Consider first the labor input.[9] The marginal productivity of labor is

---

[9] The reader who is unfamiliar with differential calculus can go directly to the final result in Equation 13.7.

equal to[10]

$$MP_L = \frac{\partial Q}{\partial L}$$

$$= \alpha \beta_1 L^{\beta_1 - 1} K^{\beta_2}$$

and the average productivity of labor is equal to

$$AP_L = \frac{Q}{L}$$

$$= \frac{\alpha L^{\beta_1} K^{\beta_2}}{L}$$

$$= \alpha L^{\beta_1 - 1} K^{\beta_2}$$

Forming the ratio of these marginal and average products, one obtains the elasticity of production for labor input:

$$E_L = \frac{MP_L}{AP_L}$$

$$= \frac{\alpha \beta_1 L^{\beta_1 - 1} K^{\beta_2}}{\alpha L^{\beta_1 - 1} K^{\beta_2}}$$

$$E_L = \beta_1 \qquad\qquad [13.7]$$

This result indicates that the elasticity of production for labor input is *constant* and is equal to the exponent of the labor variable in the production function. It shows that if the amount of labor input is increased by one percent, then output will increase by β_1 percent. A similar expression can be derived for capital input:[11]

$$E_K = \beta_2$$

The elasticity of production for capital input is likewise *constant* and is equal to the exponent of the capital variable in the production function. It indicates that output will increase by β_2 percent if the amount of capital input is increased by one percent.

Returns to Scale and Degree of Homogeneity

In Chapter 11 returns to scale was defined as the proportionate increase in output that results from a given simultaneous proportionate increase in *all* the inputs to the production process. Depending on whether the proportionate increase in output is greater than, equal to, or less than the proportionate increase in all inputs, the production process is said to exhibit increasing,

---

[10] The concept of partial differentiation is discussed in Chapter 3.
[11] The reader is asked to demonstrate this relationship as one of the problems at the end of the chapter.

constant, or decreasing returns to scale, respectively. One can determine the conditions (that is, parameter values) under which the Cobb-Douglas function will exhibit the various types of returns to scale.

Recall from Chapter 11 that, for a *homogeneous* production function, the degree of homogeneity indicates the type of returns to scale. The Cobb-Douglas production function (Equation 13.5) is a homogeneous function with a degree of homogeneity (n) equal to ($\beta_1 + \beta_2$). This can be shown as follows. Define $Q = f(L, K) = \alpha L^{\beta_1} K^{\beta_2}$. Multiplying L and K by some constant λ yields

$$
\begin{aligned}
f(L, K) &= \alpha(\lambda L)^{\beta_1}(\lambda K)^{\beta_2} \\
&= \alpha(\lambda^{\beta_1} L^{\beta_1})(\lambda^{\beta_2} K^{\beta_2}) \\
&= \lambda^{\beta_1 + \beta_2}(\alpha L^{\beta_1} K^{\beta_2}) \\
&= \lambda^{\beta_1 + \beta_2} f(L, K)
\end{aligned}
$$

Since the exponent of λ is equal to ($\beta_1 + \beta_2$), the degree of homogeneity is equal to ($\beta_1 + \beta_2$). Depending on whether $n = \beta_1 + \beta_2$ is less than, equal to, or greater than 1, the Cobb-Douglas production function will exhibit decreasing, constant, or increasing returns, respectively.

Thus once the parameters of the Cobb-Douglas model are estimated, the sum of the exponents of the labor (β_1), and capital (β_2) variables can be used to test for the presence of increasing, constant, or decreasing returns to scale.

Some Empirical Studies of the Cobb-Douglas Production Function

Since the original production function studies of Cobb and Douglas in the late 1920s,[12] literally dozens of similar studies have been undertaken.[13] Using time-series data, production functions have been developed for entire economies (for example, the United States, Norway, Finland, New Zealand), geographical regions (Massachusetts, and Victoria and New South Wales in Australia), and major sectors of the economy (manufacturing, mining, agriculture). Also, Cobb-Douglas functions have been estimated for various sectors of an economy using cross-sectional industry data (the United States, Australia, Canada) and for various industries using cross-sectional data on firms within an industry (railroads, coal, clothing, chemicals, electricity, milk, and rice).

This section examines two production function studies that illustrate the basic methodology used and the type of results obtained: first, a study employing aggregate time-series data on the economy, and second, a study using cross-sectional data on individual industries.

---

[12] P. H. Douglas, "Are There Laws of Production?" *American Economic Review* 38, no. 1 (March 1948), pp. 1–41.

[13] See Walters, "Production and Cost Functions," for a summary of many of the major studies reported in the literature. See also Paul Douglas, "The Cobb-Douglas Production Function Once Again: Its History, Its Testing, and Some New Empirical Values," *Journal of Political Economy* (October 1976), pp. 903–915.

Time-Series Analysis

In their original study, Cobb and Douglas fitted a production function of the form in Equation 13.4 to indices of production Q, labor L, and capital K in the U.S. manufacturing sector for the period from 1899 to 1922. Q was an index of physical volume of manufacturing; L was an index of the average number of employed wage earners only (that is, salaried employees, officials, and working proprietors were excluded); and K was an index of the value of plants, buildings, tools, and machinery reduced to dollars of constant purchasing power. With the sum of the exponents restricted to one (constant returns to scale), the following function was obtained:

$$Q = 1.01 \ L^{.75}K^{.25} \tag{13.8}$$

In later studies Cobb-Douglas made several modifications which altered their results somewhat. These modifications included revisions in the output and labor indices, removing the secular trend from each index by expressing each yearly index value as a percentage of its overall trend value, and dropping the assumption of constant returns to scale. With these modifications the estimated production function for the manufacturing sector was

$$Q = .84 \ L^{.63} \ K^{.30} \tag{13.9}$$

These results are fairly typical of other time-series and cross-sectional production functions developed from data collected on the U.S. manufacturing sector in the early twentieth century. A one percent increase in labor inputs results in about a $\frac{2}{3}$-percent increase in output, and a one percent increase in capital input results in approximately a $\frac{1}{3}$-percent increase in output. Also, as in this function, the sum of the exponents (that is, elasticities) of the labor and capital variables is typically slightly less than 1. Although this would seem to indicate the presence of decreasing returns to scale in the broadly defined manufacturing sector, statistically speaking the sum of the exponents was not significantly different from 1.0.

Cross-Sectional Analysis

In a study of more recent vintage, Moroney used cross-sectional data to estimate Cobb-Douglas production functions for eighteen U.S. manufacturing industries.[14] Using aggregate data on plants located within each state, the following three-variable model was fitted:

$$Q = \alpha L_p^{\beta_1}L_n^{\beta_2}K^{\beta_3} \tag{13.10}$$

where Q is the value added by the production plants, L_p is production worker work-hours, L_n is nonproduction work-years, and K is gross book values of depreciable and depletable assets.[15] The results for several of the industries are

---

[14] John R. Moroney, "Cobb-Douglas Production Functions and Returns to Scale in U.S. Manufacturing Industry," *Western Economic Journal* 6, no. 1 (December 1967), pp. 34–51.

[15] "Book values" of assets are the *historic* values of these assets as they appear on the balance sheet of the firm. Book values may differ significantly from current replacement values and hence may overstate or understate the actual amount of capital employed in the firm.

Industry	Capital Elasticity* β_1	Production Worker Elasticity β_2	Nonproduction Worker Elasticity β_3	Sum of Elasticities $\beta_1 + \beta_2 + \beta_3$
Food and	.555	.439	.076	1.070**
Beverages	(.121)	(.128)	(.037)	(.021)
Textiles	.121	.549	.335	1.004
	(.173)	(.216)	(.086)	(.024)
Furniture	.205	.802	.103	1.109**
	(.153)	(.186)	(.079)	(.051)
Petroleum	.308	.546	.093	.947
	(.112)	(.222)	(.168)	(.045)
Stone, Clay, etc.	.632	.032	.366	1.029
	(.105)	(.224)	(.201)	(.045)
Primary Metals	.371	.077	.509	.958
	(.103)	(.188)	(.164)	(.035)

Table 13.1
Production Elasticities for Several Industries

*Number in parentheses below each elasticity coefficient is the standard error.
**Significantly greater than 1.0 at the .05 level (one-tail).
Source: John R. Moroney, "Cobb-Douglas Production Functions and Returns to Scale in U.S. Manufacturing Industry," *Western Economic Journal* 6, no. 1 (December 1967), Table 1, p. 46.

shown in Table 13.1. The sum of the exponents ($\beta_1 + \beta_2 + \beta_3$), i.e., elasticities, ranged from a low of .947 for petroleum to a high of 1.109 for furniture. In thirteen of the eighteen industries studied, the statistical tests showed that the sum of the exponents was not significantly different from 1.0. This evidence supports the hypothesis that most manufacturing industries exhibit constant returns to scale.

Estimation of Cost Functions

Recall from Chapter 12 that a *cost function* is a schedule, graph, or mathematical relationship showing the total, average, or marginal cost of producing various quantities of output.[16] In that chapter two different cost functions were defined and derived—the *short-run* and the *long-run* cost functions. The short-run cost function is relevant to decisions in which one or more of the inputs to the production process are fixed or incapable of being altered. To make optimal pricing and production decisions, the firm must have a knowledge of the shape and characteristics of its short-run cost function. The long-run cost function is associated with the longer-term planning period in which all the inputs to the production process are variable and no restrictions are placed on the amount of an input that can be employed in the production process. To make optimal investment decisions in new production facilities, the firm must have a knowledge of the behavior of its long-run cost function.

As was shown in Chapter 12, the behavior of production input-output relationships and the factor markets yields a hypothesis about the shape of the *theoretical* short-run and long-run cost functions of a typical production process,

[16] Once any *one* of the total, average, or marginal cost functions is obtained, the other two can be derived by arithmetic or algebraic methods.

plant, or firm. Determination of the shape of the *actual* cost functions for a specific individual production process, plant, or firm requires the collection and analysis of cost-output data. Since different approaches are used to empirically estimate short-run and long-run cost functions, it is useful to consider the two cases separately. After completing our discussion of the estimation of short-run cost functions, we return to a discussion of the estimation of long-run cost functions.

Short-Run Cost Functions

This section discusses the statistical estimation of short-run cost functions, including the problems inherent in such estimation techniques, hypothesized cost-output relationships, and some examples of short-run cost functions.

Problems in Estimating Short-Run Cost Functions [17]

The cost function of economic theory is a *static* relationship which shows, at a given point in time, the costs that will be incurred for various output levels. The actual cost function of a firm is a *dynamic* relationship that is continually shifting throughout time. In seeking to measure statistically the static cost function of economic theory, one usually attempts to take observations of the dynamic actual cost function at different points in time. These observations must be taken in a way that allows one to estimate the average relationship between cost and output over a wide range of output values. Most of the problems in cost studies are associated with the methodology for obtaining these cost-output observations. These problems include the following:

■ Differences in the manner in which economists and accountants define and measure costs

■ Accounting for other variables (in addition to the output level) that influence costs

Differences in Cost Definition and Measurement.   Recall from the discussion of the meaning and measurement of cost in Chapter 12 that differences exist between the economic and accounting concepts of cost. Economic cost is represented by the value of opportunities foregone, whereas accounting cost is measured by the outlays that are incurred.

Since the shape of the short-run variable and total cost functions is similar,[18] either variable costs or total costs can be used to measure the cost function of the firm. One procedure is to attempt to measure variable costs by means of direct accounting costs. "Direct" costs include materials, supplies, and direct

---

[17] Much of this discussion is based on the work of Joel Dean, who pioneered the development of statistical cost functions. See Joel Dean, *Managerial Economics* (Englewood Cliffs, N.J.: Prentice-Hall, 1951), chap. 5, for a more expanded treatment of the problems associated with the measurement of cost functions.

[18] See Figure 12.3 in the preceding chapter.

labor costs, but exclude overhead costs. This approach may give unsatisfactory results if a significant portion of overhead costs (for example, staff labor costs in the head office) does indeed vary with the output level. Another procedure is to use total accounting costs in estimating the short-run variable costs of the firm. Although accounting costs may overstate or understate true economic short-run variable costs, one can argue that the two costs should behave similarly over a wide range of output levels. Given that accounting and variable costs do correlate closely over different output levels, then the cost function derived from accounting data will provide an accurate determination of the shape of the short-run cost function for the firm. Particularly troublesome accounting cost categories that must be given careful attention in a cost study are depreciation and, in the case of the multiproduct firm, overhead and joint costs.

Economic depreciation measures the decline in value of a capital asset. Conceptually, depreciation can be divided into two components—the decline in value associated with the pasage of *time* and the decline in value associated with *use*. *Time* depreciation represents the physical deterioration of an asset over time (that is not due to use) or technical progress that renders products and production processes obsolete. Time depreciation is completely independent of rate of output at which the asset (for example, plant and equipment) is operated. *Use* depreciation is the decline in value that occurs as a result of the operation of the asset in producing output. Use depreciation, in contrast with time depreciation, does vary in some manner with the rate of output.

Only use depreciation is relevant in determining the shape of the cost-output relationship. However, accounting data on depreciation are not broken down into the two components, and it is therefore usually impossible to measure use depreciation costs separately. Also, the depreciation of the value of an asset over its life cycle is usually determined by tax regulations rather than by economic criteria. As a result, the depreciation costs allocated to any period may misstate true economic depreciation costs. Finally, capital asset values (and their associated depreciation costs) are stated in terms of historical costs rather than in terms of replacement costs. In periods of rapidly increasing price levels, this will tend to understate true economic depreciation costs. These limitations need to be kept in mind when interpreting the cost-output relationship.

In the multiproduct firm, it is common practice to allocate overhead and joint costs among the various product lines and individual products. Because of the arbitrary nature of these accounting allocations, further processing of the accounting cost data may be required before the data can be used in the cost-output equation.

Accounting for Other Variables. Like most other dependent variables in economics, cost is a function of more than just one independent variable. In addition to being a function of the output level of the firm, cost is a function of such factors as output mix, the size of manufacturing lots, employee absenteeism and turnover, production methods, factor prices, and managerial efficiency. Letting C represent cost, Q represent output, and $X_1, X_2, \ldots, X_n$ represent these other factors, the cost function can be written as

$$C = f(Q, X_1, X_2, \ldots, X_n) \qquad [13.11]$$

In estimating the cost-output relationship, the objective is to isolate the influence of these other factors in the relationship. A number of methods can be used in achieving this objective:

■ Selection of an appropriate time period for analysis in which the other independent variables remain constant

■ Altering the cost-output data to remove the effects of these other variables

■ Using multiple regression analysis to hold constant the effects of these other variables

Each of these methods is examined below in more detail.

Selection of an Appropriate Time Period for Analysis. The cost-output observations should be collected during a period in which the variation in the other influencing variables is as small as possible. The data should be collected during a period in which no major changes in the product, plant, equipment, or work methods took place. Likewise, managerial methods and policies should remain constant during the collection period; for example, no major cost-cutting programs should have been instituted during the period.

Once the time period for analysis has been selected, it must be divided into a series of observation periods for collection of cost-output data. The length of an observation period can, in theory, vary from a week or less to a year or more. Several factors have to be *balanced* in choosing the length of the observation period. Use of a short observation period will ensure that the output rate within the period will be approximately constant throughout the period and that the effects (on costs) of fluctuations in the output rate will be captured in the data. Also, the use of a short observation period will permit a large number of cost-output observations to be collected. A large number of observations will improve the reliability of the statistical results. The use of a long observation period will minimize any errors and discrepancies that occur in allocating costs to the various time periods and matching output with its associated costs. It is impossible to generalize about the ideal length of the observation period since it will vary in different situations. The ideal length will depend in part on the detail and frequency of accounting records that are maintained by the firm and that are available to the investigator.

Altering the Cost-Output Data. The effects of some of the other influencing variables can be removed from the cost-output data through various rectification procedures.

One rectification procedure involves the careful definition and measurement of the output variable. In defining the theoretical cost function, output is assumed to consist of a single homogeneous product. Most plants, however, produce a variety of products if one takes into account differences in sizes, style, and quality. The effects of variations in the product mix from period to period can be reduced by constructing an output variable that is a weighted combination of the different products. Determining the weights to assign to each of the products can sometimes be difficult, particularly when the various products are significantly heterogeneous.

Another somewhat standard adjustment procedure, which can be used whenever wage rates or raw material prices change significantly over the period of analysis, is the deflation of cost data to reflect these changes in factor prices. Provided suitable price indices are available or can be constructed, costs incurred at different points in time can be restated as dollars of equivalent purchasing power. It is preferable to use separate indices to deflate each of the various cost categories (for example, wages, raw materials, and utilities) rather than using a single index to deflate total costs. Two assumptions are implicit in this approach: No substitution takes place between the inputs as prices change and changes in the output level have no influence on the prices of the inputs.

Adjustments are sometimes required to match costs with output if a time lag exists from the time a cost is incurred to the time it is reported. Maintenance costs is an example. Maintenance to equipment during peak periods of production can sometimes be postponed until subsequent periods of normal or below-normal operation. As a result, the higher costs of maintenance, which are incurred during periods of peak output due to more wear and tear on equipment, will not be recorded until later periods. A procedure for reallocating costs among different reporting periods is required in these situations.

Using Multiple Regression Analysis. If the effects of some of the other variables that influence costs cannot be removed by either of the preceding methods, a third possible method is to hold constant the effect of these variables using multiple regression techniques. One simple procedure is to use additional explanatory (independent) variables in the statistical cost equation to separate the effects of these other factors from the effect of output on costs.[19] For example, suppose a firm believes that, all other influencing factors remaining constant, costs should decline gradually over time as a result of better production methods and increased managerial efficiency. One way to incorporate this effect into the cost equation would be to include time t as an additional explanatory variable:

$$C = f(Q, t)$$

Having concluded the discussion of some of the problems associated with measuring short--run cost functions, now consider some of the various cost functions that have been hypothesized to describe the behavior of the cost-output relationship.

Hypothesized Short-Run Cost-Output Relationships

Most empirical cost studies attempt to use some form of a polynomial function—either linear, quadratic, or cubic—to represent the relationship between total costs (or variable costs) and output. Use of a polynomial function

---

[19] Other more advanced econometric procedures, which are beyond the scope of this text, have been used in dealing with the methodological problems encountered in cost studies. A number of the articles cited in the Selected References section at the end of this chapter contain discussions of these more advanced statistical techniques.

allows one to test statistically for effects of including higher powers of the output variable (Q^2 or Q^3) in the equation.[20] It is also possible to use other functional relationships (for example, exponential) to represent nonlinear cost-output behavior.

The total cost function, as hypothesized in economic theory, is an S-shaped curve that can be represented by a cubic relationship:

$$TC = a + bQ + cQ^2 + dQ^3 \qquad [13.12]$$

The familiar U-shaped marginal and average cost functions can then be derived from this relationship. The associated marginal cost function is

$$MC = \frac{d(TC)}{dQ} = b + 2cQ + 3dQ^2 \qquad [13.13]$$

and the average total cost function is

$$ATC = \frac{TC}{Q} = \frac{a}{Q} + b + cQ + dQ^2 \qquad [13.14]$$

The cubic total cost function and associated marginal and average total cost functions are shown in Figure 13.3(a).

A second hypothesis to be investigated is that total costs increase at an increasing rate throughout the typical operating range of output levels. Such a

Figure 13.3
Hypothesized Cost-Output Relationships

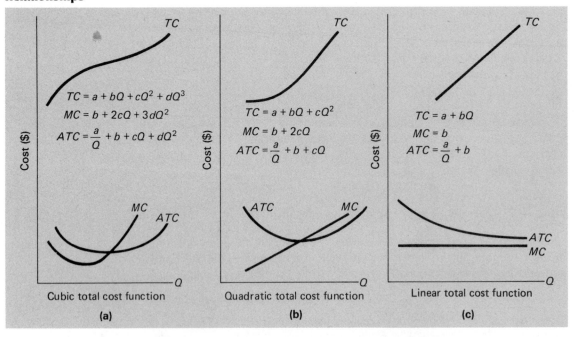

Cubic total cost function
(a)

$TC = a + bQ + cQ^2 + dQ^3$
$MC = b + 2cQ + 3dQ^2$
$ATC = \frac{a}{Q} + b + cQ + dQ^2$

Quadratic total cost function
(b)

$TC = a + bQ + cQ^2$
$MC = b + 2cQ$
$ATC = \frac{a}{Q} + b + cQ$

Linear total cost function
(c)

$TC = a + bQ$
$MC = b$
$ATC = \frac{a}{Q} + b$

---

[20] Polynomial functions are easy to fit using standard least-squares techniques. These techniques are described in Chapter 6.

relationship can be represented with a quadratic total cost function:

$$TC = a + bQ + cQ^2 \qquad [13.15]$$

Under this hypothesis, the associated marginal and average cost functions are:

$$MC = \frac{d(TC)}{dQ} = b + 2cQ \qquad [13.16]$$

$$ATC = \frac{TC}{Q} = \frac{a}{Q} + b + cQ \qquad [13.17]$$

As can be seen from Equation 13.16, this hypothesis implies that marginal costs increase linearly as the output level is increased. This second hypothesis generates the cost functions shown in Figure 13.3(b).

A final hypothesis to be considered is that total costs increase linearly with increases in the output level. Such a relationship is represented by a linear total cost function illustrated in Figure 13.3(c).

$$TC = a + bQ \qquad [13.18]$$

From this relationship, we can derive the marginal and average total cost functions:

$$MC = \frac{d(TC)}{dQ} = b \qquad [13.19]$$

$$ATC = \frac{TC}{Q} = \frac{a}{Q} + b \qquad [13.20]$$

A linear total cost function produces some interesting economic implications. First, from Equation 13.19, note that a *constant* marginal cost function is implied by the hypothesized total cost relationship. Second, Equation 13.20 indicates that average total costs are continually decreasing as output increases. Both of these implications are contrary to the law of diminishing marginal returns. Clearly, with one or more fixed inputs, short-run marginal costs will eventually begin increasing.

These implications point out an important limitation of *all* statistically derived cost-output equations, namely, that the relationship embodied in the equation may be valid only over a limited intermediate range of output values. Typically, the cost-output observations from which the cost function is statistically estimated are clustered in the middle range of output levels. Consequently, drawing conclusions based on this function about the behavior of costs at extremely high or low levels of output can be hazardous.

Examples of Statistically Estimated Short-Run Cost Functions

Short-run cost functions have been developed statistically for firms in a large number of different industries—for example, furniture, railways, gas, coal, electricity, hosiery, steel, and cement.[21] Though this discussion will not attempt

---

[21] See Walters, "Production and Cost Functions," for a summary of these studies.

to survey the results of these investigations, it may be useful to illustrate the methodology employed and the results obtained in a couple of these studies.

Multiple-Product Food Processing. In a study of a British food processing firm, Johnston constructed individual cost functions for fourteen different products and an overall cost function for the firm.[22] Weekly data for the period from September 1950 to June 1951 were obtained on the physical production of each type of product and total direct costs of each product (subdivided into the four categories of materials, labor, packing, and freight). Indirect costs (such as salaries, indirect labor, factory charges, and laboratory expenses) remained fairly constant over the time period studied and were excluded from the analysis. A factor price index for each category of direct costs for each product was constructed and used to deflate all four sets of costs, yielding a weekly total deflated direct cost for each product. For the individual products, output was measured by physical production (quantity). For the firm as a whole, an index of aggregate output was constructed by weighting the quantities of each product by its respective selling price and summing over all products produced each period.

For each of the fourteen different products and for the overall firm, the linear regression model gave an excellent fit between direct cost and output. (In a few of the regressions, autocorrelation was found to be present, but it was removed through the use of various transformations.) Therefore, Johnston concluded that total direct costs were a linear function of output and marginal costs were constant over the observed ranges of output.

Electricity Generation. A study of the costs of electric power generation in Great Britain by Johnston developed short-run cost functions for a sample of seventeen different firms from annual cost-output data on each firm for the period 1928–1947.[23] To satisfy the basic conditions underlying the short-run cost function, only those firms whose capital equipment remained constant in size over the period were included in the sample. The output variable was measured in kilowatt-hours. The cost variable was defined as the "working costs of generation" and included (1) fuel, (2) salaries and wages, and (3) repairs and maintenance, oil, water, and stores. This definition of cost does not correspond exactly with either variable costs or total costs of economic theory. It includes some fixed costs (for example, maintenance costs at zero output) and excludes some variable costs (for example, capital costs). Neither of these problems was considered serious enough to invalidate the results. Each of the three cost categories was deflated using an appropriate price index. A cubic polynomial function with an additional linear time trend variable was fitted to each of seventeen sets of cost-output observations. The results of this study did *not* lend support to the existence of a nonlinear cubic or quadratic cost function, as postulated in economic theory. The cubic term Q^3 was not statistically significant

---

[22] See Jack Johnston, *Statistical Cost Analysis* (New York: McGraw-Hill, 1960), pp. 87–97.
[23] Ibid., pp. 44–63.

in any of the regressions, and the quadratic term Q^2 was statistically significant in only five of the seventeen cost equations.

The results of the two preceding studies are similar to those found in many other cost studies—namely, that total costs tend to increase *linearly* over the ranges of output for which cost-output data are available. In other words, short-run average costs tend to decline and marginal costs tend to be constant over the "typical" or "normal" operating range of the firm. In interpreting these results, one should keep in mind that they are not necessarily inconsistent with the traditional nonlinear cost function of economic theory. If the curvature of the cost function is very slight over the typical operating output range of the firm, random variation in the cost-output data may make it impossible to detect this curvature by the usual statistical methods.

Long-Run Cost Functions

This section discusses several alternative methods for empirically estimating long-run cost-output relationships. When suitable actual cost-output data are available, *statistical methods* analogous to those used in estimating short-run cost functions can be employed in analyzing long-run cost behavior. Long-run cost functions have also been examined using *engineering cost techniques* and the *survivor technique*. These three methods are now discussed in more detail.

Statistical Estimation of Long-Run Cost Functions

In addition to many of the cost definition and measurement problems that arise in a short-run cost analysis, further difficulties of a conceptual nature are also encountered in estimating the long-run cost-output relationship by statistical methods. The long-run cost function consists of the least-cost combination of inputs for producing any level of output when *all* the inputs to the production process are variable. As is indicated in Figure 13.4, the theoretical long-run

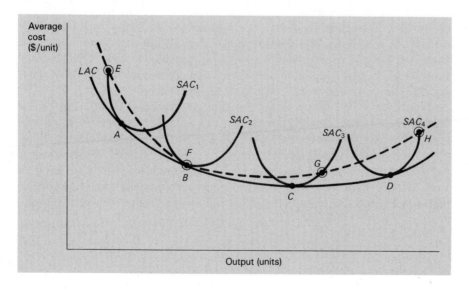

Figure 13.4
Long-Run Average Cost Function

average cost function consists of the lower boundary, or envelope, of the various short-run average cost functions.

The long-run cost function can be estimated by using either time-series cost-output data collected on a plant (or firm) whose size has been variable over time or cross-sectional cost-output data collected on a sample of various-sized plants (or firms) at a given point in time. Both approaches involve certain assumptions about technological and operating conditions that must be satisfied before the results give valid estimates of the long-run cost function.

With time-series cost-output data, one encounters the usual problems of holding constant or accounting for various factors (other than output) that affect costs. Estimating the long-run cost function from time-series data requires that observations be taken over a fairly long period of time, usually a number of years, to allow for sufficient variation in plant size. Over a long period of time, however, changes in the product and production technology are likely to occur. Such changes cause the long-run cost curve to shift over time. Without suitable methods for holding constant the effects of changes in products and technology, the cost-output data will be measuring points on *different* long-run cost functions rather than on the *same* function. Also, using time-series data requires that costs be deflated to reflect changes in prices over long periods of time.

For these reasons, the use of cross-sectional data tends to be more prevalent in estimating long-run cost functions. The use of cross-sectional data in the estimation process assumes that each firm in the sample, with its given fixed plant and equipment inputs, is operating at a point along the true long-run cost function. In effect, one is assuming that the four firms having the four short-run average cost functions labeled SAC_1, SAC_2, SAC_3, and SAC_4 in Figure 13.4 are operating at points A, B, C, and D, respectively. If, in fact, the four firms are operating at points such as E, F, G, and H, respectively, then substantial distortion of the shape of the function may occur in the estimation process. Other potential problems encountered when using cross-sectional data include merging data from firms that use different accounting techniques and deflating data for regional cost differences.

In the study of electrical power generation by British firms, which was discussed in the previous section, Johnston developed long-run cost functions using both time-series and cross-sectional data. In the time-series analysis, a cubic cost function with a linear trend variable was fitted to each of twenty-three firms whose capital equipment had *not* remained constant over the 1928–1947 period. The cubic term was not statistically significant.

In a study of U.S. electric utility companies, Christensen and Greene used a logarithmic model to test for the presence of economies and diseconomies of scale.[24] The average cost curve (using 1970 data on 114 firms) is shown in Figure 13.5. The bar below the graph indicates the number of firms in each interval. Below 19.8 billion kwh (left arrow in graph), significant economies of scale were found to exist. The 97 firms in this range accounted for almost 49 percent of the total output. Between 19.8 and 67.1 billion kwh (right arrow in the graph),

---

[24] L. R. Christensen and W. H. Greene, "Economies of Scale in U.S. Electric Power Generation," *Journal of Political Economy* 84, no. 4 (August 1976).

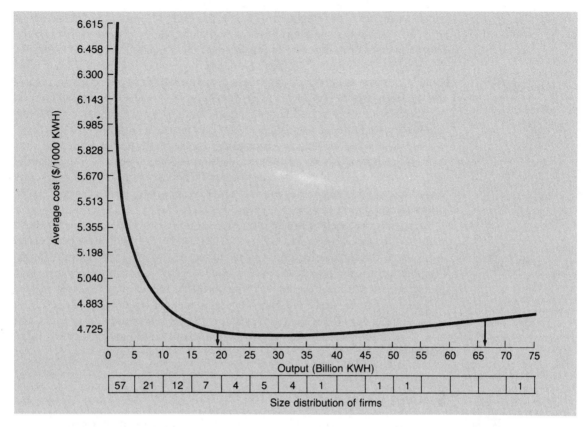

Figure 13.5
Average Cost Function for U.S. Electric Utility Firms

no significant economies of scale were present. The 16 firms in this range accounted for almost 45 percent of the total output. Above 67.1 billion kwh, diseconomies of scale (1 firm and about 7 percent of total output) were found.

These results are typical of most other statistical studies of cost-output behavior. Most studies have found an L-shaped long-run average cost curve—the average cost curve falls steeply at low levels of output and then tends to flatten out and becomes horizontal with further increases in the level of output. Significant diseconomies of scale are seldom observed in these statistical studies of long-run cost behavior.

Engineering Cost Techniques

Engineering techniques represent an alternative approach to statistical methods (least-squares) in estimating long-run cost functions. Using knowledge of production facilities and technology (such as machine speeds, worker productivity, and physical input-output transformation relationships), the engineering approach attempts to determine the most efficient (lowest average cost) combination of labor, capital equipment, and raw materials required to produce various levels of output. Engineering methods have a number of advantages over statistical methods in examining economies of scale. First, it is generally much easier with the engineering approach to hold constant such factors as input prices, product mix, and product efficiency, allowing one to isolate the effects on costs of changes in output. Second, the long-run function obtained by the engineering method is based on the production technology currently available, whereas the function obtained by the statistical approach mixes old and current production technology. Finally, use of the engineering method avoids some of the accounting cost-allocation and resource-valuation problems encountered when using statistical methods to estimate long-run cost functions.

The primary disadvantage of engineering methods is that they deal only with the technical aspects of the production process or plant. The managerial and entrepreneurial aspects, such as recruiting and training workers, marketing the product, financing the operation, and administering the organization, are not included in the analysis.

In a study designed to isolate the various sources of scale economies within a plant, Haldi and Whitcomb collected data on the cost of individual units of equipment, the initial investment in plant and equipment, and operating costs (namely, labor, raw materials, and utilities).[25] They noted that "in many basic industries such as petroleum refining, primary metals, and electric power, economies of scale are found up to very large plant sizes (often the largest built or contemplated). These economies occur mostly in the initial investment cost and in operating labor cost, with no significant economies observed in raw material cost."[26]

Survivor Technique

The "survivor technique" was first put forth by Stigler as an alternative method of determining the optimum size (or range of sizes) of firms within an industry.[27] This method involves classifying the firms in an industry by size and calculating the share of industry output coming from each size class over time. If the share of industry output of a given class decreases over time, then this size class is presumed to be relatively inefficient and to have higher average costs. Conversely, an increasing share of industry output over time indicates that the size class is relatively efficient and has lower average costs.

The rationale for this approach is that competition will tend to eliminate those firms whose size is relatively inefficient, leaving only those size firms with lower average costs to survive over time. According to Stigler, "An efficient size

---

[25] J. Haldi and D. Whitcomb, "Economies of Scale in Industrial Plants," *Journal of Political Economy* 75, no. 1 (August 1967), pp. 373–385.

[26] Ibid., p. 373.

[27] G. J. Stigler, "The Economies of Scale," *Journal of Law and Economics* 1, no. 1 (October 1958), pp. 54–81. [Reprinted as chapter 7 in G. Stigler, *The Organization of Industry* (Homewood, Ill.: Richard D. Irwin, 1968).] For other examples of the use of the survivor technique, see also William G. Shepherd, "What Does the Survivor Technique Show About Economies of Scale?" *Southern Economic Journal* (July 1967), pp. 113–122, and H. E. Ted Frech and Paul B. Ginsburg, "Optimal Scale in Medical Practice: A Survivor Analysis," *Journal of Business* (January 1974), pp. 23–26.

Company Size (percentage of total industry capacity)	Percentage of Industry Capacity			Number of Companies		
	1930	1938	1951	1930	1938	1951
Under $\frac{1}{2}$	7.16	6.11	4.65	39	29	22
$\frac{1}{2}$ to 1	5.94	5.08	5.37	9	7	7
1 to $2\frac{1}{2}$	13.17	8.30	9.07	9	6	6
$2\frac{1}{2}$ to 5	10.64	16.59	22.21	3	4	5
5 to 10	11.18	14.03	8.12	2	2	1
10 to 25	13.24	13.99	16.10	1	1	1
25 and over	38.67	35.91	34.50	1	1	1

Table 13.2
Distribution of Steel Ingot Capacity by Relative Size of Company

Source: J. S. McGee, "Efficiency and Economies of Size," in *Industrial Concentration: The New Learning*, ed. H. Goldsmid, H. Mann, and J. Weston (Boston: Little, Brown, 1974), p 76. [Adapted from George J. Stigler, "The Economies of Scale," *Journal of Law and Economics* (October 1958). Reprinted by permission.]

of firm ... is one that meets any and all problems the entrepreneur actually faces: strained labor relations, rapid innovation, government regulation, unstable foreign markets, and what not."[28] The survivor technique has some appealing characteristics. The technique is more direct and simpler to apply than are alternative techniques for examining scale economies. It avoids the accounting cost-allocation and resource-valuation problems associated with statistical methods and the hypothetical aspects of engineering cost approaches.

Despite its appeal, the survivor technique does have serious limitations. First, since the technique does not use actual cost data in the analysis, there is no way to assess the *magnitude* of the cost differentials between firms of varying size and efficiency. Also, because of legal factors, the long-run cost curve derived by this technique may be distorted and may not measure the cost curve postulated in economic theory. As McGee points out, "In some instances, law favors larger firms, especially in regulated industries. On the other hand, antitrust and other laws discourage larger firms even though 'economies,' as normally construed, persist beyond present firm sizes."[29]

The survivor technique has been used to examine the long-run cost functions in a number of different industries. One such study is Stigler's analysis of steel ingot production by open-hearth or Bessemer processes.[30] Based on the data in Table 13.2, Stigler developed the U-shaped long-run average cost function for steel ingot production shown in Figure 13.6. Because of the declining percentages, Stigler concluded that both low levels of output (less than 2.5 percent of capacity) and extremely high levels of output (25 percent or more) were relatively inefficient size classes. The intermediate size classes (from 2.5 to 25 percent of capacity) represented the range of optimum size since these size classes grew or held their shares of capacity. Stigler also applied

---

[28] Stigler, "The Economies of Scale," p. 73.

[29] J. S. McGee, "Efficiency and Economies of Size," in *Industrial Concentration: The New Learning*, ed. H. Goldsmid, H. Mann, and J. Weston (Boston: Little, Brown, 1974), pp. 82–83.

[30] Ibid., pp. 75–78.

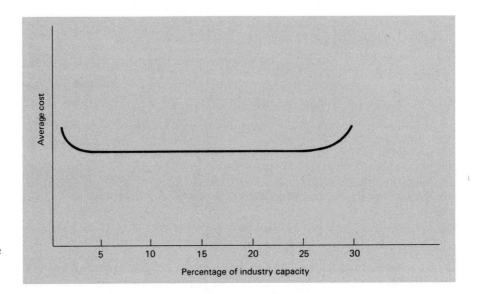

Figure 13.6
**Long-Run Average
Costs of Steel
Ingot Production**

the survivor technique to the automobile industry and found an L-shaped average cost curve (see Figure 13.3c), indicating that there was no evidence of diseconomies of scale at large levels of output.

Summary

- The Cobb-Douglas production function, which is used extensively in empirical studies, is a power (multiplicative) function in which output is a (nonlinear) monotonically increasing function of each of the inputs.

- The Cobb-Douglas production function has various properties that allow one to draw conclusions, based on parameter estimates, about economies of scale and the increase in output that will result from a given increase in any one (or more) of the inputs to the production process.

- Based on empirical production function studies, no definitive conclusions can be drawn concerning the existence of either increasing or decreasing returns to scale in the U.S. manufacturing sector.

- In estimating the behavior of short-run and long-run cost functions for firms, the primary methodological problems are (1) differences in the manner in which economists and accountants define and measure costs, and (2) accounting for other variables (in addition to the output level) that influence costs.

- Many statistical studies of *short-run* cost-output relationships suggest that total costs increase linearly with output, implying constant marginal costs over the observed ranges of output. Although the evidence is not conclusive, it tends to refute the existence of U-shaped average and marginal cost functions as postulated in economic theory.

- Many statistical studies of *long-run* cost-output relationships indicate that long-run cost functions are L-shaped. Economies of scale (declining average costs) occur at low levels of output. Thereafter, long-run average costs remain relatively constant over large ranges of output.

- *Engineering cost techniques* are an alternative approach to statistical methods in estimating long-run cost functions. With this approach, knowledge of production facilities and technology is used to determine the most efficient (lowest cost) combination of labor, capital equipment, and raw materials required to produce various levels of output.

- The *survivor technique* is a method of determining the optimum size of firms within an industry by classifying them by size and then calculating the share of industry output coming from each size class over time. Size classes whose share of industry output is increasing over time are considered to be more efficient and to have lower average costs.

Selected References

Benston, George J. "Economies of Scale in Financial Institutions," *Journal of Money, Credit and Banking* (May 1972).

Benston, George J., Gerald A. Hanweck, and David B. Humphrey, "Scale Economies in Banking: A Restructuring and Reassessment." *Journal of Money, Credit, and Banking* 14, no. 4 (November 1982, Part I), pp. 435–456.

Blair, Roger D., Jerry R. Jackson, and Ronald J. Vogel, "Economies of Scale in the Administration of Health Insurance." *Review of Economics and Statistics* 57, no. 2 (May 1975), pp. 185–189.

Caves, Douglas W., Laurits R. Christensen, and Joseph A. Swanson. "Productivity Growth, Scale Economies, and Capacity Utilization in U.S. Railroads, 1955–75, *American Economic Review* (December 1981), pp. 994–1002.

Christensen, L. R., and W. H. Greene. "Economies of Scale in U.S. Power Generation," *Journal of Political Economy* 84, no. 4 (August 1976).

Dean, Joel. *Statistical Cost Functions of a History Mill.* Chicago: University of Chicago Press 1941.

Douglas, Paul. "The Cobb-Douglas Production Once Again: Its History, Its Testing, and Some New Empirical Values." *Journal of Political Economy* (October 1976), pp. 903–915.

Frech, H. E. Ted, and Paul B. Ginsburg. "Optimal Scale in Medical Practice: A Survivor Analysis." *Journal of Business* (January 1974), pp. 23–36.

Gold, Bela. "Changing Perspectives on Size, Scale, and Returns: An Interpretive Survey." *Journal of Economic Literature* 19 (March 1981).

Houston, D. B., and R. M. Simon, "Economies of Scale in Financial Institutions: A Study of Life Insurance." *Econometrica* 38 (November 1970), pp. 856–864.

Huettner, D. A., and J. H. Landon. "Electric Utilities: Scale Economies and Diseconomies." *Southern Economic Journal* (April 1978).

Johnston, Jack. *Statistical Cost Analysis.* New York: McGraw-Hill, 1960.

Longbrake, William A. "Statistical Cost Analysis." *Financial Management* (Spring 1973)

Moroney, John R. "Cobb-Douglas Production Functions and Returns to Scale in U.S. Manufacturing Industry." *Western Economic Journal* 6, no. 1 (December 1967), pp. 34–51.

Riew, John. "Economies of Scale in High School Operation." *Review of Economics and Statistics* 48, no. 3 (August 1966), pp. 280–287.

Scherer, F. M. "Economies of Scale and Industrial Concentration." In *Industrial Concentration: The New Learning*, ed. H. Goldsmid, H. Mann, and J. Weston. Boston: Little, Brown, 1974.

Stigler, G. J. "The Economies of Scale," *Journal of Law and Economics* 1, no. 1 (October 1958), pp. 54–71. (Reprinted as chapter 7 in Stigler, G. *The Organization of Industry* Homewood, Ill.: Richard D. Irwin, 1968.)

Walters, A. A. "Production and Cost Functions: An Econometric Survey." *Econometrica* 31, no. 1–2 (January–April 1963).

Williams, Martin. "Firm Size and Operating Costs in Urban Bus Transportation." *Journal of Industrial Economics* 28, no. 2 (December 1979).

Zack, Thomas A., Cliff J. Huang, and John J. Siegfried. "Production Efficiency: The Case of Professional Basketball." *Journal of Business* 52, no. 3 (July 1979), pp. 379–392.

Zech, Charles E. "An Empirical Estimation of a Production Function: The Case of Major League Baseball." *American Economist* 25, no. 2 (Fall 1981), pp. 19–23.

Discussion Questions

1. What measurement and interpretation problems are encountered in developing production functions (a) for the individual firm and (b) for aggregates of firms such as an industry, sector of the economy, or entire economy?

2. Define *technical progress* and discuss how it can be incorporated into a production function.

3. For several decades the Cobb-Douglas power function has been the principal model used in empirical production studies. What economic and mathematical properties make it such a desirable model for use in representing the production transformation process?

4. Explain how the parameters $(\alpha, \beta_1, \beta_2)$ of the *nonlinear* Cobb-Douglas production function (Equation 13.5) can be estimated using multiple regression techniques that require a *linear* relationship between the dependent and independent variables.

5. What measurement and interpretation problems are encounted in developing short-run and long-run cost functions? What are some of the techniques used in overcoming these problems?

6. What are the advantages and disadvantages of the engineering cost technique in developing long-run cost functions?

7. Describe the survivor technique. What are its advantages and disadvantages in comparison with other techniques for estimating cost-output behavior?

8. Suppose one estimates, from cost-output data using multiple regression techniques, the following total cost function:

$$TC = \$140,000 + \$250Q + \$1.50Q^2$$

Explain why one cannot necessarily infer that fixed costs are equal to $140,000.

Problems

1. Based on the production function parameter estimates reported in Table 13.1:
   a. Which industry (or industries) appears to exhibit decreasing returns to scale (ignore the issue of statistical significance)?
   b. Which industry comes closest to exhibiting constant returns to scale?
   c. In which industry will a given percentage increase in capital result in the largest percentage increase in output?
   d. In what industry will a given percentage increase in production workers result in the largest percentage increase in output?

2. Given the following production function:

$$Q = 1.40L^{.70}K^{.35}$$

a. Determine the elasticity of production with respect to:
   (i) Labor (L)
   (ii) Capital (K)
b. Give an economic interpretation of each value determined in part (a).

3. Consider the following Cobb-Douglas production function for the bus transportation system in a particular city:

$$Q = \alpha L^{\beta_1} F^{\beta_2} B^{\beta_3}$$

where

L = labor input in man-hours

F = fuel input in gallons

B = capital input in number of buses

Q = output measured in millions of bus miles

Suppose that the parameters (α, β_1, β_2, and β_3) of this model were estimated using annual data for the past twenty-five years. The following results were obtained:

$$\alpha = .0012 \qquad \beta_1 = .45 \qquad \beta_2 = .20 \qquad \beta_3 = .30$$

a. Determine the (i) labor, (ii) fuel, and (iii) capital-input production elasticities.
b. Suppose that labor input (work-hours) is increased by 2 percent next year (with the other inputs held constant). Determine the approximate percentage change in output.
c. Suppose that capital input (number of buses) is decreased by 3 percent next year (that is, certain older buses are taken out of service). Assuming that the other inputs are held constant, determine the approximate percentage change in output.
d. What type of returns to scale appears to characterize this bus transportation system (ignore the issue of statistical significance)?
e. Discuss some of the methodological and measurement problems one might encounter in using time-series data to estimate the parameters of this model.

4. The following cost-output data were obtained as a part of a study of the economies of scale in operating a public high school in Wisconsin:[31]

Pupils in Average Daily Attendance (A)	Midpoint of Values in Column A (B)	Operating Expenditure per Pupil (C)	Number of Schools in Sample (D)
143–200	171	$531.9	6
201–300	250	480.8	12
301–400	350	446.3	19
401–500	450	426.9	17
501–600	550	442.6	14
601–700	650	413.1	13
701–900	800	374.3	9
901–1,100	1,000	433.2	6
1,101–1,600	1,350	407.3	6
1,601–2,400	2,000	405.6	7

[31] John Riew, "Economics of Scale in High School Operation," *Review of Economics and Statistics* 48 no. 3 (August 1966), pp. 280–287.

a. Plot the data in columns B and C in an output (enrollment)-cost graph and sketch a smooth curve that would appear to give a good fit to the data.

b. Based on the scatter diagram in part (a), what kind of mathematical relationship would appear to exist between enrollment and operating expenditures per pupil? In other words, do operating expenditures per pupil appear (i) to be constant (and independent of enrollment), (ii) follow a linear relationship as enrollment increases, or (iii) follow some sort of nonlinear U-shape (possibly quadratic) relationship as enrollment increases?

5. A study of the economies of scale in operating a public high school in Wisconsin (see previous problem) developed the following model:

$$C = f(Q, X_1, X_2, X_3, X_4, X_5)$$

where

C = operating expenditures per pupil in average daily attendance (measured in dollars)

Q = enrollment (number of pupils in average daily attendance)

X_1 = average teacher's salary

X_2 = number of credit units ("courses") offered

X_3 = average number of courses taught per teacher

X_4 = change in enrollment between 1957 and 1960

X_5 = percentage of classrooms built after 1950

Variables X_1, X_2, and X_3 were measures of "educational quality," that is, teacher qualifications, breadth of curriculum, and the degree of specialization in instruction, respectively. Variable X_4 measured changes in demand for school services which could cause some lagging adjustments in cost. Variable X_5 was used to reflect any differentials in the costs of maintenance and operation due to the varying ages of school properties. Statistical data on 109 selected high schools yielded the following regression equation:

$$C = 10.31 - .402Q + .00012Q^2 + .107X_1 + .985X_2 - 15.62X_3$$
$$\quad (.063)^* \quad (.000023)^* \quad (.013)^* \quad (.640) \quad (11.95)$$
$$+ .613X_4 - .102X_5$$
$$(.189)^* \quad (.109)$$

$$r^2 = .557^*$$

Notes:

(1) The numbers in parentheses are the standard deviations of each of the respective coefficients (b's).

(2) An asterisk (*) indicates that the result is statistically significant at the .01 level.

a. What type of cost-output relationship (linear, quadratic, cubic) is suggested by these statistical results?

b. What variables (other than enrollment) would appear to be most important in explaining variations in operating expenditures per pupil?

c. Holding constant the effects of the other variables (X_1 through X_5), determine the enrollment level (Q) at which average operating expenditures per pupil are minimized. (*Hint:* Find the value of Q which minimizes the $\partial C/\partial Q$ function.)

d. Again, holding constant the effects of the other variables, use the $\partial C/\partial Q$ function to determine, for a school with 500 pupils, the reduction in per-pupil operating expenditures that will occur as the result of adding one more pupil.

e. Again, holding the other variables constant, what would be the saving in per-pupil operating expenditures of an increase in enrollment from 500 to 1,000 students?

f. Based on the results of this study, what can we conclude about the existence of economies or diseconomies in operating a public high school?

6. A study of the costs of electricity generation for a sample of fifty-six British firms in 1946–47 yielded the following long-run cost function:[32]

$$AVC = 1.24 + .0033Q + .0000029Q^2 - .000046QZ - .026Z + .00018Z^2$$

where

AVC = average variable cost (that is, working costs of generation), measured in pence per kilowatt-hour. (A pence was a British monetary unit, being equals to (at that time) two U.S. cents.)

Q = output, measured in millions of kilowatt-hours per year

Z = plant size, measured in thousands of kilowatts

a. Determine the long-run variable cost function for electricity generation.

b. Determine the long-run marginal cost function for electricity generation.

c. Holding plant size constant at 150,000 kilowatts, determine the short-run average variable cost and marginal cost functions for electricity generation.

d. For a plant size equal to 150,000 kilowatts, determine the output level that minimizes short-run average variable costs.

e. Determine the short-run average variable cost and marginal cost at the output level obtained in part (d).

7. Show that elasticity of production for capital input is constant and equal to β_2 for the Cobb-Douglas production function (Equation 13.5).

8. *Extension of the Cobb-Douglas Production Function*—The Cobb-Douglas power production function (Equation 13.5) can be shown to be a special case of a larger class of production functions having the following mathematical form:[33]

$$Q = \gamma[\partial K^{-\rho} + (1 - \partial)L^{-\rho}]^{-v/\rho}$$

where γ is an efficiency parameter which shows the output that results from given quantities of inputs; ∂ is a distribution parameter $(0 \leq \partial \leq 1)$ that indicates the division of factor income between capital and labor; ρ is a substitution parameter that is a measure of substitutability of capital for labor (or vice versa) in the production process; and v is a scale parameter $(v > 0)$ that indicates the type of returns to scale (increasing, constant, or decreasing). Show that when $v = 1$, this function exhibits constant returns to scale. (*Hint:* Increase capital K and labor L each by a factor of λ—$K^* = (\lambda)K$ and $L^* = (\lambda)L$—and show that output Q also increases by a factor of λ—$Q^* = (\lambda)(Q.)$

(*Note:* The following problem requires the use of a standard regression analysis program.) Economists at the Wilson Company are interested in developing a production function for fertilizer plants. They have collected the following data on fifteen different plants that produce fertilizer.

Case Problem
Production
Function

---

[32] Jack Johnston, *Statistical Cost Analysis* (New York: McGraw-Hill, 1960), chap. 4.

[33] K. J. Arrow II, B. Chenery, B. Minhas, and R. M. Solow, "Capital-Labor Substitution and Economic Efficiency," *Review of Economics and Statistics* 43 (1961), pp. 225–235.

Plant	Output (000 tons)	Capital ($000)	Labor (000 work-hours)
1	605.3	18,891	700.2
2	566.1	19,201	651.8
3	647.1	20,655	822.9
4	523.7	15,082	650.3
5	712.3	20,300	859.0
6	487.5	16,079	613.0
7	761.6	24,194	851.3
8	442.5	11,504	655.4
9	821.1	25,970	900.6
10	397.8	10,127	550.4
11	896.7	25,622	842.2
12	359.3	12,477	540.5
13	979.1	24,002	949.4
14	331.7	8,042	575.7
15	1064.9	23,972	925.8

Questions

1. Estimate the Cobb-Douglas production function $Q = \alpha L^{\beta_1} K^{\beta_2}$ where Q = output, L = labor input, K = capital input, and α, β_1, and β_2 are the parameters to be estimated. (*Note:* If the regression program on your computer does not have a logarithmic transformation, manually transform the preceding data into the logarithms before entering the data into the computer.)

2. Test whether the coefficients of capital and labor are statistically significant.

3. Determine the percentage of the variation in output that is "explained" by the regression equation.

4. Determine the labor and capital production elasticities and give an economic interpretation of each value.

5. Determine whether this production function exhibits increasing, decreasing, or constant returns to scale (ignore the issue of statistical significance.)

The Learning Curve APPENDIX

13A

In manufacturing multiple units of a product, the quantity of resources (inputs) required to complete each successive unit of output is often observed to decrease as the cumulative volume of output increases. This reduction in inputs, and hence associated costs, is known as the *learning curve effect*.[34] This learning phenomenon is most commonly observed in the behavior of labor inputs and costs. The number of work-hours necessary to obtain one unit of output may decline for a variety of reasons as more units of the product are produced. These factors include increased familiarization with the tasks by workers and supervisors, improvements in work methods and the flow of work, reductions in the amount of scrap and rework, and the need for fewer skilled workers as the tasks become more repetitive. Raw material costs per unit may also be subject to the learning curve effect if less scrap and waste occur as workers become more familiar with the production process. Not all inputs and associated costs are subject to the learning process however. For example, shipping costs per unit normally do not decline for successive units of output.

Learning Curve Relationship

The learning curve relationship is usually expressed as a constant percentage. This percentage represents the proportion by which the amount of an input (or cost) per unit of output is reduced each time production is doubled. For example, consider a production process in which labor input and costs follow an 80 percent learning curve. Assume that the *first* unit requires labor costs of $1,000 to produce. Based on the learning curve relationship, the *second* unit costs $1,000 × .80 = $800, the *fourth* unit costs $800 × .80 = $640, the *eighth* unit costs $640 × .80 = $512, the *sixteenth* unit costs $512 × .80 = $409.60, and so on.

This learning curve relationship is shown in Figures 13A.1 and 13A.2. When plotted on an *arithmetic scale*, as shown in Figure 13A.1, the cost-output

---

[34] Other names given to this relationship include learning-by-doing, progress curve, experience curve, and improvement curve.

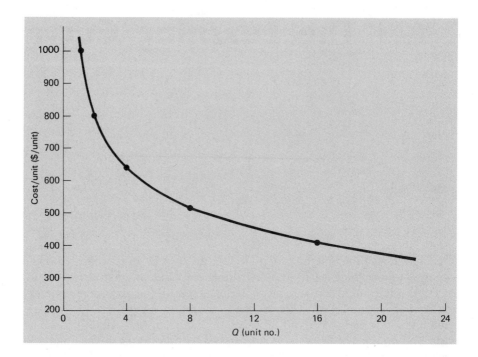

Figure 13A.1
**Learning Curve:
Arithmetic Scale**

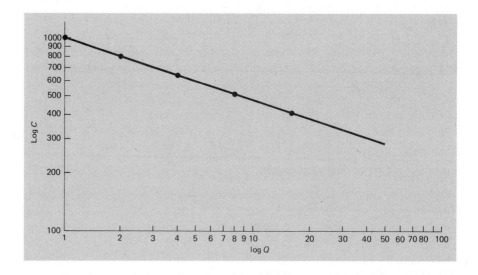

Figure 13A.2
**Learning Curve:
Logarithmic Scale**

relationship is a curvilinear function. When plotted on a *logarithmic scale*, as shown in Figure 13A.2, the cost-output relationship is a linear function.

The learning curve relationship can be expressed algebraically as follows:

$$C = aQ^b \qquad [13A.1]$$

where C is the input cost of the Qth unit of output, Q is consecutive units of output produced, a is the theoretical (or actual) input cost of the first unit of output, and b is the rate of reduction in input cost per unit of output. Since the learning curve is downward sloping, the value of b is normally negative. It should be noted that b is *not* the same as the learning curve percentage. Taking logarithms of both sides of Equation 13A.1 yields

$$\log C = \log a + b \log Q \qquad [13A.2]$$

When the learning curve is expressed in logarithmic form, b represents the slope of the function.

Estimating the Learning Curve Parameters

Application of the learning curve in forecasting costs requires that one first determine the values of the log a and b parameters in Equation 13A.2. In the absence of any historical cost-output data for the production process, one would have to make subjective estimates of these parameters based on prior experience with similar types of production operations. For a production process that has been operating for a period of time and for which historical cost-output data are available, however, statistical methods can be used to estimate the parameters. One such method is the *least-squares* technique of regression analysis.[35] In the learning curve equation (Equation 13A.2), log C is the dependent variable and log Q is the independent variable. Applying the least-squares procedure to the series of cost-output observations yields the following equations for estimating the learning curve parameters:

$$b = \frac{n\Sigma(\log Q_i \log C_i) - (\Sigma \log Q_i)(\Sigma \log C_i)}{n\Sigma(\log Q_i)^2 - (\Sigma \log Q_i)^2} \qquad [13A.3]$$

$$\log a = \frac{\Sigma \log C_i - b\Sigma \log Q_i}{n} \qquad [13A.4]$$

where n is the number of observations.

Consider the following example. The Emerson Corporation, manufacturers of airplane landing gear equipment, is trying to develop a learning curve model to help forecast labor costs for successive units of one of its products. From past data, the firm knows that labor costs of the 25th, 75th, and 125th units were $800, $600, and $500, respectively. Develop the learning curve equation from this data and use the resulting model to predict labor costs for the 200th unit of output. The preliminary calculations needed to determine log a and b are shown in Table 13A.1. Substituting the column totals from the last row of Table 13A.1 into Equations 13A.3 and 13A.4 provides the following estimates of the learning curve parameters:

$$b = \frac{3(14.92704) - (5.36991)(8.38021)}{3(9.86711) - (5.36991)^2}$$

$$= -.28724$$

---

[35] The *least-squares* technique is described in chapter 6 of this text and in the regression chapter of any basic statistics book.

Table 13A.1 **Learning Curve: Preliminary Calculations**

Observation i	Q_i (unit-no.)	C_i (dollars)	$\log Q_i$	$\log C_i$	$(\log Q_i)^2$	$(\log C_i)^2$	$(\log Q_i) \cdot (\log C_i)$
1	25	800	1.39794	2.90309	1.95423	8.42793	4.05834
2	75	600	1.87506	2.77815	3.51585	7.71811	5.20920
3($=n$)	125	500	2.09691	2.69897	4.39703	7.28444	5.65950
Sum			5.36991	8.38021	9.86711	23.43048	14.92704

$$\log a = \frac{8.38021 - (-.28724)(5.36991)}{3}$$

$$= 3.30755$$

The learning curve equation for labor costs is

$$\log C = 3.30755 - .28724 \log Q \qquad \text{[13A.5]}$$

Using this model, the estimated cost of the 200th unit of output is obtained as follows:

$$\log C = 3.30755 - .28724 \log 200$$

$$= 3.30755 - .28724(2.30103)$$

$$= 2.64660$$

$$C = \$443.20$$

The Percentage of Learning

The percentage of learning, which is defined as the proportion by which an input (or its associated cost) is reduced when output is doubled, can be estimated as follows:

$$L = \frac{C_2}{C_1} \times 100\% \qquad \text{[13A.6]}$$

where C_1 is the input (or cost) for the Q_1 unit of output and C_2 is the cost for the $Q_2 = 2Q_1$ unit of output. To illustrate the calculation of the percentage of learning, consider the Emerson Corporation example again. Using the learning curve model developed earlier (Equation 13A.5), labor costs for the $Q_1 = 50$th unit of output are $C_1 = \$659.98$ and labor costs for the $2Q_1 = 100$th unit of output are $C_2 = \$540.84$. Substituting these values into Equation 13A.6 yields

$$L = \frac{540.84}{659.98} \times 100\%$$

$$= 81.9\%$$

The percentage of learning for labor costs in the production of these landing gear units is thus approximately 82 percent—indicating that labor costs decline by about 18 percent each time output is doubled.

Uses of the Learning Curve

The learning curve principle was first applied in airplane manufacturing during the 1930s. Since then the technique has been applied in many other assembly-type production processes, including shipbuilding and appliance manufacturing. Forecasts of personnel, equipment, and raw material requirements and their associated costs based on the learning curve have been used in scheduling production, determining prices for products sold, and evaluating suppliers' price quotations.

Discussion Questions

1. Define the following terms:
   a. Learning-curve effect
   b. Percentage of learning

2. Explain how we estimate the learning curve parameters.

Problem

1. Ajax Controls Company uses a learning curve to estimate labor costs for its products. The firm recently introduced a new line of process control devices and has collected the following cost-data:

Unit no.	Labor Cost
100	$1250
300	1000
600	850

   a. Determine the learning curve for the labor costs required to produce this product.
   b. What is the percentage of learning for labor costs?
   c. Estimate the labor costs of the 800th unit based on the learning curve developed in part (a).

Pricing and Output Decisions V

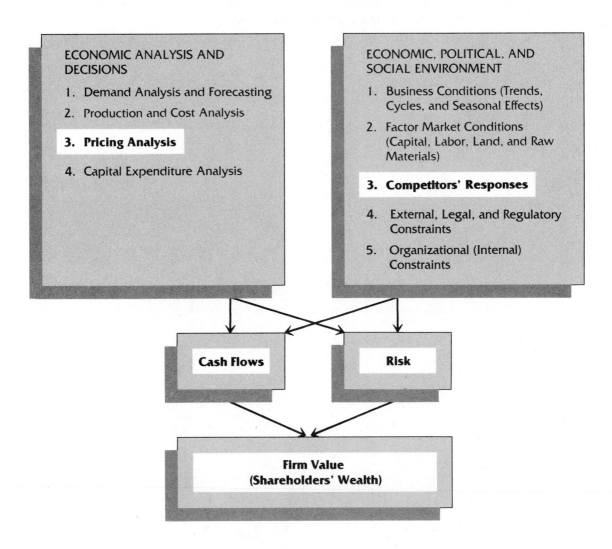

ECONOMIC ANALYSIS AND DECISIONS

1. Demand Analysis and Forecasting
2. Production and Cost Analysis
3. **Pricing Analysis**
4. Capital Expenditure Analysis

ECONOMIC, POLITICAL, AND SOCIAL ENVIRONMENT

1. Business Conditions (Trends, Cycles, and Seasonal Effects)
2. Factor Market Conditions (Capital, Labor, Land, and Raw Materials)
3. **Competitors' Responses**
4. External, Legal, and Regulatory Constraints
5. Organizational (Internal) Constraints

Cash Flows

Risk

Firm Value (Shareholders' Wealth)

In the previous chapters we developed the theories and measurement techniques useful in analyzing demand, production, and cost relationships in a firm. The optimization tools presented in Chapters 4 and 5 were used to determine the price-output levels where total revenue is maximized and the cost-output levels where total costs are minimized. In general, profits and shareholder wealth will *not* be maximized by operating at the revenue-maximizing or the cost-minimizing levels of output. Profit maximization must simultaneously consider the relationship between marginal cost and marginal revenue. In this part we consider the price-output decisions facing firms in pure competition, monopolistic competition, monopoly (Chapter 14), and oligopoly (Chapter 15). Chapter 16 examines some specialized pricing problems including pricing for the multiproduct firm, pricing when joint products are being produced, price discrimination, transfer pricing, and pricing rules used in practice by many firms. By following the correct marginal decision rules when pricing products and establishing production levels, managers can increase the firm's cash flows, control the risk of these cash flows, and thereby contribute to the goal of maximizing shareholder wealth.

Price and Output Determination: Pure Competition, Monopolistic Competition, and Monopoly

14

Wealth-maximizing managers seek a pricing and output strategy that will maximize the present value of the future profit stream to the firm. The determination of the wealth-maximizing pricing strategy depends upon the production capacity and technology available to the firm in the short-run, the potential for future changes in this production capacity, the cost of producing various levels of output, the nature of the demand for the firm's products, and the potential for immediate and longer term competition. In this chapter we develop the traditional static partial equilibrium models of price and output determination under certainty for monopoly markets, imperfectly competitive markets, and purely competitive markets. These static partial equilibrium models provide many useful insights regarding optimal price and output strategies for managers facing a wide range of market conditions.

Individual, Firm, and Market Demand Curves

Before discussing the models of price-ouput determination, it is useful to consider the relationship between individual, firm, and market demand curves. The relationship between the demand curve or function of an individual for some specific commodity at some point in time and the market demand curve is rather straightforward. The market demand curve for any commodity may be obtained, theoretically at least, by the lateral summation of the demand curves of all individual consumers of that commodity (see Figure 14.1).

Glossary of New Terms

Monopoly
A market structure characterized by one firm producing a highly differentiated product in a market with significant barriers to entry.

Pure competition
A market structure characterized by a very large number of buyers and sellers of a homogeneous (nondifferentiated) product. Entry and exit from the industry is costless, or nearly so. Information is freely available to all market participants, and there is no collusion among firms in the industry.

(Cont'd on next page)

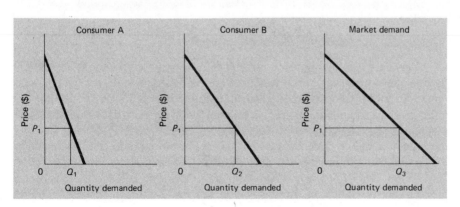

Figure 14.1
Relationship of Individual to Market Demand Curves

Glossary of New Terms (*Cont'd*)

Monopolistic competition
A market structure very much like pure competition, with the major distinction being the existence of a differentiated product.

Oligopolistic competition
A market structure in which the number of firms is so small that the actions of any one firm are likely to have noticeable impacts on the performance of other firms in the industry.

At price P_1, Consumer A demands Q_1, Consumer B demands Q_2, and total market demand (assuming only two consumers) is equal to Q_3, the sum of $Q_1 + Q_2$. For any given price of a commodity, the total industry or market demand will be exactly equal to the summation of all the quantities demanded by the individuals at that price.

The relationship between the demand function for the single firm and the industry or market demand function is more complex. The nature of the demand function for the individual firm is largely dependent on these conditions:

1. The number and relative size of firms in the industry

2. The homogeneity of the products sold by the firms of the industry; that is, the degree of product differentiation

3. The degree to which decision making by individual firms is independent; that is, noncollusive

On the basis of the nature of these conditions, four specific market structures have been traditionally defined:

1. Pure competition

2. Monopoly

3. Monopolistic competition

4. Oligopoly

Pure Competition

The *pure competition* industry model has the following characteristics:

1. A very large number of buyers and sellers, each of which buys or sells such a small proportion of the total industry output that a single buyer or seller's actions cannot have a perceptible impact on the market price

2. A homogeneous product produced by each firm, that is, no product differentiation

3. Free entry and exit from the market, that is, minimal barriers to entry and exit

4. No collusion among firms in the industry

The single firm in a purely competitive industry is, in essence, a price taker. Because the products of each producer are perfect substitutes for the products of every other producer, the single firm in pure competition can do nothing but offer its entire output at the going market price. As a result, the individual firm's demand curve approaches perfect elasticity at the market price. It can sell nothing at a higher price because all buyers (assuming rationality) will shift to other sellers. If the firm sells at a price slightly below the long-run market price, its quantity demanded approaches infinity. In the long run, at a below-market price the firm will lose money, as is demonstrated below. In addition, the firm

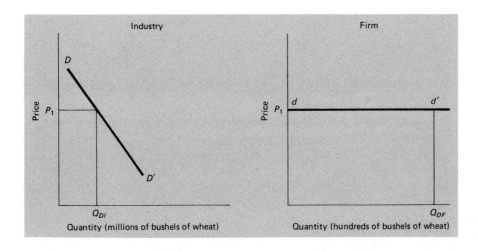

Figure 14.2
Pure Competition

has no motivation to sell below the market price because each firm may sell its entire output at the market price without having any perceptible influence on that price.

Figure 14.2 indicates the nature of the industry and firm demand curves under pure competition, as, for example, in wheat production. Line DD' represents the total industry or market demand curve for bushels of wheat. At price P_1, the market price, a total of Q_{DI} bushels of wheat will be demanded of the sum of all firms in the industry. Line dd' represents the demand curve facing each individual firm. The individual firm sells its entire output, Q_{DF}, at the market price P_1. By definition the quantity Q_{DF} represents only a small fraction of the total industry demand of Q_{DI}.

Monopoly

The *monopoly* model, the other extreme in market structure from pure competition, of an industry is characterized as follows:

1. Only one firm producing some specific commodity (in a specified market area).

2. Low cross elasticity of demand between the monopolist's product and any other product; that is, no close substitute products.

3. Substantial barriers to entry that prevent competition from entering the industry. These barriers include the following:
   a. Absolute cost advantages of the established firm, resulting from economies in securing inputs or from patented production techniques.
   b. Product differentiation advantages, resulting from consumer loyalty to established products.
   c. Scale economies, which increase the difficulty for new firms in financing an efficient-sized plant or building up a sufficient market. The need to build a large plant to compete effectively is also likely to lead to excess capacity in the industry, depressed prices, and reduced profits for all

firms. The new lower prices may not be high enough to permit the new entrant to survive and generate profits. This prospect may deter many potential entrants from actually entering a market where scale economies are substantial.

d. Large capital requirements, exceeding the financial resources of potential entrants.

Legal exclusion of potential competitors, as is the case for public utilities, may be the most effective barrier to entry.

By definition the demand curve of the individual monopoly firm is identical with the industry demand curve, since the firm is the industry. As we will see below, the identity between the firm and industry demand curves allows decision making for the monopolist to be a relatively simple matter.

Monopolistic Competition

In 1933 Chamberlin developed the theory of *monopolistic competition*. The market structure of monopolistic competition is characterized by a large number of firms each selling a product that is differentiated in some manner, real or imagined, from the products produced by its competitors. The assumptions of independent decision making by individual firms and ease of entry and exit from the market also hold. By far the most important distinguishing characteristic of monopolistic competition, however, is that the outputs of each firm are differentiated in some way from those of every other firm. In other words, the cross elasticity of demand between the products of individual firms is high, but not perfect, as in the case of pure competition. Product differentiation may be based on

certain characteristics of the product itself, such as exclusive patented features; trademarks; trade names; peculiarities of the package or container, if any; or singularity in quality, design, color or style. It may also exist with respect to the conditions surrounding its sale.[1]

These conditions may include such factors as credit terms, location of the seller, congeniality of sales personnel, after-sale service, warranties, and so on.

In the world of monopolistic competition it is difficult to define an industry demand curve because each firm produces a product differentiated in some manner from the products of other firms. Thus, "rather than well-defined industries, one tends to get something of a continuum of products, although this assertion probably overstates the situation in practice."[2] Generally, it is rather easy to identify groups of differentiated products that fall in the same industry.

The demand curve for the product of any one firm is expected to have a negative slope. Because there are by definition a large number of close but

---

[1] E. H. Chamberlin, *The Theory of Monopolistic Competition* (Cambridge: Harvard University Press, 1933), p. 56.

[2] W. J. Baumol, *Economic Theory and Operations Analysis*, 4th ed. (Englewood Cliffs, N.J.: Prentice-Hall, 1977), p. 320.

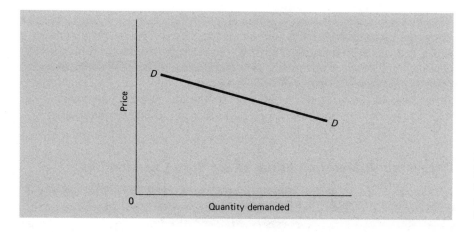

Figure 14.3
Demand Curve for the Firm under Monopolistic Competition

not perfect substitute products, the curve will usually be quite elastic (see Figure 14.3).

The more a firm differentiates its product from that of its competitors, the less elastic will be the demand curve for the differentiating firm's output (that is, the more latitude the firm has in pricing its product). The case of the monopolistic competitor's demand curve has been well summarized by Baumol:

> Under monopolistic competition the demand curve for the product of the firm may be expected to have a negative slope, even though the firm is as small as one operating under conditions of pure competition. For customers will have different degrees of loyalty to the firms from whom they make their purchases. A small reduction in one firm's price may only attract its competitors' most mercurial customers. But, as larger and larger price reductions are instituted, it may acquire more and more customers from its rivals by drawing on customers who are less anxious to switch.[3]

Oligopoly

The *oligopoly* model of an industry describes a market having few firms. The number of firms producing any commodity is so small that actions by an individual firm in the industry with respect to price, output, product style or quality, terms of sale, and so on have a perceptible impact on the sales of other firms in the industry. In other words, oligopoly is distinguished by a noticeable degree of *interdependence* between firms in the industry. The products that are produced by oligopolists may be homogeneous—as in the cases of basic steel, aluminum, and cement—or they may be differentiated—as in the cases of automobiles, cigarettes, home appliances, soaps, and detergents.

Although the degree of product differentiation is an important factor in shaping the single oligopolist's demand curve, the degree of interdependence of firms in the industry is of even greater significance. Primarily because of this

---

[3] Ibid., pp. 320–321.

interdependence, it is virtually impossible to talk in unambiguous terms of a single firm's demand curve. The relationship between price and output for a single firm is determined not only by consumer preferences, product substitutability, and level of advertising but also by the responses that other competitors may make to a price change by the firm.

Because of the conceptual difficulty in defining an unambiguous firm demand curve for oligopoly, we defer a discussion of this matter until Chapter 15.

Price-Output Determination under Pure Competition

As discussed above, the individual firm in a purely competitive industry is effectively a price taker because the products of every producer are perfect substitutes for the products of every other producer. Price takers cannot charge a price higher than their competitors since no one would buy from them. Although they can conceivably charge a price lower than the going price, they accept the going price to maximize profits. This leads to the familiar horizontal or perfectly elastic demand curve of the purely competitive firm. Although we rarely find instances where all the conditions for pure competition are met, securities exchanges and the commodity markets approach these conditions. For instance, the individual pig farmer has little choice but to accept the going price for frozen pork bellies; however, imperfections creep into even this case since the government provides price supports for farm commodities. In spite of the limited existence of purely competitive markets, individuals and smaller firms are often forced to act as price takers in their economic decisions. Pure competition also gives a basis for comparison of pricing and performance of firms in the more typical, imperfectly competitive market structures, such as oligopoly and monopolistic competition.

Short Run

A firm in a purely competitive industry may either make profits or operate at a loss in the short run. In our discussion of price and output decisions, we use the term *profits* to mean returns in excess of a normal return to compensate the entrepreneur for interest on funds invested in the firm and the value of labor services (even though the entrepreneur may not receive an explicit salary from the firm) plus an additional amount that is *just sufficient* to keep the entrepreneur producing the same product, given the special risks associated with its production and sale. In the competitive long run, all firms will operate at an equilibrium output where all profit and losses have disappeared. As more firms enter (leave) the industry in the long run, supply will increase (decrease) and the market price will be driven downward (upward), helping to eliminate profits (losses) for the remaining firms.

In addition to price changes that occur in the long run, another force also drives all firms toward equilibrium as firms enter and leave the industry. In equilibrium all firms will also have identical costs, even though they may use different production and operating techniques. A firm more efficient than its competitors may temporarily exist because some resources, such as managerial

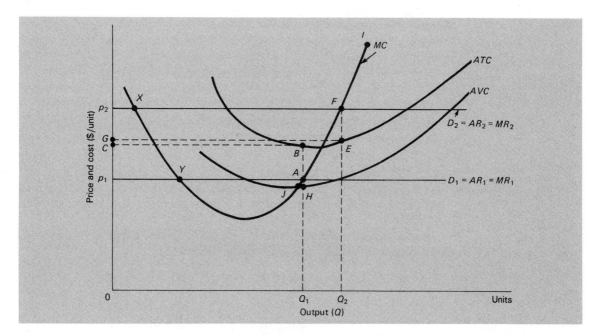

Figure 14.4
**Firm in Pure
Competition:
Short Run**

talent, firm location, and quality of raw material inputs, are not homogeneous among firms. But if Firm X has a manager whose extraordinary skills generate $5,000 more in cost savings for Firm X than a similar manager does for Firm Y, it will be in the Firm Y's interest to bid for Firm X's more efficient manager by offering a salary that fully compensates for this extraordinary effectiveness. In the world of pure competition where all firms operate under conditions of certainty and with a perfect market mechanism, all savings resulting from the use of more efficient input factors will be eliminated as the competitive bidding process rewards all on a basis equal to their marginal contributions.

The notion of a purely competitive long-run equilibrium may seem contrived. We should note that although the equilibrium conditions described here may never in fact occur, they nevertheless represent a condition toward which a purely competitive market would *tend to move* in the long run. Figure 14.4 illustrates possible short-run conditions for a purely competitive firm.

In pure competition the firm must sell at the market price (p_1 or p_2), and its demand curve is represented by a horizontal line (D_1 or D_2) at the market price. In the purely competitive case, marginal revenue MR is equal to price P, since the sale of each additional unit increases total revenue by the price of that unit (which remains constant at all levels of output). For instance, if

$$P = \$8/\text{unit}$$

then

$$\text{Total revenue} = TR = P \cdot Q$$
$$= 8Q$$

Marginal revenue is defined as the change in total revenue resulting from the sale of one additional unit, or the derivative of total revenue with respect to quantity:

$$MR = \frac{dTR}{dQ} = \$8/\text{unit}$$

and marginal revenue equals price.

The profit-maximizing firm will produce at that level of output where marginal revenue equals marginal cost. Beyond that point, the production and sale of one additional unit would add more to total cost than to total revenue ($MC > MR$), and hence total profit ($TR - TC$) would decline. Up to the point where $MC = MR$, the production and sale of one more unit increases total revenue more than total cost ($MR > MC$), and total profit would increase as an additional unit is produced and sold.

Producing at the point where marginal revenue MR equals marginal cost MC is equivalent to maximizing the total profit function. If

$$\text{Total revenue } TR = 8Q$$

and

$$\text{Total cost } TC = Q^2 + 4Q + 2$$

then

$$\text{Marginal revenue } MR = \frac{dTR}{dQ} = \$8/\text{unit}$$

and

$$\text{Marginal cost } MC = \frac{dTC}{dQ} = 2Q + 4$$

$$\text{Total profit } (\pi) = TR - TC$$
$$= 8Q - (Q^2 + 4Q + 2)$$
$$= -Q^2 + 4Q - 2$$

To maximize total profit we take the derivative of π with respect to quantity, set it equal to zero, and solve for the profit-maximizing level of Q. (It is also necessary to check the second derivative to be certain we have found a maximum, not a minimum!)[4]

$$\frac{d\pi}{dQ} = -2Q + 4 = 0$$

$$Q^* = 2 \text{ units}$$

---

[4] The check for profit maximization goes as follows:

$$\frac{d^2\pi}{dQ^2} = -2$$

Since the second derivative is negative, we know we have found a maximum value for the profit function.

But since $MR = \$8/\text{unit}$ and $MC = 2Q + 4 = [2(2) + 4] = \$8/\text{unit}$, when total profit is maximized, we are merely setting $MC = MR$.

Returning to Figure 14.4, if price $p = p_1$, the firm would produce the level of output Q_1, where $MC = MR$ (profits are maximized or losses minimized). In this case the firm would incur a loss per unit equal to the difference between average total cost ATC and average revenue or price. This is represented by BA in Figure 14.4. The total loss incurred by the firm at Q_1 level of output and price p_1 equals the rectangle p_1CBA. This may be conceptually thought of as the loss per unit (BA) times the number of units produced and sold (Q_1). At price p_1 losses are minimized, since average variable costs AVC have been covered and a contribution remains to cover part of the fixed costs (AH per unit times Q_1 units). If the firm did not produce, it would incur losses equal to the entire amount of fixed costs (BH per unit times Q_1 units). Hence we may conclude that in the short run a firm will produce and sell at that level of output where $MR = MC$, as long as the variable costs of production are being covered ($P > AVC$). If price were p_2, the firm would produce Q_2 units and make a profit per unit of EF, or a total profit represented by the rectangle $FEGp_2$.[5]

Long Run

In the long run, illustrated in Figure 14.5, all inputs are free to vary. Hence no differentiation exists between fixed and variable costs. Under long-run conditions, average cost will tend to be just equal to price and all excessive profits will be eliminated. If price exceeds average costs, more firms will enter the industry, supply will increase, and price will be driven down toward the equilibrium, zero-profit level. In addition, as more firms bid for available input resource factors (labor, capital, managerial talent), the cost of these factors will tend to rise. As mentioned earlier, if some inputs for some firms are especially productive, the competitive mechanism will result in their cost being bid up to the point where all cost savings are paid to the more productive input that made initial cost savings possible. The net result is that in the long-run equilibrium all firms will tend to have identical costs, and prices will tend to equal average costs (that is, the average cost curve AC will be tangent to the horizontal price line p_2).

Thus we may say that at the long-run profit-maximizing level of output under pure competition, equilibrium will be achieved at a point where $P = MR = MC = AC$. At this point the firm is producing at its *most efficient* (that is, lowest average cost) level of output.

---

[5] As was shown in Figure 14.4, it is quite possible for the marginal cost function to intersect marginal revenue at more than one place. In this case MC intersects D_2 at points X and F, and D_1 at points Y and A. In the graphic case we may eliminate the X and Y intersections because it is apparent that losses exceed those incurred under the F and A solutions. An algebraic solution to this problem would indicate that X and Y do not satisfy the required second-order condition.

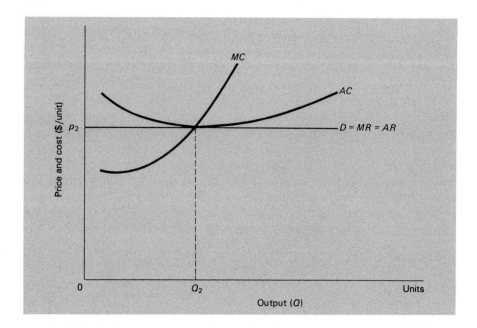

**Figure 14.5
Long-Run
Equilibrium**

Market Price Determination

We have spoken generally about the market price that a firm in pure competition is forced to accept. Let us now examine how this price is determined. Recall that the market demand curve shows the amount of a commodity that consumers would be willing to buy at some point in time at a set of specified prices (holding constant the effects of all other factors). The market supply curve may be given a similar interpretation, indicating the quantity of a product sellers *would* be willing to offer for sale at some point in time at a set of specified prices (holding constant the effects of all other factors). The supply curve may be interpreted in terms of the cost functions of firms in the industry. The short-run supply curve for any individual firm may be represented by that portion of the marginal cost curve above average variable cost AVC. If price $P(P = MR)$ intersects the marginal cost curve below AVC, the firm will shut down.

Plant shutdown under these circumstances is clearly the best alternative because losses will be limited to the total amount of fixed charges incurred. To operate when average revenue or price is less than average variable costs would result in additional losses equal to the difference between average variable cost and price times the number of units sold. When price exceeds average variable cost (even if price is less than average total cost), losses will be minimized because some contribution is made (the difference between price and average variable cost times the number of units sold) to covering fixed costs. At any point above AVC, the firm will be maximizing profit or minimizing losses by producing and selling that level of output where $MR = MC$ (remembering that in pure competition $P = MR$). In Figure 14.4 the supply curve for the firm is represented by the segment of the marginal cost curve labeled JI. The industry

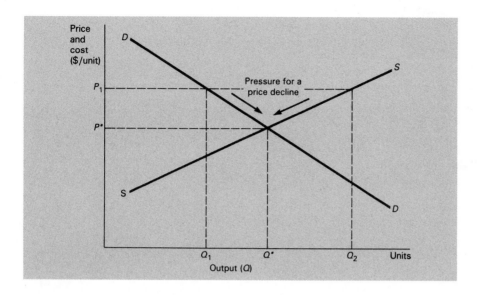

Figure 14.6
Effects of Nonequilibrium Pricing

supply curve is merely the summation of all individual firm supply curves.[6] The interaction between supply and demand curves is illustrated in Figure 14.6.

The market price will tend toward an equilibrium where the quantity demanded equals quantity supplied, for example, Q^* in Figure 14.6. If a price above the initial equilibrium price (P^*) were charged, such as P_1, the quantity consumers are willing to buy, Q_1, at that price would be less than the number of units producers would be willing to sell, Q_2, and there would be strong market pressure for a price reduction. This is often evident in local real estate markets when there is an economic downturn. The market becomes flooded with homes and prices are reduced.

Similarly, if a market price below the equilibrium price were charged, there would be upward pressure on the price back toward an equilibrium condition. Anyone who has been to a sellout athletic event and has been forced to buy tickets at scalpers' prices knows what happens when demand exceeds supply at a given price and upward-pricing pressure is brought to bear.

If the market price that is established, say p_1, results in excessive profits to firms in the industry, more firms will enter the industry, increasing supply to S_1S_1', and driving prices down to p_3. This is illustrated in Figure 14.7(a). In contrast, if some firms are operating at a loss they may cease production, reducing industry supply to S_2S_2' and boosting the price to a level where normal profits are made by the remaining firms. The supply-demand curve also shows why shifts in the demand curve (because of changing consumer tastes, changes in prices of complementary and substitute goods, and changes

[6] This condition only holds under pure competition when there is a rather wide range of outputs under which approximately constant cost conditions prevail. Under increasing or decreasing cost conditions, this simple additivity property is not strictly correct. Under either condition, the fundamentals of the market price-equilibrium mechanism, illustrated here, do apply.

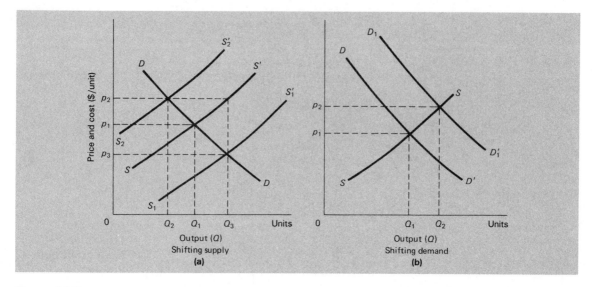

Figure 14.7
**Supply-Demand
Interaction**

in income) will result in higher or lower prices. This is illustrated in Figure 14.7 (b). If real consumer income were to increase, the demand curve for most commodities might be expected to shift upward and to the right by some amount (determined by the income elasticity of demand) to D_1D_1'. This would result in a new equilibrium level of output, Q_2, with a price increase from p_1 to p_2. Since a new, higher price has been established, it is likely that some firms will be making excess profits. As a result, new firms will enter the industry, supply will increase, prices will decline, and so the equilibrating process continues.

The notion of a market supply curve will not be encountered in our discussion of price-output determination for firms in monopoly, oligopoly, or monopolistic competition. Since the market supply curve is a representation of how much firms will produce and sell if faced with a market price of X dollars per unit, it is not a generally useful concept to develop rigorously for market structures in which firms possess considerable discretion over the prices to be charged. In addition, the market supply curve concept loses its meaning as we talk of products that are increasingly differentiated from one another.

Pure Monopoly

In the case of pure monopoly one firm is the sole producer of a good or service that has no close substitutes. The demand curve facing the pure monopolist is the same as the industry demand curve because one firm constitutes the entire industry. The price-output decision for a profit-maximizing monopolist is illustrated in Figure 14.8.

Just as in the case of pure competition, profit is maximized at the price and output combination where $MC = MR$. This corresponds to a price of P_1, output of Q_1, and total profits equal to BC profit per unit times Q_1 units. It should be evident that for a negative-sloping demand curve, the MR function is not the same as the demand function. In fact, for any linear demand function, the

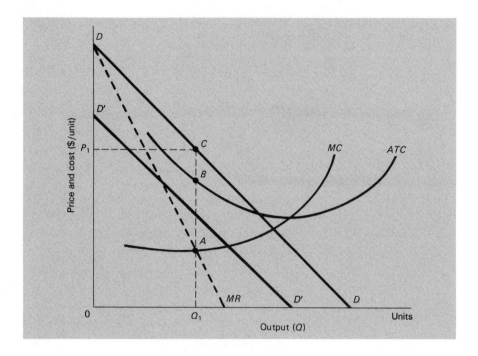

Figure 14.8
Pure Monopoly

marginal revenue function will have the same intercept on the P axis as the demand function and a slope that is twice as great as that of the demand function. If, for example, the demand function were of the form

$$P = a - bQ$$

then

$$\text{Total revenue} = TR = P \cdot Q$$
$$= aQ - bQ^2$$

and

$$MR = \frac{dTR}{dQ} = a - 2bQ$$

The slope of the demand function is $-b$, and of the MR function $-2b$.

Assume a monopolist is faced with a demand function of the form

$$Q = 400 - 20P$$

and a long-run total cost function[7] of the form

$$TC = 5Q + \frac{Q^2}{50}$$

---

[7] Because the cost function does not possess a fixed-cost component (that is, all terms contain Q), it is evident that this must represent a long-run cost function.

To maximize profits it would produce and sell that output where $MC = MR$, and charge the corresponding price:

$$MC = \frac{dTC}{dQ} = 5 + \frac{Q}{25}$$

MR may be found by rewriting the demand function in terms of Q:

$$P = \frac{-Q}{20} + 20$$

and then multiplying by Q to find TR:

$$TR = P \cdot Q$$

$$= -\frac{Q^2}{20} + 20Q$$

$$MR = \frac{dTR}{dQ} = -\frac{Q}{10} + 20$$

Setting $MR = MC$, yields

$$-\frac{Q}{10} + 20 = 5 + \frac{Q}{25}$$

$$15 = \frac{Q}{10} + \frac{Q}{25}$$

$$750 = 5Q + 2Q$$

$$Q^* = 107 \text{ units}$$

Substituting Q back into the demand equation we may solve for P:

$$P = -\frac{Q}{20} + 20$$

$$P = \frac{-107}{20} + 20$$

$$P^* = \$14.65/\text{unit}$$

Hence the profit-maximizing monopolist would produce 107 units and charge a price of $14.65 each. This yields a profit of

$$\pi = TR - TC$$

$$= (P \cdot Q) - \left(5Q + \frac{Q^2}{50}\right)$$

$$= 14.65(107) - \left(5(107) + \frac{(107)^2}{50}\right)$$

$$= 1567.55 - 764$$

$$\pi^* = \$803.55$$

A close check of Figure 14.8 shows that the monopolist produces at a level of output that is smaller than the industry output would be under pure competition since equilibrium is reached in pure competition at a point where the *ATC* curve is minimized for each firm (that is, the aggregate industry average cost curve is minimized). The profit-maximizing monopolist, faced with a negative-sloping demand curve, will always produce at an output short of that output at which average costs are minimized. As Baumol has observed, some cautions are in order when one concludes that a monopoly will produce less than a purely competitive industry, *all other things being equal.*[8] All conditions are not likely to remain equal. Both demand and cost may change when a monopolist takes over a competitive industry. For instance, the monopolist's cost function may reflect economies of scale that were not possible for the smaller firms in pure competition. Such economies might relate to more efficient plant sizes, centralizing of inventories, and the centralizing of such functions as financing, purchasing, and legal services. Because of the possibility of making excess profits, the monopolist will be able to afford to advertise, possibly increasing aggregate market demand. However, a large monopolist might require a huge administrative structure where coordination and effective communication become increasingly difficult, and diseconomies may result. On balance, a simple comparison between monopoly and pure competition can furnish little more than a possible clue about the levels of output that might be expected under each market structure.

Even if pure competition does result in a larger output than results from a monopoly, it cannot be concluded, especially under conditions of full employment, that breaking up a monopoly (which would lead to an increase in that industry's output) will be in society's best interest. Under full employment, an increase in output in the liquor industry, for example, would require that resources be drawn away from other industries and prices in those industries would possibly rise. To take an extreme example, assume that the liquor industry is a monopoly, the economy is operating under conditions of full employment, and the government seeks to break the liquor monopolist into a large number of smaller competitive firms. As a result, output in the industry increases. The new small liquor companies bid for the services of chemists to work on product development. Some chemists are attracted from drug firms, and those who remain work at a higher wage. May we conclude that society is better off because more liquor is produced? Prices of liquor perhaps are lower, but the cost of drugs may have risen. Under conditions of full employment, we must be very careful to analyze the impact of reallocating resources from one industry to another before concluding that greater output in any one industry necessarily makes society better off.[9]

---

[8] William J. Baumol, *Economic Theory and Operations Analysis*, 4th ed. (Englewood Cliffs, N.J.: Prentice-Hall, 1977), p. 402.

[9] See R. Lipsey and K. Lancaster, "The General Theory of Second Best," *Review of Economic Studies* 24, no. 1 (1956), pp. 11–32, for a more rigorous theoretical discussion of this proposition.

Elasticities and Profit Maximization

What role does the price elasticity of demand facing a profit-maximizing monopolist play in the price-output decisions of the monopolist? Intuitively we might expect that the more elastic the demand (suggesting the existence of better substitutes), the lower the price that the monopolist would charge. It can be shown that marginal revenue (MR) is equal to[10]

$$MR = P(1 + 1/E_D)$$

where E_D equals the price elaticity of demand and P equals the price per unit. Consider a monopolist with the following total cost function:

$$TC = 10 + 5Q$$

The marginal cost (MC) function is

$$MC = dTC/dQ = 5$$

The price elasticity of demand has been estimated to be -2.0. Setting $MC = MR$ results in the following pricing rule for a profit-maximizing monopolist:

$$MC = \$5 = P(1 + 1/-2.0) = MR$$

$$P = 5/(0.5) = \$10/unit$$

If, however, demand is more price elastic, such as $E_D = -4.0$, the profit-maximizing monopolist would set the price at

$$P = \$5/(0.75) = \$6.67/unit$$

Thus, the more elastic the demand function for a monopolist's output, the lower the price that will be charged, *ceteris paribus*. At the limit, consider the case of a firm in pure competition with a perfectly elastic (horizontal) demand curve. In this case the price elasticity of demand is $-\infty$, hence, one divided by the price elasticity approaches zero and marginal revenue becomes equal to price. Thus, the profit maximizing rule becomes "Set price equal to marginal cost." Of course, this is the same solution developed above in the discussion of price-output determination under pure competition.

Monopoly and Economic Profits

A common misconception is that monopolists always earn economic profits; that is, returns above those required to keep capital in the industry, given the risks being assumed by the investors. Although economic profits are more likely to be earned by monopolists than by firms operating in more competitive market structures, they are not guaranteed to the monopolist in the short run. It is possible that a monopolist can face a situation where the demand curve for the monopolist's product is located everywhere below the monopolist's average total cost function, such as demand curve D'D' in Figure 14.8. With a demand curve such as D'D', average cost always exceeds average revenue. Consequently,

---

[10] A derivation of this relationship is provided in Chapter 7, footnote 9.

there is no price the monopolist can charge that will result in a profit. This situation can persist in the short run, but in the long run the monopolist will have to lower its costs and/or take actions designed to increase demand. If this cannot be accomplished, the monopolist will cease operating and leave the business.

For example, the public transit system in most major cities operates as a monopolist. For many years these systems were operated by private, regulated companies; however, as automobiles and freeways became more generally available, demand for public transportation decreased and costs increased. Many of these companies were faced with average cost functions that were higher than average revenue functions, and losses were generated. Ultimately, these monopoly public transportation systems were taken over and operated by city or regional governments—and most continue to incur significant operating losses. In this case, no price will result in profitable operations.

Monopoly and Efficiency

In the long run, it is possible for a monopolist to end up operating an optimum scale plant. An optimum scale plant is the plant size that will lead to a maximum level of profits for the firm, but this result is not assured. The monopolist does not face the discipline of strong competition so the monopolist may install excess capacity, or alternatively, fail to install enough capacity. Indeed, a monopolist seeking to restrain entry of new competitors into the industry may install excess capacity that can be used to flood the market with supply and lower prices, thus making entry less attractive to potential competitors. Even in the case of regulated monopolists, such as electric utility companies, considerable evidence shows that regulation often provides incentives for a firm to overinvest or underinvest in generating capacity. A discussion of the tendency for regulated firms to over- or underinvest in capacity is presented in Chapter 20.

Monopolistic Competition

Chamberlin's model of monopolistic competition pictures an industry with a relatively large number of firms, each selling a product that is differentiated in some manner from the products of its competitors.[11] In such a situation it is increasingly difficult to specify precisely the bounds of an appropriate industry because no two firms produce exactly homogeneous goods or services. Instead of an easily recognizable industry, we tend to find a continuum of more or less closely substitutable products. The problem of defining an appropriate product group has been at the heart of many of the attacks on the model of monopolistic competition.[12]

---

[11] Edward H. Chamberlin, *The Theory of Monopolistic Competition* (Cambridge, Mass.: Harvard University Press, 1933).

[12] George J. Stigler, *Five Lectures on Economic Problems* (London: Longmans, Green, 1949), p. 15.

Economic Analysis and Managerial Efficiency

A MARKET SOLUTION TO CROWDED AIRSPACE*

The summer 1986 midair collision between an Aeromexico jetliner and a private plane over Los Angeles brought increased attention to the problem of crowded airspace, especially around the nation's busiest airports. A Federal Aviation Administration survey of the country's twenty-three busiest airports found that in a six-hour period, private planes intruded on restricted airspace 175 times.

The problem of crowded airspace, particularly around the busiest airports, can be viewed as a failure to use the pricing system to allocate this scarce resource. The Federal Aviation Administration (FAA) may be considered a monopolist offering a scarce resource for sale. If this resource is not priced correctly, it will be overconsumed. The result is crowded and unsafe airspace. Unfortunately, the FAA has not treated the problem with the discipline of the pricing system. Rather, the FAA has adopted new rules designed to increase the capacity of the airspace around busy airports. Even if these rules are successful, they can provide only a short-term solution to the problem. Surplus demand for flights through crowded airspace will continue to exist unless this limited resource is priced appropriately.

*Based on J. Gregory Sidak, "Marketplace Solution to Midair
*Collisions" *Wall Street Journal*, 2 March 1987.

In the near term, it is possible to limit takeoffs and landings at the most crowded airports by increasing landing and takeoff fees until a market clearing price is reached, which provides a reasonable balance between the demand for landing and takeoff slots and the limited supply. More importantly, however, is the need for a system that would allow air traffic controllers to charge a toll for any flight passing through crowded airspace. A system of fees for airspace access would send many flights to less crowded airspace and less congested airports. Airspace access at these alternative airports would then be priced at lower levels. In order to implement this system, all planes would have to be equipped with transponders, which identify the plane's altitude and location.

So far the nation's air traffic control system has made only limited use of the price system in allocating its scarcest resource—airspace in crowded air corridors. As demand for this airspace grows, the monopolistic provider of air traffic control services, the FAA, will ultimately be forced either to ration access to this airspace or to use the price system to ration access for them.

Questions

1. What factors do you feel have resulted in the FAA's unwillingness to use the price system to allocate access to the nation's air traffic control system?

2. Discuss the pros and cons of an administrative rationing system vs. the use of the price system to control access to the crowded airspace.

Product differentiation may be based on special product characteristics, trademarks, packaging, quality, design, or conditions surrounding the sale, such as location of the seller, warranties, and credit terms. The demand curve for any one firm is expected to have a negative slope and be extremely elastic because of the large number of close substitutes. The firm in monopolistic competition has limited discretion over price (as distinguished from the firm in pure competition) because of customer loyalties arising from real or perceived

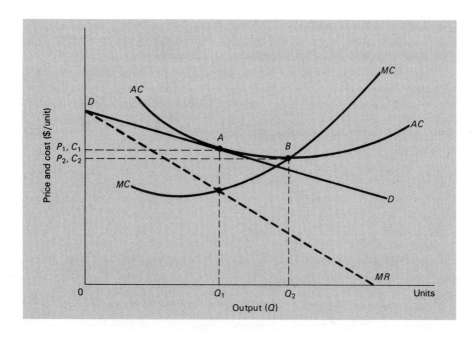

Figure 14.9
Monopolistic Competition

product differences. A price decline will attract some of the competitors' customers, and a price increase will result in a substantial loss of customers as some will shift to the close substitute offered by competitors. Profit maximization (or loss minimization) occurs when the firm produces at that level of output and charges that price where marginal revenue equals marginal cost (Figure 14.9).

Just as in the case of pure competition, a firm may or may not generate a profit in the short run. Due to relatively free entry and exit in the long run, however, average costs will be driven *toward* tangency with the demand curve at Point A. At this price, P_1, and output, Q_1, marginal cost is equal to marginal revenue. Hence the firm is producing at its optimal level of output. Any price lower or higher than P_1 will result in a loss to the firm, since average costs will exceed price.

A comparison of the price-output solution in monopolistic competition with that in pure competition indicates that because of the negatively sloping demand curve, the point of tangency A occurs at a lower-level of output, Q_1, than would occur in pure competition, Q_2. Also, *ceteris paribus*, the price P_1 charged and the cost C_1 of producing the equilibrium level of output in monopolistic competition will be higher than that of a firm in pure competition, since the purely competitive firm is in equilibrium at output level Q_2, charging a price of P_2 and incurring costs of C_2.

Because the monopolistic competitor produces at a level of output where average costs are still declining, it has been argued that society may reap savings by combining existing firms so that each of the remaining firms are producing a higher level of output (although total output of all firms remains constant) at lower costs (somewhere between Points A and B on Figure 14.9). It is conceptually possible for the same level of output to be produced at a lower cost.

Hence, a net saving may accrue to society if the number of existing firms is reduced and the equilibrium level of output for each firm thereby increases. This is called the "excess capacity theorem" of monopolistic competition.

The model of monopolistic competition has come under increasing attack with the passage of time.[13] Cohen and Cyert's attacks center around the empirical void created by the model. They conclude that markets that contain a large number of small firms are nearly always markets selling such standardized or near-standardized products as wheat and lumber. Even a moderate degree of product differentiation would likely leave demand curves for the firm so nearly horizontal that the purely competitive model is an adequate approximation. They further argue that markets where customers have strong brand preferences are typically markets better classified as oligopolies where the number of sellers is few. For markets in which firms sell a product for which there are no close substitutes, the monopoly model provides a superior basis for analysis.

The retail sector in any city (for example, grocery stores, clothing stores, gas stations, shoe stores, cleaners, and fast food outlets) is the most frequently cited example of monopolistically competitive markets. But Chamberlin assumes that any price adjustment by one firm will spread its influence over so many firms that there will be no perceptible impact on any of the other firms and hence no readjustment by them. This assumption is clearly not realistic. The effects of price changes by one firm will not be spread evenly over all other retailers but will be concentrated on those retailers in closest proximity to the initiating firm. The impact on these firms is likely to be perceptible and evoke a response. Under these circumstances the oligopoly model furnishes a better basis for analysis.

We agree with Cohen and Cyert and others that few real-world market situations are appropriately analyzed in the framework of Chamberlin's model. A more realistic model of market structure that bridges the gap between monopoly and pure competition is oligopoly. Chapter 15 discusses price-output determination in an oligopolistic market. Before considering that market model, however, let us examine the role of advertising and selling expenses in the price-output decision of a firm.

Selling and Promotional Expenses

In addition to varying price and quality characteristics of their products, firms may also vary the amount of their advertising and other promotional expenses in their search for profits. This kind of promotional activity generates two distinct types of benefits. First, demand for the general product group may be shifted upward to the right as a result of the individual firm and industry advertising activities. This general benefit of a higher level of demand presumably comes at the expense of other general product classes. As a result, a higher

---

[13] Perhaps the best brief discussion of attacks on Chamberlin's theory is in Kalman Cohen and Richard Cyert, *Theory of the Firm*, 2d ed. (Englewood Cliffs, N.J.: Prentice-Hall, 1975), pp. 225–230.

market price may prevail (at least until new competitors enter the market). This general demand-expanding effect of advertising is probably a major source of incentive for advertising when the market is more highly concentrated, as in monopoly or oligopoly. The greater the number of firms in an industry, the more diffused will be the effects of a general demand-expanding advertising campaign by any one firm. In contrast, a monopolist such as the phone company, or a highly concentrated oligopoly such as the tobacco industry, will be more inclined to undertake an advertising campaign, partially in the hope of expanding demand for the general product class, of which the individual firm provides a large share.

The second, more widespread incentive for advertising is the desire to shift the demand function of a particular firm at the expense of other firms offering similar products. This strategy will be pursued both by oligopolists and by firms in more competitive industries as long as an opportunity exists for product differentiation of some form. The level of advertising pursued by oligopolists is determined by the same considerations of mutual interdependence that influence price-output decisions. The various interdependency-based oligopoly models are discussed in more detail in the following chapter. In this section we examine a simple model of promotional expenditures for a more competitive industry structure—one that approaches the monopolistic competition model.

Determining Optimal Selling Expenses

To illustrate the effects of advertising expenditures and to determine the optimal selling expenses of a firm, consider the case where price and product characteristics have already been determined. The liquor retailing industry is an important example of such a case. In many states either prices are set by a state board, or manufacturers are permitted to set prices at which their products can be sold. Also, where some form of resale price maintenance is practiced resulting in all retailers selling a product at the manufacturer's suggested retail price, the following model offers interesting insights.

Figure 14.10 illustrates a situation that a firm may initially face under these conditions. Curve ATC_1 represents long-run average costs of production. Curve ATC_2 is equal to ATC_1 *plus* an amount of selling costs per unit of output needed to sell any given amount of output. ATC_2 is constructed under the assumption that other firms hold their selling expenses constant. Assume an initial price of P_1 that results in output for the firm of Q_1. Under these conditions the firm earns a profit of AP_1 dollars per unit sold. Also, at output level Q_1, unit selling expenses equal AB, which is the difference between ATC_1 and ATC_2. Obviously, this is not a profit-maximizing level of output.

Curve MC_2 is the marginal cost curve associated with ATC_2; that is, MC_2 represents the additional cost associated with producing *and* selling one more unit of output. Since we have assumed that price is fixed at P_1 (implying that price is also equal to marginal revenue), it follows that the profit-maximizing level of output for this firm is Q_2 units, the level at which marginal revenue equals marginal cost. At this level of output, per unit selling expenses increase to DE, and the firm earns a profit of CD dollars per unit.

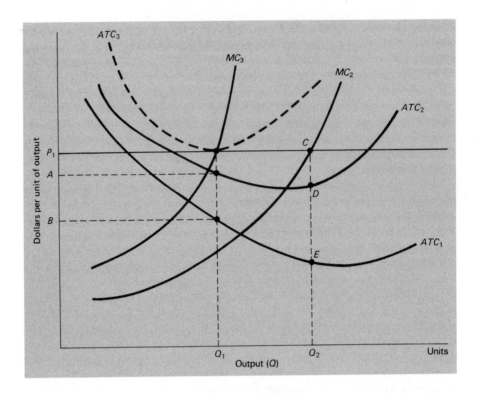

Figure 14.10
**Determination of
Selling Expense**

Unfortunately for the firm, it may not be able to earn these anticipated profits for very long. If increased selling expenses do not increase the market demand curve (cause it to shift upward to the right), or if all other firms follow a similar course of action and raise their selling expenses, the sales of the example firm may remain at Q_1 but the firm's average total costs will increase as a result of the higher selling expenses. ATC_3 represents the new average total cost curve with the increased selling expenses at each level of output. MC_3 is the marginal cost function associated with ATC_3. A long-run equilibrium is achieved when ATC_3 is just tangent to the price line. When this occurs, the firm has no incentive to change its selling expenses. This equilibrium point is brought about as firms enter and leave the industry, resulting in contracting or expanding market shares and profits (losses) for the remaining firms.

Dorfman and Steiner have developed a similar profit-maximization rule for setting the level of advertising expenditures, given that the quantity sold is a function of both price and advertising.[14] They assume that neither price nor marginal cost will change as a result of small changes in advertising expenditures, assumptions similar to those used in the preceding graphical analysis. They also assume there are diminishing returns to advertising expenditures,

---

[14] Robert Dorfman and Peter O. Steiner, "Optimal Advertising and Optimal Quality," *American Economic Review* (December 1954), pp. 826–836. See also Roger Sherman, *The Economics of Industry* (Boston: Little, Brown, 1974), especially pp. 128–131.

meaning that beyond some point successive increments of advertising outlays will result in smaller and smaller successive increments in additional sales. Under these conditions, Dorfman and Steiner prove that advertising should be carried to the point where the marginal revenue that can be obtained from an additional dollar spent on advertising, MR_A, is equal to the ratio $P \div (P - MC)$, where P is the firm's price and MC is its marginal cost. They also shows that MR_A should be equal to the absolute value of the price elasticity of demand at the optimal output level.

In addition to deciding on the total amount of selling expenses the firm should incur, it is also important for the firm to decide on an appropriate allocation of these selling expenses to different advertising media. Let ΔS_A, ΔS_B, and ΔS_C represent the increase in sales from advertising media A, B, and C, respectively. Similarly, denote ΔA_A, ΔA_B, and ΔA_C as the additional expenditures made in advertising media A, B, and C. Under these conditions an optimal advertising mix is indicated when

$$\frac{\Delta S_A}{\Delta A_A} = \frac{\Delta S_B}{\Delta A_B} = \frac{\Delta S_C}{\Delta A_C}$$

[14.1]

If this were not true and $\Delta S_A/\Delta A_A > \Delta S_B/\Delta A_B$, it would be profitable for the firm to reduce its advertising in medium B and increase it in medium A until an equilibrium is reached.

The Value of Advertising

Traditional economic analysis has tended to conclude that the primary impacts of advertising are to raise prices to consumers and to lead to the creation and maintenance of monopoly power.[15] Other research has focused on the impact of advertising on consumer tastes and preferences. Whether advertising is effective in changing consumer desires remains largely an empirically untested proposition because of the wide range of influences on consumer preferences. The analysis of the effect of advertising on the molding of consumer tastes and preferences tends to imply that this result is undesirable. This conclusion is, however, largely based on intuition. Firm evidence is scarce.

More recently, economic research has focused on the potential value of advertising from a consumer's perspective. Although it is true that advertising costs may be passed on to consumers, these increased costs may be offset by the beneficial effects of advertising. For example, if advertising is successful in expanding the market for a firm's product, and if that product is produced under conditions where the firm's average cost function is declining, then the saving in unit production costs may more than offset the unit advertising cost.

---

[15] Evidence in support of this view is presented in William Comaner and Thomas Wilson, *Advertising and Market Power* (Cambridge, Mass.: Harvard University Press, 1974).

Both Stigler[16] and Nelson [17] have used the theory of the economics of information to analyze the value of advertising. By giving consumers price information, advertising is expected to reduce the price paid by consumers. In the absence of cheaply available price information, consumers may not find the best price for a product they seek to purchase. This is because the discovery of price information may be costly and time consuming in the absence of price advertising. If, for example, it costs a consumer $10 in time to discover the store that will offer a saving of $8 on the price of an item, the search for price information is not worthwhile. But if price advertising makes all consumers aware of the lowest priced supplier of an item at an additional cost of only $1, then the great majority of consumers will be better off as a result of this advertising. For example, Benham found the price of eyeglasses to be substantially lower in states that permitted price advertising than in those that prohibited such advertising.[18] Similar results have been found for dental, medical, and legal services.

In addition, Nelson found that advertisers of all products have substantial incentives to provide useful and truthful information to customers. High-quality information can reduce the search cost for consumers as they seek to make a choice between alternative goods. Because consumers can assess the truthfulness of the information contained in an advertisement and because advertising creates brand awareness (both for good and inferior brands), advertisers who misrepresent their product will not be successful in generating future (and repeat) business.

Finally, both Nelson and Stigler have found that advertising tends to increase demand elasticities of goods. The demand for products that are not widely advertised tends to be price inelastic. The more extensive the advertising effort, the more price elastic the demand for a product becomes. In general, the more elastic the demand for a product, the more competitive is the market for that product—and frequently lower prices result.

Summary

- In general, a profit-maximizing firm will desire to operate at that level of output where marginal cost equals marginal revenue.

- In a purely competitive market structure, the firm will operate in the short run as long as price is greater than average variable cost.

- In a purely competitive market structure, the tendency is toward a long-run equilibrium condition in which firms earn just normal profits, price is equal to marginal cost and average total cost, and average total cost is minimized.

---

[16] George J. Stigler, "The Economics of Information," *Journal of Political Economy* (June 1961), pp. 213–225.

[17] Philip Nelson, "The Economic Consequences of Advertising," *Journal of Business* (April 1975), pp. 213–241.

[18] Lee Benham. "The Effect of Advertising on the Price of Eyeglasses," *Journal of Law and Economics* (October 1972), pp. 337–352.

- In a pure monopoly market structure, firms will generally produce a lower level of output and charge a higher price than would exist in a more competitive market structure. This conclusion assumes no significant economies of scale that might make a monopolist more efficient than a large group of smaller firms.

- In a monopolistically competitive industry, a large number of firms sell a differentiated product. In practice, few market structures can be best analyzed in the context of the monopolistic competition model. Most actual market structures have greater similarities to the purely competitive market model or the oligopolistic market model.

- Advertising expenditures were shown to be optimal from a profit-maximization perspective if they are carried to the point where the marginal revenue from an additional dollar spent on advertising is equal to the ratio of price divided by price minus marginal cost.

Selected References

Benham, Lee. "The Effect of Advertising on the Price of Eyeglasses." *Journal of Law and Economics* (October 1972), pp. 337–352.

Blackstone E. A. "Dentists and Denturists: The Development and Consequence of Competition in Dentures." *Antitrust Bulletin* (Winter 1980), pp. 751–776.

Chamberlin, Edward H. *The Theory of Monopolistic Competition*. Cambridge Mass.: Harvard University Press, 1933.

Cohen, Kalman and Richard Cyert. *Theory of the Firm*, 2d ed. Englewood Cliffs, N.J.: Prentice-Hall, 1975.

Comaner, William, and Thomas Wilson. *Advertising and Market Power*. Cambridge, Mass.: Harvard University Press, 1974.

Dorfman, Robert, and Peter O. Steiner. "Optimal Advertising and Optimal Quality." *American Economic Review* (December 1954), pp. 826–836.

Lipsy, R., and Lancaster, L. "The General Theory of Second Best." *Review of Economic Studies* 24, no. 1 (1956), pp. 11–32.

Nelson, Phillip. "The Economic Consequences of Advertising." *Journal of Business* (April 1975), pp. 213–241.

Shepard, William G. "Causes of Increased Competition in the United States Economy, 1939–1980." *Review of Economics and Statistics* (November 1982), pp. 613–626.

Stigler, George J. *Five Lectures on Economic Problems*. London: Longmans, Green, 1949).

Stigler, George J. "The Economics of Information." *Journal of Political Economy* (June 1961), pp. 213–225.

Williams, W. E. "Put the Brakes on Taxicab Monopolies." *Wall Street Journal*. 11 June 1984, p. 20.

Discussion Questions

1. How are above normal profits eliminated from a purely competitive or a monopolistically competitive industry?

2. Firms in competitive markets are often viewed as being price takers; that is, they must simply accept the market price as their own. Can you give examples outside of purely competitive industries where firms act as price takers?

3. How do changes in factor prices affect the short-run supply curve for the typical firm in a purely competitive market? If the same firm experiences an increase in its fixed costs, what effect will this have on its short-run supply curve?

4. What effect do you think a state law requiring gasoline stations to post their prices prominently will have on the average price of gasoline charged in the state? How can consumers benefit from such a law requiring the posting of gasoline prices?

5. In the long run, compare and contrast the size of the plant that would be built by a competitive firm with one built by a firm in a monopolistically competitive or a monopoly market.

6. At one point during the energy crisis, gasohol was viewed as one part of a solution to the problem of shortages of petroleum products. Gasohol was made from a blend of gasoline and alcohol derived from corn. What would you expect the impact of this program to be on the price of corn, soybeans, and wheat?

7. If the government sets a floor price for milk, would you expect that a need would arise for restrictions on the number of cows farmers can milk? In the absence of these restrictions, what outcome would you expect?

8. Analyze the short- and long-run effects of a quota system designed to limit steel imports into the United States.

9. At any particular level of output, a firm will always operate in such a manner as to minimize the cost of providing that output. At the same time, however, we say that it is not always in the best interests of a firm to operate at a level where average total costs are minimized. Explain.

10. What impact is a subsidy paid to a monopolist likely to have on consumer prices and output if
   a. The subsidy is a fixed amount that does not vary with the level of output;
   b. The subsidy is paid as a fixed amount on each unit produced; or
   c. The subsidy increases per unit as output increases.

11. You have been retained as an analyst to evaluate a proposal by your city's privately owned water company to increase its rates by 100 percent. The company has argued that at the present rate level, the firm is earning only a 2 percent rate of return on invested equity capital. The company believes a 16 percent rate of return is required in today's capital markets.
   Assume that you agree with the 16 percent rate of return proposed by the company.
   a. What factors need to be considered when setting rates designed to achieve this objective?
   b. Would your analysis differ if you knew that individuals were prohibited by law from drilling their own wells? What impact would this have on the price elasticity of demand?
   c. Water companies have a large proportion of fixed costs as compared with variable costs. How does this fact influence your analysis?
   d. Do you believe this firm (a monopolist) can earn its required 16 percent rate of return even if the public utility commission agrees this is a reasonable rate of return?

12. Evaluate the statement. "The reason monopolists always make excessive profits is that they face a nearly perfectly inelastic demand curve, and are thus able to charge an excessively high price."

13. Evaluate the statement, "When a firm is faced with a highly elastic demand curve for

its products, this is an indication that the firm has many competitors providing closely substitutable products. Under such conditions, it is impossible for the firm to earn anything more than a normal level of profits."

14. The Crosby Tool Company currently has a domestic monopoly position on the production of a specialty oil well servicing tool. Recently, the government has negotiated a new trade agreement that permits foreign suppliers to compete in the United States market. Discuss the likely impact of this trade agreement on the price elasticity of demand for Crosby's tool and on Crosby's prices.

15. What motivation does a monopolist have to overinvest in plant and equipment? What factors might restrain the monopolist from such overinvesting?

Problems

1. Given the demand function $P = 20 - Q$, prove that a nondiscriminating monopolist will maximize *total revenue* if the quantity sold is exactly one-half the amount that would be demanded if the good were provided free; that is, $P = 0$.

2. Assume that a firm in a perfectly competitive industry has the following total cost schedule:

Output (units)	Total Cost ($)
10	$110
15	150
20	180
25	225
30	300
35	385
40	480

a. Calculate a marginal cost and an average cost schedule for the firm.
b. If the prevailing market price is $17 per unit, how many units will be produced and sold? What are profits per unit? What are total profits?
c. Is the industry in long-run equilibrium at this price?

3. During several past wars, and more recently under programs designed to curb inflation, the government has imposed price ceilings on certain commodities. This is done to keep prices from rising to the natural level that would prevail under supply-demand equilibrium. The result is that the quantity that sellers are willing to supply at the ceiling price often falls short of the quantity demanded at that price. To bring supply and demand more into equilibrium, ration coupons are sometimes issued.

a. Show graphically, using both supply and demand curves, the effects of a ceiling price.
b. On the black market how much would you be willing to pay for a ration coupon good for the purchase of one unit of the rationed commodity?
c. If the aggregate demand curve for Commodity X is $P = 100 - 5Q$, and the industry supply curve for that same product is $P = 10 + 10Q$, calculate the following:
   (i) The equilibrium price and quantity for Commodity X
   (ii) The quantity that will be sold if a ceiling price of $60 is established
   (iii) The black market price of a ration coupon good for the purchase of one unit of X

4. Royersford Knitting Mills, Ltd. sells a line of women's knit underwear. The firm now sells about 20,000 pairs a year at an average price of $10 each. Fixed costs amount to $60,000, and total variable costs equal $120,000. The production department has estimated that a 10 percent increase in output would not affect fixed costs but would reduce average variable cost by 40 cents.

   The marketing department advocates a price reduction of 5 percent to increase sales, total revenues, and profits. The arc elasticity of demand is estimated at -2.

   a. Evaluate the impact of the proposal to cut prices on (i) total revenue, (ii) total cost, and (iii) total profits.

   b. If average variable costs are assumed to remain constant over a 10 percent increase in output, evaluate the effects of the proposed price cut on total profits.

5. The Jenkins Tool Co. has estimated the following demand equation for its product:

$$Q_D = 12,000 - 4,000P$$

where

$$P = \text{price/unit}$$
$$Q_D = \text{quantity demanded/year}$$

The firm's total costs are $4,000 when nothing is being produced. These costs increase by 50 cents for each unit produced.

   a. Write an equation for the total cost function.

   b. Specify the marginal cost function.

   c. Write an equation for total revenue in terms of Q.

   d. Specify the marginal revenue function.

   e. Write an equation for total profits, π, in terms of Q. At what level of output are total profits maximized (that is, find the maximum of the total profit function)? What price will be charged? What will total profit be?

   f. Check your answers in part (e) by equating marginal cost and marginal revenue and solving for Q.

   g. What model of market pricing behavior has been assumed in this problem?

6. If the royalties received by an author for writing a college text are set at a rate of about 15 percent of the publisher's total revenue,

   a. Demonstrate graphically that this creates an inherent conflict between the interests of a profit-maximizing publisher and those of a royalty-maximizing author.

   b. As the student consumer, whose interests would you like to see prevail?

   c. Does the magnitude of this conflict between author and publisher diminish in the case of a highly inelastic demand curve? Demonstrate graphically.

7. Ajax Cleaning Products is a medium-sized firm operating in an industry dominated by one very large firm—Tile King. Ajax produces a multi-headed tunnel wall scrubber that is very similar to a model produced by Tile King. Ajax has decided to charge the same price as Tile King to avoid the possibility of a price war. The price charged by Tile King is $20,000.

   Ajax has the following short-run cost curve:

$$TC = 800,000 - 5,000Q + 100Q^2$$

   a. Compute the marginal cost curve for Ajax.

   b. Given Ajax's pricing strategy, what is the marginal revenue function for Ajax?

   c. Compute the profit-maximizing level of output for Ajax.

   d. Compute Ajax's total dollar profits.

8. A firm operating in a purely competitive environment is faced with a market price of $250. The firm's total cost function (short-run) is

$$TC = 6,000 + 400Q - 20Q^2 + Q^3$$

a. Should the firm produce at this price in the short run?
b. If the market price is $300, what will total profits (losses) be if the firm produces ten units of output? Should the firm produce at this price?
c. If the market price is greater than $300, should the firm produce in the short run?

9. The Poster Bed Company believes that its industry can best be classified as monopolistically competitive. An analysis of the demand for its canopy bed has resulted in the following estimated demand function for the bed:

$$P = 1760 - 12Q$$

The cost analysis department has estimated the total cost function for the poster bed as

$$TC = \tfrac{1}{3}Q^3 - 15Q^2 + 5Q + 24,000$$

a. Calculate the level of output that should be produced to maximize short-run profits.
b. What price should be charged?
c. Compute total profits at this price-output level.
d. Compute the point price elasticity of demand at the profit-maximizing level of output.
e. What level of fixed costs is the firm experiencing on its bed production?
f. What is the impact of a $5,000 increase in the level of fixed costs on the price charged, output produced, and profit generated?

10. One and Only, Inc. is a monopolist. The demand function for its product is estimated to be

$$Q = 60 - .4P + 6Y + 2A$$

where

Q = quantity of units sold

P = price per unit

Y = per capita disposable personal income (thousands of dollars)

A = hundreds of dollars of advertising expenditures

The firm's average variable cost function is

$$AVC = Q^2 - 10Q + 60$$

Y is to equal 3(thousand) and A is equal to 3(hundred) for the period being analyzed.
a. If fixed costs are equal to $1,000, derive the firm's total cost function and marginal cost function.
b. Derive a total revenue function and marginal revenue function for the firm.
c. Calculate the profit-maximizing level of price and output for One and Only.
d. What profit or loss will One and Only earn?
e. If fixed costs were $1,200, how would your answers change for (a) through (d)?

11. Assume that a firm sells its product in a perfectly competitive market. The firm's fixed costs (including a "normal" return on the funds the entrepreneur has invested in the firm) are equal to $100 and its variable cost schedule is as follows:

Output (Units)	Variable Cost per Unit
50	$5.00
100	4.50
150	4.00
200	3.50
250	3.00
300	2.75
350	3.00
400	3.50

a. Find the marginal cost and average total cost schedules for the firm.
b. If the prevailing market price is $4.50, how many units will be produced and sold?
c. What are total profits and profit per unit at the output level determined in part (b)?
d. Is the industry in long-run equilibrium at this price? Explain.

12. Exotic Metals, Inc., a leading manufacturer of zirilium, which is used in many electronic products, estimates the following demand schedule for its product:

Price ($/pound)	Quantity (pounds/period)
$ 25	0
18	1,000
16	2,000
14	3,000
12	4,000
10	5,000
8	6,000
6	7,000
4	8,000
2	9,000

Fixed costs of manufacturing zirilium are $14,000 per period. The firm's variable cost schedule is as follows:

Output (pounds/period)	Variable Cost (per pound)
0	$ 0
1,000	10.00
2,000	8.50
3,000	7.33
4,000	6.25
5,000	5.40
6,000	5.00
7,000	5.14
8,000	5.88
9,000	7.00

a. Find the total revenue and marginal revenue schedules for the firm.

b. Determine the average total cost and marginal cost schedules for the firm.

c. What are Exotic Metal's profit-maximizing price and output level for the production and sale of zirilium?

d. What is Exotic's profit (or loss) at the solution determined in part (c)?

e. Suppose that the federal government announces it will sell zirilium, from its extensive wartime stockpile, to anyone who wants it at $6 per pound. How does this affect the solution determined in part (c)? What is Exotic Metal's profit (or loss) under these conditions?

13. Wyandotte Chemical Company sells various chemicals to the automobile industry. Wyandotte currently sells 30,000 gallons of polyol per year at an average price of $15 per gallon. Fixed costs of manufacturing polyol are $90,000 per year and total variable costs equal $180,000. The operations research department has estimated that a 15 percentt increase in output would not affect fixed costs but would reduce average variable costs by 60 cents per gallon. The marketing department has estimated the arc elasticity of demand for polyol to be -2.0.

a. How much would Wyandotte have to reduce the price of polyol to achieve a 15 percent increase in the quantity sold?

b. Evaluate the impact of such a price cut on (i) total revenue, (ii) total costs, and (iii) total profits.

14. Tennis Products, Inc. produces three models of high-quality tennis racquets. The following table contains recent information on the sales, costs, and profitability of the three models:

Model	Average Quantity Sold (units/ month)	Current Price	Total Revenue	Variable Cost per Unit	Contribution Margin per Unit	Contribution Margin*
A	15,000	$30	$ 450,000	$15.00	$15	$225,000
B	5,000	35	175,000	18.00	17	85,000
C	10,000	45	450,000	20.00	25	250,000
Total			$1,075,000			$565,000

*Contribution to fixed costs and profits.

The company is considering lowering the price of Model A to $27 in an effort to increase the number of units sold. Based on the results of price changes that have been instituted in the past. Tennis Products' chief economist has estimated the arc price elasticity of demand to be -2.5. Furthermore, he has estimated the arc cross-elasticity of demand between Model A and Model B to be approximately 0.5 and between Model A and Model C to be approximately 0.2. Variable costs per unit are not expected to change over the anticipated changes in volume.

a. Evaluate the impact of the price cut on the (i) total revenue, and (ii) contribution margin of Model A. Based on this analysis, should the firm lower the price of Model A?

b. Evaluate the impact of the price cut on the (i) total revenue and (ii) contribution margin for the entire line of tennis racquets. Based on this analysis, should the firm lower the price of Model A?

15. The Lumins Lamp Company, a producer of old-style oil lamps, has estimated the following demand function for its product:

$$Q = 120,000 - 10,000P$$

where Q is the quantity demanded per year and P is the price per lamp. The firm's fixed costs are $12,000 and variable costs are $1.50 per lamp.

a. Write an equation for the total revenue (TR) function in terms of Q.
b. Specify the marginal revenue function.
c. Write an equation for the total cost (TC) function in terms of Q.
d. Specify the marginal cost function.
e. Write an equation for total profits (π) in terms of Q. At what level of output (Q) are total profits maximized? What price will be charged? What are total profits at this output level?
f. Check your answers in part (e) by equating the marginal revenue and marginal cost functions, determined in parts (b) and (d), and solving for Q.
g. What model of market pricing behavior has been assumed in this problem?

16. Industry demand has been estimated as

$$Q = 5,000 - 10P + 350(T - 1)$$

Industry supply has been estimated as

$$Q = 2,200 + 18P$$

a. What will the market price be in year $T = 1$?
b. What will the market price be in year $T = 5$?

17. A monopolist faces the following demand function for its product:

$$Q = 45 - 5P$$

The fixed costs of the monopolist are $12 and the monopolist incurs variable costs of $5.00 per unit.

a. What is the profit-maximizing level of price and quantity for this monopolist? What will profits be at this price and output level?
b. If the government imposes a franchise tax on the firm of $10, what will be the profit-maximizing level of price, output, and profits?
c. If the government imposes an excise tax of 50 cents per unit of output sold, what is the impact on the profit-maximizing level of price, output, and profits?
d. If the government imposes a ceiling of $6 on the price of the firm's product, what output will the firm produce and what will be total profits?

18. Unique Creations has a monopoly position in the production and sale of magnometers. The cost function facing Unique has been estimated to be

$$TC = \$100,000 + 20Q$$

a. What is the marginal cost for Unique?
b. If the price elasticity of demand for Unique is currently -1.5, what price should Unique charge?
c. What is the marginal revenue at the price computed in part (b)?
d. If a competitor develops a substitute for the magnometer and the price elasticity increases to -3.0, what price should Unique charge?

Price and Output Determination: Oligopoly 15

Much of U.S. industry is best classified as oligopolistic in structure. An oligopoly is characterized by a relatively small number of firms producing a product. The product may be differentiated, as in the case of automobiles, or relatively undifferentiated, as in the case of oil. The distinguishing characteristic of oligopoly is that the number of firms is small enough that actions by any individual firm in the industry on price, output, product style or quality, introduction of new models, and terms of sale have a perceptible impact on the sales of other firms in the industry. Thus, the distinctive feature of oligopoly is the recognizable interdependence among the firms in the industry. Each firm is aware in its decision making that any new move, such as introducing an improved warranty for its product or the launching of a large promotional campaign, is likely to evoke a countermove from its rivals. In order to maximize wealth for the owners of a firm, the managers must consider that strategic decisions made in one firm will result in responses from other firms. Wealth maximization requires that these responses be anticipated and managed, if possible.

Glossary of New Terms

Cartel
A formal or informal agreement among firms in an oligopolistic industry. Cartel members may agree on such issues as prices, total industry output, market shares, and the division of profits.

Price leadership
A pricing strategy followed in many oligopolistic industries. One firm normally announces all new price changes. Either by an explicit or an implicit agreement, other firms in the industry regularly follow the pricing moves of the industry leader.

Interdependencies in Oligopoly

The nature of oligopoly interdependencies can be illustrated algebraically. Consider the case of a two-firm oligopoly (a duopoly) that sells a standardized product at the same market price (P). The market demand function is

$$P = f(Q_1 + Q_2) = f(Q_1, Q_2) \qquad [15.1]$$

where Q_1 and Q_2 are the outputs of the two respective firms. Total revenues for the two firms are

$$TR_1 = Q_1 P = Q_1 \cdot f(Q_1, Q_2)$$

$$TR_2 = Q_2 P = Q_2 \cdot f(Q_1, Q_2)$$

Total profits of the two firms are

$$\pi_1 = TR_1 - TC_1 = Q_1 \cdot f(Q_1, Q_2) - g_1(Q_1) \qquad [15.2]$$

$$\pi_2 = TR_2 - TC_2 = Q_2 \cdot f(Q_1, Q_2) - g_2(Q_2) \qquad [15.3]$$

where $g_1(Q_1)$ and $g_2(Q_2)$ are the respective total cost functions of two firms. From Equation 15.2 one can see that the total profits of Firm 1 are a function of (dependent on) the output decisions (Q_2) of Firm 2. Likewise, from Equation 15.3 one can see that the total profits of Firm 2 are dependent on the output decisions (Q_1) of Firm 1. Hence, in attempting to maximize profits, each firm must know (or make some assumption about) the output decisions of the other firm. In this environment of interdependence, it is virtually impossible for a firm to know its own demand function because this function is dependent on the actions of rivals.

By its very definition, the oligopolistic market structure covers a wide range of industry configurations. Some of the possibilities include a simple two-firm oligopoly, a market structure where five or ten firms produce all the industry output, or a market structure in which a small number of firms (for example, four) control most of the industry output (maybe 60 percent) but where a rather large fringe of smaller firms produce the remainder of the total output. Among the hundreds of possibilities, the only limitation is the existence of recognizable interdependencies. The recognizable interdependencies can lead to varying degrees of competition and cooperation among the oligopolistic firms. At one extreme is the case of intense rivalry (i.e., no cooperation), where a firm may seek to become a monopolist by driving its competitor(s) out of business. Alternatively, some form of informal, or tacit, cooperation may take place among the oligopolistic firms—"conscious parallelism of action"—with respect to pricing and other decisions.[1] At the other extreme is a formal collusive agreement among the firms to act as a monopolist by setting prices to maximize total industry profits. Because of the wide scope of industry configurations that fall under the oligopoly classification and the difficulty of predicting the response that rivals will take to the competitive moves of other firms, no single normative model can unambiguously prescribe oligopolists' competitive behavior regarding price, output, and other conditions surrounding the sale of their products. This chapter examines a number of possible solutions to the interdependency problem faced by the oligopolist.

Ignoring Interdependencies: Cournot Model

The easiest approach to the interdependency problem is merely to ignore it; that is, to act as if it does not exist at all and assume that your competitors will do likewise. In actual practice this probably describes the way oligopolists act in making a wide variety of routine decisions or decisions that are likely to have a rather small impact on the entire industry. In these cases tracing through the complex effects of such decisions may not be worth the time and expense required. For more significant decisions—such as the introduction of a revolutionary new model, a major price change, or the initiation of an extensive advertising campaign—the oligopolist can ill afford not to worry about the reactions of competitors.

---

[1] See F. M. Scherer, *Industrial Market Structure and Economic Performance*, 2d ed. (Chicago Ill.: Rand McNally, 1980), pp. 513–520, for a discussion of the conscious parallelism doctrine.

One oligopoly model, which ignored the interdependencies among firms, was published by the French economist Augustin Cournot in 1838. According to the Cournot model, each of the two firms (duopoly),[2] in determining its profit-maximizing output level, *assumes that the other firm's output will not change.*

The Cournot model of oligopoly decision making can be illustrated with a numerical example. Assume that two companies (A and B) produce identical products. Demand for the products is given by the following linear demand function:

$$P = 3,000 - Q_A - Q_B$$

where Q_A and Q_B are the quantities sold by the respective firms and P is the (market) selling price. For simplicity, also assume (as Cournot did) that the marginal costs of the two firms are zero,[3] that is, $MC_A = 0$ and $MC_B = 0$. Initially assume that neither firm is producing any output.

Analysis of this example is shown in Figure 15.1. Suppose Firm A makes the first decision (round 1). Since Firm B is not producing any output ($Q_B = 0$), it is faced with a demand function of $P = 3,000 - Q_A$. Being interested in maximizing profits, it sets $MR_A = MC_A = 0$ and obtains the optimal output of $Q_A^* = 1,500$ units as shown in the Q_A^* and "Solution" columns of Figure 15.1. Firm B makes the next decision (round 2). It assumes that Firm A will continue producing 1,500 units. Therefore, Firm B is faced with a demand function of $P = 1,500 - Q_B$. Also being interested in maximizing profits, Firm B sets $MR_B = MC_B = 0$ and obtains the optimal output of $Q_B^* = 750$ units as shown in the Q_B and "Solution" columns of Figure 15.1.

In the third decision-making round, Firm A observes that Firm B is now producing 750 units and assumes that Firm B will continue producing this quantity. Consequently, Firm A is faced with a new demand function: $P = 2,250 - Q_A$. As shown in Figure 15.1, its profit-maximizing output is $Q_A^* = 1,125$. In the fourth round, Firm B observes that Firm A is now producing 1,125 units and assumes that Firm A will continue producing this quantity. Firm B's new demand function is $P = 1875 - Q_B$. To maximize profits it decides to produce 937.5 units as shown in Figure 15.1.

In the Cournot model this pattern continues until equilibrium occurs. The equilibrium solution is calculated in Figure 15.1. In the equilibrium solution the optimal output for each firm is 1,000 units. In general, the optimal outputs of the two firms (with identical costs) when equilibrium is reached are equal in the Cournot model. This result occurs regardless of the initial outputs of the two firms. Note also that the selling price changes during each round of the

---

[2] The Cournot model can be extended to any number of sellers; that is, oligopoly.

[3] Cournot used the example of two firms that sell mineral water from a natural spring. Including nonzero costs in the model makes the analysis slightly more complex but does not change the conclusions of the model. See Kalman Cohen and Richard Cyert, *Theory of the Firm: Resource Allocation in a Market Economy* (Englewood Cliffs, N.J.: Prentice-Hall, 1965), pp. 234–235, for an example of the Cournot model with nonzero costs.

Decision-making Round	Decision-maker	Optimal Output Q_A^*	Q_B^*	Price P	Solution
1	Firm A	1500	0	1500	$P = 3000 - Q_A - 0 = 3000 - Q_A$
					$TR_A = PQ_A = (3000 - Q_A)Q_A = 3000Q_A - Q_A^2$
					$MR_A = \frac{d(TR_A)}{dQ_A} = 3000 - 2Q_A = 0 = MC_A$
					$Q_A^* = \frac{3000}{2} = 1500; P = 3000 - 1500 = \$1500$
2	Firm B	1500	750	750	$P = 3000 - 1500 - Q_B = 1500 - Q_B$
					$TR_B = PQ_B = (1500 - Q_B)Q_B = 1500Q_B - Q_B^2$
					$MR_B = \frac{d(TR_B)}{dQ_B} = 1500 - 2Q_B = 0 = MC_B$
					$Q_B^* = \frac{1500}{2} = 750; P = 1500 - 750 = \$750$
3	Firm A	1125	750	1125	$P = 3000 - Q_A - 750 = 2250 - Q_A$
					$TR_A = 2250Q_A - Q_A^2$
					$MR_A = 2250 - 2Q_A = 0$
					$Q_A^* = 1125; P = 2250 - 1125 = \$1125$
4	Firm B	1125	937.5	937.5	$P = 3000 - 1125 - Q_B = 1875 - Q_B$
					$TR_B = 1875Q_B - Q_B^2$
					$MR_B = 1875 - 2Q_B = 0$
					$Q_B^* = 937.5; P = 1875 - 937.5 = \$937.5$
5	Firm A	1031.25	937.5	1031.25	
6	Firm B	1031.25	984.38	984.38	Similar to analysis above.
7	Firm A	1007.81	984.38	1007.81	
8	Firm B	1007.81	996.09	996.09	
⋮	⋮	⋮	⋮	⋮	
Equilibrium		1000	1000	1000	

Equilibrium solution:

$$P = 3000 - Q_A - Q_B$$
$$TR_A = PQ_A = (3000 - Q_A - Q_B)Q_A = 3000Q_A - Q_A^2 - Q_A Q_B$$
$$TR_B = PQ_B = (3000 - Q_A - Q_B)Q_B = 3000Q_B - Q_A Q_B - Q_B^2$$
$$MR_A = \frac{\partial(TR_A)}{\partial Q_A} = \boxed{3000 - 2Q_A - Q_B = 0} = MC_A$$
$$MR_B = \frac{\partial(TR_B)}{\partial Q_B} = \boxed{3000 - Q_A - 2Q_B = 0} = MC_B$$

Solve the set of simultaneous equations in the box to obtain $Q_A^* = 1000$; $Q_B^* = 1000$; $P = 3,000 - 1,000 - 1,000 = \$1,000/\text{unit}$

Figure 15.1
Example of Cournot Duopoly Model

decision-making process as the firms adjust their output. The equilibrium price is $1,000/unit.

The Cournot model has been criticized for the unrealistic assumption made by each duopolist about the behavior of its competitor. The assumption that the other firm will keep its output constant, particularly when this independence assumption has proved incorrect on earlier decision-making rounds is not consistent with rational economic behavior. Normally, one would expect the duopolist to learn from past mistakes and either make some alternative assumption about the behavior of the competitor or, if possible, enter a (formal or informal) collusive agreement with the other firm to raise prices and increase profits.

Despite the shortcomings of the Cournot model, it provides insights into the nature of the interdependencies among oligopolists and the necessity to make *some* assumption about how competitors will react to the firm's price-output decisions.

Cartels and Other Forms of Collusion

At the other extreme, oligopolists may seek to reduce the inherent risk that exists because of the interdependencies of the industry structure by either formally or informally agreeing to cooperate or collude in decision making. Formal agreements of oligopolists are called *cartels*, such as those that are typical in much of Europe. In general, collusive agreements of any sort are illegal in the United States under the Sherman Antitrust Act of 1890; however, some important exceptions exist. For example, cooperatives set milk output quotas and prices in many parts of the country with the approval of the federal government. The International Air Transport Association (IATA), comprised of airlines flying transatlantic flights, sets uniform prices for these flights. Illegal collusive arrangements, however, have also existed in this country.[4] One of the best-known modern documented cases of this type of illegal cooperation was in the electrical equipment manufacturing industry during the 1950s. Several large firms—including General Electric, Westinghouse, and Allis Chalmers—along with some of their top executives were convicted of engaging in agreements to fix prices and divide up the markets for such items as switchgear and circuit breakers.[5]

Profit Maximization and the Division of Output

Under both legal cartels and formal secret collusive agreements, an attempt is made to increase industry profits above the level that would prevail in the absence of collusion. If the control board or directors of the cartel have a reasonably good understanding of the demand relationships for the product being controlled, then the cartel can act as a *monopolist* and *maximize total industry profits*. The profit-maximization solution for a two-firm cartel is shown graphically in Figure 15.2.

The *industry* demand, D, marginal revenue, MR, and marginal cost, ΣMC, curves are shown in the right-hand panel of Figure 15.2. The industry marginal cost curve is obtained by summing horizontally across outputs the marginal cost curves of the individual firms in the center and left-hand panels—that is, $\Sigma MC = MC_A + MC_B$. Total industry profits are maximized by setting total industry output (and consequently price) at the point where industry marginal revenue equals industry marginal cost. This yields the solution shown in the right-hand panel of Figure 15.2—the cartel should produce and sell Q_T units of output at a price of P per unit.

If the cartel seeks to maximize its profits, the market share (or quota) for each firm should be set at a level such that the marginal cost of all firms is identical. In Figure 15.2, the market share for each firm is found at the point

---

[4] See George A. Hay and Daniel Kelly, "An Empirical Survey of Price Fixing Conspiracies," *Journal of Law and Economics* 17 (April 1974), pp. 13–38.
[5] See "Collusion among Electrical Equipment Manufacturers," *Wall Street Journal*, 10 and 12 January 1962, reprinted in Edwin Mansfield, *Monopoly Power and Economic Performance* (New York: W. W. Norton, 1964).

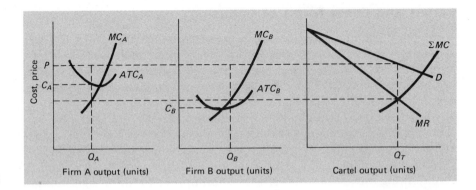

Figure 15.2
Price-Output Determination for a Two-Firm Cartel

where a horizontal line, drawn from the intersection of the ΣMC and MR curves in the right-hand panel, crosses the MC_A and MC_B curves in the left-hand and center panels, respectively. The optimal output allocation is for Firm A to produce Q_A units and for Firm B to produce Q_B units. If Firm A were producing at a level where its marginal costs exceeded Firm B's, cartel profits could be increased by shifting output from A to B until marginal costs are equal.[6] In actual practice this ideal allocation of output among firms in the cartel is rarely achieved. Each firm's share of industry output is determined by a process of negotiation so the strongest firms with the best bargaining position are likely to receive larger market shares than an optimal solution might suggest. In addition, more inefficient producers may be allocated larger shares of total profits than the optimum to convince them to participate in the cartel arrangement without "cheating." Evidence shows that often the level of output of each cartel member is based on historical patterns of sales, productive capacity, or profitability. Sometimes cartels will divide output geographically, giving each member an exclusive license to operate in a certain region.

The determination of the profit-maximizing price and output levels for a two-firm cartel can also be illustrated with a numerical example. Assume that the output of a certain industry is produced by only two firms (C and D). Demand for the product is given by the following linear demand function:

$$P = 1,000 - Q_C - Q_D \qquad [15.4]$$

where Q_C and Q_D are the quantities sold by the respective firms and P is the (market) selling price. The total cost functions for the respective firms are

$$TC_C = 90,000 + 5Q_C + .25Q_C^2 \qquad [15.5]$$

$$TC_D = 110,000 + 5Q_D + .15Q_D^2 \qquad [15.6]$$

Suppose the two firms (duopolists) decide to form a cartel and act as a monopolist to maximize total industry profits.

---

[6] Note that the average total costs of the two firms are not necessarily equal at the optimal (profit-maximizing) output level. Note also that Firm A is given a sizable share of the total output even though its average total costs are higher than Firm B's.

Total industry profits (π_T) are equal to the sum of Firm C's and Firm D's profits and are given by the following expression:

$$\pi_T = \pi_C + \pi_D$$
$$= PQ_C - TC_C + PQ_D - TC_D \qquad [15.7]$$

Substituting Equations 15.4, 15.5, and 15.6 into this expression yields

$$\begin{aligned}
\pi_T &= (1,000 - Q_C - Q_D)Q_C - (90,000 + 5Q_C + .25Q_C^2) \\
&\quad + (1,000 - Q_C - Q_D)Q_D - (110,000 + 5Q_D + .15Q_D^2) \\
&= 1,000Q_C - Q_C^2 - Q_C Q_D - 90,000 - 5Q_C - .25Q_C^2 \\
&\quad + 1,000Q_D - Q_C Q_D - Q_D^2 - 110,000 - 5Q_D - .15Q_D^2 \\
&= -200,000 + 995Q_C - 1.25Q_C^2 + 995Q_D \\
&\quad - 1.15Q_D^2 - 2Q_C Q_D \qquad [15.8]
\end{aligned}$$

To maximize π_T, take the *partial* derivatives of Equation 15.8 with respect to Q_C and Q_D:

$$\frac{\partial \pi_T}{\partial Q_C} = 995 - 2.50Q_C - 2Q_D$$

$$\frac{\partial \pi_T}{\partial Q_D} = 995 - 2.30Q_D - 2Q_C$$

Setting these expressions equal to zero yields

$$2.5Q_C + 2Q_D - 995 = 0$$
$$2Q_C + 2.3Q_D - 995 = 0$$

Solving these equations simultaneously gives the optimal output levels: $Q_C^* = 170.57$ units and $Q_D^* = 284.29$ units.

Substituting these values into Equations 15.4 and 15.8 gives an optimal selling price and total profit for the cartel of $P^* = \$545.14$ per unit and $\pi_T^* = \$26,291.43$, respectively. The marginal costs of the two firms at the optimal output level are equal to

$$MC_C^* = \frac{d(TC_C)}{dQ_C} = 5 + .50Q_C$$

$$= 5 + .50(170.57) = \$90.29$$

$$MC_D^* = \frac{d(TC_D)}{dQ_D} = 5 + .30Q_D$$

$$= 5 + .30(284.29) = \$90.29$$

As in the graphical solution illustrated earlier in Figure 15.2, the optimal output (or market share) for each firm in the cartel occurs where the marginal costs of the two firms are equal.

Factors Affecting Oligopolistic Collusion

The ability of oligopolistic firms to engage successfully in some form of formal (or informal) cooperation depends on a number of different factors. Several of these factors are examined below.[7]

Number and Size Distribution of Sellers. Effective collusion generally is more difficult as the number of oligopolistic firms involved increases. As the number of firms increases, individual firms are more likely to ignore the effects of their pricing and output decisions on the actions of rival firms. Likewise, as the number of firms increases, the chance is greater that one (or more) firm(s) will act independently and cut prices in an attempt to increase market share and profits. Finally, as the number of firms increases, a greater likelihood exists for disagreements concerning the most advantageous pricing and output policies.

Product Heterogeneity. Products manufactured by different firms are said to be *homogeneous* if they are alike in all significant physical and subjective characteristics and are viewed by customers as virtually perfect substitutes for one another. With perfect homogeneity, price is the only characteristic that differentiates the competing firms' products. In general, when the firms' products are *heterogeneous* (or differentiated), cooperation is more difficult because competition is occuring over a broad array of product characteristics, such as warranty and after-sale policies.

Cost Structures. Various firms within an industry are often faced with differing cost functions. Generally, the more cost functions differ among competing firms, the more difficult it will be for firms to collude on pricing and output decisions. Also, successful collusion is more difficult in industries where fixed costs (i.e., overhead) are a high percentage of total costs. This is particularly true during cyclical or secular declines in demand, when firms are operating well below plant capacity. With high fixed costs and correspondingly low marginal (variable) costs, firms that are operating below capacity can increase profits significantly by cutting prices and increasing output; hence, enforcing pricing agreements under such conditions can be difficult. Breakdowns in cooperation are most notable in industries that employ highly capital-intensive production processes, such as petroleum refining and steel making.

Size and Frequency of Orders. Successful oligopolistic cooperation also depends on the size distribution over time of customer orders. Effective collusion is more likely to occur when orders are small, frequent, and received regularly. When large orders are received infrequently at irregular intervals, it is more difficult for firms to collude on pricing and output decisions.

---

[7] See Sherer, *Industrial Market Structure*, pp. 199–227 for an expanded discussion of these factors.

Secrecy and Retaliation. An oligopolistic firm will be tempted to grant secret price concessions to selected customers if it feels that these price reductions will not be detected by its competitor(s). By keeping price concessions secret, a firm can forestall retaliation by its competitor(s) and hence earn additional profits. Since secret price cutting interferes with the maximization of total industry profits, oligopolistic industries sometimes attempt to make it difficult to conceal price concessions. One way this can be done is to have an industry trade association collect sales data and publish periodic reports of transactions between firms and their customers. Under such a system, information concerning price cutting by one firm will be quickly disseminated to the other firms in the industry and they can take swift retaliatory action. In general, knowledge of competitors' actions provides a favorable environment for some form of collusion to take place.

Social Structure of the Industry. Business and social contacts among industry executives at trade association and other meetings often can lead to friendship and mutual understanding that facilitates collusion among oligopolistic firms; however, such contacts do not guarantee cooperation. Personal animosity and distrust among the executives of competing firms may prevent effective collusion.

OPEC: The International Oil Producers' Cartel

The Organization of Petroleum Exporting Countries (OPEC) is a group of thirteen oil-producing nations.[8] In 1975 OPEC produced more than one-half of the world's supply of oil and more than 80 percent of the oil traded on world markets. OPEC was founded in 1960 by five large oil-producing countries that were experiencing declining oil revenues as a result of the pricing practices of the major international oil companies. At that time the international oil companies, which produced and marketed a large percentage of the world's oil, set the price of oil and paid taxes and royalties to the governments of countries in which that oil was produced.

Among OPEC's long-range goals, as set forth in a 1968 document, were that member governments should (1) determine oil prices and (2) own and control their oil resources directly.[9] This first goal was achieved by 1973, when the OPEC countries were able to increase oil prices unilaterally. During late–1973 and 1974, OPEC was able to achieve a fourfold increase in the price of petroleum. The second goal, that of government ownership and control, has been either partially or fully achieved in most OPEC countries through

---

[8] Member countries include Algeria, Ecuador, Gabon, Indonesia, Iran, Iraq, Kuwait, Libya, Nigeria, Qatar, Saudi Arabia, United Arab Emirates, and Venezuela.

[9] See Dankwart A. Rustow and John F. Mugno, *OPEC: Success and Prospects* (New York: New York University Press, 1976), appendix C, for the full text of this document.

takeovers and nationalization of the oil companies' operations. The oil companies continue to be in charge of many of the technical aspects of production and to act as worldwide distributors of OPEC oil.

OPEC is a cartel in the sense that it sets prices for oil. Prices are set at regular meetings of the oil ministers from the OPEC countries. Saudi Arabia is the most influential member of OPEC because of the tremendous size of its production capacity—almost one-half of OPEC's total output.[10] All pricing decisions are voted on by the oil ministers and are supposed to be unanimous; however, during the early 1980s, the OPEC members were unable to agree on a uniform price. The benchmark price of oil ranged from $32 to $36 per barrel among the various producing countries, with actual prices ranging from $32 to $41.[11] The conservative oil producers of the Persian Gulf (for example, Saudi Arabia and Kuwait), having large reserves expected to last well into the next century, attempted to hold prices at the low end of this range. Other countries with lesser petroleum reserves (such as Libya and Iran), along with Algeria, priced their oil at the high end of the range in an attempt to maximize their returns before their oil runs out.

Unlike many other cartels, OPEC had *not*, until recently, resorted to setting production quotas or allocating export shares among its members.[12] Despite this relatively limited amount of central direction and control, OPEC was effective in maintaining the market price of oil during the 1970s. Even during the worldwide recession of 1974–1975 (caused in part by the increase in oil prices), which saw OPEC's oil production drop by almost 22 percent from September 1973 to April 1974, OPEC was able to prevent any widespread secret price cutting that would have threatened the cartel's long-run stability. However, during the 1980s, when OPEC output fell by almost one-third, both overt and covert price cutting occurred. Because of the world oil glut during this period (due in part to conservation by consuming nations, substitution of coal for oil, and increased production from such sources as the North Sea), OPEC countries were forced to cut their prices and output. In March 1983 OPEC cut prices by 15 percent to $29 per barrel. Again, early in 1985 the official benchmark price was cut by $1 to $28. Covert price cutting took several different forms.[13] Nigeria engaged in secret price cutting by reducing royalties and income taxes for the oil companies working there. Other forms of covert price reductions included

---

[10] Rather than being a cartel, one could argue that OPEC is an example of a dominant price leadership arrangement, with Saudia Arabia acting as the dominant firm. Price leadership models are discussed in the following section. See also Armen A. Alchian and William B. Allen, *Exchange and Production*, 3d ed. (Belmont, Calif.: Wadsworth, 1983).

[11] The larger spread in actual prices compared with benchmark prices is due in part to differences in the quality of oil from various producing countries and their proximity to Western markets.

[12] Some OPEC members have individually set quotas on their own oil production "to prevent geologically premature depletion or to preserve a vanishing economic asset for future generations" (Ibid., p. 99).

[13] *Wall Street Journal*, 8 September 1981.

bartering and extending payment terms for oil purchases. Under a bartering agreement, Country A sells oil to Country B at a high price and agrees in return to purchase commodities from Country B at above-market, inflated prices. The net effect is that Country B actually pays less than the official price for the oil. Extending the payment period from the normal 15–30 days to 3–6 months reduces the effective cost of the oil to the buyer by reducing interest expenses on the funds required to finance the purchase.

During much of the 1980s, Saudia Arabia supported oil prices by acting as a "swing producer," cutting its production to as low as 2 million barrels per day (from a high of 10 million barrels per day in 1980). This was less than one-half of its authorized quota of 4.35 million barrels per day. In October 1985, however, Saudia Arabia changed its policy and began increasing its output to as much as 6 million barrels per day—which was well in excess of its quota. The objectives of this policy change were as follows:

1. To increase their own oil revenues (for example, selling twice as many barrels at 30 percent less per barrel would still yield a revenue increase of 40 percent.)

2. To encourage consumers worldwide to use more oil

3. To discipline other oil-producing countries, such as Britain, Norway, and Mexico, by making them feel the consequences of falling oil revenues

4. To force competitors in the United States, Canada, Britain, and other countries to shut down their higher-cost oil wells

Over the long run, the Saudia Arabian policy was intended to increase demand for oil, reduce oil reserves and production capacity, and induce greater co-operation on pricing and output decisions among OPEC (as well as non–OPEC) producing countries. As a result of the increase in Saudia Arabia's oil output, prices fell to as low as $6 per barrel during this period. After many months of negotiations, OPEC members (excluding Iraq who refused to participate in OPEC's quota system) agreed in July 1986 to cut oil production significantly and adopted a target price of $18 per barrel. Saudia Arabia again became OPEC's swing producer through its willingness to reduce oil output in order to support the new fixed price.

During the last few years speculation continued about an OPEC cartel collapse because of weak oil demand, surplus production capacity, and rampant price and output quota cheating by member countries. In spite of these problems, OPEC has managed to survive, even during a period when a significant price war was instigated by its largest producer and most influential member.

An awareness of cartel pricing practices is important to the managerial economist for a number of reasons. As noted in some of the examples in this section, some industries operate legally as cartels. Also, as more firms become multinational in scope, they will be forced to make decisions in an environment where cartels are permitted. Finally, an understanding of explicit cartel price-output decisions furnishes a good deal of insight into the more common domestic practice of price leadership.

Economic Analysis and Managerial Efficiency

THE NCAA: AN INTERCOLLEGIATE SPORTS CARTEL*

The National Collegiate Athletic Association (NCAA) is an organization of nearly eight hundred colleges and universities and more than one hundred related conferences (e.g., Big Ten, Southwest Conference, and Big East). Many of the rules of the NCAA have the effect of reducing economic competition among member schools, thus increasing profits (or reducing losses) that schools realize from their athletic programs. The regulations have permitted the NCAA to act like a cartel, controlling to a certain degree both the revenues and costs of its member schools.

In the past, the NCAA negotiated contracts with the major television networks. These contracts limited the number of football games that could be televised each week as well as the number of times a school could appear on television each season. In 1984, however, the U.S. Supreme Court ruled that these restrictions on televised football games were an illegal conspiracy in violation of the Sherman Antitrust Act. This ruling has significantly increased the number of college football games televised on the networks and cable carriers and has reduced the average fees per game paid to the schools. Likewise, schools such as Notre Dame and Oklahoma have increased their share of televised games at the expense of less popular schools.

While the NCAA has lost much of its power to control television revenues, it still retains control over costs through restrictions on the compensation of student athletes. Scholarships

granted to athletes are limited to tuition, room and board, and textbooks. Without this limitation, schools would undoubtedly compete openly to recruit top athletes by paying them additional money to play for their teams. Like professional athletes, the best student athletes would tend to receive the largest incomes. Under-the-table payments and other forms of cheating, which occur under the current NCAA rules, would tend to disappear. Recruiting scandals, such as the ones that led to the suspension of the football program at Southern Methodist University in 1986, would not occur.

Most economists argue that cartels raise prices, lower output, and are generally not beneficial to society. The effects on output and prices of explicit cartels, such as OPEC, are readily observable. The effects of a cartel such as the NCAA, which claims that its regulations are designed to protect student athletes and promote the financial stability of its members' athletic programs, are much more difficult to detect. Unless the courts rule that the NCAA's restraint on payments to athletes is an unlawful conspiracy, it is unlikely that the NCAA will change the present system.

Questions

1. How would an athletic administrator at a college or university determine the amount of compensation to be paid to each student athlete if the NCAA imposed no restrictions?

2. Proponents of the NCAA's present compensation rules claim that if schools could compete freely for athletes, then athletes' educations would suffer and they would be spoiled by the large incomes. In advocating the elimination of the present compensation system, how would you argue against this claim?

*Based on articles in *Business Week*, 14 September 1987 and the *Wall Street Journal*, 20 August 1985.

Price Leadership

Another model of price-output determination in some oligopolistic industries is *price leadership*. Many industries exhibit a pattern where one or a few firms normally set a price and others tend to follow, frequently with a time lag of a few days. The price pattern that is ultimately established depends very much on the degree to which products of the various firms are differentiated. In the case of basic steel products, for example, the price that finally prevails is generally uniform from one producer to another. For more differentiated products, such as automobiles, the uniform price may give way to a pricing structure among firms where recognizable differentials (within a limited range) may persist over time. Two major price leadership patterns have been observed in various industries from time to time: These are *barometric* and *dominant price leadership*. Other price leadership models not discussed in the following paragraphs are based on differential plant sizes, factor costs, technologies, and unequal market share conditions.

Barometric Price Leadership

In the case of barometric price leadership, one firm announces a change in price that it hopes will be accepted by others. The leader need not be the largest firm in the industry. In fact, this leader may actually change from time to time. The leader must, however, be reasonably correct in its interpretation of changing demand and cost conditions so that suggested price changes be accepted and stick. In essence, the barometric price leader merely initiates a reaction to changing market conditions that other firms find in their best interest to follow. These conditions might include such things as cost increases (or decreases) and sluggish (or brisk) sales accompanied by inventory buildups (or shortages) in the industry. If other firms do not agree with the leader's assessment of market conditions and changing cost patterns, a series of higher or lower prices may be announced by competitors until general agreement (via trial-and-error or explicit collusion) on a new price range is reached by all firms.

For example, on April 1, 1980, General Motors announced price increases averaging 2.2 percent on its 1980 model cars. On April 4, Ford announced similar increases of 2.2 percent. On April 7, American Motors announced increases of 2.6 percent. On April 8, Chrysler increased its prices by 2.3 percent and Volkswagen increased prices by 3.5 percent. During the severe auto industry sales slump (1981–1982), cash rebate programs initiated by one auto firm were invariably matched by the major domestic competitor firms. This pattern of comparable periodic price increases and rebate programs has repeated itself during most of the 1980s.

Dominant Price Leadership

In the case of dominant price leadership, one firm establishes itself as the leader because of its larger size, economic power, or lower cost structure in relation to other competing firms. The leader may then act as if it were a monopolist, setting prices at a level that maximizes its profits (that is, where its marginal cost

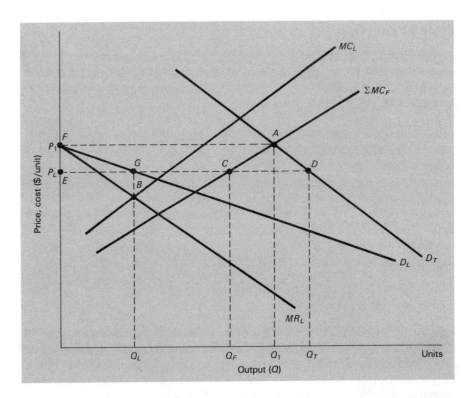

Figure 15.3
**Dominant Price
Leadership**

equals marginal revenue). In adopting this strategy, however, the leader must be reasonably certain that other firms will respond to the price change by bringing their prices in line with those of the leader.

The price-output solution for the dominant-firm model is shown in Figure 15.3. D_T shows total market demand for the product, MC_L represents the marginal cost curve for the dominant (leader) firm, and ΣMC_F constitutes the horizontal summation of the marginal cost curves for the follower firms. In the following analysis, *assume that the dominant firm sets the price and allows the follower firms to sell as much output as they wish at this price. The dominant firm then supplies the remainder of the market demand.*

Given that the follower firms can sell as much output as they wish at the price established by the dominant firm, they are faced with a horizontal demand curve and a perfectly competitive market situation. The follower firms view the dominant firm's price as their marginal revenue and, desiring to maximize profits, produce that level of output where their marginal cost equals the established price. The ΣMC_F curve therefore shows the total output that will be *supplied* at various prices by the follower firms. The dominant firm's demand curve D_L is obtained by subtracting the amount supplied by the follower firms ΣMC_F from the total market demand D_T at each price. For example, at a price of P_L, Point G on the D_L curve is obtained by subtracting EC from ED. Other points on the D_L curve are obtained in a similar manner. At a price of P_1 the quantity supplied by the follower firms Q_1 is equal to total market demand (Point A) and the dominant firm's demand is therefore zero (Point F). The dominant firm's marginal revenue curve MR_L is then obtained from its demand curve D_L.

The dominant firm maximizes its profits by setting price and output where marginal cost equals marginal revenue. As shown in Figure 15.3, $MR_L = MC_L$ at Point B. Therefore, the dominant firm should sell Q_L units of output at a price of P_L per unit. At a price of P_L, total demand is Q_T units, and the follower firms supply $Q_T - Q_L$ units of output.

What is the incentive for followers to accept the established price? In some cases it may be a fear of cutthroat retaliation from the dominant firm that keeps small firms from attempting to undercut the prevailing price. In other cases, following a price leader may be viewed as simply a convenience resulting in an accepted pattern of price leadership and followership that may operate as effectively as a formal cartel. This poses significant antitrust problems because no explicit, illegal collusion is apparent, even though the performance of the industry closely parallels what would prevail if explicit and illegal collusion had taken place.

Effective price leadership exists when price movements initiated by the leader have a high probability of sticking and no maverick or nonconforming firms exist. The fewer the number of firms in the industry (that is, the greater the interdependencies of decision outcomes among firms), the more effective price leadership is likely to be. As the number of firms expands, the relative dominance of any one firm is likely to decline, as will the interdependencies that exist among firms in the industry. It should be noted that just as in the case of cartels or illegal explicit collusion, implicit price leadership agreements may break down over time, especially in the face of substantial shifts in demand or costs that the price leader fails to reflect adequately in its established price.

The Kinked Demand Curve Model

One very popular model of oligopoly price-output behavior, known as the *kinked demand curve* model, was reported by Sweezy in 1939.[14] This model sought to explain rigidities observed in prices in oligopolistic industries. For instance, the price of steel rails had remained at $28 per ton between 1901 and 1916 and at $43 per ton between 1922 and 1933. Similarly, the price of sulphur remained at $18 per ton between 1926 and 1938, except for changes of 2 cents and 3 cents a ton in two of those years.[15]

Sweezy assumed that if an oligopolist cut its prices, competitors would quickly feel the decline in their sales and would be forced to match the price reduction. Alternatively, if one firm raised its prices, competitors would rapidly gain customers by maintaining their original prices and hence would have little or no motivation to match a price increase. In a situation such as this, the demand curve facing an individual oligopolist would be far more elastic

---

[14] Paul M. Sweezy. "Demand Under Conditions of Oligopoly," *Journal of Political Economy* 47 (1939), pp. 568–573. See also Scherer, *Industrial Market Structure*, pp. 164–168, for an expanded discussion of the model and its limitations.

[15] Marshall R. Colberg, William C. Bradford, and Richard M. Alt, *Business Economics: Principles and Cases*, rev. ed. (Homewood, Ill.: Richard D. Irwin, 1957), p. 276.

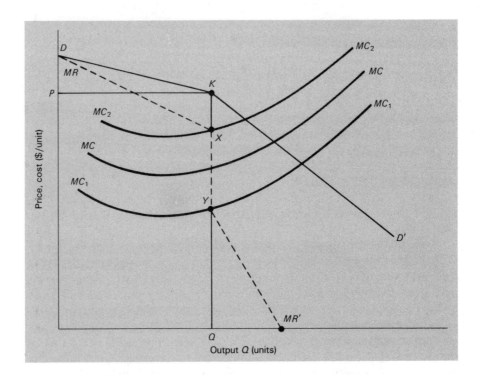

Figure 15.4
**The Kinked
Demand Curve
Model**

for price increases than for price decreases. If a firm *raises* its price and others do not follow, the increase in price will be more than offset by the decrease in sales, and total revenue received will decline. A price *reduction* that is matched by competitors would not be sufficiently offset by an increase in sales. Consequently, the total revenue received by each firm after the price reduction would be less than its original receipts. This is illustrated in Figure 15.4.

The oligopolist's demand curve is represented by DKD', with the prevailing price as P and output as Q. The marginal revenue curve is discontinuous because of the kink in the demand curve at K. Hence marginal revenue is represented by the two line segments MRX and $MR'Y$. If the marginal cost curve MC passes through the gap XY in the marginal revenue curve, the most profitable alternative is to maintain the current price-output policy.[16] The profit-maximizing level of price and output remains constant for the firm, which perceives itself to be faced with a kinked demand curve, even though costs may change over a rather wide range (for example, MC_2 and MC_1). Similarly, shifts in the demand curve either to the right (an increase in demand) or to the left (a decrease in demand) may not change the price decisions of the firm. Since the kink is determined at the *prevailing price*, a shift in demand shifts the gap XY in the marginal revenue curve to the right or left. If MC still passes through

---

[16] Profit may not be increased by increasing price (and decreasing output), since $MR > MC$, and this difference would increase with a price increase. Similarly, profit may not be increased by decreasing price (and increasing output), since $MR < MC$, and this difference would also increase with a price decrease.

the gap, the prevailing price is maintained, although output will either increase or decrease.

A number of criticisms have been made of the kinked demand curve model as a general model of oligopoly behavior. Although the model does provide a theoretical explanation for why stable prices have been observed to exist in some oligopolistic industries, it takes the prevailing price as given and offers no justification for why that price level rather than some other is the prevailing price. For this reason alone, the kinked demand model of oligopolistic pricing must be viewed as incomplete. Stigler has tested the kinked demand model empirically on seven oligopolies.[17] He found that oligopolistic rivals are just as likely to follow price increases as price decreases, indicating little empirical support for the kinked demand curve. Nevertheless, as Cohen and Cyert have suggested,[18] although the empirical evidence of Stigler indicates the theory may have little credence as a long-run explanation of oligopoly pricing, it may be a valid explanation of the way firms behave when they have little or no knowledge of how competitors will react to price changes. The cases of a new industry in its early stages of development and of an industry in which new rivals enter the market are cited by Cohen and Cyert as instances where the kinked demand model is likely to furnish a satisfactory description of pricing behavior in the short run. But as firms learn what responses to expect from their competitors and as information sources become better developed in the industry, the perceived kink in the demand curve is likely to vanish.

Game Theory Approach

Game theory is an alternative approach that can be used to formulate and analyze the interdependencies of oligopolistic decision making. With this approach, the firm does *not* try to predict or outguess the strategies or decisions of its competitor(s). Instead, the firm assumes that its competitors will choose their optimal strategies (decisions). Based on these optimal strategies (decisions), the firm then develops its own best counterstrategies (decisions). A simple example is used below to illustrate this approach.

Assume that two competing firms (duopolists) have the entire market for a given product and must determine their output for the forthcoming period.[19] Total profits from the sale of the product are fixed at $100,000 during the forthcoming period. The division of this $100,000 total profit is based solely on the respective outputs of the two firms. Assume that each firm has two possible strategies—produce either 1,000 units or 2,000 units. *Firm 1's profit* under each

---

[17] George J. Stigler, "The Kinky Oligopoly Demand Curve and Rigid Prices," *Journal of Political Economy* 55 (1947), pp. 432–449. See also George J. Stigler, "The Literature of Economics: The Case of the Kinked Oligopoly Demand Curve," *Economic Inquiry* (April 1978), pp. 185–204.

[18] Cohen and Cyert, *Theory of the Firm*, pp. 251–254.

[19] This example is based on a similar one in Robert Dorfman, Paul A. Samuelson, and Robert M. Solow, *Linear Programming and Economic Analysis* (New York: McGraw-Hill, 1958), chap. 15.

Figure 15.5
**Payoff (Profit)
Matrix for the
Duopolists
(Entries Represent
Payoffs to Firm 1)**

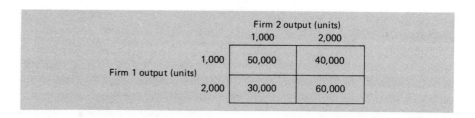

of the various combinations of strategies is shown in Figure 15.5 (*Note*: Firm 2's profit under each examination is $100,000 minus the amount shown in Figure 15.5.) This problem is an example of a *2-person, zero-sum game.*[20] These games are discussed in more detail in the appendix to this chapter.

By choosing Strategy 1 (produce 1,000 units), Firm 1 earns a minimum profit of $40,000, regardless of Firm 2's output decision. Similarly, by choosing Strategy 2 (produce 2,000 units), Firm 1's profit is at least $30,000, regardless of Firm 2's output decision. The maximum of these two profit figures is $40,000. Hence Firm 1 can earn a *guaranteed* profit of *at least* $40,000 by producing 1,000 units (Strategy 1). Using this strategy, Firm 1 could conceivably earn a profit of $50,000 if Firm 2 decides to produce 1,000 units (Strategy 1). In the terminology of game theory, Firm 1 is pursuing a *maximin* strategy, since the firm is maximizing its minimum possible profit.[21]

This example illustrates some of the limitations of game theory as a practical decision-making tool. First, the *maximin* strategy represents a very defensive approach to solving the decision-making problem. Recall that in evaluating each of Firm 1's strategies, one concentrated on the *minimum* profit that could occur. A more aggressive firm, which is willing to accept additional risk, might want to analyze the problem in a different manner. Second, it was assumed that the total profit from the sale of the product was fixed. Often, total profit is not constant—both firms may gain (or lose) depending on the strategy chosen. These are known as *2-person, nonzero-sum* games and are considerably more difficult to analyze than are zero-sum games. Finally, it was assumed that only two firms (duopolists) were competing in the market for the product. Most oligopolistic markets contain more than two competitors. Decision-making problems involving more than two participants are known as *n-person* games and are much more difficult to solve than are 2-person games. The appendix to this chapter contains a more detailed discussion of game theory, including both nonzero-sum games and *n*-person games. In general, game theory has not been too successful in solving the decision-making problems faced by oligopolists.

---

[20] Strictly speaking, this is a constant-sum, rather than a "zero-sum" game, since the sum of the profits of the two firms is $100,000 and not zero. However, both types of games are analyzed in a similar manner.

[21] Firm 2 can perform a similar analysis and choose a *minimax* strategy, since its profit is always $100,000 minus Firm 1's profit.

Economic Analysis and Managerial Efficiency

'ALL FOR ONE...ONE FOR ALL'? DON'T BET ON IT*

A group of Texas A & M University students have acquired, to their chagrin, a special insight into the difficulties of the Organization of Petroleum Exporting Countries—or any other cartel—in fixing prices.

The 27 students take the introductory course Economics 203H, and they volunteered recently to be the subjects for an experiment conducted for the *Wall Street Journal* by Prof. Raymond Battalio.

The experiment explores what economists call the "free-rider problem": In almost any effort in which a goal can be achieved only by common action, someone pays lip service to the agreement while quietly cheating for his own gain at the expense of neighbors. The experiment was devised by economists Charles Plott of California Institute of Technology, Mark Isaac of the University of Arizona and James Walker of Indiana University.

Each student in the experiment receives a mimeographed sheet showing 30 sets of figures. (See chart.) Each includes two dollar amounts.

"Each of you will write down on a slip of paper either '1' or '0,'" Prof. Battalio instructs them. The "1" votes will determine which set of figures will be used. One number in that set shows how much money Prof. Battalio will pay each student who voted "1"; the other shows how much will be paid each "0" voter.

The students are warned not to talk to each other. Without further comment a vote is taken. There are six votes for "1" and 21 for "0." The chart shows that those who voted '1' will receive 24 cents each while those who voted "0" get 74 cents each.

Obviously, voting "0" gives a bigger individual payoff than voting "1." A second vote yields only

No of People Picking No. 1	Payout For Choice of Picking	
	1	0
1	$0.04	$0.54
2	0.08	0.58
3	0.12	0.62
4	0.16	0.66
5	0.20	0.70
6	0.24	0.74
7	0.28	0.78
8	0.32	0.82
9	0.36	0.86
10	0.40	0.90
11	0.44	0.94
12	0.48	0.98
13	0.52	1.02
14	0.56	1.06
15	0.60	1.10
16	0.64	1.14
17	0.68	1.18
18	0.72	1.22
19	0.76	1.26
20	0.80	1.30
21	0.84	1.34
22	0.88	1.38
23	0.92	1.42
24	0.96	1.46
25	1.00	1.50
26	1.04	1.54
27	1.08	1.58
28	1.12	1.62
29	1.16	1.66
30	1.20	1.70

three votes for "1." The chart determines that those three each receive 12 cents while the 24 students who voted "0" each get 62 cents.

Suddenly, it dawns on the students that the figures are rigged: Students who vote "0" will always get 50 cents more than those who vote "1,"

* Source: Jerry E. Bishop. "All for One...One for All'? Don't Bet on It," *Wall Street Journal*, 4 December, 1986, p. 1. Reprinted by permission of the *Wall Street Journal.* © Dow Jones and Company 1986. All rights reserved.

(Continued on next page)

(Continued from previous page)

but the fewer "1" votes, the less money everyone gets. "Let's all put down '1,' and nobody cheat," blurts out one student, not unlike a business owner—say, an oil exporter—who tries to induce his competitors all to sell at the same price. But the conspiracy suggestion succeeds only partially. Eleven vote "1" (for 44 cents each) and 16 vote "0" (for 94 cents each).

There is a buzz of consternation among the students. "OK, if you want to talk about it, go ahead," Prof. Battalio says, lifting the rule against collusion.

"Look," says the ringleader, "if we all vote '1' we will each get $1.08." "But," retorts another student, "if 26 of us vote '1' we'll get $1.04 and the one guy who votes '0' will get $1.54." Further discussion suggests that the only fair thing is for all to vote "1." That way, the class as a whole will end up $29.16 richer—the best possible collective result.

But again the conspiracy only partially succeeds; for the fourth ballot, 14 students vote "1"; for the fifth ballot, only six do so. The class gears up for a final try, all agreeing that the common good requires a unanimous vote for "1."

After explicit agreement by all to vote "1," the final vote is taken: Four vote "1" (for 16 cents each) and 23 vote "0" (for 66 cents each).

A smiling Prof. Battalio reaches into his pocket and counts out this round's payout—$15.82, or $13.34 less than if the conspiracy had been successful. "I'll never trust anyone again as long as I live," mutters the conspiracy leader. And how did he vote? "Oh, I voted '0'" he replies.

Question

1. Compare the performance of these students with the recent peformance of OPEC member countries.

Baumol's Revenue-Maximization Model

Baumol has suggested a model of oligopoly behavior that assumes firms seek to maximize total dollar revenue from sales, subject to a minimum constraint level of profits.[22] The Baumol model essentially ignores interdependencies in decision making among oligopolists. Based on his own experience as a consultant, Baumol argues that interdependencies are ignored in virtually all decision making except in such instances when major price reductions are made, radically new products are being introduced, or large new advertising campaigns are being embarked on. This assertion is supported by his observations of the complex, clumsy, and slow-moving internal decision-making apparatus in most firms, the use of similar decision making rules of thumb from firm to firm, and the desire of corporate managers not to rock the competitive or regulatory boat—to live and let live.

Baumol argues that executives seek to maximize *sales* because of a fear that consumers may spurn a product whose popularity appears to be waning. Financing may become more difficult to arrange and the firm may lose some of its distributors as sales decline. Also, personnel management is far more difficult when people are being fired rather than hired. A declining firm (either in absolute or relative terms) loses some of its potential monopoly power, and, as a

[22] William J. Baumol, *Business Behavior, Value and Growth*, rev. ed. (New York: Harcourt, Brace and World, 1967), especially chap. 6–8.

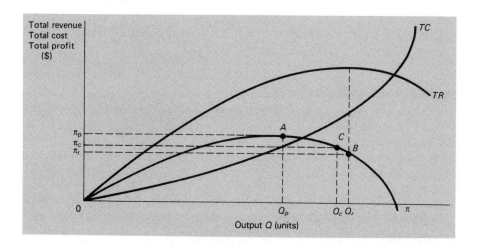

Figure 15.6
Revenue Maximization

consequence, its power to effect a strong competitive counterstrategy when one is needed. Finally, a smaller firm is probably more vulnerable to a generally depressed economy than a larger one. Up to some level of sales (that is, where $MC = MR$), no necessary conflict exists between size and profit. Baumol argues that managers have a strong motivation to want to expand sales even beyond this point, however. For instance, McGuire, Chiu, and Elbing have shown that executive salaries are more closely related to firm size than to profitability.[23] For all of these reasons, Baumol suggests that revenue maximization, subject to some minimum shareholder acceptable profit constraint, provides a better description of decision making by oligopolists than does profit maximization.

This constrained revenue-maximization concept may be illustrated graphically (see Figure 15.6). The graph shows output Q on the horizontal axis and total revenue, total costs, and total profits on the vertical axis. As can be seen by an examination of the total revenue (TR), total cost (TC), and total profit (π) curves, the profit-maximizing firm would produce at Q_p level of output and earn total profits equal to π_p. The revenue maximizer (without a profit constraint) would produce at the point where the total revenue function is maximized (where $MR = 0$). This is at output level Q_r and when total profits equal π_r. If, however, the firm is faced with a constraint level of profits, π_c, output would have to be reduced from Q_r to Q_c in order that the required level of profits be achieved.

This may also be illustrated with a numerical example. Given the demand function

$$P = 5{,}000 - 30Q \qquad [15.9]$$

and the total cost function

$$TC = 3{,}000 + 800Q \qquad [15.10]$$

---

[23] J. W. McGuire, J. S. Y. Chiu, and A. O. Elbing, "Executive Incomes, Sales and Profits," *American Economic Review* (September 1962).

one may calculate price, level of output, and profit for a firm seeking to (a) maximize total profits, (b) maximize total revenue, and (c) maximize total revenue subject to a profit constraint of $141,000.

(a) Maximization of total profits.

$$\text{Total profit} = \text{Total revenue} - \text{Total cost}$$

$$\pi = TR - TC$$
$$= P \cdot Q - TC$$
$$= 5000Q - 30Q^2 - 3000 - 800Q$$
$$= 4200Q - 30Q^2 - 3000 \qquad [15.11]$$

To maximize total profit, take the derivative of π (Equation 15.11) with respect of quantity, set it equal to zero, and solve for Q_p^*:

$$\frac{d\pi}{dQ} = 4200 - 60Q = 0$$

$$Q_p^* = 70$$

Hence,

$$P_p^* = 5000 - 30(70) = \$2900$$

$$\pi_p^* = 4200(70) - 30(70)^2 - 3000 = \$144,000$$

$$TR_p^* = 2900(70) = \$203,000$$

(b) Maximization of total revenue.

$$TR = P \cdot Q$$
$$= 5000Q - 30Q^2 \qquad [15.12]$$

To maximize total revenue, take the derivative of TR (Equation 15.12) with respect to Q, set it equal to zero, and solve for Q_r^*:

$$\frac{dTR}{dQ} = 5000 - 60Q = 0$$

$$Q_r^* = 83.3$$

Hence

$$P_r^* = 5000 - 30(83.3) = \$2500$$

$$\pi_r^* = TR - TC$$
$$= (83.3)(2500) - 3000 - 800(83.3)$$
$$= \$138,610$$

$$TR_r^* = 83.3(2500) = \$208,250$$

(c) Maximization of total revenue subject to a profit constraint. Given that

the firm has a constraint level of profits π_c equal to \$141,000, set

$$\pi_c = 141,000 = -30Q^2 + 4200Q - 3000 \qquad\qquad [15.13]$$

Simplifying this equation yields

$$Q^2 - 140Q + 4800 = 0$$

Solving this equation yields two values for Q:

$$Q = 80$$

$$Q' = 60$$

Substituting $Q = 80$ into the original demand equation (Equation 15.9) yields:

$$P = 5,000 - 30(80) = \$2,600$$

$$TR = P \cdot Q = \$208,000$$

Similarly, when $Q' = 60$,

$$P' = 5,000 - 30(60) = \$3,200$$

$$TR' = P \cdot Q' = \$192,000$$

Hence, $Q_c^* = 80$ is the level of output that would be produced by the firm under constrained revenue maximization.

The Baumol model yields some interesting conclusions. The profit-maximization model indicates that as fixed costs increase, the optimal level of price and output does not change. This is clearly at odds with observed practice, where an increase in fixed cost is an occasion for serious consideration of price increases (and a consequent reduction in output). In the Baumol model, a fixed-cost increase shifts the total profit function downward, resulting in the profit constraint line cutting the profit curve at a point signifying a diminished level of output and consequently a higher price. In essence, the constrained revenue maximizer may be viewed as having a reserve of unclaimed profits that it can fall back on as taxes or fixed costs increase.

Summary

- An *oligopoly* is an industry structure characterized by a relatively small number of firms in which recognizable *interdependencies* exist among the actions of the firms. Each firm is aware that its actions are likely to evoke countermoves from its rivals.

- No one normative model of oligopoly behavior adequately prescribes the optimal behavior (that is, price and output decisions) for firms in oligopolistic industries. Each of the models offers *some* insights that are useful in *some* decision-making situations. It is doubtful, however, whether any comprehensive model will ever be developed.

- In the *Cournot* model of oligopoly behavior, each of the firms, in determining its profit-maximizing output level, assumes that the other firm's output will remain constant.

- A *cartel* is a formal or informal agreement among oligopolists to cooperate or collude in determining outputs, prices, and profits. If the cartel members can enforce agreements and prevent cheating, they can act as a monopolist and maximize industry profits.

- A number of factors affect the ability of oligopolistic firms to engage successfully in some form of formal (or informal) cooperation. These include the number and size distribution of sellers, product heterogeneity, cost structures, size and frequency of orders, secrecy and retaliation, and the social structure of the industry.

- *Price leadership* is a pricing strategy in an oligopolistic industry in which one firm sets the price and, either by explicit or implicit agreement, the other firms tend to follow the decision. Effective price leadership exists when price movements initiated by the leader have a high probability of sticking and there are no maverick or nonconforming firms.

- In the *kinked demand curve* model, it is assumed that if an oligopolist reduces its prices, its competitors will quickly feel the decline in their sales and will be forced to match the reduction. Alternatively, if the oligopolist raises its prices, competitors will rapidly gain customers by maintaining their original prices and will have little or no motivation to match a price increase. Hence, the demand curve facing individual oligopolists is much more elastic for price increases than for price decreases and may lead oligopolists to maintain stable prices.

- In the *game theory* approach to oligopolistic behavior, the firm assumes that its competitor will choose its optimal decision-making strategy. Based on this assumption about its competitor, the firm chooses its own best counterstrategy.

- *Baumol's* model of oligopoly behavior, which is a *quasidescriptive* model rather than a normative model, assumes that the goal of the firm is to maximize revenues, subject to meeting a minimally acceptable profit constraint, rather than to maximize profits.

Selected References

Bailey, Elizabeth E. "Contestability and the Design of Regulatory and Antitrust Policy." *American Economic Review* 71 (May 1981), pp. 178–183.

Baumol, William J., John C. Panzer, and Robert D. Willig. *Contestable Markets and the Theory of Industry Structure*. New York: Harcourt Brace Jovanovich, 1982.

Cohen, Kalman, and Richard Cyert. *Theory of the Firm: Resource Allocation in a Market Economy*, 2d ed. Englewood Cliffs, N.J.: Prentice-Hall, 1975.

Dixit, A. "Recent Developments in Oligopoly Theory." *American Economic Review* (May 1982), pp. 12–17.

Henderson, James M., and Richard E. Quandt. *Microeconomic Theory: A Mathematical Approach*, 2d ed. New York: McGraw-Hill, 1971.

Johnston, Frederick I. "On the Stability of Commodity Cartels," *American Economist* (Fall 1983), pp. 34–36.

Luce, R. Duncan, and Howard Raiffa. *Games and Decisions*. New York: John Wiley, 1957.

Primeaux, W. J., and M. L. Smith. "Pricing Patterns and the Kinky Demand Curve." *Journal of Law and Economics* 19 (April 1976), pp. 181–199.

Rapoport, Anatol. *Two-Person Game Theory: The Essential Ideas*. Ann Arbor: University of Michigan Press, 1966.

Scherer, Frederic M. *Industrial Market Structure and Economic Performance*, 2d ed. Chicago: Rand McNally, 1980.

Stigler, George J. "The Kinky Oligopoly Demand Curve and Rigid Prices," *Journal of Political Economy* 55 (1947), pp. 432–449.

Telser, Lester G. *Competition, Collusion, and Game Theory*. Chicago: Aldine-Atherton, 1972.

Von Neumann, John, and Oskar Morgenstern. *Theory of Games and Economic Behavior*, 3d ed. Princeton, N.J.: Princeton University Press, 1953.

Discussion Questions

1. Define the following terms:
   a. Cartel
   b. Barometric price leadership
   c. Dominant price leadership
   d. Game theory

2. What factors differentiate oligopolistic market structures from purely competitive and monopolistic market structures?

3. Discuss why it is so difficult to develop optimal pricing and output decision-making rules for oligopolistic market structures.

4. In deriving the Cournot solution to the duopoly price-output decision-making problem, what assumption is made about the behavior of the firms? Discuss some of the criticisms of this assumption.

5. Discuss some of the factors that affect the ability of oligopolistic firms to successfully engage in cooperation or collusion.

6. In deriving the optimum price-output decisions of the dominant price leadership model, what assumptions are made about the behavior of (a) the dominant firm and (b) the follower firms?

7. What rationale is given for the existence of a kink (at the prevailing market price) in the oligopolist's demand curve?

8. What are some of the criticisms of the kinked demand curve model? Under what conditions (if any) might the model provide a valid explanation of oligopoly pricing?

9. Discuss the limitations of the use of game theory in analyzing a two-firm (duopoly) decision-making situation.

10. What reasons does Baumol give for claiming that managers are more concerned with sales (revenue) maximization than with the traditional goal of profit maximization?

Problems

1. Assume that two companies (C and D) are duopolists that produce identical products. Demand for the products is given by the following linear demand function:

$$P = 600 - Q_C - Q_D$$

where Q_C and Q_D are the quantities sold by the respective firms and P is the selling price. Total cost functions for the two companies are

$$TC_C = 25,000 + 100 \ Q_C$$
$$TC_D = 20,000 + 125 \ Q_D$$

a. Based on the Cournot model, calculate the optimum output and selling price for the first six rounds (three decisions by each firm) of decision making. Assume that Company C makes the first decision and that, initially, neither company is producing any output.

b. Based on the Cournot model, determine the equilibrium outputs and selling price for the two firms.

c. Determine the total profits for each firm at the equilibrium output found in part (b).

2. Assume that two companies (A and B) are duopolists who produce identical products. Demand for the products is given by the following linear demand function:

$$P = 200 - Q_A - Q_B$$

where Q_A and Q_B are the quantities sold by the respective firms and P is the selling price. Total cost functions for the two companies are

$$TC_A = 1500 + 55Q_A + Q_A^2$$
$$TC_B = 1200 + 20Q_B + 2Q_B^2$$

Assume that the firms act *independently* as in the Cournot model (that is, each firm assumes that the other firm's output will not change).

a. Determine the equilibrium output for each firm. (*Hint*: Develop *separate* profit functions for Firm A (π_A) and Firm B (π_B). Differentiate π_A with respect to Q_A and π_B with respect to Q_B. Set these *partial* derivatives equal to 0 and solve the set of simultaneous equations for the equilibrium values of Q_A and Q_B.

b. Determine Firm A, Firm B, and total industry profits at the Cournot equilibrium solution found in part (a).

3. Consider Problem 2 again. Assume that the firms form a *cartel* to act as a monopolist and maximize total industry profits (sum of Firm A and Firm B profits).

a. Determine the optimum output for each firm. (*Hint*: Develop a relationship for total industry profits ($\pi = \pi_A + \pi_B$) as a function of Q_A and Q_B. Differentiate π with respect to Q_A and Q_B. Set the *partial* derivatives equal to 0 and solve the set of simultaneous equations for the optimal values of Q_A and Q_B.)

b. Determine Firm A, Firm B, and total industry profits at the optimal solution found in part (a).

c. How much *additional* profit does each duopolist make by forming a cartel compared with acting independently? Is it worthwhile for the two firms to enter into a cartel agreement?

d. Show that the marginal costs of the two firms are equal at the optimal solution found in part (a).

4. Alchem (L) is the price leader in the polyglue market. All ten other manufacturers [follower (F) firms] sell polyglue at the same price as Alchem. Alchem allows the other firms to sell as much as they wish at the established price and supplies the remainder of the demand itself. Total demand for polyglue is given by the following function ($Q_T = Q_L + Q_F$):

$$P = 20,000 - 4Q_T$$

Alchem's marginal cost function for manufacturing and selling polyglue is

$$MC_L = 5,000 + 5Q_L$$

The aggregate marginal cost function for the other manufacturers of polyglue is

$$\Sigma MC_F = 2,000 + 4Q_F$$

a. To maximize profits, how much polyglue should Alchem produce and what price should they charge?

b. What is the total market demand for polyglue at the price established by Alchem in part (a)? How much of total demand do the follower firms supply?

5. Chillman Motors, Inc. believes it faces the following segmented demand function:

$$P = \begin{cases} 150 - .5Q & \text{when } 0 \leqslant Q \leqslant 50 \\ 200 - 1.5Q & \text{for } Q > 50 \end{cases}$$

a. Indicate both verbally and graphically why such a segmented demand function is likely to exist. What type of industry structure is indicated by this relationship?

b. Calculate the marginal revenue functions facing Chillman. Add these to your graph from part (a).

c. Chillman's total cost function is

$$TC_1 = 500 + 15Q + .5Q^2$$

Calculate the marginal cost function. What is Chillman's profit-maximizing price and output combination?

d. What is Chillman's profit-maximizing price-output combination if total costs increase to

$$TC_2 = 500 + 45Q + .5Q^2$$

e. If Chillman's total cost function changes to either

$$TC_3 = 500 + 15Q + 1.0Q^2$$

or

$$TC_4 = 500 + 5Q + .25Q^2$$

what price-output solution do you expect to prevail? Would your answer change if you knew that all firms in the industry witnessed similar changes in their cost functions?

6. A firm is faced with the following demand and total cost functions:

$$P = 20 - 2Q$$

$$TC = 6 + 8Q$$

a. Calculate the profit-maximizing level of price and output. What are the firm's total profits? What total revenue is received by the firm at these price and output levels?

b. Calculate the sales-maximizing values for price and output. At these levels, what would the firm's total revenue and total profit be?

c. If the firm seeks to maximize sales revenue subject to a profit constraint of $6, calculate price and output under the constrained sales-maximization objective. What are total profits and revenues?

Hint: The roots of the quadratic equation $(aX^2 + bX + c = 0)$ are

$$X = \frac{-b \pm \sqrt{b^2 - 4ac}}{2a}$$

7. a. Recalculate parts (a) and (c) of Problem 6 assuming that the firm's property taxes (that is, fixed costs) increase by $2. Compare the results with those in Problem 6.

b. Explain the reasons for any differences or similarities you find.

8. Two competing firms (duopolists) have the entire market for a given product and must determine their advertising strategies for the coming period. The payoffs (profits) to Firm A are shown in the following table (the payoff or profit to Firm B is equal to $50,000 minus the payoff to Firm A):

		Firm B Advertising Strategy	
		1	2
Firm A Advertising Strategy	1	25,000	15,000
	2	20,000	35,000

a. Determine the minimum payoff (profit) to Firm A of choosing (i) Strategy 1 and (ii) Strategy 2.

b. Which advertising strategy should Firm A choose if it is interested in maximizing its minimum possible payoff (profit)?

9. *Library Research Project.* Examine the literature on the price-fixing agreements that occurred in the electrical equipment industry during the 1950s. For example, see the article in the *Wall Street Journal* cited in footnote 5, as well as Richard Austin Smith, "The Incredible Electrical Conspiracy," *Fortune* (April, May 1961) and scattered references (see the index) to the economic aspects of this episode in Frederic M. Scherer, *Industrial Market Structure and Economic Performance*, 2d ed. (Chicago: Rand McNally, 1980). Attempt to answer the following questions:

a. What firms and products were involved in the conspiracy?

b. What measures did the executives use to keep their meetings secret?

c. How did the companies determine who should get contracts and orders?

d. What market-sharing formulas (quotas) were used in allocating demand?

e. What were some of the problems encountered in maintaining the price-fixing agreements?

10. *Library Research Project.* Examine the following articles to determine what has happened to the colluding oligopolists since the price-fixing case cited in Problem 9:

a. Bruce T. Allen, "Tacit Collusion and Market Sharing: The Case of Steam Turbine Generators," *Industrial Organization Review* 4, no. 1 (1976), pp. 48–57.

b. "A Stretched Definition of Price Fixing," *Business Week*, 15 December 1975.

Theory of Games

APPENDIX

15A

A *game* is defined as a group decision-making situation in which a *conflict of interest* exists between two or more of the participants. *Game theory* consists of a mathematical theory of decision making by the participants in such a situation.[24]

Examples of this type of decision-making situation are numerous. Card games, such as poker and bridge, are examples. Examples from economics include the price-output and related decisions of firms in oligopolistic industries and the labor contract negotiations between firms and labor unions. Military-political examples include international disarmament negotiations and tactical battlefield decision making.

Games are classified and analyzed by both the number of players involved and the compatibility of the interests of the players. Game theory distinguishes between 2-*person* games, having exactly two participants, and *n-person* games, having three or more participants. Within a 2-person game, the interests of the participants can be either strictly competitive or nonstrictly competitive. In a strictly competitive, or *zero-sum* game, the players have exactly opposite interests; that is, one player's gain is the other player's loss and vice versa. In a nonstrictly competitive, or *nonzero-sum* game, at least one outcome is preferred to other outcomes by both players. Hence, one player's gain is not necessarily the other player's loss; both players may gain or lose depending on the alternative actions the players choose to undertake. Based on this classification scheme, one can consider three cases—2-person zero-sum games, 2-person nonzero-sum games, and *n*-person games.

Two-Person Zero-Sum Games

A 2-person game can be represented in a matrix format. For example, consider the game shown in Figure 15A.1(a). Player 1 has two strategies, or alternative actions, available to him; and Player 2 has three possible actions open to her. A

[24] Two classic volumes on game theory are R. Duncan Luce and Howard Raiffa, *Games and Decisions* (New York: John Wiley, 1957) and John Von Neumann and Oskar Morgenstern, *Theory of Games and Economic Behavior*, 3d ed. (Princeton, N.J.: Princeton University Press, 1953).

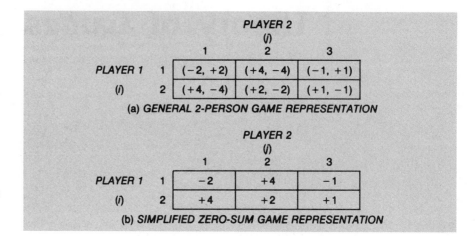

Figure 15A.1
Representation of a Game in Matrix Form

play of the game consists of each player simultaneously choosing one of his or her alternative actions.[25] The outcome or payoff that occurs from each combination of choices (i and j) by the two players is shown within the matrix. The first number within the parentheses of each entry in the matrix is the payoff to Player 1 and the second number is the payoff to Player 2. Thus, if Player 1 chooses alternative $i = 1$ and Player 2 chooses alternative $j = 3$, the payoff to Player 1 is $\$-1$ and the payoff to Player 2 is $\$+1$.[26] Since we are considering a zero-sum game, it is unnecessary to show a pair of outcomes for each entry in the matrix. If we establish the convention that each entry (a_{ij}) in the matrix shows the *payoff to Player 1 from Player 2*, then the zero-sum can be represented by the matrix shown in Figure 15A.1(b). A *negative* entry means that Player 1 receives a negative payoff from Player 2 or, in effect, makes a positive payoff to Player 2. With this representation of the game, we assume that each player has complete knowledge of the alternative actions available to him or her and the other player and the outcomes that will result from the choices made by each player.

The objective of Player 1, through his choice of an action i, is to make a_{ij} as *large* as possible. Similarly, the objective of Player 2, through her choice of an action j, is to make a_{ij} as *small* as possible. Clearly, neither player has complete control over the outcome or payoff, a_{ij} of the game. Under these circumstances, how should the players choose among alternative actions available in order to achieve their objectives?

Consider Player 1 first. If Player 1 chooses action $i = 1$, Player 2's *best* alternative is $j = 1$; and Player 1 will lose $2. Likewise, if Player 1 chooses action $i = 2$, Player 2's *best* alternative is $j = 3$; and Player 1 will receive $1. Clearly, it is possible for Player 1 to receive a payoff greater than these amounts if Player 2 *does not* choose her best alternative. However, Player 1 knows that

[25] The choices may be made sequentially as long as the second player does not know the choice made by the first player.

[26] The payoffs may represent utilities or any type of outcome and not necessarily dollars.

Player 2 is seeking to make the payoff a_{ij} as small as possible and therefore must assume that Player 2 will always choose her best alternative. Suppose we define the *minimum* payoff that Player 1 can receive from a given action i as the *security level* of that action. In the example, the security levels for Player 1 of actions $i = 1$ and $i = 2$ are $\$-2$ and $\$+1$, respectively. Given the assumptions about the objectives and choices of Player 2, a reasonable strategy for Player 1 would be to seek to maximize his minimum gain (that is, security level). Based on this criterion, Player 1 should choose action $i = 2$, since it provides the higher security level. Mathematically, this criterion can be expressed as

$$\max_{i} \left\{ \min_{j} a_{ij} \right\} = a_{23} = +1$$

It indicates that Player 1 should choose the action that maximizes the minimum payoff (or security level) associated with each *row* of the game matrix. Such a decision criterion, or strategy, is referred to as a *maximin* strategy since Player 1 is attempting to *max*imize his *min*imum payoff.

Next, consider Player 2. For each of Player 2's choices—$j = 1$, $j = 2$, and $j = 3$—Player 1's best alternatives are $i = 2$, $i = 1$, and $i = 2$, respectively; and Player 2 will *lose* (that is, receive a negative payoff) $\$+4$, $\$+4$, and $\$+1$, respectively. It is possible for Player 2 to lose less than these amounts if Player 1 does not choose his best alternative. However, the knowledge that Player 1 is seeking to make the payoff a_{ij} as large as possible forces Player 2 to assume that Player 1 will always choose his best alternative. For Player 2, define the *maximum* loss to herself of a given action j as the *security level* of that action. In the example, the security levels for Player 2 of actions $j = 1$, $j = 2$, and $j = 3$ are $\$+4$, $\$+4$ and $\$+1$, respectively. Given the assumptions about the objectives and choices of Player 1, a reasonable strategy for Player 2 would be to seek to minimize her maximum loss (that is, security level), which is equivalent to maximizing her minimum gain, except in this case the gain is negative. Based on this criterion, Player 2 should choose action $j = 3$, since it minimizes her maximum loss. Mathematically, this criterion can be represented as

$$\min_{j} \left\{ \max_{i} a_{ij} \right\} = a_{23} = +1$$

It indicates that Player 2 should choose the action that minimizes the maximum loss (that is, negative payoff or security level) associated with each *column* of the game matrix. Like Player 1, Player 2 is said to be following a *minimax* strategy since she is attempting to *min*imize her *max*imum loss. (This strategy can also be called a *maximin* strategy because Player 2 is attempting to maximize her minimum gain, where the gains are negative. For consistency we refer to the strategies of both Players 1 and 2 as *maximin* strategies.)

It is important to note that we did *not* indicate that $i = 2$ and $j = 3$ represent optimal choices for Players 1 and 2, respectively.[27] Clearly, if Player 1 expects Player 2 to choose action $j = 2$ for some reason, then Player 1's best choice of action is $i = 1$, since he receives a payoff of $\$+4$ as compared with the payoff of $\$+2$ associated with action $i = 2$. Likewise, we are *not* claiming that the solution

---

[27] Recall that the strategies were labeled "reasonable" rather than "optimal."

obtained above ($i = 2$, $j = 3$) will necessarily be observed in experiments performed on this game matrix. As Luce and Raiffa emphasize in their discussion of zero-sum games:

> It is crucial that the social scientist recognize that game theory is not *descriptive*, but rather (conditionally) *normative*. It states neither how people do behave nor how they should behave in an absolute sense, but how they should behave if they wish to achieve certain ends. It prescribes for given assumptions courses of action for the attainment of outcomes having certain formal "optimum" properties. These properties may or may not be deemed pertinent in any given real world conflict of interest. If they are, the theory prescribes the choices which *must* be made to get that optimum.[28]

The analysis of the zero-sum game in this section has assumed a very cautious or conservative attitude on the part of the players. Recall that the choice of actions for each player was based on an analysis of the *security levels* associated with the various alternatives available. Maximin is a defensive strategy. For a player who thinks that he (or she) can outguess the other player, and is willing to accept the risks associated with an offensive strategy, a maximin analysis of the game is not appealing.

Returning again to the previous example, compare the solutions obtained for Players 1 and 2. By choosing action $i = 2$, Player 1 can be assured of a payoff of at least $\$+1$. Likewise, by choosing action $j = 3$, Player 2 can be assured of a loss of no more than $\$+1$. Whenever Player 1's minimum gain is equal to Player 2's maximum loss or, in other words, when

$$\max_i \left\{ \min_j a_{ij} \right\} = \min_j \left\{ \max_i a_{ij} \right\} = a_{i^*j^*} = v$$

the game is said to have a *saddle point* or *equilibrium* at (i^*, j^*) and the *value* of the game v is equal to $a_{i^*j^*}$. Thus for the example, ($i^* = 2$, $j^* = 3$) constitutes a saddle point and the value of the game v is equal to $\$+1$. A necessary and sufficient condition for a game to have a saddle point is that an entry exists in the payoff matrix having the property of being *simultaneously* the minimum value in its row and the maximum value in its column. It is also possible for a game to have either more than one saddle point or no saddle point.

Consider a game with no saddle point. The payoff matrix in Figure 15A.2 is a slight variation of the game matrix in the earlier example. For Player 1, the security levels of his two alternatives are $\$-2$ and $\$-3$, respectively, and his maximin choice would be alternative $i = 1$. For Player 2, the security levels of her three strategies are $\$+4$, $\$+4$, and $\$+1$, respectively, and her maximin choice would be alternative $j = 3$. Under these circumstances no saddle point exists. In the previous example with a saddle point, if Player 1 believed that Player 2 would make a maximin choice, then there was no advantage to be gained from not making a maximin choice. In this example, however, that is not true. If Player 1 expects Player 2 to make a maximin choice—that is, $j = 3$—then Player 1 should *not* make his maximin choice—that is, $i = 1$—but should instead choose alternative $i = 2$. Player 1 can thus increase his payoff

---

[28]Luce and Raiffa, *Games and Decisions*, p. 63.

		PLAYER 2 (j)		
		1	2	3
PLAYER 1	1	-2	$+4$	-1
(i)	2	$+4$	-3	$+1$

Figure 15A.2
Game without a Saddle Point

from $\$-2$ to $\$+1$ by not playing a maximin strategy. Similar reasoning holds for Player 2. Thus, without the presence of an equilibrium point, an unstable (and unpredictable) situation exists.

For a game that does not contain an equilibrium point, it is important for a player to choose an alternative action in a way that makes it impossible for the other player to predict with certainty, before playing the game, what this choice will be. One technique for concealing one's choice is to use a *random process* to select an alternative action. Instead of choosing a definite alternative action, the player specifies the probabilities with which he or she wishes to play the various alternative actions available to him or her. A randomizing device is then used to choose a specific action based on these probabilities. For example, suppose Player 2 in the game shown in Figure 15A.2 decides to assign equal probabilities of $\frac{1}{3}$ to each of the three alternatives available. A die could then be rolled to choose a specific action in which alternative $j = 1$ would be chosen on a 1 or 2 roll, alternative $j = 2$ would be chosen on a 3 or 4 roll, and alternative $j = 3$ would be chosen on a 5 or 6 roll. Thus, each alternative would have an equal probability of being chosen, and neither the player nor her opponent would know beforehand the specific alternative action to be chosen. Such a strategy, in which the player specifies a probability distribution over the set of alternative actions and then uses a random process to select the actual action to play, is known as a *randomized* or *mixed strategy*. In contrast, the choice of a definite alternative action (as in the examples above) without resorting to a randomizing device is known as a *pure strategy*.

As was shown in the example just given (that is, the game in Figure 15A.2), not every game has a maximin equilibrium point that is attainable through the use of pure strategies. A fundamental contribution of Von Neumann-Morgenstern was to prove that with the introduction of mixed strategies, *every* 2-person zero-sum game has a maximin equilibrium solution. Through the adoption of an appropriate mixed strategy, the maximin player (that is, Player 1) can be assured of receiving, in terms of *expected value*, at least v. Likewise, with an appropriate mixed strategy, the maximin player (that is, Player 2) can be assured of losing, in terms of *expected value*, at most v. The expected value v is known as the value of the game. A number of methods are available for determining the appropriate (maximin) mixed strategies for the players— including graphic techniques, approximation methods, and formulation (and solution) of the game as a *linear programming* problem.[29]

---

[29] See Luce and Raiffa, *Games and Decisions*, appendix 5, for a general linear programming formulation of a game. A specific example of this formulation is contained in W. J. Baumol, *Economic Theory and Operations Analysis*, 2d ed. (Englewood Cliffs, N.J.: Prentice-Hall, 1965), pp. 538–541.

Two-Person Nonzero-Sum Games

In a 2-person zero-sum game, such as those discussed in the previous section, there is no way in which both players can increase their payoffs through joint agreements about the actions that each player will choose. One player's gain is necessarily the other player's loss and vice versa. Although a number of parlor games and possibly some competitive situations (for example, military battlefield contests) may be analyzed within the zero-sum game framework, many (if not most) real-life conflict-of-interest situations do not fit within this game model. As Luce and Raiffa indicate, "Most economic, political, and military conflicts of interest can be realistically abstracted into game form only if their non-strictly competitive nature is acknowledged."[30] In a 2-person nonzero-sum (that is, nonstrictly competitive) game, at least one outcome is preferred to other outcomes by both players, and consequently it is possible for both players to gain or lose depending on the actions chosen. The existence of a jointly preferred outcome means that both players may be able to increase their payoffs through some form of cooperation or agreement on the actions to be chosen.

For example, consider the case in which two firms have a dominant share of the market for a product, that is, a *duopoly*. Suppose the two firms are able to exercise a degree of monopoly power in the manufacture and sale of a given product. In such a situation the pricing decisions of the two firms will be interdependent. If one firm *unilaterally* lowers its prices, then it will experience increased sales (and profits) at the expense of the other firm; however, such an action will likely invoke retaliation from the other firm (that is, a similar price reduction) and may precipitate a price war. The outcome associated with neither firm's lowering its prices is definitely preferred to the outcome (that is, lower profits) associated with both firms' lowering their prices. Similar considerations exist for price increases. In such industries some form of implicit cooperation is likely to develop over time.[31] For example, one firm may take on the role as the price leader and the other may act as a follower.

Within the vast array of possible nonzero-sum games, varying degrees of cooperation exist among the participants. Well-developed analytical techniques used in solving such games are available for only two extreme forms of cooperation—the *cooperative* game and the *noncooperative* game. In a cooperative game the players have *complete freedom of communication* with the opportunity to make threats and enter into binding agreements. In a noncooperative game there is *no communication* between the participants and no way to enforce agreements. We will consider noncooperative games first.

Noncooperative Games

One form of a noncooperative game, known as the *Prisoner's Dilemma*, has received considerable attention in game-theory literature. A number of real-

---

[30] Luce and Raiffa, *Games and Decisions*, p. 88.

[31] The possibility also exists for explicit (illegal) cooperation by getting together to set prices.

		SUSPECT 2	
		NOT CONFESS	CONFESS
SUSPECT 1	NOT CONFESS	One-year prison term for each	Fifteen-year prison term for 1; suspended sentence for 2
	CONFESS	Suspended sentence for 1; fifteen-year prison term for 2	Six-year prison term for each

Figure 15A.3
Prisoner's Dilemma

world conflict-of-interest situations, such as the duopoly example discussed previously, can be represented as a Prisoner's Dilemma game.[32]

In the Prisoner's Dilemma, two suspects are accused of jointly committing a crime.[33] To convict the suspects, however, a confession is needed from one or both of them. If neither suspect confesses, the prosecutor will be unable to convict them of the crime and each suspect will receive only a minor sentence. If one suspect confesses (that is, turns state's evidence) and the other does not, then the one confessing will receive a suspended sentence and the other will receive a long-term prison sentence. If both suspects confess, then each will receive an intermediate prison sentence. Each suspect must decide, under these conditions, whether or not to confess. This conflict-of-interest situation can be represented in a game matrix such as the one shown in Figure 15A.3.

Assume that it is possible to attach numerical utilities to each of the outcomes in Figure 15A.3, thereby obtaining the game matrix shown in Figure 15A.4 where, as was indicated in the previous section, the first entry within the parentheses of each box is the utility of the outcome to Suspect 1 and the second entry is the utility of the outcome to Suspect 2.

This game can be examined by using the maximin analysis and the concept of a security level developed in the previous section on zero-sum games. For Suspect 1, the security level (that is, minimum payoff or utility) of the two alternative actions "Not Confess" and "Confess" are -10 and -8, respectively. The maximization of his security level would therefore motivate Suspect 1 to choose the second alternative action by confessing. Similar reasoning holds true for Suspect 2 and she also would, by the maximin analysis, be motivated to choose the alternative of confessing her guilt. Thus, the second alternative for each player (that is, "Confess") constitutes an equilibrium pair and, in this sense, represents the solution of the game. In this game both suspects would clearly receive a larger payoff (that is, a shorter sentence) if they both would decide to choose their first alternatives ("Not Confess"). However, in seeking to maximize

---

[32] Another real-world conflict-of-interest situation from welfare economics that falls in the Prisoner's Dilemma category is the problem of urban blight. See Otto A. Davis and Andrew B. Winston, "The Economics of Urban Renewal," *Law and Contemporary Problems* (Winter 1961).

[33] This example is discussed in more detail in Luce and Raiffa, *Games and Decisions*, sec. 5.4.

their utilities (or, more accurately, to maximize their security levels), the first alternative is not a rational choice for each player.

The Prisoner's Dilemma is only one example of a noncooperative game that has potential usefulness in analyzing real-world conflict-of-interest situations. Various other examples, such as "Chicken" and the "Battle of the Sexes," have also received considerable discussion in the game theory literature.[34]

Cooperative Games

Consider the Prisoner's Dilemma game again and assume that the two players (that is, suspects) are able to communicate with each other and are able to enter into a binding agreement on which strategy each player will choose. In this case, since the outcome associated with both suspects not confessing is preferred to the noncooperative solution (that is, has a greater utility to each player), the suspects would have an incentive to enter into a binding agreement for each to choose the strategy of not confessing. Without strong legal or moral sanctions to force the players to adhere to the agreement, however, each player would be tempted to double-cross the other player by confessing his or her guilt. The player that breaks the agreement has the possibility of increasing his or her utility, as can be seen in Figure 15A.4, from 6 to 10. However, we can rule out this possibility in the cooperative game by assuming that all agreements are binding and enforceable.

To illustrate some additional principles in analyzing cooperative games, consider the nonzero-sum game matrix shown in Figure 15A.5.[35] Unlike the cooperative version of the Prisoner's Dilemma game, which had only one outcome [that is, the outcome $(6, 6)$ associated with each suspect not confessing] that was preferred by both players, this game has two such outcomes. Each player will receive a larger payoff if he or she agrees to choose the same alternative as the other player, either $(i = 1, j = 1)$ or $(i = 2, j = 2)$ than if he or she does not agree to choose the same alternative. However, Player 1 prefers the $(i = 1, j = 1)$ outcome and Player 2 prefers the $(i = 2, j = 2)$ outcome. Suppose

Figure 15A.4
Prisoner's Dilemma with Numerical Utilities

		SUSPECT 2	
		NOT CONFESS	CONFESS
SUSPECT 1	NOT CONFESS	(6, 6)	(−10, 10)
	CONFESS	(10, −10)	(−8, −8)

[34] The game of "Chicken" is analyzed in Anatol Rapoport, *Two-person Game Theory: The Essential Ideas* (Ann Arbor: University of Michigan Press, 1966), pp. 137–142; the "Battle of the Sexes" game is discussed in Luce and Raiffa, *Games and Decisions*, pp. 91–94.

[35] This example—from Rapoport, *Two-person Game Theory*, p. 112—is the type that Luce and Raiffa have designated as the "Battle of the Sexes." See Luce and Raiffa, *Games and Decisions*, sec. 5.3 and chap. 6; and Rapoport, chap. 8, for a more detailed analysis of this type of game.

		PLAYER 2 (j)	
		1	2
PLAYER 1	1	(2, 1)	(−1, −2)
(i)	2	(−2, −1)	(1, 2)

Figure 15A.5
Nonzero-Sum Game

the two players are permitted to form an agreement to select one of the two outcomes *randomly*. If the probability of selecting outcome ($i = 1, j = 1$) is assigned a value of p and, correspondingly, the probability of selecting outcome ($i = 2, j = 2$) is assigned a value of $1 - p$, then the expected utility of each player can range from 1 to 2, depending on the numerical value of p that is agreed upon. This set of possible payoffs (that is, expected utilities) to each player that is attainable by varying the value of p from 0 to 1 is known as the *negotiation set*. Various theories have been put forth in an effort to determine which point in the negotiation set should be selected by rational players. The actual point that will be selected depends on such factors as the bargaining strengths of the players and considerations of equity.

n-Person Games

The major reason for distinguishing between 2-person and n-person games, and the reason why the latter case is so much more difficult to analyze, is due primarily to the possibility of forming *coalitions*. In the 2-person case each player attempts to get as much as he or she can either from the other player (zero-sum case) or from the system (nonzero-sum case) through whatever methods of cooperation, bargaining, and threatening are available. In the n-person case, however, the possibility exists for a subset of the players (whose numbers depend on the rules of the game) to get together and impose a solution on the rest of the players. An example of such an n-person game is a majority-rule system of the government. Although the possibility of the existence of coalitions adds greatly to the richness of the types of situations that can be considered by game theory, it also adds greatly to the complexity of the theory required to analyze such games.

In addition to the problem of coalition formation, n-person game theory must deal with the concepts of side payments, varying degrees of communication, limitations of collusion, correlation of strategies, and interpersonal comparisons and transfers of utility. Different types of games are derived depending on the assumptions made about how each of these concepts will be incorporated into the game situation. For example, consider the case of an oligopolistic industry in which the firms wish to get together to fix prices and allocate market shares. Communication is limited (for example, secret meetings must be held); prices must be set and output allocated in a manner that cannot be detected by antitrust enforcement officials; and procedures must be devised for imposing penalties on firms that cheat—that is, cut prices or exceed their allocated market shares.

The added complications of n-person games make it difficult to find solutions to these games. Indeed, the criteria for what constitutes a solution to an n-person game are much more limited than for a 2-person game. In a 2-person game we are interested in finding a set of optimal strategies for each player along with the value of the game. The theory of n-person games typically does not provide optimal strategies for playing the game, nor does it specify what coalitions should be formed. Instead, a solution often consists only of a set of *possible* coalitions that meet certain predetermined criteria along with the resulting payoffs to the members of these coalitions.[36]

In its present stage of development, game theory, both 2-person and n-person, is limited in its ability to furnish managers with straightforward solutions to conflict-of-interest decision problems. This does not mean, however, that game theory has nothing to contribute to the analysis of such problems. As Rapoport indicates:

> Game theory ... is useful in the sense that any sophisticated theory is useful, namely as a generator of ideas ... Like psychology, game theory can be a source of ideas which lead to insights—insights into the nature of conflict based upon the interplay of decisions.[37]

Discussion Questions

1. Explain the difference between zero-sum and nonzero-sum games.

2. Games with *one* saddle point (Figure 15A. 1) and *no* saddle point (Figure 15A. 2) were illustrated. Give an example of a game with *two* saddle points.

3. Explain the differences between cooperative and noncooperative nonzero-sum games.

4. Explain some of the reasons why n-person games are much more difficult to analyze and solve than 2-person games.

5. Explain the difference between a pure and a mixed strategy.

Problems

1. Determine the saddle points in the following 2-person zero-sum game. What does one note about the values of the different saddle points?

		Player 2 Strategies		
		1	2	3
Player 1	1	2	3	2
Strategies	2	0	1	−7
	3	2	8	−7

---

[36] Two examples of the application of n-person game theory to economic decision making are Martin Shubik, "Incentives, Decentralized Control, the Assignment of Joint Costs and Internal Pricing," *Management Science* 8, no. 3 (April 1962), pp. 325–343; and Luce and Raiffa, *Games and Decisions*, sections 9.4 and 10.3.

[37]. Rapoport, *Two-person Game Theory*, pp. 202–203.

2. Suppose two firms, A and B, are competing for sales in each of the two markets. Assume that Firm B has a dominant share of the sales in each market. Firm A is seeking to devise an advertising strategy to take sales away from Firm B in each of the markets, and Firm B is seeking to devise a counterstrategy to prevent Firm A from obtaining part of its sales in these markets. Assume that the total advertising budget for each firm is fixed and the firms must decide the proportions of their respective budgets to allocate to each of the two markets. Furthermore, assume that two choices are available to each firm in allocating advertising expenditures—two thirds to one market and one-third to the other market or vice versa. The payoff matrix, giving the sales *increase* to Firm A under the possible allocations, is as follows:

	Firm B	
	Allocate $\frac{2}{3}$ to Market 1, $\frac{1}{3}$ to Market 2.	Allocate $\frac{1}{3}$ to Market 1, $\frac{2}{3}$ to Market 2.
Firm A — Allocate $\frac{2}{3}$ to Market 1, $\frac{1}{3}$ to Market 2.	\$6,000	\$5,000
Allocate $\frac{1}{3}$ to Market 1, $\frac{2}{3}$ to Market 2.	\$4,000	\$3,000

The sales *decrease* to Firm B would represent the negative of each of the entries in the matrix.

a. Determine the maximin strategy for Firm A.
b. Determine the maximin strategy for Firm B.
c. Does the game have an equilibrium (or saddle point) if each firm employs a pure strategy? If so, what is the value of the game; that is, what is the sales increase to Firm A and the sales decrease to Firm B?.

3. *Mixed Strategies.* Consider the same decision-making situation as in Problem 2, except that the payoff matrix now is as follows:

	Firm B	
	Allocate $\frac{2}{3}$ to Market 1, $\frac{1}{3}$ to Market 2.	Allocate $\frac{1}{3}$ to Market 1, $\frac{2}{3}$ to Market 2.
Firm A — Allocate $\frac{2}{3}$ to Market 1, $\frac{1}{3}$ to Market 2.	\$2,000	\$5,000
Allocate $\frac{1}{3}$ to Market 1, $\frac{2}{3}$ to Market 2.	\$4,000	\$3,000

a. Employing only pure strategies, determine the maximin strategy for Firm A.
b. Employing only pure strategies, determine the maximin strategy for Firm B.
c. Does the game have an equilibrium (or saddle point) if each firm employs a pure strategy? Why or why not?

d. Observing this situation, the manager of Firm B is concerned about concealing (before adoption) his strategy from Firm A. For example, if Firm A knew for *certain* that firm B would choose Strategy 2 ($\frac{1}{3}$ to Market 1, $\frac{2}{3}$ to Market 2), then Firm A would *not* want to employ Strategy 2 ($\frac{1}{3}$ to Market 1, $\frac{2}{3}$ to Market 2), since a larger payoff—that is, \$5,000—could be obtained by choosing Strategy 1 ($\frac{2}{3}$ to Market 1, $\frac{1}{3}$ to Market 2). The manager of Firm B remembers reading in a book on game theory about the use of randomized strategies to conceal one's choice before the actual play of the game. Doing some quick calculations, he decides to employ a randomized procedure of choosing Strategy 1 with probability $\frac{1}{2}$ and Strategy 2 with probability $\frac{1}{2}$. What is Firm B's *expected* sales decrease if Firm A employs Strategy 1 and Firm B uses the randomized strategy? What is Firm B's *expected* sales decrease if Firm A employs Strategy 2 and Firm B uses the randomized strategy?

e. What do you note about the value of Firm B's expected sales decrease under each of Firm A's strategies?

f. How does this expected value compare with Firm B's maximin solution [obtained in step (b) above] when only pure strategies are used? Would a randomized strategy appear to be worthwhile to Firm B in this situation?

g. The manager of Firm A is likewise concerned about concealing (before adoption) her strategy from Firm B. She decides to employ a mixed strategy involving a $\frac{1}{4}$ probability of choosing Strategy 1 and a $\frac{3}{4}$ probability of choosing Strategy 2. What is Firm A's *expected* sales increase if Firm B employs Strategy 1 and Firm A uses a randomized strategy? What is Firm A's *expected* sales increase if Firm B employs Strategy 2 and Firm A uses the randomized strategy?

h. How does the expected value compare with Firm A's maximin solution [obtained in step (a) above] when only pure strategies are used? Would a randomized strategy appear to be worthwhile to Firm A in this situation?

i. What do you note about the value of the *expected* sales increase to Firm A and the value of the *expected* sales decrease to Firm B? Do the randomized strategies for Firms A and B [in steps (d) and (g)] satisfy the Von Neumann-Morgenstern criterion for the equilibrium solution in this game situation? Why or why not?

4. Consider the situation that exists between the United States and Russia about signing a nuclear test-ban treaty. For purposes of this analysis assume the following:

(a) Each country is intent on achieving a superior position in nuclear weapons and will seek if possible to clandestinely violate the treaty to obtain a competitive advantage.

(b) Detection of violations (particularly underground testing) is extremely difficult, if not impossible.

(c) If one side *does* violate the treaty, and the other side does not, then the violator will obtain a superior position in nuclear weapons and will be able to exert greater military-political-economic influence in the world.

(d) If both sides violate the treaty, then neither side will obtain a competitive advantage.

(e) Each side would prefer not to test (because of the costs) if it were certain that the other side would also not test weapons.

Analyze this situation as a 2-person *noncooperative* nonzero-sum game in which each side has three strategies:

(a) Not signing (N.S.)

(b) Signing, but not abiding (S.N.A.)

(c) Signing and abiding (S.A.)

A general payoff matrix for the exercise can be given by[38]

		Russia		
		N.S.	S.N.A.	S.A.
	N.S.	a, b	a, b	a, b
United States	S.N.A.	a, b	e, f	p, q
	S.A.	a, b	r, s	c, d

Examine the *relative* magnitudes of some of the payoffs to each side. In each question, state the relationship ($<$, $=$, $>$) between the two payoffs under consideration and the reason(s) for such a relationship:

a. What is the relationship between a and c and between b and d?

b. What is the relationship between c and e and between d and f?

c. What is the relationship between p and r and between q and s?

Assume now that the alternative of not signing (N.S.) is not available to each side—that is, world opinion is such that both sides are required to sign a nuclear test-ban treaty.

d. Based on the discussion in the section on 2-person nonzero-sum games in the text, which strategy (S.N.A. or S.A.) would you predict that each side will choose? Why?

[38] Thomas L. Saaty, *Mathematical Models of Arms Control and Disarmament* (New York: John Wiley, 1968).

Further Topics in Pricing 16

This chapter builds on the price and output determination models developed in Chapters 14 and 15 as it considers more complex pricing issues. In the first two sections of the chapter, the assumption that a firm produces a single product is dropped. The first section considers pricing for the multiproduct firm when the products are independent in the production process; that is, they are alternative products. The second section considers the case of products that are interdependent in the production process, that is, joint products. This chapter also develops models of price discrimination which assume that the firm sells the product at different prices at the same time. The problems of transfer pricing, that is, pricing within the firm, are considered for multiproduct and multidivision firms. Limit pricing, which is practiced by monopolists and some oligopolists in an attempt to maintain their market position, is also analyzed. Marginal pricing rules are evaluated and compared with the pricing practices actually used by firms. Finally the chapter assesses various specialized pricing methods, including skimming, prestige pricing, and price lining. Together, the pricing practices presented in this chapter provide an extensive overview of the way managers apply the pricing principles from economic models to maximize shareholder wealth.

Pricing for the Multiproduct Firm

Eli Clemens has argued that firms are not in the business of selling a product as much as they are of selling their productive capacity.[1] Since most firms produce more than one product, it is essential that we reexamine the basic model of a one-product firm, which maximized profits when the marginal cost of production for the item equaled the marginal revenue derived from its sale. This assumption breaks down if the firm has idle capacity, which may be used to produce completely new products, new models of existing products, or new and different styles, sizes, and so on. It will be shown later in the section on price discrimination that the model presented here for analyzing the pricing of

Glossary of New Terms

Joint products
Products that are interdependent in the production process, such as gasoline and fuel oil in an oil refinery. A change in the production of one produces a change in the cost or availability of the other.

Price discrimination
The act of selling the same good or service, produced by a single firm, at different prices to different buyers during the same period of time.

Transfer price
The price at which an intermediate good or service is transferred from the selling to the buying division within the same firm.

Limit price
A price, lower than the short-run profit-maximization price, charged by a monopolist firm to discourage entry into the industry by potential rivals.

(Cont'd on next page)

---

[1] Eli Clemens, "Price Discrimination and the Multiple Product Firm," *Review of Economic Studies* 19 (1950–1951), pp. 1–11; reprinted in American Economic Association. *Readings in Industrial Organization and Public Policy*, vol. 8 (Homewood, Ill.: Richard D. Irwin, 1958), pp. 262–276.

Glossary of New Terms (*Cont'd*)

Cost-plus (or full-cost) pricing
A method of determining prices in which a charge to cover overhead, plus a percentage markup or margin, is added to variable production and marketing costs to arrive at a selling price.

Target (or target return on investment) pricing
A method of pricing in which a target profit, defined as the desired profit rate on investment times total gross operating assets, is allocated to each unit of output to arrive at a selling price.

Incremental analysis
The real-world counterpart to marginal analysis. Incremental analysis requires that an estimate be made of the changes in total cost or revenue that will result from a price change or from a decision to add or delete a product, accept or reject a new order, or undertake a new investment.

Skimming
A new product-pricing strategy that results in a high initial product price. This price is reduced over time as demand at the higher price is satisfied.

Prestige pricing
The practice of charging a high price for a product to enhance its prestige value.

Price lining
The practice of producing a product that will fit in a particular price range for similar, competitive products.

multiple products may also be used for analyzing the case where price discrimination is followed; that is, one product is sold at the same time in two or more distinct markets at different prices.

When idle capacity exists, either as unused or only partially used plant facilities and equipment or as underused technical knowledge and organizational capabilities, the firm is faced with the challenge of making profitable use of these otherwise idle resources. As long as the new product (or modification of an existing product) may be sold at a price that exceeds the true marginal cost of producing and selling it, the profitability of the firm will be enhanced by its adoption. A range of alternative uses for idle resources should be examined when choosing the most profitable alternatives. In an analysis of the cost of adopting various alternatives, it is imperative that one consider true marginal costs, since the decision to add new or different products or drop some existing lines may well have an impact on the sales of a firm's remaining outputs. For instance, new products may compete with existing ones, raising the implicit cost of the new product. Failure to recognize these interdependencies may lead to a suboptimal use of available resources.

Clemens' model assumes that the productive resources of the firm may be transferred rather easily from one product to another, facilitating easy adaptation to changing markets and product demands.[2] In addition, it also assumes that the demands for the various products produced by the firm are not significantly interrelated, although this assumption is not necessary since the demand curves for each product could be adjusted for such interdependence. The market conditions that the firm faces for each of its products may range from pure competition to a near monopoly. Starting from a point where the firm is producing one product, marginal revenue equals marginal cost, and 60 to 70 percent of capacity is being used, we may now examine the decision to add additional products. This situation is illustrated in Figure 16.1.

Because the firm has excess personnel, organizational resources, and capacity, it may increase output with only a small additional cost. Instead of reducing prices and increasing output for an existing product, it will invade new markets where price is greater than marginal cost. New markets are assumed to be invaded in order of their profitability. Hence the firm does not reach an equilibrium situation until no more markets are available where the price of a product exceeds its marginal cost. Figure 16.1 illustrates a situation of a firm with five products, although that number might well be greater or less. D_1 represents the demand for Product 1, D_2 for Product 2, and so on. The number of units of Product 1 that are sold equals Q_1, of Product 2, $Q_2 - Q_1$, and so on. Profits are maximized when the firm produces and sells quantities of the five products such that marginal revenue is equal in all markets and equal to marginal cost. The line *EMR* represents a new line of *equal marginal revenue*. Since it is assumed that new product markets were entered in order of their profitability, the prices charged for the five products are arranged in declining

---

[2] This assumption probably is more generally true than one might suspect. See the cases in F. E. Folts, *Introduction to Industrial Management* (New York: McGraw-Hill, 1949) for some illustrations of this point.

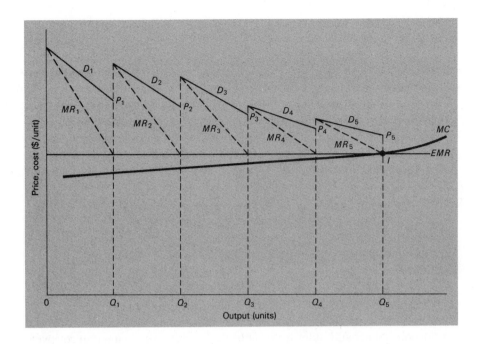

Figure 16.1
Multiple-Product Pricing

order, from P_1 to P_5, and the elasticity of demand increases from D_1 to D_5. The *EMR* line is determined by the intersection of the firm's marginal cost curve *MC* and the marginal revenue curve for the last product market that may be profitably served. Theoretically, this would be the one with the most elastic demand, D_5.[3] If D_5 is perfectly elastic, this then is the marginal market or last profitable new-product market. In such a case Price $= MR = MC$. If the marginal market is less than perfectly elastic, the possibility exists of some remaining market that may be entered where price exceeds *MC*.

The equilibrium condition where there is virtually an equivalence between P, MR, and MC in the marginal market illustrates the well-known fact that nearly all firms produce some products that generate little or no profit and are on the verge of being dropped or replaced. In some cases, such as the railway and utility industries, zero-profit products may be produced to keep the organization intact. Supermarkets provide an illustration of the multiple-product pricing model. The prices of staple items—such as coffee, soap, potatoes, and salt—are relatively lower (in terms of markups and margins) than nonstaples—such as imported foods and specialty items. This is so because of the differences in elasticities between staples and nonstaples. Even though the total market demand for many staples is probably much less elastic than for nonstaples, in any one supermarket the demand for staples is more elastic because of the

[3] The *EMR* line is determined by horizontally summing the marginal revenue curve for each product. The intersection of the combined marginal revenue curve (note that the combined marginal revenue curve is not shown in Figure 16.1) with the marginal cost curve (Point I in Figure 16.1) establishes the *EMR* line.

closeness of competition between rival supermarkets, advertising that emphasizes prices of staples, and knowledgeability of thrifty shoppers about the prices of these items. The less elastic demand for nonstaples results from their infrequent purchase and the fact that these purchases are made more on impulse where price is not nearly so important a variable. The net result is that in supermarkets, as expected, the more elastic the demand, the lower the markup.

Joint Products

Thus far our concern has been with price and output decisions for firms that produce several *alternative products* that are technically independent in the production process. *Joint products*, in contrast, are interdependent in the production process; that is, a change in the production of one produces a change in the cost (or more specifically, the marginal cost) or the availability of the other. Many examples exist of joint products that have the property that the process of producing two or more products is technically interdependent, including the production of liquid oxygen and nitrogen from air, beef and hides from steers, and gasoline and fuel oil from crude oil. In some cases, such as the production of beef and hides from cattle, the outputs are obtained in relatively fixed proportions. In other cases, such as the production of gasoline and fuel oil from crude oil, variable proportions of the outputs can be obtained through changes in the production process. Each of these cases is examined below.

Joint Products in Fixed Proportions

When outputs are produced in fixed proportions they should be analyzed as a *product package*. Since the products are jointly produced, all costs are incurred in production of the package and no conceptually correct method exists for allocating these costs to the individual products. Determination of the optimal output and prices of the products involves a comparison of the total marginal revenue from all the products with the marginal cost. In the following analysis, each unit of the product package consists of the output obtained from one unit of input. For example, the slaughtering of a steer might yield a product package consisting of five hundred pounds of beef and one hide.

Figure 16.2 (a) shows the demand functions and their respectively marginal revenue functions for two products (A and B) that make up a product package, along with the marginal cost function for the production process. The total marginal revenue function (MR_T) for the product package is obtained by *vertically* summing the marginal revenue functions for the individual products (MR_A and MR_B). The net revenue gain to the firm of producing one more unit of the product package is the additional (marginal) revenue from product A plus the additional (marginal) revenue from product B. The intersection of the total marginal revenue function (MR_T) and the marginal cost function (MC) determines the optimal output of the product package (Q^*) along with the optimal prices of the two individual products (i.e., P_A^* and P_B^*).

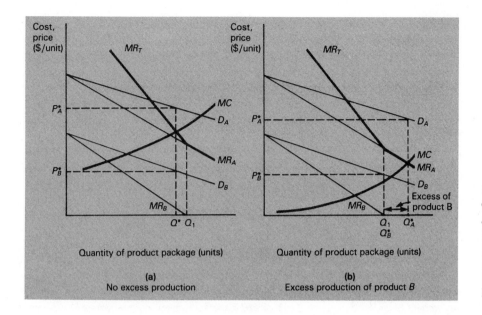

Quantity of product package (units)

(a)
No excess production

(b)
Excess production of product *B*

Figure 16.2
Optimal Price and Output Determination of Joint Products A and B Produced in Fixed Proportions

A numerical example can be used to illustrate the concepts developed above. Suppose the Williams Company is faced with the following demand functions for two joint products produced in fixed proportions:

$$P_1 = 50 - .5Q \qquad\qquad [16.1]$$

$$P_2 = 60 - 2Q \qquad\qquad [16.2]$$

Furthermore, suppose that the marginal cost function for the joint products is

$$MC = 38 + Q \qquad\qquad [16.3]$$

The two marginal revenue functions are obtained as follows:

$$TR_1 = P_1 Q = (50 - .5Q)Q = 50Q - .5Q^2$$

$$MR_1 = \frac{dTR_1}{dQ} = 50 - Q$$

$$TR_2 = P_2 Q = (60 - 2Q)Q = 60Q - 2Q^2$$

$$MR_2 = \frac{dTR_2}{dQ} = 60 - 4Q$$

Summing the two marginal revenue functions yields

$$\begin{aligned} MR_T &= MR_1 + MR_2 \\ &= (50 - Q) + (60 - 4Q) \\ &= 110 - 5Q \qquad\qquad [16.4] \end{aligned}$$

Setting the total marginal revenue function equal to the marginal cost function and solving for Q yields the optimal output

$$MR_T = MC$$

$$110 - 5Q = 38 + Q$$

$$72 = 6Q$$

$$Q^* = 12$$

or 12 units of the product package. Substituting this value into the demand functions (Equations 16.1 and 16.2) gives the optimal prices of the two products:

$$P_1^* = 50 - .5(12)$$

$$= \$44 \text{ per unit of product } A$$

$$P_2^* = 60 - 2(12)$$

$$= \$36 \text{ per unit of product } B$$

One complication in the preceding analysis can occur if the marginal cost function (MC) intersects the total marginal revenue function (MR_T) at an output in excess of Q_1 in Figure 16.2 (a). Above Q_1, the marginal revenue of product B is negative and the firm would not want to sell more than Q_1 units of product B. When this situation occurs, as shown in Figure 16.2 (b), the optimal solution is to *produce* Q_A^* units of the product package. This is determined at the intersection of the MR_A and MC functions. Q_A^* units of product A should be *sold* at a price of P_A^*. However, only $Q_B^*(= Q_1)$ units of product B should be sold at a price of P_B^*. The *excess output* of product B, namely $Q_A^* - Q_B^*$ should be destroyed or discarded so as not to depress the market price.

When solving a numerical problem, one can check to see if the marginal cost function intersects the total marginal revenue function at an output greater than Q_1 by substituting the optimal output (Q^*) into the MR_A and MR_B functions. If either marginal revenue value is negative, then the marginal cost function should be set equal to the marginal revenue function of the other product in determining the optimal price and output combination.[4] For example, if the MR_B function is negative, then one would use MR_A (rather than MR_T) to determine the optimal solution.

Joint Products in Variable Proportions

When the outputs can be produced in variable proportions, the analysis is somewhat more complex than the fixed proportions case. The decision facing the firm is illustrated in Figure 16.3. The quantities of X and Y that may be produced are indicated on the vertical and horizontal axes. The isocost or production possibility curves (labeled TC) indicate the amounts of X and Y that may be produced for the same total cost. For instance, looking at the isocost curve

---

[4] Note in the Williams Company example discussed earlier in this section, when $Q^* = 12$, $MR_1 = 50 - 12 = \$38 > 0$ and $MR_2 = 60 - 4(12) = \$12 > 0$. Hence, no excess output of either product was being produced.

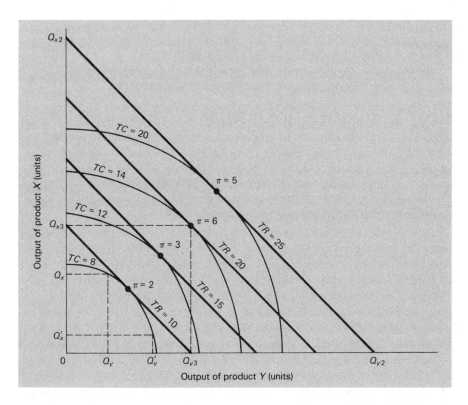

Figure 16.3
Joint Products Produced in Variable Proportions: An Optimal Price-Output Mix

labeled $TC = 8$, we see that the firm may produce Q_x units of X and Q_y units of Y, Q'_x units of X and Q'_y units of Y, or any possible combination along that curve at an equivalent total cost of $TC = 8$. Hence there are two ways of increasing the output of, say, Product X. One way is to move along the isocost curve increasing the output of X at the expense of Y. The other is to increase the amount of the inputs or factors (e.g., capital and/or labor) in the production process; that is, move in a northeast direction to a higher isocost curve. The only requirement of isocost or production possibility curves is that they be concave to the origin, indicating an imperfect adaptability of the firm's productive resources in producing X and Y.

The isorevenue lines (labeled TR) take into account the prices received by the firm for its two outputs. Each line is of equal revenue, indicating that any combination of X and Y along any particular line will yield the same total revenue. The *straight* isorevenue lines in Figure 16.3 indicate that products X and Y are being sold in *purely competitive markets*; that is, the prices of X and Y do not change as output changes. (If this were not the case, the isorevenue lines would no longer be straight; nevertheless, the general tangency solution for an optimal output combination does not change.) Line $TR = 25$ is constructed such that Q_{y2} times the price of $Y(P_y)$ equals Q_{x2} times the price of $X(P_x)$. The slope of each isorevenue line is equal to $P_y \div P_x$, because the slope of $TR = 25$ equals $Q_{x2} \div Q_{y2}$, and $P_x(Q_{x2}) = P_y(Q_{y2})$; therefore

$$\frac{P_y}{P_x} = \frac{Q_{x2}}{Q_{y2}}$$

A whole family of isorevenue lines exists that is defined by the prices and levels of output for X and Y. The further one moves in a northeast direction, the greater the total revenue associated with any isorevenue line.

The solution for an optimum combination of outputs requires a point of tangency between the isocost and isorevenue curves. This may be illustrated with the $TC = 14$ isocost curve. Under the conditions depicted in Figure 16.3, the firm should produce Q_{x3} units of X and Q_{y3} units of Y because total profit, π (the difference between TR and TC), is maximized at that point. To produce any other possible output combination along the $TC = 14$ isocost curve would result in the same costs (14), but would place the firm on a lower isorevenue curve thereby reducing profit. Since profits are maximized at the point of tangency ($\pi = 6$), the marginal cost of producing each product must be exactly equal to the marginal revenue each product generates.

The analysis presented here could be expanded considerably by dropping some of the assumptions. For instance, the two-product case could be expanded to a more general n-product case. One could also assume a far greater number of variable factors of production than the one factor (or bundle of factors) implicitly assumed. In addition, the assumption that the prices of input factors are not a function of their use and the assumption that the prices of outputs are independent of the quantity produced could be dropped. Cases such as these are capable of mathematical analysis, but in many instances the simplified model presented provides an adequate framework for analysis.[5] Linear programming also has proved to be an extremely useful tool for examining problems of allocating common productive facilities among two or more products to maximize profits.[6]

In conclusion, it should be reemphasized that the decision to add (or delete) products to a firm's product line must consider true marginal benefits as well as true marginal costs. If a new product is a reasonably close substitute for an existing product, the addition of the new product is likely to reduce sales of the existing product. This reduction must be considered in the marginal decision analysis. In addition, complementarities in demand between two or more products (that is, when a lower price or increased availability of one product stimulates an increase in demand for another) must also be considered in a multiproduct firm's price and output decisions.

Finally, in deciding whether to add, delete, or change the relative output of any one product, the impact of that action on the cost of producing the firm's other outputs must be taken into consideration. Only after true marginal costs and benefits have been accounted for may optimal strategies about the makeup of a firm's product line be adopted.

---

[5] The interested reader may wish to explore some of these more advanced models. See, for example, William Mauer and Thomas Naylor, "Monopolistic-Monopsonistic Competition: The Multi-Product Multi-Factor Firm", *Southern Economic Journal* 31 (July 1964), pp. 38–43.

[6] A discussion of linear programming is given in chapter 5 of this book.

Price Discrimination

Price discrimination is defined as the act of selling the same product (a good or service), produced under single control (that is, by one firm), at different prices to different buyers.[7] This basic definition, which assumes a homogenous product, can be broadened to a more operational level if we also include cases in which differences between prices of a firm's products exceed the differences in costs of production. Examples of price discrimination include the following:

- Doctors, dentists, hospitals, lawyers, tax consultants, and economic consultants who charge the rich more than the poor for the same quality of service

- Producers who offer large purchasers quantity discounts that exceed the difference in marginal selling costs between large and small purchasers

- Firms that sell the exact same product (e.g., appliances) under two different labels at widely varying prices

- Athletic teams that sponsor family nights and ladies' nights at discount prices, while others pay the full price

- Hotels, restaurants, and other businesses that offer discounts to senior citizens

- Airlines that offer discounted fares based on the day of the week (or time of day) of travel and the length of stay (e.g., a stay over Saturday night is normally required for the most heavily discounted "super saver" fares)

- State-supported universities that charge higher tuition to students who are not state residents

- Hotels in resort areas that offer lower off-season room rates

- Restaurants that vary their menu prices by the time of day (e.g., "early bird" specials) and day of the week (e.g., higher prices on weekends than on weekdays)

- Academic journals that charge a lower price to individuals and a higher price to institutional subscribers (e.g., libraries)

- University bookstores that offer faculty members a discount on books, which is not available to students or other customers

- Japanese TV manufacturers who sell products at a lower price in the United States than in Japan

A determination of whether price discrimination is actually being practiced requires that cost differentials be evaluated in conjunction with price differentials. It should be emphasized that the term "price discrimination" has a strictly

---

[7] Joan Robinson, *The Economics of Imperfect Competition* (London: Macmillan, 1933), p. 179.

neutral connotation in economic jargon. A determination of whether the exercise of this business practice, under any given set of circumstances, should be considered bad or good requires a more rigorous—and oftentimes value-laden—analysis. For instance, one issue that might be considered is the impact of a price-discrimination strategy on various income classes of consumers.

As far as the individual firm is concerned, the practice of charging different prices (if it is done with a proper recognition of demand elasticities) to different individuals will always result in a level of profits at least as high as would occur if only one price were charged, and usually profits may be increased through price discrimination. This is so because the price that a consumer pays for a product will never exceed that which he or she is willing to pay rather than do without it, and in many cases it does not equal this amount. As a consequence, the satisfaction or utility gained from the purchase of the product often exceeds that which is lost from paying the prevailing price. This results in a surplus of satisfaction or *consumer's surplus* that a customer may derive from the purchase. For example, if a diabetic were willing to pay $100 for a life-sustaining dose of insulin, but found that the neighborhood druggist charged only $2, the diabetic's consumer surplus would be $98. Price discrimination aims at transferring part or all of the consumer's surplus from the consumer to the producer.

Conditions Required for Successful Price Discrimination

Before examining the various degrees of price discrimination that may be practiced, consider the conditions that will enable a firm (or any organization charging a price for goods or services provided) to engage successfully in this strategy. The two basic conditions are the following:

1. It must be possible to segment the market and to prevent the transfer of the seller's product from one segment to another

2. Differences in the elasticity of demand from one segment to another must exist at the same price

The illustrations presented at the beginning of this section indicate some of the bases of price discrimination. One case is that of consumer ignorance, where Consumer A pays more than Consumer B for the same good or service, but where there is little or no communication between consumers so one consumer does not know he or she is paying a higher price. An imperfect example of this is the case of the firm that sells some of its product abroad at a lower price than it charges at home. Another example is an automobile dealer who charges different prices to different customers, depending on the relative negotiating strength of each buyer. The nature of personal services, such as medical and dental care, also permit effective price discrimination, since it is generally impossible to resell these services once they have been performed; for example, it is impossible to resell a kidney transplant operation performed under Medicare coverage to someone who does not have this coverage. Similarly, a hockey team may charge different prices to groups than to individuals. Advance purchase requirements and evidence of group affiliation are used to enforce this segmentation. Other criteria used to effect price discrimination are age, sex, educational status, income levels, and military status of the buyers.

Geographical differences in buyers' locations, alternative uses to which a product is put (for example, electric power rates for households versus industrial users), product labeling or branding, and peak versus off-peak rates (for example, discounted long-distance direct dialing telephone rates during the evening and weekends) are also used to segment the market and allow price discrimination.[8] The actual basis used for market segmentation is relatively unimportant as long as it is effective (that is, little leakage occurs among segments) and as long as different price elasticities exist between the resulting segments.

First-, Second-, and Third-Degree Price Discrimination

In the limiting case of perfect or *first-degree price discrimination*, the monopolist presumably knows not only the market demand curve but also the maximum each individual is willing to pay for any quantity.[9] The monopolist then charges each customer the highest price that purchaser is willing to pay for each unit purchased (providing this price exceeds the marginal cost of production). In this manner, the entire consumer surplus is captured by the producer. Since conditions such as these are extremely rare, consider next the more realistic cases of second- and third-degree price discrimination.[10]

Second-degree price discrimination, or "block rate-setting" as it is sometimes called, is practiced regularly by such public utilities as water companies, gas companies, and electric companies. Figure 16.4 illustrates the case of second-degree discrimination. Let DD_1 represent the household demand for natural gas in a community. If the gas company charged P_1, Q_1 cubic feet of natural gas would be demanded. If, however, the firm wished to sell Q_3 cubic feet of gas, a price of P_3 would have to be charged. In the case of second-degree discrimination, consumers would be charged a set of prices rather than a single price. For instance, the first Q_1 cubic feet used would be priced at P_1; the next block of usage, $Q_2 - Q_1$, would be priced at P_2; and the last block, $Q_3 - Q_2$, at P_3. If only one price were charged—for example P_3—total revenue received by the gas company would equal the price P_3 times Q_3 units sold. Consumer's surplus in this case is given by the triangle DP_3C. By charging three separate prices, total

---

[8] It should be emphasized that peak-load pricing is not limited to regulated public utility companies such as those that provide long-distance phone service. Many other unregulated companies, such as hotels, airlines, and restaurants, also engage in peak-load pricing. See Chapter 20 for a more detailed discussion of the peak-load pricing concept.

[9] In the discussion assume that the price-discriminating firm is a monopolist, although the practice has been frequently observed in other imperfectly competitive market structures as well. Only in highly competitive markets, where new sellers may move rapidly into higher-priced market segments thereby undermining price differentials charged, is discrimination unlikely.

[10] The practice of first-degree price discrimination is likely to be found a violation of the Clayton Antitrust Act and the Robinson Patman Act, which are discussed in Chapter 19.

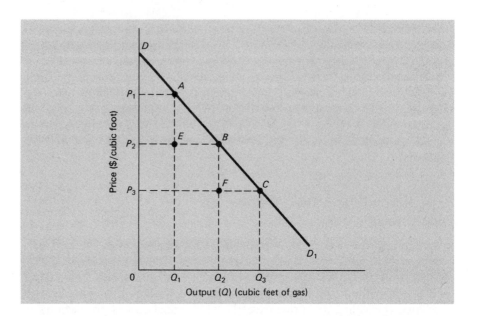

Figure 16.4
Second-Degree Price Discrimination

revenue is now represented by rectangles P_1P_2AE plus P_2P_3BF in addition to the original amount OP_3CQ_3. The remaining consumer's surplus, which the utility was unable to appropriate, is represented by the small triangles DP_1A, AEB, and BFC.

Second-degree discrimination is imperfect (in the eyes of the monopolist) because only part of the consumer's surplus may be captured. Its use is somewhat limited since it is only effective in the case of services or products that are sold in easily metered units, such as cubic feet of gas or water and kilowatt hours of electricity. Segmentation between limited users, who are charged only the higher price, and volume users, who get the benefit of lower rates as volume increases, is enforced by laws that prohibit customers from reselling gas, water, and electricity.

Third-degree price discrimination is probably the most common form of price discrimination. In addition to practicing second-degree price discrimination within markets, the utilities, for example, frequently segment their customers into several smaller groups—such as household, institutional, commercial, and industrial users—and establish a different rate schedule for each one of these groups. Likewise milk producers charge two different prices for milk, depending on whether it is to be sold as fluid milk for retail sales in a local market (where the producers' associations have a virtual monopoly) or whether it is to be sold in the more competitive surplus market, where it is used to make cheese, ice cream, powdered milk, and butter. The price of the monopoly-marketed fluid milk invariably exceeds the price in the more competitive surplus market.[11] The reasons for this are examined below.

To maximize profits, discriminating monopolists must allocate their out-

---

[11] Edmond S. Harris, *Classified Pricing of Milk*, Technical Bulletin no. 1184, U.S. Department of Agriculture (Washington, D.C.: U.S. Government Printing Office, 1958).

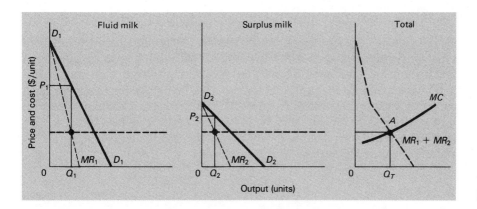

Figure 16.5
Third-Degree Price Discrimination

put in such a way as to make identical the marginal revenue in all markets. If marginal revenue derived from the fluid milk market exceeded marginal revenue derived from the surplus market, profits could be increased by transferring output from the surplus market to the fluid market. When the price rise in the surplus market (resulting from the output reduction) and the price decline in the fluid market (resulting from the output increases) settle to such a level tht MR is equal in both markets, the monopolist is at a profit-maximizing equilibrium position. The total output to be allocated among the two or more market segments is determined by setting the combined marginal revenue of all markets equal to marginal cost. This is illustrated in Figure 16.5. The marginal revenue curves for fluid milk sales (MR_1) and surplus sales (MR_2) are added together horizontally to yield the total marginal revenue curve $MR_1 + MR_2$. Total output is set at the point where total marginal revenue equals total marginal cost (that is, Point A). Total output at this point is Q_T gallons of milk. Since marginal revenue must be equal in each market to achieve profit maximization, one can determine the price and output combination that will prevail in each market at the profit-maximizing level of marginal revenue. In the fluid milk market, output will be Q_1 gallons at a price of P_1, since this is the price-output combination that corresponds to the required profit-maximizing level of marginal revenue. Similarly, in the surplus market output equals Q_2 gallons at a price of P_2 (determined from the demand curve D_2D_2). It should be noted that the sum of the outputs in these two markets equals total output ($Q_1 + Q_2 = Q_T$). Not surprisingly, one finds that the price is higher in the less competitive fluid milk market where the price elasticity of demand is less than in the more competitive surplus market. As a general rule, one would expect to find an inverse relationship between the price elasticity of demand and price in markets served by discriminating monopolists.

Mathematics of Price Discrimination[†]

This section develops the mathematics of price discrimination using some numerical examples.

[†] This section may be omitted without loss of continuity.

Price Discrimination and the Price Elasticity of Demand

It can be shown that an inverse relationship must exist between price and price elasticity in the separate markets served by a discriminating monopolist. Recall that marginal revenue must be equal in each market served by the monopolist and must equal total marginal cost for profits to be maximized. If the marginal revenues are not equal, total revenue could be increased (with no impact on total cost) by shifting sales from the low marginal revenue market to the high one. In Chapter 7 the relationship between marginal revenue (MR) and price (P) was shown to be (Equation 7.9) the following:

$$MR = P\left(1 + \frac{1}{E_D}\right) \qquad [16.5]$$

where E_D is the price elasticity of demand. If there are two markets such that P_1, P_2, E_1, and E_2 represent the prices and price elasticities in the two markets, we may equate marginal revenue in each market:

$$MR_1 = MR_2 \qquad [16.6]$$

However,

$$MR_1 = P_1\left(1 + \frac{1}{E_1}\right) \qquad \text{and} \qquad MR_2 = P_2\left(1 + \frac{1}{E_2}\right)$$

Hence

$$P_1\left(1 + \frac{1}{E_1}\right) = P_2\left(1 + \frac{1}{E_2}\right)$$

$$\frac{P_1}{P_2} = \frac{\left(1 + \dfrac{1}{E_2}\right)}{\left(1 + \dfrac{1}{E_1}\right)} \qquad [16.7]$$

To illustrate the inverse relationship between price and elasticity shown in Equation 16.7, assume that $E_1 = -2$ and $E_2 = -3$. Then

$$\frac{P_1}{P_2} = \frac{1 + \left(-\dfrac{1}{3}\right)}{1 + \left(-\dfrac{1}{2}\right)}$$

$$= \frac{\dfrac{2}{3}}{\dfrac{1}{2}}$$

$$\frac{1}{2}P_1 = \frac{2}{3}P_2$$

$$P_1 = \frac{4}{3}P_2$$

When the elasticity in Market 1 is less (in absolute value) than that in Market 2, the price in Market 1 will exceed the price in Market 2.

Price Discrimination and Profitability of the Firm

The advantages to a monopolist of engaging in price discrimination can be illustrated with the following example. Two cases are considered—Case I where the firm charges different prices for the same product in the two different markets and Case II where the firm charges the same price in the two different markets (i.e., does not engage in price discrimination).

Taiwan Instrument Company (TIC) makes computer memory chips in Formosa, which it ships to computer manufacturers in Japan (Market 1) and the United States (Market 2). Demand for the chips in the two markets is given by the following functions:

$$\text{Japan: } P_1 = 12 - Q_1 \tag{16.8}$$

$$\text{United States: } P_2 = 8 - Q_2 \tag{16.9}$$

where Q_1 and Q_2 are the respective quantities sold (in *millions* of units) and P_1 and P_2 are the respective prices (in dollars per unit) in the two markets. TIC's total cost function for these memory chips is

$$C = 5 + 2 (Q_1 + Q_2) \tag{16.10}$$

Case I: Price Discrimination. TIC's total combined profit in the two markets equals

$$\pi = P_1Q_1 + P_2Q_2 - C \tag{16.11}$$
$$= (12 - Q_1)Q_1 + (8 - Q_2)Q_2 - [5 + 2(Q_1 + Q_2)]$$
$$= 12Q_1 - Q_1^2 + 8Q_2 - Q_2^2 - 5 - 2Q_1 - 2Q_2$$
$$= 10Q_1 - Q_1^2 + 6Q_2 - Q_2^2 - 5 \tag{16.12}$$

To maximize π with respect to Q_1 and Q_2, find the partial derivatives of Equation 16.12 with respect to Q_1 and Q_2, set them equal to zero, and solve for Q_1^* and Q_2^*:

$$\frac{\partial \pi}{\partial Q_1} = 10 - 2Q_1 = 0$$

$$Q_1^* = 5 \,(\text{million}) \,\text{units}$$

$$\frac{\partial \pi}{\partial Q_2} = 6 - 2Q_2 = 0$$

$$Q_2^* = 3 \,(\text{million}) \,\text{units}$$

Substituting Q_1^* and Q_2^* into the appropriate demand and profit equations yields

$$P_1^* = \$7 \text{ per unit}$$

$$P_2^* = \$5 \text{ per unit}$$

$$\pi^* = \$29 \,(\text{million})$$

It may be noted that maximizing π with respect to Q_1 and Q_2 is equivalent to setting $MR_1 = MR_2$. The equivalence of MR_1 and MR_2 may be proved by taking the partial derivatives of the TR function:

$$\begin{aligned} TR &= P_1 \cdot Q_1 + P_2 \cdot Q_2 \\ &= (12 - Q_1)Q_1 + (8 - Q_2)Q_2 \\ &= 12Q_1 - Q_1^2 + 8Q_2 - Q_2^2 \end{aligned}$$ [16.13]

with respect to Q_1 and Q_2, and substituting the solution values, $Q_1^* = 5$ and $Q_2^* = 3$:

$$MR_1 = \frac{\partial TR}{\partial Q_1} = 12 - 2Q_1$$

$$MR_1^* = 12 - 2(5) = \$2 \text{ per unit}$$

$$MR_2 = \frac{\partial TR}{\partial Q_2} = 8 - 2Q_2$$

$$MR_2^* = 8 - 2(3) = \$2 \text{ per unit}$$

Case II: No Price Discrimination. Suppose that protectionist (anti-dumping) trade laws in the United States prohibit foreign computer chip manufacturers from selling these products for less than the prices charged in Japan. In other words, assume that TIC is not permitted to engage in price discrimination.

In order to determine the profits TIC will earn if it does not discriminate between the two markets, solve the two demand equations for Q_1 and Q_2 and add them to get a total demand function:

$$Q_1 = 12 - P_1$$

$$Q_2 = 8 - P_2$$

$$\begin{aligned} Q &= Q_1 + Q_2 \\ &= 12 - P_1 + 8 - P_2 \end{aligned}$$

Since price discrimination is no longer possible, P_1 must equal P_2, and

$$Q = 20 - 2P$$

or

$$P = 10 - \frac{Q}{2}$$ [16.14]

Total profit is now

$$\pi = PQ - C$$

$$= 10Q - \frac{Q^2}{2} - 5 - 2Q$$

$$= 8Q - \frac{Q^2}{2} - 5$$ [16.15]

To find the profit-maximizing level of Q, differentiate Equation 16.15 with

Market	Case I Price Discrimination		Case II No Price Discrimination	
	1 (Japan)	*2 (U.S.)*	*1 (Japan)*	*2 (U.S.)*
Price P^* ($/unit)	7	5	6	6
Quantity Q^* (million units)	5	3	6	2
Marginal Revenue MR ($/unit)	2	2	0	4
Profit π^* ($ million)	29		27	

Table 16.1
Taiwan Instrument Company: Effects of Price Discrimination

respect to Q, set it equal to zero, and solve for Q^*:

$$\frac{d\pi}{dQ} = 8 - Q = 0$$

$$Q^* = 8 \text{ (million) units}$$

Substituting Q^* into the appropriate equations yields:

$$P^* = 10 - \frac{Q}{2} = \$6 \text{ per unit}$$

$$\pi^* = 8Q - \frac{Q^2}{2} - 5 = \$27 \text{ (million)}$$

$$Q_1^* = 12 - 6 = 6 \text{ (million) units}$$
$$Q_2^* = 8 - 6 = 2 \text{ (million) units}$$
$$MR_1^* = 12 - 2(6) = \$0 \text{ per unit}$$
$$MR_2^* = 8 - 2(2) = \$4 \text{ per unit}$$

The two cases are summarized in Table 16.1. Note that TIC's profits ($29 million) are higher when it engages in price discrimination than when it does not engage in price discrimination ($27 million).

The example developed above shows that by charging different prices to different groups of customers, monopolists may always increase their profits above the level achieved if no market segmentation is attempted, as long as the groups of customers have differing demand functions.

Transfer Pricing[12]

Associated with the tremendous growth in the size of corporations has been a trend toward decentralized decision making and control within these organizations. Because of the exceedingly complex coordination and communication

---

[12] This section draws heavily on the contributions of J. Hirshleifer to the transfer pricing problem. See his articles "On the Economics of Transfer Pricing," *Journal of Business* 29 (1956), pp. 172–184; "Economics of the Divisionalized Firm," *Journal of Business* 30 (1957), pp. 96–108; and "Internal Pricing and Decentralized Decisions," in *Management Controls: New Directions in Basic Research,* ed. C. P. Bonini, R. K. Jaedicke, and H. M. Wagner (New York: McGraw-Hill, 1964).

problems within the large multiproduct national or international firm, such firms typically are broken up into a group of semiautonomous operating divisions. Each division constitutes a profit center with the responsibility and authority for making operating decisions. Combined with an appropriate set of rewards and incentives, division managements presumably will be oriented toward making decisions that maximize the profitability of the profit center. With all the divisions operating in this manner, it is believed that such a system will maximize the overall profitability of the firm.[13] This section examines the conditions under which such a decentralized system will in fact lead to optimal price and output decisions; that is, decisions that maximize the overall profit of the firm. Because of the complex nature of this problem, the analysis is limited to several somewhat simplified cases.

In practice, a number of conditions cause the price-output decisions made by one division of the decentralized firm to be dependent on (that is, influenced by) the price-output decisions of another division. One source of dependence occurs whenever the external demand functions of the two divisions are interrelated. For example, a degree of dependence presumably exists between the demand functions of the Chevrolet and Pontiac divisions of General Motors. In the analysis of this section, however, it is assumed that the external demand functions of each division are independent.

Another source of dependence occurs whenever the production processes of two divisions are cost dependent either through technological interdependence or through the effects of output changes on the costs of inputs employed in the production process. An example of the former type of interdependence would be the case of an oil refinery in which the mix of outputs (for example, gasoline, kerosene, heating oil, and lubricants) is limited by the production process. An example of the latter type would be two divisions that are bidding for a raw material or a labor skill that is in short supply and that are, as a result, causing the price to rise. In the ensuing analysis, it is assumed that the production processes are cost independent.

A third source of dependence, and the only one considered in this section, occurs whenever one division sells all or part of its output to another division of the same firm. For example, within the Ford Motor Company a multitude of internal transfers of goods and services takes place. The Engine and Foundry Division, Transmission and Chassis Division, Metal Stamping Division, and the Glass Division among others transfer products to the Automotive Assembly Division. The Automotive Assembly Division in turn transfers completed cars to the Ford and Lincoln-Mercury Divisions. The price at which each intermediate good or service is transferred from the selling to the buying division affects the revenues of the selling division and the costs of the buying division. Conse-

---

[13] Mathematical programming techniques have been proposed to analyze these decentralized resource allocation systems. See, for example, George Dantzig, *Linear Programming and Extensions* (Princeton, N.J. Princeton University. Press, 1963), chap. 23; and William J. Baumol and Tibor Fabian, "Decomposition Pricing for Decentralization and External Economies," *Management Science* 11 (September 1964), pp. 1–32.

quently, the price-output decisions and profitability of each division, as determined by the standard profit-maximization rule (that is, marginal cost equals marginal revenue), will be affected by the transfer price.

A *transfer price* serves two functions in the decentralized firm. One function is to act as a measure of the *marginal* value of resources used in the division when making the price and output decisions that will maximize profits. The other is to serve as a measure of the *total* value of the resources used in the division when analyzing the performance of the division. It is sometimes possible for these functions to conflict.[14] In other words, the transfer price that is correct for making optimal price-output decisions may be incorrect for measuring the overall worth of the divisions to the firm. The emphasis in this section is on determining the correct transfer price to use in making optimal (that is, profit-maximizing) price-output decisions.

In this analysis, assume that a decentralized firm consists of two separate divisions that form a two-stage process to manufacture and market a single product. The production division manufactures an intermediate product, which is sold internally to the marketing division at the transfer price. The marketing division converts the intermediate product into a final product, which it then sells in an imperfectly competitive (that is, monopolistic) external market. Depending on the nature of the external market for the intermediate product manufactured by the production division, several possible cases can be considered in deriving the transfer price that will maximize the total profits of the firm. The two cases examined here are (1) no external market for the intermediate product and (2) a perfectly competitive external market for the intermediate product.[15]

No External Market for the Intermediate Product

With no external market for the intermediate product, the production division would be unable to dispose of any excess units over and above the amount desired by the marketing division. Likewise, if demand for the final product should exceed the capacity of the production division, the marketing division would be unable to obtain additional units of the intermediate product externally. Therefore, the quantity of the product manufactured by the production division must necessarily be equal to the amount sold by the marketing division.[16] The determination of the profit-maximizing price-output combination and the resulting transfer price are shown in Figure 16.6. The marginal cost

---

[14] See J. Hirshleifer, "Internal Pricing and Decentralized Decisions," in *Management Controls*, pp. 28–29, for an example of how these functions may conflict.

[15] For a discussion of the more complicated case where there is an imperfectly competitive external market for the intermediate product, see the original Hirschleifer articles cited earlier.

[16] This analysis assumes that all units produced during the period must be sold during the period; that is, no inventories of the intermediate product can be carried over into the next period.

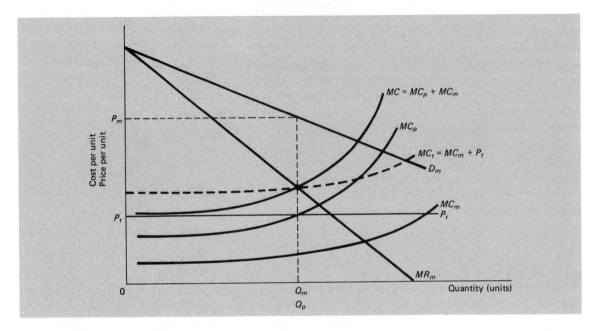

Figure 16.6
Determination of the Transfer Price When No External Market Exists for the Intermediate Product

per unit to the firm, MC, of any level of output is the sum of the marginal costs per unit of production, MC_p, and marketing, MC_m. By equating marginal cost MC to external marginal revenue MR, one obtains the firm's profit-maximizing decisions—P_m as the optimal price and Q_m as the optimal quantity of the final product to be sold by the marketing division in the external market. Therefore, a transfer price, P_t, is set equal to the marginal production cost per unit, MC_p, at the optimum output level Q_p. This will cause each division, when seeking to maximize its own divisional profit, to maximize the overall profit of the firm. This result can be demonstrated in the following manner.

Once the transfer price is established, the production division will face a *horizontal* demand curve (and corresponding marginal revenue curve) at the given transfer price for the intermediate product. The profits of the production division will be maximized at the point where its divisional marginal cost equals divisional marginal revenue—in this case where the P_t line intersects the MC_p curve. This condition yields Q_p as the optimum quantity of the intermediate product, which is identical to the optimum quantity of the final product Q_m determined previously. Similarly, once the transfer price is established, the marketing division is faced with a marginal cost curve MC_t, which is the sum of the marginal marketing cost per unit, MC_m, and the given transfer price, P_t. The profits of the marketing division will be maximized at the point were its divisional cost is equal to its divisional marginal revenue—in this case, where the MC_t and MR_m curves intersect. This condition yields the same optimal price and output decision (that is, P_m and Q_m) as was obtained previously in maximizing the overall profits of the firm.

Perfectly Competitive External Market for the Intermediate Product

With an external market for the intermediate product, the outputs of the production and marketing divisions are no longer required to be equal. If the production division has the capacity to produce more of the intermediate product than is desired by the marketing division, it can sell the excess output externally. Similarly, if the marketing division desires more of the intermediate product than can be supplied internally by the production division, it can buy additional units externally. Assume that the first case exists—namely, the production division has excess capacity and sells the intermediate product both internally to the marketing division and externally in the intermediate product market. Furthermore, assume that the external market for the intermediate product is perfectly competitive.

The derivation of the optimal price-output decisions for the firm is shown in Figure 16.7. With a perfectly competitive market for the intermediate product, the production division is faced with a horizontal external demand curve D_p for its output at the existing market price P_t. Setting divisional marginal revenue MR_p equal to the divisional marginal cost MC_p yields a profit-maximizing output of Q_p units of the intermediate product. The marketing division, which must purchase the intermediate product either internally or externally at a price of P_t, will have a marginal cost curve MC_t, which is the sum of the marginal marketing cost per unit, MC_m, and the given transfer price P_t. Again, equating divisional marginal revenue MR_m to divisional marginal cost MC_t shows that profits will be maximized when Q_m units of the final product are sold externally at a price of P_m.

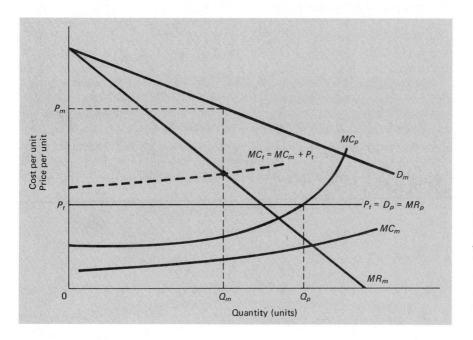

Figure 16.7
Determination of the Transfer Price When a Perfectly Competitive Market Exists for the Intermediate Product

per unit. The solution indicates that the production division should produce Q_p units of the intermediate product and sell Q_m units of its output to the marketing division and sell the difference, $Q_p - Q_m$, externally, in the intermediate product market.

A clear-cut transfer price emerges from this analysis. The competitive market price P_t becomes the transfer price for intracompany sales of the intermediate product. The production division can sell as much output as it wishes externally at this price and therefore would have no incentive to sell internally to the marketing division at a price less than P_t. Likewise, the marketing division can purchase as much of the intermediate product as it wishes externally at this price and therefore would be unwilling to make purchases from the production division at a price more than P_t.

Consider the following numerical example. Suppose that the production division (p) of Portland Electronics Company manufactures a component that it can sell either internally to the marketing division (m), which promotes and distributes the product through its own domestic retail outlets, or externally in a perfectly competitive wholesale market to foreign distributors. The product division can sell the component externally to these distributors at $50 per unit. The marketing division's demand function for the component is

$$P_m = 100 - .001Q_m \qquad [16.16]$$

where P_m is the selling price (in dollars per unit) and Q_m is the quantity sold (in units). The marketing division's total cost function (in dollars) is (excluding the cost of the component)

$$C_m = 300,000 + 10Q_m \qquad [16.17]$$

The production division's total cost function (in dollars) is

$$C_p = 500,000 + 15Q_p + .0005Q_p^2 \qquad [16.18]$$

where Q_p is the quantity produced (in units) and sold either internally or externally.

The task is to determine the profit-maximizing outputs for the production and marketing divisions and the optimal transfer price for intracompany sales. The production division's optimal output occurs at the point where divisional marginal revenue equals divisional marginal cost. Since the production division can sell as much output as it wishes (externally) at the competitive market price of $50, its marginal revenue (MR_p) is equal to $50 per unit. Its marginal cost (MC_p) is equal to the first derivative of C_p (Equation 16.18) with respect to Q_p, or

$$MC_p = \frac{dC_p}{dQ_p} = 15 + .0010Q_p$$

Setting $MC_p = MR_p$ yields the optimal output for the production division:

$$15 + .0010Q_p = 50$$

$$Q_p^* = 35,000 \text{ units}$$

The marketing division's optimal output occurs where divisional marginal revenue equals divisional marginal cost. Marginal cost for the marketing division (MC_t) is equal to the sum of its own marginal marketing costs (MC_m) plus the cost per unit of the components purchased from the production division (P_t) or

$$MC_t = MC_m + P_t \qquad [16.19]$$

Since the external wholesale market for the component is perfectly competitive, the production division would not be willing to sell components to the marketing division for less than the market price of $50 per unit. Likewise, since the market is perfectly competitive, the marketing division would be unable to purchase components from outside suppliers for less than the going price of $50. Therefore, the optimal transfer price (P_t^*) is the competitive market price of $50 per unit. Marginal marketing costs (MC_m) are equal to the first derivative of C_m (Equation 16.17) with respect to Q_m:

$$MC_m = \frac{dC_m}{dQ_m} = 10$$

Hence by Equation 16.19, MC_t is equal to $60 (i.e., 10 + 50). The marketing division's total revenue (TR_m) function is equal to

$$
\begin{aligned}
TR_m &= P_m Q_m \\
&= (100 - .001Q_m)Q_m \\
&= 100Q_m - .001Q_m^2 \qquad [16.20]
\end{aligned}
$$

Taking the first derivative of TR_m (Equation 16.20) with respect to Q_m gives the marginal revenue function for the marketing division:

$$MR_m = \frac{d(TR_m)}{dQ_m} = 100 - .002Q_m$$

Setting $MR_m = MC_t$ yields the optimal output for the marketing division:

$$100 - .002Q_m = 60$$

$$Q_m^* = 20,000 \text{ units}$$

Thus to maximize profits, Portland's production division should produce 35,000 units of the component and sell 20,000 units internally to the marketing division and the remaining 15,000 units (35,000 − 20,000) externally to other distributors. The marketing division should distribute 20,000 units of the component through its retail outlets. The optimal transfer price for the intracompany sales is the competitive market price of $50 per unit.

In summarizing these cases, one should use the market-determined price on intracompany sales when the external market for the intermediate product is perfectly competitive. In other cases the appropriate profit-maximizing transfer price is dependent on the marginal costs and revenues of the respective divisions. When no external market exists for the intermediate product, the transfer price should be set equal to marginal production cost at the overall optimal level of output.

Limit Pricing

Recall from the discussion of monopoly in Chapter 14 that the monopolist firm's *short-run* profits are maximized by setting marginal revenue equal to marginal cost. As shown in Figure 16.8, this yields an optimal output of Q_1 and an optimal price of P_1. Such a solution, however, may not necessarily maximize the *long-run* profits (or shareholder wealth) of the firm. By keeping prices high and earning monopoly profits, the monopolist firm encourages potential competitors to commit resources in an effort to obtain a share of these profits. For example, if a monopoly is based on a patented product (or production process), potential competitors may invest funds in research and development in order to design an alternative to the monopolist firm's product (or production process). Instead of charging the short-run profit-maximizing price, the monopolist firm may decide to engage in *limit pricing*, where it charges a lower price, such as P_L in Figure 16.8, in order to discourage entry into the industry by potential rivals.[17] With a limit-pricing strategy, the firm foregoes some of its short-run monopoly profits in order to maintain its monopoly position in the long run. The limit price, such as P_L in Figure 16.8, which was determined at the minimum point on the average total cost curve, is illustrative only. The appropriate limit price is a function of many different factors.[18]

The effect of the two different pricing strategies on the monopolist firm's profit stream is illustrated in Figure 16.9. By charging the (higher) short-run

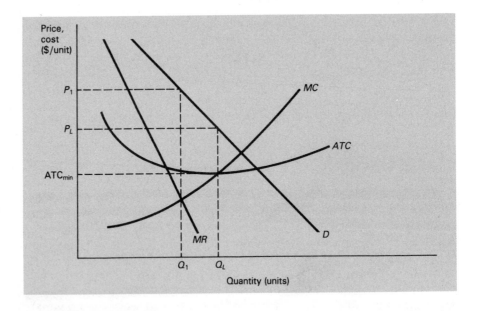

Figure 16.8
Limit-Pricing Strategy

---

[17] The limit-pricing model illustrates the importance of *potential* competition as a control device on existing firms. This concept is examined further in the discussion of contestable markets in Chapter 19.

[18] See F. H. Scherer, *Industrial Market Structure and Economic Performance*, 2d ed. (Chicago: Rand McNally, 1980), Chapter 8, for an expanded discussion of the limit pricing concept.

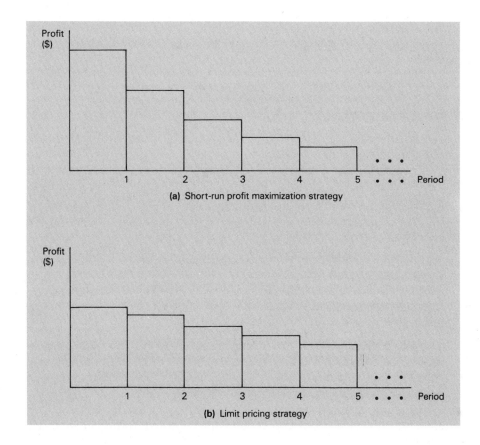

(a) Short-run profit maximization strategy

(b) Limit pricing strategy

Figure 16.9
Effect of Pricing Strategies on Profit Streams

profit-maximizing price, the firm's profits are likely to decline over time at a faster rate (Panel a) than by charging a limit price (Panel b). The firm should engage in limit pricing if the present value of the profit stream from the limit-pricing strategy exceeds the present value of the profit stream associated with the short-run profit-maximization rule of equating marginal revenue and marginal cost. Such a decision is a function of the discount rate used in calculating the present values. Choosing a high discount rate will place relatively higher weight on near-term profits and relatively lower weight on profits that occur further into the future. A high discount rate is justified when the firm's long-term pricing policy, and hence profits, are subject to a high degree of risk or uncertainty.[19]

Finally, it should be noted that limit pricing can be practiced by firms in oligopolistic industries as well as by firms in monopolistic industries. In an oligopolistic industry, limit pricing can be used by a dominant firm to discourage expansion by smaller firms in the industry as well as to deter entry

---

[19] Recall from Chapter 3 that when using risk-adjusted discount rates, the relevant rate employed in calculating the present value of future cash (or income) flows is a function of the risk associated with these flows—namely, the greater the risk, the higher the discount rate.

by firms outside the industry. In an oligopoly, limit pricing requires that the competing firms engage in some form of formal or informal collusion in setting prices.

Pricing in Practice

To this point, with the exception of the discussion of Baumol's sales-maximization model, the pricing chapters have been concerned with normative models of firm behavior. The basic underlying assumption of these traditional models is that the firm seeks to maximize its profits. Recall that Chapter 1 discussed some of the weaknesses and criticisms of decision making based on the profit-maximization objective. Two of the most substantive objections are the following:

1. The firm is assumed to have the information necessary to make the marginal calculations and decisions that profit maximization demands. In a world where information is not free and uncertainty is more the rule than the exception, one should not be surprised to see some divergence between normative theory and actual business practice.

2. The model has an inherent short-run bias in that no time dimension is placed on the profits being maximized. In spite of this, many problems may be analyzed using the calculus of profit maximization when the long-run profitability impacts are either insignificant or nonexistent. However, many decisions *do* have longer-run implications, accounting for some of the observed divergence between business practice and normative short-run theory.

Also, one would expect to see some additional divergence between economic theory and business practice to the extent that profit maximization is not the major or only objective pursued by management. Herbert Simon, for instance, has argued that in the face of uncertainty, management may abandon its goal of profit maximization and seek only a satisfactory or satisficing level of performance that assures survival and acceptable profits.[20] Others—such as Cyert and March,[21] Reid,[22] and Williamson[23]—believe profitability is only one of several possible goals that management can pursue. Other goals include market-share goals, production goals, inventory goals, sales goals, utility of the managers, professional recognition and status, and firm survival.

In the face of some practical objections to the profit-maximization model and a broad diversity of alternative descriptive models, the remainder of this

---

[20] Herbert A. Simon, "Theories of Decision Making in Economics," *American Economic Review* 49 (June 1959), pp. 253–283.

[21] Richard M. Cyert and James G. March, *A Behavioral Theory of the Firm* (Englewood Cliffs, N.J.: Prentice-Hall, 1963).

[22] Samuel R. Reid, *Mergers, Managers and the Economy* (New York: McGraw-Hill, 1968).

[23] Oliver E. Williamson, "Managerial Discretion and Business Behavior," *American Economic Review* (December 1963), pp. 1032–1057.

section examines what some of the empirical studies of pricing behavior have concluded.

A survey by Hall and Hitch emphasized the use of *cost-plus* or *full-cost pricing*.[24] *Full-cost pricing* requires that estimates be made of the variable costs of production and marketing. A charge to cover overhead, plus a percentage markup or margin, is then added to variable costs to arrive at a final price. Overhead or indirect costs may be allocated among a firm's several products in a number of ways. One typical method is to estimate total indirect costs assuming the firm operates at a standard level of output. This is frequently set in the range of 70 to 80 percent of capacity. These standard costs are then allocated among the various products on some basis such as a percentage of average variable cost. For example, if the average variable cost of producing and selling a small electronic calculator is $50, the manufacturer might add a charge of 120 percent of variable costs to cover indirect or overhead charges. To this full average cost of $110, a markup of, say, 20 percent is added, yielding a final price of $132. This could be modified slightly to reflect traditional industry pricing practice or the firm's own standard pricing rules.[25]

It is immediately apparent that full-cost pricing violates the marginal pricing rules of traditional theory since fixed costs enter explicitly into the price determination formula. It has been argued, however, that when average (unit) costs remain nearly constant over the relevant output range and when the price elasticity remains fairly constant over time, the use of cost-plus pricing may lead to nearly optimal decisions. These conditions are frequently encountered in the retail trades.[26] Furthermore, Earley has noted that the size of the markup employed for different products by "excellently managed firms" is frequently a function of demand elasticities and the degree of competition.[27] So it *may* be that in its responsiveness to varying demand conditions, full-cost pricing approaches the marginal solution.

Markup or full-cost pricing rules have also been criticized for being based on historical accounting costs rather than costs actually incurred at the time prices are set and the product is sold. To the extent that actual costs vary from the historical standard used in determining prices, full-cost pricing necessarily results in a suboptimal set of prices. In addition, accounting costs do not consider the opportunity cost of the resources being used.

Another study by Kaplan, Dirlam, and Lanzillotti of twenty large U.S. industrial firms concluded that the markup percentage is frequently set to

---

[24] R. L. Hall and C. J. Hitch, "Price Theory and Business Behavior," *Oxford Economic Papers*, no. 2 (May 1939), pp. 12–45.

[25] A full discussion of some typical product-pricing practices, such as charging $9.95 rather than $10, may be found in Joel Dean, *Managerial Economics* (Englewood Cliffs, N.J.: Prentice-Hall 1951), chap. 8.

[26] Philip Kotler, *Marketing Decision Making: A Model-Building Approach* (New York: Holt, Rinehart Winston, 1971), pp. 702–703.

[27] J. S. Earley, "Recent Developments in Cost Accounting," *Journal of Political Economy* (June 1955), pp. 227–242; and "Marginal Policies of 'Excellently Managed' Companies," *American Economic Review* (March 1956), pp. 44–70.

achieve a *target return on investment*.[28] Under target return-on-investment pricing, or simply target pricing, the firm selects an acceptable profit rate on investment. This is usually defined as earnings before interest and depreciation divided by total gross operating assets. This return is then prorated over the number of units expected to be produced over the planning horizon. Target pricing rules may be expressed in equation form as

$$P = VC_l + VC_m + VC_{mk} + \frac{F}{Q} + \frac{\pi K}{Q}$$ [16.21]

where

P = price per unit

VC_l = unit labor cost

VC_m = unit material cost

VC_{mk} = unit marketing cost

F = total fixed or indirect costs

Q = number of units to be produced during the planning horizon

K = total gross operating assets

π = desired profit rate on investment

At least three advantages have been enumerated for the use of target return-on-investment pricing. It has been argued that it leads to price stability because it is based on cost standards that vary much less than actual costs.[29] Price stability is advantageous for two reasons. First, price changes are costly. New price lists must be prepared and sales persons informed. Second, in an oligopolistic market structure, explicit price changes are likely to evoke unknown competitive responses. A second advantage of target return pricing is that it is well suited to use in an industry where price leadership is prevalent.[30] As variations between actual and standard costs increase, the price leader feels increasing pressure to either raise or lower prices. Finally, it has been argued that target pricing enables the firm to plan and manage its profits.[31]

Full-cost and target pricing are by no means the only pricing strategies followed by business firms. Some firms, such as A & P, place major emphasis on maintenance of market share. This was clearly evident in the 1972–1973 price

---

[28] A. D. H. Kaplan, J. B. Dirlam, and R. F. Lanzillotti, *Pricing in Big Business* (Washington, D.C.: Brookings Institution, 1958).

[29] Otto Eckstein, "A Theory of the Wage-Price Process in Modern Industry," *Review of Economic Studies* (October 1964), p. 269.

[30] Otto Eckstein and G. Fromm, "The Price Equation," *American Economic Review* (December 1968), p. 1165.

[31] R. F. Lanzillotti, "Pricing Objectives in Large Companies," *American Economic Review* (December 1958), p. 938.

war it engaged in with other grocers to regain a slipping market share. A & P suffered huge losses during this period, which it hoped to regain over the long run once market share was increased.

Other pricing practices are considered in the sections that follow.

Full-Cost Pricing versus Marginal Analysis

This section attempts to resolve the conflict between those who advocate the use of *marginal pricing rules* and those who argue for the use of such "short-cut" rules as *full-cost pricing* and *target pricing*. Advocates of full-cost and target pricing argue that it is important to allocate all fixed costs among the various products produced by the firm and that each product should be forced to bear its fair share of the fixed-cost burden. In contrast, marginalists say that any allocation of fixed costs between products is impossible to carry out adequately and that requiring each product to cover a fair share of fixed costs may be clearly suboptimal. Each product should instead be viewed in light of the proportion that it contributes to fixed costs and profits of the firm as a whole. This provides a sounder basis for considering whether the manufacture and sale of a product should be expanded, maintained, or discontinued in favor of some alternative that may make a greater contribution. If, for example, a typewriter manufacturer's Aztec model accounts for 40 percent of sales but only 10 percent of the contribution to fixed costs and profits, the firm should seek ways to increase its contribution or replace it with a more profitable alternative. In this example, the full-cost pricing criteria might indicate that the product should be quickly discontinued because it is not covering a fair share of fixed costs and is not providing an adequate profit margin. In the short run, however, any contribution to fixed costs is more consistent with profit maximization (although ways should be sought to increase this contribution) than dropping the product and merely shifting the burden of covering fixed costs to the remaining products of the firm. A longer-run analysis *might* indicate that dropping the Aztec model will result in actual fixed-cost savings that are greater than the maximum fixed-cost contribution that Aztec may be expected to generate. Also, in the long run the firm has the flexibility of altering its product line by substituting more profitable models for some of the firm's poorer performers.

One criticism that advocates of full-cost pricing aim at the marginalists is that if fixed costs are not allocated in some manner among products, some products are likely to be overlooked and prices for them set too low. This can happen only if the firm lacks an effective control system in which one person continually monitors the overall contribution of a firm's complete product line. This person can then ensure that prices are set sufficiently high in relation to both the variable cost of each product and the total fixed costs of the firm. In addition, marginal pricing gives the firm far more flexibility in setting appropriate prices, evaluating offers to buy below this price, and comparing alternative uses for the firm's productive capacity.

One may conclude that there is nothing full-cost pricing can do that marginal pricing, properly controlled, cannot also accomplish.[32] In addition, however, marginalism gives the firm far more flexibility and insight into evaluating alternative opportunities for the profitable use of the firm's productive resources. Costs are divided on a basis relevant to such decisions and are not arbitrarily assigned to one product or another. This permits the opportunity costs of various actions to be considered at all production output levels, not just at the standard level as does full-cost analysis.

Incrementalism: Marginalism in Practice

In the real world, demand and cost functions are not known with certainty but must be approximated. In addition, accumulating better information on the exact nature of these functions and their variations can be quite costly. These costs must be weighed against the benefits to be realized from more complete knowledge. In such a case, it is impossible (or impractical) to estimate the marginal impact of the last dollar spent on advertising or to calculate precisely the marginal cost of each unit which is produced, and then to attempt to produce up to a point where estimated marginal cost equals estimated marginal revenue.

Faced with these limitations, many business decisions are based on *incremental analysis*. In its broadest sense, incrementalism requires that an estimate be made of *changes in total cost, changes in total revenues, or changes in both total costs and revenues* that are likely to result from a decision to change prices, drop or add a product, accept or reject a new order, or undertake an investment. The concept of incremental reasoning is simple, but its application requires care. For instance, the decision to drop an item from the firm's product line requires that the loss in revenue from this action should be evaluated in light of the total *actual* cost savings that may occur. The following questions must be addressed: (1) How much, if any, will sales of other items in the firm's product line increase because this item is dropped? (2) To what extent will some overhead or fixed costs be reduced? (3) Are there more profitable alternative uses for the firm's productive capacity? (4) What is the long-run sales and profit outlook for this item versus the alternatives being considered? Successful use of incremental analysis requires that all these factors be considered in relation to their impact on total revenues received and total costs incurred by the company. Only then can decisions be made that will lead toward greater profits.

One frequently cited example of the business use of incremental reasoning is the case of Continental Airlines.[33] In 1962 Continental was filling only about 50

---

[32] In a market where marginal cost is approximately equal to averge cost and demand is relatively stable, the use of cost-plus pricing may not violate marginal pricing principles if the price is equal to $\dfrac{1}{1+\dfrac{1}{E_D}}$ times the average cost, where E_D is the price elasticity of demand.

[33] This example is adapted from "Airline Takes the Marginal Route", *Business Week*, 20 April, 1963.

percent of its available seats, or about 15 percent less than the industry average. Eliminating only 5 percent of its flights would have resulted in a substantial increase in this load factor, but would have reduced profits as well. The airline industry is characterized by extremely high fixed costs, which are incurred whether a plane flies or not. There are depreciation costs, interest charges, and the cost of maintaining ground crews, not to mention headquarters staff overhead. Consequently, Continental has found it profitable to operate a flight as long as it covers variable or out-of-pocket costs plus a small contribution to fixed costs.

The analysis of whether to operate a flight proceeds as follows: First, management examines the majority of scheduled flights to be certain that depreciation, overhead, and insurance expenses are met for this basic schedule. Then the possibility of scheduling additional flights is considered, based on their impact on corporate net profit. If revenues on a flight exceed *actual operating costs*, the flight should be added. Actual operating costs are determined by soliciting inputs from every operating department that specify exactly what extra expenses are incurred as a result of the additional flight's operation. For instance, if a ground crew that can service the additional flight is already on duty, none of the costs of this service is included in actual operating costs.

Another example of such analysis is the case of a late-night Continental flight from Colorado Springs to Denver and a very early morning return flight. Even though the flight often goes without a passenger and very little freight, the cost of operating it is less than an overnight hanger rental in Colorado Springs. Hence the flight is maintained.

There are numerous other cases of the type of incremental analysis reasoning used by Continental and other firms. Two important points, however, must be stressed. First, it is essential that someone in management have coordinating authority to ensure that overall objectives are met before facing decisions based solely on incremental analysis. In the case of Continental, the vice president of economic planning assumed this task. Second, every reasonable attempt must be made to identify *actual* incremental costs or revenues that are associated with a particular decision. Once this has been accomplished, incremental analysis becomes a useful and powerful tool in considering a wide range of decision problems facing the firm.

Other Pricing Strategies

In addition to marginal, incremental, and full-cost pricing strategies, several other pricing methods are used under certain circumstances. *Skimming* is often used in the pricing of new products. Also some goods are deliberately priced very high to increase their prestige demand (*prestige pricing*). Finally, *price lining* is used in the pricing of certain categories of goods. These techniques are considered next.

Skimming

When a new product is introduced by a firm, pricing for that product is a difficult and critical decision, especially if the product is a durable good—one that has a

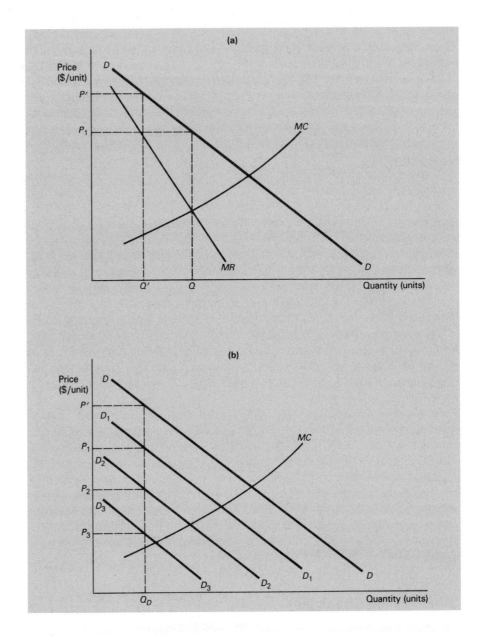

Figure 16.10
**Example of
Demand
Skimming**

relatively long useful life. The difficulty of pricing the new product arises from the fact that demand may not be known with confidence. If the price is initially set too low, some potential customers will be able to buy the product below what they are willing to pay. These lost profits will be gone forever. This problem is accentuated when the firm initially has limited production capacity for the new product. In contrast, if the firm sets a high price and maintains this price over a long time period, new competition will be encouraged.

Under these circumstances, many firms have adopted a strategy of skimming, or pricing down along the demand curve. The initial price is set at a high level, even though the firm fully intends to make later price reductions. When the product is first introduced, there will be a group of customers who are willing to pay the high price established by the firm. Once this source of demand has been exhausted, the price is reduced and a new group of customers is attracted. This strategy is readily apparent in the microcomputer hardware and software industries. For example, since its initial introduction, several price reductions have been made on the IBM-PC and the Apple Macintosh computers.

This pricing strategy can be illustrated using Figure 16.10. Panel (a) shows the estimated demand curve DD and the marginal revenue curve MR for the IBM-PC computer as well as the marginal cost curve MC. As a monopolist for the IBM-PC, IBM would set price P and produce output Q.

Suppose, however, that IBM chooses to follow the skimming strategy for its personal computer. It could initially set a price higher than P, such as P'. At that price, only Q' units would be demanded and sold. By setting the initial price at P', all consumers who are willing to pay that price or more will buy the product. Once this has occurred, IBM can then lower the price to capture the demand from the next segment of customers.

Panel (b) shows new demand curves, such as D_1D_1. The new demand curve is less than the initial demand curve DD—it is shifted to the left—by an amount equal to the Q' units that have already been purchased at price P'. A new lower price is now established, such as P_1, and Q' units are sold at this price. The new price P_1 may be set in such a manner that it approximately matches the firm's production capacity. When demand has been exhausted at this price, the price is lowered again, to a level such as P_2. The new demand curve D_2D_2 is lower and to the left of D_1D_1 by an amount equal to the Q' units that were sold at the previous price. (Although panel (b) shows quantity demanded to be the same amount for each price level, this is not necessary. The figure is merely drawn that way for ease of presentation).

This strategy can be continued many times to capitalize on the unique product characteristics and availability until competition forces the firm to a "permanently" more competitive price level. The rate at which reductions are made may depend on production capacity, the speed of competitive product introductions, and the trade-off between receiving profits now and deferring them into the future by use of the skimming strategy. In the case of IBM, price reductions were strongly resisted until true IBM "clone" microcomputers became available from firms such as Compaq and Zenith.

Prestige Pricing

Some products are priced to increase their perceived value to potential consumers. By establishing a high price, potential buyers are limited and the product often is perceived to be of higher quality than similar, lower-priced products. For example, in the automotive market, the sporty European sedans, such as the Mercedes, Audi, and BMW are priced in the $20,000 to $50,000 range. These cars have been highly successful in attracting a loyal, prestige-oriented clientele. At the same time, a car like the Toyota Camry has received wide acclaim from impartial panels such as the Consumers Union when it was compared with these more expensive vehicles. Its price is considerably less than

(*Continued on page 559*)

Economic Analysis and Managerial Efficiency

AIRLINE FARE WARS*

Judging by a recent session, the daily pricing meeting at Delta Air Lines would make a good setting for an aspirin commercial.

Seated around an L-shaped desk, a group of Delta tariff experts hash over possible countermoves to the fare changes reported by the competition overnight. "What are the yields on those new Braniff fares again?" says Robert Coggin, assistant vice president for marketing development, wanting to know how much the fares equal per mile.

"It's bad," replies an associate. "They start at 4.7 cents."

Slumping his burly frame, Mr. Coggin looks pained. "Damn. I hate to match that," he moans. "It's like a rerun of a horror movie."

Nevertheless, it is a decision the 47-year-old Mr. Coggin has to face often. He is responsible for all of Delta's pricing, and the airline leans heavily on his judgment in charting a course through the industry's often turbulent fare wars. "I'm the guy who tries to make sense out of chaos," Mr. Coggins says, with only a thin smile.

The task gets harder all the time. On a typical day, the tariff department compares at least 5,000 industry pricing changes against Delta's more than 70,000 fares. And although most of the adjustments are minor, cumulatively they have a significantly effect on the airline's profitability. Currently, for instance, Delta's system breaks even when it yields an average of 15 cents a mile from every passenger. In the past 12 months, the company has had banner operating results with an average yield of just 15.5 cents.

"Pricing has become the key battle-ground in this industry," says Joseph Cooper, Delta's senior vice president for marketing. The fight is intensifying, with 7% more seats aloft than a year ago and with a seasonal downturn coming after

Labor Day. And this week, People Express Airlines launched a long-expected, low-priced assault on the lucrative Chicago-to-New York run.

But the battle of the airlines increasingly is being won and lost in tiny, day-to-day skirmishes, not just in the widely publicized fare discounts. For every headline-making donnybrook, thousands of unpublicized adjustments occur on shorter runs, on connecting flights and even in the number of seats available for discount on an individual airplane. Analyzing the constantly changing fares of more than 50 competitors has become a high-technology game so complex that only No. 4-ranked Delta and a handful of other major airlines can begin to do a thorough job of it. And that, of course, only widens their advantage over weaker carriers.

"It's like a nonstop poker game with the same few players," Mr. Coggin says. "The more you get to know each other, the more complicated it gets."

Airline pricing is menacingly complex because supply and demand can change so drastically from day to day, from city to city and from flight to flight. A traveler jetting between Atlanta and Charlotte, N.C., for instance, currently pays the equivalent of 48.1 cents a mile, while another flying virtually the same distance between Dallas and Tulsa, Okla., can make the trip for just 11.7 cents a mile. A coast-to-coast flight can be cheaper than one crossing a single state line. Fares typically are higher on Tuesday, lower on Wednesday, and downright cheap on Saturday, reflecting some of the patterns of business travel.

Because air carriers' arcane route structures often are entwined in unseen ways, a change in the fare of one flight can have unintended consequences for another. Piedmont recently cut the fare between Chicago and Columbia, S.C., so deeply that when Delta matched, on a connecting flight through Atlanta, it discovered that a passenger flying only as far as Atlanta could do so at less cost by buying a ticket all the way through to Columbia.

There's a delicate balance in air fares," says Michael Exstein, an airline analyst at the Ford Foundation. "When one domino falls, they all can

---

* Source: John Koten, "In Airlines' Rate War, Small Daily Skirmishes often Decide Winners," *Wall Street Journal*, 24 August, 1984, p. 1.

go." It is a phenomenon of which Delta is acutely aware. "If vacationers start flocking into United flights to Hawaii, other carriers might try to lure them back by lowering fares to Miami," says Richard Lowry, a tariff analyst.

The person that Delta selected to keep track of all the variables is Mr. Coggin, a hard-bitten, shirt-sleeve antacid addict. "This is easily the toughest job I've had," says the 23-year veteran, who joined Delta as a baggage handler. "Some days you just think all hell has broken loose."

But adroit fare management has helped make Delta one of the most formidable competitors in the sky. Without putting more planes in the air, entering new markets or launching expensive promotions, Delta has increased its share of the dollars paid to all airlines to 16.3% in May from 14.9% a year earlier. The difference, worth some $300 million in annual revenue, was a major factor in Delta's profit of $175.6 million, or $4.42 a share, in the fiscal year ended June 30, compared with an $86.7 million net loss in fiscal 1983.

Until recently, Delta had nowhere to go but up. Although it entered deregulation with a reputation as the industry's best-managed airline, Delta was slow to catch on to the sensitivity of pricing. "We didn't know what we were doing," says one of the airline's tariff experts. An internal study in 1982 showed that few travelers called Delta's reservation officers first because the airline wasn't viewed as an aggresive pricer. But then Delta went too far the other way.

On the advice of its advertising agency, Batten Barton Durstline & Osborn Inc., Delta twice kicked off programs, in 1982 and 1983, offering to match any lower fare on any of its more than 5,000 routes. Passengers swarmed onto its planes, but the number paying full fares dropped to a disastrous 8% of all seats sold. Combined with the effects of the recession, selling all those cheap seats resulted in the huge fiscal 1983 loss, Delta's first annual deficit in 47 years.

Embarassed by the failure of their broad strategies, Delta officials began concentrating on the small, day-to-day pricing battles. That required not only more computer power but also many more people: Mr. Coggin's tariff department, only since airline deregulation, has grown to 147 members from 27.

The day begins at 7 a.m. EDT, when a Delta computer begins disgorging a list, sometimes several hundred pages long, showing the new fares filed the prior day with Air Tariff Publishing Co., whose computers redistribute the information. Searching for tip-offs to major changes, six tariff analysts flip quickly through the pages looking for price adjustments on monopoly routes. Knowing, for instance, that United is the only carrier between Canton, Ohio, and Little Rock, Ark., the analysts figure that if the Chicago-based airline adjusts that fare between those cities, it must be making a system-wide change.

The department also compiles a daily list, circulated to Delta's top executives, showing the number of fare adjustments by the industry. The airline business's equivalent of stock-market volume reports, the summaries are analyzed for trends to gauge whether competitors are getting together by making an increasing number of adjustments. On a recent Monday, the list showed United Airlines with 5,282, Republic Airlines with 2,946 and Eastern Airlines with 3,709. That day, Delta had an unusually low 151.

Delta's intelligence-gathering efforts go well beyond the computers. During the day, the tariff department gets a steady stream of telexes from tipsters in company field offices, alerting it to price changes announced in local newspapers or picked up by reservation agents when customers tell them about a good deal at another carrier.

The so-called match messages are important because such carriers as American and Braniff may try to get a jump with a discount fare by waiting a few days before disclosing it through the Air Tariff Publishing system. Mr. Coggin and other department members also place regular calls to other airlines' reservation offices, posing as prospective customers.

"You can find out a lot of good things that way," he says, smiling devilishly. To get an idea of how many discounted seats a competitor may be offering on a particular flight, for instance, Delta and other airlines may phone in reservations until they are told that only full-price seats remain. They then cancel the reservations.

Once Delta learns of a competitor's pricing move, it can put a matching fare into its reservation system within two hours. "If you don't move fast," Mr. Coggin says, "your phones will stop ringing."

Although Delta usually matches a lower price, it
(Continued on next page)

(Continued from previous page)

rarely initiates a fare cut. It also hesistates to loosen the strings attached to the sale of a discount ticket, such as a requirement that the passenger remain at a destination through Saturday. Most of the restrictions help control the use of discount fares by business travelers, who usually aren't all that sensitive about how they spend their companies' money.

Delta also tries to match cut-rate prices on flights that are less likely to spread fare wars. For instance, given a choice of matching a discount fare with a flight that connects through Atlanta or one that connects through Cincinnati, Mr. Coggin will choose the latter because it is a much smaller Delta hub.

Delta also developed a successful tactic for use against such "no-frills" carriers as People Express. When the cut-rate carrier announced a $99 one-way fare between New York and Miami last winter, Delta responded with a $119 fare and moved more efficient aircraft onto the route; a survey had shown that travelers were willing to pay $20 more for such conveniences as baggage handling and food service. And the higher price enabled Delta to earn a profit with one half its seats filled, compared with the 72% load needed by People Express.

The inner sanctum of Delta's tariff department is a room of 50 former reservation agents seated at computer terminals monitoring minute-by-minute booking patterns on more than 475,000 flights a year. The purpose of the system is to help the staff divide the number of discount and full-fare seats on particular flights in a way that will maximize revenue.

The year-old system continuously compares reservation levels of all flights departing within 45 days against historical patterns. If more passengers than usual are booking space at a given moment, the computer console instructs its attendant to cut back the number of discount seats available. Then, if bookings on the same flight fall below expectations—whether five minutes or five weeks

later—the computer recommends adding discount seats. (That means that a potential passenger told in one phone call that no discount seats are available may find such fares suddenly available later.)

"We don't have to know if a balloon race in Albuquerque or a rodeo in Lubbock is causing an increase in demand for a flight," says Robert Cross, Delta's manager of system marketing. A former attorney, he says that part of the seat-analysis strategy came from theories expressed by F. A. Hayek, a Nobel laureate, in a 1945 essay about how the price system can teach companies more about consumers. "It's pure supply and demand," Mr. Cross says.

The system also aids Delta's cloak-and-dagger tactics. When a tour group requests a discount, the computer helps decide whether to refer the customers to another airline. That helps to fill up a competitor's plane with low-fare passengers and, potentially, drive other passengers into the full-fare seats waiting at Delta. Similarly, the computer forecasts how many seats Delta should hold for last-minute, full-fare business travelers, a big advantage in lucrative markets such as Washington, D.C., and New York, where often more than half the passengers book their reservations in the 72 hours before departure.

The day may come, Mr. Coggin says, when airlines will, in effect, "auction" off seats, charging prices that continually change with supply and demand, the same way that stock prices move. "For a long time I prayed the industry would go back to the good old days of simple pricing," he says. "Now I realize it could get a heck of a lot worse."

Question

1. What market structure best characterizes the U.S. airline industry? Why do you feel there is a tendency for this industry to become increasingly concentrated?

the European alternatives, yet it has not attracted the loyal following of prestige-oriented consumers that the European sedans have.

The DeBeers diamond cartel, which controls at least 80 percent of the world's uncut diamond market, effectively sets prices for diamonds by greatly restricting their availability. For example, in the early 1980s, it appeared that the South African cartel might collapse. A sharp decline in demand, coupled with the withdrawal of Zaire (the world's largest producer of diamonds) from the cartel and huge new discoveries in Australia threatened to undercut the cartel. But by holding nearly $1 billion in diamonds off the market, DeBeers was able to avoid a price decline and bring Zaire and Australia back into the cartel. This pricing strategy has assured potential diamond buyers of the value of their investment and it has prevented diamonds from becoming too commonplace.

Prestige pricing is sometimes abused by selling firms. In many cases customers equate price with quality, particularly in those instances where objective product quality information is difficult or expensive to acquire. Two physically identical products may be packaged differently and priced differently to take advantage of the tendency of consumers to equate high price with high quality. The pages of *Consumers Reports* are full of examples suggesting that this relationship between high price and high quality does not exist.

Price Lining

In normal circumstances, profit-maximizing firms will attempt to set a price that maximizes the profits the firm generates from the sales of a particular product. The product and its particular quality characteristics are assumed to be known, but in some circumstances this process is reversed. For example, a price target may be established and the firm attempts to develop a product with a set of quality characteristics that will allow it to maximize profits at the target price; that is, given a price constraint, the firm attempts to develop a product with a set of quality characteristics that will lead to maximum profits in that product price line. This practice is called *price lining*. It is not inconsistent with the notion of profit maximization. Price lining simply reverses the typical profit-maximization decision process.

The automobile industry has a set of price lines that have been established over time among the major producers. For example, the Ford Motor Company sells its Ford-brand vehicles as the basic car with broad appeal. The Mercury brand is designed to appeal to a somewhat more affluent group of customers. The Lincoln brand is aimed at the wealthiest or most prestige-conscious group of consumers. Within the Ford brand are a number of sublines. The subcompact line, the Escort, competes with subcompacts of other U.S. and foreign producers. The compact line is represented by the Tempo; the sporty line is represented by Mustang; the mid-size line is represented by the Taurus; and the full-size line is represented by the Crown Victoria. In each of these lines, Ford competes with similar cars from General Motors. Each subline in the Ford model group is priced closely in line with the price of similar-sized General Motors vehicles. The objective of each auto producer is to create a distinctively high-quality vehicle in that price and model range. If price must be increased significantly, the product will not sell well, regardless of its quality.

Other examples of strong price lining exist in the pricing of snack foods for vending machines and canned soft drinks. Vending companies will be reluctant to sell a product that requires special machines for dispensing. As a consequence, candy makers often compete on product quality and product size, rather than on price.

Summary

- The multiproduct firm with a profit-maximizing goal will set prices such that marginal revenue received in each product market is the same and equal to the firm's marginal cost.

- *Joint products* are products that are technically interdependent in the production process; that is, a change in the production of one produces a change in the cost or availability of another. When the joint products are produced in *fixed proportions*, the optimal output of the product package (consisting of the individual products) and optimal prices of the individual products is found at the intersection of the total marginal revenue function and the marginal cost function of producing the product package. When joint products are produced in *variable proportions*, the optimal output occurs where the marginal cost of producing each product is equal to the marginal revenue of each product. This occurs at the point of tangency between the isocost and isorevenue curves for the products.

- *Price discrimination* is the act of selling the same good or service produced by a given firm at different prices to different customers. Two conditions are required for effective price discrimination:
  1. One must be able to segment the market and prevent the transfer of the product (or service) from one segment to another.
  2. There must be differences in the elasticity of demand at a given price between the market segments.
  In order to maximize profits using price discrimination, the firm must allocate output in such a way that marginal revenue is equal in the different market segments.

- A firm is often faced with the problem of pricing items that are produced and used internally in the firm. This is the emphasis of *transfer pricing* analysis. When the external market for the intermediate product is perfectly competitive, the firm should use the market-determined price on intracompany sales. In other cases an appropriate profit-maximizing transfer price is a function of the marginal costs and revenues of the respective divisions in the firm.

- With a *limit-pricing* strategy, the monopolist firm charges a lower price than the short-run profit-maximization price (determined by equating marginal revenue with marginal cost) in order to discourage entry into the industry by potential rivals. By employing a limit-pricing strategy, the firm foregoes some of its short-run monopoly profits to maintain its monopoly position in the long run. The monopolist firm should engage in limit pricing if the present value of the profit stream associated with this pricing strategy exceeds the present value of the profit stream associated with the short-run profit-maximization pricing strategy.

■ Many actual business pricing practices, such as *full-cost pricing* and *target return pricing*, can be consistent with the marginal pricing rules of economic theory. *Incrementalism* is a widely applicable method of economic analysis that may help management to achieve a more efficient and profitable level of operation.

■ When new products are introduced, firms may use the *skimming* strategy to price the product and increase total profits. *Prestige pricing* is often used in pricing various products and in segmenting markets. *Price lining* requires the firm to develop products with specific product quality characteristics that will maximize profits, given a price constraint.

Selected References

Cyert, Richard M., and James G. March. *A Behavioral Theory of the Firm.* Englewood Cliffs, N.J.: Prentice-Hall, 1963.

Earley, J. S. "Marginal Policies of 'Excellently Managed' Companies." *American Economic Review* (March 1956), pp. 44–70.

Hirshleifer, J. "On the Economics of Transfer Pricing." *Journal of Business* 29 (1956), pp. 172–184.

Hirshleifer, J. "Economics of the Divisionalized Firm." *Journal of Business* 30 (1957), pp. 96–108.

Kaplan, A. D. H., J. B. Dirlam, and R. F. Lanzillotti. *Pricing in Big Business.* Washington, D. C.: Brookings Institution, 1958.

Lanzilloti, R. F. "Pricing Objectives in Large Companies." *American Economic Review* (December 1958), p. 938.

Lazear, Edward P. "Retail Pricing and Clearance Sales." *American Economic Review* (March 1986), pp. 14–32.

Nayle, Thomas. "Economic Foundations for Pricing." *Journal of Business* (January 1984), pp. 23–53.

Ross, T. W. "The Costs of Regulating Price Differences." *Journal of Business* (January 1986), pp. 143–156.

Simon, Herbert A. "Theories of Decision Making in Economics." *American Economic Review* 49 (June 1959), pp. 253–283.

Discussion Questions

1. Define the following terms:
   a. Joint products
   b. Price discrimination
   c. Block rate-setting
   d. Transfer price
   e. Limit price
   f. Cost-plus pricing
   g. Full-cost pricing
   h. Target return pricing
   i. Incremental analysis
   j. Skimming
   k. Prestige pricing
   l. Price lining

2. Explain the difference between *joint products* and *alternative products*.

3. Joint products can be produced in either *fixed proportions or variable proportions*. Explain the difference between fixed and variable proportions and give examples of each type of joint products.

4. Name the two required conditions under which a firm would engage in effective price discrimination. Explain why *both* conditions are required.

5. Under what condition(s) would a firm producing joint products in fixed proportions withhold part of the output of one product from the market in order to maximize the profit from the sale of the two products?

6. Explain why and how present value analysis is used in evaluating a limit-pricing strategy.

7. If a firm follows a cost-plus pricing practice, how is it possible for such a firm to ever show a loss on its income statement?

8. What functions does the transfer price serve within the decentralized firm? To maximize the profits of the overall firm, what price should be charged for *intracompany* sales (that is, Division A to Division B) of intermediate products when the external market for the intermediate product is *perfectly competitive*?

9. Associated with the tremendous growth in the size of corporations has been a trend toward decentralized (that is, *divisionalized*) decision making and control within many of these organizations. Explain some of the conditions that cause the price-output decisions of one division to be dependent on the price-output decisions of another division.

10. Some people argue that a firm can lower its costs of doing business by purchasing its suppliers and thus eliminating the need for *double* profits. Do you agree with this conclusion?

11. Why does the phone company offer different pricing structures for business and personal phone lines? Compare this with the reasons why a bank has a different pricing structure for business and personal checking accounts.

12. A company produces both oil and natural gas from a well in the panhandle of West Texas. If these products are produced from the well in fixed proportions, what would one expect the impact of an increase in the price of oil to be on the rate of gas production?

13. Why would a grocery store want to have a lower markup on poinsettia plants than on potatoes?

14. Discuss the decision of a multiproduct firm to add an additional product when the firm has excess capacity. How does this decision change in the short run when it is operating at full capacity?

15. What conditions are necessary if a monopolist is to be successful in practicing price discrimination?

16. Why do publishers often offer discounts to professors but not to students?

17. What types of price discrimination are often used by electric utility firms? Does this amount to an abuse of their monopoly power?

18. Compare the appropriate transfer price when the external market for the intermediate product is perfectly competitive to the case where no external market exists for the intermediate product.

19. Compare the practice of *price skimming* with *first-degree price discrimination*.

20. Using the domestic automotive market as an example, give an illustration of *prestige pricing*.

21. How has *price lining* been used in the microcomputer industry?

22. a. Many university bookstores offer to professors price discounts that are generally not available to students. What conditions make this sort of price discrimination feasible and profitable for the bookstore?
b. Similarly, students are often given discounts to attend cultural and athletic events, whereas professors do not receive these discounts. What conditions make this sort of price discrimination possible and desirable?

23. In the face of stable (or declining) enrollments and increasing costs, many colleges and universities, both public and private, have found themselves in progressively tighter financial dilemmas. This has led to a basic reexamination of the pricing schemes used by institutions of higher learning. One proposal recently advocated by the Committee for Economic Development (CED) and others has been for the use of more nearly full-cost pricing of higher education, combined with the government provision of sufficient loan funds to students who would not otherwise have access to reasonable loan terms in private markets. Advocates of such proposals argue that the private rate of return to student investors is sufficiently high to stimulate socially optimal levels of demand for education, even with the higher tuition rates. Others have argued against the existence of significant external benefits to undergraduate education to warrant the current high levels of public support.

As with current university pricing schemes, proponents of full-cost pricing generally argue for a standard fee (albeit higher than at present) for all students. Standard-fee proposals ignore relative cost and demand differences among activities in the university.

a. Discuss several possible rationales for charging different prices for different courses of study.
b. What are the income-distribution effects of a pricing scheme that charges the same fee to all students?
c. If universities adopted a system of full-cost (or marginal cost) pricing for various courses, what would you expect the impact on the efficiency of resource allocations within the university to be?
d. Would you complain less about large lecture sections taught by graduate students if these were priced significantly lower than small seminars taught by outstanding scholars?
e. What problems could you see arising from a university that adopted such a pricing scheme?

Problems

1. Refer to the Williams Company joint products example (Equations 16.1–16.4) discussed in the chapter:
a. On a graph with quantity on the horizontal axis and price (and cost) on the vertical axis, plot the demand and marginal revenue functions for the two products and the marginal cost function for the product package.
b. From the graph in part (a), determine the optimal output and price for each of the two products. Compare the graphical solution with the algebraic solution in the chapter.

2. Referring again to the Williams Company joint products example (Equations 16.1–16.4) discussed in the chapter, assume that the marginal cost function (Equation 16.3) is replaced with the following one:

$$MC = 22 + .5Q$$

Determine the optimal output and selling prices for each of the two products.

3. East Publishing has best-selling textbooks in both the fields of managerial economics and corporate finance. Each book accounts for roughly 60 percent of the estimated yearly market in its field. Text A sells about twice as many copies as Text B each year.

East has recently completed a series of market pricing experiments in which it estimated that the price elasticity of demand, E_D, for both texts is about equal. In addition, East believes that the marginal cost of production for these two books is about constant over the current range of sales.

In spite of the fact that about twice as many copies of Text A than Text B are sold, the firm charges the same price for both books.

As economist for the firm, you have been asked to prepare an analysis of the firm's pricing policy. $\left[\textit{Hint:} \text{ Remember the relationship } MR = P\left(1 + \dfrac{1}{E_D}\right). \right]$

4. American Export-Import Shipping Company operates a general cargo carrier service between New York and several Western European ports. It hauls two major categories of freight: manufactured items and semimanufactured raw materials. The demand functions for these two classes of goods are

$$P_1 = 100 - 2Q_1$$
$$P_2 = 80 - Q_2$$

where Q_i = tons of freight moved. The total cost function for American is

$$TC = 20 + 4(Q_1 + Q_2)$$

a. Calculate the firm's total profit function.
b. What are the profit-maximizing levels of price and output for the two freight categories?
c. At these levels of output, calculate the marginal revenue in each market.
d. What are American's total profits if it is effectively able to charge different prices in the two markets?
e. If American is required by law to charge the same per ton rate to all users, calculate the new profit-maximizing level of price and output. What are the profits in this situation?
f. Explain the difference in profit levels between the discriminating and nondiscriminating cases. To do this one should calculate the point price elasticity of demand under the nondiscriminating price-output solution.

5. The price elasticity of demand for a textbook sold in the United States is estimated to be -2.0, whereas the price elasticity of demand for books sold overseas is -3.0. The U.S. market requires hardcover books with a marginal cost of $6; the overseas market is normally served with softcover texts, having a marginal cost of only $4.50. Calculate the profit-maximizing price in each market. $\left[\textit{Hint:} \text{ Remember that} \right.$

$$MR = P\left(1 + \frac{1}{E_D}\right) \Big]$$

6. Phillips Industries manufactures a certain product that can be sold directly to retail outlets or to the Superior Company for further processing and eventual sale by them

as a completely different product. The demand function for each of these markets is

$$\text{Retail Outlets: } P_1 = 60 - 2Q_1$$
$$\text{Superior Company: } P_2 = 40 - Q_2$$

where P_1 and P_2 are the prices charged and Q_1 and Q_2 are the quantities sold in the respective markets. Phillips' total cost function for the manufacture of this product is

$$TC = 10 + 8(Q_1 + Q_2)$$

a. Determine Phillips' total profit function.

b. What are the profit-maximizing price and output levels for the product in the two markets?

c. At these levels of output, calculate the marginal revenue in each market.

d. What are Phillips' total profits if the firm is effectively able to charge different prices in the two markets?

e. Calculate the profit-maximizing level of price and output if Phillips is required to charge the same price per unit in each market? What are Phillips' profits under this condition?

7. Referring back to the Portland Electronics Company transfer pricing example discussed in the chapter, complete the following table (based on the optimal solution):

	Production Division	Marketing Division
Total Revenue		
Total Cost		
Total Profit		

8. In Figure 16.7 the optimal quantity of the intermediate product manufactured by the product division (Q_p) exceeded the optimal quantity required by the marketing division (Q_m). The excess output ($Q_p - Q_m$) was sold in the perfectly competitive external market. Construct a diagram similar to Figure 16.7 to illustrate the optimal values of Q_p, Q_m, and P_t (transfer price) for the case where Q_m exceeds Q_p.

9. Consolidated Sugar Company has two divisions, a farming-preprocessing (p) division and a processing-marketing (m) division. The farming-preprocessing division grows sugar cane and crushes it into juice, which it may sell to the processing-marketing division or sell externally in the perfectly competitive open market. The processing-marketing division buys cane juice, either from the farming-preprocessing division or externally in the open market, and then evaporates and purifies it and sells it as processed sugar.

The processing-marketing division's demand function for processed sugar is

$$P_m = 24 - Q_m$$

where P_m is the price, in dollars per unit, and Q_m is the quantity sold, in units, and its cost function (excluding cane juice) is

$$C_m = 8 + 2Q_m$$

The farming-preprocessing division's total cost function for cane-juice is

$$C_p = 10 + 2Q_p + Q_p^2$$

where Q_p is the quantity produced, in units. Assume that one unit of cane juice is converted into one unit of processed sugar. Furthermore, assume that the open market price for cane juice is $14.

a. What is the profit-maximizing price and output level for the farming-preprocessing division?

b. What is the profit-maximizing price and output level for the processing-marketing division?

c. How much of its output (cane juice) should the farming-preprocessing division sell (i) internally to the processing-marketing division and (ii) externally on the open market?

d. How much of its input (cane juice) should the processing-marketing division buy (i) internally from the farming-preprocessing division and (ii) externally on the open market.

e. What is the minimum price that the farming-preprocessing division would be willing to sell cane juice to the processing-marketing division? Explain.

f. What is the maximum price that the processing-marketing division would be willing to pay to buy cane juice from the farming-preprocessing division? Explain.

g. To maximize the overall profits of Consolidated Sugar, what price should the company use for intracompany transfers of cane juice from the farming-preprocessing division to the processing-marketing division?

10. General Medical makes disposable syringes, which it sells to hospitals and doctor supply companies. The company uses cost-plus pricing and currently charges 150 percent of average variable costs. General Medical has learned of an opportunity to sell 300,000 syringes to the Department of Defense if they can be delivered within three months at a price not in excess of $1 each. General Medical normally sells its syringes for $1.20 each.

If General Medical accepts the Defense Department order, it will have to forego sales of 100,000 syringes to its regular customers over this time period, although this loss of sales is not expected to affect future sales.

a. Should General Medical accept the Defense Department order?

b. If sales for the balance of the year are expected to be 50,000 units less because of some lost customers who do not return, should the order be accepted (ignore any effects beyond one year)?

11. Sales of the auto industry in 1957 were about 6 million cars at an average price of $2,500 each. Union president Walter Reuther suggested at that time that if the auto companies reduced their prices by $100, an additional one million cars would be sold. He also claimed that the industry's profits would be maintained at the $2 billion level.

Assume that the industry is operating under conditions where the marginal cost curve is approximately constant over the range of sales from 6 to 7 million cars. If you know that estimates of the demand for automobiles indicate an arc price elasticity between -0.5 and -1.5, evaluate Mr. Reuther's statement.

12. Cullinary Products, Inc. (CPI) performs a target return pricing calculation as part of its analysis of any proposed new products. CPI's research and development department has provided the following information concerning a new food processor it has designed:

- Labor costs (per unit) $22
- Material costs (per unit) $11
- Marketing costs (per unit) $2
- Fixed overhead costs (per year) $1,500,000
- Gross investment (operating assets) $6,000,000
- Required rate of return on investment (per year) 25%

Determine the target price based on projected sales per year of

a. 80,000 units

b. 100,000 units

c. 60,000 units

13. The Pear Computer Company has just developed a totally revolutionary new personal computer. It estimates that it will take competitors at least two years to produce equivalent products. The demand function for the computer has been estimated to be

$$P = 2,500 - .0005Q$$

The marginal (and average variable) cost of producing the computer is $900.

a. Compute the profit-maximizing price and output levels assuming Pear acts as a monopolist for its product.

b. Determine the total contribution to profits and fixed costs from the solution generated in part (a).

Pear Computer is considering an alternative pricing strategy of sliding down the demand curve. It plans to set the following schedule of prices over the coming two years.

Time period	Price	Quantity Sold
1	$2,400	200,000
2	2,200	200,000
3	2,000	200,000
4	1,800	200,000
5	1,700	200,000
6	1,600	200,000
7	1,500	200,000
8	1,400	200,000
9	1,300	200,000
10	1,200	200,000

c. Calculate the contribution to profit and overhead for each of the ten time periods and prices.

d. Compare your result in part (c) with your answer in part (b).

e. Explain the major advantages and disadvantages of "sliding down the demand curve" as a pricing strategy.

Case Problem
Transfer Pricing

DeSoto Engine, a division of International Motors, produces automobile engines. It sells these engines to the automobile assembly division within the corporation. A dispute has arisen between the managers of the DeSoto division and the assembly division concerning the appropriate transfer price for intracompany sales of engines. The current transfer price of $385 per unit was arrived at by taking the standard cost of the engine ($350) and adding a 10 percent profit margin ($35), based on an estimated volume of 450,000 engines per year. The manager of the DeSoto division argues that the transfer price should be raised since the division's average profit margin on other products is 18 percent. The manager of the assembly division claims that the transfer price should be lowered since an assembly division manager at a competing automobile company indicated that engines only cost his division $325 per unit. The corporation's chief economist has been asked to settle this intracompany pricing problem.

The economist collected the following demand and cost information. Demand for automobiles is given by the following function:

$$P_m = 10,000 - .01Q_m$$

where P_m is the selling price (in dollars) per automobile and Q_m is the number of vehicles sold. (Assume for simplicity that price is the only variable that affects demand.) The total cost function for the assembly division is (*excluding* the cost of the engines)

$$C_m = 1,150,000,000 + 2500Q_m$$

where C_m is the cost (in dollars). The DeSoto division's total cost function is

$$C_p = 30,000,000 + 275Q_p + .000125Q_p^2$$

where Q_p is the number of engines produced and C_p is the cost (in dollars).

Questions

Assume that no external market exists for these engines (that is, the DeSoto division cannot sell any excess engines to outside buyers and the assembly division cannot obtain additional engines from outside suppliers).

1. Determine the profit-maximizing output (vehicles) for the assembly division.
2. Determine the profit-maximizing output (engines) for the DeSoto division.
3. Determine the optimal transfer price for intracompany sales of engines.
4. Calculate (a) total revenue, (b) total cost, and (c) total profits for each division at the optimal solution found in questions 1, 2, and 3.

The manager of the DeSoto division is dissatisfied with the solution to the transfer-pricing problem. On further investigation, he finds that a *perfectly competitive external market exists for automobile engines*, with many automobile manufacturers and suppliers willing to sell or purchase engines at the going market price. Specifically, a large German automobile company (BW Motors) has offered to purchase all of DeSoto's engine output (up to 700,000 engines per year) at a price of $425 per unit.

5. Determine the profit-maximizing output for the assembly division.
6. Determine the profit-maximizing output for the DeSoto division.
7. Determine the optimal transfer price for intracompany sales of engines.
8. Determine how many engines the DeSoto division should sell (a) internally to the assembly division and (b) externally to BW Motors.
9. Calculate (a) total revenue, (b) total costs, and (c) total profits for each division at the optimal solution found in questions 5, 6, 7, and 8.

Long-Term Investment Decisions

ECONOMIC ANALYSIS AND
DECISIONS

1. Demand Analysis and Forecasting

2. Production and Cost Analysis

3. Pricing Analysis

4. Capital Expenditure Analysis

ECONOMIC, POLITICAL, AND
SOCIAL ENVIRONMENT

1. Business Conditions (Trends,
   Cycles, and Seasonal Effects)

**2. Factor Market Conditions
   (Capital, Labor, Land, and Raw
   Materials)**

3. Competitors' Responses

4. External, Legal, and Regulatory
   Constraints

5. Organizational (Internal)
   Constraints

Cash Flows

Risk

**Firm Value
(Shareholders' Wealth)**

This part of the book looks at the capital investment decision for a firm. Investments in new, long-term assets have a major impact on a firm's future stream of cash flows and the risk of those cash flows. As such, the long-term investment decision has a significant impact on the value of the firm. Capital investment decisions can be viewed as the link between the short-run price and output decisions made by managers of a firm and the long-run decisions made by those managers. A capital investment involves a change in the production technology used by the firm and/or a change in the scale of operations of the firm. Because it is difficult, or very expensive, to change capital investment decisions once resources have been committed, these decisions should be given especially close scrutiny by wealth-maximizing managers. In Chapter 17, we introduce the concept of a project's net present value. The net present value of a project can be viewed as the increment to shareholder wealth that is expected to accrue as a result of undertaking a capital investment project. The same tools that are relevant to capital investment analysis by private sector managers also can be used, with minor modifications, by managers in public and not-for-profit enterprises. These are examined in Chapter 18.

Capital Budgeting and the Cost of Capital 17

Capital budgeting is the process of planning for the purchases of assets whose returns (cash flows) are expected to continue beyond one year. When making capital budgeting decisions, the managers of a firm are committing the firm's resources to the expansion of its productive capacity, an improvement in its cost efficiency, or a diversification in its asset base. Each of these decisions has important implications for the future cash flows the firm can be expected to generate and the risk of those cash flows. Capital expenditures may be viewed as a bridge between the short-term price and output determination decisions facing managers daily and the longer-term strategic decisions that wealth-maximizing managers must make to remain competitive. In this chapter we review the techniques that have been found to be helpful in making these capital investment decisions.

The Nature of Capital Expenditure Decisions[1]

Previous chapters in the text have been primarily concerned with analytical tools and decision models that may assist the firm in making the most efficient use of its existing resources. This chapter considers decisions to replace or expand the firm's resource base.

Decisions to replace aging or technologically obsolete assets have the effect of changing the technology employed by the firm. This leads to an alteration of the relevant production and cost functions. Most replacement decisions are made with the expectation that a sufficiently lower cost function will prevail after the replacement to justify the required outlays.

Decisions to expand the firm's asset base lead to an increase in the scale or size of the productive facilities. Expansion decisions must be based on forecasts of future demand and costs after the expansion. If quantity demanded is suitably high or costs sufficiently low, the resulting profits may justify the expansion decision. Other types of decisions that can be analyzed using capital-budgeting

---

[1] Chapter 2 discussed discounting and the present-value concept. Students who are unfamiliar with this subject or who wish to review their understanding of the material should read Chapter 2 *before* proceeding through this chapter.

Glossary of New Terms

Capital expenditure
A cash outlay designed to generate a flow of future cash benefits over a period of time extending beyond one year.

Capital budgeting
The process of planning for and evaluating capital expenditure decisions.

Cost of capital
The cost of funds that are supplied to a firm. The cost of capital is the minimum rate of return that must be earned on the capital supplied by a firm's various groups of investors.

Capital rationing
A situation that exists when a firm has more acceptable investment projects than it has funds available to invest.

Internal rate of return (IRR)
The discount rate that equates the present value of the stream of net cash flows from a project with the project's net investment.

(Cont'd on next page)

Glossary of New Terms (*Cont'd*)

Net present value (NPV)
The present value of the stream of net cash flows resulting from a project, discounted at the required rate of return (cost of capital), minus the project's net investment.

Profitability index (PI)
The ratio of the present value of net cash flows over the life of a project, discounted at the cost of capital, to the net investment. Frequently, it is used in conjunction with resource allocation decisions in capital rationing situations.

Dividend valuation model
A model (or formula) stating that the value of a firm (i.e., shareholder wealth) is equal to the present value of the firm's future dividend payments, discounted at the shareholder's required rate of return. It provides one method of estimating a firm's cost of equity capital.

Capital Asset Pricing Model (CAPM)
A theory that formally describes the nature of the risk-required return tradeoff. It provides one method of estimating a firm's cost of equity capital.

techniques include research and development expenditures, investments in employee education and training, and lease-versus-buy decisions.

In general, *a capital expenditure* may be defined as a cash outlay that is expected to generate a flow of future cash benefits. Future here is defined as a period of time extending beyond one year.

The importance of capital expenditures to a firm is derived from the fact that current capital outlays, by definition, have a long-range impact on the performance of the enterprise. These current outlays affect future profitability and in aggregate they plot the future direction of the firm by determining products that will be produced, markets to be entered, the location of plants and facilities, and the type of technology (with its associated costs) to be used.

Finally, it is important to recognize that many capital expenditures are both costly to make and difficult to reverse without incurring considerable costs. Highly specialized production facilities and equipment may have no ready secondhand market in which they may be disposed. For these reasons, it is imperative for management to have procedures to aid in analyzing and selecting the most desirable capital expenditure projects of the available alternatives. Choosing from among such projects is the objective of *capital-budgeting* models.

Some Basic Definitions

Before proceeding to trace through the capital-budgeting process, some terms and concepts that will be encountered in the next few sections are defined.

Cost of Capital

A firm's *cost of capital* is the cost of funds that are supplied to the firm. The cost of capital is also called the investor's *required rate of return* since it specifies a minimum necessary rate of return that must be earned on the capital supplied to the firm by its various groups of investors. In this context, the cost of capital, or required rate of return, provides a basis for choosing among various capital investment projects. The cost of capital for a firm is a function of the riskiness of that firm and its investments. A procedure for computing the cost of capital for a firm is presented later in the chapter.

Project Classifications

An *independent project* may be defined as one whose acceptance or rejection does not necessarily eliminate other projects from consideration. An example of two independent projects might be the decision to install a new telephone communication system in the headquarters building of a firm and the decision to replace a drill press. In the absence of a constraint on the amount of funds available for investment, both projects could be adopted if they met minimum investment criteria.

A *mutually exclusive* project is one whose acceptance precludes the acceptance of one or more alternative proposals. Two mutually exclusive projects have the capacity to perform the same function for a firm. For example, if a firm needs additional plant space to expand its operations and two alternative plant sites were being considered, the acceptance of one plant site automatically precludes the acceptance of the alternative site.

A *contingent project* is one whose acceptance is dependent on the adoption of one or more other projects. For example, the decision to acquire a new printing press that is dependent on a new plant addition being built to house the press may be considered as a contingent project. The installation of pollution control equipment in a new plant is contingent upon the acceptance of that new plant as a desirable investment. In the case of contingent projects, it is preferable to lump together all projects that are dependent on one another and treat them as a single project for purposes of evaluation.

Funds Availability

When a firm has a sufficient amount of funds available to invest in all projects meeting some capital-budgeting selection criterion, we say the firm is operating *without a funds constraint*. Many times, however, the amount of funds required to undertake all acceptable investment projects in the absence of a funds constraint is greater than the total amount of dollars the firm has chosen to allocate for capital investment. This is a situation called *capital rationing*, and it leads to some special capital-budgeting problems.

A Basic Framework for Capital Budgeting

Recall from Chapter 2 that the economic theory of the firm indicates that a firm should operate at the point where the marginal cost of an additional unit of output just equals the marginal revenue derived from that output. Following this rule will lead to profit maximization by a firm. As shown in Chapter 2 this principle may be applied to the capital-budgeting decisions of the firm. In the context of capital budgeting, the marginal revenue may be thought of as the rates of return earned on successive investments (i.e., investment opportunity curve). Marginal cost may be interpreted as the firm's weighted marginal cost of capital—that is, the cost of successive increments of capital acquired by the firm, weighted by the proportions in which these funds are expected to be used in the firm's capital structure. This concept is illustrated in Figure 17.1.

The projects are indicated by lettered bars on the graph. For example, Project A requires an investment of $2 million and is expected to generate a 24 percent rate of return. Project B will cost $1 million ($3 million minus $2 million on the horizontal axis) and generate a 22 percent rate of return, and so on. Graphically, the projects are arranged in descending order by their rates of return, indicating that no firm has a limitless number of possible investment projects that all generate very high rates of return. As new products are produced, new markets entered, and cost-saving technologies adopted, the number of highly profitable investment opportunities tends to decline. The marginal cost of capital curve represents the marginal cost of capital to the firm; that is, the cost of each additional dollar raised in the capital markets.

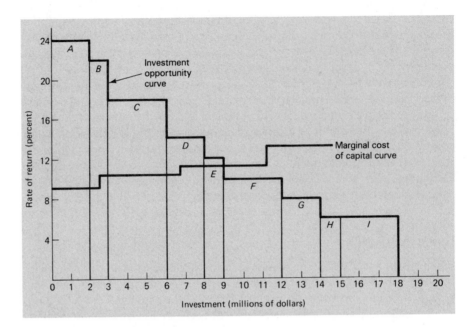

Figure 17.1
**A Simplified
Capital-Budgeting
Model**

Using this basic model, the firm should undertake Projects A, B, C, D, and E, since their returns exceed the firm's marginal cost of capital. Although there are some practical difficulties in implementing this conceptual model, it furnishes a guideline for optimal decision making. The remainder of this chapter considers some analytical tools that are useful in making long-term investment decisions.

The Capital Expenditure Selection Process

The process of selecting the capital investment projects that the firm will implement, like any rational decision-making process, consists of several important steps. To help assure that all the relevant factors will be considered, the process should consist of the following:

1. Generate alternative capital investment project proposals

2. Estimate cash flows for the project proposals

3. Evaluate and choose, from the alternatives available, those investment projects to implement

4. Review the investment projects after they have been implemented

Generating Capital Investment Projects

Ideas for new capital investments can come from many sources both inside and outside the firm. Proposals can originate at all levels in the organization, from factory workers all the way up to the board of directors. Most medium- and large-sized firms have staff groups whose responsibilities include searching for and analyzing capital expenditure projects. Among these staff groups may be cost accounting, industrial engineering, marketing research, research and development, and corporate planning personnel. Systematic procedures often exist for aiding in the research and analysis steps.

Capital expenditure projects can be classified into various types, depending on the nature of the benefits expected. One type would be projects generated by *growth* opportunities. If increased demand for a product line is forecasted, and if existing manufacturing and distribution facilities will be inadequate to meet this demand, then corporate planning (or another staff group) should develop proposals for expanding capacity. Since most existing products will eventually become obsolete in time, sustained growth also requires that firms develop and market new products. This should generate proposals for product research and development investment and possibly for investment in new plants and equipment. The desire for growth in the extractive industries (oil, natural gas, coal, and minerals) requires that investment proposals be generated to explore new sources of supply. Another type of project would be investments generated by *cost reduction* opportunities. Like products that become obsolete, technological progress also renders plants, equipment, and production processes obsolete. Normal wear and tear makes older plants and equipment more costly to operate (due to, for example, more downtime and higher maintenance costs). Obsolescence and deterioration should generate proposals to replace older facilities with new plants and equipment that are more efficient to operate. A final type would be investment projects that are generated by the need to meet *legal requirements and health and safety standards*, such as proposals for pollution control, ventilation, and fire-protection equipment.

Estimating Cash Flows

One of the most important and difficult steps in the selection process is estimation of the cash flows associated with investment projects. Because the cash flows will occur in the future, varying degrees of *uncertainty* exist about the values of these flows. Consequently, it is difficult to predict with complete accuracy what the actual cash flows for the project will be. In the ensuing analysis, we assume that the decision maker is able to estimate cash flows with accuracy sufficient enough to use these estimates in deciding whether to undertake the capital investment. Another difficulty arises from the intentional or unintentional introduction of *bias* in cash-flow estimates. It is often difficult for individuals to determine objective cash-flow estimates when they have a vested interest in seeing the project undertaken. The natural tendency is for some individuals to be overly optimistic in their estimates; that is, to underestimate the costs and to overestimate the benefits of an investment project. Therefore, besides holding individuals accountable for their estimates, it is also helpful to have the estimates reviewed by someone outside the department or division proposing the expenditure.

Certain basic guidelines have been found helpful in approaching the analysis of investment alternatives. First, cash flows should be measured on an *incremental* basis. In other words, the cash-flow stream for the project should represent the difference between the cash-flow streams to the firm with and without acceptance of the investment project. Second, cash flows should be measured on an *after-tax* basis, using the firm's marginal tax rate. Such noncash expenses associated with the project as depreciation are excluded from the analysis except to the extent that they affect the firm's cash outflow for income taxes. Third, all the *indirect effects* of the project throughout the firm should be included in the cash-flow calculations. If a department or division of the firm is contemplating a capital investment that will alter the revenues or costs of other departments or divisions, then these external effects should be incorporated into the cash-flow estimates. One such example is the investment in a new product that competes with the existing products of another division. The increased sales of the division that introduces the product may come at the expense of reduced sales in another division. Although the investment may be profitable to the one division, it may not be profitable to the firm as a whole. Fourth, *sunk costs* should not be considered when evaluating the project. A sunk cost is an outlay that has been made (or committed to be made). Since sunk costs cannot be recovered, they should not be considered in the decision to accept or reject a project. Fifth, the value of resources used in the project should be measured in terms of their *opportunity costs*. Recall from Chapter 12 that opportunity cost is the value of a resource in its next best alternative use. In the context of capital budgeting, opportunity costs of resources (assets) are the cash flows that these resources could generate if they are not used in the project under consideration.

For a typical investment project, an initial investment is made in year 0, which generates a series of yearly net cash flows over the life of the project (n). The net investment ($NINV$) of a project is defined as the initial net cash outlay in year 0. It includes the acquisition cost of any new assets plus installation and shipping costs and tax effects.[2]

The incremental, after-tax net cash flows (NCF) of a particular investment project are equal to cash inflows minus cash outflows. For any year during the life of the project, these may be defined as the difference in net income after tax ($\Delta NIAT$) with and without the project plus the difference in depreciation (ΔD):

$$NCF = \Delta NIAT + \Delta D \qquad\qquad [17.1]$$

$\Delta NIAT$ is equal to the difference in net income before tax ($\Delta NIBT$) times $(1 - t)$, where t is the corporate (marginal) income tax rate:

$$\Delta NIAT = \Delta NIBT(1 - t) \qquad\qquad [17.2]$$

$\Delta NIBT$ is defined as the difference in revenues (ΔR) minus the differences in operating costs (ΔC) and depreciation (ΔD):

$$\Delta NIBT = \Delta R - \Delta C - \Delta D \qquad\qquad [17.3]$$

---

[2] When the new asset is replacing an existing asset, one must also include in the net investment calculation the net proceeds from the sale of the existing asset and the taxes associated with its sale. See R. Charles Moyer, James R. McGuigan, and William J. Kretlow, *Contemporary Financial Management*, 3d rev. ed. (St. Paul: West, 1988), pp. 292–300, for a discussion of the cash-flow calculations for replacement decisions.

Substituting Equation 17.3 into Equation 17.2 yields

$$\Delta NIAT = (\Delta R - \Delta C - \Delta D)(1 - t) \qquad [17.4]$$

Substituting this equation into Equation 17.1 yields the following definition of net cash flow:

$$NCF = (\Delta R - \Delta C - \Delta D)(1 - t) + \Delta D \qquad [17.5]$$

To illustrate the cash-flow calculations, consider the following example. Suppose that Ace Electric, a manufacturer of small electric appliances, has been offered a contract to supply a regional merchandising company with a line of food blenders to be sold under the retail company's private brand name. Ace Electric's treasurer estimates that the initial investment in new equipment required to produce the blenders would be $1,000,000. The equipment would be depreciated (using the straight-line method)[3] over five years with a zero (0) estimated salvage value at the end of the five year contract period. Based on the contract specifications, the treasurer estimates that incremental revenues (additional sales) would be $800,000 per year. The incremental costs if the contract is accepted would be $450,000 per year. These include cash outlays for direct labor and materials, transportation, utilities, building rent, and *additional* overhead. The firm's marginal income tax rate is 40 percent and its cost of capital is 12 percent.

Based on the information, $NINV$ and NCF can be calculated for the project. The net investment ($NINV$) is equal to the $1,000,000 initial outlay for the new equipment. The difference in revenues (ΔR) with and without the project is equal to $800,000 per year and the difference in operating costs (ΔC) is equal to $450,000 per year. The difference in depreciation (ΔD) is equal to the initial outlay ($1,000,000) divided by 5, or $200,000 per year. Substituting these values, along with $t = .40$, into Equation 17.5 yields

$$NCF = (800,000 - 450,000 - 200,000)(1 - .40) + 200,000$$
$$= \$290,000$$

Ace Electric must decide whether it wants to invest $1,000,000 now to receive $290,000 per year in net cash flows over the next five years. The next section illustrates three of the criteria used in evaluating investment proposals such as this one.

Evaluating and Choosing the Investment Projects to Implement

Once a capital expenditure project has been identified and the cash flows have been estimated, a decision is required on whether to accept the project. The

---

[3] This depreciation method is just one of several possible methods that can be used. See Moyer, McGuigan and Kretlow, *Contemporary Financial Management*, Chap. 9 and Appendix A, for a discussion of the various depreciation methods.

level in the organization at which the decision is made varies among firms. In general, decisions on smaller projects, such as the purchase of a new machine, are likely to be made at the plant or division level, whereas larger projects, such as a major plant expansion, may require a decision by the board of directors or a finance committee made up of officers and directors of the firm.

The decision to accept a capital-expenditure project will result in a cash-flow stream to the firm; that is, a series of either cash inflows or outflows for a number of years into the future. Typically, a project will result in an initial (first-year) outflow (investment) followed by a series of cash inflows (returns) over a number of succeeding years. To compare and choose among alternative projects with their associated cash-flow streams, a measure of the desirability of each project must be obtained. The basic problem in measuring and comparing the desirability of investment projects to the firm is assessing the value of cash flows that occur at different points in time.

Various criteria can be employed in measuring the desirability of investment projects. This section focuses on three discounted cash-flow methods:[4]

- Internal rate of return (r)

- Net present value (NPV)

- Profitability index (PI)

Internal Rate of Return. The internal rate of return (IRR) is defined as the discount rate that equates the present value of the net cash flows from the project with the net investment. The following equation is used to find the internal rate of return:

$$\sum_{t=1}^{n} \frac{NCF_t}{(1+r)^t} = NINV \qquad [17.6]$$

where n is the life of the investment and r is the internal rate of return.

An investment project should be accepted if the internal rate of return is greater than or equal to the firm's required rate of return (cost of capital); if not, the project should be rejected.

For example, the internal rate of return for the Ace Electric investment project is calculated as follows:

$$\sum_{t=1}^{5} \frac{290,000}{(1+r)^t} = 1,000,000$$

$$\sum_{t=1}^{5} \frac{1}{(1+r)^t} = \frac{1,000,000}{290,000} = 3.4483$$

---

[4] Other investment decision-making criteria, which do not employ discounting, include the payback period and the average (or accounting) rate of return. These criteria are generally considered to be inferior to discounted cash-flow methods because they do not consider the *timing* of the cash flows.

The term $\left[\sum_{t=1}^{5} 1/(1+r)^t\right]$ represents the present value of a $1 annuity for 5 years discounted at r percent and is equal to 3.4483. Looking up 3.4483 in the Period = 05 row of Table 5 in Appendix A, this value falls between 3.5172 and 3.4431, which corresponds to discount rates of 13 and 14 percent, respectively. Interpolating between these values yields an internal rate of return of

$$r = .13 + \frac{3.5172 - 3.4483}{3.5172 - 3.4331}(.14 - .13)$$

$$= .1382$$

or 13.8 percent. Since the internal rate of return for this period exceeds Ace Electric's cost of capital ($k = 12$ percent), the project (contract) should be accepted.

Net Present Value. The net present value of an investment is defined as the present value, discounted at the firm's required rate of return (cost of capital), of the stream of net cash flows from the project minus the project's net investment. Algebraically, the net present value is equal to

$$NPV = \sum_{t=1}^{n} \frac{NCF_t}{(1+k)^t} - NINV \qquad [17.7]$$

where n is the expected life of the project and k is the firm's required rate of return (cost of capital).

An investment project should be accepted if the net present value is greater than or equal to zero and rejected if its net present value is less than zero. This is so because a positive net present value translates directly into increases in stock prices and increases in shareholder wealth.

In the Ace Electric Company investment project described earlier, the net present value is calculated as follows:

$$NPV = \sum_{t=1}^{5} \frac{290,000}{(1+.12)^t} - 1,000,000$$

The term $\left[\sum_{t=1}^{5} 290,000/(1+.12)^t\right]$ represents the present value of an annuity of $290,000 for five years discounted at 12 percent. From Table 5 in Appendix A, the present value of an annuity of $1 for five years discounted at 12 percent is 3.6048. The net present value for the project therefore is

$$NPV = 290,000(3.6048) - 1,000,000$$

$$= + \$45,392$$

Since the net present value is positive, the project (contract) should be accepted.

Both the net present value and the internal rate of return methods result in identical decisions to either accept or reject an *independent* project. This is true because the net present value is greater than (less than) zero if and only if the

Table 17.1
Net Present Value vs. Internal Rate of Return for Mutually Exclusive Investment Projects

	Project X	Project Y
Net investment	$1000	$1000
Net cash flows		
Year 1	667	0
Year 2	667	1400
Net present value at 5%	$ 240	$ 270
Internal rate of return	21.5%	18.3%

internal rate of return is greater than (less than) the required rate of return k. In the case of *mutually exclusive* projects, however, the two methods may yield contradictory results; one project may have a *higher* internal rate of return than another and, at the same time, a *lower* net present value.

Consider, for example, mutually exclusive projects X and Y shown in Table 17.1. Both require a net investment of $1,000. Based on the internal rate of return, Project X is preferred, with a rate of 21.5 percent compared with Project Y's rate of 18.3 percent. Based on the net present value with a discount rate of 5 percent, Project Y ($270) is preferred to Project X ($240). Thus it is necessary to determine which of the two criteria is the correct one to use in this situation. The outcome depends on what *assumptions* the decision maker chooses to make about the *implied reinvestment rate* for the net cash flows generated from each project. This can be seen in Figure 17.2. For discount (reinvestment) rates below 10 percent, Project Y has a higher net present value than Project X and is therefore preferred. For discount rates greater than 10 percent, Project X is preferred using both the net present value and internal rate of return approaches. Hence, a conflict only occurs in this case for discount (cost-of-capital) rates below 10 percent. The net present value method assumes that cash flows are *reinvested at the firm's cost of capital*, whereas the internal rate of return method assumes that these cash flows are *reinvested at the computed internal rate of return.*[5] Generally, the cost of capital is considered to be a more realistic reinvestment rate than the computed internal rate of return because this is the rate the next (marginal) investment project can be assumed to earn. This can be seen in Figure 17.1. The last project invested in, Project E, offers a rate of return nearly equal to the firm's marginal cost of capital.

Consequently, in the absence of capital rationing, the net present value approach is normally superior to the internal rate of return when choosing among mutually exclusive investments.

Profitability Index. The profitability index (PI), or benefit-cost ratio, is the ratio of the present value of future net cash flows over the life of a project to the

---

[5] A more thorough discussion of this problem and the underlying assumptions is found in J. Hirshleifer, "On the Theory of the Optimal Investment Decision," *Journal of Political Economy* 66 (Aug. 1958): 95–103; and James H. Lorie and Leonard J. Savage, "Three Problems in Rationing Capital," *Journal of Business* 23 (Oct. 1955): 229–239.

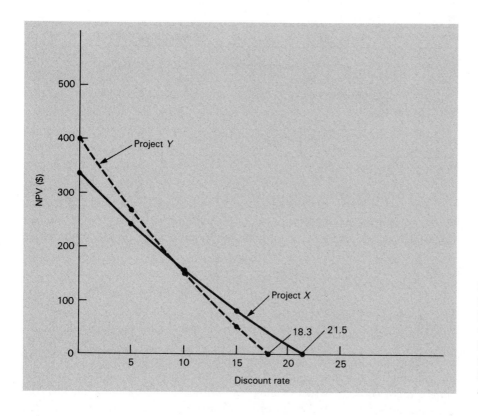

Figure 17.2
NPV Profiles: Net Present Value versus Internal Rate of Return for Mutually Exclusive Alternatives

net investment. It is expressed as follows:

$$PI = \frac{\sum_{t=1}^{n} NCF_t/(1+k)^t}{NINV}$$ [17.8]

The profitability index is interpreted as the present value return *for each dollar of initial investment*. In comparison, the net present value measures the *total* present value dollar return.

An investment project should be accepted if its profitability index is greater than or equal to 1.0 and rejected if its profitability index is less than 1.0.[6]

In the Ace Electric Company investment project described earlier, the profitability index is calculated as follows:

$$PI = \frac{\sum_{t=1}^{5} \frac{290,000}{(1+.12)^t}}{1,000,000}$$

---

[6] When a project has a profitability index equal to 1.0, the present value of the net cash flows is exactly equal to the net investment. Thus, the project has a net present value of zero, meaning that it is expected to earn the investors' required rate of return and nothing more.

Table 17.2
Net Present Value vs. Profitability Index for Mutually Exclusive Investments

	Project J	Project K
Present value of net cash flows	$25,000	$14,000
Less: Net investment	−20,000	−10,000
Net present value	$ 5,000	$ 4,000
$PI = \dfrac{\text{Present value of net cash flows}}{\text{Net investment}}$	1.25	1.40

As in the net present value calculation discussed earlier, the term $[\sum_{t=1}^{5} 290,000/(1 + .12)^t]$ represents the present value of an annuity of $290,000 for five years discounted at 12 percent. The profitability index for the project is therefore

$$PI = \frac{290,000(3.6048)}{1,000,000}$$

$$= 1.045$$

Since the profitability index is greater than 1.0, the project (contract) should be accepted.

The profitability index, net present value, and internal rate of return criteria all will yield identical accept-reject decisions when dealing with two or more *independent* projects. When dealing with *mutually exclusive* investments, conflicts may arise between the net present value and profitability index criteria. This conflict is most likely to occur if the alternative projects require significantly different net investments.

Consider, for example, the following information on Projects J and K shown in Table 17.2. According to the net present value criterion, Project J would be preferred because of its larger net present value. According to the profitability index criterion, Project K would be preferred.

When a conflict arises, the final decision must be made on the basis of other factors. For example, if a firm has no constraint on the funds available to it for capital investment—that is, no capital rationing—the net present value approach is preferred, since it will select the projects that are expected to generate the largest *total dollar* increase in the firm's wealth and, by extension, maximize shareholder wealth. If, however, the firm is in a capital rationing situation, and capital budgeting is being done for only one period, the profitability index approach may be preferred, since it will indicate which projects will maximize the returns *per dollar of investment*—an appropriate objective when a funds constraint exists.

Table 17.3 presents a summary of the three capital budgeting decision criteria discussed in the chapter.

Reviewing Investment Projects after Implementation

A very important but often neglected step in the selection process is the review of investment projects *after* they have been implemented. The purpose of this

Table 17.3 **Summary of the Capital Budgeting Decision Criteria**

Criterion	Project Acceptance Decision Rule	Benefits	Weaknesses
Net present value (NPV)	Accept project if project has a positive or zero NPV; that is, if the present value of net cash flows, evaluated at the firm's cost of capital, equals or exceeds the net investment required	Considers the timing of cash flows. Provides an objective, return-based criterion for acceptance or rejection Most conceptually accurate approach.	Difficulty in interpreting the meaning of the NPV computation.
Internal rate of return (IRR)	Accept project if IRR equals or exceeds the firm's cost of capital.	Same benefits as the NPV. Easy to interpret the meaning of IRR.	Sometimes gives decision that conflicts with NPV. Multiple rates of return problem.*
Profitability index (PI)	Accept project if PI is greater than or equal to 1.0.	Same benefits as the NPV. Useful to guide decisions in capital-rationing problems.	Sometimes gives decision that conflicts with NPV.

* See Moyer, McGuigan, and Kretlow, *Contemporary Financial Management*, pp. 326–327, for a discussion of the multiple internal rates of return problem.

review should be to provide information on the effectiveness of the selection process. In the review, the actual cash flows from an accepted project would be compared with the estimated cash flows at the time the project was proposed. This type of analysis requires the firm to keep some additional information in its accounting records to be able to associate specific costs and revenues with various investment projects. Since estimating future cash inflows and outflows is uncertain, one would not expect the actual values to agree perfectly with the estimated values. The analysis therefore should be concerned with checking for any large or systematic discrepancies in the cash-flow estimates by individual departments, plants, or divisions, and attempting to ascertain the reasons for these discrepancies. An analysis such as this will enable decision makers to make better evaluations of investment proposals submitted in the future.

Capital Rationing and the Capital Budgeting Decision

For each of the selection criteria previously discussed, the decision rule is to undertake *all* independent investment projects that meet the acceptance standard. This rule places no restrictions on the total amount of acceptable capital projects a company may undertake in any particular period.

Many firms, however, do not have unlimited funds available for investment. Rather than letting the size of their capital budget be determined by the number of profitable investment opportunities available, many companies choose to place an upper limit, or *constraint*, on the amount of funds allocated to capital investments. This constraint may be either *self-imposed*—by the firm's management—or *externally imposed*—by conditions in the capital markets.

For example, a very conservative firm may be reluctant to use debt or external equity to finance capital expenditures. Instead, it would limit capital expenditures to cash flows from continuing operations minus any dividends paid. Another firm may feel that it lacks the managerial resources to successfully undertake all acceptable projects in a given year and may choose to limit capital expenditures for this reason.

A number of externally imposed constraints might limit a firm's capital expenditures. For example, a firm's loan agreements may contain restrictive covenants that limit future borrowing. Similarly, a weak financial position, conditions in the securities markets, or both may make the flotation of a new bond or stock issue by the firm impossible or prohibitively expensive. Examples of such market-imposed constraints include depressed stock market prices, unusually high interest rates due to a "tight money" policy on the part of the Federal Reserve, or a reluctance on the part of investors to purchase new securities if the firm has a large percentage of debt in its capital structure.

Several different methods can be used in making capital budgeting decisions under capital rationing. When the initial outlays occur in two (or more) periods, the methods are quite elaborate and require the use of linear, integer, or goal programming.[7] However, for a single-period capital budgeting constraint, a relatively simple approach employing the profitability index can be used. Briefly, the approach consists of the following steps:

- **Step 1:** Calculate the profitability index for each of a series of investment projects.

- **Step 2:** Rank the projects according to their profitability indexes (from highest to lowest).

- **Step 3:** Beginning with the project having the highest profitability index, proceed down through the list and accept projects having profitability indexes greater than or equal to 1.0 until the entire capital budget has been utilized.

At times a firm may not be able to utilize its entire capital budget because the next acceptable project on its list is too large, given the remaining available funds. In this case, the firm's management should choose among the following three alternatives:

- **Alternative 1:** Search for another combination of projects, perhaps including some smaller, less profitable ones that will more fully utilize all available funds *and* increase the net present value of the combination of projects.

- **Alternative 2:** Attempt to relax the funds constraint so that sufficient resources are available to accept the last project for which funds were not fully available.

---

[7] The following references contain information on the use of these more advanced models: H. Martin Weingartner, *Mathematical Programming and the Analysis of Capital Budgeting Problems*, Englewood Cliffs, N. J.: Prentice-Hall, 1963. See also Sang M. Lee and A. J. Lerro, "Capital Budgeting for Multiple Objectives," *Financial Management* 3 (Spring 1974): 58–66; and Richard H. Bernhard, "Mathematical Programming Models for Capital Budgeting: A Survey, Generalization, and Critique," *Journal of Financial and Quantitative Analysis* 4 (June 1969): 111-158. See also Chapter 5 of this text for a discussion of the linear programming solution to a two-period capital rationing problem.

- **Alternative 3:** Accept as many projects as possible and either invest any excess funds in short-term securities until the next period,[8] pay out the excess funds to shareholders as dividends, use the funds to reduce outstanding debt, or do a combination of the above.

The following example illustrates how these alternatives can be applied to an actual budgeting decision. Suppose that the management of Leonard Savage Company has decided to limit next year's capital expenditures to $550,000. Eight capital expenditures projects have been proposed—P, Q, R, S, T, U, V and W—and ranked according to their profitability indexes, as shown in Table 17.4. Given the $550,000 ceiling, the firm's management proceeds down the list of projects, selecting, P, R, S, and U, in that order. Project T cannot be accepted, since this would require a capital outlay of $25,000 in excess of the $550,000 limit. Projects P, R, S, and U together yield a net present value of $114,750 but require a total investment outlay of $525,000, leaving $25,000 from the capital budget that is not invested in projects. Management is considering the following three alternatives:

- **Alternative 1:** It could attempt to find another combination of projects, perhaps including some smaller ones, that would allow for a full utilization of available funds and increase the cumulative net present value. In this case, a likely combination would be Projects P, R, S, T, and V. This combination

Table 17.4 Sample Ranking of Proposed Projects According to Their Profitability Indexes

Project (1)	Net Investment (2)	Net Present Value (3)	Present Value of Net Cash Flows (4)	$PI = (4) \div (2)$	Cumulative Net Investment	Cumulative Net Present Value
P	$100,000	$25,000	$125,000	1.25	$100,000	$ 25,000
R	150,000	33,000	183,000	1.22	250,000	58,000
S	175,000	36,750	211,750	1.21	425,000	94,750
U	100,000	20,000	120,000	1.20	525,000	114,750
T	50,000	9,000	59,000	1.18	575,000	123,750
V	75,000	12,500	87,500	1.17	650,000	136,250
Q	200,000	30,000	230,000	1.15	850,000	166,250
W	50,000	−10,000	40,000	0.80	900,000	156,250

[8] If a firm does not invest a portion of its available capital resources in projects earning a rate of return at least equal to the cost of capital, an implicit opportunity cost of lost earnings is incurred. For example, suppose a firm cannot invest a portion of its capital budget because the next acceptable project requires a larger net investment than is available in remaining funds. If the firm's after-tax cost of capital is 15 percent and the unutilized funds can only be invested in short-term securities earning 5 percent after taxes, the opportunity cost of this action is a 10 percent difference, representing a loss in potential earnings. Thus, as long as profitable investment alternatives exist, the firm should seek ways to fully utilize all available capital funds.

would fully utilize the $550,000 available and create a net present value of $116,250—an increase of $1,500 over the net present value of $114,750 from projects P, R, S, and U.

- **Alternative 2:** It could attempt to increase the capital budget by another $25,000 to allow Project T to be added to the list of adopted projects.

- **Alternative 3:** It could merely accept the first four projects—P, R, S, and U—and invest the remaining $25,000 in a short-term security until the next period. This alternative is not especially desirable, however, since the return on the short-term investment would surely be less than the firm's cost of capital (required rate of return). Thus, the difference between the firm's cost of capital and the return on the short-term investment would constitute an *opportunity cost*.

In this case, *Alternative 1* seems to be the most desirable of the three. In rearranging the capital budget, however, the firm should never accept a project, such as W, that does not meet the minimum acceptance criterion of a positive net present value (a profitability index greater than 1.0).

Capital Budgeting and Risk

In the discussion above of capital-budgeting decision criteria, the assumption was made that investment projects could be evaluated and selected solely on the basis of the best estimate or most likely value of the future cash flows. Although these models can be quite useful, they suffer from a major shortcoming; namely, they ignore the possibility that different projects may have different levels of risk. Because the cash-flow estimates used in capital budgeting are forecasted values, they are subject to error. The risk of a project is represented by the possibility that actual cash flows will deviate from forecasted cash flows.

Several methods for dealing with risk, described in Chapter 3, are directly applicable to investment decision making. Other methods, which are based on the capital asset pricing model (CAPM), can also be used when analyzing the projects having varying degrees of risk.[9] The CAPM is introduced later in this chapter.

The decision to employ some risk analysis technique to evaluate an investment project depends on the project size and the additional cost of applying such a technique as compared with the perceived benefits. For small projects, only the simpler risk adjustment techniques should be used. For major projects, which have above- or below-normal risk, it is worthwhile to analyze the project's risk as precisely as possible. Failure to analyze fully the risk of a large project could result in bad investment decisions and even substantial losses for the firm.

---

[9] See James Van Horne, *Financial Management and Policy*, 7th ed. (Englewood Cliffs, N.J.: Prentice-Hall, 1986), for a discussion of the use of the CAPM in risk analysis for capital budgeting.

Risk-Adjusted Discount Rate Approach

Chapter 3 discussed the use of risk-adjusted discount rates in evaluating capital-budgeting problems. The application of this approach can be illustrated using the Ace Electric Company example examined in the previous section. Suppose that Ace uses the risk-adjusted discount rates shown in Table 17.5 when making capital investment decisions. The risk premium (θ) for each risk class (determined subjectively) is added to the firm's cost of capital ($k = 12$ percent) to arrive at the risk-adjusted discount rate.

If the investment project (contract for food blenders) is considered to be of average risk, then a risk-adjusted discount rate (k^*) of 12 percent is used in the discounted cash-flow analysis. As shown earlier, the NPV for the project at a discount rate or 12 percent was $45,392 and the project (contract) should be accepted. However, if management decides that the project is of above-average risk and evaluates it at a rate (k^*) of 15 percent, the NPV is

$$NPV = \sum_{t=1}^{5} \frac{290,000}{(1 + .15)^t} - 1,000,000$$

$$= 290,000\,(3.3522) - 1,000,000$$

$$= \$ - 27,862$$

Since the NPV of the project is negative at a 15 percent discount rate, it should *not* be accepted.

Thus, the assessment of the project's risk affects its desirability (as measured by NPV) and determines whether it is accepted.

Estimating the Firm's Cost of Capital

As mentioned earlier, the firm's cost of capital is an important input in the capital-budgeting analysis procedure. The theory and measurement of a firm's cost of capital is a complex topic that is more appropriately dealt with at length in financial management texts. The purpose of this section is to provide an introduction to the topic and to summarize some of its most important elements.

Firms raise funds in the capital markets by issuing common stock, by retaining a portion of past earnings, by selling bonds, and by borrowing both long and short term from banks and other financial institutions. Although there are other sources of funds such as leasing, sale of preferred stock, and sale of

Project Risk	Risk Premium (θ)	Risk-Adjusted Discount Rate ($k^* = k + \theta$)	
Average risk	0%	12%	Table 17.5 **Risk-Adjusted Discount Rates: Ace Electric Company**
Above-average risk	3	15	
High risk	8	20	

convertible securities and warrants, the following discussion focuses on the two major sources of funds for most firms—debt and common equity. Each of these sources of funds has a cost. The cost of each of the various component sources of capital is an important input in the calculation of a firm's overall cost of capital.

Cost of Debt

The cost of debt capital to the firm is the rate of return required by investors. For a debt issue, this rate of return k_d equates the present value of all expected future receipts—interest I and principal repayment M—with the offering price V_0 of the debt security:

$$V_0 = \sum_{t=1}^{n} \frac{I}{(1+k_d)^t} + \frac{M}{(1+k_d)^n} \qquad [17.9]$$

The cost of debt k_d can be found by using the methods for finding the discount rate (that is, yield to maturity) discussed in Chapter 2.

Most *new* long-term debt (bonds) issued by companies is sold at or close to par value (normally $1,000 per bond), and the coupon interest rate is set at the rate required by investors.[10] When debt is issued at par value, the pretax cost of debt, k_d, is equal to the coupon interest rate. Interest payments made to investors, however, are deductible from the firm's taxable income. Therefore, the *aftertax* cost of debt issued at par is computed by multiplying the coupon interest rate by 1 minus the firm's marginal tax rate t:

$$k_i = k_d(1-t) \qquad [17.10]$$

In principle, the cost of external capital to the firm should be adjusted for flotation costs; however, many types of debt, such as bank loans and private placements, have virtually zero flotation costs. In addition, flotation costs on most large debt issues sold through underwriters are small, about 1 to 2 percent of the issue total. In these instances, flotation cost adjustments have an insignificant effect on debt costs.

To illustrate the cost of debt computation, suppose that National Telephone and Telegraph sells $100 million of 8.5 percent first-mortgage bonds at par. Assuming a corporate marginal tax rate of 40 percent, the aftertax cost of debt is computed as

$$k_i = k_d(1-t)$$
$$= 8.5 \ (1 - .40) = 5.1\%$$

---

[10] When debt is issued at par value, the coupon interest rate is equal to the yield to maturity. The yield to maturity calculation involves finding the discount rate that equates the stream of interest and principal payments to the par value or cost of the bond. See Moyer, McGuigan, and Kretlow, *Contemporary Financial Management*, pp. 109–112 for an example of the yield to maturity calculation for a bond.

Cost of Internal Equity

Like the cost of debt, the cost of equity capital to the firm is the equilibrium rate of return required by the firm's common stock investors.

Firms raise equity capital in two ways: (1) *internally*, through retained earnings and (2) *externally*, through the sale of new common stock. The cost of internal equity to the firm is less than the cost of new common stock because the sale of new stock requires the payment of flotation costs.

The concept of the cost of internal equity (or simply "equity," as it is commonly called) can be developed using several different approaches. The first considered here is based on the *dividend valuation model*.

Dividend Valuation Model. Recall from Chapter 1 that shareholder wealth was defined as the present value, discounted at the shareholder's required rate of return k_e, of the expected future returns generated by the firm. For the typical firm, these future returns can take two forms—the payment of dividends to the shareholder or an increase in the market value of the firm's stock (capital gain). For the shareholder who plans to hold the stock indefinitely, the value of the firm (shareholder wealth) is (Equation 1.2)

$$V_0 = \sum_{t=1}^{\infty} \frac{D_t}{(1 + k_e)^t}$$

[17.11]

where D_t is the dividend paid by the firm in period t.[11] If the shareholder chooses to sell the stock after n years, his (or her) wealth (V_0) is

$$V_0 = \sum_{t=1}^{\infty} \frac{D_t}{(1 + k_e)^t} + \frac{V_n}{(1 + k_e)^n}$$

[17.12]

where V_n is the market value of the shareholder's holdings in period n. However, Equation 17.12 can be shown to be identical to 17.11, since the value of the firm in period n is based on the future returns (dividends) of the firm in period $n + 1$, $n + 2$, ...[12]

If the dividends of the firm are expected to grow *perpetually* at a *constant compound rate* of g per year, then the value of the firm (Equation 17.11) can be

---

[11] A profitable firm that reinvests all its earnings and never distributes any dividends would still have a positive value to stockholders since its market value would be increasing and shareholders could sell their stock and obtain a capital gain on their investment in the firm.

[12] The value of the firm in period n is

$$V_n = \sum_{t=n+1}^{\infty} \frac{D_t}{(1 + k_e)^{t-n}}$$

When this expression is substituted in Equation 17.12, Equation 17.11 is obtained.

expressed as[13]

$$V_0 = \frac{D_1}{k_e - g} \qquad [17.13]$$

where D_1 is the dividend paid in period 1 and V_0 is the value of the firm (expected market value). If D_1 is the dividend *per share* (rather than total dividends) paid in period 1, then V_0 represents the market price *per share* of common stock. Solving Equation 17.13 for k_e yields

$$k_e = \frac{D_1}{V_0} + g \qquad [17.14]$$

An example illustrates how Equation 17.14 can be applied in estimating the cost of equity capital. Suppose that the current price of the common stock of Fresno Company (V_0) is \$32. The dividend per share of the firm next year, D_1, is expected to be \$2.14. Dividends have been growing at an average compound annual rate of 7 percent over the past ten years, and this growth rate is expected to be maintained for the foreseeable future. Based on this information, the cost of equity capital is estimated as

$$k_e = \frac{2.14}{32} + .07 = .137$$

or 13.7 percent.

Capital Asset Pricing Model. Another technique that can be used to estimate the cost of equity capital is the *capital asset pricing model* (CAPM). The CAPM is a theory that formally describes the risk-required return tradeoff for securities. According to the CAPM theory, the rate of return required by investors consists of a risk-free return r_f plus a premium compensating the investor for bearing the risk. The risk premium varies from stock to stock.

Obviously less risk is associated with an investment in a stable stock, such as AT&T, than in the stock of a small, wildcat oil drilling firm W. As a result, an investor in the drilling stock requires a higher return than the AT&T investor. Figure 17.3 illustrates the difference in required rates of return (or the cost of internal equity) for the two securities. The relationship illustrated in this figure is called the *security market line* (SML). The SML depicts the risk-return relationship in the market for all securities.

The cost of equity capital can be quantified using the CAPM. The CAPM assumes that a single risk-free rate exists, and the risk-required return tradeoff for stocks is characterized by a straight line sloping upward from the risk-free rate. The required return can be obtained by calculating the risk associated with a stock.

---

[13] Equation 17.13 is often referred to as the *Gordon model*, for Myron J. Gordon, who pioneered its use. See Myron J. Gordon. *The Investment, Financing, and Valuation of the Corporation*. Homewood, Ill.: Irwin, 1962.

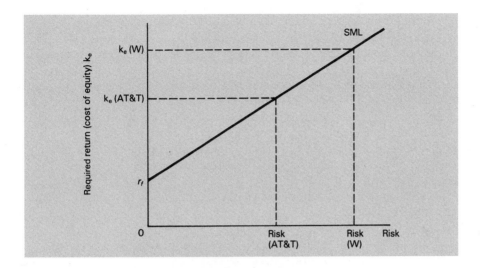

Figure 17.3
**The Security
Market Line (SML)**

Recall from Chapter 3 that risk was defined as the variability of outcomes (e.g., returns). The variability of returns for individual stocks is closely related to the variability of stock prices. In the context of the CAPM and the SML, *total* variability of returns is not considered to be the relevant measure of risk, however. Instead, total variability can be divided into two components:

- The variability of returns that is *unique* to a security. This is called *unsystematic risk*, and it includes variability caused by such factors as differing management skills, strikes, natural disasters, effects of new competition, and so on.

- The variability of returns that affects *all* securities. This is called *systematic* or *nondiversifiable* risk. It is measured by the co-movement or covariation of a security's returns with the returns of the overall market. The overall market movement is usually measured by some broad market index such as the S&P 500 stock index. Systematic variability is caused by factors like changes in the level of interest rates, the impact of recessions or business expansions, and so on.

If an investor holds a well-diversified portfolio of individual securities, it is possible to minimize or eliminate the variability of returns arising from unique factors affecting individual securities, leaving only systematic risk.

In order to use the SML to estimate the cost of equity, it is necessary to estimate the systematic risk of individual securities. One measure of the systematic risk of a stock is the stock's *beta*, b. (Beta is estimated as the slope of a regression line between an individual security's returns and the returns for a market index.)[14]

---

[14] See Moyer, McGuigan, and Kretlow, *Contemporary Financial Management*, Chapters 5 and 12, for a more detailed discussion of the CAPM theory and its use in calculating the cost of equity capital.

The stock market as a whole has a beta of 1.0; stocks whose prices fluctuate less than the market as a whole have betas of less than 1.0; and stocks with price fluctuations greater than the market have betas greater than 1.0. For example, if a stock has a beta equal to 1.0, a 5 percent increase (or decrease) in the returns on the market index would be expected to be associated with a 5 percent increase (or decrease) in that security's returns. If a stock has a beta of 2.0, a 5 percent increase (or decrease) in market returns would be expected to be associated with a 10 percent increase (or decrease) in that security's returns. Finally, a beta of 0.5 implies that a 5 percent increase (or decrease) in market returns would be expected to be associated with a 2.5 percent increase (or decrease) in that security's returns.

Given this simplified introduction to the CAPM, the cost of equity calculation can now be illustrated as:

$$k_e = r_f + b(k_m - r_f) \qquad\qquad [17.15]$$

where k_m is the expected return on the market as a whole. This equation shows that the risk premium portion of a firm's cost of equity is proportional to its beta.

To illustrate the k_e calculation using the CAPM, suppose that the Midwestern Power Company common stock has a beta of 0.8 and the present risk-free rate is 7 percent. If the expected return on the market k_m is 13 percent, the following value for k_e is obtained:

$$
\begin{aligned}
k_e &= r_f + b(k_m - r_f) \\
&= 7.0 + 0.8(13.0 - 7.0) \\
&= 11.8\%
\end{aligned}
$$

For many stocks, the cost of equity capital obtained from the dividend capitalization model and the CAPM will generally be in approximate agreement with each other. If substantial differences do exist, further analysis is required. It should be emphasized that the calculation of the cost of equity capital requires the exercise of good judgment by the financial manager.

Cost of External Equity

The cost of external equity is greater than the cost of internal equity for the following reasons:

- Flotation costs associated with new shares are usually high enough that they cannot realistically be ignored.

- The selling price of the new shares to the public must be less than the market price of the stock before announcement of the new issue, or the shares cannot be expected to sell. Before any announcement, the current market price of a stock usually represents an equilibrium between supply and demand. If supply is increased (all other things being equal), the new equilibrium price will be lower.

When a firm's future dividend payments are expected to grow forever at a constant per period rate of g, the cost of external equity k'_e is defined as

$$k'_e = \frac{D_1}{V_{net}} + g$$

[17.16]

where V_{net} is the net proceeds to the firm on a per share basis.

To illustrate, consider the Fresno Company example used in the cost of internal equity discussion, where $V_0 = \$32$, $D_1 = \$2.14$, $g = .07$, and $k_e = 13.7\%$. Assuming that new common stock can be sold at $31 to net the company $30 a share after flotation costs, k'_e is calculated as:

$$k'_e = \frac{2.14}{30} + 0.07$$

$$= 0.141 \text{ or } 14.1\%$$

Because of the relatively high cost of newly issued equity, many companies try to avoid this means of raising capital. The question of whether a firm should raise capital with newly issued common stock depends on its investment opportunities.

Weighted Cost of Capital

Firms calculate their cost of capital to determine a discount rate that may be used for evaluating proposed capital expenditure projects. Recall that the purpose of capital expenditure analysis is basically to determine which *proposed* projects the firm should *actually* undertake. Therefore, it is logical that *the capital whose cost is measured and compared with the expected benefits from these proposed projects should be the next or marginal capital the firm raises.* Typically, companies estimate the cost of each capital component as the cost they expect to have to pay on these funds during the coming year.[15]

In addition, as a firm evaluates proposed capital expenditure projects, it normally does not specify the proportions of debt and equity financing for each individual project. Instead, each project is presumed to be financed with the same proportion of debt and equity contained in the company's target capital structure.

Thus the appropriate cost of capital figure to be used in capital budgeting is not only based on the next capital to be raised but is also weighted by the proportions of the capital components in the firm's long-range target capital structure. This figure is called the *weighted*, or *overall, cost of capital.*

---

[15] Stated another way, the cost of the capital acquired by the firm in earlier periods—that is, the *historical* cost of capital—is *not* used as the discount rate in determining next year's capital expenditures.

The general expression for calculating the weighted cost of capital k_a is

$$
k_a = \begin{bmatrix} \text{equity} \\ \text{fraction} \\ \text{of capital} \\ \text{structure} \end{bmatrix} \begin{bmatrix} \text{cost} \\ \text{of} \\ \text{equity} \end{bmatrix} + \begin{bmatrix} \text{debt} \\ \text{fraction} \\ \text{of capital} \\ \text{structure} \end{bmatrix} \begin{bmatrix} \text{cost} \\ \text{of} \\ \text{debt} \end{bmatrix}
$$

$$
= \begin{bmatrix} \dfrac{E}{D+E} \end{bmatrix} (k_e) + \begin{bmatrix} \dfrac{D}{D+E} \end{bmatrix} (k_i)
$$

[17.17]

where D is the amount of debt and E the amount of equity in the target capital structure.[16]

To illustrate, suppose that a company has a current (and target) capital structure of 75 percent equity and 25 percent debt. (The proportions of debt and equity should be the proportions in which the firm intends to raise funds in the future.) For a firm that is not planning a change in its target capital structure, these proportions should be based on the current *market value weights* of the individual components (debt and common equity). The company plans to finance next year's budget with $75 million of retained earnings ($k_e = 12\%$) and $25 million of long-term debt ($k_d = 8\%$). Assume a 40 percent marginal tax rate. Using these figures, the weighted cost of capital being raised to finance next year's capital budget is calculated as

$$
k_a = 0.75 \times 12.0 + 0.25 \times 8.0 \times (1 - 0.40)
$$
$$
= 10.2\%
$$

Determining the Optimal Capital Budget and the Marginal Cost of Capital

In the previous section the computation of the weighted cost of capital was based on the assumption that the firm would only get equity funds from internal sources and that all debt could be acquired at an 8 percent pretax cost. This procedure for computing the weighted cost of capital must be modified if the firm anticipates selling new common stock (having a higher component cost) or issuing additional increments of debt securities at successively higher costs to finance its capital budget.

To illustrate, suppose that the Major Foods Corporation is developing its capital expenditure plans for the coming year. The company's schedule of

---

[16] If the target capital structure contains preferred stock, a preferred stock term is added to Equation 17.17. In this case Equation 17.17 becomes

$$
k_a = \left(\frac{E}{E+D+P} \right)(k_e) + \left(\frac{D}{E+D+P} \right)(k_i) + \left(\frac{P}{E+D+P} \right)(k_p)
$$

where P is the amount of preferred stock in the target capital structure and k_p is the component cost of preferred stock.

Project	Amount (million $)	Internal rate of return (%)
A	$ 4.0	22
B	8.0	20
C	6.0	18
D	16.0	16
E	18.0	14
F	10.0	10

Table 17.6
Schedule of Capital Expenditures: Major Foods Corporation

potentially acceptable capital expenditure projects (defined by management as projects having an internal rate of return greater than or equal to 10 percent) for next year is shown in Table 17.6. These projects are all closely related to the company's present business and have the same degree of risk as its existing assets.

The firm's current capital structure (as well as its target capital structure) consists of 25 percent long-term debt and 75 percent common equity measured on the basis of the current market value of debt and equity in the capital structure. The company can raise up to $10 million in long-term debt at a pretax cost of 9 percent; debt amounts exceeding this $10 million will cost 11 percent. The company's marginal tax rate is 40 percent.

Major Foods expects to generate $30 million of retained earnings next year. Next year's dividend rate (D_1) is $2.12 per share. The firm's common stock is presently selling at $29 per share, and new common stock can be sold to net the firm $27.50 per share.[17]

Over the past several years Major Foods' earnings and dividends have grown at an average of 6 percent per year, and this growth rate is expected to continue for the foreseeable future. The company's dividend payout ratio has been, and is expected to remain, more or less constant.

Given this information, Major Foods' weighted cost of capital can be calculated and the company's optimal capital budget for the coming year can be determined by means of the following steps:[18]

Step 1 Calculate the cost of capital for each individual component—the cost of debt and the cost of equity:

Cost of debt:

$k_i = k_d(1 - t) = 9.0 \times 0.6 = 5.4\%$ for the first $10 million

$k_i = k_d(1 - t) = 11.0 \times 0.6 = 6.6\%$ for debt exceeding $10 million

---

[17] The net proceeds per share depend on the number of shares sold. As a very general rule, underwriters are reluctant to sell new shares in an amount that exceeds 10–15 percent of a company's existing shares.

[18] For purposes of simplicity, this example does not consider depreciation. No long-term debt is retired, and working capital is assumed to remain unchanged from this year to the next. The cost of funds obtained from depreciation, the sale of assets, and so on is equal to the weighted cost of capital, however, so it does not influence these computations.

Cost of equity:

Internal (retained earnings):

$$k_e = \frac{2.12}{29} + 0.06 = 0.133, \text{ or } 13.3\%$$

External (new common stock):

$$k'_e = \frac{2.12}{27.50} + 0.06 = 0.137, \text{ or } 13.7\%$$

Step 2 Compute the weighted cost of capital.

For the first $40 million of capital raised ($10 million in debt and $30 million in retained earnings):

$$k_a = 0.25 \times 5.4 + 0.75 \times 13.3 = 11.3\%$$

For capital amounts exceeding $40 million:

$$k_a = 0.25 \times 6.6 + 0.75 \times 13.7 = 11.9\%$$

Any capital raised in excess of the first $40 million will have a higher k_a than the first $40 million because the second package will consist of higher cost debt and external equity.

This cost of capital figure is a *marginal cost of capital* because it represents the cost of the *next* capital raised after the first $40 million.

Step 3 The *optimal capital budget* can be determined by comparing the expected project returns to the company's marginal cost of capital. This is accomplished by first plotting the returns expected from the proposed capital expenditure projects against the cumulative funds required. This gives the investment opportunity curve. Next, the previously calculated k_a for the two capital packages are combined to determine the company's marginal cost of capital curve. The optimal capital budget is indicated by the point at which the investment opportunities curve and the marginal cost of capital curve intersect, as shown in Figure 17.4.

Specifically, the Major Foods Corporation's optimal capital budget totals $52 million and includes projects $A, B. C. D,$ and $E.$ Project F is excluded because its return is expected to be 10 percent and the necessary funds cost 11.9 percent. Acceptance of project F would result in a decrease in the firm's value. In principle, the optimal capital budget maximizes the value of the firm.

Summary

- A *capital expenditure* is defined as a current outlay of funds that is expected to provide a flow of future cash benefits.

- To ensure that all relevant factors are considered, the capital expenditure decision process should consist of the following steps: generating

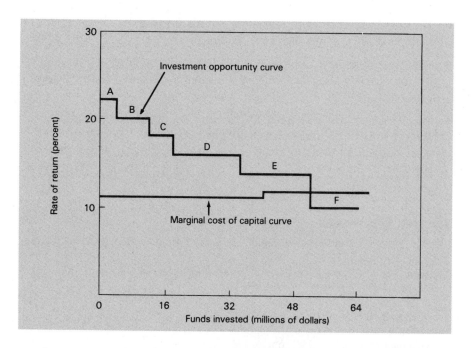

Figure 17.4
Determining the Optimal Capital Budget

alternative investment proposals, estimating cash flows, evaluating and choosing the projects to undertake, and reviewing the projects after implementation.

■ The *internal rate of return* (*IRR*) is defined as the discount rate that equates the present value of the net cash flows from the project with the net investment. An investment project should be accepted (rejected) if its internal rate of return is greater than or equal to (less than) the firm's required rate of return (that is, cost of capital).

■ The *net present value* (*NPV*) of an investment is defined as the present value of the net cash flows from the project, discounted at the firm's required rate of return (that is, cost of capital), minus the project's net investment. An investment project should be accepted (rejected) if its net present value is greater than or equal to (less than) zero.

■ The *profitability index* (*PI*) of an investment is defined as the ratio of the present value of future net cash flows over the life of a project to the net investment. An investment project should be accepted (rejected) if the profitability index is greater than or equal to (less than) 1.0.

■ *Capital rationing* is the process of limiting the number of capital expenditure projects because of insufficient funds to finance all projects that otherwise meet the firm's criteria for acceptability, or because of a lack of sufficient managerial resources to undertake all otherwise acceptable projects.

■ The *cost of capital* is defined as the cost of funds that are supplied to the firm. It is influenced by the riskiness of the firm, both in terms of its capital structure and its investment strategy.

- The aftertax cost of debt (issued at par) is equal to the coupon rate multiplied by 1 minus the firm's marginal tax rate.

- The cost of equity can be estimated using a number of different approaches, including the dividend valuation model and the capital asset pricing model.

- The weighted cost of capital is calculated by weighting the costs of specific sources of funds, such as debt and equity, by the proportions of each of the capital components in the firm's long-range target capital structure.

Selected References

Bierman, Harold, Jr., and Seymour Smidt. *The Capital Budgeting Decision*, 4th ed. New York: Macmillan, 1975.

Copeland, Thomas E., and J. Fred Weston. *Financial Theory and Corporate Policy*, 3d ed. Reading, Mass.: Addison-Wesley, 1988.

Gordon, Myron, and Paul J. Halpern, "Cost of Capital for a Division of a Firm." *Journal of Finance* 29 (Sept. 1974), pp. 1153–64.

Hirshleifer, J. "On the Theory of the Optimal Investment Decision." *Journal of Political Economy* 66 (August 1958), pp. 95–103.

Lorie, James H., and Leonard J. Savage. "Three Problems in Rationing Capital." *Journal of Business* 23 (October 1955), pp. 229–239.

Moyer, R. Charles, James R. McGuigan, and William J. Kretlow. *Contemporary Financial Management*, 3d rev. ed. St. Paul: West, 1988.

Solomon, Ezra. *The Theory of Financial Management*. New York: Columbia University Press, 1963.

Van Horne, James. *Financial Management and Policy*, 7th ed. Englewood Cliffs, N.J.: Prentice-Hall, 1986.

Discussion Questions

1. Define the following terms:
   a. Capital expenditure
   b. Capital budgeting
   c. Cost of capital
   d. Capital rationing
   e. Net present value
   f. Internal rate of return
   g. Profitability index

2. Define and give examples of the following types of investment projects:
   a. Mutually exclusive projects
   b. Independent projects
   c. Contingent projects

3. Describe the steps in the capital expenditure selection process.

4. What are the primary types of capital investment projects?

5. Cash flows of an investment project should be measured on an incremental, after-tax

basis and should consider all the indirect effects of the project. Explain what this involves.

6. When dealing with mutually exclusive investment projects, the internal rate of return and net present value decision criteria sometimes give conflicting decisions (see Table 17.1). Which decision criterion is considered more appropriate under these conditions and why?

7. Explain why the costs of internal and external equity capital differ.

8. Explain how shareholder wealth and the cost of equity capital are related in the context of the dividend capitalization model.

9. Explain how the weighted cost of capital is calculated and how it is used in making capital investment decisions.

10. Discuss the meaning of an *optimal* capital budget.

11. Since depreciation is a noncash expense, why is it considered when estimating a project's net cash flows?

12. Why is it generally incorrect to consider interest charges when computing a project's net cash flows?

13. Explain how the profitability index can be used to determine which investment projects the firm should accept when it is subject to a one-period constraint on the amount of funds available for investment.

14. Distinguish between systematic and unsystematic risk. Under what conditions are investors likely to ignore the unsystematic risk characteristics of a security?

15. The stock of Intec Corporation has a beta, b, value estimated to be 1.20. How would one interpret this value?

Problems

1. A firm has the opportunity to invest in a project having an initial outlay of $20,000. Net cash inflows (before depreciation and taxes) are expected to be $5,000 per year for five years. The firm uses the straight-line depreciation method with a zero salvage value and has a (marginal) income-tax rate of 40 percent. The firm's cost of capital is 12 percent.

   a. Compute the following quantities:
      (i)   Internal rate of return
      (ii) Net present value
      (iii) Profitability index

   b. Should the firm accept or reject the project?

2. A machine that costs $12,000 is expected to operate for ten years. The estimated salvage value at the end of ten years is $0. The machine is expected to save the company $2,331 per year before taxes and depreciation. The company depreciates its assets on a straight-line basis and has a marginal tax rate of 40 percent. The firm's cost of capital is 14 percent. Based on the internal-rate-of-return criterion, should this machine be purchased?

3. A company is planning to invest $75,000 (before tax) in a personnel training program. The $75,000 outlay will be charged off as an expense by the firm this year (Year 0). The returns estimated from the program in the form of greater productivity

and a reduction in employee turnover, are estimated as follows (on an after-tax basis):

Years 1–10: $7,500 per year

Years 11–20: $22,500 per year

The company has estimated its cost of capital to be 15 percent. Assume that the entire $75,000 is paid at time zero (the beginning of the project). The marginal tax rate for the firm is 40 percent.

Based on the net-present-value criterion, should the firm undertake the training program?

4. Alliance Manufacturing Company is considering the purchase of a new, automated drill press to replace an older one. The machine now in operation has a book value of zero and a salvage value of zero. However, it is in good working condition with an expected life of ten additional years. The new drill press is more efficient than the existing one and, if installed, will provide an estimated cost savings (in labor, materials, and maintenance) of $6,000 per year. The new machine costs $25,000 delivered and installed. It has an estimated useful life of ten years, and a salvage value of $1,000 at the end of this period. The firm's cost of capital is 14 percent and its marginal income tax rate is 40 percent. The firm uses the straight-line depreciation method.

   a. What is the net cash flow in year zero (that is, initial outlay)?
   b. What are the net cash flows after taxes in each of the next ten years?
   c. What is the net present value of the investment?
   d. Should Alliance replace its existing drill press?

5. Sam's Cleaners is considering opening a new store. The store will be owned by Sam and will cost $200,000 to build. It will be located on a piece of land that will be leased at a rate of $2,000 per year, payable at the end of each year. For planning purposes, the store is expected to have a maximum 20-year life. Cleaning equipment for the new store will cost an additional $40,000 and have an economic life of 20 years. The equipment will be depreciated on a straight-line basis to an estimated salvage value of $0 at the end of 20 years. The building will be depreciated on a straight-line basis to an estimated salvage value of $40,000.

   Operating revenues are expected to be $60,000 per year during the first 10 years. These revenues are expected to equal $100,000 per year for years 11–20. Cash operating costs, exclusive of lease payments, are expected to be $20,000 per year during the first 10 years of operation and to increase to $26,000 per year for years 11–20. The firm's marginal tax rate is 40 percent.

   a. Compute the net investment for the new cleaning store.
   b. Compute the annual net cash flows for the new cleaning store.
   c. Compute the project's net present value assuming a 12-percent cost of capital (required rate of return).
   d. Should Sam's Cleaners open the new store?

6. The Pittsburgh Condors, a recent expansion basketball team, has been offered the opportunity to purchase the contract of an aging superstar basketball player from another team. The general manager of the Condors wants to analyze the offer as a capital-budgeting problem. The Condors would have to pay the other team $800,000 to obtain the superstar. Being somewhat old, the basketball player is expected to be able to play for only four more years. The general manager figures that attendance, and hence revenues, would increase substantially if the Condors obtain the superstar. He estimates that *incremental* returns (additional ticket revenues less the superstar's

salary) would be as follows over the four-year period:

Year	Incremental Returns
1	$450,000
2	350,000
3	275,000
4	200,000

The general manager has been told by the owners of the team that any capital expenditures must yield at least 12 pecent after taxes. The firm's (marginal) income tax rate is 40 percent. Furthermore, a check of the tax regulations indicates that the team can depreciate the $800,000 initial expenditure over the four-year period.

a. Determine the following measures of the desirability of this investment:

(i) Internal rate of return
(ii) Net present value
(iii) Profitability index

b. Should the Condors sign the superstar?

7. An acre planted with walnut tress is estimated to be worth $15,000 in 25 years. If you want to realize a 12 percent rate of return on your investment, how much can you afford to invest per acre? (Ignore all taxes and assume that annual cash outlays to maintain your stand of walnut trees are nil.)

8. Fill in the missing items:

	NINV	NPV	PI
a.	$ 500,000	$ 200,000	_____
b.	$1,000,000	_____	1.50
c.	_____	$ 100,000	1.40

9. The Audio Warehouse Company, a wholesale distributor of stereo equipment, has decided to purchase a small computer system to automate the accounting department. Two computer companies are bidding for the order—each requiring an initial investment of $7,500 with an expected life of five years and a zero salvage value at the end of this period. One of the computers uses more advanced technology and is expected to be more efficient than the other computer. However, the more advanced computer has not been fully tested in an operational setting and, consequently, the estimated annual savings are more uncertain. The probability distributions of the estimated cost savings for each computer are given below. The firm uses the risk-adjusted discount rate approach in evaluating investment projects and has assigned a risk premium of 5 percent to the computer whose estimated savings are more uncertain. Audio Warehouse's cost of capital is 9 percent and its marginal income tax rate is 40 percent. The firm uses the straight-line depreciation method.

| Computer A | | Computer B | |
Annual Savings	Probability	Annual Savings	Probability
$2,000	.1	$0	.2
2,500	.4	3,000	.3
3,000	.4	4,000	.3
3,500	.1	5,000	.2

a. What are the expected annual savings for each computer?

b. What are the expected annual net cash flows after taxes for each computer?

c. Calculate the standard deviation of the annual savings for each computer. Based on the standard deviation as a measure of risk, which computer has more uncertain annual savings?

d. What is the net present value of each investment when evaluated at its appropriate risk-adjusted discount rate?

e. Which computer (*A* or *B*) would you recommend that Audio Warehouse purchase?

10. Panhandle Industries, Inc. currently pays an annual common stock dividend of $2.20 per share. The company's dividend has grown steadily over the past ten years at 8 percent per year; this growth trend is expected to continue for the foreseeable future. The company's present dividend payout ratio, also expected to continue, is 40 percent. In addition, the stock presently sells at eight times current earnings (that is, its "multiple" is 8).

Calculate the company's cost of equity capital using the dividend capitalization model approach.

11. Panhandle Industries, Inc. (see Problem 10) stock has a beta, *b*, of 1.15 as computed by a leading investment service. The present risk-free rate is 7 percent, and the expected return on the stock market is 13 percent. Compute the company's cost of equity capital using the capital asset pricing model. How does this value compare with the one determined in Problem 10 using the dividend capitalization model?

12. The Gordon Company currently pays an annual common stock dividend of $4.00 per share. Its dividend payments have been growing at a steady rate of 6 percent per year and this rate of growth is expected to continue for the forseeable future. Gordon's common stock is currently selling for $65.25 per share. The company can sell additional shares of common stock after flotation costs at a net price of $60.50 per share.

Based on the dividend capitalization model, determine the cost of

a. Internal equity (retained earnings)

b. External equity (new common stock)

13. Baker Manufacturing Company has a beta, *b*, estimated at 1.10. The risk-free rate is 6 percent and the expected market return is 12 percent. Compute the company's cost of equity capital.

14. The Williams Company has a present capital structure (that it considers optimal) consisting of 30 percent long-term debt and 70 percent common equity. The company plans to finance next year's capital budget with additional long-term debt and retained earnings. New debt can be issued at a coupon interest rate of 10 percent. The cost of retained earnings (internal equity) is estimated at 15 percent. The company's marginal tax rate is 40 percent.

Calculate the company's weighted cost of capital for the coming year.

15. Pacific Intermountain Utilities Company has a present capital structure (that the company feels is optimal) of 50 percent long-term debt, 10 percent preferred stock, and 40 percent common equity. For the coming year, the company has determined that its optimal capital budget can be externally financed with $70 million of 10 percent first-mortgage bonds sold at par and $14 million of preferred stock costing the company 11 percent. The remainder of the capital budget will be financed with retained earnings. The company's common stock is presently selling at $25 a share, and next year's common dividend D_1 is expected to be $2 a share. The company has 25 million common shares outstanding. Next year's net income available to common stock (including net income from next year's capital budget) is expected to be $106 million. The company's past annual growth rate in dividends and earnings has been 6 percent. However, a 5 percent annual growth in earnings and dividends is expected for the foreseeable future. The company's marginal tax rate is 40 percent.

Calculate the company's weighted cost of capital for the coming year. (*Hint: See footnote 16.*)

16. The Jamison Company has the following capital expenditure projects available for possible investment next year:

Project	Initial Investment	Internal Rate of Return
A	$2,000,000	18%
B	1,200,000	9
C	1,400,000	16
D	1,800,000	14
E	800,000	11
F	1,600,000	12
G	1,200,000	15

The company has developed the following schedule for the cost of various increments of capital needed to finance its capital budget for next year:

Amount of Capital Raised	Cost of Capital
Up to $4,000,000	9.5%
$4,000,000–$7,500,000	10.5
Over $7,500,000	11.5

a. Plot Jamison's investment opportunity curve.
b. On the same graph from part (a), plot the company's marginal cost of capital curve.
c. Determine the optimal capital budget for the company.

The Athens Corporation, a large manufacturer of mufflers, tail pipes, and shock absorbers, is presently carrying out its financial planning for next year. In about two weeks, at the next meeting of the firm's board of directors, Frank Masters, vice-president of finance, is scheduled to present his recommendations for next year's overall financial plan. He has asked Don James, Manager of Financial Planning, to gather the necessary information and perform the calculations for the financial plan.

Case Problem
Capital
Budgeting

The company's divisional staffs, together with corporate finance department personnel, have analyzed several proposed capital expenditure projects. The following is a summary schedule of acceptable projects (defined by the company as projects having internal rates of return greater than 8 percent):

Project	Investment Amount (million $)	Internal Rate of Return (%)
A	$10.0	24
B	20.0	20
C	30.0	18
D	35.0	16
E	40.0	14
F	40.0	12
G	40.0	10
H	20.0	9

All projects are expected to have one year of negative cash flow followed by positive cash flows over their remaining years. In addition, next year's projects involve modifications and expansion of the company's existing facilities and products. As a result these projects are considered to have approximately the same degree of risk as the company's existing assets.

Mr. James feels that the preceding summary schedule and detailed supporting documents give him the necessary information about the possible capital expenditure projects for next year. He can now direct his attention to obtaining the data necessary to determine the cost of the capital required to finance next year's proposed projects.

The company's investment bankers indicated to Mr. Masters in a recent meeting that they feel the company could issue up to $50 million of 10 percent first-mortgage bonds at par next year. The investment bankers also feel that any additional debt would have to be subordinated debentures with a coupon of 11 percent, also to be sold at par. The investment bankers rendered their opinion after Mr. Masters gave an approximate estimate of the size of next year's capital budget and after he estimated that approximately $100 million of retained earnings would be available next year.

Both the company's financial management and the investment bankers consider the present capital structure of the company, shown below, to be optimal (assume that book value and market value are equal):

Debt	$ 400,000,000
Stockholders' equity	
Common stock	150,000,000
Retained earnings	450,000,000
	$1,000,000,000

Mr. James has assembled additional information, as follows:

- Athens' common stock is presently selling at $100 a share.
- The investment bankers have also indicated that an additional $75 million in new common stock could be issued at a total flotation cost of 10 percent to net the company $90 a share.
- The company's present annual dividend is $6.80 a share; however, Mr. Masters feels fairly certain that the board will increase it to $7.20 a share next year.

- The company's earnings and dividends have grown at 6 percent per annum over the past 12 years. Growth has been fairly steady, and this rate is expected to continue for the foreseeable future.
- The company's marginal tax rate is 40 percent.

Questions

Using the information provided, answer the following questions. (*Note:* Disregard depreciation in this case.)

1. Calculate the marginal cost of capital for the various intervals or packages of capital the company can raise next year. Plot the marginal cost of capital curve.
2. Using the marginal cost of capital curve from Question 1 and plotting the investment opportunities curve, determine the company's optimal capital budget for next year.
3. What factors do you feel might cause Mr. Masters to recommend a different capital budget than the one obtained in Question 2?

Cost-Benefit Analysis and Public Sector Management 18

Up to this point, the emphasis of the book has been on problems of decision making and resource allocation in the private sector. The tools of analysis developed in Part II as well as the principles of normative microeconomic theory discussed in Parts III through VI may also be of use in formulating many of the problems and in guiding the managerial decision making in public and not-for-profit agencies and enterprises. It is important to recognize at the outset, however, that public and not-for-profit institutions may pursue a set of normative goals rather than concentrate solely on the efficiency objective that is generally assumed to be predominant in the private sector. Other public sector goals include achieving an equitable distribution of income, maintaining economic stability and full employment, controlling the balance of payments, and satisfying the demands of the primary contributors to a not-for-profit organization. Within the context of these normative goals, the objective of allocating resources most efficiently is very important in all organizations.

Introduction

The range of problems addressed by the public and not-for-profit sectors include those relating to the provision of public and private education, transportation services, recreational facilities, national defense, and health-care services for the poor, the military, and the aged. In addition, public and not-for-profit insitutions are actively involved in managing hospitals, natural resources, income maintenance and income transfer programs, research support programs, power production, police and fire protection, and many others.[1] These and similar programs have many problems common to the private sector that require nearly identical solutions. The problems run the gamut from financing (presumably as cheaply as possible), to marketing (for example, selling new coins at the mint, selling rapid transit to the commuting public, or selling individuals on the value of seatbelts), to inventory management, facility location analysis, construction management, optimal maintenance service, capital

---

[1] Quasi-public enterprises such as COMSAT (Communications Satellite Corporation) and FNMA (Federal National Mortgage Association) are probably best evaluated in the framework of regulated private monopolies.

Glossary of New Terms

Externalities
Impacts that occur whenever a third party receives benefits or bears costs arising from an economic transaction in which he or she is not a direct participant. An example would be the effects of industrial pollution on area residents.

Cost-benefit analysis
An analytical tool designed to assist public and private decision makers in their resource-allocation decisions. It requires the measurement of all benefits and costs arising from a particular project or program.

Social discount rate
The discount rate to be used when evaluating benefits and costs from public sector investments.

Benefit-cost ratio
The ratio of the present value of the benefits from a project or program (discounted at the social discount rate) to the present value of the costs (similarly discounted).

(Cont'd on next page)

Glossary of New Terms (*Cont'd*)

Cost-effectiveness analysis
An analytical tool designed to assist public decision makers in their resource-allocation decisions when benefits cannot be easily measured in dollar terms but costs can be monetarily quantified.

replacement, and hundreds of similar day-to-day decisions. In most of these cases the efficiency objective would seem quite important; hence, normative economic theory has much to contribute.[2]

Although managers in various sectors of the economy face substantially similar economic decisions, some significant differences do exist which require specific attention. This chapter focuses first on the scope and rationale for public involvement (either through government agencies or not-for-profit institutions) in the economy. Then the techniques of cost-benefit and cost-effectiveness analysis are presented as aids in the public resource allocation decision process.

Public Involvement in the Economy: A Rationale

The traditional rationale for public involvement in the economy is the case of private market failure to allocate resources efficiently or to provide consumers with particular goods and services effectively. In order to examine the market failure rationale in more detail, it is useful to distinguish between *pure private goods* and *pure public goods*.

Private Goods Defined

Pure private goods (and services) possess the following characteristics which assure that the private sector will perform reasonably well in providing these goods (and services).

Divisibility and Excludability. First, pure private goods are *divisible* and *excludable*. Divisibility implies that the good or service may be divided into finite units for consumption. Nearly all consumer products—dishwashers, pencils, desks, haircuts—are divisible. Excludability implies that both buyers and sellers may *easily* exclude nonbuyers from receiving the benefits of consumption. Property-rights law in this country, for example, is designed to provide excludability for many private goods and services.

Externalities. Recall from Chapter 14 that societal resources are efficiently allocated in a market system when the price of some commodity (that is, the market measure of relative private benefits or values received by consumers for a good or service) is just equal to the marginal cost (that is, the measure of relative sacrifice incurred by a firm in producing and distributing a commodity) of providing it. This is true, however, only if there is an *absence of significant externalities* (side effects) of production or consumption associated with the pure private good in question. *Externalities* occur when a third party is

---

[2] Our emphasis remains on normative decision making, fully recognizing that public managers (just as private managers) frequently deviate from the normative standard to pursue objectives more nearly consistent with the maximization of their personal utility.

substantially affected by an economic transaction in which he or she does not directly participate. Externalities may be either detrimental or beneficial to the third party. For instance, a paper mill's decision to dump effluent upstream from a fishery has detrimental side effects on the fishery. Similarly, your neighbor's decision to landscape and refurbish the exterior of his house may confer benefits to you because the neighborhood is now more attractive, making your home more valuable. Many goods that are produced and sold in private markets do not carry with them significant externality impacts; however, when substantial side effects *do* exist, there is no guarantee that the private-market solution will be an efficient one. Appendix 19A discusses the notion of economic externalities and the resulting divergence between private and social costs and benefits in much greater detail. The Appendix also specifically considers the alternatives open to and problems associated with government attempts at correcting private market failure to deal with externalities.

Monopoly Power. Pure private goods must also be produced under conditions characterized by an *absence of monopoly power* if resources are to be most efficiently allocated. When economies of large-scale production and distribution confer a cost advantage on firms that are very large relative to the total market, a few highly efficient firms, each possessing a degree of market power, are likely to emerge. The result is that resources may be inefficiently allocated since prices are not set at a level equal to marginal costs but rather at a level where marginal cost equals marginal revenue. All other things being equal, this leads to higher prices and lower consumption than the efficiency criteria directs. Antitrust action, as discussed in Chapter 19, may be useful in controlling monopoly power, which is based on advantages other than those accruing from technical or administrative efficiency. Other controllable sources of monopoly power include artificial entry barriers, financial advantages of size, and the use of predatory practices. In cases where true resource economies of scale exist, attempting to maintain the conditions of competition by limiting the size of individual firms is quite likely to be self-defeating *and* inefficient.

Information Availability. A final characteristic of pure private goods is that consumers have *access to complete, low-cost information* concerning the quality of competing products. If buyers do not have this information available (or if it is prohibitively expensive to procure), they are likely to pay too much for low-quality products, thereby subsidizing inefficient producers. Federal (primarily through the Federal Trade Commission) as well as state and local truth-in-advertising laws, together with the actions of groups such as Consumers Union and the Better Business Bureaus, seek to ensure that accurate and inexpensive consumer information is furnished for a wide range of goods and services.

In summary, when a good or service possesses the characteristics of divisibility and excludability, when no significant externalities of production or consumption are associated with it, when it is produced under nonmonopoly conditions, and when consumers have access to low-cost product information, the private market system is likely to provide efficiently for these goods and services.

Public Goods Defined

Many products are produced and sold under conditions that fall somewhat short of the ideal of pure private goods defined above. The extreme opposite of pure private goods is *pure public goods*. Roland McKean points out that the distinctive feature of public goods

> ... is that they can be consumed by more than one person at the same time at no extra expense; and it actually costs something to exclude potential consumers.... The feature that makes these goods different is that certain light, sound, scent, health, domestic security and national security "emissions" cover an area rather than a spot the size of a human body.[3]

In contrast to pure private goods, public goods are *indivisible* and *imperfectly excludable*. Imperfect excludability arises because in many instances A's consumption of Public Good X leads to no reduction in what remains for consumption by B, C, and D (that is, it shares the characteristic of nonexhaustive consumption). Examples of pure public goods include radio and television programs (costing the same to produce and transmit in an area whether one or a thousand people listen to or watch them), the services of a lighthouse beacon, foreign aid, and national defense. These goods all share the characteristic that once they are provided for anyone, others may reap the benefits at no cost, either to them or to other consumers. It is actually prohibitively expensive to exclude some individuals from the benefits of consumption.

Other Characteristics of Public Goods

In addition to (and partly because of) being indivisible and imperfectly excludable, public goods share some or all of three other characteristics. First, they may have *significant, unavoidable externalities* associated with their production or consumption. These arise because the cost of excluding potential beneficiaries (for example, charging admission or collecting tolls) or the cost of preventing damage to those not willing to sustain it is so great that exclusion will be uneconomical. If the good or service is provided, externalities will also be necessarily generated.

In addition to externality effects, public goods are often *produced under conditions of decreasing costs of production*. When fixed costs are quite large in relation to total costs, significant economies of scale are likely over the range in which the enterprise operates. When such economies do exist, it means that a small increase in output will cause unit cost to fall. If unit or average cost

---

[3] Roland McKean, *Public Spending* (New York: McGraw-Hill, 1968), p. 68. See also Paul A. Samuelson, "The Pure Theory of Public Expenditure," *Review of Economics and Statistics* (November 1954).

declines with an increase in output, the marginal cost (that is, the additional cost of producing one more unit) must be less than the unit cost.[4] For the allocation to be efficient, output should be increased to the point where price equals marginal cost. But since marginal cost is less than unit cost, at the *efficient* level of output, price must also be less than unit cost so the firm would operate at a loss. Depending on the magnitude of the disparity between the *efficient* level of output and the profit-maximizing level of output (if one exists) for a profit-maximizing monopolist (who sets prices where $MC = MR$, not where $P = MC$), the output may be provided in the public sector or its production in the private sector may be regulated. Where it is impossible to earn a profit at any level of production (perhaps because of the indivisible and nonexcludable characteristics of the good or service), the only alternative is public supply.

An extreme example of this sort of situation is the production of bridge crossings. Assuming that actual depreciation of the bridge is a function of time rather than the number of crossings, and that the demand for bridge use is such that excessive crowding never occurs (that is, no negative externalities of consumption exist), it can be shown that the efficient price for bridge crossings is zero. Any price that discourages even one crossing is inefficient since an additional free crossing can make someone better off without hurting others. This is another way of saying that the opportunity cost of an additional crossing is zero. Since the marginal cost is equal to zero, price should also be set at zero. This example is illustrative of many investments where there is a high initial fixed cost and very low relative variable costs—such as roads, dams, harbors, railroads, airports, and parks. Although it may be possible for a monopolist to set a price that will result in a profit, that price is necessarily not an efficient one since it is at a level above, rather than equal to, marginal cost. In these cases the market system does not provide for an efficient use of resources, and public intervention, either direct or regulatory, may be required.

Finally, *accurate* and *inexpensive market information* about the supply and demand conditions for a particular good or service *may not exist* because consumers have no market mechanism to express their preferences adequately. Such a situation generally arises because of the indivisibility and inexcludability characteristics of public goods. Because the benefits that accrue to any one individual consumer of a public good are typically quite small in relation to the costs of production, it is necessary to aggregate the demand of many consumers so that the desired output may be estimated and produced efficiently. But consumers, in the absence of collective public action, are likely to understate their true preferences for public goods. A consumer pays 40¢ for a grapefruit because he or she knows the only way to obtain the benefits of grapefruit consumption is to buy one. The consumer will buy additional grapefruit up to the point where the satisfaction received from the last grapefruit purchased is

---

[4] If the average or unit cost of producing ten units is $2.00 each, and the marginal cost of producing unit #11 is $1.00, the average cost of producing eleven units must decline, since

$$\text{Average cost} = \frac{\text{Total cost}}{\text{Number of units}} = \frac{10 \times \$2 + 1 \times \$1}{11} = \$1.91$$

just enough to compensate for not buying an additional 40¢ worth of some other good, such as a mango or avocado. But grapefruit are not the same as mosquito-control programs, fireworks displays, or national defense. Rational consumers of these goods may understate their willingness to pay for public goods in the hope that others will subscribe to these public goods in sufficient numbers to provide the public benefits to the nonsubscribers, without rational consumers' having to pay an amount equivalent to the satisfaction they themselves will gain. This makes the estimation of true consumer demand for public goods a difficult and expensive task. The net impact of such collective reasoning is that less than an optimal supply of these public goods will be supplied in the absence of coercive activity.

Public Policy Choices

Most goods and services fit neither in the category of *pure* private goods nor *pure* public goods, yet many do possess a *degree* of "publicness," expressed in the characteristics listed for public goods. Examples of goods with some, but not exclusive, public characteristics include urban renewal, hospital facilities, parks, basic research programs, highways, immunization programs, police and fire services, education, and the judicial system. When a good or service possesses a degree of publicness, even if only in the form of side effects that have some impact on some people although they pay nothing to receive the benefits, then the private market allocation decision will generate inefficiencies.

Determining the appropriate form (if any) of public intervention in the economy requires that the reasons for private market failure be defined as clearly as possible. Public policy should differ significantly depending on the source of market imperfections: monopoly power, decreasing costs of production, externalities, product indivisibility and excludability, or unavailability of good, low-cost demand and supply information. When more than one of these market shortcomings exists, justifying, developing, and financing public programs becomes a complex, often politically muddied task. This may be illustrated with the case of public trash collection. The additional cost of collecting trash at one more house may be very small, but it is not zero. Public intervention in the supply of this service may be justified either because of the decreasing cost of additional collection or because this service provides significant general external benefits and hence might be undersupplied if left to the private market allocation process. Some communities provide this service via a regulated private supplier, whereas others provide it directly and pay for it out of general tax revenues. These two different approaches reflect different evaluations of the nature of the problem.

The foregoing discussion has provided one rationale for public involvement in the economy due to market failure. Programs to deal with this problem are designed primarily to improve the efficiency of societal resource allocation.

Although they are not discussed here, it should be recognized that many goods and services provided by the public and not-for-profit sectors are designed to meet objectives that are not efficiency oriented. These objectives include giving assistance to various groups—such as the poor, the sick, and the uneducated—redistributing income, stabilizing the growth of the economy, and providing for the national defense. However, when even one of these alternative objectives is the primary concern of a governmental program, the efficiency objective enters the picture. The government has an obligation, just as the private sector does, to pursue in the most efficient fashion any program it commits funds to. The techniques of cost-benefit and cost-effectiveness analysis can be useful to the public or not-for-profit enterprise administrator in the evaluation of programs.[5]

Cost-Benefit Analysis

The remainder of this chapter is devoted to some techniques of analysis that may be used to assist in public resource-allocation decisions. The primary analytical model examined is cost-benefit analysis, although cost-effectiveness studies are also discussed.

Cost-benefit analysis is the logical public sector counterpart to the capital-budgeting techniques discussed in Chapter 17. In this chapter the focus is on the additional problems that arise in attempting to allocate resources and make other economic decisions in the public sector. These include the measurement of benefits and costs, the determination of an appropriate discount rate, and the uses and limitations of the model. Finally, some examples of the use and abuse of cost-benefit analysis are presented. It should be noted that even though we have focused our attention on cost-benefit analysis in the public and not-for-profit sectors, the broad framework for analyzing a problem that is advocated by this technique is also of value in making private sector resource-allocation decisions.

Uses of Cost-Benefit Analysis

In general, *cost-benefit analysis* is a method for assessing the desirability of projects when it is necessary to take both a long and a wide view of the repercussions of a particular program expenditure or policy change.[6] As in the case of private sector capital budgeting, cost-benefit analysis is often used in cases where the economic consequences of a project or a policy change are likely to extend beyond one year in time. Unlike capital budgeting, however, cost-benefit analysis seeks to measure all economic impacts of the project; that is, side effects as well as direct effects.

The cost-benefit model of program evaluation is not new; the notion first emerged in France back in 1844. In this century, cost-benefit analysis was widely used in the evaluation of river and harbor projects as early as 1902. The 1936 Flood Control Act authorized federal assistance in developing flood-control

---

[5] For a more complete discussion of program objectives, see Leonard Merewitz and Stephen Sosnick, *The Budget's New Clothes* (Chicago: Markham, 1971), especially chap. 9.

[6] A. R. Prest and R. Turvey, "Cost-Benefit Analysis: A Survey," *Economic Journal* (December 1965), p. 683.

programs "if the benefits to whomsoever they may accrue are in excess of the estimated costs." By 1950 federal agency practice required that secondary or indirect benefits and costs, as well as direct impacts, be considered and that the intangible effects at least be enumerated.

Despite the rather long history of widespread use of cost-benefit analysis in the water-resources area, it has only been in the past twenty-five years or so that economists have sought to apply the principles of analysis to such diverse areas as rapid transit, highways, urban renewal, recreation, job training, health care, education, research and development, and defense.

Accept-Reject Decisions

Cost-benefit analysis may be used for a number of purposes, depending on the nature of the project, the constraints of public policy, and the requirements of the information user or decision maker. One use is to determine whether a specific expenditure is economically justifiable. For instance, one might examine a program designed to eradicate syphilis in light of the current costs of the disease, which could be averted by a specific expenditure of funds. Following the framework used by Klarman,[7] benefits (averted costs) may be divided into four categories:

1. Expenditures on medical care, including physician and nurse fees, drug costs, and hospital and equipment charges

2. Loss of gross earnings during the disease

3. Reduction in gross earnings after the disease because of decreased employment opportunities resulting from the social stigma attached to the illness

4. The pain and discomfort associated with having the disease

Suppose a particular program designed to aid syphilis eradication is proposed that requires a one-time outlay of $250 million (Table 18.1). Assume

Table 18.1
Net Benefit-Cost Analysis

End of Year (1)	Actual Dollar Benefit (Cost) (2)	Discount Factor at 15 Percent (3)	Discounted Benefits and Costs ($ million) (4) = (2) × (3)
0	($250,000,000)	1.000	($250.00)
1	150,000,000	.870	130.50
2	125,000,000	.756	94.50
3	100,000,000	.658	65.80
4	50,000,000	.572	28.60
5	25,000,000	.497	12.43
			Net benefits = $81.83

[7] H. E. Klarman, "Syphilis Control Programs" in *Measuring Benefits of Government Investments*, ed. Robert Dorfman (Washington, D.C.: Brookings Institution, 1965).

that the total benefits (averted disease costs) of this one-year program are expected to accrue for a period of five years. If one accepts, for the moment, that an appropriate discount rate is 15 percent for this project, the program may be evaluated in the present-value analysis framework developed in Chapter 17. Because the program has a positive calculated net discounted benefit, in this case $81.83 million, it is an acceptable project. (An equivalent acceptance criterion is to accept all projects with a ratio of discounted benefits to discounted costs that is greater than or equal to 1.0.)

Program-Level Analysis

In addition to being used to evaluate whether an entire program is economically justifiable, cost-benefit analysis may also be used to determine whether the size of an existing program should be increased (or reduced) and, if so, by what amount. This determination may be made using traditional marginal analysis as developed earlier in the text.

Returning again to the syphilis-control program, assume that, because of strong lobbying from antisyphilis groups, a number of expenditure levels beyond the originally proposed $250 million are being considered. Table 18.2 summarizes these proposed programs and their expected benefits. It can be seen that an analysis that looked in isolation at only one of these proposed program expenditure levels would have concluded that any of the program levels was worthwhile because each proposal generates positive expected net program benefits.

If these program levels are analyzed as a group, however, it becomes clear that there is a limit to the economically justifiable expenditure of funds for syphilis control. The required analysis is summarized in Table 18.3. A level of

Program Cost (millions of dollars)	Discounted Program Benefits (millions of dollars)	Net Program Benefits (millions of dollars)
$250	$331.83	$ 81.83
300	496.00	196.00
350	540.00	190.00
400	565.00	165.00

Table 18.2
Schedule of Program Benefits for Various Cost Levels

Program Cost (millions of dollars)	Marginal Cost (millions of dollars)	Discounted Marginal Benefit (millions of dollars)
$ 0	—	—
250	$250	$331.83
300	50	164.17
350	50	44.00
400	50	25.00

Table 18.3
Marginal Analysis of Benefits and Costs

expenditure of $300 million is best because it generates an additional (marginal) $164.17 million in benefits, but the marginal program cost (in comparison to the $250 million program level) is only $50 million. To increase the program to $350 million would be counterproductive, since only $44 million in benefits are generated for the additional $50 million outlay (marginal costs exceed marginal benefits).

An Overall Resource-Allocation Model

A final use for cost-benefit analysis is as the structure of a general theory of government resource allocation. As such, the results of cost-benefit studies would serve as a guide for resource-allocation decisions both within and between such major program areas as health, defense, education, and welfare. The objective of such a comprehensive system would be to maximize the discounted benefits minus the costs of all government programs. Although this is a conceptually appealing model, it suffers from a number of serious flaws. First, measuring techniques have not been sufficiently refined or standardized to permit meaningful comparisons between such diverse areas as cancer research and "Star Wars" defense system development. A second problem arises because cost-benefit analysis is primarily restricted to a consideration of the efficiency objective. As noted earlier in this chapter, significant problems arise when a program is designed to meet more than one objective, such as income distribution and balance of payments objectives.

For these and other reasons, cost-benefit analysis will be viewed in the narrower context of a decision technique that may help focus on the economic impacts of a proposed project. Its greatest uses are in comparing projects that are designed to achieve the same or similar objectives and in focusing on the optimal level of expenditures for a particular project. In this context, the results of a cost-benefit analysis become *one* important input both in the administrative and the political decision-making process.

It should be emphasized that the term *project* or *program* that we have used may be very generally applied, not only to major government outlays, but also to such undertakings as a proposed change in the law, new pricing guidelines, and so on. For example, a law requiring that airbags be installed on all cars requires a very small government outlay of funds but can be evaluated by comparing the costs of airbag installation and maintenance with the value of the expected reduction in deaths and injuries in automobile accidents.

Steps in Cost-Benefit Analysis

The general principles of cost-benefit analysis may be summarized by answering the following set of questions:[8]

1. What is the objective function to be maximized?

2. What are the constraints placed on the analysis?

---

[8] The next two sections of this chapter draw heavily on the review article by Prest and Turvey, "Cost-Benefit Analysis: A Survey," p. 683.

3. What costs and benefits are to be included and how may they be valued?

4. What investment evaluation criterion should be used?

5. What is the appropriate discount rate?

The decision-making process in cost-benefit analysis may be traced in the flowchart presentation of Figure 18.1. Program objectives are set by the public through their political representatives. Alternatives are enumerated, explored,

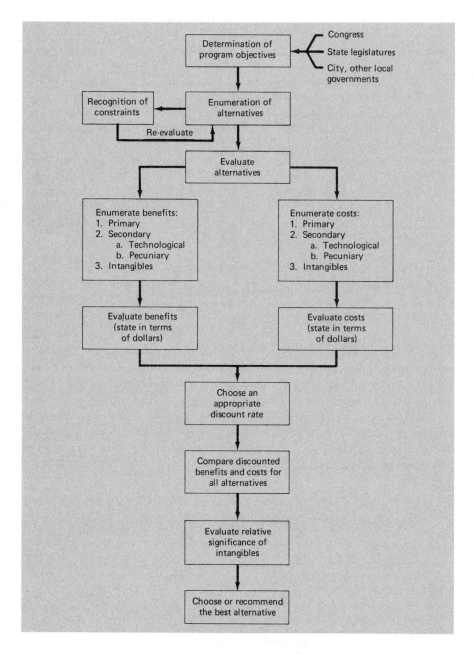

Figure 18.1
Schematic of the Cost-Benefit Analysis Process

and revised in light of constraints that may be operative in the system. These alternatives are then compared by enumerating and evaluating program benefits and costs in a present-value framework. Discounted benefits are compared with discounted costs, and intangibles are considered so a recommendation may be made about the merits of one or more alternative programs.

Objectives and Constraints in Cost-Benefit Analysis

Cost-benefit analysis is merely an application of resource-allocation theory. As such, we need to examine it in the light of several criteria that have been proposed by welfare economists for evaluating the desirability of alternative social and economic states. One such criterion is Pareto optimality:[9] A change is said to be desirable or consistent with Pareto optimality if at least one person is made better off (in his or her own judgment) and no one is made worse off (in their own judgments). Although this criterion seems to be relatively value free, as well as potentially verifiable,[10] it suffers from the severe weakness that few changes are likely to leave some individuals better off and *no one* worse off. In addition, it assumes that we know, a priori, how people affected by a program will evaluate its effects on them.

Cost-benefit analysis is tied to a weaker notion of social improvement, sometimes called the Kaldor-Hicks criterion, or merely the notion of a "potential" Pareto improvement. Under this criterion, a change (or an economic program) is desirable either (1) if it is consistent with the Pareto criterion or (2) if a potential Pareto improvement may be made by redistributing the gains such that all people in the community are at least as well off as they were before the change. This is the notion of cost-benefit analysis. A project is desirable if the benefits exceed the costs of the project because the project could be completed and the gainers *could* be made to compensate the losers. The fact that there is no compensation from gainers to losers is not a matter of direct consideration in cost-benefit analysis, but the income distributional impacts of a program are an extremely important side issue. All that cost-benefit analysis requires for a project to be acceptable is that total discounted societal benefits exceed the total discounted societal costs.

In addition to recognizing that the maximization of society's wealth is the primary objective function in cost-benefit analysis, it is also important to establish the constraints that may exist or be placed upon the achievement of this objective. According to Otto Eckstein's classification system,[11] these include the following:

1. *Physical constraints*—The type of program alternatives considered is ultimately limited by the currently available state of technology and by the

---

[9] A further discussion of the Pareto criterion is provided in W. J. Baumol, *Economic Theory and Operations Analysis*, 4th ed. (Englewood Cliffs, N.J.: Prentice-Hall, 1977), chap. 21.

[10] Merewitz and Sosnick, *The Budget's New Clothes*, pp. 78–80.

[11] Otto Eckstein, "A Survey of the Theory of Public Expenditure Criteria," in *Public Finances: Needs, Sources and Utilization*, ed. James M. Buchanan (Princeton, N.J. Princeton University Press, 1961).

production possibilities derived from the relationship between physical inputs and outputs. For example, it is not yet possible to prevent cancer; hence, major emphasis, beyond research programs, must be directed toward early detection and treatment.

2. *Legal constraints*—These may include domestic as well as international laws relating to property rights, the right of eminent domain, due process, constitutional limits on a particular agency's activities, and so on.

3. *Administrative constraints*—Effective programs require that individuals are available, or can be hired and trained, to carry out the program objectives. Even the best-conceived program is worthless unless individuals with the proper mix of technical and administrative skills are available.

4. *Distributional constraints*—Programs affect different groups in different ways because gainers are rarely the same as losers. When distributional impacts are of concern, the objective of cost-benefit analysis might be presented in terms of maximizing total benefits less total costs, subject to the constraint that benefits-less-costs for a particular group reach a prespecified level.

5. *Political constraints*—What may be optimal may not be feasible because of the slowness and inefficiency of the political process. Many times what is *best* is tempered by what is *possible*, given the existence of strong competing interest groups as well as an often cumbersome political mechanism.

6. *Financial or budget constraints*—More often than not, agencies work within the bounds of a predetermined budget. This requires that the objective function be altered to the suboptimizing form of maximizing benefits given a fixed budget. Virtually all programs have some absolute financial ceiling above which the program may not be expanded, in spite of the magnitude of social benefits.

7. *Social and religious constraints*—It is futile to tell Indians to eat sacred cattle to solve their nutritional problems. This is just one example of the social and religious constraints which may limit the range of feasible program alternatives.

All problems of public-resource allocation should be analyzed in a framework that recognizes the realities of constrained decision making. We must caution against carrying this realization too far, however, since it may unnecessarily narrow the range of considered alternatives. Somewhere between these two extremes is a compromise ground that provides for both *realistic* and *creative* program analysis.

Analysis and Valuation of Benefits and Costs

Cost-benefit analysis is quite similar to traditional private sector profit-and-loss accounting. In the private sector the firm is guided by the criterion that private revenues must be equal to or exceed private costs over the long run for the firm to survive. In contrast, in cost-benefit analysis the economist asks whether society as a whole will be better off by the adoption or nonadoption of a specific project or by the acceptance of one project to the exclusion of other alternatives. As Ezra Mishan points out:

> ... For the more precise concept of the revenue of the private concern, the economist substitutes the less precise, yet meaningful, concept of the social benefit. For the costs of the private concern, the economist will substitute the concept of opportunity cost... or social value foregone elsewhere in moving factors into a projected economic activity.[12]

Rather than considering profit of the firm as the objective in program evaluation, the economist seeks to maximize, or at least move toward a maximization of, the excess of social benefit over social cost. With this goal in mind, the context of benefit-cost analysis and valuation should have little impact on the outcome of the analysis. For example, if the city of Houston sought to build a rapid-transit system costing $1.2 billion, it makes no difference whether the city pays the entire cost or whether the city, the state of Texas, and the federal government split the costs. The entire social cost of the system needs to be considered, not merely local costs. Similarly, if Houston seeks to expand its port in the hope that shippers will come to Houston instead of Beaumont or Brownsville, the benefits of increased port traffic in Houston that has merely been diverted from other ports should *not* be counted in a cost-benefit analysis. Once again, the proper realm of concern is an increase in aggregate societal wealth, not aggregate local wealth. The consideration of net *local* impacts of a project instead of net *societal* impacts is one of the most frequent sins committed in the name of local resource-allocation decision making. In their consultant role, economists may be asked to perform such analyses in a strictly local context. When this is the case, it is important to spell out all the assumptions as well as the scope of benefit-cost considerations so that decision makers are fully aware of the limitations of the analyses.

Because of the multitude of areas in which the techniques of cost-benefit analysis have been applied, this section furnishes only a general introduction to the various classes of and problems associated with estimating benefits and costs in any particular case. A fuller appreciation of these issues may be gained when some individual studies are reviewed later in this chapter.[13]

The starting point for evaluating benefits and costs of a project is the observable market valuations. This assumes that the following conditions are met (or at least approximately met):

■ Consumers equate the value of the marginal unit of each commodity consumed to the value of foregone alternatives.

■ Producers operate so that each commodity is produced in a manner that sacrifices the lowest value of foregone alternatives.[14]

---

[12] Ezra J. Mishan, *Cost-Benefit Analysis: An Introduction* (New York: Praeger, 1971), pp. 7–8.

[13] See also several of the works cited at the end of this chapter, such as Mishan, *Cost-Benefit Analysis*, and the Prest and Turvey, "Cost-Benefit Analysis: A Survey," review article.

[14] Jesse Burkhead and Jerry Miner, *Public Expenditure* (Chicago: Aldine-Atherton, 1971), p. 208.

These are the conditions present in a competitive economy. With this assumption in mind, benefits may be measured by the market price of the outputs from a public program or by the price consumers would be *willing* to pay if they were charged. Similarly, costs are measured as the monetary expenditures necessary to undertake a project. When the assumed conditions of competition do not exist—for example, when externalities or economies of scale are present—then the estimate of benefits and costs must be modified to take account of this situation. Unfortunately for economists, many investments are made in the public sector precisely because the market mechanism has failed in one or more of the ways enumerated earlier in this chapter.

Direct Benefits

Benefits and costs may be categorized in a number of ways. *Primary* or *direct* benefits of a project "consist of the value of goods or services that result from conditions with the project as compared to conditions without the project."[15] The primary benefit of an irrigation project is the value of the additional crops produced on the irrigated land less the cost of seeds, labor, and equipment required to produce the crops. The primary benefits attributable to a college education might be considered as the increase in gross earnings of the graduate over what would have been earned without a college degree. In sum, the value of primary or direct benefits of a project may be taken as the total amount users pay (assuming pure competition) or would be willing to pay (total revenue if a charge is made, plus the consumer's surplus—discussed in Chapter 16—when pure competition does not prevail). Although this principle of evaluating direct benefits may be reasonably straightforward for irrigation projects, the estimation of direct benefits in the case of recreational resources (see Chapter 8) or the valuation of human life, as in health-care or accident prevention[16] programs, poses serious conceptual problems.

Direct Costs

Direct or *primary costs* are generally easier to measure than direct benefits. They include the capital costs necessary to undertake the project, operating and maintenance costs incurred over the life of the project, and personnel expenses. Once again the estimation of these costs is generally much easier for investments in physical assets—such as dams, canals, and so on—than it is for human resource investments. Remember that the costs being measured are opportunity costs, or the social value foregone elsewhere because factors of production have been moved into the projected area of activity. If a proposed project will draw 20

---

[15] Ibid., p. 225.

[16] For a summary of this problem, see Ezra J. Mishan, "Evaluation of Life and Limb: A Theoretical Approach," *Journal of Political Economy* (July–August 1971), pp. 687–705. See also the application on "The Valuation of Human Life" in this chapter.

Economic Analysis and Managerial Efficiency

THE ECONOMIC VALUATION OF HUMAN LIFE*

The economic valuation of human life has consequences for a broad range of management decisions in both the private and public sectors. For example, companies have to decide how much to spend to make products and the workplace safer. Government agencies have to decide the amount to spend on highway designs for reducing automobile deaths and the requirement for high-cost clean-air policies for reducing death rates due to pulmonary and other diseases. Since resources are limited both within a company and within society, a rational decision maker cannot argue that a company or society should spend "whatever it takes" to save a life. With limited resources, money spent in one area (e.g., investments in medical technology) cannot be used in other areas (e.g., investments in air traffic control facilities). In evaluating expenditures and policies to save human lives, the decision maker must make some determination, using either subjective or objective approaches, of the value of a life in society.

*Based on "How Much Is Your Life Worth?" *Fortune*, 3 March 1986, pp. 25–27.

Several different methods have been proposed over the years for calculating the value of a human life. One method, the human capital approach, determines the value of a human life as the discounted present value of a person's expected lifetime earnings. Obvious disadvantages of this approach are that it is somewhat one-dimensional (i.e., focusing only on earning power) and it implies that the lives of nonworkers have no economic value.

Another method, the "willingness to pay" approach, bases the life value on the payments one would require to accept a small risk of death or, alternatively, the payments one would be willing to make to reduce the risk of death. In implementing this approach, questionnaires have been used to determine the amount people would be willing to pay to participate in a program that would reduce the risk of death due to a given disease. In general, the results of these surveys are not totally reliable because the hypothetical nature of the questions makes it difficult for people to answer truthfully and accurately.

An alternative to questionnaires is to estimate life values from actual behavior. One study derived estimates based on people's willingness to pay extra for houses located in areas with lower levels of pollution. Another study estimated life values from data on the risk versus time tradeoffs associated with automobile seat belt usage (those

percent of the required labor from the ranks of the unemployed, the market cost (wage payments) of these workers' services will overstate the true social cost.[17] A similar conclusion applies for the use of idle land. With *no* alternative use, the opportunity cost of the use of this land is zero (for as long as no productive alternative uses exist), no matter what the government happens to actually pay

[17] A discussion of this issue is provided by Robert Haveman, "Evaluating Public Expenditures under Conditions of Unemployment," in *Public Expenditures and Policy Analysis*, ed. Robert Haveman and Julius Margolis (Chicago: Markham, 1970).

who buckle up and those who do not). The most credible estimates, based on actual behavior, have been developed using labor-market data on the relationship between job safety and pay. The primary advantages of these types of studies are that they are based on the judgments of large numbers of individual workers and that workers are generally found to be knowledgeable with respect to pay versus safety tradeoffs. A shortcoming of some of these labor-market studies is that they focus on workers who have chosen to engage in especially dangerous occupations. These individuals may not be representative of typical workers with respect to risk-reward tradeoffs.

Life-value estimates based on labor-market studies are in the $3 million range; however, a wide range of life-value estimates are used by different federal government agencies in evaluating programs. The Occupational Safety and Health Administration (OSHA) uses a range of $2 million to $5 million; the Environmental Protection Agency (EPA) uses a range of $1 million to $7.5 million; and the Federal Aviation Administration (FAA) uses $650,000. One can argue that these agencies protect different kinds of people, with different priorities and risk preferences, and that it would not be sensible to impose the same life-value estimate on all of them. Others argue, however, that these discrepancies in life-value estimates reflect a certain amount of

sloppiness in the analysis. According to Robert Bedell of the Office of Management and Budget (OMB), "Ultimately we will evolve a more uniform way of evaluating the benefits and risks and also come up with a much tighter range than now exists between agencies and even within agencies."

Since many government regulations imposed on the firm, as well as jury awards when the firm is a defendant in product-liability and workplace-safety suits, are based on the economic valuation of human life, management must have an understanding of how these estimates are determined.

Question

1. Union Carbide was faced with potentially billions of dollars in lawsuits as the result of the massive gas leak at its Bhopal, India chemical plant in 1984, which killed about 2,000 people. The relatives of the people who died wanted the case tried in the U.S. courts, where jury awards for "wrongful death" are often $1 million or more. Union Carbide wanted the trial to be held in India, where jury awards would be much less. Justify these differences in life valuations using the (a) human capital approach and (b) willingness to pay approach.

its owner in compensation. Such compensation to the owner only affects the *distribution* of the benefits derived from land usage.

Indirect Costs and Benefits

In addition to the primary impacts of a project, government investment invariably creates *secondary* or *indirect* effects. Secondary costs and benefits may be of two types: *real* or *technological* effects, and *pecuniary* effects. Real secondary benefits may include reductions in necessary outlays for other government projects, as for example when a glaucoma-detection campaign reduces the number of people who go blind, thereby reducing the need for job retraining as well as the need for future government disability transfer payments. Similarly, an irrigation dam may reduce flooding and create a recreational area. These secondary benefits should be counted in a cost-benefit study. The same argument applies in accounting for secondary costs. For example, the Wallisville Dam Project in Texas was alleged to cause in excess of $500,000 in damages annually to saltwater fishing because of its impacts on the tidal marshlands. This real secondary cost should have been counted in the cost-benefit analysis of the Wallisville Project.

Pecuniary benefits should generally not be included in the enumeration of "countable" benefits in a study. They generally arise in the form of lower input costs, increased volumes of business, or changes in land values resulting from a project. For example, an improved highway may lead to greater business volume and profitability of gas stations, souvenir shops, and restaurants along that road, as well as higher land values and consequently higher rents to the landlords. Many of these benefits are purely distributional in nature because some business will be drawn from firms along other roads once the new road is completed.

If the economy is operating under conditions of full employment, secondary impacts of the multiplier effect and induced investment which may occur as a result of a particular government investment also should not be counted. Under full employment, these benefits must be presumed to occur whether the expenditure of funds is public or private. The objective of a regional project may be to induce local investment, generate multiplier effects, and reduce regional unemployment. Under special circumstances some of these secondary effects may be appropriate to include in the analysis.

Intangibles

A final group of program benefits and costs is intangibles. These are recognizable impacts of a project for which it is either extremely difficult or impossible to calculate a dollar value. Intangibles may include such notions as quality of life, esthetic contributions (or detriments), and balance of payments impacts. Intangibles may be merely listed if it proves impossible to translate them into reasonable estimates of dollar benefits and costs. Alternatively, they may be analyzed by making trade-offs against tangibles in such a manner that the cost of additional increments of intangible improvement, for instance, may be compared with the foregone tangible benefits of a project. An example of this sort of trade-off analysis can be seen in the U.S. Maritime program. One objective of the U.S. Maritime subsidies is to reduce the U.S. balance of payments deficit. A comparison of real program costs with balance of payments impacts can provide the basis for a choice among the commitment of various levels of real resources to gain foreign exchange savings. As one study of this matter concludes, "It is scarcely credible...that the Nation would have been willing to spend $1 to save $1 of foreign exchange."[18]

---

[18] Gerald R. Jantscher, "Federal Aids to the Maritime Industries," *The Economics of Federal Subsidy Programs*, Joint Economic Committee (Washington, D.C.: U.S. Government Printing Office, 26 February 1973).

Investment Evaluation Models

In choosing an appropriate model for evaluating the economic worth of a public program, we are faced with problems very similar to those of the private firm in its capital-budgeting decision. As was discussed in Chapter 17, the model must be able to offer guidance in answering three types of investment questions. First, it must indicate whether a particular project should be adopted, assuming adequate funds are available for all economically justifiable programs. Second, if two or more alternatives are being compared that will accomplish the same purpose—that is, if one is dealing with mutually exclusive investments—the model must answer the question of which should be accepted. In its choice of a rapid-transit system, Pittsburgh, for example, had to choose among two competing systems—a steel wheel-on-rail system versus a rubber-tired Skybus system. Only one of these alternatives could eventually be selected because Pittsburgh needs and can afford only one system. Finally, if adequate resources are not available to fund all economically acceptable projects, the investment model must aid in the ordering and selection of projects so that net social benefits are maximized subject to the available funds constraint.

Since a number of alternative investment evaluation models were discussed at some length in Chapter 17, the discussion here is limited to restating these models in terms of program benefits and costs, rather than private cash inflows and outflows.[19]

Internal Rate of Return

The *internal rate of return* method calculates a discount rate that equates the net benefits of a project over its life with the original cost. This method has been used rather extensively in evaluating human resource programs, such as the investment in education. One advantage of this approach is that it avoids making explicit an appropriate *social discount rate* in the calculation procedure. As shown in the following section, the choice of an appropriate social discount rate (a "public cost of capital") is open to considerable controversy. This method does not ultimately avoid the social discount rate problem; it merely defers it to the end of the analysis. Ultimately a decision about the economic worth of a program must be made by comparing the calculated internal rate of return with the social discount rate. If a program's internal rate of return is greater than or equal to the social discount rate, it is an acceptable investment. If not, it is unacceptable.

Net Present Value

Another method is the determination of the *net present value* of a project. Using this method, program benefits and program costs for each year during the life of the project are discounted back to the present time, using the social rate of

---

[19] The problems of capital rationing and the evaluation of mutually exclusive investment alternatives are identical for both public and private investment analysis. These problems are discussed in Chapter 17.

discount. The project is acceptable (if not mutually exclusive) if the present value of benefits is greater than or equal to the present value of costs (that is, if the net present value is greater than or equal to zero, the project is acceptable).

Benefit-Cost Ratio

A third criterion, the *benefit-cost ratio* method, is the same as the profitability index method defined in the previous chapter. A project is acceptable, using this criterion, if the ratio of the present value of the benefits (discounted at the social rate of discount) to the present value of the costs (similarly discounted) is greater than or equal to 1.0. Otherwise, the project should be rejected. This method is logically equivalent to the net present value method, since the benefit-cost ratio will be greater than or equal to 1.0 only when the benefits are greater than or equal to the costs. The advantage of this method over the net present value method is that in a capital-rationing situation, net present value has an inherent bias in favor of large projects. The use of the benefit-cost ratio places all projects on an equal footing by indicating how much benefit can be achieved for *each dollar* of program outlay.

The Social Rate of Discount

When the benefits or costs of a program extend beyond a one-year time limit, it is essential that they be discounted back to some common point in time for purposes of comparison. This is so because most people prefer current consumption to future consumption. The discount rate is used to adjust for this preference.[20] The choice of the appropriate discount rate to evaluate public investments is critical to the conclusions of any cost-benefit analysis. Projects that may appear to be justified at a low discount rate, say 5 percent, may seem to be a gross misallocation of resources at a higher rate, such as 15 percent. The choice of a discount rate is likely to have a profound impact on the type of projects to be accepted. A low rate favors investments with long lives, most of which will be of the durable "bricks and mortar" variety, whereas a high rate favors those whose benefits become available soon after the initial investment. When urgent public needs are apparent, a high rate will tend to be more appropriate. To take an extreme example, when automobile deaths are rising at an alarming rate, it does little good to invest in a dam, even though at a low rate of discount this may appear to be a better alternative than investing to reduce the automobile accident rate.

A higher rate may completely switch investment priorities. In spite of the fact that the choice of a discount rate may completely alter the outcome of a careful benefit-cost analysis, it is given little attention in many studies. In some cases the researcher may select a rate merely because it has been used in the past (probably with equally little justification). Other studies merely select some

---

[20] A review of discounting and present-value concepts is provided in Chapter 2.

arbitrary rate, or rates, and perform the analysis, letting the reader decide which is best.[21]

The literature on the social discount rate is extensive and, in many cases, contradictory. Rather than attempt to synthesize and summarize the many points of view that have been expressed, the following discussion focuses on the opportunity cost criterion for estimating the social discount rate. This approach has been most clearly enunciated by Baumol.[22] Baumol's discussion is based on a recognition of the fact that resources invested in a particular manner in one sector could be withdrawn from that sector and invested elsewhere to yield either a higher or lower rate of return.

Once it is recognized that the discount rate performs the function of allocating resources between the public and private sectors, then a discount rate should be chosen that will properly indicate when resources should be transferred from one sector to another. This simply means that if resources can earn 20 percent in the private sector, then they should not be transferred to the public sector unless they can earn something greater than 20 percent on the invested resources. As Baumol explains:

> The correct discount rate for the evaluation of a government project is the percentage rate of return that the resources utilized would otherwise provide in the private sector.[23]

In calculating the opportunity cost of funds withdrawn from the private sector, it is important to recognize that funds withdrawn from corporate investment will generally incur a higher opportunity rate than funds taken from consumption. If funds used by a firm generally yield a 20 percent rate of return *before taxes*,[24] then this is the opportunity cost to society of these funds. The cost of funds withdrawn from consumption may be estimated by reference to the rate of return on risk-free bonds, such as U.S. government securities. Consumers

---

[21] Weisbrod, for example, used both 10 percent to represent the opportunity cost of capital in the private sector and 4 percent to represent the cost of government borrowing to perform his analysis. See Burton A. Weisbrod, *Economics of Public Health: Measuring the Economic Impact of Diseases* (Philadelphia: University of Pensylvania Press, 1960).

[22] William J. Baumol, "On the Social Rate of Discount," *American Economic Review* (September 1968), pp. 788–802; also, "On the Discount Rate for Public Projects" in Haveman and Margolis, *Public Expenditures and Policy Analysis*, pp. 272–290; also "On the Appropriate Discount Rate for Evaluation of Public Projects," statement in *The Planning-Programming-Budgeting System: Progress and Potentials*, Subcommittee on Economy in Government, Joint Economic Committee, 90th Congress, 1st Session (Washington, D.C.: U.S. Government Printing Office, 1967).

[23] W. J. Baumol, "On the Discount Rate for Public Projects," p. 274.

[24] The opportunity cost of funds withdrawn from corporate investment must be on a before-tax basis, since that is the true rate of return these resources generate. The fact that the corporate income tax may transfer up to 34 percent of this directly to the government is a distributional matter and not an efficiency consideration. This pretax perspective may seem at odds with the after-tax analysis advocated in Chapter 17 in the discussion of capital budgeting. The perspective in Chapter 17 is that of private enterprise, however, while the perspective in this chapter is a broader societal one.

investing in such securities which pay, say a 10 percent rate of interest, are actually indicating their preference between current consumption and future consumption. Those consumers who do not invest in these risk-free securities are indicating that they place a higher implied personal opportunity value on current consumption than the risk-free security rate. For nonbondholders, one must conclude that the opportunity cost of present consumption to them is at least as high if not higher than that of investors in risk-free securities.

We conclude, as does Baumol, that

> the correct discount rate for a project will be a weighted average of the opportunity cost rate for the various sectors from which the project would draw its resources, and the weight for each such sector in this average is the proportion of the total resources that would come from that sector.[25]

This approach to arriving at the appropriate discount rate for public projects implies that the discount rate used is not independent of the method of financing. Thus the opportunity cost of any particular project may be reduced by carefully planning the manner in which resources are acquired.[26]

In practice, public agencies have a long history of favoring low discount rates because they tend to result in the acceptance of more projects. For example, Fox and Herrfindahl found that for federal water resource projects in 1962, when a 2.625 percent discount rate was allowed, an increase in the discount rate to a mere 6 percent would have resulted in an unsatisfactory benefit-cost ratio for 64 percent of the projects evaluated.[27]

In the past, agencies have diverged considerably in their use of discount rates. Indeed, in 1969 thirteen agencies reported that they *do not* use a discount rate in evaluating proposed projects.[28] Among these agencies were the Department of Housing and Urban Development, the Department of the Treasury, and the Department of Labor. A wide range of different rates were reported for those agencies that did use a discount rate in evaluating projects in fiscal year 1969. For example, the Department of Agriculture used a 4.875 percent rate for a wide range of projects. The Job Corps program was evaluated using two rates—3 and 5 percent. The Department of Defense used a 10 percent rate for some projects, while the Atomic Energy Commission used 5 percent for some programs, 7.5 percent for others, 9 percent for others, and 15 percent for still others. Such a wide range of rates hardly seems justified and is unlikely to lead

---

[25] W. J. Baumol, "On the Discount Rate for Public Projects," p. 279.

[26] Baumol raises a number of other important issues in his development of an appropriate social discount rate, such as the role of risk in public versus private investments, the problem of externalities not accounted for in both the public and private sectors, and income distribution issues. None of these however, alters the fundamental arguments presented above.

[27] Irving K. Fox and Orris C. Herrfindahl, "Attainment of Efficiency in Satisfying Demands for Water Resources," *American Economic Review* (May 1964), pp. 198–206.

[28] Elmer B. Staats, "Survey of Use by Federal Agencies of the Discounting Technique in Evaluating Future Programs," Statement of the Comptroller General to the Joint Economic Committee, U.S. Congress (1968), in Harley Hinrichs and Graeme M. Taylor, *Program Budgeting and Benefit-Cost Analysis* (Pacific Palisades, Calif.: Goodyear, 1969), p. 218.

toward an efficient allocation of resources. In 1970 it was concluded, as a result of the Bureau of the Budget's (now the Office of Management and Budget) study of the opportunity costs of public investment, that a rate of 7.8 percent was appropriate. In the inflationary context of the early 1970s, all agencies were ordered to use at least a 10 percent rate in discounting program costs and benefits. Water-resource agencies, however, were successful in negotiating the continued use of 4.875 percent for most of their projects. In the late 1980s, a rate in the range of 9–11 percent is easily justified.

Cost-Benefit Analysis: A Critique

As the foregoing discussion has indicated, cost-benefit analysis is not without its shortcomings. This section summarizes the weaknesses and strengths of cost-benefit analysis so that we can draw some conclusions about its potential usefulness. First, it was noted that two types of problems are encountered in estimating costs and benefits—problems of enumeration and problems of evaluation.[29] The larger the project under scrutiny, the more diverse are the benefits and costs that must be enumerated. But as the number of beneficiaries of the project increases, it becomes exceedingly difficult to aggregate the generated costs and benefits without falling into the trap of double counting.

On the evaluation side, all sorts of practical, as well as conceptual, problems may be encountered. Even if we are lucky enough to have a market-price basis for measuring costs and benefits, the formidable task of estimating demand functions and measuring the consumer's surplus associated with various price levels still faces the eager analyst. In the unhappy situation where market price surrogates for benefits and costs are not available or when market valuations must be modified to take account of externalities, it becomes most difficult, though usually not impossible, to get reasonably valid dollar estimates of costs and benefits.

Another problem of cost-benefit analysis arises when there are major interrelationships in the private and public sectors or of programs within the public sector; that is, serious problems of analysis arise when the decisions of one public agency have a significant impact on the performance of others. These interrelationships may either be complementary, as in the case of public education and public library programs, or conflicting, as with farm price-support programs and the Corps of Engineers irrigation projects. When such interrelationships exist, it is necessary to determine *jointly* appropriate levels of program activity. This requires a high degree of centralized decision making and also probably a more sophisticated level of analysis than is yet possible.

Since the problem of an appropriate discount rate was discussed at length in the preceding section, it is necessary only to reiterate the importance that the discount rate may play in final project approval or rejection. Partly for this reason and partly because of a lack of unanimity among economists concerning the appropriate rate, this is still an issue of considerable concern.

---

[29] Prest and Turvey, "Cost-Benefit Analysis: A Survey," pp. 729–731.

A final problem arises when the intangible impacts of a project are significant. These may be in the form of esthetic considerations, balance of payments impacts, national defense, and income distribution. If one remembers that cost-benefit analysis is a tool designed *only* to judge the *economic efficiency impacts* of public programs in terms of the resulting changes in national income, then the problem of intangibles can be placed in an appropriate perspective. The greatest danger of cost-benefit studies here, however, is the natural tendency of decision makers to place more weight on those aspects of a program for which dollar values can be assigned and to nearly ignore the unquantifiable intangibles.

Cost-Benefit Analysis: Justification for Use

Before dismissing the technique of cost-benefit analysis as an impractical economic fantasy, some additional issues should be considered. First, the bitter reality is that decisions must be made by public agencies one way or another. A significant advantage of cost-benefit studies is that it forces costs and benefits to be quantified as far as possible rather than be estimated solely by hunch and intuition or parochial, logrolling interests. One could argue that, although cost-benefit analysis is not perfect, some information is far superior to none.

Cost-benefit analysis may play an important, though limited, negative role in screening out programs that are obviously not justifiable. When it is made clear that the discounted costs of a program exceed the discounted benefits, it is difficult for even the most astute political logroller to argue convincingly for program acceptance.

Once the strengths and weaknesses of cost-benefit analysis are recognized, this analysis may be applied in those areas where its potential utility is greatest. It may be most effectively employed at lower levels of decision making where the range of programs being considered is reasonably narrow. When alternative projects are being considered that have nearly the same purpose, and when the externalities and intangibles associated with each alternative are roughly of the same magnitude, cost-benefit analysis can be an extremely valuable tool for making resource-allocation decisions. For example, cost-benefit analysis is probably well suited to evaluating alternative locations for the new superports, but it is of limited usefulness in indicating whether defense programs should be cut in favor of the school-lunch program or whether resources should be shifted from transportation projects to health-care projects. Even with these broader program categories, cost-benefit analysis attempts to make explicit the economic considerations associated with various programs, reducing the level of subjectivity involved in resource-allocation decisions.

As long as expectations about the usefulness of cost-benefit analysis are tempered by the reality of its limitations, and if it is performed correctly and not misused—either by the advocates or the opponents of a particular project—this technique will continue to provide significant economic insights into program analysis and resource-allocation decisions.

Cost-Benefit Analysis: Some Examples

In this section the results of three cost-benefit analyses drawn from the areas of education, health, and water resources are summarized. The water resources example was chosen to illustrate the bias that may easily creep into such a study when the analysis is performed by the same agency proposing the project.

Higher Education

A paper by Duncan Bailey and Charles Schotta examined the private and social rates of return to the education of academicians.[30] The private rates of return accruing to the individual from the investment in a doctoral degree were calculated by comparing lifetime income patterns of those with the degree with similar incomes of those who hold only a bachelor's degree. Individual costs include opportunity costs of earnings foregone while in graduate school as well as direct outlays that would not have been made if the individual were not in graduate school (for example, for tuition and books). Social rates of return include, in addition to private costs and benefits, the cost of social resources provided in most graduate education programs. This recognizes the fact that in most universities tuition covers only a small part of the cost of instructional and research resources.

Using a series of reasonable assumptions relating to the average length of time in a doctoral program and to dropout rates, Bailey and Schotta found a private real rate of return to graduate education of *zero* to *one percent*. The social real rate of return was also found to be zero to one percent. Bailey and Schotta argue that in view of findings by Becker and Wilkinson of rates of return to undergraduate education in excess of 10 percent,[31] it seems reasonable that some resources might be shifted from graduate to undergraduate education. This is especially true in such areas as the humanities, education, and certain social sciences, where returns to doctoral degree holders are extremely low in comparison to holders of bachelor's degrees. They also suggest that because of the high social cost of dropouts from graduate degree programs, more attention should be devoted to preselection and early quality-control measures to avoid the cost of carrying unsuitable students too long. One limitation of their study that the authors note is that it merely examines the future monetary benefits to be gained from graduate education.

---

[30] Duncan Bailey and Charles Schotta, "Private and Social Rates of Return to the Education of Academicians," *American Economic Review* (March 1972), pp. 19–31.

[31] Gary Becker, *Human Capital* (New York: Columbia University Press, 1964) and Bruce Wilkinson, "Present Values of Lifetime Earnings for Different Occupations," *Journal of Political Economy* (December 1966), pp. 556–573.

Polio Research

The second cost-benefit analysis reviewed is a case study completed by Burton Weisbrod of the costs and benefits of polio research.[32] The major contribution of this study is that it provides a checklist of items to be considered when a public decision maker is seeking information before allocating funds to competing research programs. The approach used involved estimating the following:[33]

1. The time stream of research expenditures directed toward poliomyelitis

2. The time stream of benefits resulting from (or predicted to result from) the application of the knowledge gained by the research

3. The cost of applying that knowledge

The benefits from prevention of polio were taken to include:

1. The market value of production lost because of premature death due to polio

2. The market value of production lost due to illness and disability from polio

3. The resource costs devoted to treatment and rehabilitation of victims

This excludes estimates of the costs of pain and suffering that those afflicted with the disease had to bear. Thus the rates of return generated probably underestimate the true rates of return.

The internal rate of return on medical (in this case polio) research is the discount rate that equates the time stream of research costs with the stream of benefits. It is calculated by solving the following equation for r:

$$\sum_{t=0}^{T} \frac{R_t - [B_t(N_t - W_t) - V_t]}{(1 + r)^t} = 0$$

where

R = research costs

B = benefit per case of disease prevented (or the loss per case occurring)

N = number of cases occurring in the absence of a successful research and application program

W = number of cases occurring after a successful program

V = cost of applying research findings (for example, the cost of a vaccination program)

t = a particular year

T = the time horizon of benefits and costs, beyond which the time value of these benefits and costs are insignificant due to discounting.

---

[32] Burton A. Weisbrod, "Costs and Benefits of Medical Research: A Case Study of Poliomyelitis," *Journal of Political Economy* (May–June 1971), pp. 527–544.
[33] Ibid., p. 528.

Weisbrod concludes that on the basis of his analyses, the resources devoted to polio research and the application of this research are generating returns in the form of increased output and reduced treatment expenditures of about 11–12 percent. Because no figures are imputed for the value to the individual of reduced illness and increased longevity, the real value of this medical research program is undoubtedly higher than the 11–12 percent estimate.

Water Resources

The final example of cost-benefit analysis is in the area of water resource development. Specifically, the proposed Trinity River Basin Project in Texas is examined.[34] The basic purposes of this project were navigation (that is, construction of a channel from Galveston Bay to Fort Worth, Texas, a distance of 363 miles), flood control, water conservation, and irrigation. The navigation channel would require twenty locks and sixteen dams and would pass through Lake Livingston, Tennessee Colony Reservoir, and the proposed Wallisville Dam Reservoir. Total project costs were estimated at $1.35 billion. The Wallisville portion of the project had the objectives of salinity control, navigation, water supply, recreation, and fish and wildlife enhancement. The cost of the Wallisville Dam was estimated at $28.8 million. This dam would create a reservoir of water which is 4 feet deep, covering about 19,700 acres. The status of both these projects was in limbo because of the following:

1. Voters in the counties affected by the project rejected by a substantial margin the proposed financing arrangements for the entire Trinity River Basin Project

2. In spite of the fact that the Wallisville Dam was about 75 percent completed, work was halted under an indefinite restraining order

As will be seen, cost-benefit analysis played a significant role in both these occurrences.

The following discussion illustrates both the strengths and weaknesses of cost-benefit analyses. It should be apparent that when such a study is undertaken by the sponsoring agency (in this case the Corps of Engineers), it may be badly biased in favor of project acceptance. On the positive side, the fact that a systematic analysis of project costs and benefits was undertaken enabled intelligent discussion and criticism to take place based on a common set of assumptions.

In 1962, when the Wallisville Dam Project was authorized, the benefit-cost ratio was estimated at 2.5 (assuming a 50-year life and a 2.5 percent discount rate). Using 1970 price data and an interest rate of just 3.125 percent reduced this ratio to a marginal 1.11 to 1. The Trinity River benefit-cost ratio was estimated at 1.5 to 1, using a 3.125 percent discount rate. It should be immediately apparent that these discount rates are far too low. At a time (1973)

---

[34] The authors wish to acknowledge the assistance of Larry Hartley, who gathered the information necessary for this example.

when the cost of government borrowing exceeded 6 percent, and when private opportunity rates were more nearly on the order of 15 percent, a 3.125 percent discount rate is not reasonable. Using just a 7 percent discount rate for the Trinity River Basin Project, assuming all other Corps of Engineers figures to be correct, the benefit-cost ratio declines to an unacceptable .74 to 1.

An additional problem of the analysis of Trinity River arose because the 1.5 to 1 ratio estimated in 1968 was assumed to remain constant through 1973. Using the corps' own estimates, costs were assumed to rise at about 25 percent annually. To maintain the constant ratio, benefit estimates were increased at the same rate, in spite of the fact that no systematic study was done.

In estimating the direct benefits of the project, the corps sent a questionnaire to business executives to estimate how much they would use the channel. Taking the difference between railroad shipping rates and barge rates, the corps multiplied this by the tonnage estimated from the survey—*plus* 10 percent. It was argued by opponents of the Trinity Project that 10 percent should have been *subtracted* since business executives would be inclined to overestimate to increase the probability of getting a free canal. Deducting the 10 percent "fudge" factor supplied by the corps and using a 7 percent discount rate reduced the benefit-cost ratio even further—to .64 to 1.

Similar problems arose in estimating the recreational benefits of the project. Although benefits were based on increased motorboating and other water sports resulting from the river-straightening project, no account was taken of the loss in benefits to those who currently use this virgin river basin for fishing, canoeing, hunting, and camping—much of which use would be destroyed by the project. If one assumed that losses to current recreational users equaled gains to the motorboaters, the benefit-cost ratio is reduced even further to .62 to 1.

A detailed analysis of the Wallisville Project shows even greater abuses committed in the name of cost-benefit analysis. These include an overestimation of salinity-control benefits; imputing a value to increased area water supplies, even though there is no need for them; dubious recreational benefits for a dam that the corps, by its own admission, claims will have only *one* foot of depth much of the year, and counting freshwater fish and wildlife enhancement but failing to subtract the even greater detriments to saltwater fish and wildlife.

These two projects clearly illustrate that even in the area where cost-benefit analysis experience is the greatest, in an absence of clearly defined acceptable cost-benefit accounting standards the technique is open to much abuse. However, the poor analysis performed in this case provided a common basis on which the projects could be evaluated and criticized and ultimately resulted in the rejection of clearly unacceptable proposals.

Cost-Effectiveness Analysis

Although cost-benefit analysis may be benefically applied in wide range of areas, in many types of government activity it is simply not feasible because of the problems of measuring the value of program outputs. For instance, program analyses in the fields of defense, environmental protection, crime prevention,

Economic Analysis and Managerial Efficiency

COSTS AND BENEFITS OF A TOYOTA AUTOMOBILE PLANT TO KENTUCKY*

Toyota is building an assembly plant near Lexington, Kentucky that will be able to produce 200,000 automobiles annually beginning in the early 1990s. In order to get Toyota to locate the plant in Kentucky, the state agreed to invest approximately $325 million over a twenty-year period. These expenditures include the following:

- Land and site preparation $33 million
- Local highway construction   47 million
- Employee training center and education of workers   65 million
- Education of Japanese workers and families   5 million
- Interest on economic development bonds   167 million

The returns to the state over the twenty-year period are estimated at $632 million in income, sales, and payroll taxes from Toyota, its suppliers, and related businesses.

These numbers yield an internal rate of return

*Based on an article in the *Wall Street Journal*, 9 June, 1987.

of 25 percent, according to a University of Kentucky research team. Since the state's economic resources are limited, one must consider whether these resources could be invested in other projects that would generate even higher rates of return. However, as Brinton Milward, director of the university's center for business and economic research, explains, "Could you put these funds into improvements in education and transportation and come up with a better benefit-cost ratio? My guess is no. Manufacturing has a pretty high multiplier" (in terms of the repeated turnover of money in the form of jobs and sales).

Question

1. In 1976 Pennsylvania agreed to invest millions of dollars in order to get Volkswagen to locate its U.S. automotive assembly plant in New Stanton (near Pittsburgh). In 1987, after several years of low sales and profits, Volkswagen decided to close the plant and cease producing automobiles in the United States. How can state officials like those in Pennsylvania and Kentucky, faced with making large-scale commitments of funds to get businesses to locate in their area, protect themselves against premature plant closures?

industry regulation, and income redistribution are more frequently conducted using the cost-effectiveness framework than the cost-benefit one. Cost-benefit analysis asks the questions: "What is the dollar value of program costs and benefits, and do the benefits exceed the costs by a sufficient amount, given the timing of these outcomes, to justify undertaking the program?" In contrast, the question asked by *cost-effectiveness analysis* is: "Given that some prespecified objective is to be attained, what are the costs associated with various alternative means for reaching that objective?" In essence, cost-effectiveness analysis *begins* with the premise that some identified program outputs are useful, and proceeds to explore (1) how these may be most efficiently achieved *or* (2) what the costs are of achieving various levels of the prespecified output.

In many governmental programs, the outputs can be specified and measured, but difficulty in evaluating these outputs in dollar terms precludes the use of cost-benefit analysis. A prime example is in the area of pollution abatement. It is a rather simple matter to measure levels of various pollutants being emitted from factories and cars. It is far more difficult, however, to evaluate the societal benefit derived from various levels of discharge reduction. Likewise, it is quite easy to measure or prespecify the number of families placed in adequate housing as a result of low-income housing programs. But it is far more difficult to evaluate the societal benefits accruing from this program since its major impacts are income redistributional.

Cost-effectiveness analysis is widely applied in Department of Defense program studies. The benefits of most defense activities may be thought of as providing levels of deterrence. But for any specific program, such as the strategic nuclear bomber force, it is virtually impossible to quantify and evaluate benefits in dollar terms. Such an evaluation would require a knowledge of the difference in probability of enemy attack with and without the bomber force. It would also require an estimate of the expected dollar damage that would be inflicted by an enemy attack. Even if these data were readily available, debate over the objective of defense programs would still be considerable. Is the balance of expected program benefits and costs appropriate in this case? In cases such as these, cost-effectiveness analysis may be useful.

The problems of cost estimation for cost-effectiveness analyses are the same as those encountered in cost-benefit studies. Primary or direct costs may include outlays for personnel services, capital expenditures, and planning expenses. These should be evaluated at their market prices in most cases; however, when otherwise unemployed or underemployed resources are used, the opportunity cost of these will be less than the market rate. An attempt should be made to estimate the secondary or indirect costs that the program generates. Although it may be difficult to place a dollar figure on some of these secondary costs because they are often in the form of difficult-to-measure externalities (such as pollution), any cost-effectiveness study is incomplete without at least enumerating the secondary impacts of the project.

Constant-Cost Studies

With these general remarks about cost-effectiveness analysis in mind, three more specific types of these studies are examined. *Constant-cost studies* attempt to specify the output that may be achieved from a number of alternative programs, assuming all are funded at the same level (costs are constant between alternatives). In essence, constant-cost studies measure what may be acquired for a specific outlay of funds. Constant-cost studies differ from benefit-cost studies as there is no attempt to place dollar values on the outputs of alternative programs. The greatest use of constant-cost studies is in cases where program outputs have multiple dimensions (there may be income distribution effects, esthetic effects, or impacts on future economic development). This is the case in many urban renewal programs. Decision makers may examine several alternatives for land provided by urban renewal. They might choose on the basis of what uses—industrial, commercial, or residential—offer the greatest potential profitability. Alternatively, an explicit attempt may be made to provide for planned development considering the esthetics of development, the impacts of current development on surrounding areas and future development potential, and the desire to provide a mix of different cultures and income groups within the city. For projects such as these, all one can do is attempt to spell out all the impacts of several alternative, equal-cost schemes. This in itself is likely to be a monumental task. With impacts clearly identified, it becomes the decision maker's responsibility to weigh (subjectively) the outputs of each alternative and to make a choice.

Least-Cost Studies

The second type of cost-effectiveness analysis is *least-cost studies*.[35] As might be expected, the emphasis of these studies is to identify the least expensive way of generating some quantity of an output. For instance, a city might decide that it wishes to reduce by 20 percent the number of burglaries occurring each year within its jurisdictional limits. One approach could be to expand the size of the police force, increase the number of foot patrol officers, and increase the number of squad cars on the streets at any one time. Another possibility might be to require builders to install security bars on the windows of all new homes and to provide cash or tax incentives for current homeowners to improve their personal security systems. A third alternative might be a community drive supporting Operation Identification, where individuals place permanent identifying marks on their belongings to make fencing of this merchandise more difficult. If it is recognized that drug addicts are responsible for many burglaries, a drug rehabilitation program may be considered. Combinations of these programs are also possible. Each of these alternatives is evaluated in terms of the expenditure required to achieve the desired objective—a 20 percent reduction in burglaries.

Objective-Level Studies

A third type of cost-effectiveness analysis is *objective-level* studies. These studies attempt to estimate the costs of achieving several alternative performance levels of the same objective. This may be illustrated with the case of reducing automobile emission levels. Table 18.4 provides some hypothetical data relating to various emission-control standards.

In addition to the increased fuel and maintenance costs and the added new car costs, other impacts of a program to reduce auto emissions must be considered. For instance, what is the relative impact of such a program on various income groups? In areas where the automobile is a necessity, a program that substantially increases the cost of driving without simultaneously providing feasible alternative means of transportation could be disastrous. Given the current domestic energy situation, it is important to examine the effects of

---

[35] The discussion of both constant-cost and least-cost studies is based largely on Neil M. Singer, *Public Microeconomics* (Boston: Little, Brown & Co., 1972), chap. 12.

Table 18.4
Hypothetical Data Relating to the Cost of Achieving Various Levels of Auto Emission Reductions

Percentage of 19X8 emission levels	Costs (millions of dollars—including fuel consumption, more frequent maintenance, and added new car costs)
90	$ 200
70	250
40	500
20	2,500
10	7,500
5	38,000
1	140,000

increased fuel consumption by less-efficient engines on the balance of payments. Finally, in performing objective-level studies, we must be aware of the state of technology assumptions that are being made. Although the estimates in Table 18.4 may be realistic for the reciprocating engine, they may far overstate actual costs if alternative technology were assumed—such as the diesel, turbine, or Wankel engines. Table 18.4 *does* illustrate one economic fact of life for many programs; that is, as the level of objective achievement increases, the associated costs frequently increase at a much more rapid rate. Objective-level studies do not directly measure program benefits, but they do measure intermediate program outputs or objectives. This may give the decision maker the information needed to make more rational decisions. For instance, it may be clear that the $2.5 billion expenditure needed to reduce emissions to 20 percent of their 19X8 levels is reasonable. It may be far less clear whether an additional 19 percent (from 20 percent to 1 percent) emissions reduction is worth the required incremental expenditure of $137.5 billion (140 less 2.5 billion).

Thus it can be seen that in comparison to cost-benefit analyses, cost-effectiveness analyses provide less positive inputs on which economic decisions can be made. They furnish decision makers with disciplined studies relating program costs with some measurable but unvalued estimates of program outputs.

Summary

- *Public goods* are goods that may be consumed by more than one person at the same time with no additional expense, that is, goods that are indivisible and imperfectly excludable. Public goods are likely to have significant and unavoidable externalities associated with their production and/or consumption.

- *Externalities* occur whenever a third party receives benefits or bears costs arising from an economic transaction in which the individual (or group) is not a direct participant.

- *Cost-benefit analysis* is the public sector counterpart of capital-budgeting techniques used in private sector resource-allocation decisions.

- Cost-benefit analysis involves the following steps:

  1. Determining the program objectives

  2. Enumerating the alternative means of achieving the objectives, subject to the legal, political, technological, budgetary, and other constraints that limit the scope of action

  3. Evaluating all primary, secondary, and intangible benefits and costs associated with each alternative

  4. Discounting the benefits and costs using a social discount rate to arrive at an overall measure of the desirability of each alternative (for example, benefit-cost ratio)

  5. Choosing (or recommending) the best alternative based on the overall measure of desirability and the relative magnitude of the nonquantifiable intangibles

- Because of the measurement problems arising from intangible impacts and economic externalities of many public programs, cost-benefit analysis is most useful in comparing projects with similar objectives and similar magnitudes of intangibles and externalities.

- In cases where it is not feasible to place dollar values on final program outputs, *cost-effectiveness analysis* may be used. Cost-effectiveness analysis assumes a priori that the program objectives are worth achieving and focuses on the least-cost method of achieving them.

Selected References

Arrow, Kenneth J. *Social Choice and Individual Values*. New York: John Wiley, 1951.

Baumol, William J. "On the Discount Rate for Public Projects." In *Public Expenditures and Policy Analysts*, edited by Robert Haveman and Julius Margolis. Chicago: Markham, 1970.

Becker, Gary. *Human Capital*. New York: Columbia University Press, 1964.

Burkhead, Jesse, and Jerry Miner. *Public Expenditure*. Chicago: Aldine-Atherton, 1971.

Dorfman, Robert, ed. *Measuring Benefits of Government Investments*. Washington, D.C.: Brookings Institution, 1965.

Due, John F., and Ann F. Friedlander. *Government Finance: Economics of the Public Sector*, 6th ed. Homewood, Ill.: Richard D. Irwin, 1977.

Hausman, J. A., and P. L. Joskow. "Evaluating the Costs and Benefits of Appliance Efficiency Standards." *AEA Papers and Proceedings* (May 1982), pp. 220–225.

Haveman, Robert, and Julius Margolis, eds. *Public Expenditures and Policy Analysis* Chicago: Markham, 1970.

Hinrichs, Harley, and Graeme M. Taylor, eds. *Program Budgeting and Benefit-Cost Analysis*. Pacific Palisades, Calif.: Goodyear, 1969.

McKean, Roland. *Public Spending*. New York: McGraw-Hill, 1968.

Merewitz, Leonard, and Stephen Sosnick. *The Budget's New Clothes*. Chicago: Markham, 1971.

Mishan, Ezra J. *Cost-Benefit Analysis: An Introduction*, rev. ed. New York: Praeger, 1977.

Mishan, Ezra J. "Evaluation of Life and Limb: A Theoretical Approach." *Journal of Political Economy* (July–August 1971).

Musgrave, R. A., and Peggy B. Musgrave. *Public Finance in Theory and Practice*, 2d ed. New York: McGraw-Hill, 1975.

Pearce, D. W., and C. A. Nash. *The Social Appraisal of Projects; A Text in Cost-Benefit Analysis*. New York: Wiley, 1981.

Samuelson, Paul A. "The Pure Theory of Public Expenditure." *Review of Economics and Statistics* (November 1954).

Snyder, R., and A. Williams. *The Principles of Cost-Benefit Analysis*. Oxford: Oxford University Press, 1978.

Discussion Questions

1. Define the following terms:
   a. Externalities
   b. Public goods
   c. Social benefits
   d. Social costs
   e. Direct benefits
   f. Direct costs
   g. Secondary effects
   h. Intangibles
   i. Benefit-cost ratio
   j. Social discount rate

2. Describe the major steps in a cost-benefit study.

3. What is the function of the social discount rate in cost-benefit analysis?

4. How do the goals pursued by public and not-for-profit institutions differ from the normative goal (shareholder wealth maximization) pursued by private, profit-oriented firms?

5. Describe the characteristics that differentiate pure private goods from pure public goods.

6. Explain the difference between the Pareto optimality criterion and the Kaldor-Hicks criterion in the context of cost-benefit analysis.

7. A Harvard public policy professor, Steven Kelman, objects to the use of cost-benefit analysis in evaluating environmental programs. He states, "Subjecting decisions about clean air or water to the cost-benefit analysis tests that determine the general run of decisions removes those matters from the realm of specially valued things." Evaluate this statement. Do you agree or disagree? Why?

8. Several studies have reported very low private and social rates of return on an investment in securing (providing) graduate education in many disciplines. In spite of this evidence, an increasing number of schools have been offering advanced-level degrees. (Surprisingly, in spite of normative prescriptions of economic theory, economics falls into the category of these low-return disciplines.)
   a. How can you explain this seeming contradiction to an efficient allocation of societal resources?
   b. Can you suggest some alternatives that could help direct more resources away from low-return educational programs toward higher-return alternatives?

9. In a *Wall Street Journal* editorial (September 18, 1981), the cost of producing a Ph.D. graduate in history at Columbia University was estimated at $222,159—considering the direct cost of schooling, the opportunity cost of foregone income during school, and the risk of unemployment after school. Assume this figure is a reasonable approximation of the true present-value cost of educating each new Ph.D. graduate in history.

   a. Under what circumstances does this type of investment make *economic* sense?
   b. Can you justify this level of investment even if the present value of benefits is less than the present value of costs?

10. The Committee for Economic Development released a report in 1973 that urged state universities to increase their tuition fees substantially, forcing the student to pay a higher percentage of the cost of education. Similarly, the Nixon administration had proposed cutting financial assistance available to medical students, even though the overall supply and distribution of doctors was probably insufficient.

    In both cases it was urged that more financial assistance be made available to students from low-income backgrounds.

    Discuss these proposals in terms of their impacts on the following:

    a. Economic efficiency and improving the allocation of societal resources
    b. Income distribution

Problems

1. Refer to Tables 18.2 and 18.3 in this chapter. Reconcile the relationship between the net program benefits in Table 18.2 and the marginal figures in Table 18.3. What do you think the true optimal level of expenditure is?

2. The state of Glottamora has $100 million remaining in its budget for the current year. One alternative is to give Glottamorans a one-time tax rebate. Two proposals have been made for expenditures of these funds.

   The first proposed project is to invest in a new power plant, costing $100 million and having an expected useful life of twenty years. Projected benefits accruing from this project are as follows:

Years	Benefits per Year (millions of dollars)
1–5	$ 0
6–20	20

   The second alternative is to undertake a job-retraining program, also costing $100 million and generating the following benefits:

Years	Benefits per Year (millions of dollars)
1–5	$20
6–10	14
11–20	4

   The State Power Department has argued that a 5 percent discount factor should be used in evaluating the projects, since that is the government's borrowing rate. The Human Resources Department suggests using a 12 percent rate, since that more nearly equals society's true opportunity rate.

a. What is implied by the various departments' desires to use different discount rates?
b. Evaluate the projects using both the 5 percent and the 12 percent rates.
c. What rate do you believe to be more appropriate?
d. Make a choice between the projects and the tax-refund alternative. Why did you choose the alternative you did?

3. The Department of Transportation wishes to choose among two alternative accident prevention programs. It has identified three benefits to be gained from such programs:
a. Reduced property damage, both to the vehicles involved in an accident and to other property (for example, real estate that may be damaged at the scene of an accident)
b. Reduced injuries
c. Reduced fatalities

The department's experts are willing to make dollar estimates of property damage savings that are expected to accrue from any program, but they will only estimate the number of injuries and fatalities that may be averted.

The first program is relatively moderate in its costs and will be concentrated in a large city. It involves upgrading traffic signals, improving road markers, and repaving some potholed streets. Because of the concentration and value of property in the city, savings from reduced property damage are expected to be substantial. Likewise, a moderate number of traffic-related deaths and injuries should be avoided.

The second program is more ambitious. It involves straightening long sections of dangerous rural roads and installing improved guardrails. Although the property damage savings are expected to be small in relation to total cost, the reduction in traffic-related deaths and injuries should be substantial.

The following table summarizes the expected costs and payoffs of the two programs:

Year	1	2	3	4	Total
Alternative #1					
Cost ($000)	200	200	100	50	550
Reduced property damage ($000)	50	100	250	100	500
Lives saved	60	40	35	25	160
Injuries prevented	500	425	300	150	1,375
Alternative #2					
Cost ($000)	700	1,800	1,100	700	4,300
Reduced property damage ($000)	150	225	475	300	1,150
Lives saved	50	75	100	125	350
Injuries prevented	800	850	900	900	3,450

Assume that a 10 percent discount rate is appropriate for evaluating government programs:
a. Calculate the net present costs of the two programs.
b. Generate any other tables that you may find useful in choosing among the programs.
c. Can you arrive at any unambiguous choice between the two alternatives? What factors are likely to weigh on the ultimate choice made?

4. One study completed for the American Enterprise Institute estimated the cost per life saved in several programs supported or mandated by the government. The following

results were reported:

Estimates of cost per life saved

Recommended for cost-benefit analysis by the National Safety Council for traffic
 safety $37,500
Kidney dialysis at home $99,000
Instructions to military pilots on when to crash-land airplanes $270,000
Consumer Product Safety Commission's proposed lawn-mower safety
 standards .... $240,000 to $1,920,000
OSHA-proposed acrylonitrile exposure standard .... $1,963,000 to $624,976,000
OSHA coke-oven emission standard .... $4,500,000 to $158,000,000

Other analyses have indicated that a proposed plan to further reduce carbon
monoxide auto emissions would cost $1 billion in increased costs of production and
costs to the consumer and that the plan would prolong two lives in twenty years. This
could be compared with the $200 it would cost to prevent each of 24,000 premature
deaths per year by installing cardiac care units in ambulances.

Some studies of the value of a human life have computed an implicit value in the
range of $200,000 to $700,000. These studies have examined wage differentials for
hazardous jobs and provide estimates of what people are willing to pay for a small
decrease in risk.

a. Given these estimates of the value of a human life, which of the programs discussed
 do you think should be pursued?

b. How can you explain the actions of a mine operator who may spend $5 million to
 free a trapped miner?

5. *Campus Research Project*

Select a program that has recently been established at your college or university
(for example, a new degree program or a new department). If your school or campus
is a relatively new one (five years old or less), you might wish to use the entire school
as your example.

On the basis of discussions with officials involved in the establishment or direction
of the program, define as clearly as possible the following:

a. The program objectives as they were perceived at the time of the program's
 establishment.

b. The basis on which a need for the new program was established? What objective
 data were used to justify the program?

c. The projected future growth and resource requirements of the program. Were
 actual estimates of these made at the time the program was established?

d. Has the program been reevaluated in light of its original objectives and actual
 resources available since its adoption?

e. What consideration was given to alternatives to establishing this new program on
 your campus; for example, providing greater support for other schools that already
 have a similar program, encouraging a sharing of resources between and among
 schools, and so on?

f. Based on the information you have been able to gather, would you have been
 willing to commit the resources necessary to establish the new program? Why or
 why not?

6. *College or Community Project*

Choose a program conducted by a local government agency or by some local
not-for-profit organization. On the basis of your discussions with the administrators of

that program, identify the following:

a. Program objectives in an operational manner. What attempts are made by the organization to measure its achievement of these objectives?

b. If the organization has multiple, shared objectives, try to identify areas of potential conflict. Which objectives are primary and which are secondary?

c. What impact does this program have on other programs sponsored by the organization? Can you identify areas of overlap? Conflict?

d. Has this agency made any long-range (five-year) forecasts of its resource requirements?

Case Problem
Cost-Benefit
Analysis *

The Michigan State Fairgrounds is centrally located in the Detroit Standard Metropolitan Statistical Area (SMSA) which consists of Wayne, Oakland, and Macomb counties. The population within the SMSA numbered 4,197,931 persons in 19X0—over 47 percent of the state's total population. More than 59 percent and 75 percent of the state's population reside within 60 and 100 miles, respectively, of the fairground site. The site is located near an efficient freeway system that connects many areas of the state. The State Fairgrounds is operated by the Agriculture Department and is currently in a deplorable state of disrepair. Costs have exceeded revenues by a substantial margin every year in the recent past. A redevelopment program has been proposed for the fairgrounds that would serve several purposes:

1. Revitalization of the fairgrounds would prevent further economic deterioration of the existing facilities, increase attendance and consequently revenues, and perhaps make the fairgrounds an economically viable entity.

2. A further benefit to be realized would be an economic stimulus to the area resulting from increased employment from the initial construction program, as well as increased revenues realized from the additional business that the proposed new facilities would generate.

3. Finally, aesthetic value could be realized from the upgrading and redevelopment of what is currently a marginal area of the city.

The redevelopment program would consist of the overall rehabilitation of the grounds and buildings as well as the construction of several income-producing buildings, including a hotel and convention facility and a dog track (providing dog racing is legalized in Michigan and the fairgrounds can obtain the necessary license). Either a new coliseum would be constructed or the present one redesigned and refurbished. The cost of the redevelopment program would be $20 million. Construction would take three years with 50 percent of the cost incurred in year 0, 30 percent in year 1, and 20 percent in year 2. The redevelopment program would require funding by the state and/or federal government. The following estimated benefits would be derived from the project:

1. *Initial construction benefits.* Previous studies showed that 38 worker-years of employment are derived from each $1 million in construction. Assuming an hourly rate of $6, 40 hours per week, and 50 weeks per year, and relating this to the $20 million cost of the redevelopment program, results in $9,120,000 of economic benefit to be derived through increased employment. Like the construction costs, these benefits would be spread over three years ($4.560 million in year 0, $2.736 million in year 1, and $1.824 million in year 2).

---

* Adapted from an unpublished paper by Eric Hartshom of Wayne State University, "Cost-Benefit Analysis Concerning the Proposed Redevelopment Program For the Michigan State Fairgrounds."

2. *Coliseum*. An appropriate coliseum facility could generate, in excess of current levels, an additional $500,000 annually (years 3–20) from shows and events not currently available in the Detroit area.

3. *Increased state fair attendance*. With improved facilities (such as those planned in the redevelopment program), attendance at the state fair is expected to increase from 700,000 presently to 1,000,000 people annually. Assuming present per capita expenditures ($3.33) at the Michigan State Fair, the increased attendance would result in an additional $1 million in revenue annually (years 3–20).

4. *Convention and hotel facility*. It is estimated that a 200-room hotel, convention, and dining facility located at the fairgrounds would generate nearly $1.5 million in additional revenue annually (years 3–20).

5. *Dog-racing track*. It is estimated that an average dog-racing facility will produce $1.5 million in revenue annually. However, it must be realized that dog racing is similar to horse racing, and it is expected that a portion of the revenues generated by a dog track would be realized owing to a transfer of funds from local horse racing facilities. Since this transfer of funds should not be considered in the analysis, it will be assumed that one-third of the dog racing revenues will result from the redistribution of funds from local horse-racing tracks. Consequently only $1 million in annual revenues (years 3–20) will be attributed to the proposed dog-racing track.

The cost and benefits of the proposed redevelopment are summarized in the following table. Assume that a 10 percent interest rate is appropriate for discounting the costs and benefits of the proposed project.

Type of Cost or Benefit	Year(s)	Annual Benefit (+) or Cost (−)(million $)
Construction outlay	0	$−10.000
Construction outlay	1	−6.000
Construction outlay	2	−4.000
Increased employment	0	+4.560
Increased employment	1	+2.736
Increased employment	2	+1.824
Coliseum	3–20	+0.500
State Fair attendance	3–20	+1.000
Convention and hotel facility	3–20	+1.500
Dog-racing track	3–20	+1.000

Questions

1. Determine the benefit-cost ratio for the proposed fairground development.

2. Based on this analysis, should the redevelopment program be undertaken?

3. List some of the secondary benefits and costs, as well as intangibles, associated with the project.

In calculating the benefits of the fairground redevelopment program, increased employment opportunities were included.

4. What assumption about employment in the Detroit area must be made in associating these benefits with the project?

5. Recalculate the benefit-cost ratio, assuming that these benefits are not included in the analysis. How does this affect the desirability of the project?

In calculating the benefits of the fairground redevelopment project, it was assumed that $1.5 million in additional annual revenue would be generated from the convention and hotel facility.

6. What assumption is being made about the effects of this facility on other hotel and conventional facilities? Is this a realistic assumption?

7. Suppose that only $500,000 of the facility's annual revenues can be attributed to "new" convention and hotel business. Recalculate the benefit-cost ratio under this assumption (also exclude employment benefits). How does this affect the desirability of the project?

8. Suppose that the fairground is unable to obtain a license to operate a dog-racing track. Assume that construction costs are reduced by 15 percent if a dog-racing track is not built. Recompute the benefit-cost ratio under this assumption (also exclude employment and convention facility benefits). How does this affect the desirability of the proposed redevelopment project?

Government Responses to Market Failure

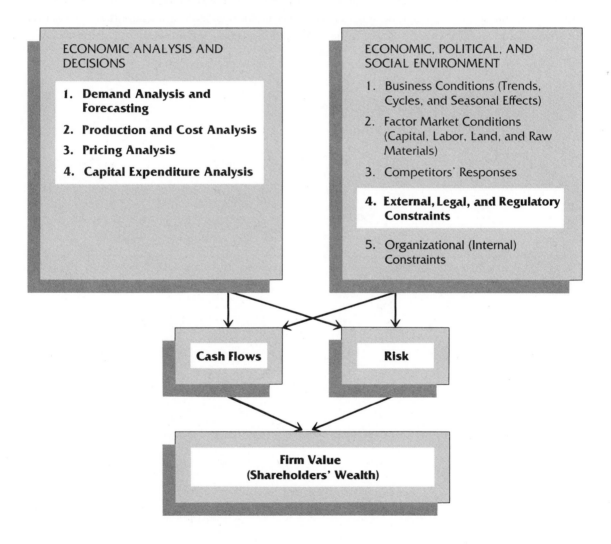

ECONOMIC ANALYSIS AND DECISIONS

1. **Demand Analysis and Forecasting**
2. **Production and Cost Analysis**
3. **Pricing Analysis**
4. **Capital Expenditure Analysis**

ECONOMIC, POLITICAL, AND SOCIAL ENVIRONMENT

1. Business Conditions (Trends, Cycles, and Seasonal Effects)
2. Factor Market Conditions (Capital, Labor, Land, and Raw Materials)
3. Competitors' Responses
4. **External, Legal, and Regulatory Constraints**
5. Organizational (Internal) Constraints

Cash Flows

Risk

Firm Value (Shareholders' Wealth)

Part VII (Government Responses to Market Failure) considers the extent and consequences of government regulation of the private sector. Although the United States' economy is predominantly a free market economy, the federal and state governments have traditionally played an active role in regulating the activities of business enterprises. The rationales for government intervention and regulation include the desire to encourage competition, to substitute regulation for the marketplace in the case of "natural monopolies," to protect consumers, particularly in those cases where information is difficult or expensive to obtain, and to assure that "optimal" levels of output be produced in the case of public goods or goods with significant externalities. Chapter 19 looks at government policies designed to restrict competition, to promote competition, to protect and inform consumers, and to pursue antitrust activities. Appendix 19A also considers solutions to the externality problem. Chapter 20 looks at the regulation of utilities in detail and identifies problems which have arisen as a result of the regulation of utility firms. Government regulation is an important constraint that managers must deal with if they are to be successful in maximizing the wealth of shareholders.

Government Regulation and Support of the Private Sector

19

As managers make decisions designed to lead to the maximization of shareholder wealth, they are faced with many constraints. Some of these constraints are external social pressures that may be brought to bear on the firm. Those which have not been codified into law but are loosely described as "moral obligations" have been referred to as the social responsibilities of business. Other constraints have been codified into legal obligations of all firms in a similar industry or class. These constraints include a wide array of government regulations designed to ensure a smooth, efficient, and competitive functioning of the economy. Government intervention into the functioning of the economy is a very important element in the resource allocation decisions made by managers in nearly every firm. As we shall see in Chapter 20, this regulation has taken an extreme form in some industries, such as the electric and natural gas utilities, the telephone industry, and various parts of the transportation industry. To allocate efficiently the resources of an enterprise and to make wealth maximizing price-output decisions, managers must fully understand both the competitive and the regulatory aspects of their environment. This chapter begins an exploration of these regulatory issues.

Policies to Support Business by Restricting Competition

Many examples of public policies pursued by government have the effect, if not always the intent, of restricting competition. These take numerous forms, including the issuance of licenses and patents and the restrictions on price competition. Although not discussed here, import controls in the form of tariffs and quotas have the same impact of restricting competition.

Licensing

When the government requires and issues a license permitting someone to practice a particular business, profession, or trade, it is by definition restricting the entry of some potential new competitors into that practice. Licensing is generally used to protect the public from fraud or incompetence in those cases where the potential for harm is quite large. Thus, doctors are required to meet

Glossary of New Terms

Patent
A legal government grant of monopoly power that prevents others from manufacturing or selling a patented article.

Antitrust laws
A series of laws passed since 1890 to prevent monopoly power and to maintain competition in most American industries.

Merger
A combination of two or more companies into one surviving company.

Market failure
The failure of market-oriented institutions to generate optimal levels of desirable outputs (activities) and to eliminate suboptimal levels of undesirable outputs (activities) through the signals provided by the market price system.

certain educational standards of professional competence; restaurants need to meet public health standards; real estate agents must meet certain standards of professional knowledge; financial trustees must be bonded to ensure the public against fraud; and cab drivers are licensed to protect the public from problem drinkers, accident-prone drivers, and the like.

In most of these cases the reason for requiring a license is to protect the public *and* the industry by establishing some minimal, acceptable criteria for participation in cases where consumers may find it difficult and/or prohibitively expensive to gather the information needed to make a rational choice. In other cases, however, the rationale for, or the type of, licensing is not so clear. In fact, in many instances the effect of licensing is to restrict unnecessarily entry into the trade and therefore to deter competition. In some cities, like Washington, D.C., taxicab licensing is intended solely to protect the public from the dangers of poor or incompetent drivers. The result is that fares are generally quite low and service is abundant. Other cities have severely restricted the number of cabs by selling only a small number of cab permits, as is the case in Chicago, or by giving an exclusive franchise to only one or a few companies, as in Houston. In such instances the effect of licensing goes well beyond the bounds of protecting the public. Those who have been privileged to receive such a license are protected against new competition, and the public pays in the form of poorer service and higher than necessary monopoly prices.

Patents

Patents are by definition a legal government grant of monopoly power. The holder of a patent may prevent others from manufacturing or selling a patented product or from using some patented process. The patent holder may grant a license permitting others to make limited use of the patent, and in exchange some sort of royalty arrangement is usually made. The monopoly granted by a patent is not, however, an absolute one. First, it is limited to a seventeen-year period, and no renewal privilege is permitted. Second, competing firms are not prohibited from engineering around an existing patent and bringing out a closely competitive, alternative design. Third, many patents are successfully challenged by competitors, placing a further limitation on the monopoly grant of power. It may be noted that even an unsuccessful legal challenge of a patent, particularly a challenge by a large firm on patents held by a smaller firm, may be successful in forcing the challenged firm to relent and perhaps sell or license its patent since such lengthy legal battles can be quite expensive for an individual or small firm.

Society pays two definite costs when it grants monopoly power to an individual or firm. Once an invention is made, it may cost very little for others to duplicate it, except for the necessary production costs. Yet the monopoly grant entitles the inventor to receive a premium above the cost of production, either in the form of higher-than-competitive-level prices, or as a royalty payment from licenses for a period of seventeen years. Hence we witness the same resource misallocation problems as are evident in any other form of monopoly. It is possible that a shorter patent monopoly period would provide sufficient incentives to encourage a high level of inventive activity in many areas.

Second, it has been observed that critical patents frequently help create strong monopoly positions that remain long after the original patent expires because of other barriers to entry that are built up in the interim. This has been the case in such industries as aluminum, shoe manufacturing, braking systems, rayon, cigarettes, metal containers, photographic equipment and supplies, and gypsum products.[1]

Offsetting these monopoly costs is the increase in inventive activity that the patent monopoly is alleged to encourage. Unfortunately, it is impossible to assess this impact in any meaningful, quantitative manner. Although doubtlessly some reduction in inventive activity would occur if the patent right were abolished, it is important to note that firms may protect the profits from inventions in other ways, including the following:

1. By keeping the technical aspects of the invention secret

2. By taking full advantage of the lead time over competitors that a new invention provides

Patents are used quite extensively by such industries as electronics, drugs, and chemicals, whereas auto manufacturers, paper, machinery, and rubber processors use them very little.

Restrictions on Price Competition

Restrictions on price competition have taken many forms in various industries. Agricultural prices have long been a function of government-guaranteed parity prices. Similarly, rates for scheduled ocean freight services by U.S. flagships are set by the international shipping conferences and approved and defended by the U.S. Maritime Commission.

Over the years a number of more general pieces of legislation have been enacted that have had the effect of limiting price competition. The most important remaining example of this type of legislation is the Robinson-Patman Act of 1936, which prohibits certain forms of price discrimination.

The Robinson-Patman Act of 1936 can be discussed both as antitrust legislation aimed at controlling the pricing aspects of market conduct and as an expression of a government policy aimed at restricting certain forms of price competition, thereby benefiting a special group of sellers. In this section the focus is on the latter objective of the act.

Robinson-Patman arose during the Depression when independent retailers and wholesalers, particularly grocers and druggists, were under strong pressures from the emerging large chain stores. These chain stores, by virtue of their size, possessed certain operating economies not realized by the small independents. More important, the chains were frequently able to wield their economic muscle to secure special low prices or brokerage concessions from sellers. Supported by the threat of moving their sizable orders elsewhere, the chains received special price concessions that were not based on inherent

---

[1] A. E. Kahn, "The Role of Patents," in *Competition, Cartels and Their Regulation,* ed. J. P. Miller (Amsterdam: North Holland, 1962).

operating economies of scale. For example, A & P received price concessions from food manufacturers by threatening to take its business elsewhere if they were not granted. Wholly owned, nonfunctioning dummy brokerage firms were established by businesses such as A & P to exact additional concessions in the form of a broker's price discount. The broker performed a useful intermediary function as a wholesale distributor for smaller firms, but in the case of A & P no services were provided, yet compensation in the form of brokers' discounts was still received. This situation further threatened the existence of the small independents, and a massive lobbying effort was mounted. The Robinson-Patman Act was finally passed in an attempt to preserve small business by regulating price discrimination.

Section 2 of the act has had the greatest impact. Its provisions are summarized below:

1. Section 2(a) makes it illegal to discriminate in price when selling goods of "like grade and quality" where the effect may be to "substantially lessen competition or tend to create a monopoly" or "to injure, destroy, or prevent competition with any person who either grants or knowingly receives the benefits of such discrimination, or with customers of either of them." This section not only declares price discrimination to be illegal when it *injures competition*, but also when it tends to *injure competitors*. In addition, it applies not only to injury to competition with respect to the one who grants the lower price but also to the one who receives it.

   A seller who is charged with price discrimination under Section 2(a) has two legal defenses. First the "cost defense" permits differentials in price that "make only due allowance for differences in the cost of manufacture, sale or delivery." The "good faith" defense permits a lower price to be charged to meet "an equally low price of a competitor." These defenses are outlined in Section 2(b).

2. Section 2(c) prohibits the payment of a brokerage commission to anyone but an independent broker. This section has been interpreted to make such payments illegal per se, without having to show proof of competitive injury.

3. Sections 2(d) and 2(e) prohibit the seller from allowing discounts to a buyer for merchandising services rendered the seller by the buyer. It also prohibits the seller from rendering such services to the buyer, unless these services or allowances are "accorded to all purchasers on proportionately equal terms." Advertising or promotional allowances, for example, must be made available to all sellers, not just a few selected large firms. Generally, these services have had to be made available proportionate to the dollar volume of purchases made by individual customers.

The Robinson-Patman Act is a curious piece of legislation that has probably deterred many price reductions that otherwise would have been made if it were not for the fear of prosecution. Under the Reagan Administration, the act has not been aggressively enforced because of the belief that it discourages competition by not encouraging the efficiencies of high volume transactions. In a May 1988 Supreme Court decision, however, the court upheld the right of Sharp Electronics to stop selling its products to a Houston discount retailer who refused to sell them at the higher markups suggested by Sharp. This decision has been described as a green light for high-markup retailers who may pressure manufacturers to stop supplying discount retailers. At this writing, it is not clear if Congress will attempt to enact legislation designed to override this recent decision.

Import Quotas

Another major policy that has supported domestic businesses by restricting competition is the use of import quotas. Faced with tough competition from producers abroad, many U.S. industries have sought restrictions on imports of products from abroad. Most vocal among these industries have been the textile, sugar, steel, and automobile industries. These industries have argued that without restrictions on foreign competition, thousands of U.S. workers would lose their jobs and critical domestic industries could be faced with extinction.

Import quotas inevitably lead to higher prices being paid for goods subject to the import restrictions. For example, in the automobile industry, the U.S. International Trade Commission estimates that the Japanese auto import restrictions had the effect in the early 1980s of increasing the average price for a Japanese car by $1,300, or about 30 percent. Under the import restrictions, the supply of Japanese-made cars fell short of the demand and many dealers were able to charge as much as $1,000 more than the official sticker price for some of the most popular models. In addition, because of the higher prices being charged for Japanese-made vehicles, U.S. manufacturers were able to charge higher prices for their products. Similar restrictions on the importation of microcomputer chips have resulted in significant price increases and shortages of many popular chips.

Government Policies of Subsidy and Promotion

In addition to the assistance that government gives private business by restricting certain forms of competition, it also undertakes more direct support programs. These take the form of the payment of subsidies, either as cash or as special tax treatments, as well as the conferring of special privileges on certain favored activities.[2] This kind of support to business occurs at all levels of government and may be granted for a wide variety of motives. The most convincing of these is that the favored activity confers significant external benefits, which firms operating independently in the private sector could not

---

[2] The government also assists private business by entering into partnerships with it, as in the case of Amtrak, the Federal Land Bank (which makes farm loans), the Federal National Mortgage Association (which finances Federal Housing Authority mortgages), the Communications Satellite Corporation, the Federal Deposit Insurance Corporation, the Federal Savings and Loan Insurance Corporation, the Export-Import Bank, and others. Some of these draw funds solely from the public sector, whereas others tap both the private and public sectors. They all operate in private markets in one way or another, frequently by insuring private risks in the financial markets.

confer or would not take into account in their profit-and-loss performance statements.[3] Nevertheless, these external benefits are deemed appropriate as social benefits by the government and therefore warrant some sort of subsidy support.

In this section we discuss but a few cases of government subsidy and promotion in our economy. Practically from the beginning of this country, the transportation industry has been the recipient of substantial economic subsidies. The rationale for this subsidization includes providing common carrier service to all parts of the nation as a stimulus to regional economic development, providing a militarily usable large-scale transportation network in case of war or national disaster, and assisting industrial development by furnishing inexpensive and plentiful logistical support. The earliest recipients of these subsidies were the railroads, and the subsidies were primarily in the form of free land provided along rights of way. Railroad subsidies had all but ceased when the formation of Amtrak to salvage rail passenger service reversed the trend. Other rail subsidies have resulted from the reorganization of six bankrupt Eastern railroads, headed by the Penn Central, into Conrail.

The airline industry is also the recipient of many forms of government subsidy. Airframe manufacturers have long benefited from government-sponsored research and development to discover new technologies for use by the military. Perhaps the most significant such example is the case of the development of the jet engine, which has revolutionized commercial airline transportation.

Government subsidy and promotional activities have been widespread in other industries as well. The electric power industry has received invaluable research and development assistance from the Atomic Energy Commission as well as generalized R & D aid aimed at developing and perfecting alternative power sources to reduce the impact of the energy crisis. And the domestic shipping industry receives substantial aid in the form of free operation and maintenance of our navigable water-ways. These examples of the wide array of government activities designed to promote private business give some indication of the extent of government involvement.

Tax Policy as a Regulatory Tool

In addition to providing direct subsidies in support of various industries, tax policy has also been used to support certain industries or economic activities. For example, the extractive industries such as oil, gas, and coal mining have received favorable tax treatment in the form of depletion allowances. Investment in capital equipment has also been encouraged through the provision of investment tax credits and accelerated depreciation allowances to investing firms. (Investment tax credits are no longer provided to business.) And small companies are subject to lower effective tax rates than are large companies, reflecting the government's belief that small business is a valuable institution in a democratic society and that small business provides competition for larger

---

[3] A thorough discussion of externalities is presented in Appendix 19A.

enterprises, thereby keeping prices in check. From time to time Congress has imposed "windfall profits taxes" on various industries in an attempt to limit potential abuses of market power. Most recently, for example, the oil industry has been subject to windfall profit taxes in response to the rapid increase in oil prices that occurred during the 1970s and early 1980s. Also, by permitting individuals to deduct home mortgage interest expenses, tax policy has provided strong support for the housing industry. These are a few of the many examples of direct and indirect subsidy, support, and regulation of various industries through the tax code. Therefore, managers must pay close attention to the tax consequences of their actions when making pricing and resource allocation decisions in their firms.

Operating Controls: An Economic Analysis

Rather than attempt to exhaustively enumerate the various operating controls that are placed on business firms, we focus primarily in this section on the usefulness of economic analysis in assessing the impact of such controls. Operating controls cover a wide range of constraints, such as those relating to environmental pollution, and to product quality and safety (for example, the Pure Food and Drug Act and automobile safety requirements). A wide variety of laws regulate industrial working conditions, further constraining the firm's decision-making flexibility. These include safety, noise, and internal plant pollution levels. The interest in providing truly equal employment opportunities has led to changes in recruiting and hiring practices. Certain labor laws, as well as union contracts, regulate working hours and require compensation for overtime work. Some industries, such as regulated monopolies, have been subject to price controls, whereas more general wage and price controls were used under the various phases of the 1972–1973 anti-inflation efforts. There are numerous other specific examples of constraints that have been imposed on the operating policies of individual firms, entire industries, and on the economy as a whole.

Economic analysis may often help in assessing the impacts of controls. In some instances, a linear-programming model may help to assess the impact of a constraint on the firm. The linear-programming technique was discussed in Chapter 5. In other cases a reasonably straightforward use of our knowledge about market structure and the relevant firm or industry demand and cost functions can offer helpful insights. The following example is an illustration of the usefulness of this latter type of analysis.

Example: The Palladium Metal-Casting Industry [4]

The palladium metal-casting industry is composed of about twenty-five firms that operate foundries engaged in making palladium castings. These foundries have

---

[4] The palladium metal-casting industry is a hypothetical example of the type of economic analysis that may be useful in assessing the impact of a wide variety of constraints. The data presented in this example are purely hypothetical and are not intended to be associated with any particular industry.

recently been under attack because of the heavy pollution they cause in the communities where they operate. Consequently, the EPA is considering standards to force a reduction in particulate emissions.

The industry makes various sizes and shapes of castings; however, production levels in individual firms are measured by hundred-pound weights of castings poured, and prices and costs vary roughly in accordance with the weight of the casting. Current industry employment is about 12,000 workers.

In an effort to assess the impact of proposed standards on the industry, the EPA has agreed to work with the trade association's economists to make these estimates. Industry demand has been estimated at

$$P = \$15,000 - .3Q$$

where P = price per hundred pounds of castings poured
Q = hundreds of pounds of castings poured

Hence, total revenue TR equals

$$TR = P \cdot Q$$
$$= \$15,000Q - .3Q^2$$

and marginal revenue MR equals

$$MR = \frac{dTR}{dQ}$$
$$= \$15,000 - .6Q$$

Similarly, the industry's total cost function TC has been estimated as

$$TC = \$100,000,000 + 6Q + .05Q^2$$

Hence marginal cost MC equals

$$MC = \frac{dTC}{dQ}$$
$$= 6 + 1Q$$

Because of a history of price leadership in the industry, the price-output solution that has generally evolved in the industry has been very close to that of a profit-maximizing monopoly. Consequently, price and output may be determined for the industry by equating marginal cost with marginal revenue and solving for

$$MC = MR$$
$$6 + .1Q = 15,000 - .6Q$$
$$.7Q = 14,994$$
$$Q^* = 21,420$$

Substituting in the demand equation, we find that

$$P^* = 15,000 - .3(21,420)$$
$$= \$8,574$$

Given this price-output combination, total industry profits π are estimated as

$$\pi = TR - TC$$
$$= P \cdot Q - TC$$
$$= (8,574)(21,420) - [100,000,000 + 6(21,420) + .05(21,420)1^2]$$
$$= 183,655,080 - 123,069,340$$
$$\pi^* = \$60,585,740$$

This profit of about $60.6 million represents a return on industry investment (ROI), estimated at about $840 million, of

$$ROI = \frac{\$60.6 \text{ million}}{\$840 \text{ million}} \times 100 = 7.2\%$$

This return is somewhat below average for U.S. industry, but this is merely an average return. Some firms are more efficient than others, thereby earning a higher return and vice versa.

To reduce smoke pollution within the proposed EPA limits, a total investment of $150,000,000 would be required. This will increase total industry fixed costs by about $15,000,000 (depreciation plus interest). If no variable costs were associated with the use of this pollution control equipment, the price-output solution would remain the same, but profits would drop by $15,000,000 and the return on investment (assuming no required return on the pollution control investment) would decline to

$$ROI_1 = \frac{\$45.5 \text{ million}}{\$840 \text{ million}} \times 100 = 5.4\%^5$$

This is well below the U.S. industry average. If the $150 million pollution investment were considered in the asset base, the ROI would be even less impressive.

It is unrealistic, however, to assume that only fixed costs will change. Variable costs also increase because it is costly to operate and maintain the pollution control equipment. Hence industry economists estimated a new industry total cost function:

$$TC_1 = \$115,000,000 + 8Q + .1Q^2$$

and

$$MC_1 = \frac{dTC_1}{dQ} = 8 + .2Q$$

Equating MC_1 to MR, we get

$$MC_1 = MR$$
$$8 + .2Q = 15,000 - .6Q$$
$$.8Q = 14,992$$
$$Q^* = 18,740$$

---

[5] Note that if the $150 million pollution control investment is added to the denominator, the computed ROI declines to 4.6 percent.

Substituting in the demand equation yields

$$P^* = 15,000 - .3(18,740)$$
$$= \$9,378$$

Thus we see that output declines nearly 3,000 units and prices are increased by about \$800. Under these circumstances, total industry profits π_2 equal

$$\pi_2 = TR - TC_1$$
$$= (9,378)(18,740) - [115,000,000 + 8(18,740) + .1(18,740)^2]$$
$$\pi_2^* = \$25,475,040$$

and return on investment (ignoring the pollution control investment) slips to

$$ROI_2 = \frac{\$25.5 \text{ million}}{\$840 \text{ million}} \times 100 = 3.0\%$$

Remembering that ROI_2 is an average figure, it is quite likely that some of the less-efficient firms would close. Industry and EPA economists make an admittedly crude estimation that the new industry total cost and marginal cost functions, after the exit of some firms, would equal

$$TC_2 = \$85,000,000 + 15Q + .2Q^2$$
$$MC_2 = 15 + .4Q$$

The profit-maximizing output now becomes

$$MC_2 = MR$$
$$15 + .4Q = 15,000 - .6Q$$
$$Q^* = 14,985$$

and price equals

$$P^* = 15,000 - .3(14,985)$$
$$= \$10,504$$

Thus we see that output will decline about 4,000 more units (from 18,740 to 14,985) and price will increase nearly \$1,150.

New industry profits (π_3) will be

$$\pi_3 = TR - TC_2$$
$$= (10,504)(14,985) - [85,000,000 + 15(14,985) + .2(14,985)^2]$$
$$\pi_3^* = \$27,267,620$$

The resulting industry return on investment ROI_3 will be enhanced by both the increase in profits from \$25 to \$27 million and the reduction in total industry investment as a result of the departure of the inefficient firms. Total industry investment is now estimated to equal only \$630 million. Hence

$$ROI_3 = \frac{\$27.2 \text{ million}}{\$630 \text{ million}} \times 100 = 4.3\%$$

It is also estimated that the departure of the industry's more inefficient firms will reduce total industry employment by about 3,000. The team of economists has determined that about one-half of the output reduction (from 21,420 to 14,985) will be absorbed by shifting demands to substitute domestic metal firms, and the other half will result in a negative balance-of-payments drain. The current foreign price per hundred pounds of casting is about $10,300. Thus the balance-of-payments impact of the proposed environmental standard is

$$BOP \text{ impacts} = \tfrac{1}{2}(21,420 - 14,985)(\$10,300)$$
$$= \$33,140,250$$

Armed with this and other data, such as what the regional impacts of plant closings will be on both unemployment rates and overall regional economic development, the EPA is in a far better position to assess the effect of its proposed standards.

Perhaps they will not decide on an across-the-board standard but may impose stricter limitations on firms located in densely populated areas than on those in sparsely inhabited areas. They may also decide to phase the standards in over time so their impacts will not be felt all at once. This would have the benefit of giving local communities, heavily dependent on the palladium foundries for employment, time to make necessary adjustments to expand the base of the area's economy, providing more stability in employment.

This rather simple, hypothetical example illustrates the insights that economic analysis can furnish in assessing the impact of operating controls on industry. Similar methods can be used to analyze nearly all the areas of operating constraints enumerated at the beginning of this section. The type of model chosen, as well as the complexity of that model, depends on the nature of the problem, the insights and creativity of the analyst, and the precision required in the results.

Government Policies to Protect and Inform Consumers[6]

Much government regulation of business is designed to increase the plane of competition by eliminating monopoly and attempts to monopolize an industry, as well as by attacking certain patterns of market conduct that are believed to have deleterious effects on a workably competitive market structure. Attempts to regulate business in this manner are discussed in the next section. The rationale for this type of regulation is the belief, founded on economic theory, that the more competitive the market structure, the greater the efficiency with which resources are allocated and the better the public interest will be served. Yet a reasonably competitive economy does not offer any iron-clad guarantees that the resulting business behavior will always be acceptable. Recall that one of the assumptions of the competitive market model was that consumers have free and full access to all the information needed to make rational choices among

---

[6] This section is based in part on James W. McKie, *Government Policies to Control and Assist Business* (New York: General Learning Press, 1972).

products and services. In this section we discuss some of the government measures designed to increase the quantity and quality of information available to consumers.

Policies Requiring Truthful Disclosure

Laws that forbid sellers to misrepresent their products or require manufacturers to disclose certain information about their products have been enacted on both the federal and state levels. The Federal Trade Commission Act of 1914 makes misrepresentation of products an unfair method of competition. Although this provision of the act was designed to protect competitors, it has been of significant benefit to consumers as well.

The Wheeler-Lea Act of 1938, an amendment to the FTC Act, makes illegal the use of unfair or deceptive acts or practices in the sale of goods and services in interstate commerce. The act currently provides protection to consumers for their own sakes, rather than requiring proof of injury to competition. This protection has been especially strong in the area of advertising, particularly with false advertisements of foods, drugs, medicines, corrective devices, and cosmetics. In those cases when misrepresentation is found, the FTC may ask a district court to issue an injunction to stop dissemination of the false advertisement, pending the outcome of an investigation. In the case of goods in general, the FTC may seek voluntary cooperation from a firm or it may issue a complaint and a "cease and desist" order and sue to have that order enforced if it is disobeyed. In recent years the FTC has become increasingly active in its efforts to require full disclosure of product characteristics and in its attempts to require that advertisers provide backup data supporting advertising claims.

Further consumer protection is given by the Food and Drug Act of 1906, which forbade adulteration and mislabeling of food and drugs sold in interstate commerce. The Food, Drug, and Cosmetics Act of 1938 strengthened the 1906 act considerably and expanded its coverage to include cosmetics.

Truth in Lending

In 1968 Congress passed the Consumer Credit Protection Act, which requires that borrowers be provided with complete and accurate disclosure of the terms under which credit is being granted or loans are being made. The major purpose of the act was to protect consumers by providing them with better, more intelligible information about the conditions surrounding a loan or an extension of credit. A secondary purpose was to encourage ethical standards of competition in the granting of credit or the making of loans, thereby exposing loan sharks and protecting ethical dealers and lenders.

Consumer Product Safety Commission

The Consumer Product Safety Commission began functioning in 1973. Its objective is to protect the public against unreasonable risks of injury associated with consumer products. Other objectives include helping consumers evaluate the comparative safety of various products and developing uniform safety standards for many goods.

Other Laws and Regulations

The preceding discussion focuses on the most significant laws and regulations designed to protect and inform consumers. A sampling of other related pieces of legislation and regulations is summarized in Table 19.1.

Market Performance

Ultimately what society would like from the producers of goods and services is that they perform in a satisfactory manner. *Good performance* is a multi-dimensional concept which includes these elements:

1. Resources should be allocated in an *efficient* manner within and among firms such that these resources are not needlessly wasted and that they are

Regulation	Primary Purpose
Drug Control Bill	Requires drugs to be proved effective before marketing. Also requires full reporting of relevant product information on product labels.
Truth in Packaging	Requires household products sold in grocery stores and drug stores to be clearly and accurately labeled regarding contents, net quantity, name of manufacturer, and the number of servings.
Fair Credit Reporting Act (1971)	Gives consumers the right to review their credit file, requires granters of credit to inform rejected applicants of the reasons for rejection, sets procedures for settling billing disputes, and prohibits creditors from discriminating on the basis of race, religion, color, sex, marital status, or age.
Magnuson-Moss Warranty Act (1975)	This act and related FTC rulings require that warranties be written in simple language, that they include a clear description of products and parts which are covered and uncovered, and that warranties clearly indicate how the consumer may exercise the rights granted by the warranty.
Mail orders	Mail order firms must fill orders in 30 days or give consumers their money back.
Real Estate Settlement and Procedures Act	Requires mortgage lenders to disclose in advance of a sale the settlement costs for both the buyer and seller.
Equal Employment Opportunity Commission	Investigates and conciliates complaints of employment discrimination based on race, religion, and sex.
Occupational Safety and Health Administration (OSHA)	Responsible for regulating safety and health conditions in workplaces.
National Highway Traffic Safety Administration	Regulates manufacturers of autos, trucks, buses, and tires in order to reduce the number of traffic accidents

Table 19.1
Summary of Other Major Regulatory Laws and Agencies

responsive to consumer desires. It is important, therefore, that a balance be drawn between potential scale economies of production and distribution and the output restrictions (and higher prices) that are assumed to be characteristic of monopoly power.

2. Producers should be *technologically progressive*; that is, they should attempt to develop and adopt quickly new techniques that will result in lower costs, improved quality, or a greater diversity of new and better products.

3. Producers should operate in a manner that encourages continued *full employment* of productive resources. It can be argued that unused resources are wasted resources, especially when they are perishable as in the case of human capital.

4. Productive resources should be organized in such a way as to encourage an *equitable distribution of income*. Although the notion of equity is a value-laden concept, we can say that profits should be no higher in the long run than necessary to invoke the productive use of resources in a particular endeavor. In addition, price stability should be encouraged because of the perverse ways in which inflation changes the distribution of income.[7]

Other aspects of good performance can be enumerated, including the extent to which a firm or industry promotes the conservation of natural resources and the performance and safety characteristics of products that are supplied.

Unfortunately, these elements of good market performance are not always completely compatible with one another or agreed on by everyone. This prevents the development of an unambiguous index that might be used to assess the performance characteristics of a firm or an industry. Consequently, research on market performance has tended to focus on certain specific, measurable aspects of market performance such as profit rates, price-cost margins, actual costs versus technologically possible costs, selling cost in relation to price or total costs, relative price flexibility, stability of employment throughout the business cycle, and improvements in the productivity of labor.

Market Conduct

With good performance as the ultimate objective, it is important to develop a conceptual model that will help explain the causes of good or bad performance. Both Edward Mason[8] and Joe Bain[9] have provided a general model of the factors influencing market performance. This model is illustrated in Figure 19.1.

---

[7] These aspects of good market performance have been adapted from Frederic M. Scherer, *Industrial Market Structure and Economic Performance*, 2d ed. (Chicago: Rand McNally, 1980), chap. 1.

[8] Edward S. Mason, "Price and Production Policies of Large-Scale Enterprise," *American Economic Review*, Supplement (March 1939), pp. 61–74, and "The Current State of the Monopoly Problem in the United States," *Harvard Law Review* (June 1949), pp. 1265–1285.

[9] Joe S. Bain, *Industrial Organization* (New York: John Wiley, 1959).

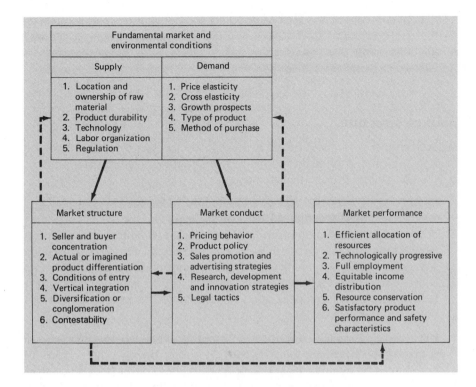

Figure 19.1
**A Conceptual
Market
Performance
Model**

Performance is viewed as dependent on the market conduct of firms in an industry. In general, market conduct includes the patterns of behavior followed by firms in the industry when adapting to a particular market situation. Included in market conduct are such things as the following:

1. *Pricing behavior of the firm or group of firms*—This includes a consideration of whether prices charged tend to maximize individual profits, whether collusive practices in use tend to result in maximum group profits, or whether price discrimination is followed.

2. *Product policy of the firm or group of firms*—For example, is product design frequently changed (as with auto style changes)? Is product quality consistent or variable? What variety of products is made available?

3. *Sales promotion and advertising policy of the firm or group*—How important are sales promotions and advertising in the firm's or industry's market policy? How is the volume of this activity determined?

4. *Research, development, and innovation strategies employed by the firm or group*—How substantial are expenditures for these purposes? To what extent is new technology available to smaller firms?

5. *Legal tactics used by the firm or group*—Are patent and trademark rights strictly enforced or defended? Are patent rights licensed to others at fair rates?

Although the distinction between conduct and performance may sometimes be blurred, it is important to remember that performance refers to the *end results* of the policies or processes of adjustment pursued by a firm, whereas market conduct encompasses the *processes* whereby the end results are reached.

Market Structure

Market conduct is to some extent dependent on the structure of a particular market. The concept of market structure refers to three main characteristics of buyers and sellers in a particular market:

1. The degree of *seller* and *buyer concentration* in the market, as well as the size distribution of these sellers or buyers—On the seller side this determines whether an industry is classified as monopoly, oligopoly, pure competition, or some variant thereof. It is also important to know if there is a significant "fringe" of potential competitors confronting the larger firms in a concentrated industry.[10] Buyer concentration is also important because it helps determine the nature of competition between the buyer and seller and ultimately the performance in a market.

2. The degree of actual or imagined *differentiation* between the products or services of competing producers—When buyers perceive the product of one firm to be different from that of another, these buyer preferences will impart a degree of market power to the seller that ulimately affects that seller's market conduct and performance.

3. The *conditions surrounding entry* into the market—This refers to the relative ease with which new sellers may enter a market. When significant barriers to entry exist, competition may cease to become a disciplining force on existing firms, and we are likely to see performance that departs from the competitive ideal.

Other related aspects of market structure include the extent to which firms are vertically integrated back to their sources of supply or forward to the final markets, and the degree of diversification of individual firms because that is also likely to impart market power and lead to unsatisfactory conduct and performance.

Contestable Markets and the Structure-Performance Relationship

William Baumol, J. C. Panzar, and R. D. Willig[11] have developed a theory of *contestable markets* that provides additional useful insights into the structure, conduct, and performance relationship. The theory of contestable markets can

---

[10] For example, see Stephen A. Rhoades, "Market Performance and the Nature of a Competitive Fringe," *Journal of Economics and Business* (May 1985),

[11] William J. Baumol, J. C. Panzar, and R. D. Willig, *Contestable Markets and the Theory of Industry Structure* (New York: Harcourt Brace Jovanovich, 1982).

be best considered as a generalization of the theory of perfect competition. It yields the same results as the theory of perfect competition but requires substantially fewer assumptions than the perfectly competitive model. The theory of contestability provides a substitute for the theory of perfect competition in a market characterized by the existence of single or multiproduct scale economies.

A perfectly contestable market is one that is accessible to potential entrants. Freedom of entry and exit is the central behavioral postulate of contestable markets. In a perfectly contestable market, potential competitors have the same cost function as the incumbent firm(s). These potential competitors can enter and leave the market without a loss of capital. The potential competitors use the incumbent firms' pre-entry price as the basis for evaluating the profitability of entry. With freedom of entry and exit, potential competitors need not fear the pricing reactions of competitors. If profit potential disappears after initial entry, the new entrants can simply leave the industry. The possibility of hit-and-run profits by potential entrants will cause incumbent firms to set prices equal to marginal cost because at any higher price, there will be an opportunity for profitable entry.

The theory of contestable markets has shifted the focus of attention in market structure, conduct, and performance relationships to the conditions of entry and exit. The lower the barriers to entry and exit, the more nearly a market structure fits the perfectly contestable market model, and consequently, the more likely the resulting set of prices and outputs will meet the perfectly competitive market norm of price equal to marginal cost.

Condition of Entry

The condition of entry gives clues about potential rivals. The condition of entry is a measure of the height of the barriers that exist against new competitors and that protect existing firms from potential competition. The condition of entry, or the barriers to entry in an industry, may be measured conceptually as "the largest percentage by which established sellers can persistently elevate their prices above the minimized or competitive average costs of production and distribution without inducing new sellers to enter the industry."[12] The importance of entry barriers may be seen in a simple example. Consider the case of a monopolist who knows that raising prices above a level that just yields a normal rate of return on the investment will result in a large influx of new competitors in the industry. The monopolist may choose no competitors and normal profits in the short run to preserve a long-run position. Alternatively, when substantial barriers to entry exist or when entry is completely blocked, as in the case of the possession of patent rights, the monopolist may be expected to charge the highest price consistent with short-run profit maximization and still maintain the preferred position over the long run (or at least the useful life of the patent). We can see that the relative ease or difficulty of entry for new firms in an industry can have a significant impact on industry performance.

---

[12] Bain, *Industrial Organization*, p. 237.

Table 19.2
Type and Consequences of Barriers to Entry

Type	Consequences for New Entrants
A. Product differentiation barriers arise from: 1. Buyer preferences, conditioned by advertising, for established brand names 2. Patent control of superior product designs by existing firms 3. Ownership or control of favored distribution systems (for example, exclusive auto dealerships)	A. 1. New entrants cannot sell their products for as high a price as existing firms can. 2. Sales promotion costs for new entrants may be prohibitive 3. New entrants may be unable to raise sufficient capital to establish a competitive distribution system
B. Absolute superiority of established firms in the matter of production and distribution costs arise from: 1. Control of superior production techniques by patent or secrecy 2. Exclusive ownership of superior natural resource deposits 3. Inability of new firms to acquire necessary factors of production (management, labor, equipment) 4. Superior access to financial resources at lower costs	B. 1. Costs of new entrants are higher than for existing firms. Hence, while existing firms may charge a price which results in above-normal profits, new entrants may be unable to make even a normal profit at that price.
C. Economies of large-scale production and distribution (or sales promotion) arise from: 1. Capital-intensive nature of industry production processes 2. High initial start-up costs	C. 1. The entry of a new firm at a sufficient scale will result in an industry price reduction and a disappearance of the profits anticipated by the new entrants. 2. New firm may be unable to acquire a sufficient market share to sustain efficient operations.

Source: Joe S. Bain, *Industrial Organization* (New York: Wiley, 1959), pp. 237–265.

When firms are able to raise their prices somewhat above those that would prevail under competition without inducing the entry of new firms, some barriers to new entry must exist. These may be classified into three types. These general types of entry barriers and how they arise are summarized on the left side of Table 19.2; the consequences of the entry barrier on new competitors are enumerated on the right.

Market and Environmental Conditions

Market structure, conduct, and ultimately performance are also influenced by certain *fundamental market and environmental conditions*. These may be divided into factors primarily influencing the *supply* or *input side* of the production equation and those whose primary impact is on the *demand side*. The supply side includes the location and ownership distribution of essential raw materials, the durability of the product, the available technology and production techniques commonly used, the degree to which labor inputs are readily available and organized (unionized), and the extent to which the firm's activities are regulated by government. On the demand side, such factors as the price elasticity of demand, the number of close substitutes that are available (measured by the cross elasticity of demand), the growth prospects of the industry, the type of good or service being produced (intermediate, consumer, specialty, convenience, and so on), and the method of purchase by buyers (list price acceptance, negotiation or haggling, sealed bid) must be included in an analysis of fundamental conditions influencing market structure, conduct, and performance.

The solid arrows in Figure 19.1 indicate flows that are primarily causal in the model, resulting ultimately in some observable market performance. As the dotted arrows indicate, however, some secondary and feedback flows are also involved. The major concern of studies in the field of market structure, conduct, and performance is to develop the capability to predict market performance, based either on observations of the fundamental market and environmental conditions, market structure and conduct, or on some contemplated and controllable changes in these factors. Several examples of this type of empirical research are illustrated at the end of this chapter.

Before moving to a further discussion of the characteristics of market structure, we wish to emphasize one final point about the usefulness of this model in providing guidance for developing regulatory policies. The point is that there is no one place in the causal chain, from fundamental conditions to market performance, at which regulation will always work best. In some cases direct control of market structure may be an effective and efficient means of achieving desired performance. In other cases direct control over certain business practices (that is, over market conduct) will be more effective. The essential ingredient in any good regulatory policy is developing the logical chain of events between fundamental market conditions and market performance and then imposing any necessary constraints at the most appropriate point.

Antitrust: Government Regulation of Market Conduct and Structure

Since 1890, a number of federal laws have been passed with the intent of preventing monopoly and of maintaining competition in U.S. industry.[13] The ultimate objective of these laws is to protect the public from the abuses and inefficiencies that are thought to flow from the possession of monopoly power. These laws have come to be known as "antitrust laws" because they were initially directed at the large voting trusts such as Standard Oil, American Tobacco, and several coal and railroad trusts. Under a trust agreement, the voting rights to the stock of a number of directly competitive firms were conveyed to a legal trust, which managed the firms as if they were one big

---

[13] Many states have also passed antitrust laws designed to regulate *intrastate* commerce. These have been of relatively little significance, however, because of poor enforcement, as well as the overwhelming *interstate* structure of U.S. industry, which is covered more effectively by federal laws.

multiplant monopoly, thereby maximizing profits. Although extremely successful on the bottom line of the income statement, these trusts were viewed with increasing dismay because of the high price and restricted outputs that resulted. In this section we summarize the provisions of the most important of these antitrust laws.

The Sherman Act (1890)

The Sherman Act was the first national antitrust law designed to regulate monopoly and the use of monopoly power. Its important provisions are brief, but they are wide-ranging. First, it declares illegal

> every contract, combination in the form of a trust or otherwise, or conspiracy in restraint of commerce among the several States, or with foreign nations ...

This provision applies only to agreements in which two or more persons are involved. The second important provision is more general, in that it also applies to individual efforts to monopolize. It declares that

> every person who shall monopolize, or attempt to monopolize, or combine or conspire with any other person or persons, to monopolize any part of the trade or commerce among the several States, or with foreign nations, shall be deemed guilty of a misdemeanor.

This act turned the already existing common-law prohibitions against restraint of trade and monopolization into federal offenses, requiring federal enforcement. In the years following the passage of the Sherman Act, dissatisfaction with the generality of its provisions, as well as with the lack of vigor with which it was enforced, led to pressure for additional legislation.

The Clayton Act (1914)

An attempt to develop a comprehensive list of forbidden monopolistic practices was largely a failure in Congress. It was difficult to enumerate precisely and define all existing unfair business practices and guard against future practices that might evolve. Hence the Clayton Act enumerated only four such unfair practices:

1. *Price discrimination* between purchasers of commodities was illegal, except to the extent that it was based on differences in grade, quality, and quantity of the product sold. Lower prices were permitted only where they made "due allowances for differences in the cost of selling or transportation" and where they were offered "in good faith to meet competition." To discriminate otherwise in pricing was illegal if the effect was to substantially lessen competition or tend to create a monopoly. It was this section of the Clayton Act, Section 2, that was amended and strengthened by the Robinson-Patman Act during the era of the rise of the chain store.

2. Section 3 of the act forbade sellers from leasing or making "a sale or contract for the sale of ... commodities ... on the condition that the lessee or

purchaser thereof shall not use or deal in the ... commodity ... of a competitor." This is commonly referred to as a prohibition against "exclusive and *trying contracts*." As with the price discrimination section, the prohibition was not absolute but only applied to the extent that the practice substantially lessened competition or tended to create a monopoly.

3. Section 7, the *antimerger* section, forbade any corporation engaged in commerce from acquiring the shares of a competing firm or from purchasing the stocks of two or more competing firms. As with Section 2 and 3, the prohibition was not absolute but applied only in cases where substantial damage to competition could be proven or where it tended to create a monopoly.

4. *Corporate interlock*, defined as cases where the same person is on the board of directors of two or more firms, was declared illegal in Section 8, if (a) the corporations were competitive, (b) if any one had capital, surplus, and undivided profits in excess of $1 million, and (c) where "the elimination of competition ... between them would constitute a violation of any of the provisions of the antitrust laws."

The Federal Trade Commission Act (1914)

The Federal Trade Commission Act was passed as a supplement to the Clayton Act. Its major antitrust provision, found in Section 5, merely states "that unfair methods of competition in commerce are hereby declared illegal." A determination of what constitutes unfair methods of competition beyond those specified in the Clayton Act is left to the Federal Trade Commission, which the act established as an independent government antitrust agency with the goal of attacking unfair practices. The creation of a specific government antitrust agency with appropriated funds needed to initiate cases under the acts was the most significant aspect of the 1914 acts. No longer did enforcement have to be initiated at private expense and risk to curb the excesses of unfair and monopolistic practices.

The Wheeler-Lea Act (1938)

In addition to its function of protecting consumers from unfair methods of competition, the Wheeler-Lea Act also serves an important antitrust role. Before Wheeler-Lea was passed as an amendment to Section 5 of the FTC Act, the courts had severely restricted the interpretation of unfair methods of competition. In several key cases the courts not only required proof of damaging deception to a buyer but also strong evidence that the deceptive firm had competitors who were also damaged and who were not engaging in similar deceptive practices themselves. By making illegal not only unfair methods of competition but also unfair or deceptive acts or practices, whether harm to competition is proven or not, the act provides for expanded consumer protection and also makes the prosecution of such cases far easier by removing the restrictive court interpretations.

The Celler-Kefauver Antimerger Act (1950)

Several court decisions following the passage of the Clayton Act substantially weakened its antimerger prohibition as contained in Section 7. The original statute dealt only with horizontal mergers, those between directly competing companies; others were not prohibited.

Another serious weakness in the original statute was that it applied only to mergers via *stock* acquisition. Mergers via the acquisition of *assets* were not affected. The Celler-Kefauver amendment was passed to close these loopholes. Under the amended Section 7, acquisition of another corporation's *stock or assets* is prohibited where "in any line of commerce in any section of the country, the effect of such acquisition may be substantially to lessen competition, or to tend to create a monopoly." Thus the two major weaknesses of the antimerger section of the Clayton Act were overcome.

The Deregulation Movement

Throughout the late 1970s and 1980s, sentiment has increased for relying less on government regulation and more on the marketplace to achieve desired economic objectives. This sentiment for increased deregulation has been felt most significantly in the price regulation of transportation services. Such recent pieces of legislation as the Airline Deregulation Act of 1978, the Railroad Revitalization and Regulatory Reform Act of 1976, and the Motor Carrier Act of 1980 have greatly increased the flexibility of airlines, railroads, and the trucking industries to set prices and determine levels of service and areas of operation *outside* of the regulatory framework. The objectives of these pieces of legislation have been to give the affected industries greater pricing flexibility in exchange for an increased and more open level of competition.

Although the full impact of deregulation in these industries has yet to be felt, most observers believe the impact has been quite favorable. In the airline industry, deregulation has meant greater competition on many routes with fare reductions and promotional fares becoming quite common. In the trucking industry, deregulation has been credited with a reduction in the rate of increase of trucking charges and improvements in service in many areas.

In the communications industry, AT&T has faced increased competition (primarily, but not exclusively) in the long-distance market from such firms as MCI. Customers may also purchase their own phone equipment from a wide range of suppliers other than AT&T. The breakup of AT&T into seven independent regional phone companies and a long-distance company is an important step in deregulation of the telecommunications industry.[14]

Although it is probably still a number of years away, there is now serious discussion of the deregulation of the electric power generation industry. Such a possibility seemed totally unlikely just a few years ago. Deregulation of natural

---

[14] For a disscussion of the impacts of deregulation see A. E. Kahn, "Surprises from Airline Deregulation", R. W. Crandall, "Surprises from Telephone Deregulation and the AT&T Divestiture", and E. J. Kane, "Interaction of Financial and Regulatory Innovation", *American Economic Review* (May 1988), pp. 316–334.

gas pipelines is effectively a reality today. Thus, it appears as though the United States has entered a new era of less regulation and more reliance on the marketplace to achieve economic objectives.

Summary

- State and local governments and especially the federal government play an active role in regulating and supporting private sector businesses.

- A number of regulatory policies are designed to restrict (or have the impact of restricting) competition. These include licensing, issuing patents trademarks, and copyrights, and using import controls, such as tariffs and quotas. Price competition has been limited in several industries by various regulatory agencies including the Interstate Commerce Commission, the Federal Energy Regulatory Commission, and the U.S. Maritime Commission.

- The Robinson-Patman Act provides a more general form of restriction on price competition. It limits the practice of price discrimination between buyers.

- In addition to these activities, government support of business has also taken the more explicit form of direct and indirect subsidies, as in the case of Amtrak, Conrail, and the shipping industries. The rationale for such subsidy support is generally that the favored industry generates significant external benefits for which it would not normally be rewarded in the marketplace.

- A wide range of government regulations have been designed to protect consumers from potential market abuses and to assist consumers in gaining easy access to all the information needed to make rational choices among goods and services. The most important of these acts regulating business are the Federal Trade Commission Act of 1914, which makes misrepresentation of products an unfair method of competition; the Food and Drug Act of 1936, which forbids the adulteration and mislabeling of food, drugs, and cosmetics; and the Consumer Credit Protection Act of 1968, which requires that borrowers be given a complete and accurate disclosure of the terms under which credit is being granted or loans are being made.

- A group of antitrust laws have been passed to prevent monopoly and to encourage competition in U.S. industry. The most important of these acts are the Sherman Act of 1890, the FTC and Clayton acts of 1914, the Robinson-Patman Act of 1936, the Wheeler-Lea Act of 1938, and the Celler-Kefauver Antimerger Act of 1950.

- The current political and economic environment favors a significant reduction in the amount of government regulation and interference in the operation of the private sector of the economy. This has been observable in deregulation in the banking, transportation, natural gas pipeline, and telecommunications industries.

- Contestable markets are assumed to have freedom of entry and exit for potential competitors. In a perfectly contestable market, the resulting set of prices and outputs approaches those expected under perfect competition.

- *Market performance* refers to the efficiency of resource allocation within and among firms, the technological progressiveness of firms, the tendency of firms to fully employ resources, and the impact on the equitable distribution of resources.

- *Market conduct* refers to the pricing behavior, the product policy, the sales promotion and advertising policy, the research, development, and innovation strategies, and the legal tactics employed by a firm or group of firms.

- *Market structure* refers to the degree of seller and buyer concentration in a market, the degree of actual or imagined product differentiation between products or services of competing producers, and the conditions surrounding entry into the market.

Selected References

Benston, George J. "The Validity of Profit-Structure Studies with Particular Reference to the FTC's Line of Business Data." *American Economic Review* (March 1985). pp. 37–67.

Bock, Betty. *Concentration, Oligopoly, and Profit.* New York: The Conference Board, 1972.

Coase, R. H. "The Nature of the Firm." *Economics* (November 1937), pp. 386–405.

Cyert, Richard M., and James G. March. *A Behavioral Theory of the Firm.* Englewood Cliffs, N.J.: Prentice-Hall, 1965.

Dalton, J. A., and D. W. Penn. "The Concentration-Profitability Relationship: Is There a Critical Concentration Ratio?" *Journal of Industrial Economics* (December 1976).

Dao, Thi D. "Drug Innovation and Decision Economics 5, no. 2 (1984), pp. 80–84.

Gilbert, R. Alton. "Bank Market Structure and Competition: A Survey," Part 2. *Journal of Money, Credit and Banking* (November 1984). pp. 617–660.

Leonard, W. N. "Airline Deregulation: Grand Design or Gross Debacle?" *Journal of Economic Issues* (June 1983), pp. 453–462.

Miller, E. M. 'Do Economies of Scale Attract Entry?" *Antitrust Bulletin* (Fall 1980).

O'Connell, Joan M. "Do Mergers Really Work?" *Business Week*, 3 June 1985, pp. 88ff.

Porter, R. H. "The Federal Trade Commission v. The Oil Industry: An Autopsy on the Commission's Shared Monopoly Case against the Nation's Eight Largest Oil Companies." *Antitrust Bulletin* (Winter 1982), pp. 753–820.

Reid, Samuel R. *Mergers, Managers and the Economy.* New York: McGraw-Hill, 1968.

Rhoades, Stephen A. "Market Performance and the Nature of the Competitive Fringe." *Journal of Economics and Business* (May 1985), pp. 141–158.

Scherer, Frederic M. *Industrial Market Structure and Economic Performance*, 2d ed. Chicago: Rand McNally, 1980.

Schmalensee, R. "Antitrust and the New Industrial Economics." *AEA Papers and Proceedings.* (May 1982), pp. 24–28.

Smirlock, M. "Evidence of the (Non) Relationship between Concentration and Profitability in Banking" *Journal of Money, Credit and Banking* (February 1985), pp. 69–83.

Smirlock, M., T. Gilligan, and W. Marshall. "Tobin's q and the Structure-Performance Relationship." *American Economic Review* (December 1984), pp. 1051–1060.

Stigler, George J. *The Organization of Industry.* Homewood, Ill.: Richard D. Irwin, 1968.

Discussion Questions

1. Under what circumstances would you defend pure competition as the most efficient market structure? What arguments can you make to the contrary?

2. One argument that is frequently made about the U.S. economic system is that there are powerful, built-in market incentives for ever-increasing efficiency. The most efficient firms are rewarded with high profit rates, whereas poorly managed firms are faced with bankruptcy or reorganization (generally with a complete change of management and significant losses to the shareholders). As the economy has become increasingly dominated by industries controlled by a few superfirms, the traditionally stated efficiency incentive appears to have changed.

  a. Based on both your current knowledge and a brief library literature search, evaluate the action taken by the government to aid the ailing Lockheed, Chrysler, and First Republic corporations. On what basis was government aid justified?
  b. Has the government treated smaller firms in more competitive industries and smaller banks in a similar fashion?

3. Discuss the proposition that corporate "raiders," such as T. Boone Pickens of Mesa Petroleum, are a valuable element in the efficient operation of the economy and that such takeover threats result in long-run benefits to shareholders and more efficient management.

4. Discuss the elements of seller concentration in a market that can influence the performance of firms in that market.

5. How do the *conditions of entry* influence potential performance of firms already producing in an industry?

6. What factors, other than the number of sellers in a marketplace, determine the degree of competition in an industry?

7. An industry is composed of one firm (1) controlling 70 percent of the market, a second firm (2) with 15 percent of the market, and a third firm (3) with 5 percent of the market. Approximately 30 firms divide the remaining 10 percent of the market. Would you view a merger of Firm 2 with Firm 3 as procompetitive or anticompetitive? Explain.

8. How can you justify the existence of government-granted monopolies for such public utilities as local telephone service, natural gas distribution, and electricity in light of the traditional economic argument that the more competition there is, the more likely it is that an efficient allocation of resources will occur?

9. What are the major factors to be considered, for antitrust purposes, in determining the relevant market in which a firm competes?

10. Evaluate the importance of the concept of price elasticity of demand when attempting to identify the ultimate incidence of the impact of government regulations on business that (a) increase fixed costs and (b) increase variable costs.

11. Discuss the pros and cons of the regulation of oil and natural gas prices.

12. During the 1970s, many banking organizations earned rates of return on common equity that were significantly above the average earned in other U.S. industries. During the mid–1980s, earned returns in the banking industry had declined relative to other U.S. industries. What factors can you identify that might be responsible for this trend?

13. What economic arguments can be made in favor of mandatory seat-belt usage laws in automobiles and mandatory helmet laws for motorcycles?

14. What are the incentives to innovate for a monopoly firm as compared with a firm in a competitive market if patent protection is not available? Does your answer change if patent protection is available?

15. Would you consider the airline industry to be a contestable market? Explain.

Problems

1. Specific Motors Corporation is one of the Big Three auto manufacturers in Transylvania. Specific's share of the domestic auto market is 55 percent. The next two closest competitors control 25 and 15 percent of the market, respectively, and the rest may be accounted for by two small, specialized firms. Specific has been under pressure from Transylvania's Justice Department and the State Trade Commission for monopolistic practices. To discourage any attempts to break up Specific, management has decided to maintain its market share below 55 percent of the total domestic automobile sales revenues.

Specific estimates that to stay within its constraint sales of 55 percent of the market, its total sales should not exceed $2.8 billion.

The firm faces the following demand and cost functions:

$$P = 16,000 - .02Q$$

$$TC = 850,000,000 + 4,000Q$$

a. Calculate the unconstrained profit-maximizing level of price and output for Specific.

b. At this level, what will total sales revenues be? Total profits?

c. If the firm constrains its sales revenue to $2.8 billion, calculate price, output, and profit levels under the constraint.

(*Hint:* Remember the quadratic formula: $x = \dfrac{-b \pm \sqrt{b^2 - 4ac}}{2a}$

based on the equation $ax^2 + bx + c = 0$.)

d. What is the cost to the firm of this market-share constraint?

2. Seidman Products, Inc. is a manufacturer of chocolate-flavored LTD tablets and aspirin. Each bottle of LTD costs the firm 50 cents in wages and 25 cents in materials to produce. In contrast, the wage and material costs per bottle of aspirin are 25 cents each. All LTD and aspirin that are produced in the period are sold on one-period credit terms. Labor and materials costs for the period must be paid in cash during that period. Liquid resources (cash, collections from previous periods, and bank credit), which are available to pay for labor and material expenses during the period, are expected to amount to $150. The firm has 60 hours of pill-manufacturing time available during the period and 25 hours of bottling-capacity time.

Each bottle of aspirin requires 9 minutes of manufacturing time and 6 minutes of bottling time. Each bottle of LTD requires 24 minutes of manufacturing time and 3 minutes of bottling time.

Because of the fear of misuse of the LTD if more is produced than is needed to meet pure medical research needs, the Food and Drug Administration has limited LTD output per period to a maximum of 100 bottles.

The selling price of a bottle of aspirin is $2.50. Each bottle of LTD sells for $4.75.

a. Formulate this problem in a linear-programming framework. Specify the objective function and all constraints.

b. Using the graphic method, solve for the optimal output mix between aspirin and LTD.

c. What is the cost to the firm of the FDA output restriction on LTD production?

d. As president of Seidman Products, what resources would you seek to increase to expand your firm's profits?

3. The industry demand function for bulk plastics is represented by the following equation:

$$P = 800 - 20Q$$

where Q represents millions of pounds of plastic.

The total cost function for the industry, exclusive of a required return on invested capital is

$$TC = \$300 + \$500Q + \$10Q^2$$

where Q represents millions of pounds of plastic and dollar figures represent millions of dollars.

a. If this industry acts like a monopolist in the determination of price and output, compute the profit-maximizing level of price and output.

b. What are total profits at this price and output level?

c. Assume that this industry is comprised of many (500) small firms, such that the demand function facing any individual firm is

$$P = \$620$$

Compute the profit-maximizing level of price and output under these conditions (the industry's total cost function remains unchanged).

d. What are total profits, given your answer to part (c)?

e. Because of the risk of this industry, investors require a 15 percent rate of return on the investment made in this industry. Total industry investment amounts to $2 billion. If the monopoly solution prevails [parts (a) and (b)], how would you describe the profits of the industry?

f. If the competitive solution most accurately describes the industry, is the industry operating under equilibrium conditions? Why or why not? What would you expect to happen?

g. The Clean Water Coalition has proposed pollution control standards for the industry that would change the industry cost curve to

$$TC = 400 + 560Q + 10Q^2$$

What is the impact of this change on price, output, and total profits under the monopoly solution?

h. Assume these standards are being proposed only in the state of Texas, which has 50 of the 500 producers. What impact would you expect the new standards to have on Texas firms? The rest of the industry?

4. A product you produce has the following annual demand function:

$$P = 90 - .003Q$$

The marginal cost of producing the product is $30. If the firm pays a fee of $50,000 to the General Drug Research Council, it can have its product's effectiveness certified. The demand function for a certified product is expected to be

$$P = 100 - .003Q$$

a. Calculate the price, output, and profit contribution if the product is not certified.

b. Calculate the price, output, and profit contribution if the product is certified.

c. Should the firm undergo the certification process?

5. Assume an industry produces a relatively homogeneous product, such that all sales must be made at approximately the same price. Assume also that the industry is dominated by one large firm but a fringe of smaller, competitive firms exists. Fringe competitors and potential new entrants are so small in size that they have no perceptible influence on price.

Discuss graphically or verbally the pricing strategies available to the dominant firm:

a. If the profit-maximizing price charged by the dominant firm is below the lowest attainable average total cost (including normal profits) for the smaller existing competitive firms and potential entrants.

b. If the profit-maximizing price charged by the dominant firm exceeds the competitive fringe firms' lowest attainable average costs, including a normal profit. Would you expect a different strategy to be followed if the dominant firm sought to maximize short-run rather than long-run profits?

c. If the dominant firm is relatively unsure of the industry's future or perceives a rapidly changing technology in the industry such that an optimal scale of operation can be achieved with an increasingly small plant size. What strategy would you expect the dominant firm to follow?

d. If the dominant firm adopts a long-run strategy to deter new entry. Explain how the use of full-cost pricing rules can lead to nearly maximum long-run profits.

6. Public Service Company has been disappointed by its failure to be allowed to earn what it considers to be a fair return on its investment in utility assets. The firm has averaged a return on equity of 12 percent over the past ten years, with a standard deviation of 3 percent. It is considering a series of acquisitions that, when complete, would roughly double the firm's size. The expected return on equity from these new activities is 19 percent, with a standard deviation of 7 percent. Based on past performance, the correlation between returns in the utility business and returns in the other businesses is expected to +0.3.

a. Calculate the expected return and risk of the returns for the Public Service Company before and after the acquisitions.

[*Hint:* A general formula for the risk (standard deviation) of two assets' returns is

$$\sigma_T = \sqrt{w_A^2 \sigma_A^2 + w_B^2 \sigma_B^2 + 2 w_A w_B \rho_{AB} \sigma_A \sigma_B}$$

where w_A and w_B are the proportions invested in assets A and B, respectively, and $w_A + w_B = 1$; σ_A and σ_B are the standard deviations of returns for assets A and B, respectively; and ρ_{AB} is the correlation of returns from assets A and B.]

b. Recalculate the expected return and risk of the Public Service Company after completing the acquisitions if the acquisitions are two times the size of the utility business of Public Service Company; that is, w_A = proportion of utility assets = 0.333 and w_B = proportion of acquired assets = 0.667.

c. What other potential benefits can you see being derived from this program of diversification?

d. What regulatory problems can you perceive when a utility diversifies outside of the regulated sector of the economy?

7. An industry produces its product, Scruffs, at a constant marginal cost of $50. The market demand for Scruffs is equal to

$$Q = 75,000 - 600P$$

a. What is the value to a monopolist who is able to develop a patented process for producing Scruffs at a cost of only $45?

b. If the industry producing Scruffs is purely competitive, what is the maximum benefit that an inventor of a process that will reduce the cost of producing Scruffs by $5 per unit can expect to receive by licensing her invention to the firms in the industry?

8. The demand curve in a competitive industry has been estimated to be

$$P = 1500 - 9Q$$

The industry's short-run supply curve is

$$P = 80 + 3Q$$

A single firm emerges as the dominant firm in the industry and gradually acquires all of the other firms in the industry. The marginal cost curve for the monopolist becomes

$$MC = 50 + 3Q$$

as a result of effecting a number of operating economies.

a. Calculate the competitive market's price and output levels.

b. Calculate the price and output levels for the industry once the monopolist assumes control, assuming that industry demand remains unchanged.

c. If this monopolist were regulated so that the maximum price the monopolist is allowed to charge is $450, what is the benefit to consumers and the cost to the monopolist?

9. If OPEC agrees to raise the price of oil by $3 a barrel and if all other world oil prices increase by a similar amount, is the economic cost to consumers equal to $3 a barrel, something more, or something less?

Economic Externalities and Market Failure

Externalities

Economic externalities are one of several causes of the private market mechanism's failure to achieve an efficient allocation of societal resources. This appendix takes a closer look at the problem and examines several proposed public policy remedies.

The Importance of Externalities

Managers in both the public and private sectors are faced with many decisions influenced by economic externalities. The private manager needs to be aware that economic externalities are often generated by the firm in the normal course of its business. Such an awareness allows the firm to consciously consider ways of reducing negative externalities in the normal course of its business or of emphasizing to the public the positive externalities (social benefits) that the firm generates and for which it is not compensated by the market. *Furthermore, the private manager has a strong interest in the kinds of remedies adopted by society (the government) for controlling externalities at the least cost.*

The public manager also needs to be aware of the nature and sources of economic externalities. Many public enterprises also generate these effects in the normal course of their activities. When these are negative, appropriate actions must be taken to control the problem. More importantly, perhaps, the full extent of positive externalities should be understood by the public manager because these benefits often provide the justification for maintaining or expanding a public program. In the role of a regulator, the public manager must understand the scope of remedies available and the strengths and weaknesses of each.

Glossary of New Terms

Production externalities Externalities that arise in the production process for a good or service. *Favorable* (to a third party) production externalities are called "external production economies." *Unfavorable* (to a third party) production externalities are called "external production diseconomies."

Consumption externalities Externalities that result when the actions taken by one consumer influence the satisfaction received by one or more other consumers. *Favorable* (to a third party) consumption externalities are called "external consumption economies." *Unfavorable* (to a third party) consumption externalities are called "external consumption diseconomies."

Externalities Defined

Externalities exist when a third party receives benefits or bears costs arising from an economic transaction in which he or she is not a direct participant.[1] This occurs when producers or consumers provide benefits to others (the third party) for which the market system does not enable them to receive full payment in return. Thus when a firm provides workers with new skills through job training, the firm is not only furnishing a base for its own increased productivity but is also simultaneously expanding the pool of skilled labor from which other firms may benefit; that is, when a worker moves from one employer to another, it is difficult for the first employer to charge the second for skills provided to the employee. Similarly, producers or consumers may inflict costs on a third party for which the market does not require them to bear commensurate costs in return. A commuter, for example, may decide to drive rather than use public transportation to get to work in the morning. This results in additional road congestion and costs (in terms of the opportunity cost of lost time as well as greater operating expenses) to all those who had already been using the roads. This commuter, however, looks only at personal costs, both operating costs and the value of commuting time, in deciding whether to drive or use public transportation.

Another way of viewing externalities is to say that they exist when significant interactions occur between the utility functions of individuals and the production functions of firms, or a combination of production and utility functions, not recognized by the market mechanism. For instance, in the case of an individual's utility function, an externality is said to be present if

$$u^x = u^x(W_1, W_2, W_3, \ldots, W_n, Z_1)$$

The utility of individual X is a function of Activities W_1 through W_n, which are under X's control, but also of Activity Z_1, which is under the control of some other individual. In such cases, when each individual pursues his or her own self-interest and attempts to maximize his or her personal utility function or allocate productive resources in the most profitable manner, the individual may end up less well off under the private market solution than under some modified or partially controlled market arrangement. The usual marginal conditions for an optimal allocation of resources do not apply here, and resources will likely be misallocated. That is, the economic system only gives partial signals to producers and consumers regarding their respective profit and utility-maximizing decisions. As a result, society as a whole will be less well off when externalities exist and are not recognized in resource-allocation decisions. In the case of an economy dominated by pure competition, for example, it is easy to see how the existence of externalities will result in a misallocation of resources. As we saw in Chapter 14, the equilibrium condition under pure

---

[1] In viewing the externality problem, it is important to recognize that externalities exist primarily because of an incomplete definition of property rights in the laws. As we see later in this appendix, one solution to externality problems is to define property rights more completely and to incorporate this expanded definition into the legal structure.

competition is one in which the long-run marginal costs (the costs to society and the firm) of providing one more unit of output are just equal to price (the value society or consumers place on this additional output). If, however, the producer of a product were to generate costs in the production process for which payment did not have to be made, the $P = MC$ solution is no longer ideal. The true marginal costs of production will be somewhat higher and the private market solution will allocate an inappropriately large amount of resources to the production of this commodity. Conversely, when benefits of consumption are conferred with little or no cost on others in addition to the immediate consumer, the price or societal value of this commodity will be artificially low, and output will be set at a suboptimally low level.

Thus, when externalities exist there is a divergence between private returns—those accruing to the *direct* parties in an economic transaction—and social returns—those accruing to the *indirect* parties in such a transaction.

Public Sector Externalities

Externalities occur in the public as well as the private sector. One local government may dispose of its sewage in a fashion that imposes additional treatment costs on another downstream town. This is the case of many communities located along the Schuylkill River from which Philadelphia draws much of its drinking water. Similarly, a major metropolitan power company may resort to nuclear energy to supply the metropolitan region and then expose both urban and rural areas to the dangers associated with the transportation and storage of nuclear wastes.

At the federal level, spillovers or externalities are often evident between agencies. For example, the Public Health Service Hospital at Staten Island, New York, is said to have been dumping 7,500 gallons of untreated sewage per day into upper New York Bay as well as placing a heavy burden on New York's regular sewage disposal system. In Los Angeles the buses run by the Rapid Transit District are exempt from the same smog checks that private vehicles, buses, and trucks must pass.

Production Externalities: Economies and Diseconomies

Just as the firm may experience *internal* economies or diseconomies as it changes the scale of its production processes, *externalities* arising in production may be classified as either *external economies* or *external diseconomies*.

External Production Economies

External economies are said to occur when an increase in one firm's production generates benefits accruing to others that may not normally be captured through the market mechanism by the producing firm. External economies of this sort may arise, for example, if a firm decides to increase its plant size in some locality. The new, larger plant may require that rail service be provided to handle the increased output of the firm. If this service is provided, it benefits not only the firm that induced the extended rail service but also all other firms and individuals in the community who now have access to a new, lower-cost source of transportation. Another type of external economy of production may arise when the expansion of output of one firm—for example, a large appliance manufacturer—makes it less costly for other metal fabricators to acquire needed raw material. This may occur if the appliance manufacturer buys from a steel firm operating in the range of increasing returns to scale. As a result of the new orders, prices may fall and all other steel purchasers will also benefit from these lower prices.

External Production Diseconomies

External diseconomies of production arise when a firm's production results in uncompensated costs or detriments to others. External production diseconomies are real costs of production that, until they are internalized either voluntarily or by legal requirement, are escaped by the private business firm. Thus although the associated social costs are not "relevant" costs to managerial decision making, they always have the potential to become relevant if laws are changed. These costs are borne by others dependent on the same resources for their own production processes. Once again, the market system fails to account for all relevant costs in the resource-allocation decisions of autonomous enterprises or municipalities.

Other common examples of external diseconomies of production are apparent in the case of oil spills, excessive use of dangerous pesticides, airport noise, traffic congestion, urban renewal, and many more.

Consumption Externalities

Externalities that result when the actions taken by one consumer influence the satisfaction received by one or more other consumers are called consumption externalities. Favorable and unfavorable consumption externalities are discussed in the sections that follow.

External Consumption Economies

When the utility functions of individuals are interdependent, an increase in consumption by one consumer may have either advantageous or disadvantageous effects on another. When an action taken by one consumer results in uncompensated benefits to other consumers, we say there are *external economies of consumption*. If X provides an excellent education for his children, this presumably makes them better citizens and benefits others in society. Similarly, if Y replaces her noisy, twenty-year-old central air conditioner with a new, quieter model that no longer keeps the neighbors awake at night, benefits have accrued to both Y and the neighbor, although Y alone paid for the new air conditioner.

External Consumption Diseconomies

When an action taken by one consumer results in uncompensated detriments or costs to others, we say there are *external diseconomies of consumption*. Some examples of these external diseconomies may seem quite trivial, as in the case where Mrs. Snodgrass decides that her current home is no longer adequate because her neighbor and good friend, whose home was always smaller, is now building a much bigger home down the block. In essence, Mrs. Snodgrass has been forced to alter her pattern of housing consumption to maintain her level of satisfaction. Another example is the familiar drainage problem. Mr. Jones's home stands next to a vacant lot. Because both lots are very flat, drainage is a problem. Consequently, when Jones built his home he had it placed on a slab much higher than the surrounding land and then graded and filled in his lot so that the water would run onto the vacant property. Some years passed and then Smith built on the vacant lot. Being a resonably astute man, he built his home even higher than Jones's, reversing the drainage problem. As a result of Smith's action, Jones is now forced to install an underground drain system at considerable expense—a clear case of an external diseconomy of consumption.

Interaction of Production and Consumption Externalities

Thus far we have dealt with externalities of consumption and production as completely separable phenomena. It should be apparent, however, that producers may impose externalities on consumers and vice versa. Indeed, some of the most significant pollution problems are of this kind. Pollution may, for instance, impair the usefulness of recreational sites or it may impair the health of a region's residents.

Although the isolated examples of externalities that we have cited may seem rather trivial taken by themselves, the sum of externalities generated in any one economy may assume enormous significance. They help to explain why underdeveloped countries or urban ghettos find it difficult to attract industry from more developed regions where skilled labor, easy access, well-developed financial institutions, and suppliers are all readily available. Likewise, the fact that the market system requires that little or no cost be incurred by those using air and water resources as industrial and municipal sewers explains the increased problem of, and concern with, environmental quality. Consumption externalities also play a significant role in most societies. Housing patterns, eating habits, and dress standards differ widely from country to country because the utility functions of consumers, and hence their consumption patterns, are highly interdependent. Fashion and style trends are frequently visible evidence of such interdependencies.[2]

---

[2] The sections "Production Externalities" and "Consumption Externalities" are based on the classification scheme used by William J. Baumol, *Economic Theory and Operations Analysis*, 3d ed. (Englewood Cliffs, N.J.: Prentice-Hall, 1972), pp. 392–395.

Economic Externalities and Resource Allocation

When external effects are present, resources are likely to be misallocated by producers or consumers whether the externality is beneficial to its recipients or not. If producers or consumers make a contribution to society's well-being for which they are not compensated, they are less likely to engage in the action generating the external benefit (social contribution) than if they were fully reimbursed for all benefits generated. Similarly, in the case of external diseconomies, a producer or consumer will likely overallocate resources to some production or consumption activity if part of the costs of engaging in this activity is shifted to others.[3] The reason for this likely misallocation of resources is that when externalities exist, the price system fails to provide the correct signals to firms making output and resource-allocation decisions. In the case of external diseconomies, only part of the costs of production or consumption are considered—those that the firm must pay or that it imputes in terms of its opportunity costs. Similarly, when external economies are present, market price is no longer an adequate measure of social benefit.

Resource-Allocation Effects: An Illustration

A brief example may help to illustrate these points. Mr. Bolten and Ms. Connally are next-door neighbors in a row of townhouses. To simplify matters, assume Ms. Connally owns a corner house and Mr. Bolten is her only immediate neighbor. Connally enjoys playing country-western music at a very high volume on her stereo, to the displeasure of Bolten who enjoys only the classics. The cost to Connally of playing her music is the sum of electricity costs, wear and tear (depreciation) on her record player, and wear and tear on the records. These costs can be assumed to increase with the hours she uses the stereo per day. They are shown in Figure 19A.1 as MC_C.[4] Connally's desire for country-western music is given by curve MB_C, indicating the marginal benefit derived from additional hours of music. Under these conditions Connally will play her stereo for h_1 hours per day, or out to the point where her marginal cost of playing music just equals her marginal benefit from listening to it.

Mr. Bolten, however, must bear some costs because of Connally's habits. He may choose to play his own classical music longer and louder than otherwise to drown out Connally's "bad" sounds. Or he may take more trips and eat out more often to get away from the noise. The costs imposed on Bolten by Connally's

---

[3] As Baumol, *Economic Theory and Operations Analysis*, p. 395, has pointed out, when significant external diseconomies exist, it *may* be preferable to have a monopoly market structure rather than perfect competition, since the monopoly is likely to restrict output in comparison to output under perfect competition.

[4] Graphs such as Figures 19A.1 and 19A.2 assume that something like "societal marginal benefit and cost" are measurable objects. In practice, it is often quite difficult to operationalize such concepts. Our purpose in presenting them here is to help the student conceptualize the nature of the problem.

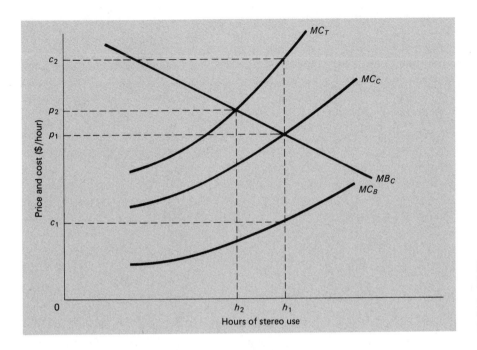

Figure 19A.1
**Resource
Allocation
and External
Diseconomies**

music are represented by MC_B. It can be seen that although h_1 hours of stereo music is efficient from Connally's viewpoint, it is obviously not satisfactory to Bolten. When Connally uses her stereo for h_1 hours, the marginal costs imposed on Bolten equal c_1, whereas his marginal benefits are obviously zero. Using the total societal marginal cost curve $MC_T(MC_T = MC_C + MC_B)$, we can again see that h_1 hours of music is inefficient because total societal marginal costs equal c_2 at that level of stereo use, whereas total societal marginal benefit (in this case, Connally's benefit alone) equals only p_1 (that is, marginal costs exceeds marginal benefit).

In the absence of any legal requirement for Connally to compensate Bolten for his discomfort, or of an arrangement whereby Bolten bribes Connally to play her stereo more softly and less frequently, Connally has no incentive to cut back her listening time to the efficient level of h_2 hours where total societal marginal cost equals total societal marginal benefit.

External Economies: A Further Illustration

Let us now graphically examine the impact of *external economies* on resource allocation. An often-cited example is the case of the neighborhood effects of home improvement. If Mr. Anagnos decides to invest in beautifying his home, his desire for additional home beautification may be represented by MB_A—that is, the marginal benefit—(in terms of increased resale value and the value of his own personal satisfaction) derived from successive increments of home improvements. The cost of each increment of home improvement is represented in Figure 19A.2 by MC_A, which rises as the number of low-cost home im-

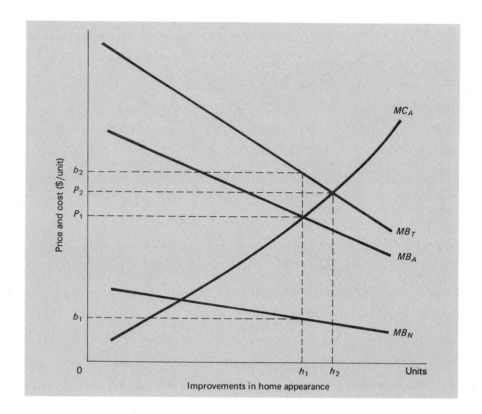

Figure 19A.2
**Resource
Allocation
and External
Economies**

provement and beautification opportunities diminishes. In this case Anagnos will be in equilibrium by making h_1 home improvements. But this level of home improvement activity is inefficient because Anagnos's neighbors also receive benefits (in terms of enhanced neighborhood real estate values and esthetic pleasure) represented by the MB_N curve. Although an h_1 level of home improvements is obviously efficient from Anagnos's point of view, it is clearly inefficient when neighborhood effects are taken into account. With h_1 home improvements neighbors receive b_1 marginal benefits, and their marginal cost is zero. Thus, it should be apparent that when external economies are present, output (or consumption) is likely to be less than socially desirable.

From a societal point of view, Anagnos should make home improvements up to point h_2, where total societal marginal benefit MB_T equals marginal cost. Just as in the case of external diseconomies, it is unlikely that Anagnos, acting on his own, will make the socially optimal allocation of his resources for home improvements, since he is unable to reap all the benefits that his expenditures generate. Some form of cooperative neighborhood organization would have to be formed, deed restrictions imposed, zoning laws passed, or tax subsidies provided for a more nearly optimal level of expenditures to be made.

In summary, we can see the difference between the allocation criterion used by a direct producer or consumer of some good or service and the socially optimal allocation criterion. The direct producer or user of a commodity should carry production or use to the point where

$$MC_P = MB_P$$

that is, where direct private marginal costs MC_P equal direct private marginal benefits MB_P.

When externalities are present, however, a socially efficient allocation of resources requires that

$$MC_T = MB_T$$

that is, total social marginal costs MC_T equal total social marginal benefits MB_T.

Total social marginal costs are made up of direct private marginal costs MC_P, plus indirect marginal costs MC_I (that is, the external diseconomies). Total social marginal benefits include both direct private marginal benefits MB_P, and indirect marginal benefits MB_I (that is, the external economies).

The Reciprocal Nature of Externalities

One additional characteristic of externalities must be emphasized before moving to a discussion of possible solutions; that is, *it takes at least two to create an externality*. In the case of Bolten and Connally, for example, if Connally lived on a 140-acre ranch, her taste for high-volume country-western music would bother no one; thus no externality would exist. Similarly, power plants located in the middle of the desert impose only minor social costs on distant areas until people move to the vicinity of the power plant. The more people who live in the area of the plant, the greater are the external costs. Thus if more residents move into the area of the power plant, they may seek an injunction against the power plant to stop polluting. But remember, the power plant imposed little or no cost on anyone until the new residents moved into the vicinity of the plant. Although the plant imposes costs on the residents, the granting of an injunction against the plant imposes costs on the power company. In an instance such as this, it is not altogether clear exactly who has caused the externality and who should bear the liability. Should the power plant be forced to pay to reduce pollution, or should the new residents have to pay the cost of installing pollution-abatement equipment?[5]

The problem of "Who should pay?" may be solved in a number of ways, although it often boils down to who has the greatest negotiating or political strength. Ronald Coase has shown that an optimal solution to externalities can generally be achieved if the creator of the externality (pollution, for example) and the recipient of the externality get together and reach an agreement through bargaining.[6] No matter who pays, however, the general principle of how much

---

[5] For a good discussion of this and related problems, see William J. Baumol, *Welfare Economies and the Theory of the State*, 2d ed. (Cambridge, Mass.: Harvard University Press, 1965), pp. 23–46.

[6] Ronald Coase, "The Problem of Social Cost," *Journal of Law and Economies* 2 (October 1960), pp. 1–44.

of society's resources should be allocated to solving the externality problem is clear. An external diseconomy, for example, should be reduced up to the point where the marginal costs of any further reduction just equal the marginal benefits to society from the reduction. Similarly, an action that generates, external benefits should be expanded to the point where the marginal benefits to all of society from such an expansion just equal the societal marginal costs of gaining the benefit.

Possible Solutions to the Externalities Problem[7]

The foregoing discussion leads to the conclusion that when externalities are present, the market mechanism is likely to fail to achieve an efficient allocation of societal resources. In such instances, intervention of some sort or another may be necessary to force firms to internalize negative externalities. Unfortunately, the range of externalities that exists, the constraints of political decision-making processes, the problems of accurately measuring the costs or benefits of any particular externality, and the existence of transaction costs incurred in applying a particular solution to a particular problem make it impossible to identify any one correct solution to the problem. Accordingly, this section enumerates several proposed solutions and discusses their relative merits.

Solution by Prohibition

One simple approach to solving problems created by externalities is merely to prohibit the action that generates the external effects. A little reflection on most externality problems, however, should indicate that in most cases this is at least nonoptimal and frequently impractical. Auto emissions could be cut to zero if autos were banned, but the effects of such a move, at least in the short run, would be disastrous. Pollution in the Houston Ship Channel or the Detroit River could practically be abolished if industries and municipalities were no longer permitted to dump any of their waste products there. But employment would also grind to a halt in the short run in these areas if such a step were taken. Furthermore, an optimal solution does not require that externalities be completely eliminated but that the *right amount* of them be eliminated. In the case of air and water, both of these resources have the capacity to assimilate wastes up to a certain level. A strict zero-pollution policy would entail a waste of some resources.

Solution by Directive

The problem of controlling externalities is to get just the right amount of them; that is, to attempt to eliminate an externality up to the point where the marginal

---

[7] This section is based largely on the treatment of Otto A. Davis and Morton I. Kamien, "Externalities, Information and Alternative Collective Action," in *Public Expenditures and Policy Analysis*, ed. Robert Haveman and Julius Margolis (Chicago: Markham, 1971), pp. 74–95.

costs of further reductions are just equal to the marginal benefits derived therefrom. Since we have seen that outright prohibition may be suboptimal, another possibility that has been suggested is to let the government decide how much of the externality may be produced. This is the approach that has been used in setting auto emission standards. This approach also suffers from serious weaknesses. First, one problem is determining just how much of an externality should be permitted. This requires in theory that costs and benefits of various levels of reduction be compared. But in many instances, estimating the benefits of various levels of pollution reduction, for example, is nearly impossible. Second, even if an overall standard could be agreed on, when multiple sources of pollution are in an area, each of the polluting entities must in turn be directed how it should act. A simple proportionate distribution of "pollution rights" is likely to be suboptimal because the costs of achieving various levels of pollution reduction may vary dramatically from industry to industry. Optimality, however, requires that the marginal effectiveness of the last dollar spent by each polluter be equated.

Solution by Voluntary Payment

Some have argued that when externalities exist, collective action may not be necessary since it is in the interest of private parties to voluntarily take the appropriate action. If a foul-smelling rendering plant is located in a community, there is likely to be a divergence between the private and social cost or the private and social benefit of livestock rendering. To avoid the foul smells, the community might seek to pay the plant to reduce or eliminate the odor discharges. Optimality (and good sense) requires that the payment not exceed the value of the damage suffered by the community. The rendering plant should accept the payment if it exceeds the costs of reducing the foul odors generated and reject the payment if it is less than the cost of odor reduction. Although the voluntary payment solution is certainly consistent with *Pareto optimality* (everyone is better off and no one is worse off in this case), some problems exist. First, how is the community to value the odor damage of the rendering plant? Individual citizens are likely to understate their willingness to pay to reduce the odors in hopes that their neighbors will provide sufficient funds to get the desired reduction. Second, in a dynamic economic system, demand for meat may rise causing the rendering plant to increase output. New and greater payments would have to be offered, and the citizens would have to monitor continually the state of odor-reducing technology to keep the firm from "cheating."

Solution by Merger

When the entities generating externalities are firms, merger is a very attractive but limited way of internalizing externalities. If a paper mill is polluting a stream so that a chemical firm downstream must make large expenditures on water purification before using the water in its processes, the problem may be eliminated by a merger of the two firms. After the merger, it is in the best interests of the new firm to consider the chemical plant's purification costs in determining what quality of effluent should be emitted from the paper mill. A merger solution has two problems. First, it is feasible only when the entities involved are firms—or perhaps municipal or regional water, air, or transportation authorities. Second, as the number of entities increases, the possibility of effecting a merger decreases.

Solution by Taxes and Subsidies

One solution to externalities problems, which has long been favored by economists, is to provide subsidies (either in the form of cash or tax relief) to those whose activities generate significant external benefits and to tax those whose activities create external costs. Such a tax and subsidy scheme, however, requires a tremendous amount of information if it is to be administered in an optimal fashion. A tax and subsidy approach differs only slightly from the solution-by-directive approach. Rather than issuing directives to individual firms about the quantities of each pollutant (or external benefits, such as clean water) that each is permitted, the tax and subsidy scheme seeks to do this indirectly by setting taxes or providing subsidies that will maximize overall societal benefit. Thus it is subject to the same weaknesses discussed in the case of solution by directive. In spite of these problems, a less than perfect attempt at achieving an optimal allocation of resources may be justified if the societal costs of a continued external diseconomy or of a less than optimal external economy are large enough. In deciding on an approach, the cost of gaining the information necessary to arrive at an optimal solution needs to be weighed against the societal losses that accrue if nothing is done or if some other imperfect solution is adopted.

One solution attempts to avoid the problems of a direct measurement of benefits and costs associated with solution by directive or the traditional tax and subsidy solution. Rather, in the case of pollution, a tax or emission charge is placed on a firm's pollutants, such as pounds of particulate matter emitted from a power plant's smokestacks. A firm may continue to pollute if it pays the tax, or it may find that it is cheaper to buy pollution control equipment (or shut down). If, after a reasonable period of time, a community still believes the level of particulate matter in the air is too high, the tax per pound of pollutant may be increased in a stepwise fashion until the community is satisfied with the result. This solution avoids the rigidity of all-or-nothing regulations and directives. A second advantage to this approach is that it is geographically flexible. If lower fees were charged in sparsely populated areas, firms would be encouraged to move from densely populated areas, where pollution damage is great, to the more sparsely settled regions, where the extent of pollution damage would be greatly reduced. A final advantage of this approach is that it forces firms to consider the costs of emissions and to weigh the benefits and costs of abatement in their production and pricing decisions. In this way, incentives are provided to seek new and lower-cost methods of reducing waste output and reducing the social harm caused by waste disposal.

The emissions-charge approach has a number of problems, however. First, the political mechanism does not always reflect community interests in an accurate and timely way. Because of their concentrated and coordinated resources, industrial firms may exert disproportionate pressures on lawmaking bodies. A second problem is that only certain types of pollution can be measured economically with metering devices. An inexpensive method of measuring pollutants is essential to such an emission-charge scheme. Third, although the scheme provides the possibility of building incentives for firms to move from densely to sparsely populated areas, this result is not likely to be greeted with universal acclaim. Those living in the sparsely populated, relatively pollution-free areas of this country have already mounted an effective attack on any additional environmental degradation to their areas. Their argument is a powerful one, since it is consistent with freedom of choice (that is, the choice of living in congested, polluted areas versus sparsely populated areas with little pollution) in our market system.

Solution by Sale of Pollution Rights

Another increasingly popular approach to the problem of pollution is the sale of pollution rights. Licenses could be sold that would give the owner a right to pollute up to some specific limit during a particular period of time. Under such a system, the government would set a maximum level of some pollutant that may be safely emitted in an area. It could then sell, at auction, licenses to individual firms giving them the right to pollute up to a specified amount. These licenses could be freely traded in an organized market, permitting their price to fluctuate with market demands. The advantage to this approach is that it is essentially market oriented, forcing pollution costs to be internally recognized in the price and production decisions of individual firms. As the demand for pollution rights rises over time (for example, as income and population grow), the cost of polluting will similarly increase and incentives for reducing pollution become stronger. This is exactly the solution that we would hope for, since the social costs of any particular source of pollution increase as the number of people in the pollution-affected area increases. This approach, however, also has a number of problems. First, setting an appropriate, initial total level of allowable pollution cannot yet be done in any precise manner. Second, the approach is limited to cases where emissions are economically measurable. Finally, this approach has an inherent bias against smaller firms, which lack the extensive financial resources of the largest corporations.

There is now an active market for pollution rights (credits) in the United States. For example, the Times Mirror Co. was able to complete a $120 million expansion of a paper-making plant near Portland, Oregon, after buying the right to emit 150 tons of additional hydrocarbons into the air annually. The pollution credits were acquired for $50,000 from the owners of a wood-coating plant that had gone out of business and a local dry-cleaning firm. Some states and a growing number of independent consultants are setting up clearinghouse arrangements to facilitate the exchange of pollution credits.

Solution by Regulation

Auto safety devices are a good example of solution by regulation. Recognizing that significant external benefits are to be gained from reducing killing and crippling automotive accidents, the federal government does not give the consumer the choice of acquiring auto safety equipment; it is simply required on all vehicles. Regulation, however, has significant implementation difficulties associated with it. In the absence of a mandatory seat-belt use law (or even in the presence of one), it is difficult to get people to use these devices.

In this section we have briefly introduced several of the approaches that have been proposed for, or used in, the solution to externalities problems. It should be apparent that no one best solution exists for all cases. Because of the great diversity of externality problems, appropriate policies must be tailored to meet the specific problem, while comparing the costs and benefits of alternative solutions. Policy makers may then be guided in their decision making to choose that alternative where net benefits are likely to be maximized and the social costs are effectively internalized, forcing firms to treat them as a part of their relevant costs for decision-making purposes.

Summary

- Economic externalities exist when a third party receives benefits or bears costs arising from an economic transaction in which he or she is not a direct participant. The impact of economic externalities is felt outside of (external to) the normal market pricing and resource-allocation mechanism.

- *External production economies* (positive externalities) occur when an increase in one firm's production generates benefits accruing to others that are not normally recaptured through the market mechanism by the producing firm.

- *External production diseconomies* (negative externalities) arise when a firm's production results in uncompensated costs or detriments to others —such as the emission of pollutants.

- *External consumption economies* (positive externalities) occur when there is an interdependence of the utility functions of individuals, so that an increase in consumption by one individual results uncompensated benefits accruing to others.

- *External consumption diseconomies* (negative externalities) occur when an action taken by one consumer, such as smoking in a crowded room, imposes uncompensated costs or detriments on others.

- When economic externalities exist, resources are likely to be misallocated through the market pricing mechanism.

- Many possible solutions to problems of economic externalities exist. These include solution by prohibition, solution by directive, solution by voluntary payment, solution by merger, solution by taxes and subsidies, solution by sale of rights to create the externality, and solution by regulation.

- Coase has shown that an optimal allocation of resources can generally be achieved in the face of externalities if the creator of the externality and the recipient of the externality get together and reach an agreement on how to handle the problem through bargaining.

Selected References

Baumol, William J. *Welfare Economics and the Theory of the State*, 2d ed. Cambridge, Mass.: Harvard University Press, 1965.

Coase, Ronald. "The Problem of Social Cost." *Journal of Law and Economics* 2 (October 1960), pp. 1–44.

R. W. Crandall, T. E. Keeler and L. B. Lave, "The Cost of Automobile Safety and Emissions Regulations to the Consumer", *AEA Papers and Proceedings* (May 1982), pp. 324–327.

Davis, Otto A., and Andrew Whinston. "The Economics of Urban Renewal," *Law and Contemporary Problems* (Winter 1961).

Dorfman, Robert. "Incidence of the Benefits and Costs of Environmental Programs." *American Economic Review* (February 1977).

Mishan, Ezra J. "The Postwar Literature on Externalities: An Interpretive Essay." *Journal of Economic Literature* (March 1971).

Pasztor, Andy. "Market Booms for 'Rights' to Pollute," *Wall Street Journal*, 18 June 1981, p. 1.

Discussion Questions

1. What do you see as the major weakness of the various solutions to the externalities problem discussed in this chapter?

2. Under what circumstances do the market prices of privately produced goods reflect the externalities created when the product is produced and consumed?

3. Using the externality concept, explain why rents for retail space in a mall generally exceed rents on retail space that is not connected with a shopping mall.

4. Discuss the problems of aircraft noise around an airport from an externality perspective and a possible solution perspective if (a) housing existed in the airport area before the airport was built and (b) housing was built adjacent to the airport after the airport was built and operating.

5. A sheep rancher has leased the mineral rights to her land to an oil company. The sheep rancher fears that discharges from the oil wells will pollute her underground water resources. Consequently, the contract for the sale of mineral rights requires that the rancher and the oil company reach a mutually agreeable solution to the problem should it occur or the mineral rights lease will be terminated and the rancher will be required to return a portion of the lease proceeds to the oil company. The portion that must be returned to the oil company is to be determined through a process of binding arbitration. Discuss possible "optimal" solutions should this problem arise.

6. Why do zoning ordinances frequently prohibit the construction of residences near industrial areas and large retail malls?

7. Using game theory, show why two adjacent rental property owners may not make a profit-maximizing level of investment in their properties.

Problems

1. Chester Country is a rural farm county in southeastern Pennsylvania. It is within thirty miles of the outer reaches of the city of Philadelphia, and as such is somewhat typical of other rural areas being affected by urban growth (sprawl). In recent years, much of the farmland in the country has been sold to real estate developers who have sold

small lots ($\frac{1}{2}$ to 1 acre) for new suburban developments. The impact of this development has been significant. Schools became overcrowded as the new, higher-density suburbias filled up. Septic systems were no longer adequate to dispose of the increased volume of sewage. The new suburbanites pushed for a public sewer and treatment system (as well as city, not well, water). Roads previously adequate for farm traffic needed to be widened. The greater volume of traffic found the slow, cumbersome farm traffic to be a dangerous nuisance. Many suburban residents complained of the odor of manure on neighboring fields.

As these and other problems developed, a great strain was placed on the county's tax revenues to meet the growing need for social services. Consequently, taxes have been raised dramatically, largely reflecting increased land values. Until recently, the remaining farms, of which there are still many, had not been assessed for taxes at the same percentage of *actual* market value of the real estate property as the new suburbanites. The new suburbanites complained, arguing that farmers should pay their fair share and that the fair share should be based on real estate values, just as the taxes on the new suburbanites are.

a. Discuss the pros and cons of increasing farm tax assessments to make them in line with other property assessments in the county in terms of (i) economic efficiency and (ii) equity.

b. What are the real externalities in this case?

c. How should the problem of compensation for externalities, both real and pecuniary, be handled?

2. Before the imposition of mandatory 55-mph speed limits on most of this nation's highways during the 1973–1974 energy crisis, motorists were asked to voluntarily reduce their driving speed to 55 mph. Those who did generally found that the majority of drivers continued along at their customary 65-75 mph.

a. Why is a program of voluntary energy conservation, particularly among small consumers, likely to be ineffective?

b. Formulate the problem of voluntary energy conservation compliance in the framework of a game theory problem. Can you show why the desired solution is unlikely to prevail?

3. Branding Iron Products, a specialty steel fabricator, operates a plant in the town of West Star, Texas. The town has grown rapidly because of recent discoveries of oil and gas in the area. Many of the new residents have expressed concern at the amount of pollution (primarily particulate matter in the area and waste water in the town's river) emitted by Branding Iron. Three proposals have been made to remedy the problem.:

a. Impose a tax on the amount of particulate matter and the amount of waste water emitted by the firm

b. Prohibit pollution by the firm

c. Offer tax incentives to the firm to clean up its production processes

Evaluate these alternatives from the perspective of economic efficiency, equity, and the likely long-term impact on the firm.

4. Middlefield, Ohio, a town with a 50,000 population, is the home of Legco Steel. Legco employs about 20 percent of the town's work force. Because of an increase in complaints from local environmentalists, the town's city council is considering taking action to reduce the firm's pollution. The following alternatives are being considered:

a. Pass an ordinance requiring the firm to reduce its discharge of particulates into the air by 95 percent.

b. Impose a tax of $5 per ton of particulates

c. Maintain the status quo

The expected payoffs to the firm and the town are as follows:

Action	Firm (impact on profits)	Town (impact on employment)
Reduce Discharge with Ordinance	−50%	20% reduction in work force employed in Middlefield
Tax Discharge	−10%	5% reduction in work force employed in Middlefield
Do Nothing	0	0

a. What action do you think the town should take? Why?

b. What other factors need to be considered?

c. Why do you think Alternative (a) has such a large impact on employment in Middlefield.

5. Lead Weight Refining, Inc. operates a large ore smelter in Junction City, Utah. The firm produces lead ingots that are later used to manufacture batteries for heavy-duty equipment. In the lead-refining process, a substantial amount of air pollution is generated.

A local mothers' organization is concerned about the health hazard posed by the emissions of the firm. After consulting with local officials, the mothers convince the city to impose a pollution tax on the discharges of the firm.

Each unit of output, Q, is comprised of one unit of lead, Q_A, and one unit of air pollution (particulates), Q_B. The total cost function of the firm is

$$TC = 25,000 + 8Q + 4Q^2$$

The demand for lead is

$$P_A = 4522 - 4Q_A$$

The demand function for the firm's particulate pollution is derived from the use of these pollutants as an input in the battery production process. The demand function for these discharges is

$$P_B = 400 - Q_B$$

a. In the absence of any pollution tax, what price, quantity, and profit levels will prevail for the firm?

b. Compute the marginal revenue for lead output and for pollution output at this price and output level.

c. What is the minimum tax that must be charged to completely eliminate pollution by the firm?

6. **a.** Discuss the reasons why it is necessary to be able to measure the damage from pollution so the affected parties may reach an optimal solution through bargaining.

b. How does your answer relate to the negative reaction of many communities to the location of a nuclear power plant in their area?

7. A local coke works operates in a competitive market where the prevailing price is $100 per ton. The marginal cost of producing coke is $20 + 2.5Q$.

a. What output will the firm produce?

b. Pollution from the production of coke causes damage of approximately $10 per ton. If an effluent charge of $10 per ton is imposed, what will be the output of the firm?

8. The demand for specialty glue is given as follows:

$$P = 1200 - 6Q$$

where P is the price per 100 pounds of specialty glue produced and Q is the amount produced and sold in hundreds of pounds.

The marginal cost of producing glue for the entire glue industry is

$$MC = 700 + 2Q$$

a. What will industry output and price be in the absence of regulation?
b. The production of specialty glue results in marginal pollution costs of

$$MC = 200 + Q$$

What is marginal social cost for the production of specialty glue?
c. If the firms in the industry attempt to achieve a *socially* optimal level of output, what price should be charged and what should be the level of output?

Public Utility Regulation[1]

20

As discussed in Chapter 19, no business enterprise in the U.S. economy is immune from the influences of government regulation. Nevertheless, individual firms in most industries make the critical decisions about prices, quantities of output, and entry into markets with an objective of maximizing shareholder wealth, subject to the constraints of regulation. In contrast, regulation of a small number of industries, known as public utilities—electric power, natural gas distribution and transmission, communication, and some elements of transportation—is more intense and includes regulation of prices, outputs, profits, and the quality of service provided. The regulation of these industries raises many challenging economic and legal issues. A consideration of these issues is important for a managerial economist for two reasons. First, the public utility industries are an important element of the American economy in their own right. As public debate is focused on regulatory reform, it is important that reform be consistent with basic economic principles in order to avoid the problems inherent in the current system of utility regulation. Second, because public utility regulation covers nearly all aspects of economic decision making in an enterprise, it provides an interesting laboratory to integrate our understanding of demand analysis, forecasting, production and cost analysis, price-output decisions, cost of capital determination, and capital expenditure analysis. Hence, this chapter serves also as a capstone review (in the context of a specific group of industries) of many of the important managerial economic concepts developed throughout the book.

The Regulated Sector of the Economy

It is difficult to describe the industries that make up the regulated sector of the economy and the agencies that exercise control over the activities of the firms in these industries because the "'regulated sector" is not a well-defined segment of the economic system made up of homogeneous firms. Important differences exist among regulated firms, even in the same industry. Moreover, there is substantial variation among the practices of the regulatory agencies with

Glossary of New Terms

Public utilities
A group of firms, mostly in the electric power, natural gas, transportation, and communications industries, that are closely regulated by one or more government agencies. The agencies control entry into the business, set prices, establish product quality standards, and influence the total profits that may be earned by the firms.

Natural monopoly
An industry in which maximum economic efficiency is obtained when one firm produces, distributes, and transmits all of the commodity or service produced in that industry. The production of natural monopolists is typically characterized by increasing returns to scale throughout the range of output demanded by the market.

(Cont'd on next page)

---

[1] A major portion of this chapter was prepared by Professor John Crockett, George Mason University, Fairfax, Virginia.

Glossary of New Terms (*Cont'd*)

Rate level
The actual dollar amount of revenue a utility is authorized to collect; also called the *Total revenue requirement*.

Rate structure
A set of prices that may be charged to various users of a regulated utility's services.

Rate base
The dollar value established by a regulatory commission of a company's plant, equipment, and intangible capital used and useful in serving the public; invested capital minus depreciation.

Rate of return
The percentage of the rate base a utility is allowed to collect to pay the cost of capital.

Peak-load pricing
The process of charging users of a utility's services a higher price during those periods of time when demand for that service is heaviest and lower prices when demand is light.

jurisdiction over particular geographical regions or types of business activity. Nevertheless, even though we make some generalizations that may result in slightly misleading impressions about the amount of similarity among regulated firms, it is useful to examine in broad terms the components of the regulated sector. This in turn leads to the search for the unique economic characteristics that set the regulated industries apart from the unregulated sector where the forces of competition are generally relied on to provide satisfactory performance.

Electric Power Companies

Investor-owned electric power companies make up one large industry subject to economic regulation. Electric power is made available to the consumer through a production process characterized by three distinct stages. First, the power is generated in generating plants. Next, in the transmission stage, the power is transmitted at high voltage from the generating site to the locality where it is used. Finally, in the distribution stage, the power is distributed to the individual users. The complete process may take place as part of the operations of a single firm, or the producing firm may sell power at wholesale rates to a second enterprise that carries out the distribution function. In the latter case, the distribution firm is usually a department within the municipal government serving the locality, or a consumers' cooperative.

Firms producing electric power are subject to regulation at several levels. Integrated firms carrying out all three stages of production are usually regulated by state public utility commissions. These commissions set the rates to be charged to the final consumers. The firms receive exclusive rights to serve individual localities through franchises granted by local governing bodies. A franchise is a long-term contract that is normally renewed when it expires. As a consequence of their franchises, electric power companies have well-defined markets within which they are the sole provider of output. Finally, the Federal Energy Regulatory Commission (FERC) has the authority to set rates on power that crosses state lines and on wholesale power sales.

Natural Gas Companies

A second energy industry characterized by regulation is the natural gas industry. The furnishing of natural gas to users also includes a three-stage process. The first stage is the production of the gas in the field. Transportation to the consuming locality through pipelines is the second stage. Distribution to the final user makes up the third stage. The FERC historically set the field price of natural gas that is to be moved out of the production stage. The regulation of natural gas prices at the wellhead has been effectively phased out. In addition, the FERC oversees the interstate transportation of gas by approving pipeline routes and by controlling the wholesale rates charged by pipeline companies to distribution firms. The distribution function may be carried out by a private firm or by a municipal government agency. In either event, the rates charged to final users are also controlled since the distribution firm normally has a monopoly in its service area.

Transportation Companies

Firms that provide transportation make up another broad area of the regulated sector. In interstate markets, the Interstate Commerce Commission (ICC) regulates the rail and trucking industries. Regulation of these industries has been drastically reduced over the past ten years.

In the interstate airline market, the Civil Aeronautics Board (CAB) historically had the power to grant carriers the right to provide scheduled passenger service between pairs of cities. Once service authority was obtained, the airline could schedule flights at whatever frequency was desired. The CAB also regulated fares to be charged. Airlines that offer scheduled service exclusively within a state are usually regulated by a state agency, whereas air safety regulation for all carriers is undertaken by the Federal Aviation Administration. The CAB has been phased out of existence and the airline industry is now unregulated (domestically) with respect to routes and fares.

Communications Companies

In the communications industry, the most important regulated activity is the provision of telephone service. Interstate telephone service, furnished largely by American Telephone and Telegraph (ATT), is subject to rates set by the Federal Communication Commission (FCC), but competitors of ATT are essentially unregulated. Local service in the intrastate markets, which may be provided either by one of the former Bell System companies or by one of the so-called independents, is regulated by state commissions. As in the case of other public utilities, authority to provide service in a locality is granted by a franchise from a local government.

The Economic Rationale for Regulation

The preceding brief survey of the regulated sector reveals the crucial nature of the regulated industries: They furnish services that are critical to the functioning of the other elements in the economic system. Apart from this factor, do the regulated industries share any other common characteristics that account for the regulation imposed upon them? This question can be answered by considering the major reasons cited as justifications for instituting economic regulation.

Natural Monopoly Argument

It is frequently asserted that the firms operating in the regulated sector are *natural monopolies*, indicating that a tendency exists for a single supplier to emerge in a given market. If this were the case, then the implementation of regulation would represent an acknowledgement of this trend. The presence of a single supplier would be sanctioned, and regulatory overview would be imposed to ensure that the firm granted a monopoly position did not behave in the fashion characteristic of an unregulated monopolist, who tends to charge excessive prices and restrict output.

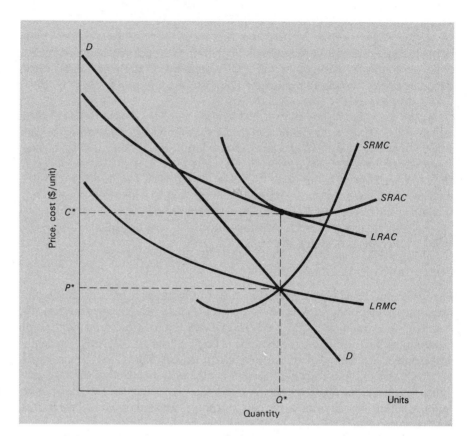

Figure 20.1
**Natural Monopoly:
Price-Output
Determination**

On economic grounds, the situation that can best be termed a "natural monopoly" is found in the case of a product whose production process is characterized by increasing returns to scale. By recalling the discussion of returns to scale in Chapters 11, 12, and 13, increasing returns to scale imply that as all inputs are increased by a given percentage, the average total cost of a unit of output decreases. Alternatively, the long-run marginal cost of output declines throughout the range of output levels that are relevant. This situation is illustrated in Figure 20.1 for a firm in long-run stable equilibrium.

Suppose that the market demand curve for output is represented by the curve DD in Figure 20.1. The socially optimal level of output would then be Q^*; at that level of output, price would be equal to short-run and long-run marginal cost, and the average total cost per unit would be C^*. In this case the firm and the market cost curves are the same; if more than one firm supplies output, the average total cost for the quantity of output produced and sold in the market would be higher than the average cost of the same level of output of a single firm. A single producer is able to realize economies of scale that are unavailable to firms in the presence of competition. From a social perspective, competition would result in inefficiency in the form of costs above their minimum level. More resources than necessary would be used in producing the output, a sign of economic waste. It is argued that if production relations exist like those in

Figure 20.1, a single supplier will eventually emerge. Competing firms will realize that their costs decrease as output expands. As a consequence, they will have an incentive to cut prices to increase quantity demanded. During this period, prices will be below average cost, resulting in losses for the producing firms. Unable to sustain such losses, the weaker firms will gradually leave the industry, until only a single producer remains. Thus competitive forces will contribute to the emergence of the natural monopoly.

If a monopolistic position were to exist in the absence of regulation, the results described in Chapter 14 would be produced. The monopolist would maximize profit by equating marginal revenue and marginal cost, leading to an excessively high price, and output would be relatively too low. Thus intervention through regulation is required to prevent monopolistic abuse while achieving the benefits of the most efficient organization of production. In its simplest form, this is the explanation of regulation based on the existence of natural monopolies.

Figure 20.1 illustrates one final problem that would arise in the presence of a genuine natural monopoly. Suppose that a regulatory agency succeeded in establishing the socially optimal price for output, P^*. As the cost curves indicate, this price would lead to losses for the producing firm, since price would be below average total cost. This is obviously an unsustainable result, illustrating a perplexing dilemma for pricing: Marginal-cost pricing in the usual sense is impossible where economies of scale exist. In this situation, several options might be considered. The regulating agency might allow prices at average cost, ensuring revenues sufficient to cover all costs. This policy would lead to a misallocation of resources, however, since customers would be unable to purchase output at prices that equal the marginal cost of the resources absorbed in making that output available. Alternatively, the regulatory authority might order pricing at marginal cost, with subsidies out of tax revenues provided to cover the operating losses such a policy would produce.

It is apparent that increasing returns to scale, the economic source of a natural monopoly, raise many issues in the theory of optimal pricing. These issues remain controversial among economists. What is important for our purposes is whether this characteristic of production is typical of all the firms that are subject to economic regulation. The answer to this question is no. After substantial amounts of empirical analysis of the behavior of the cost curves of regulated firms, researchers have concluded that many of these firms do not display the kind of static behavior shown in Figure 20.1. As a result, the explanation of the decision to regulate some industries does not lie completely in the existence of a natural monopoly determined by economies of scale.

Duplication of Facilities Arguments

Other economic reasons exist for preferring that a single supplier serve a particular market. For example, there would be an undesirable duplication of facilities if electric power, natural gas, or telephone service were provided by several firms in a given locality. The physical network required to connect the producer and user of these services requires a substantial investment before service can be provided. It would be uneconomical to have competing networks of these facilities in a locality. As a consequence, individual firms are granted franchises to furnish service. The franchise gives some assurance to the firm that demands for service will be forthcoming once the capacity is in place, justifying the investment. The alternative to regulation here is frequently public ownership of the distribution facilities, as in the case of municipally owned electric power distribution systems.

Price Discrimination Arguments

Associated with the idea of a distribution network in many regulated industries is the fact that in these industries a physical link exists between producer and user. In addition, many of these services cannot be inventoried. Rather, production and consumption take place simultaneously. Examples of these characteristics include the use of electric power, travel by commercial air carrier, and with minor exceptions, telephone use. The physical connection makes it feasible for the producer to charge different prices for virtually identical service to different users; that is, to engage in price discrimination. The physical link makes it impossible for consumers eligible for lower prices to resell output to users who would otherwise pay the higher charges imposed by the producer, thereby thwarting the producer's scheme. In fact, various types of price discrimination are common in regulated industries. For instance, residential users of electric power and telephones are billed according to rates that are different from those paid by industrial users.

In view of the ability of these firms to engage in price discrimination, one of the justifications for regulatory control over pricing is to ensure that these practices do not result in abuses. In fact, consumer discontent over what was believed to be inequitable price discrimination by the railroads was a major factor leading to the development of formal regulation in the nineteenth century. Now one of the functions of regulation is to see that no consumer is made worse off under a scheme of discriminatory pricing than he or she would be in the absence of price discrimination.

Destructive Effects of Competition Arguments

A final argument that has been used to explain regulation involves the idea that even if it were present, competition in some industries might not produce desirable results. It is recognized that at some points in time in many regulated industries, capacity exists in excess of levels required to serve expected demand. The presence of excess capacity is a result of the fact that increments to capacity must typically be installed in lumpy, nonmarginal units. Additionally, the provision of excess capacity may be required to meet unexpectedly large demands for output and to provide a margin of safety in the event of equipment failure. In an industry characterized by excess capacity, competition is often particularly intense. Firms are willing to sell output at any price above variable cost to minimize their losses. In most industries, this process is a normal one, leading to the justified elimination of excess capacity. It is argued, however, that in the regulated sector, such competition might lead to deterioration in the quality of service as firms seek to cut costs in the short run. For instance, maintenance of equipment might be postponed, leading to service failures or to unnecessary hazards to the public. The result is that some industries, although not natural monopolies in the strict sense, are characterized by factors that make competition inherently unstable. Regulation is then an appropriate policy measure.

These arguments all contain some truth. Taken individually, they are useful in calling attention to some of the characteristics of the regulated industries that raise questions about how the industries would perform in the absence of regulation. However, no single factor or set of factors clearly distinguishes all regulated industries from all nonregulated industries. The line between the two sectors is not distinct; hence, the reasons for the regulated status of any particular industry must be sought on an individual basis. Phillips has provided the most appropriate generalization:

> What determines, then, which industries are to be regulated? It is the judgment of legislatures and, ultimately, of the Supreme Court. Regulation is applied when it is felt that competition cannot be relied on to provide adequate service at a reasonable price. This decision often has been based on proper economic criteria, but it has sometimes been predicated on political or social considerations.[2]

The Regulatory Process[3]

The agencies that carry out tasks of economic regulation are specialized bodies consisting of a small number of formal decision makers supported by a professional staff of economists, lawyers, accountants, and engineers. At the federal level the members of the various regulatory commissions are appointed by the president, whereas at the state level the commissioners may be elected or appointed officials. The formal proceedings used by the regulatory agencies for determining rates are quasijudicial in character, involving an adversary process. The utilities' adversaries may be the regulatory commission's staff, consumer groups, or in some cases the state attorney general's office. Since these rate hearings are costly and time consuming, many commissions have adopted informal procedures for making periodic adjustments in rates. Finally, the decisions of regulatory agencies are subject to the review of the courts. As a result, the U.S. Supreme Court has established many of the doctrines under which regulation is carried out.

Within this general framework, the regulatory agencies control entry by firms into the regulated industries, set prices that consumers are to pay, and oversee the quality of service provided. Of these basic functions, the determination of prices accounts for the largest proportion of regulatory activity. In many

---

[2] Charles F. Phillips, Jr., *The Regulation of Public Utilities* (Arlington, Va.: Public Utilities Reports, 1984), p. 65. See also Robert W. Poole, Jr., ed., *Unnatural Monopolies: The Case for Deregulating Public Utilities* (Lexington, MA: D. C. Heath, 1985).

[3] An excellent overview of the regulatory process is found in U.S. Department of Energy, A *Consumer's Guide to the Economics of Electric Utility Ratemaking*, DOE/RG/09154, (Springfield, Va.: NTIS, May 1980).

of the regulated industries, the questions of the entry of new firms and the extension of service by established firms into new markets are closed. In other industries, such as in airline transportation and trucking, the regulation of new entrants has been almost eliminated.

Rate Determination

When carried out as part of a formal rate hearing, the process of determining the rates to be charged by a regulated firm takes place in two stages. In the first phase, the total revenue that the firm is to be allowed in a period is calculated. This sum is called the *rate level*.

In the second stage, the specific prices to be charged various users for particular services are set to produce the target revenue, assuming that users purchase estimated quantities of output. The resulting set of prices is called the *rate structure*.

In actual practice, the rate-level phase of a regulatory proceeding consumes the bulk of attention. Once the rate level is determined, the issues of the rate structure are addressed. Some of the major problems in designing a structure of rates are considered later in this chapter in the discussion of price discrimination. At this point, we focus on the problem of the rate level.

The calculation of the total revenue requirement of a firm is organized around the following formula:

$$R = C + (V - D)k \qquad [20.1]$$

where R represents the total revenue requirement, C represents all operating costs including taxes, V is the gross value of the firm's assets, D is accumulated depreciation of the assets, and k is the *rate of return* allowed on assets. The quantity $V - D$ is called the firm's *rate base*. The firm is entitled by law to have the opportunity to earn a reasonable rate of return on this rate base. As the formula suggests, the determination of a firm's revenue can be separated into three steps: estimation of operating costs, identification of the rate base, and calculation of a reasonable rate of return.

As previously mentioned, a full-scale rate-determination proceeding occurs no more frequently than annually for most firms, primarily because of the high costs that such a proceeding imposes on the firm and on the regulatory agency. A rate proceeding can be initiated by either the firm or by the regulatory commission. In recent years, the regulated firms have requested most rate hearings in an effort to have their rates increased to compensate for rising costs. The information required to determine the magnitudes of the various quantities in the formula for computing revenues to be allowed the firm is obtained by analyzing the record of a firm's actual experience over a recent period, called the *test period*. Once the magnitudes for the test period, commonly a year, have been identified, adjustments may be made to reflect forecasted changes in conditions between the test year and the period during which the new rates will be in effect. Since each of the elements in the allowed revenue formula raises different issues, we discuss them separately.

Operating Costs. The operating costs that regulated firms are allowed to recover from consumers include the usual operating expenses, depreciation, and taxes. Regulatory commissions have the power to examine operating costs to ensure that users are not penalized through higher prices as a consequence of a firm's incurring expenses that are higher than necessary. If the commission excludes certain expenses from operating costs, the allowed level of revenue is correspondingly reduced, resulting in lower profits available for common stockholders. Thus the focus of many issues involving operating costs is whether the expenses should be borne by users or by stockholders.

It is difficult for a regulatory commission to monitor accurately all the expenses associated with operating a large utility. As a consequence, only selected cost items that raise potentially serious difficulties are analyzed. For example, salaries and other benefits to management may be examined to ascertain if excessive compensation is provided. Similarly, prices paid for other inputs may be examined, particularly when obtained from a supplier that is affiliated with the regulated firm.

The most troublesome issues involving operating expenses arise in connection with items such as charitable contributions, promotional activities, lobbying activities, and the expenses associated with litigation arising out of the regulatory process itself. Practices related to these expenses vary considerably among regulatory jurisdictions, so it is difficult to offer general conclusions about their treatment. In most situations, however, each commission has adopted policies that it follows consistently in evaluating items such as these, thus eliminating uncertainty that might otherwise complicate the firm's decision making.

In treating depreciation, regulatory agencies have authority to prescribe depreciation policies for firms subject to their jurisdiction. Some commissions allow firms to charge depreciation under accelerated schedules, whereas others require the use of straight-line depreciation techniques. If accelerated depreciation is employed, a controversial issue is whether the savings associated with deferred federal income taxes should accrue to users in the form of lower rates or whether these savings should benefit the firm as higher profits. Again, agencies differ in their treatment of this item.

Taxes of various kinds represent a significant cost to regulated firms. Since the production of their services frequently requires substantial plant and equipment facilities, utilities typically have high property tax expenses which are included in the cost of service. Unlike practices in nonregulated industries, federal income taxes are also treated as an expense item in the regulated sector.

The Rate Base. The rate base of a regulated firm embodies the property, both tangible and intangible, that the firm has acquired to make service available to its users, less accrued depreciation charges on the property. The firm is entitled to rates that provide an adequate rate of return on the investment required to obtain this property. To have any lower rate would mean that the utility's property was being confiscated. In principle, the role of the rate base in determining the revenues allowed a firm is straightforward. But in practice, the rate base has been a source of continuing controversy in rate proceedings.

One aspect of this controversy has concerned items to include in the rate base. The basic rule is that the rate base should encompass all the firm's "used and useful" property. The used-and-useful standard implies that unneeded, duplicate, or abandoned property should not be a part of the rate base. Also, strictly speaking, the standard implies that a piece of property should not become a part of the rate base until it is actually placed into service. However, in view of the substantial costs of constructing many types of utility plants and in light of the lengthy periods of construction required, many regulatory agencies have procedures under which an allowance for capital costs incurred during construction is included in the rate base. Recently, some commissions have not allowed a new utility plant into a firm's rate base if the result will be a large "rate shock." This has been especially true for nuclear power plants. They are often phased into rate base gradually, and in some instances completed plants have been fully excluded from the rate base.

Since the used and useful property of a utility consists of a diverse collection of assets acquired at different points in time, the property must be expressed in common terms for purposes of determining rates. The value of the property represents an obvious common denominator so the valuation of the assets represents an integral part of the regulatory process. The difficulty is that the property can be assigned values in a number of conflicting ways. As a result, the "valuation" problem, as it is called, has long been a disputed aspect of regulation.

One area in which the property of a firm and its earnings are evaluated on a continuing basis is in the capital markets, where the firm's stocks and bonds trade at easily observed prices. It should be apparent, however, that the current market value of the firm, as seen in the capital maket, is completely unacceptable as a method of valuation for rate-making purposes. Prices that investors are willing to pay for a firm's securities depend on the stream of payments they anticipate receiving from the securities. In turn, these payment streams are a function of the revenues generated by the firm. Thus to let the rates and revenues allowed a firm depend on its market value would introduce circularity into the valuation process.

One standard of value that is more meaningful is the so-called original cost standard. Here assets are included in the rate base at values equal to the cost of acquiring them, a figure that is relatively simple to determine. Although its ease of implementation is attractive, the original cost method of valuation has been criticized by some who argue that the costs of acquiring assets is largely irrelevant as a factor determining the current value of the same assets. When price levels change through time, the value of the real assets also changes. The property of many public utilities is likely to be particularly sensitive to the effects of price level changes since many of these assets have extremely long productive lives. As a result, critics of the original cost method argue that basing current prices for service on such historical costs may lead to misallocation of resources by basing prices and decisions on incomplete or inaccurate information.

An alternative technique designed to overcome this difficulty is what is known as "reproduction cost" valuation. According to this method, the value of the rate base is adjusted for general price-level changes to produce an estimate of the present cost of acquiring the firm's assets. During periods characterized by inflation, the resulting reproduction cost rate base would be larger than the corresponding value at original cost. The primary shortcoming of the reproduction cost method is that it is extremely difficult to put into practice. It is impossible to determine unambiguously the current cost of acquiring a particular firm's collection of assets because technological change results in a steady stream of product innovations. Since much of the equipment of a firm is no longer available on the market, estimates of current acquisition costs must be based on some adjustment process that is ultimately arbitrary. Thus efforts to derive reproduction cost are quite expensive, extremely time consuming, and of questionable validity.

A third approach to valuation, representing a compromise between the original cost and the reproduction cost techniques, is called the "fair value" method. This method stems from the 1898 decision of the Supreme Court in the case of *Smyth v. Ames* [169 U.S. 466(1898)] and revolves around a measure of the value of a firm's assets that reasonable persons would find reasonable. No definitive guidelines exist explaining how such a fair value is to be reached.

The courts have ruled that no particular approach to valuing a firm's rate base must be followed. What is important, according to the Supreme Court, is not the particular technique enjoyed but the ultimate results produced as a consequence of combining some measure of the rate base with some rate of return. Actual regulatory attitudes toward the valuation problem vary subtantially. The federal commissions generally use the original cost approach, whereas state commissions use either original cost or fair value.

The Rate of Return. From the basic formula for determining allowed revenues, it is clear that a given level of revenues could be justified on the basis of many combinations of a rate base and a rate of return, with higher levels of the rate base being associated with lower rates of return. It seems natural that each of these components would receive equal attention in a regulatory proceeding. Until recently, however, this has not been the case. Determination of the rate base was taken to be the important problem, with the allowed rate of return attracting little attention. Most regulatory commissions now take a more balanced view of the matter so that the rate of return represents an important decision in rate proceedings.

The idea of a reasonable rate of return reflects the need to compensate suppliers of capital for investing in utility securities. Determining the rate of return involves the identification of an appropriate return on these investments; that is, the firm's costs of various types of capital must be estimated. In accomplishing this, information obtained from the capital market about returns available on alternative investments is an important factor.

In the 1944 Hope Natural Gas case,[4] the Supreme Court established two standards for determining a reasonable rate of return. One of these standards is the attraction-of-capital standard. Reasonable rates of return ensure that the firm will be able to attract the capital needed to finance justified investment in new capacity. The second standard is the comparable earnings standard. It states that rates should be set so that equity holders receive a return comparable to what can be obtained from alternative investments of a similar risk.

---

[4] Federal Power Commission et al. *v.* Hope Natural Gas Co., 320 U.S. 591 (1944).

Each of these standards raises interesting problems when used as a basis for establishing allowed rates of return. The ability of a firm to attract new capital depends on the expectation of investors that they will in fact receive a return sufficient to justify their investment; however, the expectations of investors about future returns are not directly observable since they are based on subjective forecasts by these investors. Thus it is difficult for regulatory agencies to estimate with precision the minimum return required to induce investors to make capital available on a continuing basis. In putting the comparable earnings standard into practice, the major difficulty lies in identifying firms that are comparable in risk to the regulated firm. This reflects the fact that major differences of opinion still exist about the appropriate way to measure the risk of a firm. Lacking well-defined rules for implementating either the capital attraction or the comparable earnings standard, the determination of a firm's rate of return relies heavily on judgmental considerations by the regulatory agencies.[5]

It is important to point out that the existence of regulation does not in itself guarantee that investors will realize an adequate rate of return on their investment. Regulation is not intended to eliminate the risks inherent in making financial investments. This fact introduces an additional element of judgment into the process of calculating the required rate of return. As a result of this and other factors that make determining the rate of return imprecise, it is common to interpret the required return in terms of an interval encompassing a range of reasonable returns rather than as a single value.

Other Dimensions of Regulation

Although the regulation of the rate level is the focus of much of the attention devoted to the regulatory process, regulatory agencies have the ability to influence many other decisions made by the firms subject to their jurisdiction. For instance, commissions require that firms employ a uniform system of accounting designed to produce the financial information necessary to carry out effective regulation. Similarly, agencies supervise the capital structure of firms within their jurisdiction in an effort to see that the firms are capitalized in a manner consistent with minimizng their costs of capital.

Another important aspect of regulatory control involves the quality of service provided by utilities. Because of the critical nature of the services produced in the regulated sector, reliability and safety of those services are of concern to consumers and regulators. The regulatory agencies may set standards for service quality and impose operating rules designed to see that these standards are achieved. In addition, the commissions monitor service quality and provide a forum within which consumer grievances can be evaluated. This is an important function in the regulated sector since in many of the regulated industries

---

[5] The FERC has recently (in 1985) adopted a "generic cost of capital" standard for all regulated electric utilities. The FERC computes a cost of equity capital for the electric utility industry in general. This number is updated quarterly. At the present time this generic standard is for advisory use only.

consumers cannot express dissatisfaction with a supplier by turning to a competing firm.

The ultimate objective of all these regulatory decisions is to see that regulated firms perform in much the same manner as they would if competition were feasible. To accomplish this, regulatory agencies attempt to ensure that the socially optimal output is produced by each firm. In addition, prices must be set to compensate producers adequately, yet not excessively. As it currently functions, the regulatory process attempts to achieve these ultimate objectives indirectly by manipulating other variables. Components of the regulatory process, such as the determination of the rate base, are important only to the extent that they provide techniques for controlling economic performance in the regulated sector.

Special Issues in Utility Regulation

Notice that, as it has been described, the process of determining the total revenue required by a regulated firm follows a sequence completely different from that in the conventional case. Usually, we think of firms setting prices, selling quantities of output at those prices, and collecting whatever amount of revenue results. In the regulated case, however, a target level of total revenue is identified before specific prices are set. In a rate proceeding, the individual prices charged by a firm make up the rate structure. This rate structure is designed to produce revenue consistent with the target level of revenue. In practice, the design of the rate structure has received much less attention in rate cases than the rate level issue, where the problems of identifying appropriate values of the rate base and the rate of return are the principal sources of concern. The selection of a rate structure raises interesting economic problems, however. In this section we consider two of these. First, the general problem of price discrimination is discussed, and then the so-called peak-load pricing problem is described.

Price Discrimination

It has long been common in the regulated sector to categorize users of the services provided by a single regulated firm on the basis of well-defined characteristics. Each of these categories then constitutes a separate market for output, which is sold at prices unique to that market. For example, markets for electric power and telephone services are divided between residential and commercial users. In railway and truck freight transportation, separate markets on a single route are defined by the commodities shipped. As a result, users in different markets, as defined by the producer, pay different prices for what is essentially the same output. The practice of charging different prices for the same output is called *price discrimination*.

As is evident in Table 20.1, price discrimination is quite common in the electric power industry. As this table shows, the average price charged per kilowatt-hour ranged from 4.88 cents for industrial customers to 7.17 cents for residential consumers.

Table 20.1
Average Price per kwh Charged by Investor-Owned Utilities to Various Customer Classifications

Customer Classification	Average Price per kwh (cents)
Residential	7.17
Commercial	7.03
Industrial	4.88

Source: Energy Information Administration, *Financial Statistics of Selected Electric Utilities*, 1983 (Washington, D.C.: U.S. Government Printing Office, February 1985).

Cost Justifications.   One justification for price discrimination by regulated firms lies in the fact that users in different markets may differ in the costs they impose on the supplier in providing service to them. It is argued that these cost differentials ought to be reflected in price differentials as well so that the information given by prices is accurate and can thus contribute to desirable patterns of resource allocation. In the electric power industry, for example, it may be much less costly per unit of output to serve a large industrial user than it is to serve a typical residential customer. The costs incurred in distributing power to the industrial user may be spread over a substantially larger volume of output, resulting in a lower average cost of output and justifying a lower price per unit for the large user. In the telephone industry, the typical commercial user makes a larger number of calls per telephone than does the residential user, placing a heavier burden on the system's capacity to transmit calls. The higher charges for commercial services are designed to reflect these cost differences. It should be obvious that differences in costs such as these are properly a basis for price differences. To charge a uniform price to all customers would be inefficient—encouraging high-cost users to take too much output—and unfair—penalizing low-cost users in the form of prices above cost-justified levels. In fact, narrowly defined, the term *price discrimination* does not apply to situations where cost-of-service differentials are present.

Demand Justification.   It is widely recognized, however, that cost considerations are not the only source of price discrimination in the regulated sector. Price differentials are also designed to reflect differing demand characteristics of various user groups. In particular, differences in what are called "values of service," which basically reflect differences in elasticities of demand, also lead to differences in price among consumer categories. The basic pattern is that consumers with relatively inelastic demands are charged higher prices. This produces small decreases in quantity demanded by these users. In contrast, users with relatively elastic demands pay lower prices, resulting in what may be substantial increases in output demanded. In the electric power industry, residential users, with no realistic substitutes for purchased power, have relatively inelastic demands. On the other hand, large industrial users presumably have the option of producing their own power and thus have more elastic demand. The demand or value of service considerations thus reinforces the pattern of price differentials based strictly on cost factors.

Regulated firms practicing value-of-service discrimination point out that this technique promotes greater use of their services. In turn, this may lead to a more efficient use of a given level of capacity by reducing the excess capacity present at a point in time, spreading the capacity costs over a larger quantity of output, and reducing average total costs. In addition, the promotional aspect of discriminatory pricing may lead to the realization of economies of scale in the long run as larger and more efficient plants are installed. The result is that costs for all users are lower than they would be in the absence of price discrimination. This makes possible prices for all users that are lower than the prices they would otherwise pay. This is true of higher prices for more "costly" consumers as well as lower prices for consumers whose service is less costly to provide.

The challenge raised to regulatory agencies by price discrimination is to ensure that the practice is not abused. The overall rate structure of a regulated firm must be analyzed to see that the users who receive the lowest prices actually pay the full costs of their service. It is conceivable that their prices could be set below cost, with the high-price users subsidizing the low-price consumers through excessive prices. The results of such a pattern would clearly be inefficient as well as inequitable. On the other hand, properly designed rate schedules can promote efficiency without making any users worse off than they would be in the absence of price discrimination.

Block Pricing

The price discrimination discussed thus far involves the segmentation of a firm's total market into submarkets with separate rates for each submarket. This form of third-degree price discrimination was discussed in Chapter 16. Many regulated firms also use second-degree price discrimination: The customers in a particular category pay differing prices for various units of output based on the quantity of output used per billing period. For example, electric power is typically sold under rates similar to the following pattern:

Price	Quantity
16¢ per kilowatt-hour	First 100 kilowatt-hours
12¢ per kilowatt-hour	Next 300 kilowatt-hours
9¢ per kilowatt-hour	Next 800 kilowatt-hours
5¢ per kilowatt-hour	All over 1,200 kilowatt-hours

This type of price discrimination, called block pricing, involves a type of quantity discount as use increases.

Block pricing was introduced in the early stages of the development of the electric power industry. The justification for its use was that the price pattern embodied in block pricing reflected the behavior of the costs of supplying power as produced quantity increased. Again, by spreading costs of a given level of capacity over more units of output, larger production is associated with lower unit costs. In addition, the promotional aspect of block rates, it was argued, contributes to the development of the industry by justifying the installation of larger, more efficient plants.

In recent years, declining block rates have come under considerable

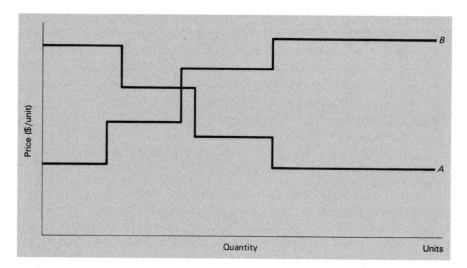

Figure 20.2
Inverted Block Pricing

criticism from those who argue that this form of pricing encourages wasteful use of increasingly scarce energy resources. It is pointed out that with increasing costs for the fuels that are used to generate electricity, what might be appropriate is actually a reversal in the pattern of block rates with higher prices for higher levels of output. In effect, the block schedule would be inverted, as depicted in Figure 20.2. Curve A shows the price schedule for output under a conventional declining block scheme, while B reflects the pattern that would result from inverting the block rates.

Whether a restructuring of the basic pattern in electric power rates is justified depends on what has happened to the basic characteristics of production in the industry. These possibilities are depicted in Figure 20.3, where

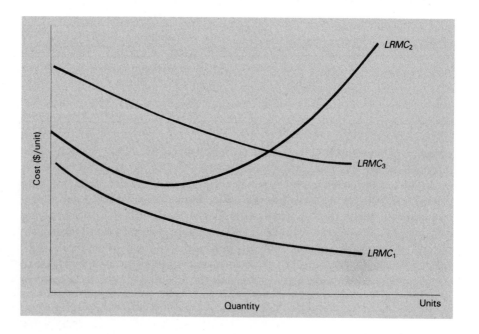

Figure 20.3
Alternative Cost Curves

$LRMC_1$ represents a historical cost curve, and $LRMC_2$ and $LRMC_3$ represent the alternatives for new curves. One possibility would be that the long-run marginal-cost curve for output does not decline over the relevant range. If marginal costs for output are increasing, then there is a need for rearranging the rate pattern (see Figure 20.3, $LRMC_2$). Alternatively, the higher costs may be associated with a roughly parallel upward adjustment in the long-run marginal-cost curve, which retains a basic downward slope. In this event, a shift upward in the complete price schedule would be indicated, but the declining pattern would persist (see Figure 20.3, $LRMC_3$). As yet, considerable disagreement exists about whether $LRMC_2$ or $LRMC_3$ is the more appropriate depiction for purposes of designing rate structures.

The future shape of block rate schedules may not depend solely on the economic factors that determine the behavior of utility cost curves. Rates in the regulated sector are made in an environment where political and other noneconomic considerations play a role in the ultimate decisions. As a result, consumer pressures might lead to the abandonment of declining block rates even if these rates were called for on strictly economic grounds. For example, so-called lifeline rates have been proposed that offer at very low prices a level of power sufficient to satisfy the minimum monthly requirements of an average household, with steep price increases for output taken in excess of this level. If these were instituted, in effect, supplying firms would represent an agent for promoting income distributional objectives. When considerations like these are introduced into the problem of setting utility rates, the task of regulation obviously becomes much more complicated.

Peak-Load Pricing

The characteristics of production in some regulated industries may give rise to another and different form of price discrimination. In situations where output cannot be stored in inventory, and where the producing firm ordinarily stands ready to satisfy whatever level of demand is imposed by users, the cost of producing a unit of output varies according to a time dimension associated with the demand for that unit of output. To see this, consider the case of an electric power company that faces varying demands for power over the course of a day. For simplicity, suppose that there are only two levels of demand, an afternoon period when the demand is high and the rest of the day when the demand is below the level of afternoon demand. Because of the way in which electricity is produced, the generating capacity required to produce power for the afternoon period stands idle for the remainder of the firm's operating cycle; that is, there is excess generating capacity except during the period when demand is at its peak. The firm can produce additional output during the morning, for instance, at a relatively low marginal cost. The only expense for additional output would be the cost of fuel used. In contrast, to produce an additional unit of output during the afternoon period, the firm would have to install an additional unit of generating capacity, implying that the marginal cost of that unit of output would be quite high.

This example illustrates the essential features of what is called the peak-load phenomenon. When demand levels fluctuate over some time period and when the same capacity produces output over this time period, excess producing capacity will exist during some phases of the cycle, called "off-peak" periods. During other phases, the "peak" periods, the system will be fully used. To expand output in the peak period requires the expansion of productive capacity and the costs associated with this expansion. The basic principle of equating prices to marginal costs suggests that peak and off-peak output be priced differently to reflect the differences in marginal cost associated with producing output in each period. The time periods appropriate here are not determined by chronological time, but are rather defined by patterns of demand for output.

A number of regulated industries face demand patterns that vary more or less regularly over a cycle. Electric power, telephone, and transportation services are all produced under conditions characterized by peak-loads. In some cases, capacity may be unavailable to serve all users at the peak. If this is the case, the available output is typically rationed by some nonprice mechanism such as queuing.

To see what type of pricing policy is appropriate in the presence of peak loads, consider the situation shown in Figure 20.4 where two independent demand periods are assumed. In the peak period (day), demand is represented by curve D_1, whereas in the off-peak period (night), demand is shown by D_2. All units of output require the use of fuel at a constant rate, assumed to be b per unit. In addition, capital or generating capacity, which costs β per unit, is also required to produce all output; however, the capacity is not fully used except in the peak period.

The supply curve relevant for determining price and output during the day is the curve $b + \beta$, which reflects the marginal (and average) cost of supplying an additional unit of output during the peak period. At price $P_1 = b + \beta$, day users

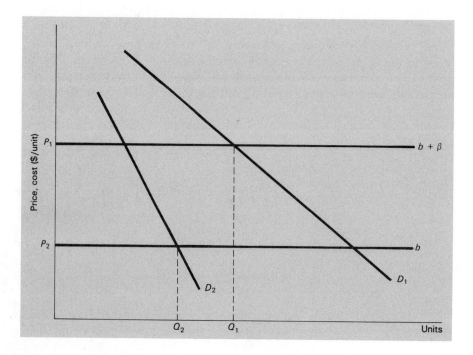

Figure 20.4
Peak-Load Pricing

are just willing to pay the cost of producing a unit of output, so this is the appropriate price for peak service. At this price, Q_1 units of output are produced, implying that Q_1 is the level of capacity installed. At what price should off-peak output be sold? Given the existence of capacity Q_1, the appropriate price of off-peak output is P_2, equal to the marginal cost of fuel. Providing off-peak service imposes no other costs. As a result, the price should be no higher than b per unit at which Q_2 units of output are sold.

This simplified example illustrates the basic principles of peak-load pricing. Peak users should bear all the costs of capacity, a rule that ensures that the optimal level of capacity is installed. At any lower price, peak service would be sold at a price not completely covering all the costs of production. In contrast, off-peak output should be priced to cover only the costs incurred in producing output, given capacity sufficient to do so. This policy encourages the most efficient use of existing capacity. Notice that in the usual case, users would be expected to purchase both peak and off-peak output.

Although principles are theoretically well established for the optimal pricing of goods subject to cyclical demands, the implementation of these principles in the regulated sector has been modest in the United States. Telephone users face lower long-distance charges in the evening and at night. Some electric power firms offer rates that vary seasonally. For instance, systems that have peak use in the summer as a result of heavy demands for air conditioning may impose higher rates during the summer months.

Many observers feel that the absence of more refined peak-load or time-of-day pricing systems represents a fundamental flaw in the way in which electric power is retailed in this country. As a consequence, electric utilities are under considerable pressure to move in the direction of more rational pricing schemes. Of course, the institution of peak-load pricing would require expenses for more sophisticated metering equipment. Nevertheless, it appears that increased attention to the peak-load aspect will be one of the results of the growing concern over energy use.

Criticism of Regulatory Performance

Even a brief survey of economic regulation such as the one given in this chapter would not be complete without a review of some of the principal criticisms of regulation and its performance. Sources of dissatisfaction with regulation fall into two broad categories. On the one hand are a number of shortcomings that seem inherent in the way in which the present set of regulatory institutions operate. On the other hand, and more broadly, a number of writers argue that the approach embodied in regulation is deficient on conceptual grounds. Therefore, simply modifying regulatory institutions and procedures would not be effective in improving regulatory performance.

Problems with the Regulatory Mechanism

It is widely believed that some of the weaknesses of regulation lie in the fact that the regulatory process is cumbersome, time consuming, and costly. Because of the adversarial nature of regulatory proceedings, the proceedings can involve lengthy periods of preparation before the hearing phase, which in itself is quite time consuming. Although some argue that the adversary process is not the most efficient way to organize a regulatory proceeding, it is difficult to design an alternative that provides adequately for the protection of the interests of all parties involved. These factors all contribute to what is commonly called regulatory lag—a frequently cited major weakness of current regulatory practice. One dimension of regulatory lag lies in the findings of a regulatory proceeding that are often based on data for some period in the past. When economic conditions are changing rapidly, the danger is that this information may not really be relevant for future pricing decisions. A second aspect of the regulatory lag problem focuses on the considerable time that may elapse between the point at which a change in rates is appropriate and the point at which a regulatory proceeding is initiated and an order is finalized. It is argued that this is most likely to happen when a downward adjustment in rates is in order. Clearly a regulated firm has no incentive to press for a rate hearing in this instance.

Apart from the difficulties associated with designing regulatory practices that are timely and cost effective, a more fundamental criticism of regulation points out that regulation may remove incentives for efficiency and innovation. Given the nature of the results that regulation attempts to produce, managers and owners of regulated firms may not benefit if costs are reduced. More important, the regulated firms may not realize benefits associated with innovation or technological change through time. Thus regulation offers little in the way of a formal mechanism for rewarding the innovative and risk-taking activities important for economic progress.

Incentives for Inefficiency

Not only may regulation fail to provide incentives for superior performance but the possibility also exists that regulation actually gives incentives for inefficient performance as a by-product of the rate-of-return approach to regulation. This possibility was first identified by Harvey Averch and Leland Johnson. As a result, the kind of behavior that they described has come to be known as the Averch-Johnson, or A-J, effect.[6]

The essential feature of the A-J effect stems from recognition of the fact that, from the point of view of the regulated firm, rate-of-return regulation as it is conventionally applied does not give the same treatment to expenditures for different kinds of productive inputs. When a firm is subject to rate-base, rate-of-return regulation for a given allowed rate of return, the volume of the firm's allowed earnings increases as the rate base increases. The rate base in turn represents the firm's capital stock or capital input. If the allowed rate of return is greater than the firm's actual cost of capital, then the larger the rate base, the larger will be the profits that the firm can earn. Finally, to increase the

---

[6] Harvey Averch and Leland Johnson, "Behavior of the Firm under Regulatory Constraint," *American Economic Review* 53 (December 1962), pp. 1052–1069.

rate base, the firm may substitute capital for labor, to the extent feasible, in producing output. The result is that, for whatever level of output the firm chooses, such output will be produced in a technically inefficient manner. In other words, if the allowed rate of return exceeds the cost of capital, the firm has an incentive to employ input combinations other than the input that produces the selected level of output at least total cost. The regulated firm will use relatively too much capital and relatively too little labor, absorbing more resources than necessary to produce the resulting level of output. In contrast, if the allowed rate of return is set at a level below the cost of capital, utilities may defer needed capital improvements and continue to operate older plants well beyond their "economic" life, resulting in high operating costs.

The A-J analysis is useful because it calls attention to the way in which regulatory institutions can affect the incentives that face regulated firms. It provides an example of how optimizing behavior appropriate for the regulated environment may lead to effects that are socially undesirable on economic grounds. Although the actual empirical significance of the A-J effect is still uncertain, the analysis emphasizes the necessity for including a consideration of possible firm reactions to regulatory practices as part of the process of economic regulation.

The Revisionist View of Regulation

Finally, we have a set of criticisms of regulation that challenges the basic idea that regulation ultimately serves as an instrument to benefit the public in general. Rather, the thrust of the revisionist view of regulation is that the results of regulation are to bestow benefits on the firms in the regulated sector at the expense of broader economic interests. Associated most prominently with conservative economists of the University of Chicago, this approach to regulation emphasizes the role that political factors play in establishing and implementing regulation in any particular industry. It is argued that a regulated industry may use political strength to influence regulatory decisions in directions that serve the interests of the firms in the industry, for instance, by prohibiting the entry of new firms and by structuring rates to produce excessive rates of return. This outcome may be feasible as a consequence of the way in which the political process works. An interest group may be able to favorably influence decisions that affect it simply because the potential benefits justify the commitment of resources required to have a significant impact on the political and regulatory processes. In contrast, the costs of these decisions to the system in general are likely to be so widely distributed that the effective cost to each consumer is quite low, resulting in little incentive at the individual level to exert countervailing demands.[7]

One implication of this view of regulation is that the regulatory agencies are likely to be "captured" by the industries they oversee. As a result, regulatory commissions will attempt to protect the industries from competition. In this case

---

[7] See Robert W. Poole, ed., *Unnatural Monopolies*, for an excellent survey of this literature.

industry stability becomes a goal more important than economic efficiency. Proponents of this approach point out that frequently the most vocal opposition to deregulation of an industry comes from the very firms subject to the regulation, an observation inconsistent with the idea that regulation promotes general economic welfare at the expense of the regulated firms.

From this brief survey of some of the major lines of criticism on regulation, it is apparent that regulation is not without its shortcomings. In fact, it is a simple task to note deficiencies of regulation; it is more difficult, however, to propose alternatives that will lead to unambiguous improvements in the performance of regulated industries. Thus regulation will continue to be important in some industries. For other industries, however, there appears to be a growing feeling that some experimentation with deregulation is appropriate. The most likely prospects for deregulation are industries where the justification for regulation was weakest in the first place, particularly the trucking and airline industries. Both of these industries have been substantially "deregulated" in the last few years and the FERC is currently experimenting with limited deregulation of the natural gas transmission and electric power generation industries.

Summary

- Public utilities are a group of firms, mostly in the electric power, natural gas distribution, natural gas pipeline, transportation, and communications industries, that are closely regulated with respect to entry into the business, prices, service quality, and total profits.

- Regulation is designed to fairly compensate investors for the risks assumed on their investment in the assets of a utility. In a properly functioning regulatory environment, no utility should consistently earn a rate of return on its assets that is either above or below that required by investors. Regulation can be thought of as a process that is designed to make all investment projects undertaken by utilities to be projects having a net present value equal to zero (rate of return equals cost of capital).

- The rationales for public utility regulation are many. The *natural monopoly* argument is applied in cases where a product is characterized by increasing returns to scale. The one large firm can theoretically furnish the good or service at a lower cost than a group of smaller competitive firms.

- The *duplication of facilities* argument is applied in cases where it would be undesirable to have more than one provider of a service because that would result in unnecessary duplication of facilities, such as phone, gas, or electric lines in a city.

- Because of the potential for *price discrimination* by many utilities, regulation is often justified to protect consumers from abuses that may be associated with unregulated price discrimination.

- The regulatory process requires the determination of the *level* of rates as well as the *structure* of rates that will be charged to various user groups.

Public utility regulatory commissions have wide latitude in the determination of rate levels, allowable costs, and rate structures.

- Price discrimination by utilities is often economically desirable on the basis of cost justifications and demand justifications.

- Many utilities engage in the practice of *block pricing*, charging higher rates for the first X units of a good or service and successively lower prices for subsequent units of the good or service. This is designed to encourage greater use and therefore spread the fixed costs of the utility's plant over a larger number of units of output.

- *Peak-load pricing* is designed to charge customers a greater amount for the services they purchase, if these services are used during periods of greatest demand. Long-distance phone services typically have been priced on a peak-load basis.

- Because of many problems that have been encountered in making the regulatory process serve the interests of the public and investors, the current trend is toward increased deregulation of formerly regulated firms. Deregulation is nearly complete in the transportation industries. It is progressing swiftly in the telecommunications industry and the natural gas pipeline industry. Movement toward increased deregulation in the natural gas distribution and electric utility industries can be expected in the future.

Selected References

Averch, Harvey, and Leland Johnson. "Behavior of the Firm Under Regulatory Constraint." *American Economic Review* 53 (December 1962), pp. 1052–1069.

Berg, Stanford V. *Innovative Electric Rates*. Lexington, Mass.: Lexington Books, 1983.

Boonbright, James C. *Principles of Public Utility Rates*. New York: Columbia University Press, 1961.

Douglas, George W., and James C. Miller III. *Economic Regulation of Domestic Air Transport: Theory and Policy*. Washington D. C.: Brookings Institution, 1974.

Joskow, Paul L., and Richard Schmalensee. *Markets for Power: An Analysis of Electric Utility Deregulation*. Cambridge, Mass.: M.I.T. Press, 1983.

Kahn, Alfred E. *The Economics of Regulation*, 2 vols. New York: John Wiley 1971.

Lehr, R. L., and R. Touslee. "What Are We Bid? Stimulating Electric Generation Resources through The Auction Method." *Public Utilities Fortnightly* (12, November 1987), pp. 11–17.

Phillips, Charles F., Jr. *The Regulation of Public Utilities*. Arlington, Va.: Public Utilities Report, 1984.

Poole, Robert W., Jr. *Unnatural Monopolies: The Case for Deregulating Public Utilities*. Lexington, Mass.: D. C. Health, 1985.

Public Utilities Reports. *Utility Restructuring: Strategies, Issues and Cases:* New York: Public Utilities Reports, 1987.

Stigler, George J. "The Theory of Economic Regulation." *Bell Journal of Economics and Management Science* 2 (Spring 1971).

U.S. Department of Energy. *A Consumer's Guide to the Economics of Electric Utility Ratemaking*, DOE/RG/09154. Springfield, Va.: NTIS, May 1980.

Discussion Questions

1. Discuss the role played and the importance of each of the following areas of managerial economics in the regulation of public utilities:
   a. Demand theory
   b. Forecasting
   c. Cost theory and cost measurement
   d. Pricing
   e. Capital budgeting
   f. Cost of capital
   g. Opportunity cost concept
   h. Price discrimination

2. Discuss at least three economic rationales for the regulation of the public utilities.

3. Discuss the three key decisions in the regulatory process.

4. Why has price discrimination become so widespread among firms in the public utility sector of the economy? Why is price discrimination generally supported by the regulatory bodies?

5. Discuss the differences between third-degree and second-degree price discrimination as it is normally practiced by electric power companies.

6. Under what circumstances could you reasonably argue in favor of an inverted block-pricing scheme?

7. What are the strongest economic arguments that can be presented in favor of a peak-load pricing scheme by electric utilities?

8. What is the Averch-Johnson effect? What is the impact of this phenomenon on the efficiency of resource allocation in the regulated utility industries?

9. If the regulatory process is working effectively, the aggregate of all projects undertaken by a nondiversified electric utility firm should have a net present value that equals zero. Why is this true?

10. Southwestern Power Company has a cost of equity capital of 16 percent. The firm has consistently been authorized a return on equity capital below this cost. Also, the effects of regulatory lag and attrition have further reduced the realized return to the 13 percent range. If the utility expects this problem to continue, what actions would you expect Southwestern to take?

11. Northwestern Power Company has a cost of equity capital of 12 percent, but it has been continuously successful in earning a 17 percent return on the portion of its equity capital that is committed to utility operations. If Northwestern expects this situation to continue for the foreseeable future, would you expect its next power plant to be a large coal plant or a series of several smaller natural gas-fired plants? Why?

12. What are the major differences between industrial users of natural gas and residential users that allow natural gas utilities to discriminate between the two groups of customers in price?

Problems

1. The Public Service Company of the Southwest is regulated by an elected state utility commission. The firm has total assets of $500,000. The demand function for its

services has been estimated as

$$P = \$250 - \$.15Q$$

The firm faces the following total cost function:

$$TC = \$25,000 + \$10Q$$

(The total cost function does not include the firm's cost of capital.)

a. In an unregulated environment, what price would this firm charge, what output would be produced, what would total profits be, and what rate of return would the firm earn on its asset base?

b. The firm has proposed charging a price of $100 for each unit of output. If this price is charged, what will be the total profits and the rate of return earned on the firm's asset base?

c. The commission has ordered the firm to charge a price that will provide the firm with no more than a 10 percent return on its assets. What price should the firm charge, what output will be produced, and what dollar level of profits will be earned?

2. *Library Research Project.* Attend the public hearings of a local or state utility commission as it considers the request of a utility for a rate increase. As an alternative you might get a copy of the proceedings from a recent rate hearing. (An excellent source of summary findings in public utility rate cases is *Public Utility Reports.*) Identify the following issues in the case:

a. What was the lag between the utility's application and the commission's final decision?

b. What was the basis for the commission's granting or denying the utility's request?

c. Were any costs disallowed by the commission?

d. What was the basis of the commission's valuation of the firm's rate base?

e. What is the firm's allowable rate of return? How was this determined? What rate of return is the firm actually earning?

f. How large a role did the question of the firm's rate structure, as compared with the firm's rate level, play in the case?

3. A firm faces a demand function per day of

$$P = 29 - 2Q$$

and a total cost function of

$$TC = 20 + 7Q$$

a. Calculate the profit-maximizing price, output, and profit levels for this firm if it is not regulated.

b. If regulators set the maximum price the firm may charge equal to the firm's marginal cost, what output level will be produced and what will be the level of profits?

f. If regulators seek to equate total costs (including a fair return to invested capital) with total revenues, what output level will be produced and what price will be charged?

4. The Odessa Independent Phone Company (OIPC) is currently engaged in a rate case that will set rates for its Midland-Odessa area customer base. OIPC has total assets of $20 million. The Texas Public Utility Commission has determined that an 11 percent return on its assets is fair. OIPC has estimated its annual demand function as follows:

$$P = 3,514 - 0.08Q$$

Its total cost function (not including the cost of capital) is

$$TC = 2,300,000 + 130Q$$

a. OIPC has proposed a rate of $250 per year for each customer. If this rate is approved, what return on assets will OIPC earn?

b. What rate can OIPC charge if the commission wants to limit the return on assets to 11 percent?

c. What problem of utility regulation does this exercise illustrate?

Tables APPENDIX A

Table 1*
Values of the Standard Normal Distribution Function

Z	0	1	2	3	4	5	6	7	8	9
−3.	.0013	.0010	.0007	.0005	.0003	.0002	.0002	.0001	.0001	.0000
−2.9	.0019	.0018	.0017	.0017	.0016	.0016	.0015	.0015	.0014	.0014
−2.8	.0026	.0025	.0024	.0023	.0023	.0022	.0021	.0021	.0020	.0019
−2.7	.0035	.0034	.0033	.0032	.0031	.0030	.0029	.0028	.0027	.0026
−2.6	.0047	.0045	.0044	.0043	.0041	.0040	.0039	.0038	.0037	.0036
−2.5	.0062	.0060	.0059	.0057	.0055	.0054	.0052	.0051	.0049	.0048
−2.4	.0082	.0080	.0078	.0075	.0073	.0071	.0069	.0068	.0066	.0064
−2.3	.0107	.0104	.0102	.0099	.0096	.0094	.0091	.0089	.0087	.0084
−2.2	.0139	.0136	.0132	.0129	.0126	.0122	.0119	.0116	.0113	.0110
−2.1	.0179	.0174	.0170	.0166	.0162	.0158	.0154	.0150	.0146	.0143
−2.0	.0228	.0222	.0217	.0212	.0207	.0202	.0197	.0192	.0188	.0183
−1.9	.0287	.0281	.0274	.0268	.0262	.0256	.0250	.0244	.0238	.0233
−1.8	.0359	.0352	.0344	.0336	.0329	.0322	.0314	.0307	.0300	.0294
−1.7	.0446	.0436	.0427	.0418	.0409	.0401	.0392	.0384	.0375	.0367
−1.6	.0548	.0537	.0526	.0516	.0505	.0495	.0485	.0475	.0465	.0455
−1.5	.0668	.0655	.0643	.0630	.0618	.0606	.0594	.0582	.0570	.0559
−1.4	.0808	.0793	.0778	.0764	.0749	.0735	.0722	.0708	.0694	.0681
−1.3	.0968	.0951	.0934	.0918	.0901	.0885	.0869	.0853	.0838	.0823
−1.2	.1151	.1131	.1112	.1093	.1075	.1056	.1038	.1020	.1003	.0985
−1.1	.1357	.1335	.1314	.1292	.1271	.1251	.1230	.1210	.1190	.1170
−1.0	.1587	.1562	.1539	.1515	.1492	.1469	.1446	.1423	.1401	.1379
− .9	.1841	.1814	.1788	.1762	.1736	.1711	.1685	.1660	.1635	.1611
− .8	.2119	.2090	.2061	.2033	.2005	.1977	.1949	.1922	.1894	.1867
− .7	.2420	.2389	.2358	.2327	.2297	.2266	.2236	.2206	.2177	.2148
− .6	.2743	.2709	.2676	.2643	.2611	.2578	.2546	.2514	.2483	.2451
− .5	.3085	.3050	.3015	.2981	.2946	.2912	.2877	.2843	.2810	.2776
− .4	.3446	.3409	.3372	.3336	.3300	.3264	.3228	.3192	.3156	.3121
− .3	.3821	.3783	.3745	.3707	.3669	.3632	.3594	.3557	.3520	.3483
− .2	.4207	.4168	.4129	.4090	.4052	.4013	.3974	.3936	.3897	.3859
− .1	.4602	.4562	.4522	.4483	.4443	.4404	.4364	.4325	.4286	.4247
− .0	.5000	.4960	.4920	.4880	.4840	.4801	.4761	.4721	.4681	.4641

*Note: Table values give the probability of a value occurring which is *less than* Z standard deviations from the mean.

Note 1: If a random variable X is not "standard," its values must be "standardized": $Z = (X - \mu)/\sigma$. That is:

$$P(X \leq x) = N\left(\frac{x - \mu}{\sigma}\right)$$

Note 2: For $z \geq 4$, $N(z) = 1$ to 4 decimal places; for $z \leq -4$, $N(z) = 0$ to 4 decimal places.

Table 1 (*cont'd*)
**Values of the
Standard Normal
Distribution
Function**

Z	0	1	2	3	4	5	6	7	8	9
.0	.5000	.5040	.5080	.5120	.5160	.5199	.5239	.5279	.5319	.5359
.1	.5398	.5438	.5478	.5517	.5557	.5596	.5636	.5675	.5714	.5753
.2	.5793	.5832	.5871	.5910	.5948	.5987	.6026	.6064	.6103	.6141
.3	.6179	.6217	.6255	.6293	.6331	.6368	.6406	.6443	.6480	.6517
.4	.6554	.6591	.6628	.6664	.6700	.6736	.6772	.6808	.6844	.6879
.5	.6915	.6950	.6985	.7019	.7054	.7088	.7123	.7157	.7190	.7224
.6	.7257	.7291	.7324	.7357	.7389	.7422	.7454	.7486	.7517	.7549
.7	.7580	.7611	.7642	.7673	.7703	.7734	.7764	.7794	.7823	.7852
.8	.7881	.7910	.7939	.7967	.7995	.8023	.8051	.8078	.8106	.8133
.9	.8159	.8186	.8212	.8238	.8264	.8289	.8315	.8340	.8365	.8389
1.0	.8413	.8438	.8461	.8485	.8508	.8531	.8554	.8577	.8599	.8621
1.1	.8643	.8665	.8686	.8708	.8729	.8749	.8770	.8790	.8810	.8830
1.2	.8849	.8869	.8888	.8907	.8925	.8944	.8962	.8980	.8997	.9015
1.3	.9032	.9049	.9066	.9082	.9099	.9115	.9131	.9147	.9162	.9177
1.4	.9192	.9207	.9222	.9236	.9251	.9265	.9278	.9292	.9306	.9319
1.5	.9332	.9345	.9357	.9370	.9382	.9394	.9406	.9418	.9430	.9441
1.6	.9452	.9463	.9474	.9484	.9495	.9505	.9515	.9525	.9535	.9545
1.7	.9554	.9564	.9573	.9582	.9591	.9599	.9608	.9616	.9625	.9633
1.8	.9641	.9648	.9656	.9664	.9671	.9678	.9686	.9693	.9700	.9706
1.9	.9713	.9719	.9726	.9732	.9738	.9744	.9750	.9756	.9762	.9767
2.0	.9772	.9778	.9783	.9788	.9793	.9798	.9803	.9808	.9812	.9817
2.1	.9821	.9826	.9830	.9834	.9838	.9842	.9846	.9850	.9854	.9857
2.2	.9861	.9864	.9868	.9871	.9874	.9878	.9881	.9884	.9887	.9890
2.3	.9893	.9896	.9898	.9901	.9904	.9906	.9909	.9911	.9913	.9916
2.4	.9918	.9920	.9922	.9925	.9927	.9929	.9931	.9932	.9934	.9936
2.5	.9938	.9940	.9941	.9943	.9945	.9946	.9948	.9949	.9951	.9952
2.6	.9953	.9955	.9956	.9957	.9959	.9960	.9961	.9962	.9963	.9964
2.7	.9965	.9966	.9967	.9968	.9969	.9970	.9971	.9972	.9973	.9974
2.8	.9974	.9975	.9976	.9977	.9977	.9978	.9979	.9979	.9980	.9981
2.9	.9981	.9982	.9982	.9983	.9984	.9984	.9985	.9985	.9986	.9986
3.	.9987	.9990	.9993	.9995	.9997	.9998	.9998	.9999	.9999	1.0000

Source: *Statistical Analysis: With Business and Economic Applications,* by Ya-lun Chou. Copyright © 1969 by Holt, Rinehart and Winston, Inc. Reprinted by permission of Holt, Rinehart and Winston, Inc.

Table 2*
Table of "Students" Distribution—Value of t

Degrees of Freedom	Probability												
	0.9	0.8	0.7	0.6	0.5	0.4	0.3	0.2	0.1	0.05	0.02	0.01	0.001
1	0.158	0.325	0.510	0.727	1.000	1.376	1.963	3.078	6.314	12.706	31.821	63.657	636.619
2	0.142	0.289	0.445	0.617	0.816	1.061	1.386	1.886	2.920	4.303	6.965	9.925	31.598
3	0.137	0.277	0.424	0.584	0.765	0.978	1.250	1.638	2.353	3.182	4.541	5.841	12.924
4	0.134	0.271	0.414	0.569	0.741	0.941	1.190	1.533	2.132	2.776	3.747	4.604	8.610
5	0.132	0.267	0.408	0.559	0.727	0.920	1.156	1.476	2.015	2.571	3.365	4.032	6.869
6	0.131	0.265	0.404	0.553	0.718	0.906	1.134	1.440	1.943	2.447	3.143	3.707	5.959
7	0.130	0.263	0.402	0.549	0.711	0.896	1.119	1.415	1.895	2.365	2.998	3.499	5.408
8	0.130	0.262	0.399	0.546	0.706	0.889	1.108	1.397	1.860	2.306	2.896	3.355	5.041
9	0.129	0.261	0.398	0.543	0.703	0.883	1.100	1.383	1.833	2.262	2.821	3.250	4.781
10	0.129	0.260	0.397	0.542	0.700	0.879	1.093	1.372	1.812	2.228	2.764	3.169	4.587
11	0.129	0.260	0.396	0.540	0.697	0.876	1.088	1.363	1.796	2.201	2.718	3.106	4.437
12	0.128	0.259	0.395	0.539	0.695	0.873	1.083	1.356	1.782	2.179	2.681	3.055	4.318
13	0.128	0.259	0.394	0.538	0.694	0.870	1.079	1.350	1.771	2.160	2.650	3.012	4.221
14	0.128	0.258	0.393	0.537	0.692	0.868	1.076	1.345	1.761	2.145	2.624	2.977	4.140
15	0.128	0.258	0.393	0.536	0.691	0.866	1.074	1.341	1.753	2.131	2.602	2.947	4.073
16	0.128	0.258	0.392	0.535	0.690	0.865	1.071	1.337	1.746	2.120	2.583	2.921	4.015
17	0.128	0.257	0.392	0.534	0.689	0.863	1.069	1.333	1.740	2.110	2.567	2.898	3.965
18	0.127	0.257	0.392	0.534	0.688	0.862	1.067	1.330	1.734	2.101	2.552	2.878	3.922
19	0.127	0.257	0.391	0.533	0.688	0.861	1.066	1.328	1.729	2.093	2.539	2.861	3.883
20	0.127	0.257	0.391	0.533	0.687	0.860	1.064	1.325	1.725	2.086	2.528	2.845	3.850
21	0.127	0.257	0.391	0.532	0.686	0.859	1.063	1.323	1.721	2.080	2.518	2.831	3.819
22	0.127	0.256	0.390	0.532	0.686	0.858	1.061	1.321	1.717	2.074	2.508	2.819	3.792
23	0.127	0.256	0.390	0.532	0.685	0.858	1.060	1.319	1.714	2.069	2.500	2.807	3.767
24	0.127	0.256	0.390	0.531	0.685	0.857	1.059	1.318	1.711	2.064	2.492	2.797	3.745
25	0.127	0.256	0.390	0.531	0.684	0.856	1.058	1.316	1.708	2.060	2.485	2.787	3.725
26	0.127	0.256	0.390	0.531	0.684	0.856	1.058	1.315	1.706	2.056	2.479	2.779	3.707
27	0.127	0.256	0.389	0.531	0.684	0.855	1.057	1.314	1.703	2.052	2.473	2.771	3.690
28	0.127	0.256	0.389	0.530	0.683	0.855	1.056	1.313	1.701	2.048	2.467	2.763	3.674
29	0.127	0.256	0.389	0.530	0.683	0.854	1.055	1.311	1.699	2.045	2.462	2.756	3.659
30	0.127	0.256	0.389	0.530	0.683	0.854	1.055	1.310	1.697	2.042	2.457	2.750	3.646
40	0.126	0.255	0.388	0.529	0.681	0.851	1.050	1.303	1.684	2.021	2.423	2.704	3.551
60	0.126	0.254	0.387	0.527	0.679	0.848	1.046	1.296	1.671	2.000	2.390	2.660	3.460
120	0.126	0.254	0.386	0.526	0.677	0.845	1.041	1.289	1.658	1.980	2.358	2.617	3.373
∞	0.126	0.253	0.385	0.524	0.674	0.842	1.036	1.282	1.645	1.960	2.326	2.576	3.291

*Note: Probabilities given are for two-tailed tests. For example, a probability of .05 allows for .025 in one tail of the distribution and .025 in the other.

Table 2 is taken from Table III of Fisher and Yates: *Statistical Tables for Biological, Agricultural and Medical Research*, published by Longman Group, Ltd., London (previously published by Oliver and Boyd, Edinburgh), and by permission of the authors and publishers.

Table 3
The F Distribution—Upper 5% Points

δ_2 \ δ_1	1	2	3	4	5	6	7	8	9	10	12	15	20	24	30	40	60	120	∞
1	161.4	199.5	215.7	224.6	230.2	234.0	236.8	238.9	240.5	241.9	243.9	245.9	248.0	249.1	250.1	251.1	252.2	253.3	254.3
2	18.51	19.00	19.16	19.25	19.30	19.33	19.35	19.37	19.38	19.40	19.41	19.43	19.45	19.45	19.46	19.47	19.48	19.49	19.50
3	10.13	9.55	9.28	9.12	9.01	8.94	8.89	8.85	8.81	8.79	8.74	8.70	8.66	8.64	8.62	8.59	8.57	8.55	8.53
4	7.71	6.94	6.59	6.39	6.26	6.16	6.09	6.04	6.00	5.96	5.91	5.86	5.80	5.77	5.75	5.72	5.69	5.66	5.63
5	6.61	5.79	5.41	5.19	5.05	4.95	4.88	4.82	4.77	4.74	4.68	4.62	4.56	4.53	4.50	4.46	4.43	4.40	4.36
6	5.99	5.14	4.76	4.53	4.39	4.28	4.21	4.15	4.10	4.06	4.00	3.94	3.87	3.84	3.81	3.77	3.74	3.70	3.67
7	5.59	4.74	4.35	4.12	3.97	3.87	3.79	3.73	3.68	3.64	3.57	3.51	3.44	3.41	3.38	3.34	3.30	3.27	3.23
8	5.32	4.46	4.07	3.84	3.69	3.58	3.50	3.44	3.39	3.35	3.28	3.22	3.15	3.12	3.08	3.04	3.01	2.97	2.93
9	5.12	4.26	3.86	3.63	3.48	3.37	3.29	3.23	3.18	3.14	3.07	3.01	2.94	2.90	2.86	2.83	2.79	2.75	2.71
10	4.96	4.10	3.71	3.48	3.33	3.22	3.14	3.07	3.02	2.98	2.91	2.85	2.77	2.74	2.70	2.66	2.62	2.58	2.54
11	4.84	3.98	3.59	3.36	3.20	3.09	3.01	2.95	2.90	2.85	2.79	2.72	2.65	2.61	2.57	2.53	2.49	2.45	2.40
12	4.75	3.89	3.49	3.26	3.11	3.00	2.91	2.85	2.80	2.75	2.69	2.62	2.54	2.51	2.47	2.43	2.38	2.34	2.30
13	4.67	3.81	3.41	3.18	3.03	2.92	2.83	2.77	2.71	2.67	2.60	2.53	2.46	2.42	2.38	2.34	2.30	2.25	2.21
14	4.60	3.74	3.34	3.11	2.96	2.85	2.76	2.70	2.65	2.60	2.53	2.46	2.39	2.35	2.31	2.27	2.22	2.18	2.13
15	4.54	3.68	3.29	3.06	2.90	2.79	2.71	2.64	2.59	2.54	2.48	2.40	2.33	2.29	2.25	2.20	2.16	2.11	2.07
16	4.49	3.63	3.24	3.01	2.85	2.74	2.66	2.59	2.54	2.49	2.42	2.35	2.28	2.24	2.19	2.15	2.11	2.06	2.01
17	4.45	3.59	3.20	2.96	2.81	2.70	2.61	2.55	2.49	2.45	2.38	2.31	2.23	2.19	2.15	2.10	2.06	2.01	1.96
18	4.41	3.55	3.16	2.93	2.77	2.66	2.58	2.51	2.46	2.41	2.34	2.27	2.19	2.15	2.11	2.06	2.02	1.97	1.92
19	4.38	3.52	3.13	2.90	2.74	2.63	2.54	2.48	2.42	2.38	2.31	2.23	2.16	2.11	2.07	2.03	1.98	1.93	1.88
20	4.35	3.49	3.10	2.87	2.71	2.60	2.51	2.45	2.39	2.35	2.28	2.20	2.12	2.08	2.04	1.99	1.95	1.90	1.84
21	4.32	3.47	3.07	2.84	2.68	2.57	2.49	2.42	2.37	2.32	2.25	2.18	2.10	2.05	2.01	1.96	1.92	1.87	1.81
22	4.30	3.44	3.05	2.82	2.66	2.55	2.46	2.40	2.34	2.30	2.23	2.15	2.07	2.03	1.98	1.94	1.89	1.84	1.78
23	4.28	3.42	3.03	2.80	2.64	2.53	2.44	2.37	2.32	2.27	2.20	2.13	2.05	2.01	1.96	1.91	1.86	1.81	1.76
24	4.26	3.40	3.01	2.78	2.62	2.51	2.42	2.36	2.30	2.25	2.18	2.11	2.03	1.98	1.94	1.89	1.84	1.79	1.73
25	4.24	3.39	2.99	2.76	2.60	2.49	2.40	2.34	2.28	2.24	2.16	2.09	2.01	1.96	1.92	1.87	1.82	1.77	1.71
26	4.23	3.37	2.98	2.74	2.59	2.47	2.39	2.32	2.27	2.22	2.15	2.07	1.99	1.95	1.90	1.85	1.80	1.75	1.69
27	4.21	3.35	2.96	2.73	2.57	2.46	2.37	2.31	2.25	2.20	2.13	2.06	1.97	1.93	1.88	1.84	1.79	1.73	1.67
28	4.20	3.34	2.95	2.71	2.56	2.45	2.36	2.29	2.24	2.19	2.12	2.04	1.96	1.91	1.87	1.82	1.77	1.71	1.65
29	4.18	3.33	2.93	2.70	2.55	2.43	2.35	2.28	2.22	2.18	2.10	2.03	1.94	1.90	1.85	1.81	1.75	1.70	1.64
30	4.17	3.32	2.92	2.69	2.53	2.42	2.33	2.27	2.21	2.16	2.09	2.01	1.93	1.89	1.84	1.79	1.74	1.68	1.62
40	4.08	3.23	2.84	2.61	2.45	2.34	2.25	2.18	2.12	2.08	2.00	1.92	1.84	1.79	1.74	1.69	1.64	1.58	1.51
60	4.00	3.15	2.76	2.53	2.37	2.25	2.17	2.10	2.04	1.99	1.92	1.84	1.75	1.70	1.65	1.59	1.53	1.47	1.39
120	3.92	3.07	2.68	2.45	2.29	2.17	2.09	2.02	1.96	1.91	1.83	1.75	1.66	1.61	1.55	1.50	1.43	1.35	1.25
∞	3.84	3.00	2.60	2.37	2.21	2.10	2.01	1.94	1.88	1.83	1.75	1.67	1.57	1.52	1.46	1.39	1.32	1.22	1.00

Table 3 (*cont'd*)
The F Distribution— Upper 1% Points

δ_1 / δ_2	1	2	3	4	5	6	7	8	9
1	4052	4999.5	5403	5625	5764	5859	5928	5982	6022
2	98.50	99.00	99.17	99.25	99.30	99.33	99.36	99.37	99.39
3	34.12	30.82	29.46	28.71	28.24	27.91	27.67	27.49	27.35
4	21.20	18.00	16.69	15.98	15.52	15.21	14.98	14.80	14.66
5	16.26	13.27	12.06	11.39	10.97	10.67	10.46	10.29	10.16
6	13.75	10.92	9.78	9.15	8.75	8.47	8.26	8.10	7.98
7	12.25	9.55	8.45	7.85	7.46	7.19	6.99	6.84	6.72
8	11.26	8.65	7.59	7.01	6.63	6.37	6.18	6.03	5.91
9	10.56	8.02	6.99	6.42	6.06	5.80	5.61	5.47	5.35
10	10.04	7.56	6.55	5.99	5.64	5.39	5.20	5.06	4.94
11	9.65	7.21	6.22	5.67	5.32	5.07	4.89	4.74	4.63
12	9.33	6.93	5.95	5.41	5.06	4.82	4.64	4.50	4.39
13	9.07	6.70	5.74	5.21	4.86	4.62	4.44	4.30	4.19
14	8.86	6.51	5.56	5.04	4.69	4.46	4.28	4.14	4.03
15	8.68	6.36	5.42	4.89	4.56	4.32	4.14	4.00	3.89
16	8.53	6.23	5.29	4.77	4.44	4.20	4.03	3.89	3.78
17	8.40	6.11	5.18	4.67	4.34	4.10	3.93	3.79	3.68
18	8.29	6.01	5.09	4.58	4.25	4.01	3.84	3.71	3.60
19	8.18	5.93	5.01	4.50	4.17	3.94	3.77	3.63	3.52

δ_1 / δ_2	10	12	15	20	24	30	40	60	120	∞
1	6056	6106	6157	6209	6235	6261	6287	6313	6339	6366
2	99.40	99.42	99.43	99.45	99.46	99.47	99.47	99.48	99.49	99.50
3	27.23	27.05	26.87	26.69	26.60	26.50	26.41	26.32	26.22	26.13
4	14.55	14.37	14.20	14.02	13.93	13.84	13.75	13.65	13.56	13.46
5	10.05	9.89	9.72	9.55	9.47	9.38	9.29	9.20	9.11	9.02
6	7.87	7.72	7.56	7.40	7.31	7.23	7.14	7.06	6.97	6.88
7	6.62	6.47	6.31	6.16	6.07	5.99	5.91	5.82	5.74	5.65
8	5.81	5.67	5.52	5.36	5.28	5.20	5.12	5.03	4.95	4.86
9	5.26	5.11	4.96	4.81	4.73	4.65	4.57	4.48	4.40	4.31
10	4.85	4.71	4.56	4.41	4.33	4.25	4.17	4.08	4.00	3.91
11	4.54	4.40	4.25	4.10	4.02	3.94	3.86	3.78	3.69	3.60
12	4.30	4.16	4.01	3.86	3.78	3.70	3.62	3.54	3.45	3.36
13	4.10	3.96	3.82	3.66	3.59	3.51	3.43	3.34	3.25	3.17
14	3.94	3.80	3.66	3.51	3.43	3.35	3.27	3.18	3.09	3.00
15	3.80	3.67	3.52	3.37	3.29	3.21	3.13	3.05	2.96	2.87
16	3.69	3.55	3.41	3.26	3.18	3.10	3.02	2.93	2.84	2.75
17	3.59	3.46	3.31	3.16	3.08	3.00	2.92	2.83	2.75	2.65
18	3.51	3.37	3.23	3.08	3.00	2.92	2.84	2.75	2.66	2.57
19	3.43	3.30	3.15	3.00	2.92	2.84	2.76	2.67	2.58	2.49

Table 3 (*cont'd*)
The F Distribution— Upper 1% Points

δ_2 \ δ_1	1	2	3	4	5	6	7	8	9
20	8.10	5.85	4.94	4.43	4.10	3.87	3.70	3.56	3.46
21	8.02	5.78	4.87	4.37	4.04	3.81	3.64	3.51	3.40
22	7.95	5.72	4.82	4.31	3.99	3.76	3.59	3.45	3.35
23	7.88	5.66	4.76	4.26	3.94	3.71	3.54	3.41	3.30
24	7.82	5.61	4.72	4.22	3.90	3.67	3.50	3.36	3.26
25	7.77	5.57	4.68	4.18	3.85	3.63	3.46	3.32	3.22
26	7.72	5.53	4.64	4.14	3.82	3.59	3.42	3.29	3.18
27	7.68	5.49	4.60	4.11	3.78	3.56	3.39	3.26	3.15
28	7.64	5.45	4.57	4.07	3.75	3.53	3.36	3.23	3.12
29	7.60	5.42	4.54	4.04	3.73	3.50	3.33	3.20	3.09
30	7.56	5.39	4.51	4.02	3.70	3.47	3.30	3.17	3.07
40	7.31	5.18	4.31	3.83	3.51	3.29	3.12	2.99	2.89
60	7.08	4.98	4.13	3.65	3.34	3.12	2.95	2.82	2.72
120	6.85	4.79	3.95	3.48	3.17	2.96	2.79	2.66	2.56
∞	6.63	4.61	3.78	3.32	3.02	2.80	2.64	2.51	2.41

δ_2 \ δ_1	10	12	15	20	24	30	40	60	120	∞
20	3.37	3.23	3.09	2.94	2.86	2.78	2.69	2.61	2.52	2.42
21	3.31	3.17	3.03	2.88	2.80	2.72	2.64	2.55	2.46	2.36
22	3.26	3.12	2.98	2.83	2.75	2.67	2.58	2.50	2.40	2.31
23	3.21	3.07	2.93	2.78	2.70	2.62	2.54	2.45	2.35	2.26
24	3.17	3.03	2.89	2.74	2.66	2.58	2.49	2.40	2.31	2.21
25	3.13	2.99	2.85	2.70	2.62	2.54	2.45	2.36	2.27	2.17
26	3.09	2.96	2.81	2.66	2.58	2.50	2.42	2.33	2.23	2.13
27	3.06	2.93	2.78	2.63	2.55	2.47	2.38	2.29	2.20	2.10
28	3.03	2.90	2.75	2.60	2.52	2.44	2.35	2.26	2.17	2.06
29	3.00	2.87	2.73	2.57	2.49	2.41	2.33	2.23	2.14	2.03
30	2.98	2.84	2.70	2.55	2.47	2.39	2.30	2.21	2.11	2.01
40	2.80	2.66	2.52	2.37	2.29	2.20	2.11	2.02	1.92	1.80
60	2.63	2.50	2.35	2.20	2.12	2.03	1.94	1.84	1.73	1.60
120	2.47	2.34	2.19	2.03	1.95	1.86	1.76	1.66	1.53	1.38
∞	2.32	2.18	2.04	1.88	1.79	1.70	1.59	1.47	1.32	1.00

Source: E. S. Pearson and H. O. Hartley, *Biometrika Tables for Statisticians,* Vol. I, Table 18 with permission.

Table 4
Present Value of $1

Period	1%	2%	3%	4%	5%	6%	7%	8%	9%	10%	Period
01	.99010	.98039	.97007	.96154	.95233	.94340	.93458	.92593	.91743	.90909	01
02	.98030	.96117	.94260	.92456	.90703	.89000	.87344	.85734	.84168	.82645	02
03	.97059	.94232	.91514	.88900	.86384	.83962	.81639	.79383	.77228	.75131	03
04	.96098	.92385	.88849	.85480	.82270	.79209	.76290	.73503	.70883	.68301	04
05	.95147	.90573	.86261	.82193	.78353	.74726	.71299	.68058	.64993	.62092	05
06	.94204	.88797	.83748	.79031	.74622	.70496	.66634	.63017	.59627	.56447	06
07	.93272	.87056	.81309	.75992	.71063	.66506	.62275	.58349	.54705	.51316	07
08	.92348	.85349	.78941	.73069	.67684	.62741	.58201	.54027	.50189	.46651	08
09	.91434	.83675	.76642	.70259	.64461	.59190	.54393	.50025	.46043	.42410	09
10	.90529	.82035	.74409	.67556	.61391	.55839	.50835	.46319	.42241	.38554	10
11	.89632	.80426	.72242	.64958	.58468	.52679	.47509	.42888	.38753	.35049	11
12	.88745	.78849	.70138	.62460	.55684	.49697	.44401	.39711	.35553	.31683	12
13	.87866	.77303	.68095	.60057	.53032	.46884	.41496	.36770	.32618	.28966	13
14	.86996	.75787	.66112	.57747	.50507	.44230	.38782	.34046	.29925	.26333	14
15	.86135	.74301	.64186	.55526	.48102	.41726	.36245	.31524	.27454	.23939	15
16	.85282	.72845	.62317	.53391	.45811	.39365	.33873	.29189	.25187	.21763	16
17	.84436	.71416	.60502	.51337	.43630	.37136	.31657	.27027	.23107	.19784	17
18	.83602	.70016	.58739	.49363	.41552	.35034	.29586	.25025	.21199	.17986	18
19	.82774	.68643	.57029	.47464	.39573	.33051	.27651	.23171	.19449	.16354	19
20	.81954	.67297	.55367	.45639	.37689	.31180	.25842	.21455	.17843	.14864	20
21	.81143	.65978	.53755	.44883	.35894	.29415	.24151	.19866	.16370	.13513	21
22	.80340	.64684	.52189	.42195	.34185	.27750	.22571	.18394	.15018	.12285	22
23	.79544	.63414	.50669	.40573	.32557	.26180	.21095	.17031	.13778	.11168	23
24	.78757	.62172	.49193	.39012	.31007	.24698	.19715	.15770	.12640	.10153	24
25	.77977	.60953	.47760	.37512	.29530	.23300	.18425	.14602	.11597	.09230	25

Table 4 (cont'd)
Present Value of $1

Period	11%	12%	13%	14%	15%	16%	17%	18%	19%	20%	Period
01	.90090	.89286	.88496	.87719	.86957	.86207	.85470	.84746	.84043	.83333	01
02	.81162	.79719	.78315	.76947	.75614	.74316	.73051	.71818	.70616	.69444	02
03	.73119	.71178	.69305	.67497	.65752	.64066	.62437	.60863	.59342	.57870	03
04	.65873	.63552	.61332	.59208	.57175	.55229	.53365	.51579	.49867	.48225	04
05	.59345	.56743	.54276	.51937	.49718	.47611	.45611	.43711	.41905	.40188	05
06	.53464	.50663	.48032	.45559	.43233	.41044	.38984	.37043	.35214	.33490	06
07	.48166	.45235	.42506	.39964	.37594	.35383	.33320	.31392	.29592	.27908	07
08	.43393	.40388	.37616	.35056	.32690	.30503	.28478	.26604	.24867	.23257	08
09	.39092	.36061	.33288	.30751	.28426	.26295	.24340	.22546	.20897	.19381	09
10	.35218	.32197	.29459	.26974	.24718	.22668	.20804	.19106	.17560	.16151	10
11	.31728	.28748	.26070	.23662	.21494	.19542	.17781	.16192	.14756	.13459	11
12	.28584	.25667	.23071	.20756	.18691	.16846	.15197	.13722	.12400	.11216	12
13	.25751	.22917	.20416	.18207	.16253	.14523	.12989	.11629	.10420	.09346	13
14	.23199	.20462	.18068	.15971	.14133	.12520	.11102	.09855	.08757	.07789	14
15	.20900	.18270	.15989	.14010	.12289	.10793	.09489	.08352	.07359	.06491	15
16	.18829	.16312	.14150	.12289	.10686	.09304	.08110	.07073	.06184	.05409	16
17	.16963	.14564	.12522	.10780	.09293	.08021	.06932	.05998	.05196	.04507	17
18	.15282	.13004	.11081	.09456	.08080	.06914	.05925	.05083	.04367	.03756	18
19	.13768	.11611	.09806	.08295	.07026	.05961	.05064	.04308	.03669	.03130	19
20	.12403	.10367	.08678	.07276	.06110	.05139	.04328	.03651	.03084	.02608	20
21	.11174	.09256	.07680	.06383	.05313	.04430	.03699	.03094	.02591	.02174	21
22	.10067	.08264	.06796	.05599	.04620	.03819	.03162	.02622	.02178	.01811	22
23	.09069	.07379	.06014	.04911	.04017	.03292	.02702	.02222	.01830	.01509	23
24	.08170	.06588	.05322	.04308	.03493	.02838	.02310	.01883	.01538	.01258	24
25	.07361	.05882	.04710	.03779	.03038	.02447	.01974	.01596	.01292	.01048	25

Table 5
Present Value of an Annuity of $1

Period	1%	2%	3%	4%	5%	6%	7%	8%	9%	10%	Period
01	.9901	.9804	.9709	.9615	.9524	.9434	.9346	.9259	.9174	.9091	01
02	1.9704	1.9416	1.9135	1.8861	1.8594	1.8334	1.8080	1.7833	1.7591	1.7355	02
03	2.9410	2.8839	2.8286	2.7751	2.7233	2.6730	2.6243	2.5771	2.5313	2.4868	03
04	3.9020	3.8077	3.7171	3.6299	3.5459	3.4651	3.3872	3.3121	3.2397	3.1699	04
05	4.8535	4.7134	4.5797	4.4518	4.3295	4.2123	4.1002	3.9927	3.8896	3.7908	05
06	5.7955	5.6014	5.4172	5.2421	5.0757	4.9173	4.7665	4.6229	4.4859	4.3553	06
07	6.7282	6.4720	6.2302	6.0020	5.7863	5.5824	5.3893	5.2064	5.0329	4.8684	07
08	7.6517	7.3254	7.0196	6.7327	6.4632	6.2093	5.9713	5.7466	5.5348	5.3349	08
09	8.5661	8.1622	7.7861	7.4353	7.1078	6.8017	6.5152	6.2469	5.9852	5.7590	09
10	9.4714	8.9825	8.7302	8.1109	7.7217	7.3601	7.0236	6.7101	6.4176	6.1446	10
11	10.3677	9.7868	9.2526	8.7604	8.3064	7.8868	7.4987	7.1389	6.8052	6.4951	11
12	11.2552	10.5753	9.9589	9.3850	8.8632	8.3838	7.9427	7.5361	7.1601	6.8137	12
13	12.1338	11.3483	10.6349	9.9856	9.3935	8.8527	8.3576	7.9038	7.4869	7.1034	13
14	13.0088	12.1062	11.2960	10.5631	9.8986	9.2950	8.7454	8.2442	7.7860	7.3667	14
15	13.8651	12.8492	11.9379	11.1183	10.3796	9.7122	9.1079	8.5595	8.0607	7.6061	15
16	14.7180	13.5777	12.5610	11.6522	10.8377	10.1059	9.4466	8.8514	8.3126	7.8237	16
17	15.5624	14.2918	13.1660	12.1656	11.2740	10.4772	9.7632	9.1216	8.5435	8.0215	17
18	16.3984	14.9920	13.7534	12.6592	11.6895	10.8276	10.0591	9.3719	8.7556	8.2014	18
19	17.2201	15.2684	14.3237	13.1339	12.0853	11.1581	10.3356	9.6036	8.9501	8.3649	19
20	18.0457	16.3514	14.8774	13.5903	12.4622	11.4699	10.5940	9.8181	9.1285	8.5136	20
21	18.8571	17.0111	15.4149	14.0291	12.8211	11.7640	10.8355	10.0168	9.2922	8.6487	21
22	19.6605	17.6581	15.9368	14.4511	13.1630	12.0416	11.0612	10.2007	9.4424	8.7715	22
23	20.4559	18.2921	16.4435	14.8568	13.4885	12.3033	11.2722	10.3710	9.5802	8.8832	23
24	21.2435	18.9139	16.9355	15.2469	13.7986	12.5503	11.4693	10.5287	9.7066	8.9847	24
25	22.0233	19.5234	17.4181	15.6220	14.9039	12.7833	11.6536	10.6748	9.8226	9.0770	25

Table 5 (cont'd)
Present Value of an Annuity of $1

Period	11%	12%	13%	14%	15%	16%	17%	18%	19%	20%	Period
01	.9009	.8929	.8850	.8772	.8696	.8621	.8547	.8475	.8403	.8333	01
02	1.7125	1.6901	1.6681	1.6467	1.6257	1.6052	1.5852	1.5656	1.5465	1.5278	02
03	2.4437	2.4018	2.3612	2.3216	2.2832	2.2459	2.2096	2.1743	2.1399	2.1065	03
04	3.1024	3.0373	2.9745	2.9137	2.8550	2.7982	2.7432	2.6901	2.6386	2.5887	04
05	3.6959	3.6048	3.5172	3.4331	3.3522	3.2743	3.1993	3.1272	3.0576	2.9906	05
06	4.2305	4.1114	3.9976	3.8887	3.7845	3.6847	3.5892	3.4976	3.4098	3.3255	06
07	4.7122	4.5638	4.4226	4.2883	4.1604	4.0386	3.9224	3.8115	3.7057	3.6046	07
08	5.1461	4.9676	4.7988	4.6389	4.4873	4.3436	4.2072	4.0776	3.9544	3.8372	08
09	5.5370	5.3282	5.1317	4.9464	4.7716	4.6065	4.4506	4.3030	4.1633	4.0310	09
10	5.8892	5.6502	5.4262	5.2161	5.0188	4.8332	4.6586	4.4941	4.3389	4.1925	10
11	6.2065	5.9377	5.6869	5.4527	5.2337	5.0286	4.8364	4.6560	4.4865	4.3271	11
12	6.4924	6.1944	5.9176	5.6603	5.4206	5.1971	4.9884	4.7932	4.6105	4.4392	12
13	6.7499	6.4235	6.1218	5.8424	5.5831	5.3423	5.1183	4.9095	4.7147	4.5327	13
14	6.9819	6.6282	6.3025	6.0021	5.7245	5.4675	5.2293	5.0081	4.8023	4.6106	14
15	7.1909	6.8109	6.4624	6.1422	5.8474	5.5755	5.3242	5.0916	4.8759	4.6755	15
16	7.3792	6.9740	6.6039	6.2651	5.9542	5.6685	5.4053	5.1624	4.9377	4.7296	16
17	7.5488	7.1196	6.7291	6.3729	6.0472	5.7487	5.4746	5.2223	4.9897	4.7746	17
18	7.7016	7.2497	6.8389	6.4674	6.1280	5.8178	5.5339	5.2732	5.0333	4.8122	18
19	7.8393	7.3650	6.9380	6.5504	6.1982	5.8775	5.5845	5.3176	5.0700	4.8435	19
20	7.9633	7.4694	7.0248	6.6231	6.2593	5.9288	5.6278	5.3527	5.1009	4.8696	20
21	8.0751	7.5620	7.1016	6.6870	6.3125	5.9731	5.6648	5.3837	5.1268	4.8913	21
22	8.1757	7.6446	7.1695	6.7429	6.3587	6.0113	5.6964	5.4099	5.1486	4.9094	22
23	8.2664	7.7184	7.2297	6.7921	6.3988	6.0442	5.7234	5.4321	5.1668	4.9245	23
24	8.3481	7.7843	7.2829	6.8351	6.4338	6.0726	5.7465	5.4509	5.1822	4.9371	24
25	8.4217	7.8431	7.3300	6.8729	6.4641	6.0971	5.7662	5.4669	5.1951	4.9476	25

Table 6
Durbin-Watson Statistic for 2.5% Significance (one-tail) or 5.0% Significance (two-tail)

n	$m = 1$		$m = 2$		$m = 3$		$m = 4$		$m = 5$	
	d_L	d_U	d_L	d_U	d_L	d_U	d_L	d_U	d_L	d_U
15	0.95	1.23	0.83	1.40	0.71	1.61	0.59	1.84	0.48	2.09
16	0.98	1.24	0.86	1.40	0.75	1.59	0.64	1.80	0.53	2.03
17	1.01	1.25	0.90	1.40	0.79	1.58	0.68	1.77	0.57	1.98
18	1.03	1.26	0.93	1.40	0.82	1.56	0.72	1.74	0.62	1.93
19	1.06	1.28	0.96	1.41	0.86	1.55	0.76	1.73	0.66	1.90
20	1.08	1.28	0.99	1.41	0.89	1.55	0.79	1.72	0.70	1.87
21	1.10	1.30	1.01	1.41	0.92	1.54	0.83	1.69	0.73	1.84
22	1.12	1.31	1.04	1.42	0.95	1.54	0.86	1.68	0.77	1.82
23	1.14	1.32	1.06	1.42	0.97	1.54	0.89	1.67	0.80	1.80
24	1.16	1.33	1.08	1.43	1.00	1.54	0.91	1.66	0.83	1.79
25	1.18	1.34	1.10	1.43	1.02	1.54	0.94	1.65	0.86	1.77
26	1.19	1.35	1.12	1.44	1.04	1.54	0.96	1.65	0.88	1.76
27	1.21	1.36	1.13	1.44	1.06	1.54	0.99	1.64	0.91	1.75
28	1.22	1.37	1.15	1.45	1.08	1.54	1.01	1.64	0.93	1.74
29	1.24	1.38	1.17	1.45	1.10	1.54	1.03	1.63	0.96	1.73
30	1.25	1.38	1.18	1.46	1.12	1.54	1.05	1.63	0.98	1.73
31	1.26	1.39	1.20	1.47	1.13	1.55	1.07	1.63	1.00	1.72
32	1.27	1.40	1.21	1.47	1.15	1.55	1.08	1.63	1.02	1.71
33	1.28	1.41	1.22	1.48	1.16	1.55	1.10	1.63	1.04	1.71
34	1.29	1.41	1.24	1.48	1.17	1.55	1.12	1.63	1.06	1.70
35	1.30	1.42	1.25	1.48	1.19	1.55	1.13	1.63	1.07	1.70
36	1.31	1.43	1.26	1.49	1.20	1.56	1.15	1.63	1.09	1.70
37	1.32	1.43	1.27	1.49	1.21	1.56	1.16	1.62	1.10	1.70
38	1.33	1.44	1.28	1.50	1.23	1.56	1.17	1.62	1.12	1.70
39	1.34	1.44	1.29	1.50	1.24	1.56	1.19	1.63	1.13	1.69
40	1.35	1.45	1.30	1.51	1.25	1.57	1.20	1.63	1.15	1.69
45	1.39	1.48	1.34	1.53	1.30	1.58	1.25	1.63	1.21	1.69
50	1.42	1.50	1.38	1.54	1.34	1.59	1.30	1.64	1.26	1.69
55	1.45	1.52	1.41	1.56	1.37	1.60	1.33	1.64	1.30	1.69
60	1.47	1.54	1.44	1.57	1.40	1.61	1.37	1.65	1.33	1.69
65	1.49	1.55	1.46	1.59	1.43	1.63	1.40	1.66	1.36	1.69
70	1.51	1.57	1.48	1.60	1.45	1.63	1.42	1.66	1.39	1.70
75	1.53	1.58	1.50	1.61	1.47	1.64	1.45	1.67	1.42	1.70
80	1.54	1.59	1.52	1.63	1.49	1.65	1.47	1.67	1.44	1.70
85	1.56	1.60	1.53	1.63	1.51	1.66	1.49	1.68	1.46	1.71
90	1.57	1.61	1.55	1.64	1.53	1.66	1.50	1.69	1.48	1.71
95	1.58	1.62	1.56	1.65	1.54	1.67	1.52	1.69	1.50	1.71
100	1.59	1.63	1.57	1.65	1.55	1.67	1.53	1.70	1.51	1.72

m = number of independent variables
n = number of observations
Source: From J. Durbin and G. S. Watson, "Testing for Serial Correlation in Least-Squares Regression," *Biometrika,* Vol. 38 (1951); 159–177. With the permission of the authors and the Trustees of *Biometrika.*

Documentation for ForeProfit and the Lotus Capital Budgeting Template[1]

Getting Started

The ForeProfit computer program and the Lotus capital budgeting template are designed to assist students in the analysis of data and the solution of complex problems in a managerial economics course. Students will find both of these programs easy to use. They are menu driven and require little prior computer knowledge.

Before proceeding further, please take a few moments to complete and mail the registration form found at the end of this documentation. Assistance will be provided *only* to registered users. Only the original registration form, *no photocopies*, will be accepted.

The first thing you should do is create a backup copy of your program diskettes. You will need three blank diskettes—two for copying the ForeProfit (FP) program disks and one for storing data. You will also need a copy of your computer's DOS diskette. These programs are designed for use on an IBM or IBM compatible computer with at least 320K of memory and two floppy disk drives.

First, insert the DOS diskette in the A drive of the computer and turn on the computer. After responding to the prompts for date and time (you can simply press the RETURN [called ENTER on some computer keyboards] key rather than entering the date and time), you will get the A> prompt on the screen. Type in the following:

FORMAT A:

and press RETURN. You will be instructed to remove the DOS diskette from Drive A and insert a new diskette into Drive A. Insert one of your three blank diskettes. (Be careful not to put in your FP diskette by mistake, or your program diskette will be ruined.) Press RETURN and the computer will format the blank

---

[1] Fore Profit is a trademark of Loon Valley Software, Inc. The ForeProfit program was prepared by Professor Joseph L. Kreitzer, Department of Economics, College of St. Thomas, St. Paul, Minnesota. The capital budgeting Lotus template was prepared by Professor Phillip M. Sisneros, College of Business and Economics, Lehigh University, Bethlehem, Pennsylvania.

diskette. When formatting is complete for that diskette you will be asked if you want to format another diskette. Respond "Y" (yes) and follow the instructions to format the other two blank diskettes. When you are finished formatting the three diskettes, respond "N" (no). You will see the A> prompt again.

Next put the #1 FP master diskette into Drive A and one of your newly formatted diskettes into Drive B. Type:

COPY A:*.* B:*.*

and press RETURN. The computer will copy the contents from the master (original) diskette onto your formatted, blank, backup diskette. When this task is complete the A> prompt will reappear. Remove both diskettes and label the new backup diskette. Insert the #2 FP diskette in Drive A and another blank, formatted diskette in Drive B and repeat the process.

Put your master FP diskettes in a safe place and do all your work with the backup diskettes you just created.

Running the FP Programs

In order to run the FP programs, start by booting up your computer with the DOS diskette. At the A> prompt, remove the DOS diskette from Drive A and insert the #1 FP diskette into Drive A and the data diskette into Drive B. The #1 FP diskette contains the startup routines, the main menu, and the linear programming routines. (The #1 FP diskette also has the capital budgeting routines, discussed below.) The #2 FP diskette has the regression routines, the extrapolative forecasting routines, and the data editor. (When you choose these options from the main menu you will be instructed to remove the #1 FP diskette from Drive A and insert the #2 FP diskette into Drive A.) After inserting the #1 FP diskette type:

4PROFIT

You will see a title page screen and then the main menu screen will appear as in Figure B.1.

FP Menus

The FP menu system provides "on-line help screens" at all times. This means that the computer always shows you the options available to you and provides some basis for deciding what to do or how to respond. FP assumes that you have a basic understanding of the routines you are using.

Each screen in the FP program has four basic areas, commonly referred to as "windows." The top window has the name of the routine you are currently in. The bottom window either tells you what you can do or asks for information. The big window on the right hand side has information about the option or about what you are being asked to enter. The left hand side has a series of small windows which are alternately highlighted as you push the up and down arrow (cursor) keys. When one of these left hand side windows is highlighted (it will appear different from the others and have an arrow pointing to it), pressing RETURN will select the highlighted option.

ForeProfit Educational Version: A Forecasting & Linear Programming Package

→ Extrapolative (black box)
   forecast tools

   Regression modeling of
   deterministic models

   Optimizing linear models

   Data entry, editing, &
   listing

   Change default locations
   for data or ForeProfit.

   Return to DOS

Say you have a set of numbers (e.g. sales, prices, orders, etc.) like these:

January	120
February	150
March	160
April	140
May	130
June	160
July	170
August	160
September	190
October	170.
November	180
December	180

have no other pertinent information and wish to forecast the value for the next month.

This option has procedures that are well suited for this task.

Use ↑ & ↓ to change options, → for more information; 'enter' to select.

Figure B.1
**ForeProfit Main
Menu Screen**

Use the "up" and "down" arrow keys on your keypad to change options (these keys are found on the numeric keypad). Be certain the "Number Lock" light is off before using the arrow keys. When you press one of these arrows two things will happen: the highlighted option changes and the text in the "information window" changes to correspond to the new option.

Pressing the "right" or "left" arrow keys will provide more information about an option, *if* a right or left arrow is present in the bottom window. The information becomes more technical as you move to the right, and less so to the left. Subsequent menus do not have this deeper layer of information screens, and hence do not show right or left arrows.

Correcting Errors

If you find yourself in a routine or making a choice you later regret, simply press the ESC key. When you do this an E or other character will appear to verify that you pushed ESC. If you really wish to back out of the current command, that is, escape, press ESC a second time and you will be returned to the previous menu. If you press ESC by mistake, press any other key to ignore the first ESC.

Output Menus

At the end of the calculations for any routine an output menu will appear. The output menu allows you to view the results in any order and as many times as you want. When you have finished looking at the output, an option places you back in the main FP menu. The output menus for each routine look similar to the main menu screen in Figure B.1. You will be shown the options and provided with information to help you choose from the options. In some routines there are additional layers of menus and information windows. This arrangement keeps the number of options at any one time down to a manageable level.

Limitations

The maximum length of any one data series is 300 observations. The maximum number of independent variables for regression is 10. The maximum number of variables for linear programming is 25 and the maximum number of constraints for linear programming is 25.

ForeProfit Options—The Main Menu

FP gives you the capability to do extrapolative forecasting—simple moving averages and exponential smoothing. These options are available by selecting the "Extrapolative (black box) forecast tools" option on the main menu. Simple regression and multiple regression are available by selecting the "Regression modeling of deterministic models" option on the main menu.

In order to create and modify data sets that will be used for forecasting and regression analysis, it is necessary to use the "Data entry, editing & listing" option. Data sets can be created and saved to your blank, formatted "Data Disk", which you should place in the B Drive. *The data editor, the regression programs and the forecasting programs are on the FP#2 program diskette.*

Linear programming models are available under the "Optimizing linear models" option on the main menu. *The startup routine, the main menu, and the linear programming routine are on the FP#1 program diskette. The Lotus capital budgeting template, discussed below, is also on the FP#1 diskette.*

Finally, if you wish to change the default drives for the "Data Disk" or for the FP program diskettes, or install the program on a computer with a hard disk you should choose the "Change default locations for data or ForeProfit" option.

Operating Tips

Data Entry

When using the linear programming routine, you will be directed to enter the necessary input for the constraints and the objective function. There is no need to create a separate data series in order to use the linear programming option.

When you are using the extrapolative forecast tools option or the regression modeling option, it is necessary to enter the "Data entry, editing & listing" option first *before* you attempt to do the regression or forecasting analysis.

When using the forecasting and regression options you will be directed to enter the name of the data series you have created for use as the dependent and independent variables, or for use as the data series from which forecasts will be generated. When you are indicating the data series to be used in a regression analysis you will be given an opportunity to create a new "transformed data series" from an original data series. The transformations that are possible are:

1. **Lags:** Creates a series which contains the lagged values (up to a maximum lag of 13 periods) of the original series.

2. **Differences:** Calculates changes in the value of a series or changes in the changes in the values of a series.

3. **Logs:** Creates a series of the logarithms of the values in a series.

4. **Inverse:** Creates a series of inverse (reciprocal) values of the series.

5. **Exponential:** Creates a series of values where the original values are replaced by their exponential values. This option is limited because microcomputers cannot handle values larger than exp(88).

Remembering Filenames

If you forget the filename you used when saving a data series, FP can show you all of the files stored on your "Data Diskette" and let you choose one with the cursor (arrow) keys. Any time you are prompted for a filename to RETRIEVE you can just push the "RETURN" key instead of typing the filename. After a few moments, the big window will be filled with the filenames from your directory. Use the arrow keys to highlight the filename you want and then push the "RETURN" key.

Redirecting Output and Saving Results

Output from a routine is directed to your monitor, unless you request otherwise. Output also can be directed to your printer or to a "printfile."

Printer Output.   Redirecting output to a printer means that the results you ask for will not appear on your monitor, but rather they will be printed on a printer attached to a computer. *Be certain to have a printer connected to your computer if you redirect output to the printer.* If no computer is attached the program may "crash" and you will have to start over!

You can also print any screen (other than a graph) that appears on the computer by pressing the SHIFT and PRT SC keys.

Printfile Output.   A printfile is simply a disk file which contains an exact copy of your output as though it had been printed. The primary advantage of using a printfile is that you can "save" your findings while working at any computer, printing them at some other time when a computer/printer becomes available. For example, suppose that you have run a regression and ask for the output to be sent to a printfile you have named REGROUT. (Be sure you select each of the statistical output options that you wish to have contained in your printfile. You must select the items of output that you want to save on "Printfile" in exactly the same way you select output for your screen or printer.) The printfile can be printed by (1) booting DOS on a computer with a printer, and (2) at the A> prompt inserting the data diskette containing REGROUT in Drive A and typing:

COPY REGROUT LPT1:

Printfiles can accumulate results from several procedures. If you run several regressions and request the output from each to be sent to the printfile REGROUT, then REGROUT would contain the results of ALL of the regressions.

Technical Assistance

ForeProfit is made available to you through a licensing agreement with Loon Valley Software™, INc. Any technical questions regarding the operation of the program should be directed to:

Loon Valley Software
420 Summit Avenue, Suite #38
St. Paul, MN 55102-2699
612/227-5552

Assistance can only be made available to *registered users*. Be sure to mail in the registration form now.

The Capital Budgeting Template

The capital budgeting model that comes with this software package is accessed through Lotus 1-2-3. The capital budgeting model can be used to solve capital budgeting problems and cost-benefit analysis problems.

In order to use this model you will need a copy of the Lotus 1-2-3 system disk (version 2.0 or 2.01). After booting up your system using your DOS disk, and after you see the A> prompt, insert the Lotus system disk in Drive A and the #1 FP diskette in Drive B. Type "123" in response to the A> prompt. (Note: These instructions assume that your copy of Lotus is configured to look for the templates in Drive B. If this is not true, see your Lotus manual to make the necessary change.)

After a short time the Lotus copyright screen will appear, followed by a blank Lotus spreadsheet. In order to access the capital budgeting template you need to retrieve the template from the disk in Drive B. First type /. This will put the Lotus menu across the top of the blank spreadsheet. Using the cursor keys select the FILE command and press RETURN. A new submenu of commands will appear. Select the RETRIEVE command and press RETURN. You will be asked to choose a Lotus spreadsheet appearing on the disk in Drive B. The choices are:

MAINMENU.WK1   and   NPV.WK1

Use the cursor keys to select MAINMENU.WK1, and then press RETURN. The menu screen shown in Figure B.2 will appear. Next remove the Lotus system disk from Drive A and insert a formatted data disk.

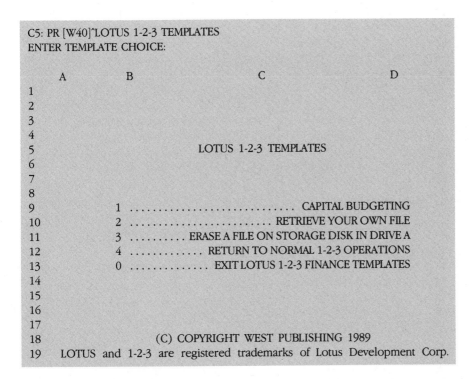

Figure B.2
Capital Budgeting Template Main Menu Screen

C5: PR [W40]'LOTUS 1-2-3 TEMPLATES
ENTER TEMPLATE CHOICE:

	A	B	C	D
1				
2				
3				
4				
5			LOTUS 1-2-3 TEMPLATES	
6				
7				
8				
9		1 .... CAPITAL BUDGETING		
10		2 .... RETRIEVE YOUR OWN FILE		
11		3 .... ERASE A FILE ON STORAGE DISK IN DRIVE A		
12		4 .... RETURN TO NORMAL 1-2-3 OPERATIONS		
13		0 .... EXIT LOTUS 1-2-3 FINANCE TEMPLATES		
14				
15				
16				
17				
18		(C) COPYRIGHT WEST PUBLISHING 1989		
19	LOTUS and 1-2-3 are registered trademarks of Lotus Development Corp.			

You will be asked to select one of the five choices on the screen by typing the number of the choice you desire and pressing RETURN. If you select choice 1, you will enter the capital budgeting template. Choice 2 will permit you to retrieve a file you have previously saved on your data disk (now in Drive A). Choice 3 allows you to erase a file on your data disk. Choice 4 returns you to the normal LOTUS 1-2-3 operation mode (that is, out of the capital budgeting template). Choice 0 exits you from LOTUS and takes you back to DOS.

The Capital Budgeting (Cost-Benefit Analysis) Template

If you select choice 1, the screen shown in Figure B.3 will appear.

When working with the capital budgeting template, you must first BUILD a spreadsheet of the appropriate size to handle your problem. Use the cursor keys to highlight the BUILD option and press RETURN. You will be asked, "ECONO-MIC LIFE OF PROJECT (3–35 YEARS)?" Type in the appropriate response and press return. The screen will now jump around quite a bit for the next few moments while the spreadsheet is being built. When this is complete, the COMMAND MENU shown in Figure B.3 will reappear.

Next, highlight the INPUT option and press RETURN. The cursor will jump down to the first entry line on the spreadsheet and you will be able to enter the appropriate data. The ECONOMIC LIFE OF INVESTMENT PROJECT line will already contain the value you specified during the BUILD routine. The first section of the spreadsheet allows you to enter data concerning the initial outlay

Figure B.3
Capital Budgeting
Spreadsheet
Screen

MENU

B6: PR [W15]
BUILD INPUT SAVE GRAPH PRINT RETRIEVE MENU QUIT
BUILD A WORKSHEET

	A	B	C
1	>> TO VIEW CMD MENU HOLD THE Alt KEY DOWN AND PRESS M <<		
2			
3			
4	CAPITAL BUDGETING INVESTMENT ANALYSIS		
5			
6			
7	INFORMATION ON INVESTMENT PROJECT		
8			
9			
10	ECONOMIC LIFE OF INVESTMENT PROJECT		0
11	AFTER-TAX SALVAGE VALUE OF INVESTMENT PROJECT		$0
12	MARGINAL TAX RATE		0.00%
13			
14	NET COST OF INVESTMENT PROJECT		$0
15	DELIVERY AND INSTALLATION		$0
16	NET WORKING CAPITAL REQUIRED FOR INVESTMENT PROJECT		$0
17			
18			
19	NET INVESTMENT		$0
20			

CMD   CALC

required for the project, the tax rate (if any), the initial working capital required for the project (if any), and the after-tax salvage value of the project. (Note: When you begin to enter data in the spreadsheet, the COMMAND MENU across the top of the spreadsheet may disappear. In order to call the COMMAND MENU back, hold down the ALT key and press M.)

As soon as you enter any data in the spreadsheet the CALC indicator will appear at the bottom right of the screen. Whenever this light is on, you can recompute the values in the spreadsheet by pressing the F9 function key.

The next section of the spreadsheet permits you to enter revenue, cost and depreciation data for each year over the life of the project. If the project has more than one revenue or cost stream you may use the two lines for entry of the two streams. Also, if the revenue or cost stream is projected to grow at a constant rate over the life of the project, you can simply enter the first period's actual amount and enter the growth rate. (Type growth rate entries in decimal form. Do not use dollar signs or commas when typing in other numerical values.) The spreadsheet will project the revenue stream out to the end of the life of the project when the F9 key is pressed.

Also, in this second section of the spreadsheet there is a row that allows you to enter ADDITIONAL NET WORKING CAPITAL AFTER YEAR 0. During the last year of the project, the template will automatically recapture any net working capital investments and the after-tax salvage value input in the first section of the template.

The final section of the template provides a place for you to input the DISCOUNT RATE to be used to compute the project's net present value. After all data have been input, you can press the F9 key and the template will compute the project's NET PRESENT VALUE (NPV), IRR (internal rate of return), PROFITA-BILITY INDEX, and PAYBACK (for the first full year after the initial investment has been fully recovered). (Note: In order for the IRR calculation to be correct, it is necessary that you enter a value for the INITIAL GUESS FOR IRR that is reasonably close to the actual IRR. An initial guess equal to the cost of capital (discount rate) will often be satisfactory.)

Correcting Errors. If you make an error inputting data you can simply input the correct values in the cell when the faulty values appear. If you choose an option in error, you can "back out of it" by pressing the ESC key one or two times.

Graphing. If you wish to see a graph of the project's NPV at various discount rates, choose the GRAPH option from the command menu at the top of the screen. (Remember, you may have to press ALT M in order to get the command menu to reappear). Press any key while the graph is showing to return to the spreadsheet.

Printing. In order to print your spreadsheet, you highlight the PRINT command in the command menu and press return. Be sure you are connected to a printer that is turned on.

Saving and Retrieving Problems. In order to save a problem you have developed using the template, highlight the SAVE option from the command menu and follow the instructions that appear on the screen. The problem you save will be saved to the data disk in Drive A. Problems can be saved using names up to eight characters in length. The first character must be a letter and no blank spaces are permitted. You may also retrieve a problem that you previously saved onto the data disk in Drive A by choosing the RETRIEVE option. Finally, if you choose the MENU option you will be returned to the main menu. Whenever you choose an option that will cause you to leave the spreadsheet you are working on, you will always be given the opportunity to SAVE the current spreadsheet before leaving it.

Quitting. The QUIT command returns you to the regular Lotus 1-2-3 mode of operation. If you wish to return to DOS, first return to the Main Menu and select option 0.

ForeProfit™
Educational Version

Owner Registration

Congratulations. You are now the owner of the Educational version of ForeProfit, the forecasting and linear programming tool for decision makers. This version does not include all of the powerful routines of the ForeProfit 1.0 but it will solve many of your analytic problems.

Stop Number Frustration

ForeProfit provides solutions to number frustration. It's an integrated data examination package to look at sets of numbers and draw conclusions, and to examine relationships between various data sets.

Please take the time to complete this owner registration card. Completion of this card entitles you to access to the user support telephone number. User help is available only to registered owners. This registration entitles you to a 30% discount on the full version of ForeProfit 1.0

Name _____

Address _____

City _____ State _____ ZIP _____

Phone _____

Job Title (if employed) _____

Major or Area of Concentration _____

College Attending _____

Computer System   XT or equiv _____   AT or equiv _____   386 _____

Return to:

ForeProfit Owner Registration
Loon Valley Software
420 Summit Avenue, Suite 38
St. Paul, MN 55102
612-227-5552

Check Answers to Selected End-of-Chapter Problems

Chapter 1

3. b. Economic profit = ($90,000)

Chapter 2

3. $PV = 10,000$
5. $r = 12\%$
7. $PV = 925.22$
9. Payment = 11,017
11. $P_0 = \$40.04$
12. a. $Q_S = 52$

Chapter 3

1. c. Coefficient of variation = 0.122
4. a. .0062
6. d. Expected return for $A_1 = \$600$
8. a. Minimum utility for $A_2 = .09$
10. a. $p = .0401$
11. d. Expected return for stocking 25 = $23.725
12. b. $\sigma_p = 5.23\%$
13. a. Net gain = $125,000

Chapter 4

1. d. $Q^* = 8$
3. c. $d(MC)/dQ = -12 + 3Q$
5. b. $Q^* = 5$ units
7. b. $Q^* = 5$
9. a. $Q^* = 180$
11. b. $S^* = 3250$
12. a. $Y^* = 7; X^* = 13; \lambda^* = 80$

Chapter 5

1. b. $X_1^* = 800$ (STD model); $X_2^* = 600$ (DEL model); Profit contribution = $155,000
4. c. $X_1^* = 12$ (small); $X_2^* = 12$ (large)
7. c. $X_1^* = 10$ oz. fortified cereal; $X_2^* = 20$ oz. dried milk; Cost = 70 cents
17. Cost = $258,000

Chapter 6

1. c. $Y = 1.565 + .7496X$
3. c. $s_e = 10.132; s_b = .396$
3. d. $R^2 = .885$
6. c. $\log Y = 2.4747 + .6965 \log X$
9. a. F value = 2.072
9. b. $b_1 = 1.2945$ (income)
11. Correlation between size and rooms = .5903

Chapter 7

2. c. $P_2 = \$454.54$
4. $E_D = -.727$
7. Chow forecast = 11.528M
9. $P = \$90$
11. b. $E_y = .16$
15. c. $E_D = -2.2$
17. b. $E_D = -2.57$
20. % change $Q_D = -3\%$
23. a. $E_X = 1.34$
25. Week 1–2 price elasticity = $-.795$; Week 9–10 income elasticity = .900

Appendix 7A

1. c. $X_1^* = 5.256$; $X_2^* = 4.496$

Chapter 8

1. b. $E_A = 1.05$
3. b. $E_A = 0.98$
6. a. $Q = 28.915 - 19.105\ P$
8. a. $E_D = -2.174$
10. a. $E_D = -.375$
12. b. $Q = 16,870$
14. b. $E_A = .197$

Chapter 9

1. b. $k = .225$
3. 19X2 ridership $= 5169$
4. $T = 286.5$
6. b. June adjustment factor $\approx +6\%$
8. a. $Q_D = 11,450$
10. b. $Y'_{10} = 259.03$ (19Y0)

Appendix 9A

1. $Y'_6 = 22.95$

Chapter 10

2. c. $16.2 million
4. b. $30,700
6. b. 11.1% market share required

Chapter 11

1. c. Stage 1: 0–6
3. b. Max $Q = 34$ at crew size of 10 or 11
5. b. $Q^* = 44$
7. b. $MFC_X = 20$
9. b. Output increases by 11.8%

Appendix 11A

1. b. 4 units of output using 14 machine hours and 6 man hours

Chapter 12

4. a. $TC = 150 + 200Q - 9Q^2 + .25\ Q^3$
5. b. i. $Q^* = 18$
8. a. TC (one plant) $= \$4,275,000$

Appendix 12A

1. d. iii. Profit $= \$50,000$
2. b. $DOL = 3.5$
4. $Q_b = 5,988$

Chapter 13

2. a. ii. $\beta_k = 0.35$
3. b. % change $Q = 0.9\%$
5. c. $Q^* = 1675$ students

Appendix 13A

1. c. $C = \$803.51$

Chapter 14

1. $Q = 20$
3. c. iii. Value of ration coupon $= \$15$
5. e. $\pi = \$2,250$
7. b. $P = MR = \$20,000$
9. a. $Q = 45$ units
11. b. $Q^* = 350$ units
13. a. $Q_2 = 34,865$ gallons
15. e. $\pi = \$263,625$
17. d. $\pi = \$3$

Chapter 15

2. a. $Q_B^* = 25$; $Q_A^* = 30$
4. a. $P^* = \$9,666.7$
6. a. $Q^* = 3$ units
6. c. $Q^* = 4.732$ units
8. a. i. $15,000

Appendix 15A

2. c. $i^* = 1$ and $j^* = 2$; Value of game $= \$5,000$

Chapter 16

2. $Q = 18.67$ units; $P_1^* = \$40.67/\text{unit}$
4. **b.** $P_1^* = \$52$ unit
6. **b.** $Q_2^* = 16$ units
7. $\pi_p = \$112,500$
9. **b.** $Q_m^* = 4$ units
12. **c.** $\$85/\text{unit}$

Chapter 17

3. $NPV = \$20,553$
5. **c.** $NPV = \$1,438$
8. **a.** $PI = 1.40$
10. $k_e = 13.4\%$
14. $k_a = 12.3\%$

Chapter 18

3. **a.** Net present cost of Alternative #1 = $\$456.39(000)$

Chapter 19

1. **b.** $\pi = \$950,000,000$
3. **d.** $\pi = \$60$ million
6. **a.** Standard deviation = 4.2%
8. **c.** Profit contribution under moonopoly = $\$50,059.52$

Appendix 19A

5. **a.** $\pi = \$645,761$
7. **a.** $Q = 32$

Chapter 20

1. **a.** $ROI = 14.2\%$
3. **a.** $\pi = \$40.5$

Index to Glossary

(NOTE: The number in parentheses indicates the chapter or appendix in which the term is discussed.)

Index